# Type Navigator

—

The Independent
Foundries Handbook

—

*Jan Middendorp &
TwoPoints.Net*

3
Preface

12
Featured
Foundries

308
Index

gestalten

Page
2

Typefaces used on the cover

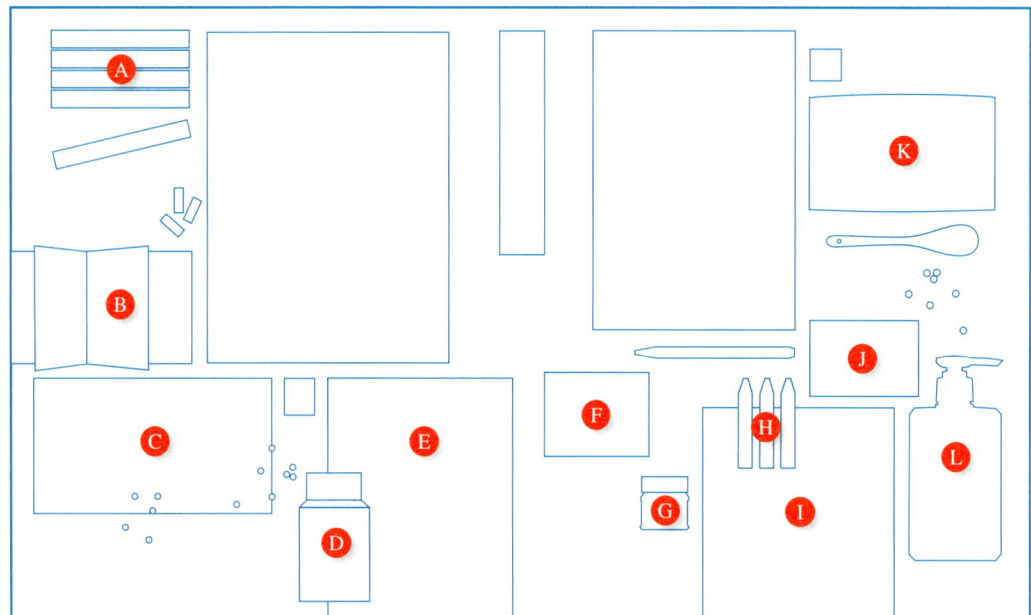

A   Grumpy
    *Suomi*

B   VLNL Bint
    *VetteLetters*

C   Burgues Script
    *Sudtipos*

D   Theinhardt
    *Optimo*

E   Klimax Std
    *Typotheque*

F   Romain BP Headline
    *b+p swiss typefaces*

G   Malaussene Translation
    *Gestalten Fonts*

H   Lokal Script 33
    *Storm Type*

I   Nitti Typewriter
    *Bold Monday*

J   TpHolaBcn
    *VetteLetters*

K   Brownstone
    *Sudtipos*

L   Acta Poster
    *DSType*

## Preface

There is something oddly attractive about letterforms. The characters of an alphabet are invariably based on a collective idea of how each letter should look; they must be, in order to be recognized. And yet the variations are endless. There is a world of possibility between the bland functionality of a no-nonsense sans-serif typeface and the funky, provocative what-letter-am-I esthetics of an elaborate graffiti piece. But for the designer the challenge remains the same: devising shapes that, regardless of whatever message or mystery is embedded in the form itself, exist to be read. It is probably this tension between constraints and freedom that attracts more and more young designers to letters: in an age that lacks a dominant style or a philosophy of form, in a period in which literally everything (at least on a visual level) seems to be possible and permitted, making things that need to resemble a shared idea of how they should look at least offers something to hold on to. And it offers a different kind of fun as well — a game with some well-established rules that designers can choose to break at their own risk.

Type and typography have become hugely popular: as a subject in design schools, as something to share in online forums and as a product to sell or buy. Typographic products come in many guises — silk-screened posters, T-shirts, letter sculptures, calendars and much more. These are all finished artifacts, commodities to use or put on a shelf.

Fonts — digital typefaces — are something different. They are half-products, building blocks to be used to make something bigger. Like the good old dry transfer sheets from companies such as Letraset, fonts aren't just bought by professional designers and printers; there is a growing number of "civilian" computer users who also want their texts to look special. They have tens of thousands of typefaces to choose from, supplied by at least a thousand large and small type foundries worldwide. MyFonts alone acts as a retail platform for over 800 companies that design, produce and sell type. This vast typographic landscape is not easy to navigate. Students and budding designers — let alone non-professional users — are often overwhelmed by the number of internet addresses where fonts can be seen and bought. This book is aimed at the people who want to know more about fonts and the companies that make them.

# Type culture

An interesting rhythm can be perceived in the development of audiovisual culture. Each medium or discipline seems to go through periods in which it is more relevant than others; then it takes a back seat again. Rock music and film took center stage in the sixties; theater in the seventies; product and furniture design in the eighties. Today, type design and lettering seem to have a privileged position. Type is the subject of hundreds of publications each year, it is a favorite among design students and is a theme of ever more conferences and seminars. It is not the first time this has happened. Two decades ago, type design made a sudden jump into prominence. What had, up to then, been a rather obscure occupation practised by a small elite, suddenly became a kind of popular art form. Affordable tools for making letterforms and producing fonts became available to anyone owning a computer, and young designers began exploring the peculiarities of these digital tools. Many post-modernist processes and strategies that were already common practice in other forms of art and design were adapted to type and typography: sampling and appropriation, layering and montage, ornament and exuberance, destruction and deconstruction. And many designers wanted to join in the fun. The number of fonts available went from hundreds to thousands in just a few years and a great many of the new fonts were experimental.

But that was then — the early 1990s — and this is now. The last few years have seen a renewed and rather frantic interest in all things typographic. However, there are some huge differences, and most of these are related to the web. In social networks, new ideas travel fast and are seen by many more people than any printed design magazine or book ever reached. Curiously, this doesn't imply that trends are more short-lived — visual ideas often stay online for a surprisingly long time and get forwarded and rediscovered for several years. They are discussed on several levels, from uncritical praise to thoughtful analysis, and inspire clueless amateurs as well as seasoned specialists. In type design, this means that trends are more visible than ever before, they are picked up by more people and they are more consciously processed — and some ideas are endlessly recycled.

Besides the above-mentioned post-modern, stylistic strategies, which have proved amazingly persistent, a different set of typographic concepts has emerged, or re-emerged. After a wild phase when everything had to be tried out, young type designers are now showing a renewed interest in functionality, technical sophistication and typographic tradition. Specialized type design courses fuel a movement that aims to innovate type design in the digital age while respecting time-honored criteria of conceptual and technical exactingness.

But possibly the most far-reaching change is on the distribution side. Just fifteen years ago, fonts were still quite literally a mail order product: they were ordered by telephone or e-mail, and supplied on diskettes or locked CD-ROMs from which single fonts could be unlocked using a code that the supplier would fax to the user. In other words, type designers would need a sound infrastructure to get their fonts out into the world. Some young visionaries ventured out on their own, but most type designers chose to contribute to one or more of the larger type libraries, from long-established companies such as Linotype to brand-new collections like FontFont or T26. All foundries depended largely on distributors such as the FontShop network to reach their retail customer base.

All of this has changed very quickly over the last decade under the influence of the web and its social networks. Hundreds of designers who published their earliest fonts with one of the major libraries ventured out on their own. Many of the newly-established "foundries" are one- or two-person companies, and offer just a small collection. Others have grown to include dozens or even hundreds of typeface families by several designers.

**From founts to fonts**

People sometimes ask why foundries are called foundries (that is the default term in English; in other languages, such as German and Dutch, the commonly used term can be translated as "type publishers"). Well, sometimes old names get carried over to new technologies. There are many examples of this. Judged solely by its name, a *smart phone* would be a thing for sound — in reality, of course, it is as much a thing for seeing.

Back in the days of metal type, founding was what foundries did. Type was made from a fluid mix of lead and other metals, either by hand or, after the introduction of Linotype and Monotype typecasting machines in the 1890s, mechanically. What the foundry produced was, in the original British spelling, *founts*: melted things. A fount was a complete set of glyphs, enough of each one to set a substantial piece of text, in one single size.

In the digital age, people use *font*, in the American spelling, to mean several different things. Sometimes it is taken to refer to a complete type family (such as Times New Roman, aka Times, the typeface you are reading now), sometimes it is used for just one weight, like Times Bold Italic. The correct way is to use the word *typeface* to designate the general design, and *type family* for all the varieties taken together. *Weight* or *style* are both good words to describe a specific variant of the typeface (e.g. Times Bold Italic), and *font* for the smallest entity that you can actually buy. In the age of the OpenType format, fonts are much larger than they used to be; a single font may contain small caps, special ligatures, diacritics (accents) for many languages, multiple numeral sets, and many more things for which one had to buy separate fonts ten years ago.

Before the advent of desktop typography, individual designers did not buy fonts at all. Until the mid to late 1980s, fonts were exclusively sold to specialized printing and typesetting companies that were equipped with one or more specific composition systems; a new font family represented a considerable investment. What a designer bought from the typesetting company was ready-made pieces of text on film or proofing paper. Depending on the total order, the price of a single page of typeset text could be in the same range as one font may cost today (say, 20–50 dollars or euros). For headlines, the alternative was to use dry transfer sheets from companies like Letraset or Mecanorma, which allowed a designer to "set" words by rubbing down the single letters from a thin plastic sheet. And of course, until well into the 1980s designers drew their own lettering — either freehand or geometrically constructed with a ruler and compass. Needless to say, non-professionals seldom ordered typeset text. Creative individuals who wanted to prepare a newsletter, invitation or leaflet resorted to dry transfer sheets, hand-drawn lettering and text from their home typewriter.

All this changed fast from 1990 onwards. Professional typesetting companies all but disappeared over the course of a decade. Those that survived, including the in-house design and typesetting departments of printing companies, were forced to write off their expensive high-end equipment and replace it with desktop computers (usually Apple Macs). These took up less space, were more cost-effective, were easier to update, and did not require much training. Buying new and fashionable fonts now cost a fraction of what platform-specific fonts had cost before, and prices kept dropping. The same equipment and fonts now became accessible to designers and regular folk alike. By the end of the 1990s, every new computer came with dozens of system fonts — as many different typefaces as a small typesetting or printing firm would have had on offer in the 1950s, or more.

With that in mind, it is fascinating to see how many non-designers now feel the urge (and the courage) to venture beyond the set of standard fonts that come with their computer system and buy some fonts of their own. Managers of small companies, scrapbookers, amateur designers of leaflets and invitations: the customer base for type has broadened in a way that until recently no type designer ever imagined. Among young designers and graphic design students, there is now also a growing awareness of type design as a discipline; not only do many of them want to try their hand at drawing letterforms, they also are more aware that fonts are products that represent a significant investment of time and talent, and are therefore worth paying for.

### Paying for fonts

Which brings us to the subject of money: price policies, copyrights and the question of whether fonts are worth paying for at all.

To begin with the last question: there are several possible answers to this, and a couple of them are plain wrong. One of those is the pirates' answer. Most fonts (like most songs, and many films) can be found online for free, and they are put out there by two kinds of people. On the one hand there are unethical businessmen who make money from the advertising on their sites; on the other, people who think of themselves as idealists and upload digital products because they are convinced that everything, or at least everything digital, should be free. A common assumption — which could be called the Robin Hood fallacy — is that fonts come from large anonymous companies that are already rich enough as it is. As this book shows, nothing could be further from the truth.

Most type designers and owners of so-called "microfoundries" are self-employed, and to them font sales represent an essential source of income. When a graphic designer or a fan of nice type decides to copy those fonts illegally, this implies a sincere "screw you" to the type designer. That's not very fair. If everyone did the same there soon there would soon cease to be new fonts, or necessary updates.

The prices of digital fonts range from a few dollars to about €300 per weight, but make no mistake: compared to the cost of strips of text in the time of lead or photo-typesetting, prices are lower than ever.

### Licenses and the EULA

Strictly speaking, fonts are not bought; what is acquired is a license to use them. In this sense fonts do not differ much from other types of software. The user acquires the right to adopt the fonts within well-defined restrictions. While typefaces that come with an operating system or program are not paid for separately, they too are commercial fonts that cannot be owned but for which the buyer receives a "permission to use."

The rules for what the user can and cannot do with the fonts are laid down in the End User License Agreement (EULA). Some of these conditions vary from one foundry to the next. For instance, the number of computers that fonts may be installed on can vary, and so may the rules for embedding fonts in PDFs or websites. Special authorization is usually required for modifying fonts — like adding a character, for example. An organization that plans to use fonts on a larger number of computers needs a group license.

Most EULAs forbid "lending" fonts to third parties. Copying a font as part of a design job or sharing a license with fellow freelancers is, strictly speaking, illegal. Many professionals have a surprisingly relaxed attitude about these rules. Even large publishers have been known to give copies of the fonts used in books to their partners in international coproductions. Should they be caught (e.g. in a Business Software Alliance audit), then this might result in costly legal proceedings.

Until recently, EULAs were invariably worded in obscure legalese; today, more and more foundries strive to make these agreements understandable to users without the need to consult a lawyer. Not surprisingly, it is often small and young companies that take the lead in humanizing the license agreement.

---

# Types of type foundries

---

Type foundries operate in many different ways. What exactly goes on behind the scenes will make little difference to casual users who acquire fonts through a distributor's web shop. But for those who have more than a passing interest in type and type design, it may be useful to gain some insight into the various models that exist.

**State of independence**

The type world is a bit like the music world in that a large part of the most popular fonts are produced by a small number of "majors" who own a series of subsidiaries and are often characterized by slow decision-making and a strong link to the past. And just like in the music world, the "indies" are smaller companies that have a well-defined program and are often more flexible and forward-thinking. That, however, is more or less where the parallel stops. The music world is full of labels that have their own management or A&R staff but still have to report to the mother company; this label model hardly exists in the typographic world. Virtually all smaller foundries are really independent and only rely on larger companies for their distribution; and some foundries with an influential program and a large collection of fonts (such as FSI/Font Shop or Font Bureau) are run by a surprisingly small staff and are, for all intents and purposes, independent.

Through a series of successive acquisitions, much of what can be called "major" in font production has ended up in the hands of one company — Monotype Imaging. Apart from its own type library, which goes back to the early 1900s, Monotype now owns some of the most significant typographic companies of the past century, notably Linotype and ITC, and have also absorbed the type division of Agfa. More recently, Monotype acquired (or more precisely, bought back) Ascender, a company most widely known as the vendor of Microsoft's system fonts and as a bunch of extremely capable technicians.

The quick transitions from one technology to the next during the 20th century (metal > photocomposition > digital systems > desktop) left many victims among historical type foundries. Apart from Monotype and Linotype, there are only a few companies that survived or were taken into the digital age by new owners. Neufville Digital in Barcelona inherited parts of the renowned German Bauer foundry; Berthold Types took the heritage of the Berlin Berthold foundry to Chicago. However, these companies that once employed hundreds and made millions manufacturing and selling huge machines (and to whom the fonts were a bit like machine parts), are now small offices run by a handful of people. Strictly speaking they are independent, but not necessarily "indies" as innovation is to be found elsewhere.

So in the digital age, it is not so easy to define "large" and "small" companies. Perceived size has become independent of the number of employees, or even the number of products. Internet-based companies, which is what most type foundries are today, can have a huge impact as well as an extensive, influential catalog of products and still be run by just two people. Producing and selling retail type may be the only thing that a company does; but in other cases, retail fonts may be the tip of the iceberg and most of a company's income is made from different sources: custom fonts, software development, lettering or design work, and more.

The model of the independent foundry was pioneered by a few, mostly American companies in the early to mid-1980s. Arguably the first independent company — i.e. with no links to a historical type foundry — to specialize in digital type was Bitstream, established in 1981 by Matthew Carter and Mike Parker after having left Linotype, taking with them most of that company's type design division (including David Berlow, who later co-founded the Font Bureau). Bitstream began doing what they thought Linotype should have been doing: developing fonts for the new digital hardware that was coming on the market (all of this is pre-standardization: each system came with its own specs and fonts). The Linotype management had refused to follow Carter's and Parker's reasoning that there was money to be made from producing type for third parties: as Linotype was still primarily a manufacturer of typesetting equipment, they did not see the point of selling fonts to competitors.

While Bitstream had its roots in established type production and was very much part of the industry, Emigre Graphics in California entered the market from left field — two graduates from Europe who started out editing, designing and publishing what was initially a (sub-)cultural magazine for outsiders and didn't become a platform for typographic theory until a few years later. After they began selling the fonts designed for *Emigre* magazine, they gradually became the model *par excellence* of the fiercely autonomous, designer-run foundry, inviting dozens of other designers over the years while staying true to a clear yet flexible vision of innovative typography.

Emigre's example inspired and empowered many designers who, from around 1990 onwards, began creating their own fonts. Many submitted their typefaces to Emigre or to one of the other emerging type libraries such as FontFont/FSI, or chose to go with established companies like Linotype, Berthold or software manufacturer Adobe. But several designers felt that they, like Emigre, would benefit from total independence and set up their own foundry. Needless to say, the emergence of the internet as a medium for promoting and selling type in the mid-1990s helped immensely. New platforms for retail, both online and off, helped young foundries reach an audience. We'll talk more about these distribution channels later.

### Foundry models

Today, a type foundry can be many things. Some are created as spin-offs of graphic design studios, selling typefaces that were originally developed as part of larger design projects (identities, magazine and book designs, signage, etc). This book profiles several foundries in this category, many of them having entered the market only recently. To mention just a few, A2-Type from London, André Baldinger from Paris, Colophon from Brighton, Optimo from Geneva and Playtype from Copenhagen are cases in point.

There is a small number of graphic designers who began marketing their own fonts in the 1990s and have managed to pursue double careers to date. Jonathan Barnbrook (VirusFonts) and Rian Hughes (Device) are two prominent British designers who, apart from running successful studios for design and illustration, release new typefaces on a regular basis (as well as publishing books and writing articles). Both have committed to remaining small: although internationally in demand, they never worked with more than a couple of assistants and interns.

To grow or not to grow can be a dilemma for owners of foundries and type design studios once their work becomes successful. For studios whose work depends largely on the vision and talent of one person, hiring additional staff can be the best way for the principal to keep focusing on concepts and design, while assistants complete character sets, design additional weights, handle kerning and do other kinds of production work. Especially in the realm of text fonts, extensive typeface families are now the norm; and even though computer-enhanced methods like interpolation can help automate part of the process, creating large families requires attention to thousands of details, and hence often involves teamwork. Among the studios centered around a single designer but working with several assistants are LucasFonts in Berlin and Darden Studio in Brooklyn. Similarly, Hoefler & Frere-Jones in New York is headed by two renowned designers who have several very competent but largely anonymous designers on staff.

Many small companies like these are first and foremost type development studios, often working for clients in the corporate and editorial field. In London, both Fontsmith and Dalton Maag are examples of studios employing a number of designers, and specializing in bespoke fonts made directly for clients or for communications agencies, which can become retail fonts once the exclusivity period is over.

One- and two-person foundries can also decide to grow in a different way — by expanding their type libraries beyond the output of the founders and publishing work by other type designers as well. During the past few years, several microfoundries have actively sought to expand their collection of personal fonts into a library of a wider scope. TypeTogether, the foundry set up by University of Reading graduates Veronika Burian (Prague) and José Scaglione (Rosario, Argentina) has rapidly developed into one of the type world's most versatile and fastest-growing collections, even including work by Dutch veteran (and Reading teacher) Gerard Unger. Peter Biľak's Typotheque has also taken in work by a growing number of freelance designers, as has OurType, the foundry established to market Fred Smeijers' typefaces. P22 in Buffalo, New York, is a special case. Having originated in Richard Kegler's personal art type projects, it has organically grown into a conglomerate of several sub-foundries or labels, including IHOF (International House of Fonts), Lanston Type and the Rimmer Type Foundry.

However, as many of the profiles in this book will show, it is very well possible not to grow and still be successful; the typographic world is open to many models and with a product as immaterial and easy to distribute as digital type, the possibilities are endless.

# Where to shop for fonts

The internet has become the default place to find and buy fonts. Several large type manufacturers have moved into the retail arena and set up their own online supermarkets, selling downloadable fonts from hundreds of foundries. A growing number of smaller foundries now have their own online store, while continuing to sell through larger or smaller distributors, with many offering their type through multiple vendors. Where a user decides to shop for fonts is a question of personal preference and habit.

Many newcomers to the typographic world are overwhelmed by the multiplicity of choices, and the following overview may help both users and aspiring type designers to get a general overview of the font retail landscape.

**Large shops and small shops**
The obvious place to go when shopping for fonts is to one of the large online distributors, who represent dozens if not hundreds of foundries. Some foundries, however, prefer not to work with outside distributors. These are, for the most part, small companies offering an exclusive collection of typefaces which they sell to the customers directly. Some of these are briefly described at the bottom of this article.

Discerning customers may find the offer of supermarket distributors such as MyFonts or Fonts.com a little overwhelming and inconsistent in quality, and opt for a boutique distributor that carries a more selective, scrupulously-monitored collection. For those who want to be able to buy a superbly drawn original font with their eyes closed, a boutique distributor like Veer or YouWorkForThem, or a small collection like that curated and sold by TypeTrust may be a better option. In between these extremes is FontShop, which offers a large but hand-picked selection of foundries and designers.

What customers don't always realize is that a font distributor (just like Amazon.com or other online shops) sells products made by other companies. It is the foundries themselves that control the quality of the fonts, which glyphs (characters and other signs) the fonts contain and what conditions of use are allowed in the EULA (the End-User Licensing Agreement, a sort of contract that governs the use of software). When a customer complains, most distributors can only transmit the complaint to the foundry, and in the worst case decide to give a refund, and discontinue the faulty font; they are not in a position to repair or alter it. For those font buyers who have special requirements or who want to use the font in special conditions, dealing directly with the foundry may be the better option. This book lists the foundry's own outlet, when available, for each featured foundry. The following is a description of the most popular and/or interesting retail websites for fonts.

**MyFonts** — *myfonts.com*
Founded in 2000 as an independent subsidiary of Bitstream, MyFonts is the marketplace where the largest number of independent foundries and labels can be found — around 800 at the time of writing, offering over 60,000 fonts (i.e. individual styles). The collections on offer range from large font libraries produced by Adobe, URW++, Berthold Types and Font Bureau, to one-person microfoundries with just one or two typefaces, and everything in between.

MyFonts is the only retailer that has absolutely no editorial filter: anyone who has produced a font that is technically usable and is not a copy of an existing font is admitted with no further ado. This means that new foundries get a quick start, without having to wait for decisions from type directors or committees. The no-frills approach also implies that fonts are made available with very little delay. A new family can be up and selling within days, where other distributors may need weeks or months. It also means that the quality of the typefaces MyFonts offers varies from mediocre to top-notch.

MyFonts positions itself as a "level playing field" where all fonts and foundries have the same chance of making it, and where promotion is based on a font's commercial success, not the staff's personal preference. Much of the online content, such as font descriptions and designers' biographies, is provided by the foundries and consequently varies heavily in both style and substance.

MyFonts is probably the place where fashions in type design can be most easily identified, through daily updated lists of bestsellers and "hot new fonts," as well as a monthly e-mail newsletter profiling current best sellers. The type designers themselves, when they are commercially inclined, also take their cues from these lists; a successful font is often followed by a string of products in a similar vein that eventually may find their way to other distributors as well.

From the start, MyFonts put an emphasis on ease of use and accessibility, putting in place an intuitive system of keywords or tags that users contribute to. For instance, in addition to searching for a specific typeface or genre (like "copperplate script"), users may instead search for a "wedding" or "invitation" font. MyFonts also developed WhatTheFont, an online application for recognizing typefaces from photos or scans the user can upload.

### Monotype Imaging — *fonts.com*

Monotype's online retail wing Fonts.com represents about 350 type foundries and labels. It claims to have 150,000 "font products" for sale; as the various font formats (TrueType, OpenType) are apparently counted separately, this number cannot be easily compared to MyFonts' total.

Monotype, originally a manufacturer of typesetting equipment with a world-renowned selection of original typefaces, branched out into the wholesale market after the advent of digital desktop publishing. Before the surge of interest in and use of the web in the late 1990s, they were among the suppliers that used a system of locked CD-ROMs holding libraries of thousands of fonts, from which single fonts could be activated using codes that were faxed to the user after payment. At that time, Monotype still relied heavily on retail networks like FontShop, who had customer-friendly local sales offices in place. Having established Fonts.com in the early 2000s, Monotype moved into the online retail market, striking distribution deals with an increasing number of small foundries that may also sell through other channels.

Monotype also began to collaborate with Linotype, their biggest competitor in the hot-metal age. Both companies started selling each others fonts, and the collaboration eventually became a fusion with the already-mentioned acquisition of Linotype by Monotype Imaging in 2006. Both firms have maintained a separate online retail presence to date.

As the result of the 1990s distribution deals between Monotype and FontShop International (FSI), Fonts.com is still one of the very few online distributors that sells fonts from FSI's selectively curated FontFont type library that is otherwise exclusive to the FontShop network. Fonts.com's other advantage over MyFonts is that Fonts.com (as well as Linotype) offers the renowned Monotype and Linotype originals, which MyFonts was forced to discontinue.

In addition, Fonts.com functions as a portal to Monotype Imaging's font services for professional uses, which include the design of bespoke fonts, customization ("localization") for specific language support and platforms, and producing logo fonts.

### Linotype — *linotype.com*

Although the Linotype website is structured differently from Monotype's Fonts.com, its collection of fonts and foundries has become very similar since the merger. While not as heavily populated with designer biographies and foundry presentations as MyFonts, the Linotype website is still quite content-rich. The Font Lounge section includes several sections featuring background information on typographic subjects and specific type designers. Much of this information focuses on Linotype's own font library; independent foundries are not presented on the same level. Linotype markets itself as "the source of the originals" and, in fact, holds the registered trademarks to many of the type world's classics, from Helvetica (the perpetual #1 bestseller) to Caecilia (the default Kindle typeface). This is partly the result of several decades of acquisitions, through which Linotype acquired the rights to many modern classics from now-defunct foundries such as Haas, Stempel, and Deberny & Peignot. Through such acquisitions, Linotype also became home to many modern classics by two of the greatest icons of late-twentieth century type, Hermann Zapf and Adrian Frutiger. Both designers have continued working with Linotype into their eighties, and have produced rigorously updated versions of their best known typefaces in collaboration with the company's Type Director, Akira Kobayashi, a gifted designer in his own right. The Linotype site offers lengthy articles on these designers, as well as articles on single type families, typographic tips and facts by Kobayashi, and more.

### FontShop — *fontshop.com*

FontShop came into being in 1989, when German designer Erik Spiekermann and his wife at the time, Joan Spiekermann, realized there was no designer-oriented, Euro-centered distribution channel for the growing wave of digital typefaces that were being produced. Having established a distribution company based in Berlin, the Spiekermanns found independent partners in several countries, and set up a network of local retailers. This was very useful in pre-web days, when fonts were delivered on physical disks and most orders were taken by telephone or fax, or even over the counter in walk-in shops. Apart from digital fonts by historical foundries like Monotype, Linotype and Berthold, the FontShop network became the first international platform for new, independent foundries including Boston's Font Bureau, California's Emigre, Barcelona's Type-Ø-Tones (which doubled as the Spanish FontShop representative) and pioneering one-person ventures such as Judith Sutcliff's Electric Typographer.

From 1990 onwards FontShop has had its own type library, FontFont, founded by Spiekermann and London designer Neville Brody. FontFont, which spun off into a separate company, FontShop International (FSI), attracted dozens of young designers of cutting-edge fonts, from quality text type to wildly experimental faces, and became a hothouse for new type designing talents. Many designers, having acquired some renown with their early FontFonts, went on to start up their own independent foundry. Fred Smeijers (OurType), Jean-François Porchez (Typofonderie), Rian Hughes (Device), Nick Shinn (ShinnType), Veronika Burian (TypeTogether), Ole Schäfer (Primetype), Luc(as) de Groot (LucasFonts), Morten Rostgaard Olsen and Ole Søndergaard (Fontpartners) all published work at FontFont before venturing out on their own.

With the advent of online shopping, the local FontShops lost some of their reason for being. Those with a firm client base, such as FontShop Germany, Benelux and USA, survived. All operate through a central website, relaying customers to local affiliates where appropriate, so that buyers receive local invoices. In order to keep its retail network attractive, the FontShop network has struck distribution agreements with a growing number of independent foundries. In its selection of partner foundries FontShop is more rigorous than the large supermarket distributors, and can therefore be recommended to those who prefer a somewhat more selective collection to choose from.

**Veer** — *veer.com*

Veer was founded as a one-stop supplier for creative companies and has a strong client base among North American design and advertising agencies. Veer sells stock photography and illustration as well as fonts, and became a division of stock art seller Corbis in 2007. For several years the Veer Ideas section of the website allowed creatives to set up personal profiles, post on community blog the Fat, and read the latest design news on the Skinny blog. The community-oriented sections of Veer Ideas (Portfolio, Groups and Fat) were shelved in mid-2011.

Veer has a relatively small but well-curated selection of quality fonts. Among others, it introduced the sophisticated packaging-oriented script fonts of Alejandro Paul's Sudtipos foundry to the advertising world, having secured an exclusive distribution deal (Sudtipos is now available elsewhere as well). Besides approximately 35 hand-picked type libraries, Veer offers the work of a number of small foundries as part of their Cabinet and Umbrella collections. While individual designers are credited on the Veer website, the fact that these fonts are part of independent type libraries is never mentioned; the fonts are presented as having been designed for Veer's boutique collections.

**Village** — *vllg.com*

Created by Brooklyn based type designer Chester Jenkins, Village is a special case. Under the Village umbrella, Jenkins united a fine choice of microfoundries (foundries, for the most part, operated by a single person) who decided "to go it alone together." In other words, these small foundries were wary of large-scale retailers because they found that their high-quality output was "getting lost in the shuffle," most of which is cheaper than theirs and which is often not nearly as good. Village is the chief outlet for a handful of interesting American, European and New Zealand foundries including Feliciano, Klim, LuxType and Kontour, plus Jenkins's own typefaces.

**Other retail websites**

**Phil's Fonts** — *philsfonts.com*. Known mostly in the USA, Phil's Fonts is one of the best known remaining smaller retail companies for fonts, representing approximately 75 foundries which, for the most part, are available at the larger platforms mentioned above as well. Phil's Fonts also offers other services such as custom font design.

**Faces** — *faces.co.uk*. A UK based web retailer offering fonts, picture fonts and clip art. Owned by Monotype Imaging, it is more designer-oriented than Monotype's Fonts.com and represents almost 200 foundries. The list includes some collections that aren't easy to find elsewhere, such as Jeremy Tankard's sophisticated type library. Faces also offers services such as custom font design.

**FontShop UK** — *www.fontshop.co.uk*. Confusingly, FontShop UK has nothing to do with the international FontShop network; established as a supplier of phototype in 1979, it simply registered its name in the UK before Spiekermann's FontShop did. The site carries almost thirty well-known type collections, as well as some that are hard to find elsewhere, such as the mid-1990s fonts by now-famous Dutch studio Lust.

**FontWorks/Type.co.uk** — *type.co.uk*. The site is part of a group that also includes web shops FontShop.co.uk and Atomictype.co.uk, focusing on the UK market. Type.co.uk is evolved from popular 1990s distributor FontWorks. They carry a number of exclusive collections, such as the Heinemann collection of fonts designed for educational publishing.

**FontHaus** — *fonthaus.com*. Established in 1990 as one of the first font retailers, FontHaus is both a foundry offering fonts by individual designers and a distributor for several dozen microfoundries and larger collections, most of which are also available through other channels.

**TypeTrust** — *typetrust.com*. A digital font distribution partnership founded by designers Silas Dilworth and Neil Summerour. Besides being the outlet for Dilworth's typefaces, it offers a small selection of fonts from other designers and microfoundries, including Okay Type, DSType and Summerour's Positype.

**Hype for Type** — *hypefortype.com*. A new UK based foundry that doubles as a distributor for a small number of microfoundries. Their unique selling point is a collection of exclusive fonts by internationally-renowned graphic designers, illustrators and lettering artists including Alex Trochut, Ariel Di Lisio, Si Scott, Luke Lucas, Jon Burgerman and Non-Format.

**T26** — *t26.com*. Founded in 1994 by maverick graphic designer Carlos Segura, whose participation in Neville Brody's FontShop-produced FUSE project popularized his work in the early 1990s, T26 Digital Type Foundry was long known for its eye-catching merchandise and packaging. When the font trade became purely web-based, Segura adjusted his concept and began including fonts by third parties in his internet offering. While the website makes no clear distinction between fonts that appear under the T26 label and those provided by other foundries, it offers fonts from URW++, Alias, FontFabric and Mark Simonson, among others.

**Ascender Fonts** — *ascenderfonts.com*. As a service provider, Ascender is known for superb technical font services like hinting and webfonts. As a foundry, it offers a growing collection of well-made originals by, mainly, its type director Steve Matteson. It is also the vendor of well-known system fonts originally designed for Microsoft, such as the ClearType collection (Calibri, Corbel, Consolas, et al.). Having recently been acquired by Monotype, Ascender is a retailer as well, carrying just over 40 collections, most of which are also available at other addresses mentioned on these pages.

**YouWorkForThem** — *youworkforthem.com*. Like Veer, YouWorkForThem is a boutique retailer that sells fonts as well as stock images (and, until recently, books as well). The company doubles as a foundry, with its own collection of display fonts.

This list is not complete, and does not include websites that cater exclusively to local markets. More and more typographic companies open their own online stores, and several have chosen to sell other collections in addition to their own work.

### Exclusivity

There is a growing number of foundries that work largely or entirely without representation by third parties. These foundries can be reached via the URLs mentioned in the index.

Most North American type foundries rely heavily on the network of established distributors, but there are some exceptions. Hoefler & Frere-Jones believe in self-distribution, as does the new transatlantic joint venture of Christian Schwartz (USA) and Paul Barnes (UK), Commercial Type.

Several foundries in Britain prefer to work directly with their customers. The Foundry is home to typefaces by David Quay, Freda Sack and Wim Crouwel, which can only be ordered through via e-mail or telephone. Jeremy Tankard, too, likes to be in touch directly with his users; even the fonts ordered through the Faces retail platform are shipped from Tankard's own office. Of the younger foundries, Colophon is one that deals directly with customers on a basis of exclusivity.

The Enschedé Font Foundry in the Netherlands is home to fonts by Gerrit Noordzij, one of the world's most influential teachers of typography, and his son Christoph Noordzij. Its bestsellers are two modern classics by Bram de Does, Lexicon and Trinité. The exclusivity of the collection is underlined by the fact that the fonts can only be obtained directly from the foundry. Another Dutch foundry that is wary of distributors is Dutch Type Library (DTL). As they have a long-standing relationship with German digital pioneers URW++, the URW website is currently the only other place where DTL fonts can be found.

In Germany, veteran type designer Georg Salden has always been one of the type world's great individualists. Refusing to have anything to do with distributors, he has entrusted the maintenance of his exclusive online outlet TypeManufactur to his young colleague Ludwig Übele.

In recent years, several boutique foundries from Switzerland have won the hearts of cutting-edge graphic designers in Europe and elsewhere. True to Swiss tradition (remember, Switzerland is the only non-EU member nation in Western Europe), these foundries generally operate alone, without outside distribution. Optimo, B+P and Grilli Type are among the Swiss foundries featured in this book who work with no outside distributors.

### Featured foundries

What follows is a personal selection of independent foundries active today, based on a loose set of criteria: variety in style and focus, quality, originality, and overall "interestingness." Some established independents whose work can be found in numerous publications were relegated to the Index; the same goes for a few foundries that were on our wishlist but chose not to contribute. In an area so extensive, it is impossible to be complete; but we hope our selection is representative, and we trust it will be useful to some.

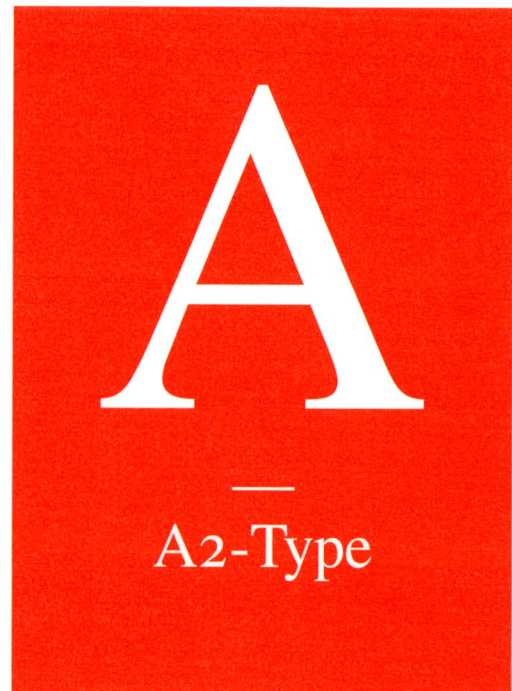

A2-Type

—

Henrik Kubel,
Scott Williams

—

London
Great Britain

—

Since
2010

A2-Type is a new type foundry set up by the London based design studio A2/SW/HK. Established to release and distribute over a decade's worth of specially crafted typefaces the foundry offers access to a unique collection of fonts. Launched in the fall of 2010 with a selection of fifteen font families specially created for print, screen and environment. The studio also provides customizing services.

Info

—Why?
As a graphic design studio we have created many fonts over the years. It's a natural development for us to release these on to the commercial market.

—People on staff
2

—Type designers on staff
2

—Font families
25

—Designers represented
2

—Web shop
a2-type.co.uk

—Distributors
www.playtype.com
www.myfonts.com

—Webfont service
WebINK + MyFonts

—Basic license
£50–£100. See individual typefaces at the website for precise costs.

Typeface selection

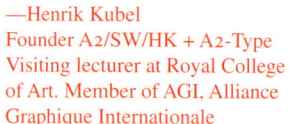

Danmark
London
Monday
New Rail Alphabet
Outsiders
Typewriter

24pt

Biographies

—Henrik Kubel
Founder A2/SW/HK + A2-Type
Visiting lecturer at Royal College of Art. Member of AGI, Alliance Graphique Internationale

—Scott Williams
Founder A2/SW/HK + A2-Type
Member of AGI, Alliance Graphique Internationale

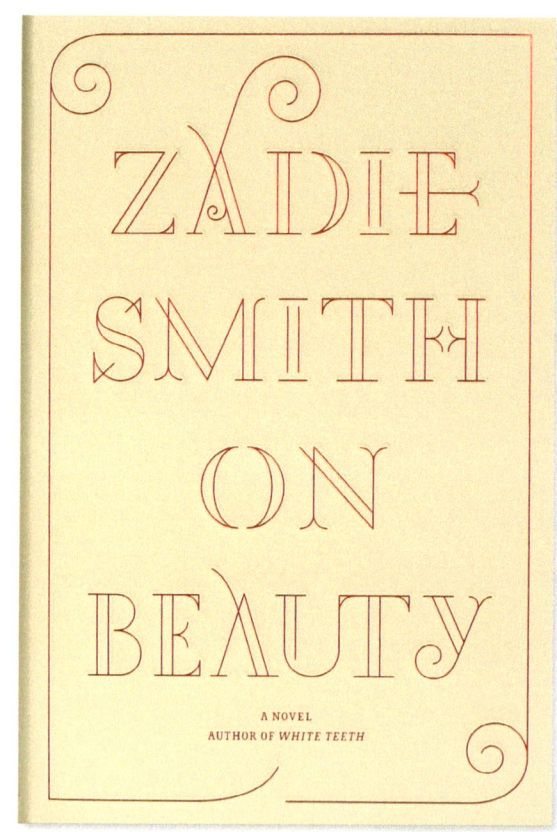

The Zadie typeface was inspired by railings from the Edwardian era at the Royal Army Medical College in London. Originally developed as a headline face for *Vogue UK*, the final version was featured on the cover of Zadie Smith's bestseller *On Beauty*, Penguin Press 2005.

Page 13

The type family A2 Beckett was specially developed for the book covers of the Faber & Faber edition of Samuel Beckett's CompleteWorks. Design by A2/SW/HK.

Foundry A2-Type

Typeface A2 Beckett
Designer Henrik Kubel
Year 2008
Format OpenType

# Sala Beckett

Thin
Regular
Medium
**SemiBold**
**Bold**

Aa Bb Cc Dd Ee Ff Gg Hh Ii Jj Kk Ll Mm Nn Oo Pp Qq Rr Ss Tt Uu Vv Ww Xx Yy Zz 0123456789

---

Typeface Danmark
Designer Henrik Kubel
Year 2008
Format OpenType

# Smørrebrød
# Kierlighed

Regular
Medium
**Bold**

Aa Bb Cc Dd Ee Ff Gg Hh Ii Jj Kk Ll Mm Nn Oo Pp Qq Rr Ss Tt Uu Vv Ww Xx Yy Zz 0123456789

---

Typeface Monday
Designer Henrik Kubel
Year 2003
Format OpenType

# Monday
# Morning
# Milk

Regular

Aa Bb Cc Dd Ee Ff Gg Hh Ii Jj Kk Ll Mm Nn Oo Pp Qq Rr Ss Tt Uu Vv Ww Xx Yy Zz 0123456789

Page 15  Foundry A2-Type

Typeface  New Rail Alphabet
Designer  Margaret Calvert, Henrik Kubel
Year  2009
Format  OpenType

Aa Bb Cc Dd Ee Ff Gg Hh Ii Jj Kk
Ll Mm Nn Oo Pp Qq Rr Ss Tt Uu
Vv Ww Xx Yy Zz
0123456789
—

New Rail Alphabet Off White 22pt
*New Rail Alphabet Off White Italic 22pt*
New Rail Alphabet White 22pt
*New Rail Alphabet White Italic 22pt*
New Rail Alphabet Light 22pt
*New Rail Alphabet Light Italic 22pt*
**New Rail Alphabet Medium 22pt**
*New Rail Alphabet Medium Italic 22pt*
**New Rail Alphabet Bold 22pt**
***New Rail Alphabet Bold Italic 22pt***
**New Rail Alphabet Black 22pt**
***New Rail Alphabet Black Italic 22pt***

---

12/14  New Rail Alphabet Light

The quick brown fox jumps over the lazy dog. Voyez le brick géant que j'examine près du wharf. Zwölf Boxkämpfer jagen Viktor quer über

12/14  New Rail Alphabet Medium

The quick brown fox jumps over the lazy dog. Voyez le brick géant que j'examine près du wharf. Zwölf Boxkämpfer jagen Viktor quer über

12/14  New Rail Alphabet Medium

The quick brown fox jumps over the lazy dog. Voyez le brick géant que j'examine près du wharf. Zwölf Boxkämpfer jagen Viktor quer über

12/14  New Rail Alphabet Bold

The quick brown fox jumps over the lazy dog. Voyez le brick géant que j'examine près du wharf. Zwölf Boxkämpfer jagen Viktor quer über den großen Sylter Deich. El veloz murciélago hindú comía feliz cardillo y kiwi. La cigüeña tocaba el saxofón detrás del palenque de pajaatur? Rissimo lorereped ex es

---

9/12  New Rail Alphabet White

The quick brown fox jumps over the lazy dog. Voyez le brick géant que j'examine près du wharf. Zwölf Boxkämpfer jagen Viktor quer über den großen Sylter Deich. El veloz murciélago hindú comía feliz cardillo y kiwi. La cigüeña

9/12  New Rail Alphabet Light

The quick brown fox jumps over the lazy dog. Voyez le brick géant que j'examine près du wharf. Zwölf Boxkämpfer jagen Viktor quer über den großen Sylter Deich. El veloz murciélago hindú comía feliz cardillo y kiwi. La

9/12  New Rail Alphabet Medium

The quick brown fox jumps over the lazy dog. Voyez le brick géant que j'examine près du wharf. Zwölf Boxkämpfer jagen Viktor quer über den großen Sylter Deich. El veloz murciélago hindú comía feliz cardillo y kiwi. La

9/12  New Rail Alphabet Bold

The quick brown fox jumps over the lazy dog. Voyez le brick géant que j'examine près du wharf. Zwölf Boxkämpfer jagen Viktor quer über den großen Sylter Deich. El veloz murciélago hindú comía feliz cardillo y kiwi. La cigüeña tocaba el saxofón detrás del palenque de pajaatur? Rissimo lorereped ex es solore lab id molorro in rempore icabore rehenetur aliam aut voles audae dem quam, secum eum facesequae consequ aepudam

---

7/10  New Rail Alphabet White

The quick brown fox jumps over the lazy dog. Voyez le brick géant que j'examine près du wharf. Zwölf Boxkämpfer jagen Viktor quer über den großen Sylter Deich. El veloz murciélago hindú comía feliz cardillo y kiwi. La cigüeña tocaba el saxofón detrás del palenque de pajaatur? Rissimo lorereped ex es solore lab id molorro in rempore icabore rehenetur aliam aut

7/10  New Rail Alphabet Light

The quick brown fox jumps over the lazy dog. Voyez le brick géant que j'examine près du wharf. Zwölf Boxkämpfer jagen Viktor quer über den großen Sylter Deich. El veloz murciélago hindú comía feliz cardillo y kiwi. La cigüeña tocaba el saxofón detrás del palenque de pajaatur? Rissimo lorereped ex es solore lab id molorro in rempore icabore rehenetur

7/10  New Rail Alphabet Medium

The quick brown fox jumps over the lazy dog. Voyez le brick géant que j'examine près du wharf. Zwölf Boxkämpfer jagen Viktor quer über den großen Sylter Deich. El veloz murciélago hindú comía feliz cardillo y kiwi. La cigüeña tocaba el saxofón detrás del palenque de pajaatur? Rissimo lorereped ex es solore lab id molorro in rempore icabore rehenetur aliam

7/10  New Rail Alphabet Bold

The quick brown fox jumps over the lazy dog. Voyez le brick géant que j'examine près du wharf. Zwölf Boxkämpfer jagen Viktor quer über den großen Sylter Deich. El veloz murciélago hindú comía feliz cardillo y kiwi. La cigüeña tocaba el saxofón detrás del palenque de pajaatur? Rissimo lorereped ex es solore lab id molorro in rempore icabore rehenetur aliam aut voles audae dem quam, secum eum facesequae consequ aepudam quia voluptiur repel in et faccustibus, nonsenis aut quisqui rero mi, ipiet lam ant ut maio et hil molupta tustis atatur, consedi tasimol orerem aut volor andipsapis sit, illaut volore officatus alicae dusdaec tatecte cearum qui accatibus restiore nulpa secaerfe-

Page 16

Foundry A2-Type

Typeface Outsiders
Designer Henrik Kubel
Year 2007
Format OpenType

Aa Bb Cc Dd Ee Ff Gg Hh Ii Jj
Kk Ll Mm Nn Oo Pp Qq Rr Ss
Tt Uu Vv Ww Xx Yy Zz
0123456789
—

Outsiders Light 24pt
*Outsiders Light Italic 24pt*
Outsiders Regular 24pt
*Outsiders Italic 24pt*
Outsiders Medium 24pt
*Outsiders Medium Italic 24pt*
**Outsiders SemiBold 24pt**
***Outsiders SemiBold Italic 24pt***
**Outsiders Bold 24pt**
***Outsiders Bold Italic 24pt***

---

12/14 Outsiders Light

The quick brown fox jumps over the lazy dog. Voyez le brick géant que j'examine près du wharf. Zwölf Boxkämpfer jagen Viktor

9/12 Outsiders Light

The quick brown fox jumps over the lazy dog. Voyez le brick géant que j'examine près du wharf. Zwölf Boxkämpfer jagen Viktor quer über den großen Sylter Deich. El veloz murciélago hindú comía feliz cardillo y kiwi. La

7/10 Outsiders Light

The quick brown fox jumps over the lazy dog. Voyez le brick géant que j'examine près du wharf. Zwölf Boxkämpfer jagen Viktor quer über den großen Sylter Deich. El veloz murciélago hindú comía feliz cardillo y kiwi. La cigüeña tocaba el saxofón detrás del palenque de pajaatur? Rissimo lorereped ex es solore lab id molorro in rempore icabore

---

12/14 Outsiders Medium

The quick brown fox jumps over the lazy dog. Voyez le brick géant que j'examine près du wharf. Zwölf Boxkämpfer jagen Vik-

9/12 Outsiders Medium

The quick brown fox jumps over the lazy dog. Voyez le brick géant que j'examine près du wharf. Zwölf Boxkämpfer jagen Viktor quer über den großen Sylter Deich. El veloz murciélago hindú comía feliz cardillo y kiwi. La

7/10 Outsiders Medium

The quick brown fox jumps over the lazy dog. Voyez le brick géant que j'examine près du wharf. Zwölf Boxkämpfer jagen Viktor quer über den großen Sylter Deich. El veloz murciélago hindú comía feliz cardillo y kiwi. La cigüeña tocaba el saxofón detrás del palenque de pajaatur? Rissimo lorereped ex es solore lab id molorro in rempore

---

12/14 Outsiders SemiBold

The quick brown fox jumps over the lazy dog. Voyez le brick géant que j'examine près du wharf. Zwölf Boxkämpfer jagen Vik-

9/12 Outsiders SemiBold

The quick brown fox jumps over the lazy dog. Voyez le brick géant que j'examine près du wharf. Zwölf Boxkämpfer jagen Viktor quer über den großen Sylter Deich. El veloz murciélago hindú comía feliz cardillo y kiwi. La

7/10 Outsiders SemiBold

The quick brown fox jumps over the lazy dog. Voyez le brick géant que j'examine près du wharf. Zwölf Boxkämpfer jagen Viktor quer über den großen Sylter Deich. El veloz murciélago hindú comía feliz cardillo y kiwi. La cigüeña tocaba el saxofón detrás del palenque de pajaatur? Rissimo lorereped ex es solore lab id molorro in rempore

---

12/14 Outsiders Bold

The quick brown fox jumps over the lazy dog. Voyez le brick géant que j'examine près du wharf. Zwölf Boxkämpfer jagen Viktor quer über den großen Sylter Deich. El veloz murciélago hindú comía feliz cardillo y kiwi. La cigüeña tocaba el saxofón detrás del palenque de pajaatur? Rissimo lo-

9/12 Outsiders Bold

The quick brown fox jumps over the lazy dog. Voyez le brick géant que j'examine près du wharf. Zwölf Boxkämpfer jagen Viktor quer über den großen Sylter Deich. El veloz murciélago hindú comía feliz cardillo y kiwi. La cigüeña tocaba el saxofón detrás del palenque de pajaatur? Rissimo lorereped ex es solore lab id molorro in rempore icabore rehenetur aliam aut voles audae dem quam, secum eum facesequae consequ aepudam

7/10 Outsiders Bold

The quick brown fox jumps over the lazy dog. Voyez le brick géant que j'examine près du wharf. Zwölf Boxkämpfer jagen Viktor quer über den großen Sylter Deich. El veloz murciélago hindú comía feliz cardillo y kiwi. La cigüeña tocaba el saxofón detrás del palenque de pajaatur? Rissimo lorereped ex es solore lab id molorro in rempore icabore rehenetur aliam aut voles audae dem quam, secum eum facesequae consequ aepudam quia voluptiur repel in et faccustibus, nonsenis aut quisqui rero mi, ipiet lam ant ut maio et hil molupta tustis atatur, consedi tasimol orerem aut volor andipsapis sit, illaut volore officatus alicae dusdaec tatecte cearum qui accatibus restiore nulpa

Page 17  
Foundry  A2-Type

Typeface  London  Year  2010
Designer  Henrik Kubel  Format  OpenType

London Light 20pt
*London Light Italic 20pt*
London Regular 20pt
*London Italic 20pt*
**London Medium 20pt**
***London Medium Italic 20pt***
**London SemiBold 20pt**
***London SemiBold Italic 20pt***
**London Bold 20pt**
***London Bold Italic 20pt***

Aa Bb Cc Dd Ee Ff Gg Hh Ii Jj Kk Ll Mm Nn Oo Pp Qq Rr Ss Tt Uu Vv Ww Xx Yy Zz
0123456789
—

12/14  London Light
The quick brown fox jumps over the lazy dog. Voyez le brick géant que j'examine près du wharf. Zwölf Boxkämpfer jagen Viktor quer über

9/12  London Light
The quick brown fox jumps over the lazy dog. Voyez le brick géant que j'examine près du wharf. Zwölf Boxkämpfer jagen Viktor quer über den großen Sylter Deich. El veloz murciélago hindú comía feliz cardillo y kiwi. La

7/10  London Light
The quick brown fox jumps over the lazy dog. Voyez le brick géant que j'examine près du wharf. Zwölf Boxkämpfer jagen Viktor quer über den großen Sylter Deich. El veloz murciélago hindú comía feliz cardillo y kiwi. La cigüeña tocaba el saxofón detrás del palenque de pajaatur? Rissimo lorereped ex es solore lab id molorro in rempore icabore rehenetur aliam

Typeface  Typewriter  Year  2000
Designer  Henrik Kubel  Format  OpenType

Typewriter Regular 24pt
**Typewriter Medium 24pt**
**Typewriter Bold 24pt**

Aa Bb Cc Dd Ee Ff Gg Hh Ii Jj Kk Ll Mm Nn Oo Pp Qq Rr Ss Tt Uu Vv Ww Xx Yy Zz
0123456789
—

9/12  Typewriter Regular
The quick brown fox jumps over the lazy dog. Voyez le brick géant que j'examine près du wharf. Zwölf Boxkämpfer jagen Viktor quer über den großen Sylter Deich. El veloz murciélago hindú comía feliz car-

9/12  Typewriter Medium
The quick brown fox jumps over the lazy dog. Voyez le brick géant que j'examine près du wharf. Zwölf Boxkämpfer jagen Viktor quer über den großen Sylter Deich. El veloz murciélago hindú comía feliz cardillo y kiwi. La cigüeña tocaba el saxofón detrás del palenque de pajaatur? Rissimo

7/10  Typewriter Regular
The quick brown fox jumps over the lazy dog. Voyez le brick géant que j'examine près du wharf. Zwölf Boxkämpfer jagen Viktor quer über den großen Sylter Deich. El veloz murciélago hindú comía feliz cardillo y kiwi. La cigüeña tocaba el saxofón detrás del palenque de pajaatur? Rissimo lorereped ex es solore lab id molorro

7/10  Typewriter Medium
The quick brown fox jumps over the lazy dog. Voyez le brick géant que j'examine près du wharf. Zwölf Boxkämpfer jagen Viktor quer über den großen Sylter Deich. El veloz murciélago hindú comía feliz cardillo y kiwi. La cigüeña tocaba el saxofón detrás del palenque de pajaatur? Rissimo lorereped ex es solore lab id molorro in rempore icabore rehenetur aliam aut voles audae dem quam, secum eum facesequae consequ aepu-

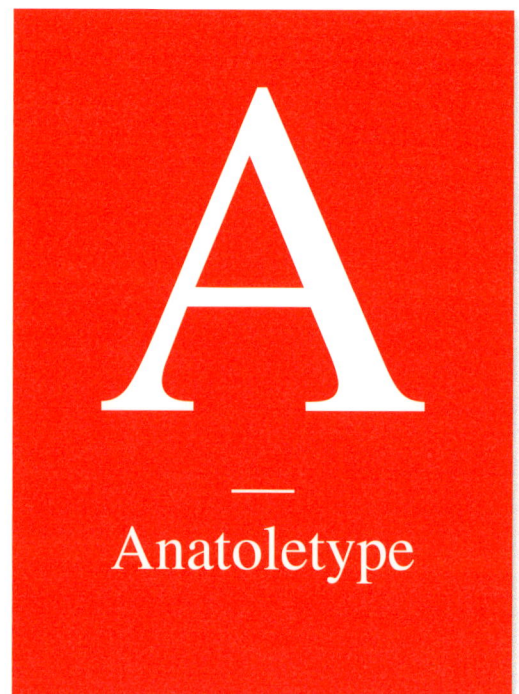

# Anatoletype

Elena Albertoni, Pascal Duez

Berlin, Germany

Since 2005

Based in Berlin, Anatoletype was founded in 2005 by Elena Albertoni (Italian) and Pascal Duez (French). They describe themselves as "enthusiastic collectors of many kinds of vernacular type and image-making." They enjoy experimenting with manual techniques such as drawing, handwriting, calligraphy and silkscreen. In the digital realm, they explore the possibilities of OpenType to give form to their ideas and make their script and handwriting fonts come alive with natural spontaneity.

## Info

—Why?
Initially our main goal was to create an online collaborative platform to publish our work and do research related to type design and type in public environments (urban epigraphy). Today our microfoundry combines lettering and handwriting expertise with the highest quality in font development and OpenType programming to offer a wide range of customized services as well as a distinctive collection of quality typefaces.

—People on staff
2

—Type designers on staff
1

—Font families
10

—Designers represented
1

—Web shop
Not yet.

—Distributors
MyFonts, FontHaus, Phil's Fonts.

—Webfont service
Typekit, MyFonts

—Basic license
The average price for a single weight is $25, the basic license covers up to 5 computers.

Typeface selection

**Acuta**
**DejaRip**
*Dolce*
*Dyna*
Scritta Nuova

24pt

## People

—Elena Albertoni is an independent type designer living in Berlin. After a thorough education in graphic and type design in Amiens and Paris, France, Italian-born Elena joined LucasFonts to perfect her type designing and programming skills. She is especially interested in the way OpenType technology can be used to enrich typographic performance. Among her own typefaces are the spirited script face Dolce and the Gregoria font for the notation of Gregorian chant, both of which won her awards in the TDC type design competition.

—Pascal Duez is a French designer and web developer. He co-founded Anatoletype with Elena in 2005 and currently runs the DZLV web design studio based in Paris, Brussels and Berlin.

Happy new type in 2010!

Page 19

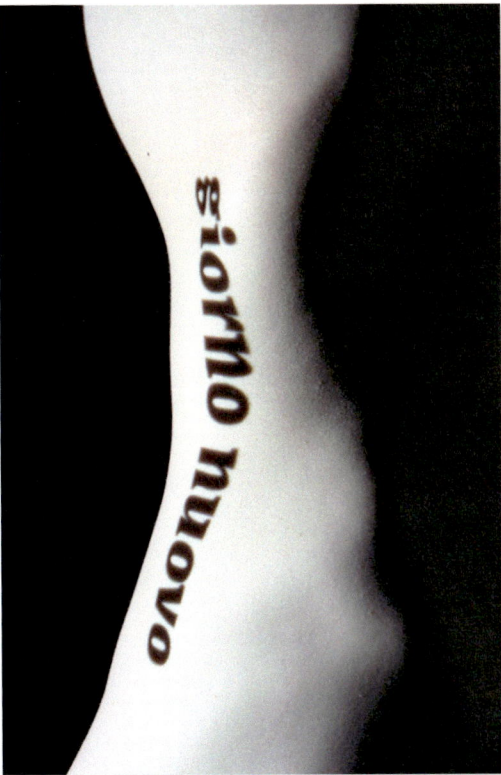

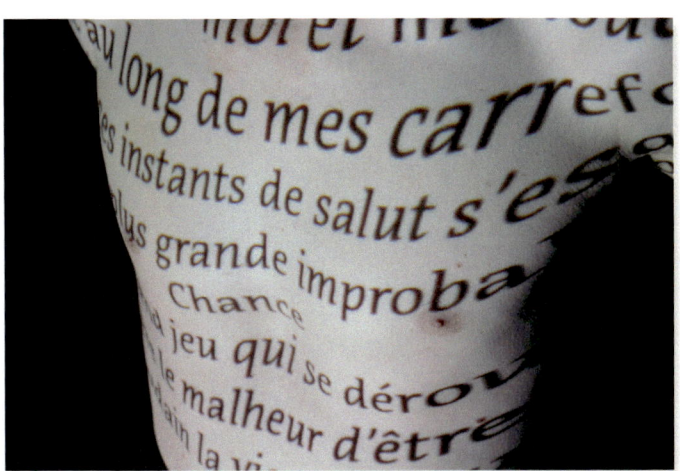

**Opposite page**
New Year's card designed with Dyna.

**Above**
Poster for film event designed with Acuta.

**Left, right**
"Tattoos" made with Acuta.

Foundry  Anatoletype

---

Typeface  Dolce  Year  2004
Designer  Elena Albertoni  Format  OpenType

# Genova cenone

Thin
Regular
Medium
**Bold**
**Black**

Aa Bb Cc Dd Ee Ff Gg Hh Ii Jj Kk Ll Mm
Nn Oo Pp Qq Rr Ss Tt Uu Vv Ww Xx Yy Zz
0123456789

---

Typeface  Scritta Nuova  Year  2011
Designer  Elena Albertoni  Format  OpenType

# Perfetta scrittrice

Regular

Aa Bb Cc Dd Ee Ff Gg Hh Ii Jj Kk Ll Mm
Nn Oo Pp Qq Rr Ss Tt Uu Vv Ww Xx Yy Zz
0123456789

---

Typeface  Dyna  Year  2003
Designer  Elena Albertoni  Format  OpenType

# Parapluie de Monsieur von Trapp

Regular

Aa Bb Cc Dd Ee Ff Gg Hh Ii Jj Kk Ll
Mm Nn Oo Pp Qq Rr Ss Tt Uu Vv Ww
Xx Yy Zz 0123456789

Page 21                Foundry   Anatoletype

---

Typeface   Acuta                Year      2010
Designer   Elena Albertoni      Format    OpenType

Aa Bb Cc Dd Ee Ff Gg Hh Ii Jj Kk
Ll Mm Nn Oo Pp Qq Rr Ss Tt Uu
Vv Ww Xx Yy Zz
0123456789
—

Acuta Thin 20pt
*Acuta Thin Italic 20pt*
Acuta Light 20pt
*Acuta Light Italic 20pt*
Acuta Book 20pt
*Acuta Book Italic 20pt*
Acuta Medium 20pt
*Acuta Medium Italic 20pt*
**Acuta Bold 20pt**
***Acuta Bold Italic 20pt***
**Acuta Black 20pt**
***Acuta Black Italic 20pt***
**Acuta Fat 20pt**
***Acuta Fat Italic 20pt***

9/12   Acuta Medium

The quick brown fox jumps over the lazy dog. Voyez le brick géant que j'examine près du wharf. Zwölf Boxkämpfer jagen Viktor quer über den großen Sylter Deich. El veloz murciélago

9/12   Acuta Medium

The quick brown fox jumps over the lazy dog. Voyez le brick géant que j'examine près du wharf. Zwölf Boxkämpfer jagen Viktor quer über den großen Sylter Deich. El veloz murciélago hindú comía feliz cardillo y kiwi. La cigüeña tocaba el saxofón detrás del palenque de pajaatur? Rissimo lorereped ex es solore lab id molorro in rempore icabore

---

Typeface   DejaRip              Year      2009
Designer   Elena Albertoni      Format    OpenType

Aa Bb Cc Dd Ee Ff Gg Hh Ii Jj Kk
Ll Mm Nn Oo Pp Qq Rr Ss Tt Uu
Vv Ww Xx Yy Zz
0123456789
—

DejaRip Regular 20pt
*DejaRip Italic 20pt*
DejaRip Medium 20pt
*DejaRip Medium Italic 20pt*
**DejaRip Bold 20pt**
***DejaRip Bold Italic 20pt***

9/12   DejaRip Medium

The quick brown fox jumps over the lazy dog. Voyez le brick géant que j'examine près du wharf. Zwölf Boxkämpfer jagen Viktor quer über den großen Sylter Deich. El veloz murciélago hindú comía feliz cardillo y kiwi. La cigüeña tocaba el saxofón detrás del palenque de pajaatur? Rissimo lorereped ex es solore lab id molorro in rempore icabore rehenetur aliam aut voles audae dem quam, secum eum facesequae consequ aepudam quia voluptiur

7/10   DejaRip Medium

The quick brown fox jumps over the lazy dog. Voyez le brick géant que j'examine près du wharf. Zwölf Boxkämpfer jagen Viktor quer über den großen Sylter Deich. El veloz murciélago hindú comía feliz cardillo y kiwi. La cigüeña tocaba el saxofón detrás del palenque de pajaatur? Rissimo lorereped ex es solore lab id molorro in rempore icabore rehenetur aliam aut voles audae dem quam, secum eum facesequae consequ aepudam quia voluptiur repel in et faccustibus, nonsenis aut quisqui rero mi, ipiet lam ant ut maio et hil molupta tustis atatur, consedi tasimol orerem aut volor andipsapis sit, illaut volore officatus alicae dusdaec tatecte cearum qui accatibus restiore nulpa secaerferum, nus dolenim in et quoddita que

André Baldinger

—

André Baldinger

—

Paris, France

—

Since 2001

André Baldinger is a Swiss graphic designer and typographer based in Paris. In 1995 he opened his own studio, where he mostly works on projects related to the cultural sphere and its institutions, as well as alternative projects, stage sets and three-dimensional works. Baldinger has created a library of new typefaces, including a wide range of bespoke fonts for specific projects.

Info

—Why?
Independence in esthetics, innovation, pricing and distribution

—People on staff
1–2

—Type designers on staff
1

—Font families
5

—Designers represented
1

—Web shop
andrebaldinger.com

—Distributors
Self-distributed

—Webfont service
Webfont service will be available soon

—Basic license
Basic license (one style) starts at $90 for one to two computers.

People

—André Baldinger
Swiss born, Baldinger studied typography and visual communication in Zurich and type design at the Atélier National de Création Typographique (ANCT) in Paris. After his graduation in 1994, he founded his own design studio. Type design is part of his professional practice; typefaces include Newut (New universal typeface), BDot, BLine, BaldingerPro, Eiffel and CitéInter. His work is regularly published, exhibited and awarded and can be found in the collections of the Design Museum Zurich, the National Library of France, the Toyama Museum of contemporary Arts in Japan and the Klingspor Museum Offenbach. In 2005, the Swiss National Bank invited him to take part in the competition for the design of the new Swiss banknotes.

Since 2006 he has been teaching typography and type design at the École Nationale Supérieure des Arts Décoratifs in Paris (ENSAD) and the Zürcher Hochschule der Künste in Zurich. He co-heads the type design unit of the Creation and Innovation Research Centre (EnsadLab) at ENSAD.

Typeface selection

AB BDot
AB BLine
AB Eiffel
AB Baldinger Pro

24pt

The artist's book *Toit du Monde* was designed using AB NewutClassic and Plain. Design and photos by André Baldinger.

Page 23

**Above**
Roof lettering for an urban train station in Lausanne. B-Dot is a pixel font based on the esthetics of classic typeface design, lending it increased legibility while maintaining the look of a matrix font.

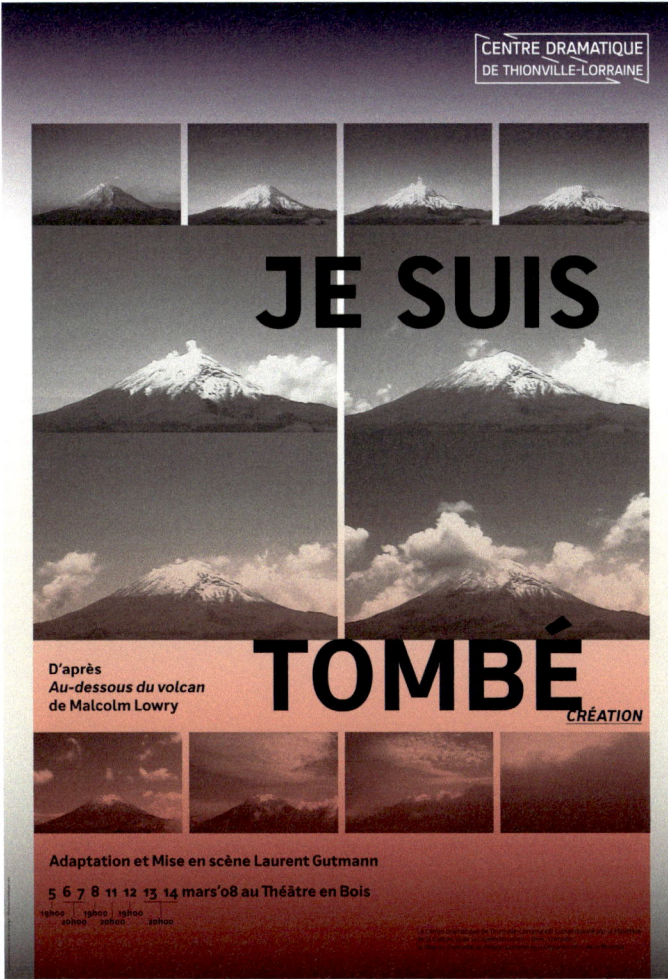

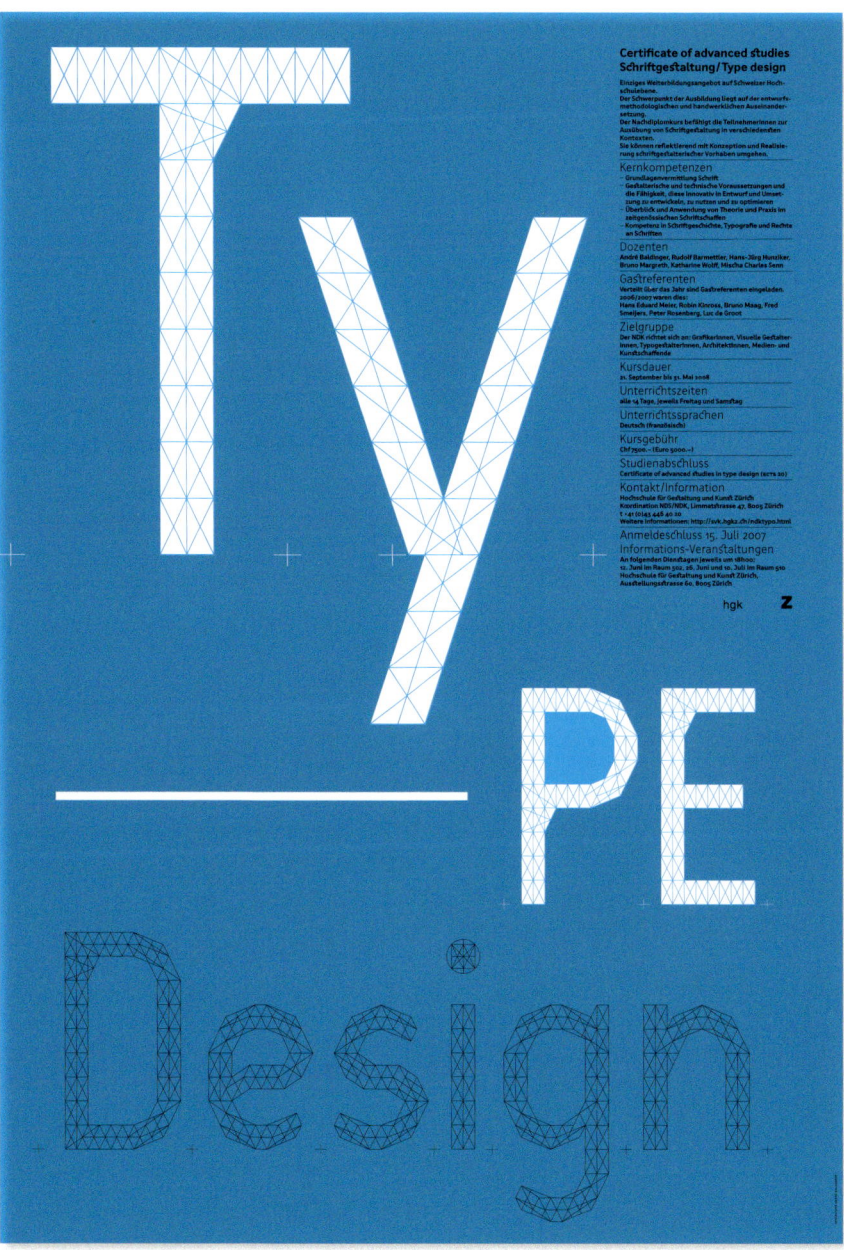

**Above and right**
Theater posters designed by André Baldinger with the typeface Baldinger Pro; two results of a long-standing working relationship with CDNTL – Centre Dramatique National de Thionville-Lorraine, France.

**Above**
Poster to promote the advanced type design studies at the Zürcher Hochschule der Künste (University of the Arts, Zurich), where Baldinger teaches. Designed by André Baldinger using the Eiffel typeface.

Typeface AB Eiffel
Designer André Baldinger
Foundry André Baldinger
Year 2004–2011
Format OpenType

Regular
**Bold**
Niveau 2

Aa Bb Cc Dd Ee Ff Gg Hh Ii Jj Kk Ll Mm
Nn Oo Pp Qq Rr Ss Tt Uu Vv Ww Xx Yy
Zz 0123456789

**Viaduc de Garabit**

Statue of Liberty

Page 25

Foundry  André Baldinger

Typeface  AB BDot, BLine
Designer  André Baldinger

Year    First Version 2000
        New Version 2011
Format  OpenType

Aa Bb Cc Dd Ee Ff Gg Hh Ii Jj
Kk Ll Mm Nn Oo Pp Qq Rr Ss Tt
Uu Vv Ww Xx Yy Zz
0123456789
—

AB BDot UltraThin 18pt
AB BDot Thin 18pt
AB BDot Light 18pt
AB BDot Regular 18pt
AB BDot Bold 18pt

AB BLine UltraThin 18pt
AB BLine Thin 18pt
AB BLine Light 18pt
AB BLine Regular 18pt
AB BLine Bold 18pt

9/12  AB BLine Regular

The quick brown fox jumps over the lazy dog. Voyez le brick géant que j'examine près du wharf. Zwölf Boxkämpfer jagen Viktor quer über den großen Sylter Deich. El veloz murciélago hindú comía feliz cardillo y kiwi. La cigüeña tocaba el saxofón detrás del palenque de pajaatur? Rissimo lorereped ex es solore lab id molorro in rempo-

7/10  AB BLine Regular

The quick brown fox jumps over the lazy dog. Voyez le brick géant que j'examine près du wharf. Zwölf Boxkämpfer jagen Viktor quer über den großen Sylter Deich. El veloz murciélago hindú comía feliz cardillo y kiwi. La cigüeña tocaba el saxofón detrás del palenque de pajaatur? Rissimo lorereped ex es solore lab id molorro in rempore icabore rehenetur aliam aut voles audae dem quam, secum eum facesequae consequ aepudam quia voluptiur repel in et faccustibus, nonsenis aut quisqui rero mi, ipiet lam ant ut maio et hil molupta tustis

Typeface  AB Baldinger Pro
Designer  André Baldinger

Year    2010
Format  OpenType

Aa Bb Cc Dd Ee Ff Gg Hh Ii Jj Kk
Ll Mm Nn Oo Pp Qq Rr Ss Tt Uu
Vv Ww Xx Yy Zz
0123456789
—

AB Baldinger Pro Hairline 24pt
AB Baldinger Pro Thin 24pt
AB Baldinger Pro Light 24pt
AB Baldinger Pro Book 24pt
AB Baldinger Pro Bold 24pt
AB Baldinger Pro Heavy 24pt

12/14  AB Baldinger Pro Book

The quick brown fox jumps over the lazy dog. Voyez le brick géant que j'examine près du wharf. Zwölf Boxkämpfer jagen Viktor quer über den großen Sylter Deich. El veloz murciélago hindú comía feliz cardillo y kiwi. La cigüeña tocaba el saxofón detrás del palenque de pajaatur? Rissimo lorereped ex es

9/12  AB Baldinger Pro Book

The quick brown fox jumps over the lazy dog. Voyez le brick géant que j'examine près du wharf. Zwölf Boxkämpfer jagen Viktor quer über den großen Sylter Deich. El veloz murciélago hindú comía feliz cardillo y kiwi. La cigüeña tocaba el saxofón detrás del palenque de pajaatur? Rissimo lorereped ex es solore lab id molorro in rempore icabore rehenetur aliam aut voles audae dem quam, secum eum facesequae consequ aepudam quia voluptiur

7/10  AB Baldinger Pro Book

The quick brown fox jumps over the lazy dog. Voyez le brick géant que j'examine près du wharf. Zwölf Boxkämpfer jagen Viktor quer über den großen Sylter Deich. El veloz murciélago hindú comía feliz cardillo y kiwi. La cigüeña tocaba el saxofón detrás del palenque de pajaatur? Rissimo lorereped ex es solore lab id molorro in rempore icabore rehenetur aliam aut voles audae dem quam, secum eum facesequae consequ aepudam quia voluptiur repel in et faccustibus, nonsenis aut quisqui rero mi, ipiet lam ant ut maio et hil molupta tustis atatur, consedi tasimol orerem aut volor andipsapis sit, illaut volore officatus alicae dusdaec tatecte cearum qui accatibus restiore nulpa secaerferum, nus do-

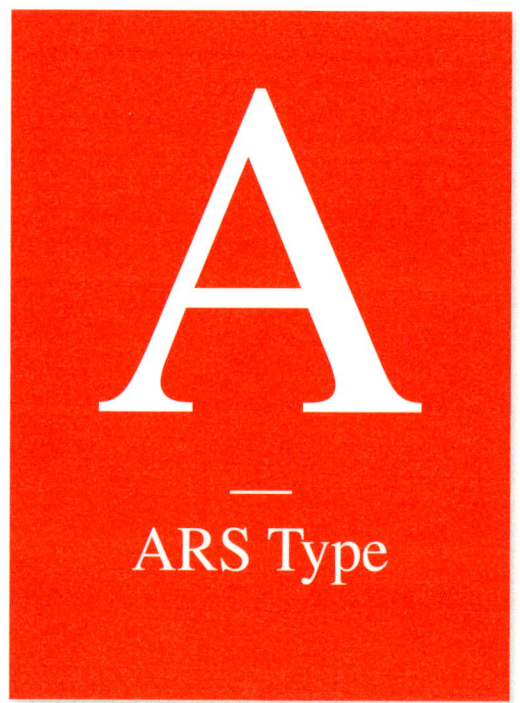

ARS Type

—

Angus R. Shamal

—

Amsterdam, Netherlands

—

Since 1994

Info

—Why?
As a graphic designer starting out in 1993, I didn't have much access to other fonts, so I started designing my own. Back then I didn't have a computer so at first everything was done by hand. The foundry began out of an increasing interest in and demand for these fonts. By then, the love of type design had already become deeply implanted.

—People on staff
Officially 1

—Type designers on staff
1

—Font families (retail)
9

—Designers represented
1

—Web shop
arstype.nl

—Distributors
FontShop

—Webfont service
TypeKit will be the webfont hosting service provider. Self-hosting licenses exclusively from ARS Type.

—Basic license
From 40 € (single font families) to 435 € (full ARS Maquette Pro family)

People

—Angus R. Shamal (1972) is a multidisciplinary creative based in Amsterdam, Netherlands. With long-time experience in graphic design and advertising, Angus decided to shift his main interest to photography in 2007, working on editorial and advertising commissions as well as his own artistic projects. He has been running his one-person type foundry ARS Type since 1994, designing and publishing his own original typefaces. His type designs are always created from a designer/user's perspective, in terms of usability in a modern environment. In early 2011, ARS Type launched its new website with its own online shop.

Typeface selection

Founded in 1994 by photographer and graphic designer Angus R. Shamal, ARS Type is an independent type foundry based in Amsterdam. Having made his first typefaces for personal use, Shamal develop a strong interest in form and legibility, leading to the production of a versatile library of high-quality text and display faces. In addition to the retail library, ARS Type specializes in developing custom type solutions for a variety of applications.

ARS Descendiaan Roman
ARS Maquette Pro
ars novelty
ARS Region
ARS Twenty

**Top**
Samples of ARS Novelty.

**Bottom**
Teaser poster for ARS Parallax.
Designed by Angus R. Shamal.

24pt

Page 27

We desgined Omagiu and we'r not so praud of it. It's nowthing special yet, but it's okeish. Aniway there is more to come.

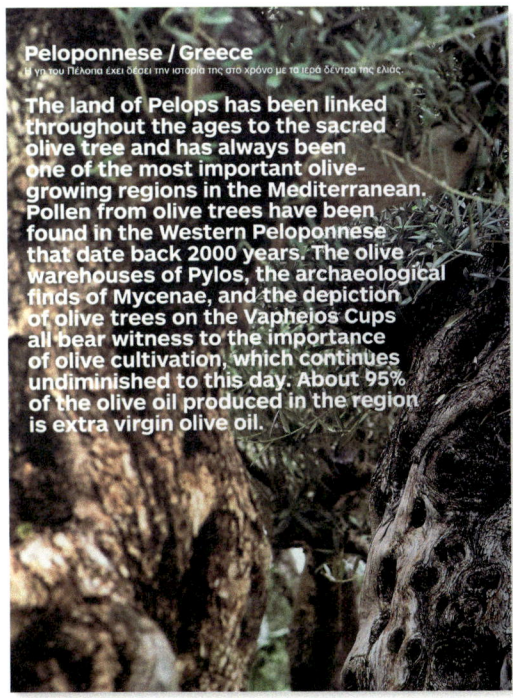

Italy
Italic
Itslike
Italice
Italick

*Italics*
ARS Maquette Pro available from ARS Type®   arstype.nl

98765432110
zyxwvutsrqp
onmlkjihgfed
cba€+£:;>?!&
ZYXWVUTS
RQPONMLK
JIHGFEDCB
ARS
Maquette
Display

**Left, top**
It's Everyday™ print ad in Omagiu#2. 2005.

**Left, bottom**
Page from a brochure for 'Greek Extra Virgin Olive Oil', using ARS Maquette Pro. Mouse Graphics 2011.

**Right**
Promotional posters for ARS Maquette Pro. 2010.

| Foundry | ARS Type |

| Typeface | ARS Region | Year | 2002 |
| Designer | Angus R. Shamal | Format | OpenType |

# Regional Trainee

Regular
**Bold**

Aa Bb Cc Dd Ee Ff Gg Hh Ii
Jj Kk Ll Mm Nn Oo Pp Qq
Rr Ss Tt Uu Vv Ww Xx Yy Zz
0123456789

| Typeface | ARS Novelty | Year | 2010 |
| Designer | Angus R. Shamal | Format | OpenType |

# moon novelty

**bold**

aa bb cc dd ee ff gg hh ii jj kk
ll mm nn oo pp qq rr ss tt uu
vv ww xx yy zz 0123456789

| Typeface | ARS Twenty | Year | 2001 |
| Designer | Angus R. Shamal | Format | OpenType |

# Twenty Five Ago

Light
Medium
**Bold**

Aa Bb Cc Dd Ee Ff Gg Hh Ii
Jj Kk Ll Mm Nn Oo Pp Qq Rr
Ss Tt Uu Vv Ww Xx Yy Zz
0123456789

Page 29

Foundry ARS Type

Typeface ARS Descendiaan Roman
Designer Angus R. Shamal
Year 1998
Format OpenType

ARS Descendiaan Roman 18pt
*ARS Descendiaan Roman Italic 18pt*
**ARS Descendiaan Roman Bold 18pt**

Aa Bb Cc Dd Ee Ff Gg Hh Ii Jj
Kk Ll Mm Nn Oo Pp Qq Rr Ss
Tt Uu Vv Ww Xx Yy Zz
0123456789
—

9/12 ARS Descendiaan Roman

The quick brown fox jumps over the *lazy dog*. Voyez le brick géant que j'examine près du wharf. Zwölf Boxkämpfer jagen Viktor quer über den großen *Sylter Deich*. El veloz murciélago hindú comía feliz cardillo y kiwi. La cigüeña tocaba el saxofón detrás del palenque de pajaatur? Rissimo lorereped ex es solore lab id molorro in rempore icabore rehenetur

7/10 ARS Descendiaan Roman

The quick brown fox jumps over the *lazy dog*. Voyez le brick géant que j'examine près du wharf. Zwölf Boxkämpfer jagen Viktor quer über den großen *Sylter Deich*. El veloz murciélago hindú comía feliz cardillo y kiwi. La cigüeña tocaba el saxofón detrás del palenque de pajaatur? Rissimo lorereped ex es solore lab id molorro in rempore icabore rehenetur aliam aut voles audae dem quam, secum eum facesequae consequ aepudam quia voluptiur repel in et faccustibus, nonsenis aut quisqui rero mi, ipiet lam ant ut maio et hil molupta tustis atatur, consedi tasimol orerem

Typeface ARS Maquette Pro
Designer Angus R. Shamal
Year 2010
Format OpenType

ARS Maquette Pro Light 18pt
*ARS Maquette Pro Light Italic 18pt*
ARS Maquette Pro Regular 18pt
*ARS Maquette Pro Regular Italic 18pt*
ARS Maquette Pro Medium 18pt
*ARS Maquette Pro Medium Italic 18pt*
**ARS Maquette Pro Bold 18pt**
***ARS Maquette Pro Bold Italic 18pt***
**ARS Maquette Pro Black 18pt**
***ARS Maquette Pro Black Italic 18pt***

Aa Bb Cc Dd Ee Ff Gg Hh Ii Jj
Kk Ll Mm Nn Oo Pp Qq Rr Ss
Tt Uu Vv Ww Xx Yy Zz
0123456789
—

12/14 ARS Maquette Pro Regular

The quick brown fox jumps over the lazy dog. Voyez le brick géant que j'examine près du wharf. Zwölf Boxkämpfer jagen Viktor quer über den großen Sylter Deich. El veloz murciélago hindú comía feliz cardillo y kiwi. La cigüeña tocaba el saxofón detrás del palenque de pajaatur? Ris-

9/12 ARS Maquette Pro Regular

The quick brown fox jumps over the lazy dog. Voyez le brick géant que j'examine près du wharf. Zwölf Boxkämpfer jagen Viktor quer über den großen Sylter Deich. El veloz murciélago hindú comía feliz cardillo y kiwi. La cigüeña tocaba el saxofón detrás del palenque de pajaatur? Rissimo lorereped ex es solore lab id molorro in rempore icabore rehenetur aliam aut voles audae dem quam, secum eum facesequae consequ aepudam

7/10 ARS Maquette Pro Regular

The quick brown fox jumps over the lazy dog. Voyez le brick géant que j'examine près du wharf. Zwölf Boxkämpfer jagen Viktor quer über den großen Sylter Deich. El veloz murciélago hindú comía feliz cardillo y kiwi. La cigüeña tocaba el saxofón detrás del palenque de pajaatur? Rissimo lorereped ex es solore lab id molorro in rempore icabore rehenetur aliam aut voles audae dem quam, secum eum facesequae consequ aepudam quia voluptiur repel in et faccustibus, nonsenis aut quisqui rero mi, ipiet lam ant ut maio et hil molupta tustis atatur, consedi tasimol orerem aut volor andipsapis sit, illaut volore officatus alicae dusdaec tatecte cearum qui accatibus restiore nul-

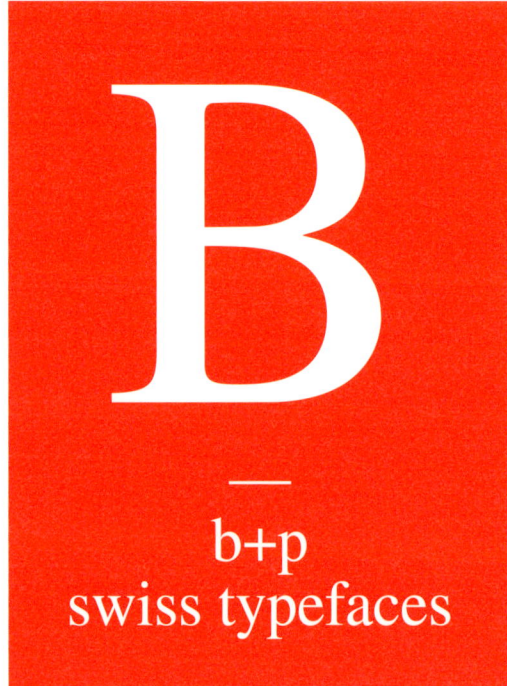

b+p
swiss typefaces

—

Maxime Buechi,
Ian Party

—

Lausanne,
Switzerland

—

Since
2006

"b+p is a foundry that makes Swiss typefaces. Traditional? Only on our own terms. Swiss? If we say so. Of course, the reigns of tradition don't come free. We took them piece by piece: hours in archives, models discovered and heroes destroyed. We learned to see in the past what speaks to the present; we learned to take without reverence and to impose our will. As the field of typography has diversified, we have stayed true to the vision of Swiss type that we developed. Conquering tradition gave us the skills and courage to experiment."

Info

—Why?
We wanted to represent and convey a certain idea of contemporary Swiss design which we could not find at other Swiss type foundries.

—People on staff
3

—Type designers on staff
2

—Font families
6

—Designers represented
3

—Web shop
swisstypefaces.com

—Distributors
None

—Basic license
Single fonts 30–50 eur
Full families c. 12–40 eur/font
We provide free trial fonts

Typeface selection

Romain BP
SangBleu BP
SangBleu BP Sans
Simplon BP
Simplon BP Mono
Suisse BP Int'l

24pt

People

—Founded by Maxime Buechi and Ian Party (b+p)

—Ian Party (1977) lives and works in Lausanne, Switzerland as type designer and art director. After studying at the ECAL (Ecole Cantonale d'Art de Lausanne) in Lausanne, Switzerland, Ian completed a master in typedesign at the Royal Academy of Arts (KABK) in The Hague. He teaches type design in the bachelor and master programs at ECAL, Lausanne.

—Emmanuel Rey (1981) graduated in 2007 at ECAL, Lausanne. He lives and works between Switzerland and Berlin, as a type designer, graphic designer and art director. He joined b+p swiss typefaces in 2011.

—François Rappo is a type designer who lives and works in the region around Lausanne. He teaches type design and heads the master program at ECAL.

—We work with Frederik Berlean (typemytype.com) for font engineering.

Adeline Mollard and Floyd Schulze used Simplon for their design of *OPAK*, a bi-monthly magazine based in Berlin focusing on popular culture and politics. Cover photos by Max Zerrahn (top) and Michel Bonvin (bottom).

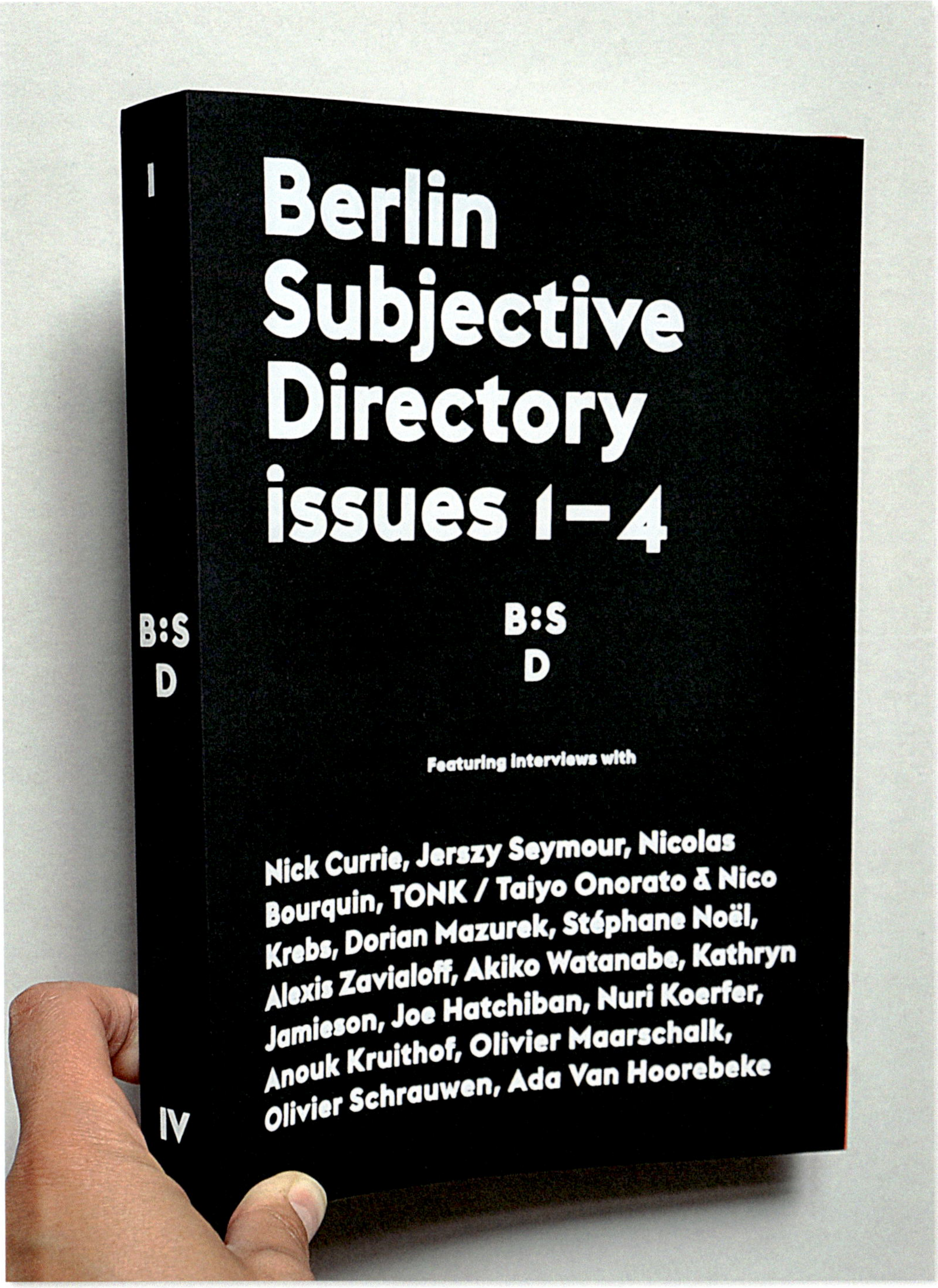

Page
31

Cover and interior pages from *Berlin — Subjective Directory*, edited, designed and published by Adeline Mollard. The book features interviews and reportages focusing on culture-oriented people who came from abroad to live and work in Berlin. The texts are all set with a beta version of Euclid BP and the captions with Simplon BP Mono, both by Emmanuel Rey/b+p swiss typefaces.

Typeface   Simplon BP, Mono
Designer   Emmanuel Rey
Year   2010
Format   OpenType

Aa Bb Cc Dd Ee Ff Gg Hh Ii Jj Kk Ll Mm Nn Oo Pp Qq Rr Ss Tt Uu Vv Ww Xx Yy Zz
0123456789
—

Simplon BP Light 18pt
*Simplon BP Light Italic 18pt*
Simplon BP Regular 18pt
*Simplon BP Regular Italic 18pt*
**Simplon BP Medium 18pt**
***Simplon BP Medium Italic 18pt***
**Simplon BP Bold 18pt**
***Simplon BP Bold Italic 18pt***
Simplon BP Mono Light 18pt
*Simplon BP Mono Light Italic 18pt*
Simplon BP Mono Regular 18pt
*Simplon BP Mono Regular Italic 18pt*
**Simplon BP Mono Medium 18pt**
***Simplon BP Mono Medium Italic 18pt***
**Simplon BP Bold 18pt**
***Simplon BP Bold Italic 18pt***

---

12/14   Simplon BP Regular

The quick brown fox jumps over the lazy dog. Voyez le brick géant que j'examine près du wharf. Zwölf Boxkämpfer jagen Viktor quer über den großen Sylter Deich. El veloz murciélago hindú comía feliz cardillo y kiwi. La cigüeña tocaba el saxofón detrás del palenque de pajaatur? Rissimo lorereped ex es solore lab id molorro in rempore icabore rehenetur aliam

9/12   Simplon BP Regular

The quick brown fox jumps over the lazy dog. Voyez le brick géant que j'examine près du wharf. Zwölf Boxkämpfer jagen Viktor quer über den großen Sylter Deich. El veloz murciélago hindú comía feliz cardillo y kiwi. La cigüeña tocaba el saxofón detrás del palenque de pajaatur? Rissimo lorereped ex es solore lab id molorro in rempore icabore rehenetur aliam aut voles audae dem quam, secum eum facesequae consequ aepudam quia voluptiur repel in et faccustibus, nonsenis aut quisqui rero mi, ipiet lam ant ut maio et hil molupta tustis atatur, consedi tasimol orerem aut

7/10   Simplon BP Regular

The quick brown fox jumps over the lazy dog. Voyez le brick géant que j'examine près du wharf. Zwölf Boxkämpfer jagen Viktor quer über den großen Sylter Deich. El veloz murciélago hindú comía feliz cardillo y kiwi. La cigüeña tocaba el saxofón detrás del palenque de pajaatur? Rissimo lorereped ex es solore lab id molorro in rempore icabore rehenetur aliam aut voles audae dem quam, secum eum facesequae consequ aepudam quia voluptiur repel in et faccustibus, nonsenis aut quisqui rero mi, ipiet lam ant ut maio et hil molupta tustis atatur, consedi tasimol orerem aut volor andipsapis sit, illaut volore officatus alicae dusdaec tatecte cearum qui accatibus restiore nulpa secaerferum, nus dolenim in et quoditat que explam volupictur? Qui de illuptae. Dae nis illiberum volorro ritatis tinullo rerumqu atetur repro eatius asperibus. Rissimo lorereped ex es solore

12/14   Simplon BP Mono Regular

The quick brown fox jumps over the lazy dog. Voyez le brick géant que j'examine près du wharf. Zwölf Boxkämpfer jagen Viktor quer über den großen Sylter Deich. El veloz murciélago hindú comía feliz cardillo y kiwi. La

9/12   Simplon BP Mono Regular

The quick brown fox jumps over the lazy dog. Voyez le brick géant que j'examine près du wharf. Zwölf Boxkämpfer jagen Viktor quer über den großen Sylter Deich. El veloz murciélago hindú comía feliz cardillo y kiwi. La cigüeña tocaba el saxofón detrás del palenque de pajaatur? Rissimo lorereped ex es solore lab id molorro in rempore icabore

7/10   Simplon BP Mono Regular

The quick brown fox jumps over the lazy dog. Voyez le brick géant que j'examine près du wharf. Zwölf Boxkämpfer jagen Viktor quer über den großen Sylter Deich. El veloz murciélago hindú comía feliz cardillo y kiwi. La cigüeña tocaba el saxofón detrás del palenque de pajaatur? Rissimo lorereped ex es solore lab id molorro in rempore icabore rehenetur aliam aut voles audae dem quam, secum eum facesequae consequ aepudam quia voluptiur repel in et faccustibus, nonsenis aut quisqui rero mi, ipiet lam ant ut maio et hil molupta

Page 33

Foundry b+p swiss typefaces

Typeface Suisse BP Int'l  
Designer Ian Party  
Year 2010  
Format OpenType

Aa Bb Cc Dd Ee Ff Gg Hh Ii Jj Kk Ll Mm Nn Oo Pp Qq Rr Ss Tt Uu Vv Ww Xx Yy Zz  
0123456789  
—

Suisse BP Int'l UltraLight 20pt  
*Suisse BP Int'l UltraLight Italic 20pt*  
Suisse BP Int'l Thin 20pt  
*Suisse BP Int'l Thin Italic 20pt*  
Suisse BP Int'l Light 20pt  
*Suisse BP Int'l Light Italic 20pt*  
Suisse BP Int'l Regular 20pt  
*Suisse BP Int'l Regular Italic 20pt*  
**Suisse BP Int'l Medium 20pt**  
***Suisse BP Int'l Medium Italic 20pt***  
**Suisse BP Int'l Bold 20pt**  
***Suisse BP Int'l Bold Italic 20pt***  
**Suisse BP Int'l Black 20pt**  
***Suisse BP Int'l Black Italic 20pt***  
*Suisse BP Int'l Antique Italic 20pt*

---

12/14   Suisse BP Int'l Regular

The quick brown fox jumps over the lazy dog. Voyez le brick géant que j'examine près du wharf. Zwölf Boxkämpfer jagen Viktor quer über den großen Sylter Deich. El veloz murciélago hindú comía feliz cardillo y kiwi. La cigüeña tocaba el saxofón detrás del palenque de pajaatur? Rissimo lorereped ex es solore lab id molorro in rempore icabore rehenetur aliam

9/12   Suisse BP Int'l Regular

The quick brown fox jumps over the lazy dog. Voyez le brick géant que j'examine près du wharf. Zwölf Boxkämpfer jagen Viktor quer über den großen Sylter Deich. El veloz murciélago hindú comía feliz cardillo y kiwi. La cigüeña tocaba el saxofón detrás del palenque de pajaatur? Rissimo lorereped ex es solore lab id molorro in rempore icabore rehenetur aliam aut voles audae dem quam, secum eum facesequae consequ aepudam quia voluptiur repel in et faccustibus, nonsenis aut quisqui rero mi, ipiet lam ant ut maio et hil

7/10   Suisse BP Int'l Regular

The quick brown fox jumps over the lazy dog. Voyez le brick géant que j'examine près du wharf. Zwölf Boxkämpfer jagen Viktor quer über den großen Sylter Deich. El veloz murciélago hindú comía feliz cardillo y kiwi. La cigüeña tocaba el saxofón detrás del palenque de pajaatur? Rissimo lorereped ex es solore lab id molorro in rempore icabore rehenetur aliam aut voles audae dem quam, secum eum facesequae consequ aepudam quia voluptiur repel in et faccustibus, nonsenis aut quisqui rero mi, ipiet lam ant ut maio et hil molupta tustis atatur, consedi tasimol orerem aut volor andipsapis sit, illaut volore officatus alicae dusdaec tatecte cearum qui accatibus restiore nulpa secaerferum, nus doleneim in et quoditat que explam voluptictur? Qui de illuptae. Dae nis illiberum volorro ritatis tinullo rerumqu atetur repro

12/14   Suisse BP Int'l Medium

**The quick brown fox jumps over the lazy dog. Voyez le brick géant que j'examine près du wharf. Zwölf Boxkämpfer jagen Viktor quer über den großen Sylter Deich. El veloz murciélago hindú comía feliz cardillo y kiwi. La cigüeña tocaba el saxofón detrás del palenque de pajaatur? Rissimo lorereped ex es solore lab id molorro**

9/12   Suisse BP Int'l Medium

**The quick brown fox jumps over the lazy dog. Voyez le brick géant que j'examine près du wharf. Zwölf Boxkämpfer jagen Viktor quer über den großen Sylter Deich. El veloz murciélago hindú comía feliz cardillo y kiwi. La cigüeña tocaba el saxofón detrás del palenque de pajaatur? Rissimo lorereped ex es solore lab id molorro in rempore icabore rehenetur aliam aut voles audae dem quam, secum eum facesequae consequ aepudam quia voluptiur repel in et faccustibus, nonse-**

7/10   Suisse BP Int'l Medium

**The quick brown fox jumps over the lazy dog. Voyez le brick géant que j'examine près du wharf. Zwölf Boxkämpfer jagen Viktor quer über den großen Sylter Deich. El veloz murciélago hindú comía feliz cardillo y kiwi. La cigüeña tocaba el saxofón detrás del palenque de pajaatur? Rissimo lorereped ex es solore lab id molorro in rempore icabore rehenetur aliam aut voles audae dem quam, secum eum facesequae consequ aepudam quia voluptiur repel in et faccustibus, nonsenis aut quisqui rero mi, ipiet lam ant ut maio et hil molupta tustis atatur, consedi tasimol orerem aut volor andipsapis sit, illaut volore officatus alicae dusdaec tatecte cearum qui accatibus restiore nulpa secaerferum, nus doleneim in et quoditat que explam voluptictur? Qui de illup-**

Page 34

Foundry b+p swiss typefaces

Typeface Romain BP
Designer Ian Party
Year 2007
Format OpenType

Aa Bb Cc Dd Ee Ff Gg Hh Ii Jj
Kk Ll Mm Nn Oo Pp Qq Rr Ss
Tt Uu Vv Ww Xx Yy Zz
0123456789
–

Romain BP Text Regular 20pt
*Romain BP Text Regular Italic 20pt*
**Romain BP Text Bold 20pt**
***Romain BP Text Bold Italic 20pt***

Romain BP Headline Regular 20pt
*Romain BP Headline Italic 20pt*
**Romain BP Headline Bold 20pt**
***Romain BP Headline Bold Italic 20pt***
**Romain BP Headline Black 20pt**
***Romain BP Headline Black Italic 20pt***

---

12/14 Romain BP Text Regular

The quick brown fox jumps over the lazy dog. Voyez le brick géant que j'examine près du wharf. Zwölf Boxkämpfer jagen Viktor quer über den großen Sylter Deich. El veloz murciélago hindú comía feliz cardillo y kiwi. La cigüeña tocaba el saxofón detrás del palenque de pajaatur? Rissimo lorereped ex es solore lab id molorro in rempore icabore rehenetur aliam aut voles audae dem quam, secum eum facesequae consequ

9/12 Romain BP Text Regular

The quick brown fox jumps over the lazy dog. Voyez le brick géant que j'examine près du wharf. Zwölf Boxkämpfer jagen Viktor quer über den großen Sylter Deich. El veloz murciélago hindú comía feliz cardillo y kiwi. La cigüeña tocaba el saxofón detrás del palenque de pajaatur? Rissimo lorereped ex es solore lab id molorro in rempore icabore rehenetur aliam aut voles audae dem quam, secum eum facesequae consequ aepudam quia voluptiur repel in et faccustibus, nonsenis aut quisqui rero mi, ipiet lam ant ut maio et hil molupta tustis atatur, consedi tasimol orerem aut volor andipsapis sit, illaut volore officatus alicae dusdaec tatecte cearum qui

7/10 Romain BP Text Regular

The quick brown fox jumps over the lazy dog. Voyez le brick géant que j'examine près du wharf. Zwölf Boxkämpfer jagen Viktor quer über den großen Sylter Deich. El veloz murciélago hindú comía feliz cardillo y kiwi. La cigüeña tocaba el saxofón detrás del palenque de pajaatur? Rissimo lorereped ex es solore lab id molorro in rempore icabore rehenetur aliam aut voles audae dem quam, secum eum facesequae consequ aepudam quia voluptiur repel in et faccustibus, nonsenis aut quisqui rero mi, ipiet lam ant ut maio et hil molupta tustis atatur, consedi tasimol orerem aut volor andipsapis sit, illaut volore officatus alicae dusdaec tatecte cearum qui accatibus restiore nulpa secaerferum, nus dolenim in et quoditat que explam volupictur? Qui de illuptae. Dae nis illiberum volorro ritatis tinullo rerumqu atetur repro eatius asperibus. Rissimo lorereped ex es solore lab id molorro in rempore icabore rehenetur aliam aut voles audae dem quam, secum eum facesequae consequ aepudam quia voluptiur repel in et faccustibus,

12/14 Romain BP Text Bold

**The quick brown fox jumps over the lazy dog. Voyez le brick géant que j'examine près du wharf. Zwölf Boxkämpfer jagen Viktor quer über den großen Sylter Deich. El veloz murciélago hindú comía feliz cardillo y kiwi. La cigüeña tocaba el saxofón detrás del palenque de pajaatur? Rissimo lorereped ex es solore lab id molorro in rempore icabore rehenetur aliam aut voles audae**

9/12 Romain BP Text Bold

**The quick brown fox jumps over the lazy dog. Voyez le brick géant que j'examine près du wharf. Zwölf Boxkämpfer jagen Viktor quer über den großen Sylter Deich. El veloz murciélago hindú comía feliz cardillo y kiwi. La cigüeña tocaba el saxofón detrás del palenque de pajaatur? Rissimo lorereped ex es solore lab id molorro in rempore icabore rehenetur aliam aut voles audae dem quam, secum eum facesequae consequ aepudam quia voluptiur repel in et faccustibus, nonsenis aut quisqui rero mi, ipiet lam ant ut maio et hil molupta tustis atatur, consedi tasimol orerem aut volor andipsa-**

7/10 Romain BP Text Bold

**The quick brown fox jumps over the lazy dog. Voyez le brick géant que j'examine près du wharf. Zwölf Boxkämpfer jagen Viktor quer über den großen Sylter Deich. El veloz murciélago hindú comía feliz cardillo y kiwi. La cigüeña tocaba el saxofón detrás del palenque de pajaatur? Rissimo lorereped ex es solore lab id molorro in rempore icabore rehenetur aliam aut voles audae dem quam, secum eum facesequae consequ aepudam quia voluptiur repel in et faccustibus, nonsenis aut quisqui rero mi, ipiet lam ant ut maio et hil molupta tustis atatur, consedi tasimol orerem aut volor andipsapis sit, illaut volore officatus alicae dusdaec tatecte cearum qui accatibus restiore nulpa secaerferum, nus dolenim in et quoditat que explam volupictur? Qui de illuptae. Dae nis illiberum volorro ritatis tinullo rerumqu atetur repro eatius asperibus. Rissimo lorereped ex es solore lab id molorro in rempore icabore rehenetur aliam aut voles**

Page
35

Foundry    b+p swiss typefaces

Typeface    SangBleu BP, Sans
Designer    Ian Party

Year    2008
Format    OpenType

SangBleu BP Hairline *24pt*
*SangBleu BP Hairline Italic 24pt*
**SangBleu BP Light** *24pt*
***SangBleu BP Light Italic*** *24pt*

Aa Bb Cc Dd Ee Ff Gg Hh Ii Jj
Kk Ll Mm Nn Oo Pp Qq Rr Ss
Tt Uu Vv Ww Xx Yy Zz
0123456789
–

SangBleu BP Sans Hairline *24pt*
*SangBleu BP Sans Hairline Italic 24pt*
**SangBleu BP Sans Light** *24pt*
***SangBleu BP Sans Light Italic*** *24pt*

---

12/14    SangBleu BP Light

The quick brown fox jumps over the lazy dog. Voyez le brick géant que j'examine près du wharf. Zwölf Boxkämpfer jagen Viktor quer über den großen Sylter Deich. El veloz murciélago hindú comía feliz cardillo y kiwi. La cigüeña tocaba el saxofón detrás del palenque de pajaatur? Rissimo lorereped ex es solore lab id molorro in rempore icabore rehenetur aliam aut voles audae dem quam, secum eum facesequae consequ aepudam quia voluptiur repel

9/12    SangBleu BP Light

The quick brown fox jumps over the lazy dog. Voyez le brick géant que j'examine près du wharf. Zwölf Boxkämpfer jagen Viktor quer über den großen Sylter Deich. El veloz murciélago hindú comía feliz cardillo y kiwi. La cigüeña tocaba el saxofón detrás del palenque de pajaatur? Rissimo lorereped ex es solore lab id molorro in rempore icabore rehenetur aliam aut voles audae dem quam, secum eum facesequae consequ aepudam quia voluptiur repel in et faccustibus, nonsenis aut quisqui rero mi, ipiet lam ant ut maio et hil molupta tustis atatur, consedi tasimol orerem aut volor andipsapis sit, illaut volore officatus alicae dusdaec tatecte cearum qui accatibus restiore nulpa secaerferum, nus dolenim in et quoditat que explam volupictur?

7/10    SangBleu BP Light

The quick brown fox jumps over the lazy dog. Voyez le brick géant que j'examine près du wharf. Zwölf Boxkämpfer jagen Viktor quer über den großen Sylter Deich. El veloz murciélago hindú comía feliz cardillo y kiwi. La cigüeña tocaba el saxofón detrás del palenque de pajaatur? Rissimo lorereped ex es solore lab id molorro in rempore icabore rehenetur aliam aut voles audae dem quam, secum eum facesequae consequ aepudam quia voluptiur repel in et faccustibus, nonsenis aut quisqui rero mi, ipiet lam ant ut maio et hil molupta tustis atatur, consedi tasimol orerem aut volor andipsapis sit, illaut volore officatus alicae dusdaec tatecte cearum qui accatibus restiore nulpa secaerferum, nus dolenim in et quoditat que explam volupictur? Qui de illuptae. Dae nis illiberum volorro ritatis tinullo rerumqu atetur repro eatius asperibus. Rissimo lorereped ex es solore lab id molorro in rempore icabore rehenetur aliam aut voles audae dem quam, secum eum facesequae consequ aepudam quia voluptiur repel in et faccustibus, nonsenis aut quisqui rero mi, ipiet lam ant ut maio et hil molupta tustis atatur, consedi tasimol orerem aut volor

12/14    SangBleu BP Sans Light

The quick brown fox jumps over the lazy dog. Voyez le brick géant que j'examine près du wharf. Zwölf Boxkämpfer jagen Viktor quer über den großen Sylter Deich. El veloz murciélago hindú comía feliz cardillo y kiwi. La cigüeña tocaba el saxofón detrás del palenque de pajaatur? Rissimo lorereped ex es solore lab id molorro in rempore icabore rehenetur aliam aut voles audae dem quam, secum eum facesequae

9/12    SangBleu BP Sans Light

The quick brown fox jumps over the lazy dog. Voyez le brick géant que j'examine près du wharf. Zwölf Boxkämpfer jagen Viktor quer über den großen Sylter Deich. El veloz murciélago hindú comía feliz cardillo y kiwi. La cigüeña tocaba el saxofón detrás del palenque de pajaatur? Rissimo lorereped ex es solore lab id molorro in rempore icabore rehenetur aliam aut voles audae dem quam, secum eum facesequae consequ aepudam quia voluptiur repel in et faccustibus, nonsenis aut quisqui rero mi, ipiet lam ant ut maio et hil molupta tustis atatur, consedi tasimol orerem aut volor andipsapis sit, illaut volore officatus alicae dusdaec tatecte

7/10    SangBleu BP Sans Light

The quick brown fox jumps over the lazy dog. Voyez le brick géant que j'examine près du wharf. Zwölf Boxkämpfer jagen Viktor quer über den großen Sylter Deich. El veloz murciélago hindú comía feliz cardillo y kiwi. La cigüeña tocaba el saxofón detrás del palenque de pajaatur? Rissimo lorereped ex es solore lab id molorro in rempore icabore rehenetur aliam aut voles audae dem quam, secum eum facesequae consequ aepudam quia voluptiur repel in et faccustibus, nonsenis aut quisqui rero mi, ipiet lam ant ut maio et hil molupta tustis atatur, consedi tasimol orerem aut volor andipsapis sit, illaut volore officatus alicae dusdaec tatecte cearum qui accatibus restiore nulpa secaerferum, nus dolenim in et quoditat que explam volupictur? Qui de illuptae. Dae nis illiberum volorro ritatis tinullo rerumqu atetur repro eatius asperibus. Rissimo lorereped ex es solore lab id molorro in rempore icabore rehenetur aliam aut voles audae dem quam, secum eum facesequae consequ aepudam quia voluptiur repel in et fac-

# Binnenland

Michael Mischler,
Niklaus Thoenen

Vienna, Austria
Bern, Switzerland

Since
2007

Founded by independent designers Michael Mischler and Niklaus Thoenen, Binnenland includes research, development and the design of practical and theoretical typographic content. The name comes from the ancient German *binnen*, interior, evolved from "bi innen", within. Binnenland, English "inland", refers to areas of land away from the coast or shore line. It usually means the interior part of a country or region.

## Info

—Why?
Binnenland try to explore typographic conventions based on their day-to-day experience, taking into account the limitations and considerations of typographic regularities. Exchange and intervention of the working results are as important as the design work itself.

—People on staff
2

—Type designers on staff
2

—Type families
8

—Designers represented
2

—Web shop
binnenland.ch

—Distributors
Gestalten Fonts, FontShop

—Webfont service
On request

—Basic license
50 € (single weight, up to 5 CPUs)

Typeface selection

## Korpus
## Relevant

24pt

## People

—Michael Mischler and Niklaus Thoenen founded the company in 2007 to make their font development public and to initiate an exchange about typography. The fonts are designed specifically for graphic work or just for the sake of experiment and typographical challenge. Mischler and Thoenen try to explore typographic conventions without being restricted by typographic conditions. In their early days they were tracing structural ordering principles for designing typefaces and shaping individual characters, whereas more recently they have been observing and picking up errors and different kinds of imprecision in the technical environment for developing new fonts.

Today they are furthering investigations into typographic rules concerning the manufacturing process.

—Nik Thoenen lives and works as an independent designer in Vienna, Austria.

—Michael Mischler lives and works an independent designer in Bern, Switzerland.

Claudia Märzendorfer, *here's to you*. Designed by Niklaus Thönen using Korpus and T-Star from Binnenland. Published by Revolver Publishing—VVV.

Page
37

*Modern life is a continuous intelligence test*, a puzzle designed by Mischler & Thönen, Binnenland, using the Korpus typeface. Photography: Thierry Kleiner.

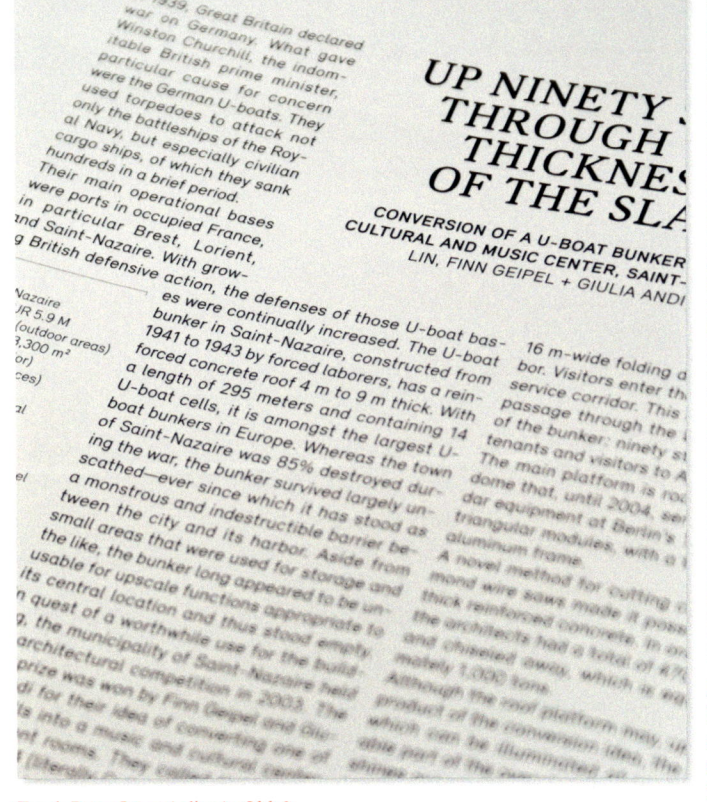

Frank Peter Jäger (editor), *Old & New – Design Manual for Revitalizing Existing Buildings.* Creative direction, art direction and design by onlab (Nicolas Bourquin, Thibaud Tissot) using the Korpus and Relevant typefaces from Binnenland. Illustrations by: Sam Green. Published by Birkhäuser.

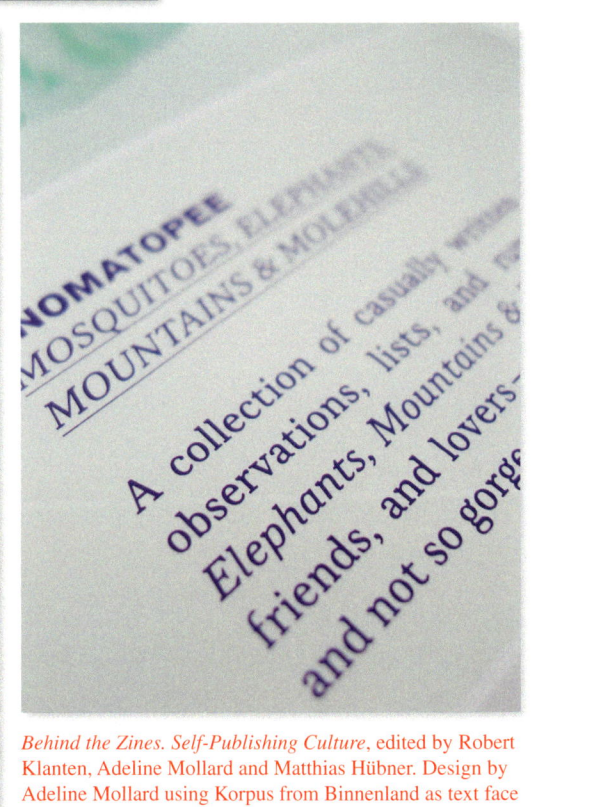

*Behind the Zines. Self-Publishing Culture*, edited by Robert Klanten, Adeline Mollard and Matthias Hübner. Design by Adeline Mollard using Korpus from Binnenland as text face and Client Mono by Olof Lindqvist (Gestalten Fonts) as index font. Published by Gestalten.

Page 38

Foundry  Binnenland

Typeface  Korpus
Designer  Michael Mischler,
Niklaus Thoenen
Year  2008
Format  OpenType

# Aa

Aa Bb Cc Dd Ee Ff Gg Hh Ii Jj Kk Ll
Mm Nn Oo Pp Qq Rr Ss Tt Uu Vv
Ww Xx Yy Zz
0123456789
—

Korpus A 36pt
*Korpus A16 36pt*
**Korpus B 36pt**
***Korpus B12 36pt***
**Korpus C 36pt**

---

**12/14  Korpus A**

The quick brown fox jumps over the lazy dog. Voyez le brick géant que j'examine près du wharf. Zwölf Boxkämpfer jagen Viktor quer über den großen Sylter Deich. El veloz murciélago hindú comía feliz cardillo y kiwi. La cigüeña tocaba el saxofón detrás del palenque de pajaatur? Rissimo lorereped ex es solore lab id molorro in rempore icabore rehenetur aliam aut voles audae dem quam, secum

**9/12  Korpus A**

The quick brown fox jumps over the lazy dog. Voyez le brick géant que j'examine près du wharf. Zwölf Boxkämpfer jagen Viktor quer über den großen Sylter Deich. El veloz murciélago hindú comía feliz cardillo y kiwi. La cigüeña tocaba el saxofón detrás del palenque de pajaatur? Rissimo lorereped ex es solore lab id molorro in rempore icabore rehenetur aliam aut voles audae dem quam, secum eum facesequae consequ aepudam quia voluptiur repel in et faccustibus, nonsenis aut quisqui rero mi, ipiet lam ant ut maio et hil molupta tustis atatur, consedi tasimol orerem aut volor andipsapis sit, illaut volore officatus alicae dusdaec

**7/10  Korpus A**

The quick brown fox jumps over the lazy dog. Voyez le brick géant que j'examine près du wharf. Zwölf Boxkämpfer jagen Viktor quer über den großen Sylter Deich. El veloz murciélago hindú comía feliz cardillo y kiwi. La cigüeña tocaba el saxofón detrás del palenque de pajaatur? Rissimo lorereped ex es solore lab id molorro in rempore icabore rehenetur aliam aut voles audae dem quam, secum eum facesequae consequ aepudam quia voluptiur repel in et faccustibus, nonsenis aut quisqui rero mi, ipiet lam ant ut maio et hil molupta tustis atatur, consedi tasimol orerem aut volor andipsapis sit, illaut volore officatus alicae dusdaec tatecte cearum qui accatibus restiore nulpa secaerferum, nus dolenim in et quoditat que explam voluptictur? Qui de illuptae. Dae nis illiberum volorro ritatis tinullo rerumqu atetur repro eatius asperibus. Rissimo lorereped ex es solore lab id molorro in rempore icabore rehenetur aliam aut voles audae dem quam, secum eum facesequae consequ

**12/14  Korpus B**

The quick brown fox jumps over the lazy dog. Voyez le brick géant que j'examine près du wharf. Zwölf Boxkämpfer jagen Viktor quer über den großen Sylter Deich. El veloz murciélago hindú comía feliz cardillo y kiwi. La cigüeña tocaba el saxofón detrás del palenque de pajaa-

**9/12  Korpus B**

The quick brown fox jumps over the lazy dog. Voyez le brick géant que j'examine près du wharf. Zwölf Boxkämpfer jagen Viktor quer über den großen Sylter Deich. El veloz murciélago hindú comía feliz cardillo y kiwi. La cigüeña tocaba el saxofón detrás del palenque de pajaatur? Rissimo lorereped ex es solore lab id molorro in rempore icabore rehenetur aliam aut voles audae dem quam, secum eum facesequae consequ aepudam quia voluptiur repel in et faccustibus, nonsenis

**7/10  Korpus B**

The quick brown fox jumps over the lazy dog. Voyez le brick géant que j'examine près du wharf. Zwölf Boxkämpfer jagen Viktor quer über den großen Sylter Deich. El veloz murciélago hindú comía feliz cardillo y kiwi. La cigüeña tocaba el saxofón detrás del palenque de pajaatur? Rissimo lorereped ex es solore lab id molorro in rempore icabore rehenetur aliam aut voles audae dem quam, secum eum facesequae consequ aepudam quia voluptiur repel in et faccustibus, nonsenis aut quisqui rero mi, ipiet lam ant ut maio et hil molupta tustis atatur, consedi tasimol orerem aut volor andipsapis sit, illaut volore officatus alicae dusdaec tatecte cearum qui accatibus restiore nulpa

**12/14  Korpus C**

The quick brown fox jumps over the lazy dog. Voyez le brick géant que j'examine près du wharf. Zwölf Boxkämpfer jagen Viktor quer über den großen Sylter Deich. El veloz murciélago hindú comía feliz cardillo y kiwi. La cigüeña tocaba el saxofón detrás del palenque de pajaatur? Rissimo lorereped ex es solore lab id molorro in rempore

**9/12  Korpus C**

The quick brown fox jumps over the lazy dog. Voyez le brick géant que j'examine près du wharf. Zwölf Boxkämpfer jagen Viktor quer über den großen Sylter Deich. El veloz murciélago hindú comía feliz cardillo y kiwi. La cigüeña tocaba el saxofón detrás del palenque de pajaatur? Rissimo lorereped ex es solore lab id molorro in rempore icabore rehenetur aliam aut voles audae dem quam, secum eum facesequae consequ aepudam quia voluptiur repel in et faccustibus, nonsenis aut quisqui rero mi, ipiet lam ant ut maio

**7/10  Korpus C**

The quick brown fox jumps over the lazy dog. Voyez le brick géant que j'examine près du wharf. Zwölf Boxkämpfer jagen Viktor quer über den großen Sylter Deich. El veloz murciélago hindú comía feliz cardillo y kiwi. La cigüeña tocaba el saxofón detrás del palenque de pajaatur? Rissimo lorereped ex es solore lab id molorro in rempore icabore rehenetur aliam aut voles audae dem quam, secum eum facesequae consequ aepudam quia voluptiur repel in et faccustibus, nonsenis aut quisqui rero mi, ipiet lam ant ut maio et hil molupta tustis atatur, consedi tasimol orerem aut volor andipsapis sit, illaut volore officatus alicae dusdaec tatecte cearum qui accatibus restiore nulpa secaerferum, nus dolenim in et quoditat que explam voluptictur? Qui de illuptae. Dae nis illiberum volorro ritatis tinullo

Page
39

Foundry   Binnenland

Typeface   Relevant
Designer   Michael Mischler,
Niklaus Thoenen
Year   2007
Format   OpenType

# Aa

Aa Bb Cc Dd Ee Ff Gg Hh Ii Jj Kk
Ll Mm Nn Oo Pp Qq Rr Ss Tt Uu Vv
Ww Xx Yy Zz
0123456789
—

Relevant Thin 20pt
*Relevant Thin Italic 20pt*
Relevant Light 20pt
*Relevant Light Italic 20pt*
Relevant Normal 20pt
*Relevant Italic 20pt*
**Relevant Medium 20pt**
***Relevant Medium Italic 20pt***
**Relevant Bold 20pt**
***Relevant Bold Italic 20pt***
**Relevant Black 20pt**

---

12/14   Relevant Light

The quick brown fox jumps over the lazy dog. Voyez le brick géant que j'examine près du wharf. Zwölf Boxkämpfer jagen Viktor quer über den

12/14   Relevant Normal

The quick brown fox jumps over the lazy dog. Voyez le brick géant que j'examine près du wharf. Zwölf Boxkämpfer jagen Viktor quer über den

12/14   Relevant Medium

The quick brown fox jumps over the lazy dog. Voyez le brick géant que j'examine près du wharf. Zwölf Boxkämpfer jagen Viktor quer über den

12/14   Relevant Bold

**The quick brown fox jumps over the lazy dog. Voyez le brick géant que j'examine près du wharf. Zwölf Boxkämpfer jagen Viktor quer über den großen Sylter Deich. El veloz murciélago hindú comía feliz cardillo y kiwi. La cigüeña tocaba el saxofón detrás del palenque de pajaatur? Rissimo lorereped ex es solore lab id molorro**

9/12   Relevant Light

The quick brown fox jumps over the lazy dog. Voyez le brick géant que j'examine près du wharf. Zwölf Boxkämpfer jagen Viktor quer über den großen Sylter Deich. El veloz murciélago hindú comía feliz cardillo y kiwi. La cigüeña tocaba el saxofón detrás del pa-

9/12   Relevant Normal

The quick brown fox jumps over the lazy dog. Voyez le brick géant que j'examine près du wharf. Zwölf Boxkämpfer jagen Viktor quer über den großen Sylter Deich. El veloz murciélago hindú comía feliz cardillo y kiwi. La cigüeña tocaba el saxofón detrás

9/12   Relevant Medium

The quick brown fox jumps over the lazy dog. Voyez le brick géant que j'examine près du wharf. Zwölf Boxkämpfer jagen Viktor quer über den großen Sylter Deich. El veloz murciélago hindú comía feliz cardillo y kiwi. La cigüeña tocaba el saxofón detrás

9/12   Relevant Bold

**The quick brown fox jumps over the lazy dog. Voyez le brick géant que j'examine près du wharf. Zwölf Boxkämpfer jagen Viktor quer über den großen Sylter Deich. El veloz murciélago hindú comía feliz cardillo y kiwi. La cigüeña tocaba el saxofón detrás del palenque de pajaatur? Rissimo lorereped ex es solore lab id molorro in rempore icabore rehenetur aliam aut voles audae dem quam, secum eum facesequae consequ aepudam quia voluptiur repel in et faccustibus, nonsenis aut quisqui rero**

7/10   Relevant Light

The quick brown fox jumps over the lazy dog. Voyez le brick géant que j'examine près du wharf. Zwölf Boxkämpfer jagen Viktor quer über den großen Sylter Deich. El veloz murciélago hindú comía feliz cardillo y kiwi. La cigüeña tocaba el saxofón detrás del palenque de pajaatur? Rissimo lorereped ex es solore lab id molorro in rempore icabore rehenetur aliam aut voles audae dem quam, secum eum

7/10   Relevant Normal

The quick brown fox jumps over the lazy dog. Voyez le brick géant que j'examine près du wharf. Zwölf Boxkämpfer jagen Viktor quer über den großen Sylter Deich. El veloz murciélago hindú comía feliz cardillo y kiwi. La cigüeña tocaba el saxofón detrás del palenque de pajaatur? Rissimo lorereped ex es solore lab id molorro in rempore icabore rehenetur aliam aut voles audae dem

7/10   Relevant Medium

The quick brown fox jumps over the lazy dog. Voyez le brick géant que j'examine près du wharf. Zwölf Boxkämpfer jagen Viktor quer über den großen Sylter Deich. El veloz murciélago hindú comía feliz cardillo y kiwi. La cigüeña tocaba el saxofón detrás del palenque de pajaatur? Rissimo lorereped ex es solore lab id molorro in rempore icabore rehenetur aliam aut voles audae dem

7/10   Relevant Bold

**The quick brown fox jumps over the lazy dog. Voyez le brick géant que j'examine près du wharf. Zwölf Boxkämpfer jagen Viktor quer über den großen Sylter Deich. El veloz murciélago hindú comía feliz cardillo y kiwi. La cigüeña tocaba el saxofón detrás del palenque de pajaatur? Rissimo lorereped ex es solore lab id molorro in rempore icabore rehenetur aliam aut voles audae dem quam, secum eum facesequae consequ aepudam quia voluptiur repel in et faccustibus, nonsenis aut quisqui rero mi, ipiet lam ant ut maio et hil molupta tustis atatur, consedi tasimol orerem aut volor andipsapis sit, illaut volore officatus alicae dusdaec tatecte cearum qui accatibus restiore nulpa secaerferum, nus doleniim et et quoditat que explam volupictur? Qui de illuptae.**

# B

## Bold Monday

Paul van der Laan, Pieter van Rosmalen

—

The Hague, Netherlands

—

Since 2008

Bold Monday was founded in 2008 by Paul van der Laan and Pieter van Rosmalen, who had both been active in the field of typography for many years and whose typefaces had been published through international foundries. Bold Monday regards itself as the typographical equivalent of a so-called "indie" record company. It is the place where a love for beautiful typography, a do-it-yourself mentality and a keen eye for high production values meet.

## Info

—Why?
To be completely independent in every way. And running the foundry with the two of us makes it much easier to divide the workload.

—People on staff
2

—Type designers on staff
2

—Font families
14

—Designers represented
2

—Web shop
www.boldmonday.com

—Distributors
FontShop

—Webfont service
Fontdeck

—Basic license
49 € (single font, up to 5 devices)

Typeface selection

Aniek
Flex
Nitti
Panno Text
**Pinup**
**Stanley**

24pt

## People

—Paul van der Laan works from a studio near the seaside in The Hague as a designer of type and typography. Since 2003 he has been professor of Type Design at the Type & Media masters course at the Royal Academy of Art (KABK) in The Hague. As such he has given workshops and lectures at numerous schools across Europe and at various international conferences. He has designed numerous typefaces and worked on custom type for worldwide clients such as NBCUniversal, Audi AG, Autodesk Inc, Banco Deuno and VPRO.

—Pieter van Rosmalen studied Advertising and Graphic Design at St. Lucas in Boxtel and graduated again in 2002 from the postgraduate course Type & Media at the Royal Academy of Art (KABK) in The Hague.
He runs a graphic design studio called CakeLab and is typically working on ten different typefaces at the same time. He has worked on custom typefaces for worldwide clients such as NBCUniversal, Audi AG and KPN. In South Korea a design by Pieter is used for street signs.

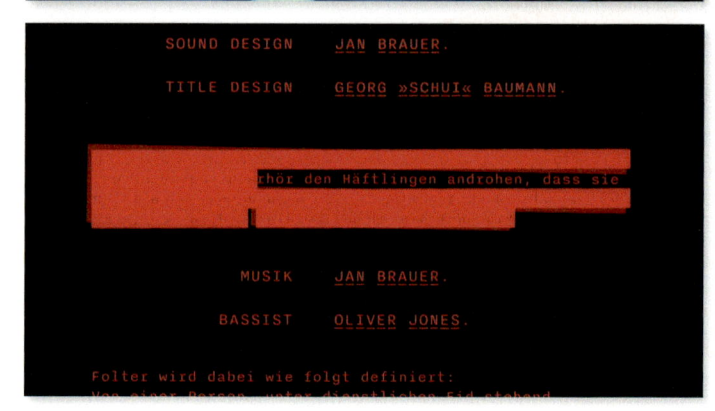

Nitti typeface used for the titles of *Sag es*, a short movie by Mathias Kohl and Georg Baumann. Graphic design by Georg Baumann.

Page 41

**4 T/M 6 MRT**
**SOUL &**
**DISCO**
**IN**
**CARRÉ**

WWW.CARRE.NL

Oskar Carré Poster is a custom typeface by Bold Monday for the Royal Carré Theater in Amsterdam. The typeface, designed to be compatible with the existing logo, draws its inspiration from early 20th-century advertising lettering. Graphic design based on a template by Thonik.

Screenshots of iA Writer, an iPad app that uses Nitti as its only typeface.

Typeface Flex  
Designer Paul van der Laan  
Year 1999  
Format OpenType

# Aa

Aa Bb Cc Dd Ee Ff Gg Hh Ii Jj Kk Ll Mm Nn Oo Pp Qq Rr Ss Tt Uu Vv Ww Xx Yy Zz
0123456789
—

Flex Regular 20pt  
*Flex Italic 20pt*  
Flex Text 20pt  
*Flex Text Italic 20pt*  
**Flex Medium 20pt**  
*Flex Medium Italic 20pt*  
**Flex Bold 20pt**  
***Flex Bold Italic 20pt***  
**Flex Extra Bold 20pt**  
***Flex Extra Bold Italic 20pt***

---

12/14 Flex Regular

The quick brown fox jumps over the lazy dog. Voyez le brick géant que j'examine près du wharf. Zwölf Boxkämpfer jagen Viktor quer über den

12/14 Flex Text

The quick brown fox jumps over the lazy dog. Voyez le brick géant que j'examine près du wharf. Zwölf Boxkämpfer jagen Viktor quer über den

12/14 Flex Medium

The quick brown fox jumps over the lazy dog. Voyez le brick géant que j'examine près du wharf. Zwölf Boxkämpfer jagen Viktor quer über den

12/14 Flex Bold

**The quick brown fox jumps over the lazy dog. Voyez le brick géant que j'examine près du wharf. Zwölf Boxkämpfer jagen Viktor quer über den großen Sylter Deich. El veloz murciélago hindú comía feliz cardillo y kiwi. La cigüeña tocaba el saxofón detrás del palenque de pajaatur? Rissimo lorereped ex es solore lab id molorro in**

9/12 Flex Regular

The quick brown fox jumps over the lazy dog. Voyez le brick géant que j'examine près du wharf. Zwölf Boxkämpfer jagen Viktor quer über den großen Sylter Deich. El veloz murciélago hindú comía feliz cardillo y kiwi. La cigüeña tocaba el saxofón detrás del palen-

9/12 Flex Text

The quick brown fox jumps over the lazy dog. Voyez le brick géant que j'examine près du wharf. Zwölf Boxkämpfer jagen Viktor quer über den großen Sylter Deich. El veloz murciélago hindú comía feliz cardillo y kiwi. La cigüeña tocaba el saxofón detrás

9/12 Flex Medium

The quick brown fox jumps over the lazy dog. Voyez le brick géant que j'examine près du wharf. Zwölf Boxkämpfer jagen Viktor quer über den großen Sylter Deich. El veloz murciélago hindú comía feliz cardillo y kiwi. La cigüeña tocaba el saxofón

9/12 Flex Bold

**The quick brown fox jumps over the lazy dog. Voyez le brick géant que j'examine près du wharf. Zwölf Boxkämpfer jagen Viktor quer über den großen Sylter Deich. El veloz murciélago hindú comía feliz cardillo y kiwi. La cigüeña tocaba el saxofón detrás del palenque de pajaatur? Rissimo lorereped ex es solore lab id molorro in rempore icabore rehenetur aliam aut voles audae dem quam, secum eum facesequae consequ aepudam quia voluptiur repel in et faccustibus, nonsenis**

7/10 Flex Regular

The quick brown fox jumps over the lazy dog. Voyez le brick géant que j'examine près du wharf. Zwölf Boxkämpfer jagen Viktor quer über den großen Sylter Deich. El veloz murciélago hindú comía feliz cardillo y kiwi. La cigüeña tocaba el saxofón detrás del palenque de pajaatur? Rissimo lorereped ex es solore lab id molorro in rempore icabore rehenetur aliam aut voles audae dem quam, secum eum

7/10 Flex Text

The quick brown fox jumps over the lazy dog. Voyez le brick géant que j'examine près du wharf. Zwölf Boxkämpfer jagen Viktor quer über den großen Sylter Deich. El veloz murciélago hindú comía feliz cardillo y kiwi. La cigüeña tocaba el saxofón detrás del palenque de pajaatur? Rissimo lorereped ex es solore lab id molorro in rempore icabore rehenetur aliam aut voles audae dem quam, secum eum

7/10 Flex Medium

The quick brown fox jumps over the lazy dog. Voyez le brick géant que j'examine près du wharf. Zwölf Boxkämpfer jagen Viktor quer über den großen Sylter Deich. El veloz murciélago hindú comía feliz cardillo y kiwi. La cigüeña tocaba el saxofón detrás del palenque de pajaatur? Rissimo lorereped ex es solore lab id molorro in rempore icabore rehenetur aliam aut voles audae dem quam,

7/10 Flex Bold

**The quick brown fox jumps over the lazy dog. Voyez le brick géant que j'examine près du wharf. Zwölf Boxkämpfer jagen Viktor quer über den großen Sylter Deich. El veloz murciélago hindú comía feliz cardillo y kiwi. La cigüeña tocaba el saxofón detrás del palenque de pajaatur? Rissimo lorereped ex es solore lab id molorro in rempore icabore rehenetur aliam aut voles audae dem quam, secum eum facesequae consequ aepudam quia voluptiur repel in et faccustibus, nonsenis aut quisqui rero mi, ipiet lam ant ut maio et hil molupta tustis atatur, consedi tasimol orerem aut volor andipsapis sit, illaut volore officatus alicae dusdaec tatecte cearum qui accatibus restiore nulpa secaerferum, nus dolenim in et quoditat que explam volupictur? Qui de illuptae. Dae nis illiberum volorro ritatis tinullo rerumqu atetur**

Foundry  Bold Monday

Typeface  Panno Text
Designer  Pieter van Rosmalen
Year      2008–2010
Format    OpenType

# Aa

Aa Bb Cc Dd Ee Ff Gg Hh Ii Jj Kk Ll Mm Nn Oo
Pp Qq Rr Ss Tt Uu Vv Ww Xx Yy Zz
0123456789
—

Panno Text Light 20pt
*Panno Text Light Italic 20pt*
Panno Text Semi Light 20pt
*Panno Text Semi Light Italic 20pt*
Panno Text Normal 20pt
*Panno Text Normal Italic 20pt*
**Panno Text Medium 20pt**
*Panno Text Medium Italic 20pt*
**Panno Text Semi Bold 20pt**
***Panno Text Semi Bold Italic 20pt***
**Panno Text Bold 20pt**
***Panno Text Bold Italic 20pt***

---

12/14  Panno Text Light

The quick brown fox jumps over the lazy dog. Voyez le brick géant que j'examine près du wharf. Zwölf Boxkämpfer jagen Viktor quer über den großen Sylter Deich. El veloz murciélago

12/14  Panno Text Normal

The quick brown fox jumps over the lazy dog. Voyez le brick géant que j'examine près du wharf. Zwölf Boxkämpfer jagen Viktor quer über den großen Sylter Deich. El veloz

12/14  Panno Text Medium

The quick brown fox jumps over the lazy dog. Voyez le brick géant que j'examine près du wharf. Zwölf Boxkämpfer jagen Viktor quer über den großen Sylter Deich. El veloz

12/14  Panno Text Bold

**The quick brown fox jumps over the lazy dog. Voyez le brick géant que j'examine près du wharf. Zwölf Boxkämpfer jagen Viktor quer über den großen Sylter Deich. El veloz murciélago hindú comía feliz cardillo y kiwi. La cigüeña tocaba el saxofón detrás del palenque de pajaatur? Rissimo lorereped ex es solore lab id molorro in rempore icabore rehenetur aliam aut voles**

9/12  Panno Text Light

The quick brown fox jumps over the lazy dog. Voyez le brick géant que j'examine près du wharf. Zwölf Boxkämpfer jagen Viktor quer über den großen Sylter Deich. El veloz murciélago hindú comía feliz cardillo y kiwi. La cigüeña tocaba el saxofón detrás del palenque de pajaatur? Rissimo lorereped ex es solore

9/12  Panno Text Normal

The quick brown fox jumps over the lazy dog. Voyez le brick géant que j'examine près du wharf. Zwölf Boxkämpfer jagen Viktor quer über den großen Sylter Deich. El veloz murciélago hindú comía feliz cardillo y kiwi. La cigüeña tocaba el saxofón detrás del palenque de pajaatur? Rissimo lorereped ex es

9/12  Panno Text Medium

The quick brown fox jumps over the lazy dog. Voyez le brick géant que j'examine près du wharf. Zwölf Boxkämpfer jagen Viktor quer über den großen Sylter Deich. El veloz murciélago hindú comía feliz cardillo y kiwi. La cigüeña tocaba el saxofón detrás del palenque de pajaatur? Rissimo lorereped

9/12  Panno Text Bold

**The quick brown fox jumps over the lazy dog. Voyez le brick géant que j'examine près du wharf. Zwölf Boxkämpfer jagen Viktor quer über den großen Sylter Deich. El veloz murciélago hindú comía feliz cardillo y kiwi. La cigüeña tocaba el saxofón detrás del palenque de pajaatur? Rissimo lorereped ex es solore lab id molorro in rempore icabore rehenetur aliam aut voles audae dem quam, secum eum facesequae consequ aepudam quia voluptiur repel in et faccustibus, nonsenis aut quisqui rero mi, ipiet lam ant ut maio et hil molupta tustis**

7/10  Panno Text Light

The quick brown fox jumps over the lazy dog. Voyez le brick géant que j'examine près du wharf. Zwölf Boxkämpfer jagen Viktor quer über den großen Sylter Deich. El veloz murciélago hindú comía feliz cardillo y kiwi. La cigüeña tocaba el saxofón detrás del palenque de pajaatur? Rissimo lorereped ex es solore lab id molorro in rempore icabore rehenetur aliam aut voles audae dem quam, secum eum facesequae consequ aepudam quia voluptiur repel in et faccustibus, nonsenis aut quisqui

7/10  Panno Text Normal

The quick brown fox jumps over the lazy dog. Voyez le brick géant que j'examine près du wharf. Zwölf Boxkämpfer jagen Viktor quer über den großen Sylter Deich. El veloz murciélago hindú comía feliz cardillo y kiwi. La cigüeña tocaba el saxofón detrás del palenque de pajaatur? Rissimo lorereped ex es solore lab id molorro in rempore icabore rehenetur aliam aut voles audae dem quam, secum eum facesequae consequ aepudam quia voluptiur repel

7/10  Panno Text Medium

The quick brown fox jumps over the lazy dog. Voyez le brick géant que j'examine près du wharf. Zwölf Boxkämpfer jagen Viktor quer über den großen Sylter Deich. El veloz murciélago hindú comía feliz cardillo y kiwi. La cigüeña tocaba el saxofón detrás del palenque de pajaatur? Rissimo lorereped ex es solore lab id molorro in rempore icabore rehenetur aliam aut voles audae dem quam, secum eum facesequae consequ aepudam quia voluptiur

7/10  Panno Text Bold

**The quick brown fox jumps over the lazy dog. Voyez le brick géant que j'examine près du wharf. Zwölf Boxkämpfer jagen Viktor quer über den großen Sylter Deich. El veloz murciélago hindú comía feliz cardillo y kiwi. La cigüeña tocaba el saxofón detrás del palenque de pajaatur? Rissimo lorereped ex es solore lab id molorro in rempore icabore rehenetur aliam aut voles audae dem quam, secum eum facesequae consequ aepudam quia voluptiur repel in et faccustibus, nonsenis aut quisqui rero mi, ipiet lam ant ut maio et hil molupta tustis atatur, consedi tasimol orerem aut volor andipsapis sit, illaut volore officatus alicae dusdaec tatecte cearum qui accatibus restiore nulpa secaerferum, nus dolenim in et quoditat que explam voluptict? Qui de illuptae. Dae nis illiberum volorro ritatis tinullo rerumqu atetur repro eatius asperibus. Rissimo lorereped ex es**

Page 44

Foundry  Bold Monday

Typeface  Aniek
Designer  Pieter van Rosmalen
Year  2009
Format  OpenType

## Anieketje! Kom eens.

Light
Book
Medium
Semi Bold
Bold
Extra Bold
Black

Aa Bb Cc Dd Ee Ff Gg Hh Ii Jj Kk Ll Mm Nn Oo Pp Qq Rr Ss Tt Uu Vv Ww Xx Yy Zz 0123456789

---

Typeface  Stanley
Designer  Pieter van Rosmalen
Year  2009
Format  OpenType

## Nope! Don't! Never!

**Normal**
**Stencil**
**Stencil Rough**

**Aa Bb Cc Dd Ee Ff Gg Hh Ii Jj Kk Ll Mm Nn Oo Pp Qq Rr Ss Tt Uu Vv Ww Xx Yy Zz 0123456789**

---

Typeface  Pinup
Designer  Pieter van Rosmalen
Year  2009
Format  OpenType

## Wat heb jij een lekker fontje, zeg!

**Regular**

**Aa Bb Cc Dd Ee Ff Gg Hh Ii Jj Kk Ll Mm Nn Oo Pp Qq Rr Ss Tt Uu Vv Ww Xx Yy Zz 0123456789**

Page 45

Foundry  Bold Monday

Typeface  Nitti
Designer  Pieter van Rosmalen
Year  2008
Format  OpenType

# Aa

Nitti Light 20pt
Nitti Normal 20pt
**Nitti Medium 20pt**
**Nitti Bold 20pt**
**Nitti Black 20pt**

Aa Bb Cc Dd Ee Ff Gg Hh
Ii Jj Kk Ll Mm Nn Oo Pp
Qq Rr Ss Tt Uu Vv Ww Xx
Yy Zz
0123456789
—

Nitti Typewriter Normal 20pt
Nitti Typewriter Underlined 20pt
N̶i̶t̶t̶i̶ ̶T̶y̶p̶e̶w̶r̶i̶t̶e̶r̶ ̶C̶o̶r̶r̶e̶c̶t̶e̶d̶ ̶2̶0̶p̶t̶
Nitti Typewriter Cameo 20pt
Nitti Typewriter Open 20pt

---

12/14  Nitti Light

The quick brown fox jumps over the lazy dog. Voyez le brick géant que j'examine près du wharf.

12/14  Nitti Normal

The quick brown fox jumps over the lazy dog. Voyez le brick géant que j'examine près du wharf.

12/14  Nitti Medium

The quick brown fox jumps over the lazy dog. Voyez le brick géant que j'examine près du wharf.

12/14  Nitti Bold

The quick brown fox jumps over the lazy dog. Voyez le brick géant que j'examine près du wharf. Zwölf Boxkämpfer jagen Viktor quer über den großen Sylter Deich. El veloz murciélago hindú comía feliz cardillo y kiwi. La

9/12  Nitti Light

The quick brown fox jumps over the lazy dog. Voyez le brick géant que j'examine près du wharf. Zwölf Boxkämpfer jagen Viktor quer über den großen Sylter Deich. El veloz mur-

9/12  Nitti Normal

The quick brown fox jumps over the lazy dog. Voyez le brick géant que j'examine près du wharf. Zwölf Boxkämpfer jagen Viktor quer über den großen Sylter Deich. El veloz mur-

9/12  Nitti Medium

The quick brown fox jumps over the lazy dog. Voyez le brick géant que j'examine près du wharf. Zwölf Boxkämpfer jagen Viktor quer über den großen Sylter Deich. El veloz mur-

9/12  Nitti Bold

The quick brown fox jumps over the lazy dog. Voyez le brick géant que j'examine près du wharf. Zwölf Boxkämpfer jagen Viktor quer über den großen Sylter Deich. El veloz murciélago hindú comía feliz cardillo y kiwi. La cigüeña tocaba el saxofón detrás del palenque de pajaatur? Rissimo lorereped ex es solore lab id molorro in rempore icabore

7/10  Nitti Light

The quick brown fox jumps over the lazy dog. Voyez le brick géant que j'examine près du wharf. Zwölf Boxkämpfer jagen Viktor quer über den großen Sylter Deich. El veloz murciélago hindú comía feliz cardillo y kiwi. La cigüeña tocaba el saxofón detrás del palenque

7/10  Nitti Normal

The quick brown fox jumps over the lazy dog. Voyez le brick géant que j'examine près du wharf. Zwölf Boxkämpfer jagen Viktor quer über den großen Sylter Deich. El veloz murciélago hindú comía feliz cardillo y kiwi. La cigüeña tocaba el saxofón detrás del palenque

7/10  Nitti Medium

The quick brown fox jumps over the lazy dog. Voyez le brick géant que j'examine près du wharf. Zwölf Boxkämpfer jagen Viktor quer über den großen Sylter Deich. El veloz murciélago hindú comía feliz cardillo y kiwi. La cigüeña tocaba el saxofón detrás del palenque

7/10  Nitti Bold

The quick brown fox jumps over the lazy dog. Voyez le brick géant que j'examine près du wharf. Zwölf Boxkämpfer jagen Viktor quer über den großen Sylter Deich. El veloz murciélago hindú comía feliz cardillo y kiwi. La cigüeña tocaba el saxofón detrás del palenque de pajaatur? Rissimo lorereped ex es solore lab id molorro in rempore icabore rehenetur aliam aut voles audae dem quam, secum eum facesequae consequ aepudam quia voluptiur repel in et faccustibus, nonsenis aut quisqui rero mi, ipiet lam ant ut maio et hil molup-

# B

## Büro Dunst

Christoph Dunst

—

Berlin, Germany

—

Since 2006

Büro Dunst is an independent font foundry and design studio based in Berlin, Germany. Dedicated to fine typography, the studio works on typefaces for both retail and custom purposes, as well as on applied typography projects such as editorial, corporate and brand design. Christoph Dunst founded the studio in The Hague in 2006, moved to Berlin in 2009, renaming it Büro Dunst.

## Info

—Why?
After finishing the first typeface, I was considering going to an established label. But what frightened me a bit was the idea they could just pick what they thought would sell or would set up their promotion adjusted to politics. My idea was to establish a small collection of typefaces that I would enjoy working with.

—People on staff
2

—Type designers on staff
1

—Font families
4

—Designers represented
1

—Web shop
burodunst.com

—Distributors
FontShop, MyFonts

—Basic license
Depending on the typeface, single weights are about $50, families c. $300.

### Typeface selection

Heimat Sans
Novel Pro
Novel Sans Pro

24pt

## People

—Christoph Dunst studied at the Royal Academy of Fine Arts in The Hague, Netherlands, where he graduated with a degree in Graphic and Typographic Design and an MA in Type Design. In 2009 the Type Directors Club of New York awarded the Certificate of Excellence in Type Design to his Novel font family. Novel was also nominated by the German Ministry of Economy and Technology for the Design Prize of Germany 2010.

Christoph Dunst, type specimens for Novel Pro and Novel Sans Pro.

Page
47

Karin Bucher, Matthias Kuhn: *Die Mona Lisa von Trogen.* In the eighteenth and nineteenth centuries the textile trade was huge in the eastern part of Switzerland. A large collection of portraits from this era formed the foundation of this book. The designers, GG Hafen Senn Stieger from St.Gallen, used Novel Pro for their award-winning design. Appenzeller Verlag, 2010.

Novel Pro and Novel Sans Pro were used throughout *Typoversity,* edited by Nadine Roßa, Andrea Schmidt, Patrick Marc Sommer. Design by Andrea Schmidt and Patrick Marc Sommer. Norman Beckmann Verlag, 2011.

Page
48

Foundry  Büro Dunst

Typeface   Heimat Sans
Designer   Christoph Dunst

Year     2009
Format   OpenType

# Aa

Aa Bb Cc Dd Ee Ff Gg Hh Ii Jj Kk Ll
Mm Nn Oo Pp Qq Rr Ss Tt Uu Vv
Ww Xx Yy Zz
0123456789
—

Heimat Sans Extra Light 20pt
*Heimat Sans Extra Light Italic 20pt*
Heimat Sans Light 20pt
*Heimat Sans Light Italic 20pt*
Heimat Sans Regular 20pt
*Heimat Sans Italic 20pt*
**Heimat Sans Semi Bold 20pt**
***Heimat Sans Semi Bold Italic 20pt***
**Heimat Sans Bold 20pt**
***Heimat Sans Bold Italic 20pt***
**Heimat Sans Extra Bold 20pt**
***Heimat Sans Extra Bold Italic 20pt***

---

12/14   Heimat Sans Light

The quick brown fox jumps over the lazy dog. Voyez le brick géant que j'examine près du wharf. Zwölf Boxkämpfer jagen Viktor quer über den

12/14   Heimat Sans Regular

The quick brown fox jumps over the lazy dog. Voyez le brick géant que j'examine près du wharf. Zwölf Boxkämpfer jagen Viktor quer über den

12/14   Heimat Sans Semi Bold

The quick brown fox jumps over the lazy dog. Voyez le brick géant que j'examine près du wharf. Zwölf Boxkämpfer jagen Viktor quer über

12/14   Heimat Sans Bold

The quick brown fox jumps over the lazy dog. Voyez le brick géant que j'examine près du wharf. Zwölf Boxkämpfer jagen Viktor quer über den großen Sylter Deich. El veloz murciélago hindú comía feliz cardillo y kiwi. La cigüeña tocaba el saxofón detrás del palenque de pajaatur? Rissimo Lorereped ex es

---

9/12   Heimat Sans Light

The quick brown fox jumps over the lazy dog. Voyez le brick géant que j'examine près du wharf. Zwölf Boxkämpfer jagen Viktor quer über den großen Sylter Deich. El veloz murciélago hindú comía feliz cardillo y kiwi. La cigüeña tocaba el saxofón detrás

9/12   Heimat Sans Regular

The quick brown fox jumps over the lazy dog. Voyez le brick géant que j'examine près du wharf. Zwölf Boxkämpfer jagen Viktor quer über den großen Sylter Deich. El veloz murciélago hindú comía feliz cardillo y kiwi. La cigüeña tocaba el

9/12   Heimat Sans Semi Bold

The quick brown fox jumps over the lazy dog. Voyez le brick géant que j'examine près du wharf. Zwölf Boxkämpfer jagen Viktor quer über den großen Sylter Deich. El veloz murciélago hindú comía feliz cardillo y kiwi. La cigüeña tocaba

9/12   Heimat Sans Bold

The quick brown fox jumps over the lazy dog. Voyez le brick géant que j'examine près du wharf. Zwölf Boxkämpfer jagen Viktor quer über den großen Sylter Deich. El veloz murciélago hindú comía feliz cardillo y kiwi. La cigüeña tocaba el saxofón detrás del palenque de pajaatur? Rissimo Lorereped ex es solore lab id molorro in rempore icabore rehenetur aliam aut voles audae dem quam, secum eum facesequae consequ aepudam quia voluptiur repel

---

7/10   Heimat Sans Light

The quick brown fox jumps over the lazy dog. Voyez le brick géant que j'examine près du wharf. Zwölf Boxkämpfer jagen Viktor quer über den großen Sylter Deich. El veloz murciélago hindú comía feliz cardillo y kiwi. La cigüeña tocaba el saxofón detrás del palenque de pajaatur? Rissimo Lorereped ex es solore lab id molorro in rempore icabore rehenetur aliam aut voles audae dem

7/10   Heimat Sans Regular

The quick brown fox jumps over the lazy dog. Voyez le brick géant que j'examine près du wharf. Zwölf Boxkämpfer jagen Viktor quer über den großen Sylter Deich. El veloz murciélago hindú comía feliz cardillo y kiwi. La cigüeña tocaba el saxofón detrás del palenque de pajaatur? Rissimo Lorereped ex es solore lab id molorro in rempore icabore rehenetur aliam aut voles

7/10   Heimat Sans Semi Bold

The quick brown fox jumps over the lazy dog. Voyez le brick géant que j'examine près du wharf. Zwölf Boxkämpfer jagen Viktor quer über den großen Sylter Deich. El veloz murciélago hindú comía feliz cardillo y kiwi. La cigüeña tocaba el saxofón detrás del palenque de pajaatur? Rissimo Lorereped ex es solore lab id molorro in rempore icabore rehenetur

7/10   Heimat Sans Bold

The quick brown fox jumps over the lazy dog. Voyez le brick géant que j'examine près du wharf. Zwölf Boxkämpfer jagen Viktor quer über den großen Sylter Deich. El veloz murciélago hindú comía feliz cardillo y kiwi. La cigüeña tocaba el saxofón detrás del palenque de pajaatur? Rissimo Lorereped ex es solore lab id molorro in rempore icabore rehenetur aliam aut voles audae dem quam, secum eum facesequae consequ aepudam quia voluptiur repel in et faccustibus, nonsenis aut quisqui rero mi, ipiet lam ant ut maio et hil molupta tustis atatur, consedi tasimol orerem aut volor andipsapis sit, illaut volore officatus alicae dusdaec tatecte cearum qui accatibus restiore nulpa secaerferum,

Page 49

Typeface  Novel Pro, Sans Pro  Year    2008–2010
Designer  Christoph Dunst      Format  OpenType

# Aa

Aa Bb Cc Dd Ee Ff Gg Hh Ii Jj Kk Ll Mm Nn Oo Pp Qq Rr Ss Tt Uu Vv Ww Xx Yy Zz
0123456789
—

Novel Pro ExtraLight 20pt
*Novel Pro ExtraLight Italic 20pt*
Novel Pro Light 20pt
*Novel Pro Light Italic 20pt*
Novel Pro Regular 20pt
*Novel Pro Italic 20pt*
**Novel Pro SemiBold 20pt**
***Novel Pro SemiBold Italic 20pt***
**Novel Pro Bold 20pt**
***Novel Pro Bold Italic 20pt***
**Novel Pro ExtraBold 20pt**
***Novel Pro ExtraBold Italic 20pt***
Novel Sans Pro ExtraLight 20pt
*Novel Sans Pro ExtraLight Italic 20pt*
Novel Sans Pro Light 20pt
*Novel Sans Pro Light Italic 20pt*
Novel Sans Pro Regular 20pt
*Novel Sans Pro Italic 20pt*
**Novel Sans Pro SemiBold 20pt**
***Novel Sans Pro SemiBold Italic 20pt***
**Novel Sans Pro Bold 20pt**
***Novel Sans Pro Bold Italic 20pt***
**Novel Sans Pro Extra Bold 20pt**
***Novel Sans Pro Extra Bold Italic 20pt***

---

12/14  Novel Pro Extra Light

The quick brown fox jumps over the lazy dog. Voyez le brick géant que j'examine près du wharf. Zwölf Boxkämpfer jagen Viktor quer über

12/14  Novel Pro Light

The quick brown fox jumps over the lazy dog. Voyez le brick géant que j'examine près du wharf. Zwölf Boxkämpfer jagen Viktor quer

12/14  Novel Pro SemiBold

The quick brown fox jumps over the lazy dog. Voyez le brick géant que j'examine près du wharf. Zwölf Boxkämpfer jagen Vik-

12/14  Novel Pro Regular

The quick brown fox jumps over the lazy dog. Voyez le brick géant que j'examine près du wharf. Zwölf Boxkämpfer jagen Viktor quer über den großen Sylter Deich. El veloz murciélago hindú comía feliz cardillo y kiwi. La cigüeña tocaba el saxofón detrás del palenque de pajaatur? Rissimo lorereped ex

12/14  Novel Sans Pro Regular

The quick brown fox jumps over the lazy dog. Voyez le brick géant que j'examine près du wharf. Zwölf Boxkämpfer jagen Viktor quer über den großen Sylter Deich. El veloz murciélago hindú comía feliz cardillo y kiwi. La cigüeña tocaba el saxofón detrás del palenque de pajaatur? Rissimo lorereped ex es solore

7/10  Novel Pro Regular

The quick brown fox jumps over the lazy dog. Voyez le brick géant que j'examine près du wharf. Zwölf Boxkämpfer jagen Viktor quer über den großen Sylter Deich. El veloz murciélago hindú comía feliz cardillo y kiwi. La cigüeña tocaba el saxofón detrás del palenque de pajaatur? Rissimo lorereped ex es solore lab id molorro in rempore icabore rehenetur aliam aut voles audae dem quam, secum eum facesequae consequ aepudam quia voluptiur repel in et faccustibus, nonsenis aut quisqui rero mi, ipiet lam ant ut maio et hil molupta tustis atatur, consedi tasimol orerem aut volor andipsapis sit, illaut volore officatus alicae dusdaec tatecte cearum qui accatibus restiore nulpa secaerferum, nus dole-

# C

— Canada Type

—

Patrick Griffin,
Rebecca Alaccari

—

Toronto, Canada

—

Since
2004

Canada Type is an independent digital type design and development firm based in Toronto. After its humble artistic start with a few retail typefaces and some custom publishing work in early 2004, the quality and affordability of Canada Type's work made it popular with graphic designers all around the world. The foundry continues to expand its library on a monthly basis, as well as to provide custom work, technical support, and multiple type licensing to a large list of publishing clients.

## Info

—Why?
Canada Type was originally founded as a specialty type design resource for creative firms, as well as an outlet to retail a few fonts we had designed previously. We still work every day under the same aims of our founding, but the operation is much more efficient and on an entirely higher level now.

—People on staff
3

—Type designers on staff
3

—Font families
Approx. 220

—Designers represented
10

—Web shop
Not yet! Next year.

—Distributors
MyFonts, Veer, Fontshop, Fonts.com, Fontbros, Fontspring, Hype For Type, YouWorkForThem, Fonthaus.

—Webfont services
MyFonts, Fontspring.

—Basic license
Prices vary by design. Typical price of a single font: $24.95

## People

—Patrick Griffin: Worked in film production design for 16 years before finally following his heart and giving in to a lifelong obsession with the alphabet. Co-founder in 2004.

—Rebecca Alaccari: Worked at a variety of design agencies around Toronto before coming up with the idea of founding Canada Type in 2004.

—Kevin King: Graduated from the extended design program at Humber College, as part of which he studied type design under Patrick Griffin. Joined Canada Type in 2010.

—Philip Bouwsma: American calligraphy maestro who studied under the legendary Arthur Baker in the 1970s, and came into his own brilliant individualism over four decades of inimitable alphabet design. With Canada Type since 2005.

—Hans van Maanen: Dutch science writer and lifelong type enthusiast. Specializes in reviving early- to mid-20th century Dutch type treasures. With Canada Type since 2006.

## Typeface selection

Didot
Informa Pro
Maestro Pro
Memoriam Pro
Orpheus

Roos
Serena
Sol Pro
Taboo Pro

24pt

Page
51

Selection of type samples designed by Canada Type for their typefaces.

**Previous page**
Diploma.

**Right** Mayfair.

**Below**
Gala.

**Bottom right**
Ambassador.

**Left**
Each December, the last issue of *New York Times Magazine* is dedicated to the people who passed away during the year. Canada Type's Patrick Griffin designed the Memoriam typeface for the 2008 edition of this special issue. Title page. Art direction: Nancy Harris Rouemy.

Foundry Canada Type

Typeface Memoriam Pro
Designer Patrick Griffin
Year 2011
Format OpenType

*Uh Lala*

Pro Regular
Pro Headline
Pro Inline
Pro Outline

Aa Bb Cc Dd Ee Ff Gg Hh
Ii Jj Kk Ll Mm Nn Oo Pp
Qq Rr Ss Tt Uu Vv Ww Xx
Yy Zz 0123456789

Typeface Maestro Pro
Designer Philip Bouwsma, Patrick Griffin
Year 2009
Format OpenType

*Maestro Vivaldini*

Regular
Bold

Aa Bb Cc Dd Ee Ff Gg Hh Ii Jj Kk Ll Mm
Nn Oo Pp Qq Rr Ss Tt Uu Vv Ww Xx Yy Zz
0123456789

Typeface Serena
Designer Stefan Schlesinger, Hans van Maanen
Year 2007
Format OpenType

*Serena Williams*

Regular

Aa Bb Cc Dd Ee Ff Gg Hh Ii Jj Kk
Ll Mm Nn Oo Pp Qq Rr Ss Tt Uu
Vv Ww Xx Yy Zz 0123456789

Foundry  Canada Type

Typeface  Roos
Designer  Sjoerd Hendrik de Roos,
          Hans van Maanen,
          Patrick Griffin
Year      2009
Format    OpenType

# Aa

Aa Bb Cc Dd Ee Ff Gg Hh Ii Jj Kk Ll
Mm Nn Oo Pp Qq Rr Ss Tt Uu Vv
Ww Xx Yy Zz
0123456789
—

Roos Roman Regular 20pt
*Roos Roman Italic 20pt*
Roos Roman Semi Bold Regular 20pt
*Roos Roman Semi Bold Italic 20pt*
Roos Display Sc Regular 20pt
Roos Semi Bold Sc Regular 20pt
Roos Initials Regular

9/12  Roos Roman Regular

The quick brown fox jumps over the lazy dog. Voyez le brick géant que j'examine près du wharf. Zwölf Boxkämpfer jagen Viktor quer über den großen Sylter Deich. El veloz murciélago hindú comía feliz cardillo y kiwi. La cigüeña tocaba el saxofón detrás del palenque de pajaatur? Rissimo lorereped ex es solore lab id molorro in rempore icabore rehenetur aliam aut voles audae dem quam, secum eum facesequae consequ aepudam quia

7/10  Roos Roman Regular

The quick brown fox jumps over the lazy dog. Voyez le brick géant que j'examine près du wharf. Zwölf Boxkämpfer jagen Viktor quer über den großen Sylter Deich. El veloz murciélago hindú comía feliz cardillo y kiwi. La cigüeña tocaba el saxofón detrás del palenque de pajaatur? Rissimo lorereped ex es solore lab id molorro in rempore icabore rehenetur aliam aut voles audae dem quam, secum eum facesequae consequ aepudam quia voluptiur repel in et faccustibus, nonsenis aut quisqui rero mi, ipiet lam ant ut maio et hil molupta tustis atatur, consedi tasimol orerem aut volor andipsapis sit, illaut volore officatus alicae dusdaec tatecte cearum

---

Typeface  Orpheus
Designer  Patrick Griffin &
          Kevin King
          (based on a design by
          Walter Tiemann)
Year      2011
Format    OpenType

# Aa

Aa Bb Cc Dd Ee Ff Gg Hh Ii Jj Kk Ll
Mm Nn Oo Pp Qq Rr Ss Tt Uu Vv
Ww Xx Yy Zz
0123456789
—

Orpheus Regular 20pt
*Orpheus Italic 20pt*
Orpheus Sc Regular 20pt
Orpheus Alts
ABCDEFGHIJKLMNORSTUVWXYZ
No No No ffffififfifflfbfhfjfkft✦✧

9/12  Orpheus Regular

The quick brown fox jumps over the lazy dog. Voyez le brick géant que j'examine près du wharf. Zwölf Boxkämpfer jagen Viktor quer über den großen Sylter Deich. El veloz murciélago hindú comía feliz cardillo y kiwi. La cigüeña tocaba el saxofón detrás del palenque de pajaatur? Rissimo lorereped ex es solore lab id molorro in rempore icabore rehenetur aliam aut voles audae dem quam, secum eum facesequae consequ aepudam quia voluptiur repel in et faccustibus, nonsenis aut quisqui rero mi, ipiet

7/10  Orpheus Regular

The quick brown fox jumps over the lazy dog. Voyez le brick géant que j'examine près du wharf. Zwölf Boxkämpfer jagen Viktor quer über den großen Sylter Deich. El veloz murciélago hindú comía feliz cardillo y kiwi. La cigüeña tocaba el saxofón detrás del palenque de pajaatur? Rissimo lorereped ex es solore lab id molorro in rempore icabore rehenetur aliam aut voles audae dem quam, secum eum facesequae consequ aepudam quia voluptiur repel in et faccustibus, nonsenis aut quisqui rero mi, ipiet lam ant ut maio et hil molupta tustis atatur, consedi tasimol orerem aut volor andipsapis sit, illaut volore officatus alicae dusdaec tatecte cearum qui accatibus restiore nulpa secaerferum, nus dolenim in et quoditat que explam volupictur? Qui de illuptae. Dae nis illiberum voloro ritatis tinullo

Foundry Canada Type

Typeface Sol Pro
Designer Patrick Griffin, Kevin Allan King
Year 2010
Format OpenType

# Solaris Station

Light
*Light Italic*
Regular
*Italic*
Medium
*Medium Italic*
**Bold**
***Bold Italic***
**Black**
***Black Italic***

Aa Bb Cc Dd Ee Ff Gg Hh Ii
Jj Kk Ll Mm Nn Oo Pp Qq Rr
Ss Tt Uu Vv Ww Xx Yy Zz
0123456789

---

Typeface Didot
Designer Bill Troop
Year 1999–2009
Format OpenType

# Encyclopédie universelle

Display Regular
Display Demi
**Display Bold**

Aa Bb Cc Dd Ee Ff Gg Hh Ii Jj Kk Ll
Mm Nn Oo Pp Qq Rr Ss Tt Uu Vv
Ww Xx Yy Zz 0123456789

---

Typeface Taboo Pro
Designer Patrick Griffin
Year 2009
Format OpenType

# islands

Regular
*Italic*
Medium
*Medium Italic*
**Bold**
***Bold Italic***

Foundry  Canada Type

Typeface  Informa Pro         Year     2009
Designer  Patrick Griffin     Format   OpenType

# Aa

Aa Bb Cc Dd Ee Ff Gg Hh Ii Jj Kk
Ll Mm Nn Oo Pp Qq Rr Ss Tt Uu
Vv Ww Xx Yy Zz
0123456789
—

Informa Pro Light 20pt
*Informa Pro Light Italic 20pt*
Informa Pro Regular 20pt
*Informa Pro Italic 20pt*
**Informa Pro Medium 20pt**
***Informa Pro Medium Italic 20pt***
**Informa Pro Bold 20pt**
***Informa Pro Bold Italic 20pt***
Informa Pro Light Condensed 20pt
Informa Pro Condensed 20pt
**Informa Pro Medium Condensed 20pt**
**Informa Pro Bold Condensed 20pt**

---

12/14   Informa Pro Light

The quick brown fox jumps over the lazy dog. Voyez le brick géant que j'examine près du wharf. Zwölf Boxkämpfer jagen Viktor quer über den

12/14   Informa Pro Regular

The quick brown fox jumps over the lazy dog. Voyez le brick géant que j'examine près du wharf. Zwölf Boxkämpfer jagen Viktor quer über den

12/14   Informa Pro Medium

The quick brown fox jumps over the lazy dog. Voyez le brick géant que j'examine près du wharf. Zwölf Boxkämpfer jagen Viktor quer über

12/14   Informa Pro Bold

The quick brown fox jumps over the lazy dog. Voyez le brick géant que j'examine près du wharf. Zwölf Boxkämpfer jagen Viktor quer über den großen Sylter Deich. El veloz murciélago hindú comía feliz cardillo y kiwi. La cigüeña tocaba el saxofón detrás del palenque de pajaatur? Rissimo lorereped ex es solore

9/12   Informa Pro Light

The quick brown fox jumps over the lazy dog. Voyez le brick géant que j'examine près du wharf. Zwölf Boxkämpfer jagen Viktor quer über den großen Sylter Deich. El veloz murciélago hindú comía feliz cardillo y kiwi. La cigüeña tocaba el

9/12   Informa Pro Regular

The quick brown fox jumps over the lazy dog. Voyez le brick géant que j'examine près du wharf. Zwölf Boxkämpfer jagen Viktor quer über den großen Sylter Deich. El veloz murciélago hindú comía feliz cardillo y kiwi. La cigüeña tocaba el

9/12   Informa Pro Medium

The quick brown fox jumps over the lazy dog. Voyez le brick géant que j'examine près du wharf. Zwölf Boxkämpfer jagen Viktor quer über den großen Sylter Deich. El veloz murciélago hindú comía feliz cardillo y kiwi. La cigüeña tocaba

9/12   Informa Pro Bold

The quick brown fox jumps over the lazy dog. Voyez le brick géant que j'examine près du wharf. Zwölf Boxkämpfer jagen Viktor quer über den großen Sylter Deich. El veloz murciélago hindú comía feliz cardillo y kiwi. La cigüeña tocaba el saxofón detrás del palenque de pajaatur? Rissimo lorereped ex es solore lab id molorro in rempore icabore rehenetur aliam aut voles audae dem quam, secum eum facesequae consequ aepudam quia voluptiur repel in et fac-

7/10   Informa Pro Light

The quick brown fox jumps over the lazy dog. Voyez le brick géant que j'examine près du wharf. Zwölf Boxkämpfer jagen Viktor quer über den großen Sylter Deich. El veloz murciélago hindú comía feliz cardillo y kiwi. La cigüeña tocaba el saxofón detrás del palenque de pajaatur? Rissimo lorereped ex es solore lab id molorro in rempore icabore rehenetur aliam aut voles audae dem

7/10   Informa Pro Regular

The quick brown fox jumps over the lazy dog. Voyez le brick géant que j'examine près du wharf. Zwölf Boxkämpfer jagen Viktor quer über den großen Sylter Deich. El veloz murciélago hindú comía feliz cardillo y kiwi. La cigüeña tocaba el saxofón detrás del palenque de pajaatur? Rissimo lorereped ex es solore lab id molorro in rempore icabore rehenetur aliam aut voles au-

7/10   Informa Pro Medium

The quick brown fox jumps over the lazy dog. Voyez le brick géant que j'examine près du wharf. Zwölf Boxkämpfer jagen Viktor quer über den großen Sylter Deich. El veloz murciélago hindú comía feliz cardillo y kiwi. La cigüeña tocaba el saxofón detrás del palenque de pajaatur? Rissimo lorereped ex es solore lab id molorro in rempore icabore rehenetur aliam aut voles

7/10   Informa Pro Bold

The quick brown fox jumps over the lazy dog. Voyez le brick géant que j'examine près du wharf. Zwölf Boxkämpfer jagen Viktor quer über den großen Sylter Deich. El veloz murciélago hindú comía feliz cardillo y kiwi. La cigüeña tocaba el saxofón detrás del palenque de pajaatur? Rissimo lorereped ex es solore lab id molorro in rempore icabore rehenetur aliam aut voles audae dem quam, secum eum facesequae consequ aepudam quia voluptiur repel in et faccustibus, nonsenis aut quisqui rero mi, ipiet lam ant ut maio et hil molupta tustis atatur, consedi tasimol orerem aut volor andipsapis sit, illaut volore officatus alicae dusdaec tatecte cearum qui accatibus restiore nulpa secaerferum, nus doleinim in et quoditat que explam

# C
—
Colophon

—
Anthony Sheret,
Edd Harrington
—
Brighton,
UK
—
Since
2009

Colophon is an independent type foundry set up by the Brighton based design studio The Entente (Anthony Sheret & Edd Harrington). As well as distributing and acting as a platform for fonts designed by The Entente, it selects fonts designed by other designers to distribute and create products for. Working in a similar way to a publisher, some of Colophon's typefaces will be limited edition releases.

## Info

—Why?
The foundry was set up as an addition to our main studio practice. We wanted to initially release our typefaces that we had created for projects, as well as our for our friends. From there we started to develop the esthetic and catalog of the foundry.

—People on staff
2

—Type designers on staff
1

—Font families
11

—Designers represented
4 (soon to be 7)

—Web shop
colophon-foundry.org

—Distributors
None

—Webfont service
Fontdeck

—Basic license
Single weights £40–£50 (3 devices at a single location).

—Special conditions
Online calculator for multi-user licenses.

Typeface selection

Apercu
Fortescue
Monosten
Pantograph
**Raisonne**
Reader
**Transcript**

24pt

## People

—Anthony Sheret, partner–designer. Born Redhill, Surrey, UK. London College of Communication 2005–2006, Brighton University 2006–2008.

—Edd Harrington, type designer CRC Cambridge 2005–2006; Brighton University 2006–2009. Self-taught in type design.

Page
57

**Left and below**
Promotional brochures for Monosten
created by The Entente, 2010–2011.

**Bottom left**
Promotional postcard,
The Entente 2010.

**Right**
Specimen for Apercu,
The Entente 2010.

---

Light & *Light Italic*
Alfa Bravo Charlie
*Delta Echo Foxtrot*
Regular & *Regular Italic*
Golf Hotel India Juliet
*Kilo Lima Mike November*
Medium & *Medium Italic*
Oscar Papa Quebec
*Romeo Sierra Tango*
**Bold & *Bold Italic***
**Uniform Victor Whiskey**
***X-ray Yankee Zulu***

p.04: Echo Sierra Sierra Alfa Yankee
p.05: Family Overview

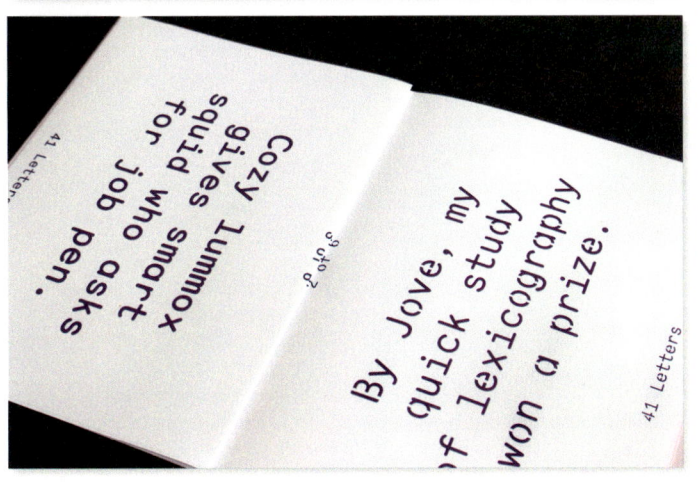

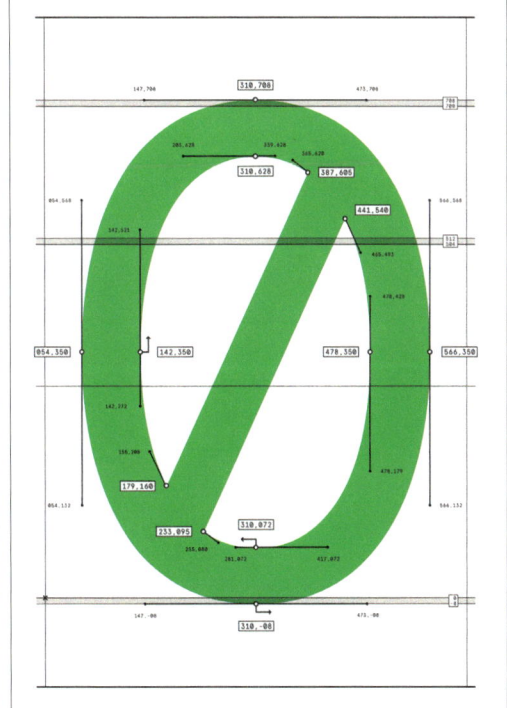

| | | |
|---|---|---|
| Typeface Apercu | Year | 2010 |
| Designer The Entente (Anthony Sheret, Edd Harrington) | Format | OpenType |

# Aa

Aa Bb Cc Dd Ee Ff Gg Hh Ii Jj Kk
Ll Mm Nn Oo Pp Qq Rr Ss Tt Uu
Vv Ww Xx Yy Zz
0123456789
—

Apercu Light 24pt
*Apercu Light Italic 24pt*
Apercu Regular 24pt
*Apercu Italic 24pt*
**Apercu Medium 24pt**
***Apercu Medium Italic 24pt***
**Apercu Bold 24pt**
***Apercu Bold Italic 24pt***

Apercu Mono 24pt

---

**12/14 Apercu Light**

The quick brown fox jumps over the lazy dog. Voyez le brick géant que j'examine près du wharf. Zwölf Boxkämpfer jagen Viktor quer über

**12/14 Apercu Regular**

The quick brown fox jumps over the lazy dog. Voyez le brick géant que j'examine près du wharf. Zwölf Boxkämpfer jagen Viktor quer über

**12/14 Apercu Medium**

The quick brown fox jumps over the lazy dog. Voyez le brick géant que j'examine près du wharf. Zwölf Boxkämpfer jagen Viktor quer über den

**12/14 Apercu Bold**

The quick brown fox jumps over the lazy dog. Voyez le brick géant que j'examine près du wharf. Zwölf Boxkämpfer jagen Viktor quer über den großen Sylter Deich. El veloz murciélago hindú comía feliz cardillo y kiwi. La cigüeña tocaba el saxofón detrás del palenque de pajaatur? Rissimo lorereped ex es

**9/12 Apercu Light**

The quick brown fox jumps over the lazy dog. Voyez le brick géant que j'examine près du wharf. Zwölf Boxkämpfer jagen Viktor quer über den großen Sylter Deich. El veloz murciélago hindú comía feliz cardillo y kiwi. La cigüe-

**9/12 Apercu Regular**

The quick brown fox jumps over the lazy dog. Voyez le brick géant que j'examine près du wharf. Zwölf Boxkämpfer jagen Viktor quer über den großen Sylter Deich. El veloz murciélago hindú comía feliz cardillo y kiwi. La

**9/12 Apercu Medium**

The quick brown fox jumps over the lazy dog. Voyez le brick géant que j'examine près du wharf. Zwölf Boxkämpfer jagen Viktor quer über den großen Sylter Deich. El veloz murciélago hindú comía feliz cardillo y kiwi. La

**9/12 Apercu Bold**

The quick brown fox jumps over the lazy dog. Voyez le brick géant que j'examine près du wharf. Zwölf Boxkämpfer jagen Viktor quer über den großen Sylter Deich. El veloz murciélago hindú comía feliz cardillo y kiwi. La cigüeña tocaba el saxofón detrás del palenque de pajaatur? Rissimo lorereped ex es solore lab id molorro in rempore icabore rehenetur aliam aut voles audae dem quam, secum eum facesequae consequ aepudam quia voluptiur

**7/10 Apercu Light**

The quick brown fox jumps over the lazy dog. Voyez le brick géant que j'examine près du wharf. Zwölf Boxkämpfer jagen Viktor quer über den großen Sylter Deich. El veloz murciélago hindú comía feliz cardillo y kiwi. La cigüeña tocaba el saxofón detrás del palenque de pajaatur? Rissimo lorereped ex es solore lab id molorro in rempore icabore rehenetur aliam

**7/10 Apercu Regular**

The quick brown fox jumps over the lazy dog. Voyez le brick géant que j'examine près du wharf. Zwölf Boxkämpfer jagen Viktor quer über den großen Sylter Deich. El veloz murciélago hindú comía feliz cardillo y kiwi. La cigüeña tocaba el saxofón detrás del palenque de pajaatur? Rissimo lorereped ex es solore lab id molorro in rempore icabore rehenetur aliam

**7/10 Apercu Medium**

The quick brown fox jumps over the lazy dog. Voyez le brick géant que j'examine près du wharf. Zwölf Boxkämpfer jagen Viktor quer über den großen Sylter Deich. El veloz murciélago hindú comía feliz cardillo y kiwi. La cigüeña tocaba el saxofón detrás del palenque de pajaatur? Rissimo lorereped ex es solore lab id molorro in rempore icabore rehenetur aliam

**7/10 Apercu Bold**

The quick brown fox jumps over the lazy dog. Voyez le brick géant que j'examine près du wharf. Zwölf Boxkämpfer jagen Viktor quer über den großen Sylter Deich. El veloz murciélago hindú comía feliz cardillo y kiwi. La cigüeña tocaba el saxofón detrás del palenque de pajaatur? Rissimo lorereped ex es solore lab id molorro in rempore icabore rehenetur aliam aut voles audae dem quam, secum eum facesequae consequ aepudam quia voluptiur repel in et faccustibus, nonsenis aut quisqui rero mi, ipiet lam ant ut maio et hil molupta tustis atatur, consedi tasimol orerem aut volor andipsapis sit, illaut volore officatus alicae dusdaec tatecte cearum qui accatibus restiore nulpa secaerferum, nus dolenim in et quoditat que explam volupictur? Qui de illuptae.

Foundry Colophon

Typeface Reader
Designer The Entente (Anthony Sheret, Edd Harrington)
Year 2009–2010
Format OpenType

# Aa

Aa Bb Cc Dd Ee Ff Gg Hh Ii Jj Kk Ll Mm Nn Oo Pp Qq Rr Ss Tt Uu Vv Ww Xx Yy Zz
0123456789
—

Reader Regular 24pt
*Reader Italic 24pt*
**Reader Medium 24pt**
***Reader Medium Italic 24pt***
**Reader Bold 24pt**
***Reader Bold Italic 24pt***

**READER BLACK 24PT**

---

**12/14 Reader Regular**

The quick brown fox jumps over the lazy dog. Voyez le brick géant que j'examine près du wharf. Zwölf Boxkämpfer jagen Viktor quer über den großen Sylter Deich. El veloz murciélago hindú comía feliz cardillo y kiwi. La cigüeña tocaba

**9/12 Reader Regular**

The quick brown fox jumps over the lazy dog. Voyez le brick géant que j'examine près du wharf. Zwölf Boxkämpfer jagen Viktor quer über den großen Sylter Deich. El veloz murciélago hindú comía feliz cardillo y kiwi. La cigüeña tocaba el saxofón detrás del palenque de pajaatur? Rissimo lorereped ex es solore lab id molorro in rempore icabore rehenetur aliam

**7/10 Reader Regular**

The quick brown fox jumps over the lazy dog. Voyez le brick géant que j'examine près du wharf. Zwölf Boxkämpfer jagen Viktor quer über den großen Sylter Deich. El veloz murciélago hindú comía feliz cardillo y kiwi. La cigüeña tocaba el saxofón detrás del palenque de pajaatur? Rissimo lorereped ex es solore lab id molorro in rempore icabore rehenetur aliam aut voles audae dem quam, secum eum facesequae consequ aepudam quia voluptiur repel in et faccustibus, nonsenis aut quisqui rero mi, ipiet lam ant ut maio et hil molupta tustis atatur, consedi tasimol orerem aut volor

**12/14 Reader Medium**

The quick brown fox jumps over the lazy dog. Voyez le brick géant que j'examine près du wharf. Zwölf Boxkämpfer jagen Viktor quer über den großen Sylter Deich. El veloz murciélago hindú comía feliz cardillo y kiwi. La

**9/12 Reader Medium**

The quick brown fox jumps over the lazy dog. Voyez le brick géant que j'examine près du wharf. Zwölf Boxkämpfer jagen Viktor quer über den großen Sylter Deich. El veloz murciélago hindú comía feliz cardillo y kiwi. La cigüeña tocaba el saxofón detrás del palenque de pajaatur? Rissimo lorereped ex es solore lab id molorro in rempore icabore

**7/10 Reader Medium**

The quick brown fox jumps over the lazy dog. Voyez le brick géant que j'examine près du wharf. Zwölf Boxkämpfer jagen Viktor quer über den großen Sylter Deich. El veloz murciélago hindú comía feliz cardillo y kiwi. La cigüeña tocaba el saxofón detrás del palenque de pajaatur? Rissimo lorereped ex es solore lab id molorro in rempore icabore rehenetur aliam aut voles audae dem quam, secum eum facesequae consequ aepudam quia voluptiur repel in et faccustibus, nonsenis aut quisqui rero mi, ipiet lam ant ut maio et hil molupta tustis atatur, consedi tasimol

**12/14 Reader Bold**

**The quick brown fox jumps over the lazy dog. Voyez le brick géant que j'examine près du wharf. Zwölf Boxkämpfer jagen Viktor quer über den großen Sylter Deich. El veloz murciélago hindú comía feliz cardillo y kiwi. La cigüeña tocaba el saxofón detrás del palenque de pajaros.**

**9/12 Reader Bold**

**The quick brown fox jumps over the lazy dog. Voyez le brick géant que j'examine près du wharf. Zwölf Boxkämpfer jagen Viktor quer über den großen Sylter Deich. El veloz murciélago hindú comía feliz cardillo y kiwi. La cigüeña tocaba el saxofón detrás del palenque de pajaatur? Rissimo lorereped ex es solore lab id molorro in rempore icabore rehenetur aliam aut voles audae dem quam, secum eum facesequae**

**7/10 Reader Bold**

**The quick brown fox jumps over the lazy dog. Voyez le brick géant que j'examine près du wharf. Zwölf Boxkämpfer jagen Viktor quer über den großen Sylter Deich. El veloz murciélago hindú comía feliz cardillo y kiwi. La cigüeña tocaba el saxofón detrás del palenque de pajaatur? Rissimo lorereped ex es solore lab id molorro in rempore icabore rehenetur aliam aut voles audae dem quam, secum eum facesequae consequ aepudam quia voluptiur repel in et faccustibus, nonsenis aut quisqui rero mi, ipiet lam ant ut maio et hil molupta tustis atatur, consedi tasimol orerem aut volor andipsapis sit, illaut volore officatus alicae dusdaec**

Typeface  Raisonne
Designer  Benjamin Critton
Year  2011
Format  OpenType

# Catalogue raisonné

**Demi Bold**

Aa Bb Cc Dd Ee Ff Gg Hh
Ii Jj Kk Ll Mm Nn Oo Pp Qq
Rr Ss Tt Uu Vv Ww Xx Yy Zz
0123456789

---

Typeface  Transcript
Designer  The Entente
          (Anthony Sheret,
          Edd Harrington)
Year  2011
Format  OpenType

# Transcript Files

**Bold**

Aa Bb Cc Dd Ee Ff Gg Hh Ii Jj Kk
Ll Mm Nn Oo Pp Qq Rr Ss Tt Uu Vv
Ww Xx Yy Zz 0123456789

---

Typeface  Pantograph
Designer  StudioMakgill
Year  2008–2010
Format  OpenType

# Pantograph Reader

Regular

Aa Bb Cc Dd Ee Ff Gg Hh Ii Jj Kk Ll
Mm Nn Oo Pp Qq Rr Ss Tt Uu Vv Ww
Xx Yy Zz 0123456789

Foundry Colophon

---

| | | | |
|---|---|---|---|
| Typeface | Monosten | Year | 2010–2011 |
| Designer | The Entente (Anthony Sheret, Edd Harrington) | Format | OpenType |

# Aa

Monosten A 20pt
Monosten B 20pt
**Monosten C 20pt**
Monosten D 20pt
Monosten E 20pt
Monosten F 20pt

Aa Bb Cc Dd Ee Ff Gg Hh
Ii Jj Kk Ll Mm Nn Oo Pp
Qq Rr Ss Tt Uu Vv Ww Xx
Yy Zz
0123456789
—

**9/12   Monosten A**

The quick brown fox jumps over the lazy dog. Voyez le brick géant que j'examine près du wharf. Zwölf Boxkämpfer jagen Viktor quer über den großen Sylter Deich. El veloz murciélago hindú comía feliz cardillo y kiwi. La cigüeña tocaba el saxofón detrás del palenque

**7/10   Monosten A**

The quick brown fox jumps over the lazy dog. Voyez le brick géant que j'examine près du wharf. Zwölf Boxkämpfer jagen Viktor quer über den großen Sylter Deich. El veloz murciélago hindú comía feliz cardillo y kiwi. La cigüeña tocaba el saxofón detrás del palenque de pajaatur? Rissimo lorereped ex es solore lab id molorro in rempore icabore rehenetur aliam aut voles audae dem quam,

---

| | | | |
|---|---|---|---|
| Typeface | Fortescue | Year | 2009–2011 (On going) |
| Designer | The Entente (Anthony Sheret, Edd Harrington) | Format | OpenType |

# *Aa*

Fortescue Regular 20pt
*Fortescue Italic 20pt*
**Fortescue Semi Bold 20pt**
***Fortescue Semi Bold Italic 20pt***
**Fortescue Bold 20pt**
***Fortescue Bold Italic 20pt***

Aa Bb Cc Dd Ee Ff Gg Hh Ii Jj Kk
Ll Mm Nn Oo Pp Qq Rr Ss Tt Uu
Vv Ww Xx Yy Zz
0123456789
—

**9/12   Fortescue Regular**

The quick brown fox jumps over the lazy dog. Voyez le brick géant que j'examine près du wharf. Zwölf Boxkämpfer jagen Viktor quer über den großen Sylter Deich. El veloz murciélago hindú comía feliz cardillo y kiwi. La cigüeña tocaba el saxofón detrás del palenque de pajaatur? Rissimo lorereped ex es solore lab id molorro in rempore icabore rehenetur aliam aut voles audae dem quam, secum eum facesequae consequ aepudam quia voluptiur repel in et faccustibus, nonsenis aut quisqui rero mi, ipiet lam ant ut maio et hil molupta tustis atatur, consedi tasimol orerem aut volor andipsapis sit, illaut volore officatus alicae dusdaec tatecte cearum qui accatibus restiore

**7/10   Fortescue Regular**

The quick brown fox jumps over the lazy dog. Voyez le brick géant que j'examine près du wharf. Zwölf Boxkämpfer jagen Viktor quer über den großen Sylter Deich. El veloz murciélago hindú comía feliz cardillo y kiwi. La cigüeña tocaba el saxofón detrás del palenque de pajaatur? Rissimo lorereped ex es solore lab id molorro in rempore icabore rehenetur aliam aut voles audae dem quam, secum eum facesequae consequ aepudam quia voluptiur repel in et faccustibus, nonsenis aut quisqui rero mi, ipiet lam ant ut maio et hil molupta tustis atatur, consedi tasimol orerem aut volor andipsapis sit, illaut volore officatus alicae dusdaec tatecte cearum qui accatibus restiore nulpa secaerferum, nus dolenim in et quoditat que explam volupictur? Qui de illuptae. Dae nis illiberum volorro ritatis tinullo rerumqu atetur repro eatius asperibus. Rissimo lorereped ex es solore lab id molorro in rempore icabore rehenetur aliam aut voles audae dem quam, secum eum facesequae consequ aepudam quia voluptiur repel in et faccustibus, nonsenis aut quisqui rero mi, ipiet lam ant

# D

Darden Studio

—

Joshua Darden

—

New York, USA

—

Since 2004

The Darden Studio produces and publishes the typeface designs of Joshua Darden and his collaborators. Housed in a former telephone switching station in Greenpoint, Brooklyn, New York, they create new typefaces and lettering for publications, institutions, corporate brands and private clients. "Working closely with our clients, we pursue typography that is the result of earnest inquiry, appropriate for current editorial standards and technology, and rooted in the values and practices of five centuries of type founding."

## Info

—Why?
We like to meet the people who use our type. Working directly with clients allows us to do better work, which in turn informs and improves our retail catalog.

—People on staff
5–10, depending on the project at hand.

—Type families (retail)
9

—Designers represented
1

—Web shop
dardenstudio.com

—Distributors
Phil's Fonts, FontShop

—Webfont services
All

—Basic license
$39–499 for one computer, with cumulative discounts for larger licenses.

## People

—Joshua Darden, Chief Designer. Born and raised in suburban Los Angeles, Joshua Darden published his first typeface at the age of 15. He spent the next decade assisting in the development and production of typefaces for a broad range of commercial and cultural institutions. Since establishing his Brooklyn based studio in 2004, he has collaborated with clients in dozens of markets to invent rich, communicative typography.
Joshua has developed custom typefaces for Latin-based, Cyrillic, and Greek alphabets. He has taught the history, design, & use of typography at Parsons the New School for Design & the School of Visual Arts, lectured at the University of California, Santa Barbara, sat on panels at the TypeCon and South by Southwest Interactive conferences, juried the Type Directors Club Type Design Competition, and visited the Rhode Island School of Design as a Guest Critic.
In addition to guiding the creative work of the studio, Joshua is an avid amateur photographer, commuter by bicycle, and tireless collector, accumulating and cataloging books, small objects, and awesomely bad pop music.

—Nick Kwiatek, Tech Director. Nick (aka Bachelor Number Four), has thus far enjoyed an extraordinarily fascinating life, the details of which are still being proofread and/or censored.

—Noam Berg, Senior Draftsman. Born in Los Angeles and raised in Israel, Noam's type career began with an aborted port of Kid Pix's blackletter font to IBM's Storyboard Live. It picked up years later with a family of stencil fonts designed for easy cutting. He's been a printmaker and programmer, guitar player and singer in less-than-seminal Israeli Punk band Fishyboom, and managed to get court martialled not once but twice during his service as a medic in the IDF. Having recently completed his MFA thesis, Noam aspires to be a crotchety old man who hits people over the head with his cane for using inferior typefaces.

Typeface selection

Jubilat
**Birra**
Omnes
Freight Big
Freight Display
Freight Text
Freight Micro
Freight Sans

24pt

For his redesign of the French independent magazine *Courrier International*, Mark Porter used a combination of Freight and Omnes.

Page 63

Birra Stout used on merchandising designed for the Mexican brand Mouscacho by designer Jasho Salazar.

| | | | |
|---|---|---|---|
| Typeface | Jubilat | Year | 2005–2008 |
| Designer | Darden Studio | Format | OpenType |

# Aa

Aa Bb Cc Dd Ee Ff Gg Hh Ii Jj Kk Ll Mm Nn Oo Pp Qq Rr Ss Tt Uu Vv Ww Xx Yy Zz 0123456789

Jubilat Extra Light 20pt
*Jubilat Extra Light Italic 20pt*
Jubilat Light 20pt
*Jubilat Light Italic 20pt*
Jubilat Regular 20pt
*Jubilat Regular Italic 20pt*
**Jubilat Medium 20pt**
***Jubilat Medium Italic 20pt***
**Jubilat Bold 20pt**
***Jubilat Bold Italic 20pt***
**Jubilat Black 20pt**
***Jubilat Black Italic 20pt***

---

**12/14  Jubilat Light**

The quick brown fox jumps over the lazy dog. Voyez le brick géant que j'examine près du wharf. Zwölf Boxkämpfer jagen Viktor quer über den

**12/14  Jubilat Regular**

The quick brown fox jumps over the lazy dog. Voyez le brick géant que j'examine près du wharf. Zwölf Boxkämpfer jagen Viktor über den

**9/12  Jubilat Light**

The quick brown fox jumps over the lazy dog. Voyez le brick géant que j'examine près du wharf. Zwölf Boxkämpfer jagen Viktor quer über den großen Sylter Deich. El veloz murciélago hindú comía feliz cardillo y kiwi. La cigüeña tocaba el

**9/12  Jubilat Regular**

The quick brown fox jumps over the lazy dog. Voyez le brick géant que j'examine près du wharf. Zwölf Boxkämpfer jagen Viktor quer über den großen Sylter Deich. El veloz murciélago hindú comía feliz cardillo y kiwi. La cigüeña

**7/10  Jubilat Light**

The quick brown fox jumps over the lazy dog. Voyez le brick géant que j'examine près du wharf. Zwölf Boxkämpfer jagen Viktor quer über den großen Sylter Deich. El veloz murciélago hindú comía feliz cardillo y kiwi. La cigüeña tocaba el saxofón detrás del palenque de pajaatur? Rissimo lorereped ex es solore lab id molorro in rempore icabore rehenetur aliam aut voles au-

**7/10  Jubilat Regular**

The quick brown fox jumps over the lazy dog. Voyez le brick géant que j'examine près du wharf. Zwölf Boxkämpfer jagen Viktor quer über den großen Sylter Deich. El veloz murciélago hindú comía feliz cardillo y kiwi. La cigüeña tocaba el saxofón detrás del palenque de pajaatur? Rissimo lorereped ex es solore lab id molorro in rempore icabore rehenetur aliam

---

| | | | |
|---|---|---|---|
| Typeface | Birra | Year | 2008 |
| Designer | Joshua Darden | Format | OpenType |

# Bottoms UP!

**Stout**

Aa Bb Cc Dd Ee Ff Gg Hh Ii Jj Kk Ll Mm Nn Oo Pp Qq Rr Ss Tt Uu Vv Ww Xx Yy Zz 0123456789

Page
65

Foundry   Darden Studio

Typeface   Omnes
Designer   Darden Studio

Year   2006
Format   OpenType

# Aa

Aa Bb Cc Dd Ee Ff Gg Hh Ii Jj Kk Ll Mm Nn Oo Pp Qq Rr Ss Tt Uu Vv Ww Xx Yy Zz
0123456789

Omnes Hairline Regular 20pt
*Omnes Hairline Italic* 20pt
Omnes Thin 20pt
*Omnes Thin Italic* 20pt
Omnes ExtraLight 20pt
*Omnes ExtraLight Italic* 20pt
Omnes Light 20pt
*Omnes Light Italic* 20pt
Omnes Regular 20pt
*Omnes Regular Italic* 20pt
Omnes Medium 20pt
*Omnes Medium Italic* 20pt
**Omnes Semibold** 20pt
***Omnes Semibold Italic*** 20pt
**Omnes Bold** 20pt
***Omnes Bold Italic*** 20pt
**Omnes Black** 20pt
***Omnes Black Italic*** 20pt

---

12/14   Omnes Regular

The quick brown fox jumps over the lazy dog. Voyez le brick géant que j'examine près du wharf. Zwölf Boxkämpfer jagen Viktor quer über den

12/14   Omnes Medium

The quick brown fox jumps over the lazy dog. Voyez le brick géant que j'examine près du wharf. Zwölf Boxkämpfer jagen Viktor quer über den

12/14   Omnes Bold

**The quick brown fox jumps over the lazy dog. Voyez le brick géant que j'examine près du wharf. Zwölf Boxkämpfer jagen Viktor**

9/12   Omnes Regular

The quick brown fox jumps over the lazy dog. Voyez le brick géant que j'examine près du wharf. Zwölf Boxkämpfer jagen Viktor quer über den großen Sylter Deich. El veloz murciélago hindú comía feliz cardillo y kiwi. La cigüeña tocaba el saxofón detrás

9/12   Omnes Medium

The quick brown fox jumps over the lazy dog. Voyez le brick géant que j'examine près du wharf. Zwölf Boxkämpfer jagen Viktor quer über den großen Sylter Deich. El veloz murciélago hindú comía feliz cardillo y kiwi. La cigüeña tocaba el sa-

9/12   Omnes Bold

**The quick brown fox jumps over the lazy dog. Voyez le brick géant que j'examine près du wharf. Zwölf Boxkämpfer jagen Viktor quer über den großen Sylter Deich. El veloz murciélago hindú comía feliz cardillo y kiwi.**

7/10   Omnes Regular

The quick brown fox jumps over the lazy dog. Voyez le brick géant que j'examine près du wharf. Zwölf Boxkämpfer jagen Viktor quer über den großen Sylter Deich. El veloz murciélago hindú comía feliz cardillo y kiwi. La cigüeña tocaba el saxofón detrás del palenque de pajaatur? Rissimo lorereped ex es solore lab id molorro in rempore icabore rehenetur aliam aut voles audae dem

7/10   Omnes Medium

The quick brown fox jumps over the lazy dog. Voyez le brick géant que j'examine près du wharf. Zwölf Boxkämpfer jagen Viktor quer über den großen Sylter Deich. El veloz murciélago hindú comía feliz cardillo y kiwi. La cigüeña tocaba el saxofón detrás del palenque de pajaatur? Rissimo lorereped ex es solore lab id molorro in rempore icabore rehenetur aliam aut voles

7/10   Omnes Bold

**The quick brown fox jumps over the lazy dog. Voyez le brick géant que j'examine près du wharf. Zwölf Boxkämpfer jagen Viktor quer über den großen Sylter Deich. El veloz murciélago hindú comía feliz cardillo y kiwi. La cigüeña tocaba el saxofón detrás del palenque de pajaatur? Rissimo lorereped ex es solore lab id molorro in rempore icabore**

Page 66

Foundry  Darden Studio

---

Typeface  Freight Big
Designer  Joshua Darden
Year  2008
Format  OpenType

# Poster
# *KingSize*

Light *Italic*
Book *Italic*
Medium *Italic*
Semibold *Italic*
**Bold** *Italic*
**Black** *Italic*

Aa Bb Cc Dd Ee Ff Gg Hh Ii Jj Kk Ll Mm Nn Oo Pp Qq Rr Ss Tt Uu Vv Ww Xx Yy Zz  0123456789

---

Typeface  Freight Display
Designer  Joshua Darden
Year  2008
Format  OpenType

# Making
# *Headlines*

Light *Italic*
Book *Italic*
Medium *Italic*
Semibold *Italic*
**Bold** *Italic*
**Black** *Italic*

Aa Bb Cc Dd Ee Ff Gg Hh Ii Jj Kk Ll Mm Nn Oo Pp Qq Rr Ss Tt Uu Vv Ww Xx Yy Zz  0123456789

---

Typeface  Freight Micro
Designer  Joshua Darden
Year  2005–2008
Format  OpenType

# Aa

Aa Bb Cc Dd Ee Ff Gg Hh Ii Jj Kk Ll Mm Nn Oo Pp Qq Rr Ss Tt Uu Vv Ww Xx Yy Zz
0123456789
—

Freight Micro Light 14pt
*Freight Micro Light Italic 14pt*
Freight Micro Book 14pt
*Freight Micro Book Italic 14pt*
Freight Micro Medium 14pt
*Freight Micro Medium Italic 14pt*
**Freight Micro Semibold 14pt**
***Freight Micro Semibold Italic 14pt***
**Freight Micro Bold 14pt**
***Freight Micro Bold Italic 14pt***
**Freight Micro Black 14pt**
***Freight Micro Black Italic 14pt***

---

7/10  Freight Micro Regular

THE QUICK BROWN FOX JUMPS over the lazy dog. Voyez le brick géant que j'examine près du wharf. Zwölf Boxkämpfer jagen Viktor quer über den großen Sylter Deich. El veloz murciélago hindú comía feliz cardillo y kiwi. La cigüeña tocaba el saxofón detrás del palenque de pajaatur? Rissimo lorereped ex es solore lab id molorro in rempore icabore rehenetur aliam aut voles

7/10  Freight Micro Medium

THE QUICK BROWN FOX jumps over the lazy dog. Voyez le brick géant que j'examine près du wharf. Zwölf Boxkämpfer jagen Viktor quer über den großen Sylter Deich. El veloz murciélago hindú comía feliz cardillo y kiwi. La cigüeña tocaba el saxofón detrás del palenque de pajaatur? Rissimo lorereped ex es solore lab id molorro in rempore icabore rehenetur aliam

7/10  Freight Micro Bold

**THE QUICK BROWN FOX jumps over the lazy dog. Voyez le brick géant que j'examine près du wharf. Zwölf Boxkämpfer jagen Viktor quer über den großen Sylter Deich. El veloz murciélago hindú comía feliz cardillo y kiwi. La cigüeña tocaba el saxofón detrás del palenque de pajaatur? Rissimo lorereped ex es solore lab id molorro**

Typeface   Freight Text, Sans          Year     2004–2009
Designer   Joshua Darden               Format   OpenType

# Aa

Aa Bb Cc Dd Ee Ff Gg Hh Ii Jj Kk Ll Mm Nn Oo Pp Qq Rr Ss Tt Uu Vv Ww Xx Yy Zz
0123456789
—

Freight Text Light 14pt
*Freight Text Light Italic 14pt*
Freight Text Book 14pt
*Freight Text Book Italic 14pt*
Freight Text Medium 14pt
*Freight Text Medium Italic 14pt*
**Freight Text Semibold 14pt**
***Freight Text Semibold Italic 14pt***
**Freight Text Bold 14pt**
***Freight Text Bold Italic 14pt***
**Freight Text Black 14pt**
***Freight Text Black Italic 14pt***

# Aa

Aa Bb Cc Dd Ee Ff Gg Hh Ii Jj Kk Ll Mm Nn Oo Pp Qq Rr Ss Tt Uu Vv Ww Xx Yy Zz
0123456789
—

Freight Sans Light 14pt
*Freight Sans Light Italic 14pt*
Freight Sans Book 14pt
*Freight Sans Book Italic 14pt*
Freight Sans Medium 14pt
*Freight Sans Medium Italic 14pt*
**Freight Sans Semibold 14pt**
***Freight Sans Semibold Italic 14pt***
**Freight Sans Bold 14pt**
***Freight Sans Bold Italic 14pt***
**Freight Sans Black 14pt**
***Freight Sans Black Italic 14pt***

---

12/14   Freight Text Book

The quick brown fox jumps over the lazy dog. Voyez le brick géant que j'examine près du wharf. Zwölf Boxkämpfer jagen Viktor quer über den

9/12   Freight Text Book

The quick brown fox jumps over the lazy dog. Voyez le brick géant que j'examine près du wharf. Zwölf Boxkämpfer jagen Viktor quer über den großen Sylter Deich. El veloz murciélago hindú comía feliz cardillo y kiwi. La cigüeña tocaba el saxofón

9/12   Freight Sans Book

The quick brown fox jumps over the lazy dog. Voyez le brick géant que j'examine près du wharf. Zwölf Boxkämpfer jagen Viktor quer über den großen Sylter Deich. El veloz murciélago hindú comía feliz cardillo y kiwi. La cigüeña tocaba el saxofón detrás del palenque

12/14   Freight Text Medium

The quick brown fox jumps over the lazy dog. Voyez le brick géant que j'examine près du wharf. Zwölf Boxkämpfer jagen Viktor quer über den

9/12   Freight Text Medium

The quick brown fox jumps over the lazy dog. Voyez le brick géant que j'examine près du wharf. Zwölf Boxkämpfer jagen Viktor quer über den großen Sylter Deich. El veloz murciélago hindú comía feliz cardillo y kiwi. La cigüeña tocaba el saxofón detrás

9/12   Freight Sans Medium

The quick brown fox jumps over the lazy dog. Voyez le brick géant que j'examine près du wharf. Zwölf Boxkämpfer jagen Viktor quer über den großen Sylter Deich. El veloz murciélago hindú comía feliz cardillo y kiwi. La cigüeña tocaba el saxofón detrás

12/14   Freight Text Bold

**The quick brown fox jumps over the lazy dog. Voyez le brick géant que j'examine près du wharf. Zwölf Boxkämpfer jagen Viktor quer über den**

9/12   Freight Text Bold

**The quick brown fox jumps over the lazy dog. Voyez le brick géant que j'examine près du wharf. Zwölf Boxkämpfer jagen Viktor quer über den großen Sylter Deich. El veloz murciélago hindú comía feliz cardillo y kiwi. La cigüeña tocaba el**

9/12   Freight Sans Bold

**The quick brown fox jumps over the lazy dog. Voyez le brick géant que j'examine près du wharf. Zwölf Boxkämpfer jagen Viktor quer über den großen Sylter Deich. El veloz murciélago hindú comía feliz cardillo y kiwi. La cigüeña**

# D
## DSType

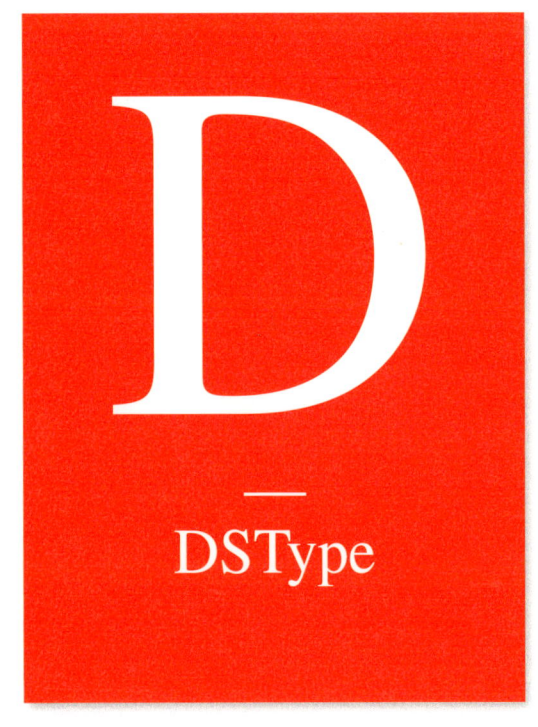

Dino dos Santos

Matosinhos, Portugal

Since 1994

DSType was founded in late 1994 by Dino dos Santos and since then has designed typefaces for several corporations, magazines and cultural projects. The studio specializes in creating custom typefaces, including completely new typefaces as well as improving and finetuning existing typefaces and logotypes.

## Info

—Why?
I began designing typefaces in the early 1990s because there was not much available to us in those days, just the Macintosh system fonts and dry transfer sheets from Letraset and Mecanorma. So I started designing fonts that matched the new typographic experience.

—People on staff
3

—Type designers on staff
2

—Type families
Approx. 30

—Designers represented
2

—Web shop
dstype.com

—Distributors
MyFonts, TypeTrust, FontShop, Veer, Fontworks, Luth, Monotype, and others.

—Webfont services
License extension for self-hosting

—Basic license
17–40 € (single fonts, 5 devices)
Clients can build personalized font packages with discounts.

### Typeface selection

Acta
Dobra
Estilo Pro
Penna
Prelo
Prelo Slab
Ventura

24pt

## People

—Dino dos Santos graduated in Graphic Design from ESAD, Escola Superior de Artes e Design in Matosinhos, and obtained an MA in Multimedia Arts at FBAUP, Porto. He teaches Typographic Studies at ESAD. His work has been featured in many international design magazines. Several of Dino dos Santos's typefaces have been internationally successful, such as Andrade, winner of the Creative Review Type Design Awards, for the Best Revival/Extension Family in 2005 and Ventura, awarded with the Certificate of Excellence in Type Design from the Type Directors Club of New York in 2008. The studio's work was selected for the Schrift in Form exhibition at the Klingspor-Museum in Offenbach, Germany. Dos Santos regularly contributes to conferences, seminars and publications. His typefaces are used in prestigious Portuguese and international magazines.

The Ventura typeface's "V".

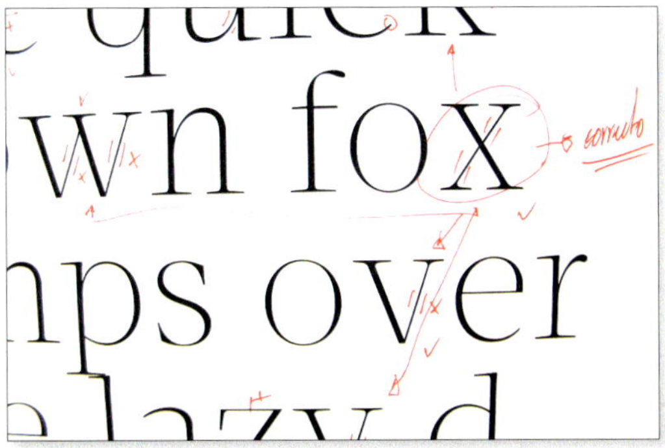

Page
69

"Zi" ligature from Penna.

**Left and below**
Dino dos Santos, corrected proofs.

*leMag*, magazine section of the French daily *Libération*, was designed using DSType's Andrade Pro.

Andrade used for the identity of Portuguese design agency Maga.

"ffk" ligature from Acta Poster Swashes.

Page 70

Foundry DSType

Typeface Estilo Pro
Designer Dino dos Santos
Year 2010
Format OpenType

# La cigüeña tocaba

Hairline
Light
Book
**Medium**
**Bold**

Aa Bb Cc Dd Ee Ff Gg Hh Ii Jj Kk Ll Mm Nn Oo Pp Qq Rr Ss Tt Uu Vv Ww Xx Yy Zz 0123456789

Typeface Penna
Designer Pedro Leal
Year 2011
Format OpenType

*El veloz murciélago*

Regular
Swashes
Connected
Connected Swashes

Aa Bb Cc Dd Ee Ff Gg Hh Ii Jj Kk Ll Mm Nn Oo Pp Qq Rr Ss Tt Uu Vv Ww Xx Yy Zz 0123456789

Typeface Ventura
Designer Joaquim José Ventura da Silva, Dino dos Santos
Year 2007
Format OpenType

*Las Aventuras*

Regular

Aa Bb Cc Dd Ee Ff Gg Hh Ii Jj Kk Ll Mm Nn Oo Pp Qq Rr Ss Tt Uu Vv Ww Xx Yy Zz 0123456789

Typeface   Acta
Designer   Dino dos Santos

Year     2010
Format   OpenType

# Aa

Aa Bb Cc Dd Ee Ff Gg Hh Ii Jj Kk Ll Mm Nn Oo Pp Qq Rr Ss Tt Uu Vv Ww Xx Yy Zz
0123456789

Acta Light 20pt
*Acta Light Italic 20pt*
Acta Book 20pt
*Acta Book Italic 20pt*
Acta Medium 20pt
*Acta Medium Italic 20pt*
**Acta Bold 20pt**
***Acta Bold Italic 20pt***
**Acta Extra Bold 20pt**
***Acta Extra Bold Italic 20pt***
**Acta Black 20pt**
***Acta Black Italic 20pt***
Acta Poster Regular
*Acta Poster Regular Italic*
*Acta Poster Swashes*

---

**12/14   Acta Light**

The quick brown fox jumps over the lazy dog. Voyez le brick géant que j'examine près du wharf. Zwölf Boxkämpfer jagen Viktor quer über

**12/14   Acta Book**

The quick brown fox jumps over the lazy dog. Voyez le brick géant que j'examine près du wharf. Zwölf Boxkämpfer jagen Viktor quer über den

**12/14   Acta Medium**

The quick brown fox jumps over the lazy dog. Voyez le brick géant que j'examine près du wharf. Zwölf Boxkämpfer jagen Viktor quer über den großen Sylter Deich. El veloz murciélago hindú comía feliz cardillo y kiwi. La cigüeña tocaba el saxofón detrás del palenque de pajaatur? Rissimo lorereped ex es solore

**9/12   Acta Light**

The quick brown fox jumps over the lazy dog. Voyez le brick géant que j'examine près du wharf. Zwölf Boxkämpfer jagen Viktor quer über den großen Sylter Deich. El veloz murciélago hindú comía feliz cardillo y kiwi. La cigüeña to-

**9/12   Acta Book**

The quick brown fox jumps over the lazy dog. Voyez le brick géant que j'examine près du wharf. Zwölf Boxkämpfer jagen Viktor quer über den großen Sylter Deich. El veloz murciélago hindú comía feliz cardillo y kiwi. La

**9/12   Acta Medium**

The quick brown fox jumps over the lazy dog. Voyez le brick géant que j'examine près du wharf. Zwölf Boxkämpfer jagen Viktor quer über den großen Sylter Deich. El veloz murciélago hindú comía feliz cardillo y kiwi. La cigüeña tocaba el saxofón detrás del palenque de pajaatur? Rissimo lorereped ex es solore lab id molorro in rempore icabore rehenetur aliam aut voles audae dem quam, secum eum facesequae consequ aepudam quia voluptiur

**7/10   Acta Light**

The quick brown fox jumps over the lazy dog. Voyez le brick géant que j'examine près du wharf. Zwölf Boxkämpfer jagen Viktor quer über den großen Sylter Deich. El veloz murciélago hindú comía feliz cardillo y kiwi. La cigüeña tocaba el saxofón detrás del palenque de pajaatur? Rissimo lorereped ex es solore lab id molorro in rempore icabore rehenetur aliam aut voles

**7/10   Acta Book**

The quick brown fox jumps over the lazy dog. Voyez le brick géant que j'examine près du wharf. Zwölf Boxkämpfer jagen Viktor quer über den großen Sylter Deich. El veloz murciélago hindú comía feliz cardillo y kiwi. La cigüeña tocaba el saxofón detrás del palenque de pajaatur? Rissimo lorereped ex es solore lab id molorro in rempore icabore rehenetur aliam aut voles

**7/10   Acta Medium**

The quick brown fox jumps over the lazy dog. Voyez le brick géant que j'examine près du wharf. Zwölf Boxkämpfer jagen Viktor quer über den großen Sylter Deich. El veloz murciélago hindú comía feliz cardillo y kiwi. La cigüeña tocaba el saxofón detrás del palenque de pajaatur? Rissimo lorereped ex es solore lab id molorro in rempore icabore rehenetur aliam aut voles audae dem quam, secum eum facesequae consequ aepudam quia voluptiur repel in et faccustibus, nonsenis aut quisqui rero mi, ipiet lam ant ut maio et hil molupta tustis atatur, consedi tasimol orerem aut volor andipsapis sit, illaut volore officatus alicae dusdaec tatecte cearum qui accatibus restiore nulpa secaerferum, nus doleniim in et quoditat que

Foundry DSType

Typeface  Prelo, Slab
Designer  Dino dos Santos
Year      2007–2008
Format    OpenType

# Aa

Aa Bb Cc Dd Ee Ff Gg Hh Ii Jj Kk Ll
Mm Nn Oo Pp Qq Rr Ss Tt Uu Vv
Ww Xx Yy Zz
0123456789
—

Prelo Hairline 14pt
*Prelo Hairline Italic* 14pt
Prelo Extra Light 14pt
*Prelo Extra Light Italic* 14pt
Prelo Light 14pt
*Prelo Light Italic* 14pt
Prelo Book 14pt
*Prelo Book Italic* 14pt
Prelo Medium 14pt
*Prelo Medium Italic* 14pt
**Prelo Semi Bold** 14pt
***Prelo Semi Bold Italic*** 14pt
**Prelo Bold** 14pt
***Prelo Bold Italic*** 14pt
**Prelo Extra Bold** 14pt
***Prelo Extra Bold Italic*** 14pt
**Prelo Black** 14pt
***Prelo Black Italic*** 14pt

Prelo Slab Hairline 14pt
*Prelo Slab Hairline Italic* 14pt
Prelo Slab Extra Light 14pt
*Prelo Slab Extra Light Italic* 14pt
Prelo Slab Light 14pt
*Prelo Slab Light Italic* 14pt
Prelo Slab Book 14pt
*Prelo Slab Book Italic* 14pt
Prelo Slab Medium 14pt
*Prelo Slab Medium Italic* 14pt
**Prelo Slab Semi Bold** 14pt
***Prelo Slab Semi Bold Italic*** 14pt
**Prelo Slab Bold** 14pt
***Prelo Slab Bold Italic*** 14pt
**Prelo Slab Extra Bold** 14pt
***Prelo Slab Extra Bold Italic*** 14pt
**Prelo Slab Black** 14pt
***Prelo Slab Black Italic*** 14pt

---

12/14  Prelo Book

The quick brown fox jumps over the lazy dog. Voyez le brick géant que j'examine près du wharf. Zwölf Boxkämpfer jagen Viktor quer über den großen Sylter Deich. El veloz murciélago hindú comía feliz cardillo y kiwi. La cigüeña tocaba el saxofón detrás del palenque de pajaatur? Rissimo lorereped ex es solore lab id molorro in rempore icabore rehenetur aliam

12/14  Prelo Slab Book

The quick brown fox jumps over the lazy dog. Voyez le brick géant que j'examine près du wharf. Zwölf Boxkämpfer jagen Viktor quer über den großen Sylter Deich. El veloz murciélago hindú comía feliz cardillo y kiwi. La cigüeña tocaba el saxofón detrás del palenque de pajaatur? Rissimo lorereped ex es solore lab id

9/12  Prelo Book

The quick brown fox jumps over the lazy dog. Voyez le brick géant que j'examine près du wharf. Zwölf Boxkämpfer jagen Viktor quer über den großen Sylter Deich. El veloz murciélago hindú comía feliz cardillo y kiwi. La cigüeña tocaba el saxofón detrás

9/12  Prelo Medium

The quick brown fox jumps over the lazy dog. Voyez le brick géant que j'examine près du wharf. Zwölf Boxkämpfer jagen Viktor quer über den großen Sylter Deich. El veloz murciélago hindú comía feliz cardillo y kiwi. La cigüeña tocaba el saxofón detrás

9/12  Prelo Bold

**The quick brown fox jumps over the lazy dog. Voyez le brick géant que j'examine près du wharf. Zwölf Boxkämpfer jagen Viktor quer über den großen Sylter Deich. El veloz murciélago hindú comía feliz cardillo y kiwi. La cigüeña tocaba el saxofón detrás del palenque de pajaatur? Rissimo lorereped ex es solore lab id molorro in rempore icabore rehenetur aliam aut voles audae dem quam, secum eum facesequae consequ aepudam quia voluptiur repel in et faccustibus, nonsenis aut quisqui rero**

9/12  Prelo Slab Book

The quick brown fox jumps over the lazy dog. Voyez le brick géant que j'examine près du wharf. Zwölf Boxkämpfer jagen Viktor quer über den großen Sylter Deich. El veloz murciélago hindú comía feliz cardillo y kiwi. La cigüeña tocaba el

9/12  Prelo Slab Medium

The quick brown fox jumps over the lazy dog. Voyez le brick géant que j'examine près du wharf. Zwölf Boxkämpfer jagen Viktor quer über den großen Sylter Deich. El veloz murciélago hindú comía feliz cardillo y kiwi. La cigüeña tocaba

9/12  Prelo Slab Bold

**The quick brown fox jumps over the lazy dog. Voyez le brick géant que j'examine près du wharf. Zwölf Boxkämpfer jagen Viktor quer über den großen Sylter Deich. El veloz murciélago hindú comía feliz cardillo y kiwi. La cigüeña tocaba el saxofón detrás del palenque de pajaatur? Rissimo lorereped ex es solore lab id molorro in rempore icabore rehenetur aliam aut voles audae dem quam, secum eum facesequae consequ aepudam quia voluptiur repel in et faccustibus,**

Typeface  Dobra  
Designer  Dino dos Santos  
Year  2009  
Format  OpenType  
Foundry  DSType

# Aa

Aa Bb Cc Dd Ee Ff Gg Hh Ii Jj Kk Ll Mm
Nn Oo Pp Qq Rr Ss Tt Uu Vv Ww Xx
Yy Zz
0123456789
—

Dobra Light 24pt
*Dobra Light Italic* 24pt
Dobra Book 24pt
*Dobra Book Italic* 24pt
**Dobra Medium** 24pt
***Dobra Medium Italic*** 24pt
**Dobra Bold** 24pt
***Dobra Bold Italic*** 24pt
**Dobra Black** 24pt
***Dobra Black Italic*** 24pt

---

12/14  Dobra Light

The quick brown fox jumps over the lazy dog. Voyez le brick géant que j'examine près du wharf. Zwölf Boxkämpfer jagen Viktor quer über den großen Sylter

12/14  Dobra Book

The quick brown fox jumps over the lazy dog. Voyez le brick géant que j'examine près du wharf. Zwölf Boxkämpfer jagen Viktor quer über den

12/14  Dobra Medium

**The quick brown fox jumps over the lazy dog. Voyez le brick géant que j'examine près du wharf. Zwölf Boxkämpfer jagen Viktor quer über den**

12/14  Dobra Bold

**The quick brown fox jumps over the lazy dog. Voyez le brick géant que j'examine près du wharf. Zwölf Boxkämpfer jagen Viktor quer über den großen Sylter Deich. El veloz murciélago hindú comía feliz cardillo y kiwi. La cigüeña tocaba el saxofón detrás del palenque de pajaatur? Rissimo lorereped ex es solore lab id molorro**

9/12  Dobra Light

The quick brown fox jumps over the lazy dog. Voyez le brick géant que j'examine près du wharf. Zwölf Boxkämpfer jagen Viktor quer über den großen Sylter Deich. El veloz murciélago hindú comía feliz cardillo y kiwi. La cigüeña tocaba el saxofón detrás del

9/12  Dobra Book

The quick brown fox jumps over the lazy dog. Voyez le brick géant que j'examine près du wharf. Zwölf Boxkämpfer jagen Viktor quer über den großen Sylter Deich. El veloz murciélago hindú comía feliz cardillo y kiwi. La cigüeña tocaba el saxofón detrás

9/12  Dobra Medium

**The quick brown fox jumps over the lazy dog. Voyez le brick géant que j'examine près du wharf. Zwölf Boxkämpfer jagen Viktor quer über den großen Sylter Deich. El veloz murciélago hindú comía feliz cardillo y kiwi. La cigüeña tocaba el saxofón detrás**

9/12  Dobra Bold

**The quick brown fox jumps over the lazy dog. Voyez le brick géant que j'examine près du wharf. Zwölf Boxkämpfer jagen Viktor quer über den großen Sylter Deich. El veloz murciélago hindú comía feliz cardillo y kiwi. La cigüeña tocaba el saxofón detrás del palenque de pajaatur? Rissimo lorereped ex es solore lab id molorro in rempore icabore rehenetur aliam aut voles audae dem quam, secum eum facesequae consequ aepudam quia voluptiur repel in et faccustibus, nonsenis**

7/10  Dobra Light

The quick brown fox jumps over the lazy dog. Voyez le brick géant que j'examine près du wharf. Zwölf Boxkämpfer jagen Viktor quer über den großen Sylter Deich. El veloz murciélago hindú comía feliz cardillo y kiwi. La cigüeña tocaba el saxofón detrás del palenque de pajaatur? Rissimo lorereped ex es solore lab id molorro in rempore icabore rehenetur aliam aut voles audae dem quam, secum eum facesequae

7/10  Dobra Book

The quick brown fox jumps over the lazy dog. Voyez le brick géant que j'examine près du wharf. Zwölf Boxkämpfer jagen Viktor quer über den großen Sylter Deich. El veloz murciélago hindú comía feliz cardillo y kiwi. La cigüeña tocaba el saxofón detrás del palenque de pajaatur? Rissimo lorereped ex es solore lab id molorro in rempore icabore rehenetur aliam aut voles audae dem quam, secum eum

7/10  Dobra Medium

**The quick brown fox jumps over the lazy dog. Voyez le brick géant que j'examine près du wharf. Zwölf Boxkämpfer jagen Viktor quer über den großen Sylter Deich. El veloz murciélago hindú comía feliz cardillo y kiwi. La cigüeña tocaba el saxofón detrás del palenque de pajaatur? Rissimo lorereped ex es solore lab id molorro in rempore icabore rehenetur aliam aut voles audae dem**

7/10  Dobra Bold

**The quick brown fox jumps over the lazy dog. Voyez le brick géant que j'examine près du wharf. Zwölf Boxkämpfer jagen Viktor quer über den großen Sylter Deich. El veloz murciélago hindú comía feliz cardillo y kiwi. La cigüeña tocaba el saxofón detrás del palenque de pajaatur? Rissimo lorereped ex es solore lab id molorro in rempore icabore rehenetur aliam aut voles audae dem quam, secum eum facesequae consequ aepudam quia voluptiur repel in et faccustibus, nonsenis aut quisqui rero mi, ipiet lam ant ut maio et hil molupta tustis atatur, consedi tasimol orerem aut volor andipsapis sit, illaut volore officatus alicae dusdaec tatecte cearum qui accatibus restiore nulpa secaerferum, nus dolenim in et quoditat que explam voluptiur? Qui de**

# E
## Emtype

Eduardo Manso

Barcelona, Spain

Since 1997

Having published a number of typefaces through T26, ITC, Bitstream and Linotype, Argentinian-born Eduardo Manso founded Emtype as a one-person type foundry in 1997.

## Info

—Why?
In the past, a type designer had to go to a large foundry to publish a typeface, convince them that your project was commercially viable and in some cases you had to accept changes to fit in with their marketing strategies. The popularization of the internet allowed many independent authors like me to get in touch directly with the customers, either through distributors or our own websites. As a result of that, type design became more dignified. I do not publish fonts to get a bestseller, I publish because I believe in what I do and want to share it with people who think in the same way. That is the real difference between an independent type foundry and a huge font company, and this was the main reason I created Emtype.

—People on staff
1

—Type designers on staff
1

—Type families
7

—Designers represented
None

— Web shop
www.emtype.net

—Distributors
MyFonts, FontShop, FontWorks

—Webfont services
MyFonts

—Basic license
Style (1–5 Users) : From 35 to 39€,
Family (1–5 Users) : From 60 to 569€

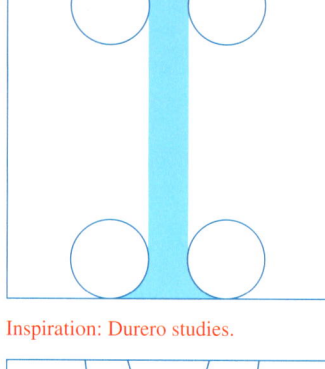

Typeface selection

## People

—Born in Argentina, Eduardo Manso has been living in Barcelona since 2000. He studied graphic design at the Martín Malharro School of Visual Arts in Mar del Plata and completed a postgraduate degree in visual communication at the National University of Mar del Plata. Among other awards, his Bohemia typeface won first prize in the text category of the International Type Design Contest 2003 organized by Linotype. He has received a Certificate of Excellence from the Type Directors Club of New York on three occasions. He currently gives typography classes at several schools in Barcelona and works as a freelance type designer.

Design principle of Relato Serif.

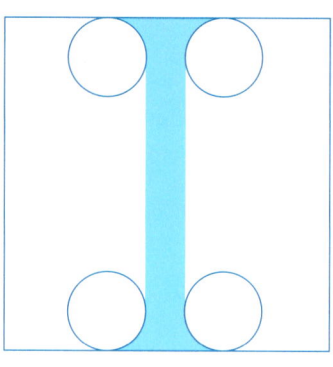

Inspiration: Durero studies. 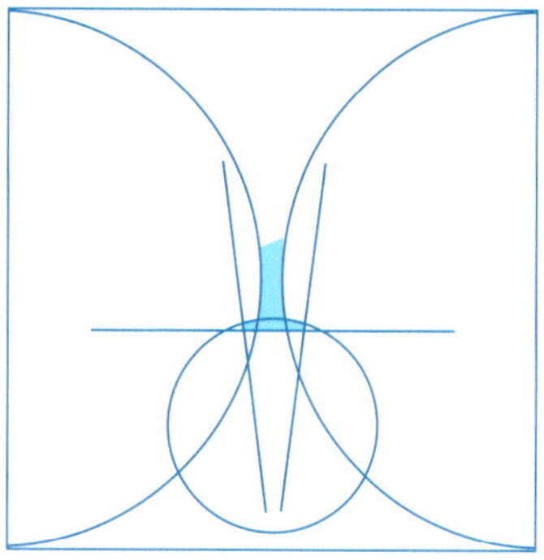 | Formal principle of serif.

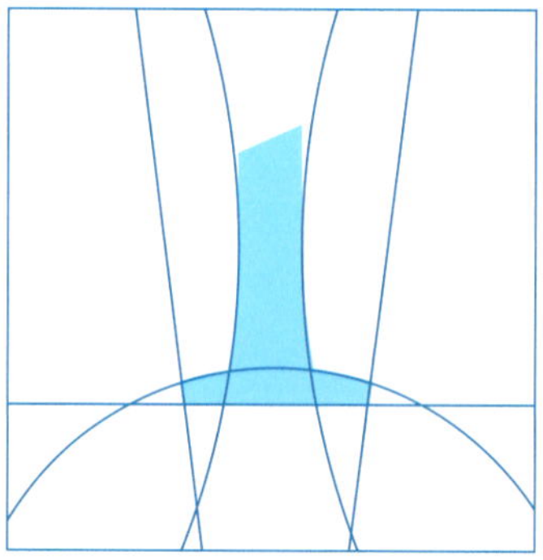

Zoom  | Serif

Geogrotesque
Geogrotesque Stencil
Relato Serif
Relato Sans
Periódico Display
Periódico Text

24pt

Page
75

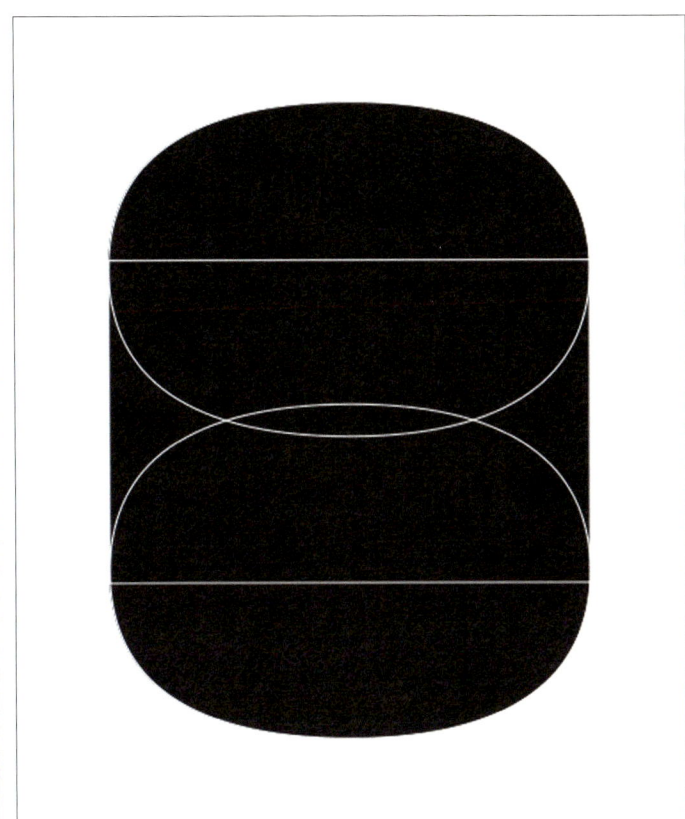

Sketches for Periódico.

Formal principle of Geogrotesque.

Corrected proofs of the Geogrotesque family.

Page 76

Foundry Emtype

Typeface  Geogrotesque, Stencil
Designer  Eduardo Manso
Year      2009
Format    OpenType

# Aa

Aa Bb Cc Dd Ee Ff Gg Hh Ii Jj Kk Ll
Mm Nn Oo Pp Qq Rr Ss Tt Uu Vv Ww
Xx Yy Zz
0123456789
—

Geogrotesque Thin 18pt
*Geogrotesque Thin Italic 18pt*
Geogrotesque Ultra Light 18pt
*Geogrotesque Ultra Light Italic 18pt*
Geogrotesque Light 18pt
*Geogrotesque Light Italic 18pt*
Geogrotesque Regular 18pt
*Geogrotesque Regular Italic 18pt*
**Geogrotesque Medium 18pt**
*Geogrotesque Medium Italic 18pt*
**Geogrotesque Semi Bold 18pt**
***Geogrotesque Semi Bold Italic 18pt***
**Geogrotesque Bold 18pt**
***Geogrotesque Bold Italic 18pt***
**Geogrotesque Stencil A 18pt**
**Geogrotesque Stencil B 18pt**
**Geogrotesque Stencil C 18pt**

---

12/14  Geogrotesque Light

The quick brown fox jumps over the lazy dog. Voyez le brick géant que j'examine près du wharf. Zwölf Boxkämpfer jagen Viktor quer über den

12/14  Geogrotesque Regular

The quick brown fox jumps over the lazy dog. Voyez le brick géant que j'examine près du wharf. Zwölf Boxkämpfer jagen Viktor quer über den

12/14  Geogrotesque Medium

The quick brown fox jumps over the lazy dog. Voyez le brick géant que j'examine près du wharf. Zwölf Boxkämpfer jagen Viktor quer über den

12/14  Geogrotesque Bold

**The quick brown fox jumps over the lazy dog. Voyez le brick géant que j'examine près du wharf. Zwölf Boxkämpfer jagen Viktor quer über den großen Sylter Deich. El veloz murciélago hindú comía feliz cardillo y kiwi.**

---

9/12  Geogrotesque Light

The quick brown fox jumps over the lazy dog. Voyez le brick géant que j'examine près du wharf. Zwölf Boxkämpfer jagen Viktor quer über den großen Sylter Deich. El veloz murciélago hindú comía feliz cardillo y kiwi. La cigüeña tocaba el saxofón detrás

9/12  Geogrotesque Regular

The quick brown fox jumps over the lazy dog. Voyez le brick géant que j'examine près du wharf. Zwölf Boxkämpfer jagen Viktor quer über den großen Sylter Deich. El veloz murciélago hindú comía feliz cardillo y kiwi. La cigüeña tocaba el saxofón detrás

9/12  Geogrotesque Medium

The quick brown fox jumps over the lazy dog. Voyez le brick géant que j'examine près du wharf. Zwölf Boxkämpfer jagen Viktor quer über den großen Sylter Deich. El veloz murciélago hindú comía feliz cardillo y kiwi. La cigüeña tocaba el saxofón detrás

9/12  Geogrotesque Bold

**The quick brown fox jumps over the lazy dog. Voyez le brick géant que j'examine près du wharf. Zwölf Boxkämpfer jagen Viktor quer über den großen Sylter Deich. El veloz murciélago hindú comía feliz cardillo y kiwi. La cigüeña tocaba el saxofón detrás del palenque de pajaatur? Rissimo lorereped ex es solore lab id molorro in rempore**

---

7/10  Geogrotesque Light

The quick brown fox jumps over the lazy dog. Voyez le brick géant que j'examine près du wharf. Zwölf Boxkämpfer jagen Viktor quer über den großen Sylter Deich. El veloz murciélago hindú comía feliz cardillo y kiwi. La cigüeña tocaba el saxofón detrás del palenque de pajaatur? Rissimo lorereped ex es solore lab id molorro in rempore icabore rehenetur aliam aut voles audae dem

7/10  Geogrotesque Regular

The quick brown fox jumps over the lazy dog. Voyez le brick géant que j'examine près du wharf. Zwölf Boxkämpfer jagen Viktor quer über den großen Sylter Deich. El veloz murciélago hindú comía feliz cardillo y kiwi. La cigüeña tocaba el saxofón detrás del palenque de pajaatur? Rissimo lorereped ex es solore lab id molorro in rempore icabore rehenetur aliam aut voles audae dem

7/10  Geogrotesque Medium

The quick brown fox jumps over the lazy dog. Voyez le brick géant que j'examine près du wharf. Zwölf Boxkämpfer jagen Viktor quer über den großen Sylter Deich. El veloz murciélago hindú comía feliz cardillo y kiwi. La cigüeña tocaba el saxofón detrás del palenque de pajaatur? Rissimo lorereped ex es solore lab id molorro in rempore icabore rehenetur aliam aut voles audae dem

7/10  Geogrotesque Bold

**The quick brown fox jumps over the lazy dog. Voyez le brick géant que j'examine près du wharf. Zwölf Boxkämpfer jagen Viktor quer über den großen Sylter Deich. El veloz murciélago hindú comía feliz cardillo y kiwi. La cigüeña tocaba el saxofón detrás del palenque de pajaatur? Rissimo lorereped ex es solore lab id molorro in rempore icabore rehenetur aliam aut voles audae dem quam, secum eum facesequae consequ aepudam quia voluptiur repel in et faccustibus, nonsenis aut quisqui rero**

Foundry Emtype

Typeface  Relato Sans, Serif
Designer  Eduardo Manso
Year      2005
Format    OpenType

# Aa

Aa Bb Cc Dd Ee Ff Gg Hh Ii Jj Kk Ll Mm Nn Oo Pp Qq Rr Ss Tt Uu Vv Ww Xx Yy Zz
0123456789
—

Relato Sans Light 18pt
*Relato Sans Light Italic 18pt*
Relato Sans Regular 18pt
*Relato Sans Regular Italic 18pt*
Relato Sans Medium 18pt
*Relato Sans Medium Italic 18pt*
**Relato Sans Semi Bold 18pt**
***Relato Sans Semi Bold Italic 18pt***
**Relato Sans Bold 18pt**
***Relato Sans Bold Italic 18pt***
**Relato Sans Black 18pt**
***Relato Sans Black Italic 18pt***
Relato Serif Regular 18pt
*Relato Serif Italic 18pt*
**Relato Serif Semi Bold 18pt**
**Relato Serif Bold 18pt**

---

12/14 Relato Sans Light

The quick brown fox jumps over the lazy dog. Voyez le brick géant que j'examine près du wharf. Zwölf Boxkämpfer jagen Viktor quer über den großen Sylter Deich.

12/14 Relato Sans Regular

The quick brown fox jumps over the lazy dog. Voyez le brick géant que j'examine près du wharf. Zwölf Boxkämpfer jagen Viktor quer über den großen Sylter

12/14 Relato Sans Medium

The quick brown fox jumps over the lazy dog. Voyez le brick géant que j'examine près du wharf. Zwölf Boxkämpfer jagen Viktor quer über den

12/14 Relato Sans Bold

**The quick brown fox jumps over the lazy dog. Voyez le brick géant que j'examine près du wharf. Zwölf Boxkämpfer jagen Viktor quer über den großen Sylter Deich. El veloz murciélago hindú comía feliz cardil-**

---

9/12 Relato Sans Light

The quick brown fox jumps over the lazy dog. Voyez le brick géant que j'examine près du wharf. Zwölf Boxkämpfer jagen Viktor quer über den großen Sylter Deich. El veloz murciélago hindú comía feliz cardillo y kiwi. La cigüeña tocaba el saxofón detrás del palen-

9/12 Relato Sans Regular

The quick brown fox jumps over the lazy dog. Voyez le brick géant que j'examine près du wharf. Zwölf Boxkämpfer jagen Viktor quer über den großen Sylter Deich. El veloz murciélago hindú comía feliz cardillo y kiwi. La cigüeña tocaba el saxofón detrás del

9/12 Relato Sans Medium

The quick brown fox jumps over the lazy dog. Voyez le brick géant que j'examine près du wharf. Zwölf Boxkämpfer jagen Viktor quer über den großen Sylter Deich. El veloz murciélago hindú comía feliz cardillo y kiwi. La cigüeña tocaba el saxofón detrás

9/12 Relato Sans Bold

**The quick brown fox jumps over the lazy dog. Voyez le brick géant que j'examine près du wharf. Zwölf Boxkämpfer jagen Viktor quer über den großen Sylter Deich. El veloz murciélago hindú comía feliz cardillo y kiwi. La cigüeña tocaba el saxofón detrás del palenque de pajaatur? Rissimo lorereped ex es solore lab id**

---

7/10 Relato Sans Light

The quick brown fox jumps over the lazy dog. Voyez le brick géant que j'examine près du wharf. Zwölf Boxkämpfer jagen Viktor quer über den großen Sylter Deich. El veloz murciélago hindú comía feliz cardillo y kiwi. La cigüeña tocaba el saxofón detrás del palenque de pajaatur? Rissimo lorereped ex es solore lab id molorro in rempore icabore rehenetur aliam aut voles audae dem quam, secum eum facesequae consequ ae-

7/10 Relato Sans Regular

The quick brown fox jumps over the lazy dog. Voyez le brick géant que j'examine près du wharf. Zwölf Boxkämpfer jagen Viktor quer über den großen Sylter Deich. El veloz murciélago hindú comía feliz cardillo y kiwi. La cigüeña tocaba el saxofón detrás del palenque de pajaatur? Rissimo lorereped ex es solore lab id molorro in rempore icabore rehenetur aliam aut voles audae dem quam, secum eum

7/10 Relato Sans Medium

The quick brown fox jumps over the lazy dog. Voyez le brick géant que j'examine près du wharf. Zwölf Boxkämpfer jagen Viktor quer über den großen Sylter Deich. El veloz murciélago hindú comía feliz cardillo y kiwi. La cigüeña tocaba el saxofón detrás del palenque de pajaatur? Rissimo lorereped ex es solore lab id molorro in rempore icabore rehenetur aliam aut voles audae dem quam, secum eum

7/10 Relato Sans Bold

**The quick brown fox jumps over the lazy dog. Voyez le brick géant que j'examine près du wharf. Zwölf Boxkämpfer jagen Viktor quer über den großen Sylter Deich. El veloz murciélago hindú comía feliz cardillo y kiwi. La cigüeña tocaba el saxofón detrás del palenque de pajaatur? Rissimo lorereped ex es solore lab id molorro in rempore icabore rehenetur aliam aut voles audae dem quam, secum eum facesequae consequ aepudam quia voluptiur repel in et faccustibus, nonsenis aut quisqui**

| | | | |
|---|---|---|---|
| Page | | Foundry | Emtype |
| 78 | | | |
| Typeface | Periódico Display | Year | 2011 |
| Designer | Eduardo Manso | Format | OpenType |

# Newspaper
# Tageszeitung

Periódico Display Thin 22pt
*Periódico Display Thin Italic* 22pt
Periódico Display Ultra Light 22pt
*Periódico Display Ultra Light Italic* 22pt
Periódico Display Light 22pt
*Periódico Display Light Italic* 22pt
Periódico Display Regular 22pt
*Periódico Display Regular Italic* 22pt
Periódico Display Medium 22pt
*Periódico Display Medium Italic* 22pt
**Periódico Display Semi Bold** 22pt
***Periódico Display Semi Bold Italic*** 22pt
**Periódico Display Bold** 22pt
***Periódico Display Bold Italic*** 22pt
**Periódico Display Black** 22pt
***Periódico Display Black Italic*** 22pt
**Periódico Display Ultra Black** 22pt
***Periódico Display Ultra Black Italic*** 22pt

| | | | |
|---|---|---|---|
| Typeface | Periódico Text | Year | 2011 |
| Designer | Eduardo Manso | Format | OpenType |

# Aa

Aa Bb Cc Dd Ee Ff Gg Hh Ii Jj Kk Ll Mm Nn Oo Pp Qq Rr Ss Tt Uu Vv Ww Xx Yy Zz
0123456789

Periódico Text Light 22pt
*Periódico Text Light Italic 22pt*
Periódico Text Regular 22pt
*Periódico Text Regular Italic 22pt*
**Periódico Text Medium 22pt**
***Periódico Text Medium Italic 22pt***
**Periódico Text Semi Bold 22pt**
***Periódico Text Semi Bold Italic 22pt***
**Periódico Text Bold 22pt**
***Periódico Text Bold Italic 22pt***

---

**12/14 — Periódico Text Light**

The quick brown fox jumps over the lazy dog. Voyez le brick géant que j'examine près du wharf. Zwölf Boxkämpfer jagen Viktor quer über

**12/14 — Periódico Text Regular**

The quick brown fox jumps over the lazy dog. Voyez le brick géant que j'examine près du wharf. Zwölf Boxkämpfer jagen Viktor quer

**12/14 — Periódico Text Medium**

The quick brown fox jumps over the lazy dog. Voyez le brick géant que j'examine près du wharf. Zwölf Boxkämpfer jagen Vik-

**12/14 — Periódico Text Bold**

The quick brown fox jumps over the lazy dog. Voyez le brick géant que j'examine près du wharf. Zwölf Boxkämpfer jagen Viktor quer über den großen Sylter Deich. El veloz murciélago hindú comía feliz cardillo y kiwi. La cigüeña tocaba el saxofón detrás del palenque de pajaatur?

---

**9/12 — Periódico Text Light**

The quick brown fox jumps over the lazy dog. Voyez le brick géant que j'examine près du wharf. Zwölf Boxkämpfer jagen Viktor quer über den großen Sylter Deich. El veloz murciélago hindú comía feliz cardillo y kiwi. La

**9/12 — Periódico Text Regular**

The quick brown fox jumps over the lazy dog. Voyez le brick géant que j'examine près du wharf. Zwölf Boxkämpfer jagen Viktor quer über den großen Sylter Deich. El veloz murciélago hindú comía feliz cardillo y kiwi. La

**9/12 — Periódico Text Medium**

The quick brown fox jumps over the lazy dog. Voyez le brick géant que j'examine près du wharf. Zwölf Boxkämpfer jagen Viktor quer über den großen Sylter Deich. El veloz murciélago hindú comía feliz cardillo y kiwi. La

**9/12 — Periódico Text Bold**

The quick brown fox jumps over the lazy dog. Voyez le brick géant que j'examine près du wharf. Zwölf Boxkämpfer jagen Viktor quer über den großen Sylter Deich. El veloz murciélago hindú comía feliz cardillo y kiwi. La cigüeña tocaba el saxofón detrás del palenque de pajaatur? Rissimo lorereped ex es solore lab id molorro in rempore icabore rehenetur aliam aut voles audae dem quam, secum eum facesequae

---

**7/10 — Periódico Text Light**

The quick brown fox jumps over the lazy dog. Voyez le brick géant que j'examine près du wharf. Zwölf Boxkämpfer jagen Viktor quer über den großen Sylter Deich. El veloz murciélago hindú comía feliz cardillo y kiwi. La cigüeña tocaba el saxofón detrás del palenque de pajaatur? Rissimo lorereped ex es solore lab id molorro in rempore icabore rehenetur aliam

**7/10 — Periódico Text Regular**

The quick brown fox jumps over the lazy dog. Voyez le brick géant que j'examine près du wharf. Zwölf Boxkämpfer jagen Viktor quer über den großen Sylter Deich. El veloz murciélago hindú comía feliz cardillo y kiwi. La cigüeña tocaba el saxofón detrás del palenque de pajaatur? Rissimo lorereped ex es solore lab id molorro in rempore icabore rehenetur

**7/10 — Periódico Text Medium**

The quick brown fox jumps over the lazy dog. Voyez le brick géant que j'examine près du wharf. Zwölf Boxkämpfer jagen Viktor quer über den großen Sylter Deich. El veloz murciélago hindú comía feliz cardillo y kiwi. La cigüeña tocaba el saxofón detrás del palenque de pajaatur? Rissimo lorereped ex es solore lab id molorro in rempore

**7/10 — Periódico Text Bold**

The quick brown fox jumps over the lazy dog. Voyez le brick géant que j'examine près du wharf. Zwölf Boxkämpfer jagen Viktor quer über den großen Sylter Deich. El veloz murciélago hindú comía feliz cardillo y kiwi. La cigüeña tocaba el saxofón detrás del palenque de pajaatur? Rissimo lorereped ex es solore lab id molorro in rempore icabore rehenetur aliam aut voles audae dem quam, secum eum facesequae consequ aepudam quia voluptiur repel in et faccustibus, nonsenis aut quisqui rero mi, ipiet lam ant ut maio et hil molupta tustis atatur, consedi tasimol orerem aut volor andipsapis sit, illaut volore officatus alicae dusdaec tatecte

# E
## exljbris

—

## Jos Buivenga

—

## Arnhem, Netherlands

—

## Since 2008

exljbris is the personal foundry of self-taught type designer Jos Buivenga. Before launching his first commercial typeface in 2008, Buivenga shared his explorations in type with a growing circle of online friends and fans for fifteen years, allowing them to follow the development of his typefaces and download the results at no cost.

## Info

—Why?
Because I no longer wanted to work for someone else.

—People on staff
1

—Type designers on staff
1

—Type familys
15

—Designers represented
1

— Web shop
No

—Distributors
MyFonts, Ascender, FontShop, Fontspring

—Webfont services
Typekit, WebINK, Fontdeck, Fontspring

—Basic license
About $16 (single font, 1 computer)

Typeface selection

Calluna
**Geotica**
Museo
Museo Sans
Museo Sans Rounded
Museo Slab

24pt

## People

—Jos Buivenga can be passionate about a lot of things. He loves to paint, listen to music, brew an almost perfect espresso… but nothing challenges and rewards him more than designing type. If ever he was stranded on a desert island he would still draw alphabets in the sand, even if there was no one else to see them. He is the founder of exljbris, the one-man Dutch font foundry through which he releases and offers his typefaces. In 2008, while still working as an art director at an advertising agency, he released his first commercial typeface, Museo, with several weights offered for free. That strategy paid off and Museo became a huge bestseller. Partly thanks to that success he now calls himself a full time type designer.

F is for Fonts. The exljbris logo.

Page
81

# Deo
# Machina
# Questions
# For a
# Hectic
# Orb

Demonstration of the layering possibilities of Geotica, using a separate Fill font to create the different colors.

# Machina
# for only £4,00?
# WOW
# Add Céruleum & be
# Astonished
# ZELHEM
# Best of Luck

Based on simple geometric design principles, Geotica has a several varieties that can be combined or layered.

# g1

Ligature in Calluna.

Typeface  Geotica
Designer  Jos Buivenga

Year    2010
Format  OpenType

# Geometry
# Chaos Theory
# Cheops Sphynx
# Cheops Sphynx
# Cheops Sphynx

**Geotica One Regular**
Geotica One Open
Geotica One Fill
Geotica One Engraved

**Geotica Two Regular**
Geotica Two Open
Geotica Two Fill
Geotica Two Engraved

**Geotica Three Regular**
Geotica Three Open
Geotica Three Fill
Geotica Three Engraved

**Geotica Four Regular**
Geotica Four Open
Geotica Four Fill
Geotica Four Engraved

Page 83

Foundry  exljbris

Typeface  Calluna
Designer  Jos Buivenga
Year  2009
Format  OpenType

# Aa

Aa Bb Cc Dd Ee Ff Gg Hh Ii Jj Kk Ll Mm Nn Oo Pp Qq Rr Ss Tt Uu Vv Ww Xx Yy Zz
0123456789
—

Calluna Light 24pt
Calluna Regular 24pt
*Calluna Italic* 24pt
**Calluna Semi Bold** 24pt
***Calluna Semi Bold Italic*** 24pt
**Calluna Bold** 24pt
***Calluna Bold Italic*** 24pt
**Calluna Black** 24pt

---

12/14  Calluna Light

The quick brown fox jumps over the lazy dog. Voyez le brick géant que j'examine près du wharf. Zwölf Boxkämpfer jagen Viktor quer über den

12/14  Calluna Regular

The quick brown fox jumps over the lazy dog. Voyez le brick géant que j'examine près du wharf. Zwölf Boxkämpfer jagen Viktor quer über den

12/14  Calluna SemiBold

The quick brown fox jumps over the lazy dog. Voyez le brick géant que j'examine près du wharf. Zwölf Boxkämpfer jagen Viktor quer über den

12/14  Calluna Bold

The quick brown fox jumps over the lazy dog. Voyez le brick géant que j'examine près du wharf. Zwölf Boxkämpfer jagen Viktor quer über den großen Sylter Deich. El veloz murciélago hindú comía feliz cardillo y kiwi. La cigüeña tocaba el saxofón detrás del palenque de pajaatur? Rissimo lorereped ex es solore

---

9/12  Calluna Light

The quick brown fox jumps over the lazy dog. Voyez le brick géant que j'examine près du wharf. Zwölf Boxkämpfer jagen Viktor quer über den großen Sylter Deich. El veloz murciélago hindú comía feliz cardillo y kiwi. La cigüeña tocaba el saxofón detrás

9/12  Calluna Regular

The quick brown fox jumps over the lazy dog. Voyez le brick géant que j'examine près du wharf. Zwölf Boxkämpfer jagen Viktor quer über den großen Sylter Deich. El veloz murciélago hindú comía feliz cardillo y kiwi. La cigüeña tocaba el saxofón

9/12  Calluna SemiBold

The quick brown fox jumps over the lazy dog. Voyez le brick géant que j'examine près du wharf. Zwölf Boxkämpfer jagen Viktor quer über den großen Sylter Deich. El veloz murciélago hindú comía feliz cardillo y kiwi. La cigüeña tocaba el saxofón

9/12  Calluna Bold

The quick brown fox jumps over the lazy dog. Voyez le brick géant que j'examine près du wharf. Zwölf Boxkämpfer jagen Viktor quer über den großen Sylter Deich. El veloz murciélago hindú comía feliz cardillo y kiwi. La cigüeña tocaba el saxofón detrás del palenque de pajaatur? Rissimo lorereped ex es solore lab id molorro in rempore icabore rehenetur aliam aut voles audae dem quam, secum eum facesequae consequ aepudam quia voluptiur repel in et faccustibus, nonsenis

---

7/10  Calluna Light

The quick brown fox jumps over the lazy dog. Voyez le brick géant que j'examine près du wharf. Zwölf Boxkämpfer jagen Viktor quer über den großen Sylter Deich. El veloz murciélago hindú comía feliz cardillo y kiwi. La cigüeña tocaba el saxofón detrás del palenque de pajaatur? Rissimo lorereped ex es solore lab id molorro in rempore icabore rehenetur aliam aut voles audae dem

7/10  Calluna Regular

The quick brown fox jumps over the lazy dog. Voyez le brick géant que j'examine près du wharf. Zwölf Boxkämpfer jagen Viktor quer über den großen Sylter Deich. El veloz murciélago hindú comía feliz cardillo y kiwi. La cigüeña tocaba el saxofón detrás del palenque de pajaatur? Rissimo lorereped ex es solore lab id molorro in rempore icabore rehenetur aliam aut voles audae dem

7/10  Calluna SemiBold

The quick brown fox jumps over the lazy dog. Voyez le brick géant que j'examine près du wharf. Zwölf Boxkämpfer jagen Viktor quer über den großen Sylter Deich. El veloz murciélago hindú comía feliz cardillo y kiwi. La cigüeña tocaba el saxofón detrás del palenque de pajaatur? Rissimo lorereped ex es solore lab id molorro in rempore icabore rehenetur aliam aut voles audae

7/10  Calluna Bold

The quick brown fox jumps over the lazy dog. Voyez le brick géant que j'examine près du wharf. Zwölf Boxkämpfer jagen Viktor quer über den großen Sylter Deich. El veloz murciélago hindú comía feliz cardillo y kiwi. La cigüeña tocaba el saxofón detrás del palenque de pajaatur? Rissimo lorereped ex es solore lab id molorro in rempore icabore rehenetur aliam aut voles audae dem quam, secum eum facesequae consequ aepudam quia voluptiur repel in et faccustibus, nonsenis aut quisqui rero mi, ipiet lam ant ut maio et hil molupta tustis atatur, consedi tasimol orerem aut volor andipsapis sit, illaut volore officatus alicae dusdaec tatecte cearum qui accatibus restiore nulpa secaerferum, nus dolenim in et quoditat que explam voluptur?

Foundry exljbris

Typeface Museo, Slab
Designer Jos Buivenga
Year 2008
Format OpenType

# Aa

Aa Bb Cc Dd Ee Ff Gg Hh Ii Jj Kk
Ll Mm Nn Oo Pp Qq Rr Ss Tt Uu
Vv Ww Xx Yy Zz
0123456789

Museo 100 14pt
*Museo 100 Italic 14pt*
Museo 300 14pt
*Museo 300 Italic 14pt*
Museo 500 14pt
*Museo 500 Italic 14pt*
**Museo 700 14pt**
*Museo 700 Italic 14pt*
**Museo 900 14pt**
***Museo 900 Italic 14pt***

Museo Slab 100 14pt
*Museo Slab 100 Italic 14pt*
Museo Slab 300 14pt
*Museo Slab 300 Italic 14pt*
Museo Slab 500 14pt
*Museo Slab 500 Italic 14pt*
**Museo Slab 700 14pt**
***Museo Slab 700 Italic 14pt***
**Museo Slab 900 14pt**
***Museo Slab 900 Italic 14pt***
**Museo Slab 1000 14pt**
***Museo Slab 1000 Italic 14pt***

---

12/14  Museo 100

The quick brown fox jumps over the lazy dog. Voyez le brick géant que j'examine près du wharf. Zwölf Boxkämpfer jagen Viktor quer über den großen Sylter Deich. El veloz murciélago hindú comía feliz cardillo y kiwi. La cigüeña tocaba el saxofón detrás del palenque de pajaatur? Rissimo lorereped ex es solore lab id molorro in rempore icabore rehenetur aliam aut voles

12/14  Museo Slab 100

The quick brown fox jumps over the lazy dog. Voyez le brick géant que j'examine près du wharf. Zwölf Boxkämpfer jagen Viktor quer über den großen Sylter Deich. El veloz murciélago hindú comía feliz cardillo y kiwi. La cigüeña tocaba el saxofón detrás del palenque de pajaatur? Rissimo lorereped ex es solore lab id molorro in rempore icabore rehen-

9/12  Museo 100

The quick brown fox jumps over the lazy dog. Voyez le brick géant que j'examine près du wharf. Zwölf Boxkämpfer jagen Viktor quer über den großen Sylter Deich. El veloz murciélago hindú comía feliz cardillo y kiwi. La cigüe-

9/12  Museo 300

The quick brown fox jumps over the lazy dog. Voyez le brick géant que j'examine près du wharf. Zwölf Boxkämpfer jagen Viktor quer über den großen Sylter Deich. El veloz murciélago hindú comía feliz cardillo y kiwi. La

9/12  Museo 500

The quick brown fox jumps over the lazy dog. Voyez le brick géant que j'examine près du wharf. Zwölf Boxkämpfer jagen Viktor quer über den großen Sylter Deich. El veloz murciélago hindú comía feliz cardillo y kiwi.

9/12  Museo 700

**The quick brown fox jumps over the lazy dog. Voyez le brick géant que j'examine près du wharf. Zwölf Boxkämpfer jagen Viktor quer über den großen Sylter Deich. El veloz murciélago hindú comía feliz cardillo y**

9/12  Museo 900

**The quick brown fox jumps over the lazy dog. Voyez le brick géant que j'examine près du wharf. Zwölf Boxkämpfer jagen Viktor quer über den großen Sylter Deich. El veloz murciélago hindú comía feliz cardillo y kiwi. La cigüeña tocaba el saxofón detrás del palenque de pajaatur? Rissimo**

9/12  Museo Slab 100

The quick brown fox jumps over the lazy dog. Voyez le brick géant que j'examine près du wharf. Zwölf Boxkämpfer jagen Viktor quer über den großen Sylter Deich. El veloz murciélago hindú comía feliz cardillo y

9/12  Museo Slab 300

The quick brown fox jumps over the lazy dog. Voyez le brick géant que j'examine près du wharf. Zwölf Boxkämpfer jagen Viktor quer über den großen Sylter Deich. El veloz murciélago hindú comía feliz cardillo y

9/12  Museo Slab 500

The quick brown fox jumps over the lazy dog. Voyez le brick géant que j'examine près du wharf. Zwölf Boxkämpfer jagen Viktor quer über den großen Sylter Deich. El veloz murciélago hindú comía feliz car-

9/12  Museo Slab 700

**The quick brown fox jumps over the lazy dog. Voyez le brick géant que j'examine près du wharf. Zwölf Boxkämpfer jagen Viktor quer über den großen Sylter Deich. El veloz murciélago hindú comía feliz car-**

9/12  Museo Slab 900

**The quick brown fox jumps over the lazy dog. Voyez le brick géant que j'examine près du wharf. Zwölf Boxkämpfer jagen Viktor quer über den großen Sylter Deich. El veloz murciélago hindú comía feliz cardillo y kiwi. La cigüeña tocaba el saxofón detrás del palenque de pajaa-**

Typeface  Museo Sans, Sans Rounded   Year    2008, 2011
Designer  Jos Buivenga               Format  OpenType

Museo Sans 100 14pt
*Museo Sans 100 Italic 14pt*
Museo Sans 300 14pt
*Museo Sans 300 Italic 14pt*
Museo Sans 500 14pt
*Museo Sans 500 Italic 14pt*
**Museo Sans 700 14pt**
***Museo Sans 700 Italic 14pt***
**Museo Sans 900 14pt**
***Museo Sans 900 Italic 14pt***

Museo Sans Rounded 100 14pt
Museo Sans Rounded 300 14pt
Museo Sans Rounded 500 14pt
**Museo Sans Rounded 700 14pt**
**Museo Sans Rounded 900 14pt**
**Museo Sans Rounded 1000 14pt**

---

9/12  Museo Sans 100

The quick brown fox jumps over the lazy dog. Voyez le brick géant que j'examine près du wharf. Zwölf Boxkämpfer jagen Viktor quer über den großen Sylter Deich. El veloz murciélago hindú comía feliz cardillo y kiwi. La

9/12  Museo Sans 300

The quick brown fox jumps over the lazy dog. Voyez le brick géant que j'examine près du wharf. Zwölf Boxkämpfer jagen Viktor quer über den großen Sylter Deich. El veloz murciélago hindú comía feliz cardillo y kiwi. La

9/12  Museo Sans 500

The quick brown fox jumps over the lazy dog. Voyez le brick géant que j'examine près du wharf. Zwölf Boxkämpfer jagen Viktor quer über den großen Sylter Deich. El veloz murciélago hindú comía feliz cardillo y kiwi. La ci-

9/12  Museo Sans 700

**The quick brown fox jumps over the lazy dog. Voyez le brick géant que j'examine près du wharf. Zwölf Boxkämpfer jagen Viktor quer über den großen Sylter Deich. El veloz murciélago hindú comía feliz cardillo y kiwi.**

9/12  Museo Sans 900

**The quick brown fox jumps over the lazy dog. Voyez le brick géant que j'examine près du wharf. Zwölf Boxkämpfer jagen Viktor quer über den großen Sylter Deich. El veloz murciélago hindú comía feliz cardillo y kiwi. La cigüeña tocaba el saxofón detrás del palenque de pajaatur? Rissimo lorer-**

9/12  Museo Sans Rounded 100

The quick brown fox jumps over the lazy dog. Voyez le brick géant que j'examine près du wharf. Zwölf Boxkämpfer jagen Viktor quer über den großen Sylter Deich. El veloz murciélago hindú comía feliz cardillo y kiwi. La cigüe-

9/12  Museo Sans Rounded 300

The quick brown fox jumps over the lazy dog. Voyez le brick géant que j'examine près du wharf. Zwölf Boxkämpfer jagen Viktor quer über den großen Sylter Deich. El veloz murciélago hindú comía feliz cardillo y kiwi. La cigüe-

9/12  Museo Sans Rounded 500

The quick brown fox jumps over the lazy dog. Voyez le brick géant que j'examine près du wharf. Zwölf Boxkämpfer jagen Viktor quer über den großen Sylter Deich. El veloz murciélago hindú comía feliz cardillo y kiwi. La

9/12  Museo Sans Rounded 700

**The quick brown fox jumps over the lazy dog. Voyez le brick géant que j'examine près du wharf. Zwölf Boxkämpfer jagen Viktor quer über den großen Sylter Deich. El veloz murciélago hindú comía feliz cardillo y kiwi. La**

9/12  Museo Sans Rounded 900

**The quick brown fox jumps over the lazy dog. Voyez le brick géant que j'examine près du wharf. Zwölf Boxkämpfer jagen Viktor quer über den großen Sylter Deich. El veloz murciélago hindú comía feliz cardillo y kiwi. La cigüeña tocaba el saxofón detrás del palenque de pajaatur? Rissimo lorereped ex**

12/14  Museo Sans 300

The quick brown fox jumps over the lazy dog. Voyez le brick géant que j'examine près du wharf. Zwölf Boxkämpfer jagen Viktor quer über den großen Sylter Deich. El veloz murciélago hindú comía feliz cardillo y kiwi. La cigüeña tocaba el saxofón detrás del palenque de pajaatur? Rissimo lorereped ex es solore lab id molorro in rempore icabore rehenetur aliam aut

12/14  Museo Sans Rounded 300

The quick brown fox jumps over the lazy dog. Voyez le brick géant que j'examine près du wharf. Zwölf Boxkämpfer jagen Viktor quer über den großen Sylter Deich. El veloz murciélago hindú comía feliz cardillo y kiwi. La cigüeña tocaba el saxofón detrás del palenque de pajaatur? Rissimo lorereped ex es solore lab id molorro in rempore icabore rehenetur aliam aut

# F

## FaceType

— Marcus Sterz
— Vienna, Austria
— Since 2008

Founded in 2008, the FaceType foundry is constantly working on expanding its library. "Our goal is to provide high quality fonts at a reasonable price. Although interested in digitizing old type gems like Ivory, Aeronaut and Letterpress, our primary focus is to develop new designs such as Lignette, Brilliant and Marlowe."

## Info

—Why?
Marcus Sterz: "I was fed up with the conditions in the field of 'normal' graphic design. Making fonts is like paradise: No negotiations with clients, no meetings — in short: I finally felt really independent."

—People on staff
1

—Type designers on staff
1

—Type families
30

—Designers represented
3

— Web shop
www.facetype.org

—Distributors
MyFonts, Veer, YouWorkForThem, Fontspring, HypeForType, Fonts.com, Monotype Imaging, Linotype

—Webfont services
Fontspring, MyFonts

—Basic license
Family prices depend on complexity of designs, Single fonts $8 and up (some free); 3-style familes $38–$90, etc.

## People

—Marcus Sterz
Marcus Sterz, one of FaceType's founders, is following his passion: designing typefaces. With a background in graphic design he loves to see his work being transformed into something new through the hands of others.

—Georg Herold-Wildfellner
"What I would set my heart on is graphic design, what I would sell my soul for is type design. Thank God I have a family who occupies both."

—Igor Labudovic
Igor Labudovic is an Austrian graphic design student with a passion for typefaces. He is currently studying at the 'die Graphische' masterclass for graphic design in Vienna. He created Brilliant as a graduation project in 2009–10.

## Typeface selection

IVORY
Lignette
MOTTO
STRANGELOVE
Weingut

Lignette

24pt

Page
87

Weingut

Motto

Motto

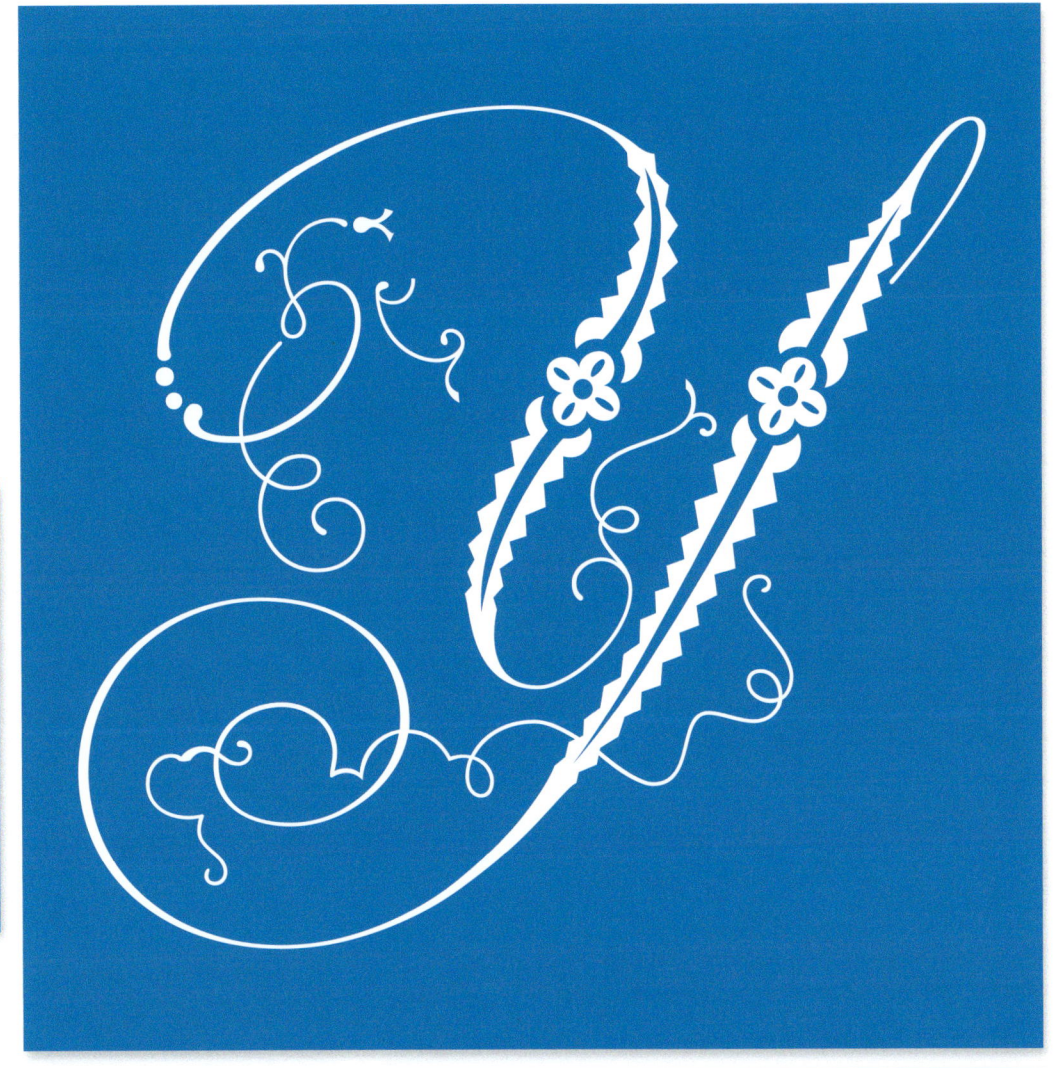

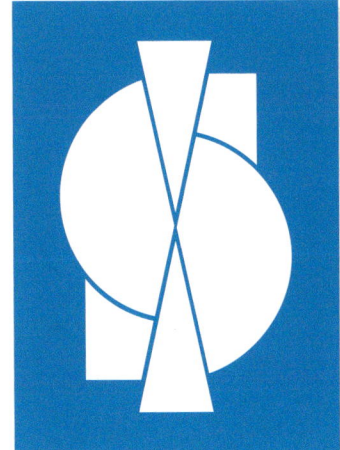

Strangelove

| Page | Foundry | FaceType |
| --- | --- | --- |
| 88 | | |

| Typeface | Ivory | Year | 2009 |
| --- | --- | --- | --- |
| Designer | Marcus Sterz | Format | OpenType |

# ELFENBEIN
# EBONY KEYS
# EBONY KEYS
# EBONY KEYS

HEADLINE
NO SWASHES
WITH

Aa Bb Cc Dd Ee Ff
Gg Hh Ii Jj Kk Ll Mm
Nn Oo Pp Qq Rr Ss Tt
Uu Vv Ww Xx Yy Zz
0123456789

| Typeface | Weingut | Year | 2011 |
| --- | --- | --- | --- |
| Designer | Marcus Sterz | Format | OpenType |

*Wozu Reize?*

*Weingut Script*
*Weingut Script Flourish*

*Aa Bb Cc Dd Ee Ff*
*Gg Hh Ii Jj Kk Ll*
*Mm Nn Oo Pp Qq Rr*
*Ss Tt Uu Vv Ww Xx*
*Yy Zz 0123456789*

| | | | |
|---|---|---|---|
| Page | | Foundry | FaceType |
| 89 | | | |

| | | | |
|---|---|---|---|
| Typeface | Motto | Year | 2009 |
| Designer | Marcus Sterz | Format | OpenType |

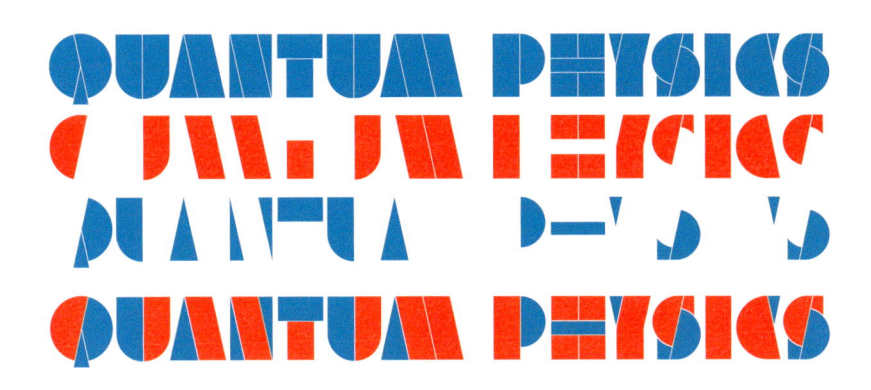

**QUANTUM PHYSICS**

REGULAR

AA BB CC DD EE FF GG HH II
JJ KK LL MM NN OO PP QQ
RR SS TT UU VV WW XX YY ZZ
0123456789

| | | | |
|---|---|---|---|
| Typeface | Strangelove | Year | 2009 |
| Designer | Marcus Sterz | Format | OpenType |

**LOVE THE BOMB**

WIDE
NARROW
MIX

AA BB CC DD EE FF GG HH II
JJ KK LL MM NN OO PP QQ RR
SS TT UU VV WW XX YY ZZ
0123456789

| | | | |
|---|---|---|---|
| Typeface | Lignette | Year | 2011 |
| Designer | Marcus Sterz | Format | OpenType |

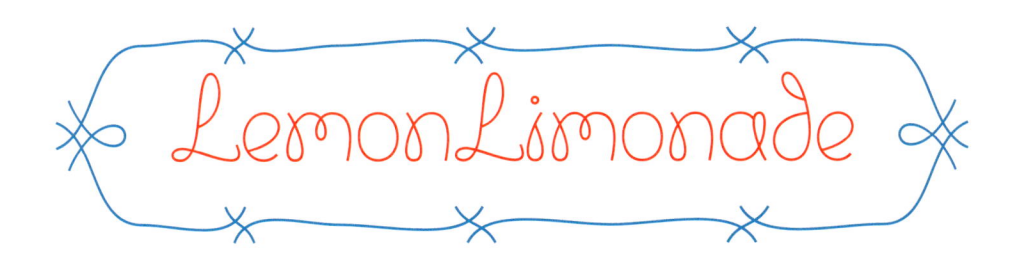

*LemonLimonade*

*StrawberryJam*

Script
Deco

Aa Bb Cc Dd Ee Ff Gg Hh Ii Jj Kk Ll Mm
Nn Oo Pp Qq Rr Ss Tt Uu Vv Ww Xx Yy
Zz 0123456789

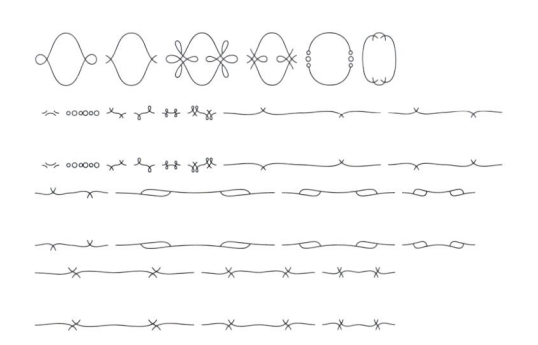

# F
Feliciano

—

Mário Feliciano

—

Lisbon, Portugal

—

Since 2001

The Feliciano Type Foundry represents the type designs of Portuguese designer Mário Feliciano.

## Info

—Why?
I was running a design company but I wanted to concentrate more on type design. Being able to do things on my own terms was one of the reasons to start a foundry alone. But it was also maybe down to being relatively isolated.

—People on staff
1

—Type designers on staff
1

—Type families
17

—Designers represented
1

— Web shop
www.felicianotypefoundry.com

—Distributors
Village, MyFonts

—Webfont services
To be announced

—Basic license
35€ (single fonts), 1 user

## People

—Mário Feliciano drew his first fonts in the early 1990s for two Portuguese surf magazines which he art-directed, under the influence of cutting-edge typography by David Carson, Emigre and others. Having decided to become a type designer he went through a long process of investigation. Between 1997 and 1999 he released his first typefaces through Chicago-based foundry T26 and Adobe. He got involved in the world-wide typographic association ATypI, becoming its Portuguese delegate. His meetings with renowned type designers such as Peter Matthias Noordzij, Matthew Carter and Gerard Unger were crucial to his evolution as a type designer and radically changed his perspective of typography, urging him to deepen his studies of type design history. In 1999 Feliciano became the Portuguese agent for The Enschedé Font Foundry. Shortly therafter, he launched the Feliciano Type Foundry with two very different concepts, a large type family — The Morgan Project — and a collection of small display families and single fonts — the B-sides modular series.

## Typeface selection

Eudald News
Flama
GARĐA
Merlo
MORGAN TW
MORGAN POSTER AVEC
Stella

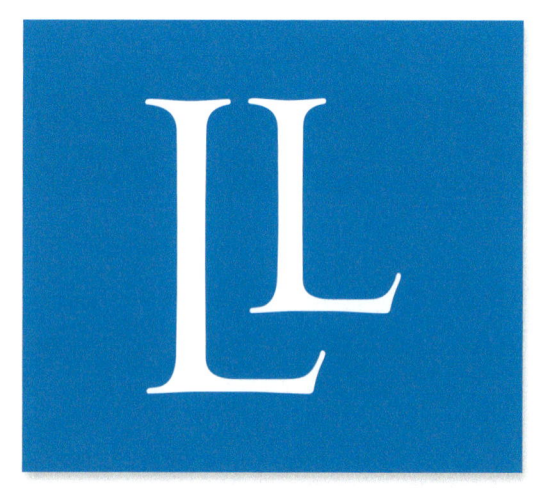

24pt

Merlo

Page
91

The Morgan Project

Stella

Monogram: Feliciano Type Foundry

Eudald News

Page 92

Foundry  Feliciano

---

Typeface  Eudald News
Designer  Mário Feliciano
Year  1998–2009
Format  OpenType

# Aa

Aa Bb Cc Dd Ee Ff Gg Hh Ii Jj Kk
Ll Mm Nn Oo Pp Qq Rr Ss Tt Uu
Vv Ww Xx Yy Zz
0123456789
—

Eudald News Regular 18pt
*Eudald News Regular Italic 18pt*
**Eudald News Medium 18pt**
*Eudald News Medium Italic 18pt*
**Eudald News Semibold 18pt**
***Eudald News Semibold Italic 18pt***
**Eudald News Bold 18pt**
***Eudald News Bold Italic 18pt***

9/12  Eudald News Regular

The quick brown fox jumps over the lazy dog. Voyez le brick géant que j'examine près du wharf. Zwölf Boxkämpfer jagen Viktor quer über den großen Sylter Deich. El veloz murciélago hindú comía feliz cardillo y kiwi. La cigüeña tocaba el saxofón detrás del palenque de pajaatur? Rissimo lorereped ex es solore lab id molorro in rempore icabore rehenetur aliam aut voles audae dem quam, secum eum facesequae consequ aepudam quia voluptiur repel in et faccustibus, nonsenis aut quisqui rero mi, ipiet lam ant ut maio et hil molupta tustis atatur, consedi tasimol orerem aut

7/10  Eudald News Regular

The quick brown fox jumps over the lazy dog. Voyez le brick géant que j'examine près du wharf. Zwölf Boxkämpfer jagen Viktor quer über den großen Sylter Deich. El veloz murciélago hindú comía feliz cardillo y kiwi. La cigüeña tocaba el saxofón detrás del palenque de pajaatur? Rissimo lorereped ex es solore lab id molorro in rempore icabore rehenetur aliam aut voles audae dem quam, secum eum facesequae consequ aepudam quia voluptiur repel in et faccustibus, nonsenis aut quisqui rero mi, ipiet lam ant ut maio et hil molupta tustis atatur, consedi tasimol orerem aut volor andipsapis sit, illaut volore officatus alicae dusdaec tatecte cearum qui accatibus restiore nulpa secaerferum, nus dolenim in et quoditat que explam volupictur? Qui de illuptae. Dae nis illiberum volorro ritatis tinullo rerumqu atetur repro eatius asperibus. Rissimo lorereped ex es solore lab id mo-

---

Typeface  Merlo
Designer  Mário Feliciano
Year  1998–2009
Format  OpenType

# Aa

Aa Bb Cc Dd Ee Ff Gg Hh Ii Jj Kk
Ll Mm Nn Oo Pp Qq Rr Ss Tt Uu
Vv Ww Xx Yy Zz
0123456789
—

Merlo Roman 18pt
*Merlo Italic 18pt*

9/12  Merlo Roman

The quick brown fox jumps over the lazy dog. Voyez le brick géant que j'examine près du wharf. Zwölf Boxkämpfer jagen Viktor quer über den großen Sylter Deich. El veloz murciélago hindú comía feliz cardillo y kiwi. La cigüeña tocaba el saxofón detrás del palenque de pajaatur? Rissimo lorereped ex es solore lab id molorro in rempore icabore rehenetur aliam aut voles audae dem quam, secum eum facesequae consequ aepudam quia voluptiur repel in et faccustibus, nonsenis aut quisqui rero mi, ipiet lam ant ut maio et hil molupta tustis atatur, consedi tasimol orerem aut volor andipsapis sit, illaut volore officatus alicae dusdaec tatecte cearum qui accatibus restiore nulpa secaerferum, nus

7/10  Merlo Roman

The quick brown fox jumps over the lazy dog. Voyez le brick géant que j'examine près du wharf. Zwölf Boxkämpfer jagen Viktor quer über den großen Sylter Deich. El veloz murciélago hindú comía feliz cardillo y kiwi. La cigüeña tocaba el saxofón detrás del palenque de pajaatur? Rissimo lorereped ex es solore lab id molorro in rempore icabore rehenetur aliam aut voles audae dem quam, secum eum facesequae consequ aepudam quia voluptiur repel in et faccustibus, nonsenis aut quisqui rero mi, ipiet lam ant ut maio et hil molupta tustis atatur, consedi tasimol orerem aut volor andipsapis sit, illaut volore officatus alicae dusdaec tatecte cearum qui accatibus restiore nulpa secaerferum, nus dolenim in et quoditat que explam volupictur? Qui de illuptae. Dae nis illiberum volorro ritatis tinullo rerumqu atetur repro eatius asperibus. Rissimo lorereped ex es solore lab id molorro in rempore icabore rehenetur aliam aut voles audae dem quam, secum eum facesequae consequ aepudam quia voluptiur repel in et faccustibus, nonsenis aut quisqui rero mi, ipiet lam ant ut maio et hil molupta tustis

Page
93

Foundry  Feliciano

Typeface  Flama
Designer  Mário Feliciano

Year  2002–2006
Format  OpenType

# Aa

Aa Bb Cc Dd Ee Ff Gg Hh Ii Jj Kk
Ll Mm Nn Oo Pp Qq Rr Ss Tt Uu
Vv Ww Xx Yy Zz
0123456789
—

Flama Thin 18pt
*Flama Thin Italic 18pt*
Flama Ultra Light 18pt
*Flama Ultra Light Italic 18pt*
Flama Light 18pt
*Flama Light Italic 18pt*
Flama Book 18pt
*Flama Book Italic 18pt*
Flama Basic 18pt
*Flama Basic Italic 18pt*
**Flama Medium 18pt**
*Flama Medium Italic 18pt*
**Flama Semi Bold 18pt**
***Flama Semi Bold Italic 18pt***
**Flama Bold 18pt**
***Flama Bold Italic 18pt***
**Flama Extra Bold 18pt**
***Flama Extra Bold Italic 18pt***
**Flama Black 18pt**
***Flama Black Italic 18pt***

---

12/14  Flama Book

The quick brown fox jumps over the lazy dog. Voyez le brick géant que j'examine près du wharf. Zwölf Boxkämpfer jagen Viktor quer über

12/14  Flama Medium

The quick brown fox jumps over the lazy dog. Voyez le brick géant que j'examine près du wharf. Zwölf Boxkämpfer jagen Viktor quer über

12/14  Flama Bold

**The quick brown fox jumps over the lazy dog. Voyez le brick géant que j'examine près du wharf. Zwölf Boxkämpfer jagen Viktor quer über den großen Sylter Deich. El veloz murciélago hin-**

9/12  Flama Book

The quick brown fox jumps over the lazy dog. Voyez le brick géant que j'examine près du wharf. Zwölf Boxkämpfer jagen Viktor quer über den großen Sylter Deich. El veloz murciélago hindú comía feliz cardillo y kiwi. La cigüeña tocaba el

9/12  Flama Medium

The quick brown fox jumps over the lazy dog. Voyez le brick géant que j'examine près du wharf. Zwölf Boxkämpfer jagen Viktor quer über den großen Sylter Deich. El veloz murciélago hindú comía feliz cardillo y kiwi. La

9/12  Flama Bold

**The quick brown fox jumps over the lazy dog. Voyez le brick géant que j'examine près du wharf. Zwölf Boxkämpfer jagen Viktor quer über den großen Sylter Deich. El veloz murciélago hindú comía feliz cardillo y kiwi. La cigüeña tocaba el saxofón detrás del palenque de pajaatur? Rissimo lorereped ex**

7/10  Flama Book

The quick brown fox jumps over the lazy dog. Voyez le brick géant que j'examine près du wharf. Zwölf Boxkämpfer jagen Viktor quer über den großen Sylter Deich. El veloz murciélago hindú comía feliz cardillo y kiwi. La cigüeña tocaba el saxofón detrás del palenque de pajaatur? Rissimo lorereped ex es solore lab id molorro in rempore icabore rehenetur aliam aut voles

7/10  Flama Medium

The quick brown fox jumps over the lazy dog. Voyez le brick géant que j'examine près du wharf. Zwölf Boxkämpfer jagen Viktor quer über den großen Sylter Deich. El veloz murciélago hindú comía feliz cardillo y kiwi. La cigüeña tocaba el saxofón detrás del palenque de pajaatur? Rissimo lorereped ex es solore lab id molorro in rempore icabore

7/10  Flama Bold

**The quick brown fox jumps over the lazy dog. Voyez le brick géant que j'examine près du wharf. Zwölf Boxkämpfer jagen Viktor quer über den großen Sylter Deich. El veloz murciélago hindú comía feliz cardillo y kiwi. La cigüeña tocaba el saxofón detrás del palenque de pajaatur? Rissimo lorereped ex es solore lab id molorro in rempore icabore rehenetur aliam aut voles audae dem quam, secum eum facesequae consequ aepudam quia**

| | | | |
|---|---|---|---|
| Page | 94 | Foundry | Feliciano |

---

Typeface  Garda
Designer  Mário Feliciano
Year  1998–2005
Format  OpenType

# SAVE WALLY

TITLING N 01
TITLING N 02
TITLING N 03

A✶ B✶ C✶ DD EE FfI G✶ HH
ITY JlL K✶ LlA MM N✶ OO P✶
Q✶ RR S✶ TTH UU V✶ W✶ X✶
YY Z✶ 0123456789

---

Typeface  Morgan TW
Designer  Mário Feliciano
Year  2001
Format  OpenType

# HOCHHAUS

TW 1
TW 2
TW 3

AA BB CC DD EE FF GG HH II JJ KK LL
MM NN OO PP QQ RR SS TT UU VV
WW XX YY ZZ 0123456789

---

Typeface  Morgan Poster Avec
Designer  Mário Feliciano
Year  2003
Format  OpenType

# BAUHAUS HAUSBAU

POSTER AVEC REGULAR
**POSTER AVEC BOLD**
**POSTER AVEC BLACK**

AA BB CC DD EE FF GG
HH II JJ KK LL MM
NN OO PP QQ RR SS TT
UU VV WW XX YY ZZ
0123456789

Typeface Stella
Designer Mário Feliciano
Year 1999–2010
Format OpenType

# Aa

Aa Bb Cc Dd Ee Ff Gg Hh Ii Jj Kk Ll
Mm Nn Oo Pp Qq Rr Ss Tt Uu Vv
Ww Xx Yy Zz
0123456789
—

Stella ExtraLight 18pt
*Stella ExtraLight Italic 18pt*
Stella Light 18pt
*Stella Light Italic 18pt*
Stella Regular 18pt
*Stella Regular Italic 18pt*
Stella Medium 18pt
*Stella Medium Italic 18pt*
**Stella SemiBold 18pt**
***Stella SemiBold Italic 18pt***
**Stella Bold 18pt**
***Stella Bold Italic 18pt***
**Stella ExtraBold 18pt**
***Stella ExtraBold Italic 18pt***

---

12/14 Stella Light

The quick brown fox jumps over the lazy dog. Voyez le brick géant que j'examine près du wharf. Zwölf Boxkämpfer jagen Viktor quer über den

12/14 Stella Regular

The quick brown fox jumps over the lazy dog. Voyez le brick géant que j'examine près du wharf. Zwölf Boxkämpfer jagen Viktor quer über den

12/14 Stella Medium

The quick brown fox jumps over the lazy dog. Voyez le brick géant que j'examine près du wharf. Zwölf Boxkämpfer jagen Viktor quer über den

12/14 Stella Bold

**The quick brown fox jumps over the lazy dog. Voyez le brick géant que j'examine près du wharf. Zwölf Boxkämpfer jagen Viktor quer über den großen Sylter Deich. El veloz murciélago hindú comía feliz cardil-**

9/12 Stella Light

The quick brown fox jumps over the lazy dog. Voyez le brick géant que j'examine près du wharf. Zwölf Boxkämpfer jagen Viktor quer über den großen Sylter Deich. El veloz murciélago hindú comía feliz cardillo y kiwi. La cigüeña tocaba el saxofón

9/12 Stella Regular

The quick brown fox jumps over the lazy dog. Voyez le brick géant que j'examine près du wharf. Zwölf Boxkämpfer jagen Viktor quer über den großen Sylter Deich. El veloz murciélago hindú comía feliz cardillo y kiwi. La cigüeña tocaba el

9/12 Stella Medium

The quick brown fox jumps over the lazy dog. Voyez le brick géant que j'examine près du wharf. Zwölf Boxkämpfer jagen Viktor quer über den großen Sylter Deich. El veloz murciélago hindú comía feliz cardillo y kiwi. La cigüeña tocaba el

9/12 Stella Bold

**The quick brown fox jumps over the lazy dog. Voyez le brick géant que j'examine près du wharf. Zwölf Boxkämpfer jagen Viktor quer über den großen Sylter Deich. El veloz murciélago hindú comía feliz cardillo y kiwi. La cigüeña tocaba el saxofón detrás del palenque de pajaatur? Rissimo lorereped ex es solore lab id molorro in**

7/10 Stella Light

The quick brown fox jumps over the lazy dog. Voyez le brick géant que j'examine près du wharf. Zwölf Boxkämpfer jagen Viktor quer über den großen Sylter Deich. El veloz murciélago hindú comía feliz cardillo y kiwi. La cigüeña tocaba el saxofón detrás del palenque de pajaatur? Rissimo lorereped ex es solore lab id molorro in rempore icabore rehenetur aliam aut voles audae dem

7/10 Stella Regular

The quick brown fox jumps over the lazy dog. Voyez le brick géant que j'examine près du wharf. Zwölf Boxkämpfer jagen Viktor quer über den großen Sylter Deich. El veloz murciélago hindú comía feliz cardillo y kiwi. La cigüeña tocaba el saxofón detrás del palenque de pajaatur? Rissimo lorereped ex es solore lab id molorro in rempore icabore rehenetur aliam aut voles au-

7/10 Stella Medium

The quick brown fox jumps over the lazy dog. Voyez le brick géant que j'examine près du wharf. Zwölf Boxkämpfer jagen Viktor quer über den großen Sylter Deich. El veloz murciélago hindú comía feliz cardillo y kiwi. La cigüeña tocaba el saxofón detrás del palenque de pajaatur? Rissimo lorereped ex es solore lab id molorro in rempore icabore rehenetur aliam aut voles

7/10 Stella Bold

**The quick brown fox jumps over the lazy dog. Voyez le brick géant que j'examine près du wharf. Zwölf Boxkämpfer jagen Viktor quer über den großen Sylter Deich. El veloz murciélago hindú comía feliz cardillo y kiwi. La cigüeña tocaba el saxofón detrás del palenque de pajaatur? Rissimo lorereped ex es solore lab id molorro in rempore icabore rehenetur aliam aut voles audae dem quam, secum eum facesequae consequ aepudam quia voluptiur repel in et faccustibus, nonsenis aut quisqui rero**

# F

— Fontsmith

—

Jason Smith

—

London, UK

—

Since 1999

Fontsmith is a leading London-based type design studio founded in 1999 by Jason Smith. The studio consists of a team dedicated to designing and developing high quality typefaces for both independent release as well as bespoke fonts for international clients.

## Info

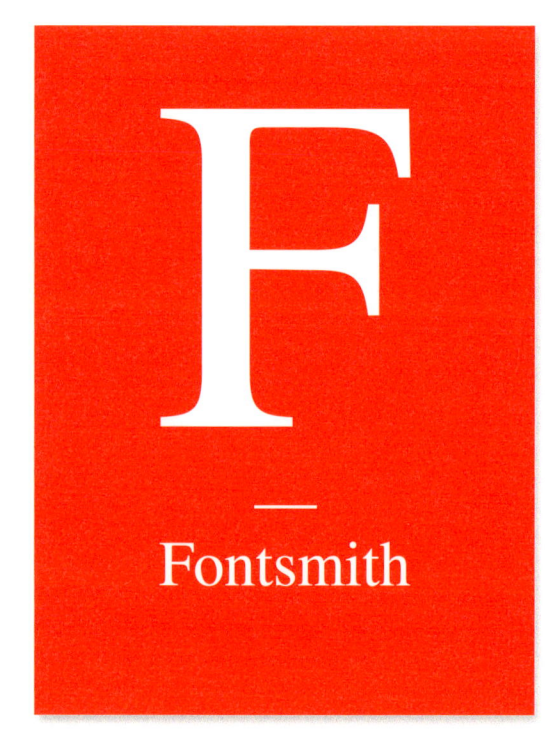

—People on staff
4

—Type designers on staff
4

—Type families
Retail: 20+

—Designers represented
5

— Web shop
Yes

—Distributors
FontShop

—Webfont services
Fontdeck

—Basic license
From £30 to £250

## Typeface selection

FS Blake
FS Dillon
FS Jack
FS Rufus
FS Sally

24pt

## People

—Jason Smith
Jason Smith is the founder of Fontsmith, with a background in hand-lettering and calligraphy. His work has a distinct quality that combines warmth and modernity with an intense eye for finely crafted letter-forms.

—Phil Garnham
Phil is the typeface design director at Fontsmith, with a penchant for asymmetric doodles and alphabets of all shapes and sizes. A creator of type to use and type to admire, Phil designs functional forms from abstract ideas.

—Fernando Mello
Fernando Mello joined Fontsmith in the summer of 2008. His background in multiple visual areas — architecture, typography, graphic design and illustration — influences his search for creating innovative and original, yet functional and well-constructed typefaces.

—Emanuela Conidi
Manu joined Fontsmith in 2008 after studying typeface design. With a background in graphic design, experience in hot-metal type hand composition and letterpress printing, she is passionate about typographic history, 19th century typefaces and Arabic typography.

Double-page spread from *The Collection*, showing FS Conrad.

Page
97

*The Collection.* An inspirational overview of the Fontsmith font library designed by Spin, 2010.

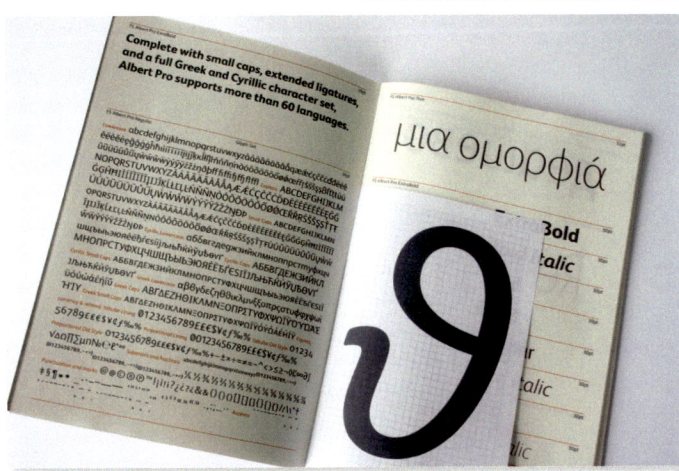

Double-page spread from *The Collection*, showing FS Albert Pro and FS Dillon. Graphic design by Spin.

**Center right**
*FS Blake - A Striking Type*. A finely tuned, mechanical and organical booklet designed by Spin.

**Below right**
*Bespoke Broadcast Type*, a showcase of some of custom-made fonts for television brands in the UK.

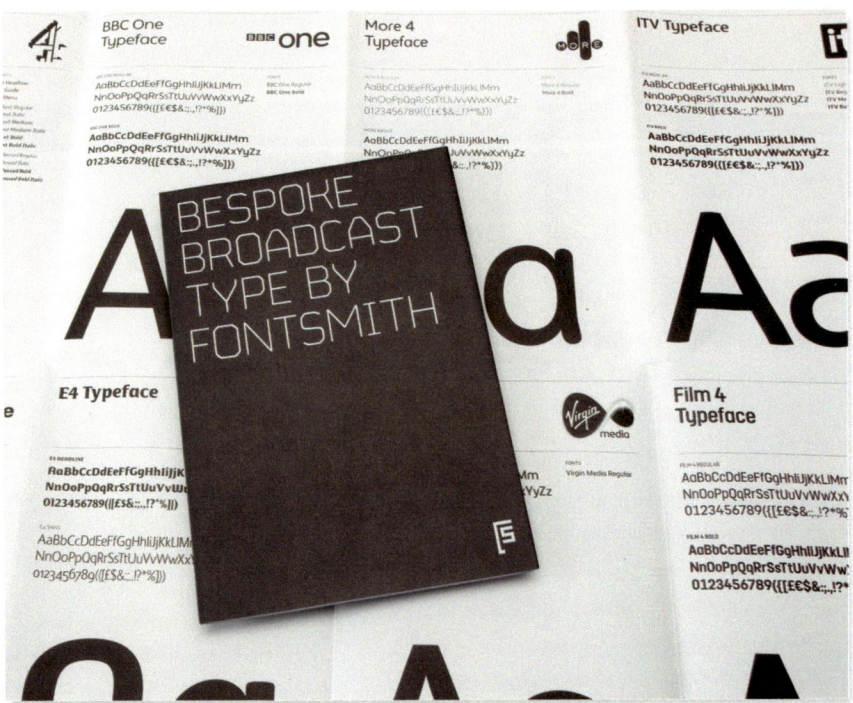

Page Foundry Fontsmith
98

Typeface FS Blake  Year 2010
Designer Emanuela Conidi Format OpenType

# Aa

Aa Bb Cc Dd Ee Ff Gg Hh Ii Jj Kk Ll
Mm Nn Oo Pp Qq Rr Ss Tt Uu Vv
Ww Xx Yy Zz
0123456789
—

FS Blake Light 24pt
*FS Blake Light Italic 24pt*
FS Blake Regular 24pt
*FS Blake Italic 24pt*
**FS Blake Bold 24pt**
***FS Blake Bold Italic 24pt***
**FS Blake Heavy 24pt**
***FS Blake Heavy Italic 24pt***

---

12/14 FS Blake Light

The quick brown fox jumps over the lazy dog. Voyez le brick géant que j'examine près du wharf. Zwölf Boxkämpfer jagen Viktor quer über den großen

12/14 FS Blake Regular

The quick brown fox jumps over the lazy dog. Voyez le brick géant que j'examine près du wharf. Zwölf Boxkämpfer jagen Viktor quer über den

12/14 FS Blake Bold

**The quick brown fox jumps over the lazy dog. Voyez le brick géant que j'examine près du wharf. Zwölf Boxkämpfer jagen Viktor quer über**

12/14 FS Blake Heavy

**The quick brown fox jumps over the lazy dog. Voyez le brick géant que j'examine près du wharf. Zwölf Boxkämpfer jagen Viktor quer über den großen Sylter Deich. El veloz murciélago hindú comía feliz cardillo y kiwi. La cigüeña tocaba el saxofón detrás del palenque de pajaatur? Rissimo lorereped ex es**

9/12 FS Blake Light

The quick brown fox jumps over the lazy dog. Voyez le brick géant que j'examine près du wharf. Zwölf Boxkämpfer jagen Viktor quer über den großen Sylter Deich. El veloz murciélago hindú comía feliz cardillo y kiwi. La cigüeña tocaba el saxofón detrás del

9/12 FS Blake Regular

The quick brown fox jumps over the lazy dog. Voyez le brick géant que j'examine près du wharf. Zwölf Boxkämpfer jagen Viktor quer über den großen Sylter Deich. El veloz murciélago hindú comía feliz cardillo y kiwi. La cigüeña tocaba el saxofón detrás

9/12 FS Blake Bold

**The quick brown fox jumps over the lazy dog. Voyez le brick géant que j'examine près du wharf. Zwölf Boxkämpfer jagen Viktor quer über den großen Sylter Deich. El veloz murciélago hindú comía feliz cardillo y kiwi. La cigüeña tocaba el**

9/12 FS Blake Heavy

**The quick brown fox jumps over the lazy dog. Voyez le brick géant que j'examine près du wharf. Zwölf Boxkämpfer jagen Viktor quer über den großen Sylter Deich. El veloz murciélago hindú comía feliz cardillo y kiwi. La cigüeña tocaba el saxofón detrás del palenque de pajaatur? Rissimo lorereped ex es solore lab id molorro in rempore icabore rehenetur aliam aut voles audae dem quam, secum eum facesequae consequ aepudam quia voluptiur**

7/10 FS Blake Light

The quick brown fox jumps over the lazy dog. Voyez le brick géant que j'examine près du wharf. Zwölf Boxkämpfer jagen Viktor quer über den großen Sylter Deich. El veloz murciélago hindú comía feliz cardillo y kiwi. La cigüeña tocaba el saxofón detrás del palenque de pajaatur? Rissimo lorereped ex es solore lab id molorro in rempore icabore rehenetur aliam aut voles audae dem quam, secum eum

7/10 FS Blake Regular

The quick brown fox jumps over the lazy dog. Voyez le brick géant que j'examine près du wharf. Zwölf Boxkämpfer jagen Viktor quer über den großen Sylter Deich. El veloz murciélago hindú comía feliz cardillo y kiwi. La cigüeña tocaba el saxofón detrás del palenque de pajaatur? Rissimo lorereped ex es solore lab id molorro in rempore icabore rehenetur aliam aut voles audae dem quam, secum

7/10 FS Blake Bold

**The quick brown fox jumps over the lazy dog. Voyez le brick géant que j'examine près du wharf. Zwölf Boxkämpfer jagen Viktor quer über den großen Sylter Deich. El veloz murciélago hindú comía feliz cardillo y kiwi. La cigüeña tocaba el saxofón detrás del palenque de pajaatur? Rissimo lorereped ex es solore lab id molorro in rempore icabore rehenetur aliam aut voles**

7/10 FS Blake Heavy

**The quick brown fox jumps over the lazy dog. Voyez le brick géant que j'examine près du wharf. Zwölf Boxkämpfer jagen Viktor quer über den großen Sylter Deich. El veloz murciélago hindú comía feliz cardillo y kiwi. La cigüeña tocaba el saxofón detrás del palenque de pajaatur? Rissimo lorereped ex es solore lab id molorro in rempore icabore rehenetur aliam aut voles audae dem quam, secum eum facesequae consequ aepudam quia voluptiur repel in et faccustibus, nonsenis aut quisqui rero mi, ipiet lam ant ut maio et hil molupta tustis atatur, consedi tasimol orerem aut volor andipsapis sit, illaut volore officatus alicae dusdaec tatecte cearum qui accatibus restiore nulpa secaerferum, nus do-**

Foundry  Fontsmith

Typeface  FS Dillon
Designer  Jason Smith
Year  2009
Format  OpenType

# Aa

FS Dillon Regular 18pt
*FS Dillon Italic 18pt*
**FS Dillon Medium 18pt**
***FS Dillon Medium Italic 18pt***
**FS Dillon Bold 18pt**
***FS Dillon Bold Italic 18pt***

Aa Bb Cc Dd Ee Ff Gg Hh Ii Jj Kk Ll Mm Nn Oo Pp Qq Rr Ss Tt Uu Vv Ww Xx Yy Zz
0123456789
—

9/12  FS Dillon Regular

The quick brown fox jumps over the lazy dog. Voyez le brick géant que j'examine près du wharf. Zwölf Boxkämpfer jagen Viktor quer über den großen Sylter Deich. El veloz murciélago hindú comía feliz cardillo y kiwi. La cigüeña tocaba el saxofón detrás del palenque de pajaatur? Rissimo lorereped ex es solore lab id molorro in rempore icabore rehenetur aliam aut voles audae dem quam, secum eum facesequae consequ aepudam quia voluptiur repel in et faccustibus, nonsenis aut

7/10  FS Dillon Regular

The quick brown fox jumps over the lazy dog. Voyez le brick géant que j'examine près du wharf. Zwölf Boxkämpfer jagen Viktor quer über den großen Sylter Deich. El veloz murciélago hindú comía feliz cardillo y kiwi. La cigüeña tocaba el saxofón detrás del palenque de pajaatur? Rissimo lorereped ex es solore lab id molorro in rempore icabore rehenetur aliam aut voles audae dem quam, secum eum facesequae consequ aepudam quia voluptiur repel in et faccustibus, nonsenis aut quisqui rero mi, ipiet lam ant ut maio et hil molupta tustis atatur, consedi tasimol orerem aut valor andipsapis sit, illaut volore officatus alicae dusdaec tatecte cearum qui accatibus restiore nulpa secaerferum, nus dolenim in et quoditat que explam volupictur? Qui de illuptae. Dae nis

Typeface  FS Rufus
Designer  Mitja Miklavčič,
          Emanuela Conidi,
          Jason Smith,
          Phil Garnham
Year  2009
Format  OpenType

# Aa

FS Rufus Light 18pt
*FS Rufus Light Italic 18pt*
FS Rufus Regular 18pt
*FS Rufus Italic 18pt*
**FS Rufus Bold 18pt**
***FS Rufus Bold Italic 18pt***

Aa Bb Cc Dd Ee Ff Gg Hh Ii Jj Kk Ll Mm Nn Oo Pp Qq Rr Ss Tt Uu Vv Ww Xx Yy Zz
0123456789
—

9/12  FS Rufus Regular

The quick brown fox jumps over the lazy dog. Voyez le brick géant que j'examine près du wharf. Zwölf Boxkämpfer jagen Viktor quer über den großen Sylter Deich. El veloz murciélago hindú comía feliz cardillo y kiwi. La cigüeña tocaba el saxofón detrás del palenque de pajaatur? Rissimo lorereped ex es solore lab id molorro in rempore icabore rehenetur aliam aut voles audae dem quam, secum eum facesequae

7/10  FS Rufus Regular

The quick brown fox jumps over the lazy dog. Voyez le brick géant que j'examine près du wharf. Zwölf Boxkämpfer jagen Viktor quer über den großen Sylter Deich. El veloz murciélago hindú comía feliz cardillo y kiwi. La cigüeña tocaba el saxofón detrás del palenque de pajaatur? Rissimo lorereped ex es solore lab id molorro in rempore icabore rehenetur aliam aut voles audae dem quam, secum eum facesequae consequ aepudam quia voluptiur repel in et faccustibus, nonsenis aut quisqui rero mi, ipiet lam ant ut maio et hil molupta tustis atatur, consedi tasimol orerem aut valor andipsapis sit, illaut volore officatus alicae

Typeface FS Jack
Designer Jason Smith, Fernando Mello
Year 2009
Format OpenType

# Aa

Aa Bb Cc Dd Ee Ff Gg Hh Ii Jj Kk Ll Mm Nn Oo Pp Qq Rr Ss Tt Uu Vv Ww Xx Yy Zz
0123456789
—

FS Jack Light 24pt
*FS Jack Light Italic 24pt*
FS Jack Regular 24pt
*FS Jack Italic 24pt*
FS Jack Medium 24pt
*FS Jack Medium Italic 24pt*
**FS Jack Bold 24pt**
***FS Jack Bold Italic 24pt***
**FS Jack Poster Regular 24pt**

---

12/14 FS Jack Light

The quick brown fox jumps over the lazy dog. Voyez le brick géant que j'examine près du wharf. Zwölf Boxkämpfer jagen Viktor quer über den großen Sylter

12/14 FS Jack Regular

The quick brown fox jumps over the lazy dog. Voyez le brick géant que j'examine près du wharf. Zwölf Boxkämpfer jagen Viktor quer über den

12/14 FS Jack Medium

The quick brown fox jumps over the lazy dog. Voyez le brick géant que j'examine près du wharf. Zwölf Boxkämpfer jagen Viktor quer über den

12/14 FS Jack Bold

**The quick brown fox jumps over the lazy dog. Voyez le brick géant que j'examine près du wharf. Zwölf Boxkämpfer jagen Viktor quer über den großen Sylter Deich. El veloz murciélago hindú comía feliz cardillo y kiwi. La cigüeña tocaba el saxofón detrás del palenque de pajaatur? Rissimo lorereped ex es solore lab id molorro in**

9/12 FS Jack Light

The quick brown fox jumps over the lazy dog. Voyez le brick géant que j'examine près du wharf. Zwölf Boxkämpfer jagen Viktor quer über den großen Sylter Deich. El veloz murciélago hindú comía feliz cardillo y kiwi. La cigüeña tocaba el saxofón detrás del palenque

9/12 FS Jack Regular

The quick brown fox jumps over the lazy dog. Voyez le brick géant que j'examine près du wharf. Zwölf Boxkämpfer jagen Viktor quer über den großen Sylter Deich. El veloz murciélago hindú comía feliz cardillo y kiwi. La cigüeña tocaba el saxofón detrás

9/12 FS Jack Medium

The quick brown fox jumps over the lazy dog. Voyez le brick géant que j'examine près du wharf. Zwölf Boxkämpfer jagen Viktor quer über den großen Sylter Deich. El veloz murciélago hindú comía feliz cardillo y kiwi. La cigüeña tocaba el saxofón detrás

9/12 FS Jack Bold

**The quick brown fox jumps over the lazy dog. Voyez le brick géant que j'examine près du wharf. Zwölf Boxkämpfer jagen Viktor quer über den großen Sylter Deich. El veloz murciélago hindú comía feliz cardillo y kiwi. La cigüeña tocaba el saxofón detrás del palenque de pajaatur? Rissimo lorereped ex es solore lab id molorro in rempore icabore rehenetur aliam aut voles audae dem quam, secum eum facesequae consequ aepudam quia voluptiur repel in et faccustibus, nonsenis**

7/10 FS Jack Light

The quick brown fox jumps over the lazy dog. Voyez le brick géant que j'examine près du wharf. Zwölf Boxkämpfer jagen Viktor quer über den großen Sylter Deich. El veloz murciélago hindú comía feliz cardillo y kiwi. La cigüeña tocaba el saxofón detrás del palenque de pajaatur? Rissimo lorereped ex es solore lab id molorro in rempore icabore rehenetur aliam aut voles audae dem quam, secum eum

7/10 FS Jack Regular

The quick brown fox jumps over the lazy dog. Voyez le brick géant que j'examine près du wharf. Zwölf Boxkämpfer jagen Viktor quer über den großen Sylter Deich. El veloz murciélago hindú comía feliz cardillo y kiwi. La cigüeña tocaba el saxofón detrás del palenque de pajaatur? Rissimo lorereped ex es solore lab id molorro in rempore icabore rehenetur aliam aut voles audae dem quam, secum eum

7/10 FS Jack Medium

The quick brown fox jumps over the lazy dog. Voyez le brick géant que j'examine près du wharf. Zwölf Boxkämpfer jagen Viktor quer über den großen Sylter Deich. El veloz murciélago hindú comía feliz cardillo y kiwi. La cigüeña tocaba el saxofón detrás del palenque de pajaatur? Rissimo lorereped ex es solore lab id molorro in rempore icabore rehenetur aliam aut voles audae dem quam, secum

7/10 FS Jack Bold

**The quick brown fox jumps over the lazy dog. Voyez le brick géant que j'examine près du wharf. Zwölf Boxkämpfer jagen Viktor quer über den großen Sylter Deich. El veloz murciélago hindú comía feliz cardillo y kiwi. La cigüeña tocaba el saxofón detrás del palenque de pajaatur? Rissimo lorereped ex es solore lab id molorro in rempore icabore rehenetur aliam aut voles audae dem quam, secum eum facesequae consequ aepudam quia voluptiur repel in et faccustibus, nonsenis aut quisqui rero mi, ipiet lam ant ut maio et hil molupta tustis atatur, consedi tasimol orerem aut volor andipsapis sit, illaut volore officatus alicae dusdaec tatecte cearum qui accatibus restiore nulpa secaerferum, nus dolenim in et quoddiat que explam volupictur? Qui de illup-**

Foundry  Fontsmith

Typeface  FS Sally
Designer  Jason Smith, Phil Garnham
Year  2009
Format  OpenType

# Aa

Aa Bb Cc Dd Ee Ff Gg Hh Ii Jj Kk Ll Mm Nn Oo Pp Qq Rr Ss Tt Uu Vv Ww Xx Yy Zz
0123456789
—

FS Sally Regular 24pt
*FS Sally Italic 24pt*
FS Sally Medium 24pt
*FS Sally Medium Italic 24pt*
**FS Sally Semi Bold 24pt**
***FS Sally Semi Bold Italic 24pt***
**FS Sally Bold 24pt**
***FS Sally Bold Italic 24pt***
**FS Sally Heavy 24pt**
***FS Sally Heavy Italic 24pt***

---

12/14  FS Sally Regular

The quick brown fox jumps over the lazy dog. Voyez le brick géant que j'examine près du wharf. Zwölf Boxkämpfer jagen Viktor quer über den großen

12/14  FS Sally Medium

The quick brown fox jumps over the lazy dog. Voyez le brick géant que j'examine près du wharf. Zwölf Boxkämpfer jagen Viktor quer über den

12/14  FS Sally Semi Bold

**The quick brown fox jumps over the lazy dog. Voyez le brick géant que j'examine près du wharf. Zwölf Boxkämpfer jagen Viktor quer über den**

12/14  FS Sally Bold

**The quick brown fox jumps over the lazy dog. Voyez le brick géant que j'examine près du wharf. Zwölf Boxkämpfer jagen Viktor quer über den großen Sylter Deich. El veloz murciélago hindú comía feliz cardillo y kiwi. La cigüeña tocaba el saxofón detrás del palenque de pajaatur? Rissimo lorereped ex es solore lab id molorro in**

---

9/12  FS Sally Regular

The quick brown fox jumps over the lazy dog. Voyez le brick géant que j'examine près du wharf. Zwölf Boxkämpfer jagen Viktor quer über den großen Sylter Deich. El veloz murciélago hindú comía feliz cardillo y kiwi. La cigüeña tocaba el saxofón detrás del pa-

9/12  FS Sally Medium

The quick brown fox jumps over the lazy dog. Voyez le brick géant que j'examine près du wharf. Zwölf Boxkämpfer jagen Viktor quer über den großen Sylter Deich. El veloz murciélago hindú comía feliz cardillo y kiwi. La cigüeña tocaba el saxofón detrás

9/12  FS Sally Semi Bold

**The quick brown fox jumps over the lazy dog. Voyez le brick géant que j'examine près du wharf. Zwölf Boxkämpfer jagen Viktor quer über den großen Sylter Deich. El veloz murciélago hindú comía feliz cardillo y kiwi. La cigüeña tocaba el saxofón detrás**

9/12  FS Sally Bold

**The quick brown fox jumps over the lazy dog. Voyez le brick géant que j'examine près du wharf. Zwölf Boxkämpfer jagen Viktor quer über den großen Sylter Deich. El veloz murciélago hindú comía feliz cardillo y kiwi. La cigüeña tocaba el saxofón detrás del palenque de pajaatur? Rissimo lorereped ex es solore lab id molorro in rempore icabore rehenetur aliam aut voles audae dem quam, secum eum facesequae consequ aepudam quia voluptiur repel in et faccustibus, nonsenis**

---

7/10  FS Sally Regular

The quick brown fox jumps over the lazy dog. Voyez le brick géant que j'examine près du wharf. Zwölf Boxkämpfer jagen Viktor quer über den großen Sylter Deich. El veloz murciélago hindú comía feliz cardillo y kiwi. La cigüeña tocaba el saxofón detrás del palenque de pajaatur? Rissimo lorereped ex es solore lab id molorro in rempore icabore rehenetur aliam aut voles audae dem quam, secum eum

7/10  FS Sally Medium

The quick brown fox jumps over the lazy dog. Voyez le brick géant que j'examine près du wharf. Zwölf Boxkämpfer jagen Viktor quer über den großen Sylter Deich. El veloz murciélago hindú comía feliz cardillo y kiwi. La cigüeña tocaba el saxofón detrás del palenque de pajaatur? Rissimo lorereped ex es solore lab id molorro in rempore icabore rehenetur aliam aut voles audae dem quam, secum eum

7/10  FS Sally Semi Bold

**The quick brown fox jumps over the lazy dog. Voyez le brick géant que j'examine près du wharf. Zwölf Boxkämpfer jagen Viktor quer über den großen Sylter Deich. El veloz murciélago hindú comía feliz cardillo y kiwi. La cigüeña tocaba el saxofón detrás del palenque de pajaatur? Rissimo lorereped ex es solore lab id molorro in rempore icabore rehenetur aliam aut voles audae dem**

7/10  FS Sally Bold

**The quick brown fox jumps over the lazy dog. Voyez le brick géant que j'examine près du wharf. Zwölf Boxkämpfer jagen Viktor quer über den großen Sylter Deich. El veloz murciélago hindú comía feliz cardillo y kiwi. La cigüeña tocaba el saxofón detrás del palenque de pajaatur? Rissimo lorereped ex es solore lab id molorro in rempore icabore rehenetur aliam aut voles audae dem quam, secum eum facesequae consequ aepudam quia voluptiur repel in et faccustibus, nonsenis aut quisqui rero mi, ipiet lam ant ut maio et hil molupta tustis atatur, consedi tasimol orerem aut volor andipsapis sit, illaut volore officatus alicae dusdaec tatecte cearum qui accatibus restiore nulpa secaerferum, nus dolenim in et quoditat que explam volupictur? Qui de illuptae. Dae nis illiberum volorro ritatis tinullo rerumqu atetur**

# F
## Fountain

Peter Bruhn

Malmö, Sweden

Since 1993

Fountain started out as the personal foundry of type and graphic designer Peter Bruhn. As one of the first one-man foundries in Europe, it soon grew to accommodate work by over 20 type designers.

## Info

—Why?
In the early 90s there were almost no small foundries around, and the fonts I wanted weren't there. So I started making the ideas in my head a reality.

—People on staff
1

—Type designers on staff
1

—Type families
67

—Designers represented
23

— Web shop
www.fountaintype.com

—Distributors
Fontshop, MyFonts, Veer

—Webfont services
MyFonts, Fontdeck, Typekit, Fontspring

—Basic license
From $29 upwards for 3 CPUs

## People

—Peter Bruhn, born in Malmö, Sweden, founded Fountain in 1993. MFA&D graduate, 1997. "I am possessed with type, and I love browsing through the second-hand book shops for old type books and specimens."

—Stefan Hattenbach is an espresso-fueled art director and graphic designer specializing in type and logo solutions. After two decades in the industry, a third of that running his own studio, he has managed to keep his work strong and compelling via a dynamic balance of experimentation and traditionalism: a blend which has worked to the benefit of clients such as Greenpeace, Amnesty International, Telia, and Hennes & Mauritz.

—Göran Söderström is a self-taught Swedish type designer and font developer. His obsession with type began in 1994 when doing the initial sketches for his first typeface, Exemplar, but it was not until 2006 that he took this obsession seriously and started his own type studio, Autodidakt.

—Gábor Kóthay is a multi-disciplinary artist and type designer from Hungary. He is a graduate of the Academy of Fine Arts, Budapest, and has been designing professionally since 1991. His work has been showcased in several books, annuals and magazines and he has won multiple awards for his installations.

—Rui Abreu is a Portuguese type and graphic designer. He graduated in 2003 from the FBAUP (Faculdade de Belas Artes da Universidade do Porto), where he studied graphic design. He has been working as an interactive media designer in different design and advertising agencies alongside his type design activity.

—Martin Lexelius (alias Martin Fredrikson) was born in Gothenburg, Sweden. Having started out as a graffiti and comic book artist, he pursued a career as an artist and freelance illustrator in the mid-1990s and rapidly became fascinated by typography and type design. Under Peter Bruhn's mentorship Martin has developed numerous fonts.

—Randy Jones is a California based freelance graphic designer and principal of Aquatoad Design. Having learned to draw letters under the guidance of Ed Benguiat at the School of Visual Arts, he now spends much of his time hunched over his Mac adjusting kerning pairs. Fortunately it is a laptop so he can get his fix of mountains and trees as needed.

—Lucas Brusquini, born in Sweden, was a calligraphy and type geek as early as the age of 10. Later he moved on to study graphic communication at The Graphic Arts Institute of Denmark. As a designer and art director he has worked in the UK, Denmark and Sweden.

## Typeface selection

Aria Pro
Catacumba Pro
Foral Pro
Malmo Sans Pro
ORBE PRO

24pt

Specimen for Incognito by Hungarian designer Gábor Kóthay.

Regular, Medium, **Bold**, **Extra Bold**, **Black**, Condensed, Condensed Medium, **Condensed Bold & Condensed Extra Bold**

FOUNTAIN & AUTODIDAKT
Proudly Presents

Special Appearance by

*Swashes*, *Alternate letters*, *Stylistic alternates*, SMALL CAPS & *special ligatures*

# Heroine

Starring

Bezier Artist   Goran Soderstrom
Glyph Stylist   Peter Bruhn
Assistant to Mr. Bruhn   Jon Jurt
Inspiration   Eleisha Pechey

Stills from a short film made for the launch of the Heroine typeface, produced by Göran Söderström's Autodidakt type design studio.

Page
104

Foundry  Fountain

Typeface  Orbe Pro
Designer  Rui Abreu
Year  2008
Format  OpenType

# FANTASY WORLD

**REGULAR**

AA BB CC DD EE FF GG HH
II JJ KK LL MM NN OO PP
QQ RR SS TT UU VV WW XX
YY ZZ 0123456789

Typeface  Aria Pro
Designer  Rui Abreu
Year  2011
Format  OpenType

# Opéra

Regular
*Italic*

Aa Bb Cc Dd Ee Ff Gg Hh Ii
Jj Kk Ll Mm Nn Oo Pp Qq
Rr Ss Tt Uu Vv Ww Xx Yy Zz
0123456789

Typeface  Catacumba Pro
Designer  Rui Abreu
Year  2009
Format  OpenType

# CATACUMBA EXCELSA

Regular
*Italic*
**Bold**
***Bold Italic***
MODERATA
EXCELSA

Aa Bb Cc Dd Ee Ff Gg Hh Ii
Jj Kk Ll Mm Nn Oo Pp Qq
Rr Ss Tt Uu Vv Ww Xx Yy Zz
0123456789

Foundry Fountain

Typeface  Malmo Sans Pro     Year    2001
Designer  Peter Bruhn        Format  OpenType

# Aa

Malmo Sans Pro Regular 18pt
*Malmo Sans Pro Oblique* 18pt
**Malmo Sans Pro Bold** 18pt
***Malmo Sans Pro Bold Oblique*** 18pt
**MALMO SANS PRO HEADLINE 18PT**
***MALMO SANS PRO HEADLINE OBLIQUE 18PT***

Aa Bb Cc Dd Ee Ff Gg Hh Ii Jj Kk Ll Mm Nn Oo Pp Qq Rr Ss Tt Uu Vv Ww Xx Yy Zz
0123456789
—

9/12   Malmo Sans Pro Regular

The quick brown fox jumps over the lazy dog. Voyez le brick géant que j'examine près du wharf. Zwölf Boxkämpfer jagen Viktor quer über den großen Sylter Deich. El veloz murciélago hindú comía feliz cardillo y kiwi. La cigüeña tocaba el saxofón detrás del palenque de pajaatur? Rissimo lorereped ex es solore lab id molorro in rempore icabore rehenetur aliam aut voles audae dem quam, secum eum

7/10   Malmo Sans Pro Regular

The quick brown fox jumps over the lazy dog. Voyez le brick géant que j'examine près du wharf. Zwölf Boxkämpfer jagen Viktor quer über den großen Sylter Deich. El veloz murciélago hindú comía feliz cardillo y kiwi. La cigüeña tocaba el saxofón detrás del palenque de pajaatur? Rissimo lorereped ex es solore lab id molorro in rempore icabore rehenetur aliam aut voles audae dem quam, secum eum facesequae consequ aepudam quia voluptiur repel in et faccustibus, nonsenis aut quisqui rero mi, ipiet lam ant ut maio et hil molupta tustis atatur, consedi tasimol orerem aut volor andipsapis sit, illaut volore officatus alicae dusdaec tatecte cearum qui accatibus

Typeface  Foral Pro      Year    2010
Designer  Rui Abreu      Format  OpenType

# Aa

Foral Pro Light 18pt
*Foral Pro Light Italic* 18pt
Foral Pro Regular 18pt
*Foral Pro Italic* 18pt
**Foral Pro Bold** 18pt
***Foral Pro Bold Italic*** 18pt
**Foral Pro Extra Bold** 18pt
***Foral Pro Extra Bold Italic*** 18pt

Aa Bb Cc Dd Ee Ff Gg Hh Ii Jj Kk Ll Mm Nn Oo Pp Qq Rr Ss Tt Uu Vv Ww Xx Yy Zz
0123456789
—

9/12   Foral Pro Regular

The quick brown fox jumps over the lazy dog. Voyez le brick géant que j'examine près du wharf. Zwölf Boxkämpfer jagen Viktor quer über den großen Sylter Deich. El veloz murciélago hindú comía feliz cardillo y kiwi. La cigüeña tocaba el saxofón detrás del palenque de pajaatur? Rissimo lorereped ex es solore lab id molorro in rempore icabore rehenetur aliam aut voles audae dem quam, secum eum facesequae consequ aepudam quia voluptiur repel in et faccustibus, nonsenis aut quisqui rero mi, ipiet lam ant ut maio

7/10   Foral Pro Regular

The quick brown fox jumps over the lazy dog. Voyez le brick géant que j'examine près du wharf. Zwölf Boxkämpfer jagen Viktor quer über den großen Sylter Deich. El veloz murciélago hindú comía feliz cardillo y kiwi. La cigüeña tocaba el saxofón detrás del palenque de pajaatur? Rissimo lorereped ex es solore lab id molorro in rempore icabore rehenetur aliam aut voles audae dem quam, secum eum facesequae consequ aepudam quia voluptiur repel in et faccustibus, nonsenis aut quisqui rero mi, ipiet lam ant ut maio et hil molupta tustis atatur, consedi tasimol orerem aut volor andipsapis sit, illaut volore officatus alicae dusdaec tatecte cearum qui accatibus restiore nulpa secaerferum, nus dolenim in et quoditat que explam volupictur? Qui de illuptae. Dae nis illiberum volorro ritatis tinullo rerumqu atetur

# G

## Gestalten Fonts

Robert Klanten, Michael Mischler, Critzla

Berlin, Germany

Since 2003

Gestalten Fonts is the type founding division of Gestalten in Berlin.

## Info

—Why?
Gestalten specializes in developing content for aficionados of cutting-edge visual culture worldwide. Keeping with the Gestalten philosophy, firmly committed to presenting design excellence in visual culture, Gestalten Fonts was founded in 2003 to offer a versatile selection of contemporary typefaces by designers for designers. Handpicked by the in-house graphic design and editorial team, the independent font foundry now features over 120 contemporary typefaces that range in style from refined, elegant, and minimal text fonts to more experimental display, ornamental, script, blackletter, monospaced, stencil and typewriter fonts.

—People on staff
6

—Type designers on staff
3

—Type families
Approx. 120

—Designers represented
50

—Web shop
www.gestaltenfonts.com

—Webfont services
In development

### Typeface selection

Calcine
Maksim
Malaussene Translation
Nautinger
Sensaway PRO
T-Star Pro
Treza

24pt

## People

—Robert Klanten, founder. As publisher and editor-in-chief of Gestalten, Klanten founded Gestalten Fonts as an offshoot of the publishing house. Klanten has always kept a sharp eye on choosing typography for his own publications—even designing bespoke fonts by in-house designers at times. At a time when there were few foundries offering cutting-edge and experimental fonts and with many book buyers inquiring about where they can purchase these fonts, starting a small foundry to sell and distribute fonts was a logical step.

—Michael Mischler, co-fouder. Hailing from Bern, Switzerland, Michael Mischler is a graduate of Schule für Gestaltung Biel where he studied graphic design. One of the first graphic designers and editors at Gestalten, Mischler conceived, edited, and designed over 20 publications on graphic design, typography and visual culture while working at Gestalten between 1998 and 2006. Mischler co-founded Gestalten Fonts in 2003 and continues to scout fresh type designing talent for the foundry. In 2006, together with Nik Thönen, he also founded the independent font platform Binnenland.ch. He currently lives and works in Bern.

—Critzla, co-founder. Critzla started out as a sign and poster painter in East Germany. Deeply rooted in the Berlin music scene, he became an independent designer in 1994 — designing flyers, record sleeves, and posters, not to mention the first 12 issues of *Flyer*, a magazine about Berlin's club scene. Critzla is a founding member of Pfadfinderei, a graphic and motion design studio that doubles as one of the world's most popular groups of VJs. Having designed the typeface Localizer for the book of the same name — Gestalten's first release — Critzla released many other fonts through Gestalten Fonts, for which he has been a contributing editor since 2003.

—Laure Afchain is a graphic designer and type designer living in Paris. Having graduated from the Fine Arts School of Toulouse, she went on to study Type & Media at the Royal Academy (KABK) in The Hague.

—Martin Aleith is a contemporary graphic designer whose fonts, design work and video installations are closely associated with music. Since 1998, he has been a founding member of the Berlin-based collective Pfadfinderei.

—Sofie Beier is a designer, researcher, and lecturer currently employed at the Danish Design School, where she teaches graphic and type design. She has written extensively on the subject of typeface legibility.

—Matthieu Cortat is a typographer currently working at the Museum of Print and Banking in Lyon and is also on the graphic design team at the Swiss publisher Éditions de la Société jurassienne d'Émulation.

—Boris Dworschak is a graphic designer whose main focuses are corporate design, editorial, poster and type design. He describes his approach as clear, conceptual, multi-disciplinary and type-oriented.

—S. W. Bugten & S. P. Egli. Stian Ward Bugten lives in Trondheim, Norway, working as an art director at HK Reklamebyra. His main areas of work are in advertising and developing concepts in film, web, and print. Simon Egli graduated from Central Saint Martins in London and subsequently worked for clients including MTV, TESS supermodel agency and Studio Achermann. He works and lives in London and in Zürich.

—Benjamin Gomez studied in Valence and Strasbourg before graduating from the Ecole Nationale Supérieure des Arts Décoratifs in Paris. In 2007 he founded the design collective Dépli Design Studio with Aurelie Gasche and Vadim Bernard.

—Aron Jancso was scouted by Gestalten Fonts as an amazingly fresh talent from Budapest. A self-confessed type addict, he devotes his time to meticulously drawing and designing alphabets.

—Joerg Schmitt is constantly searching for new ideas for typefaces. At the moment he is working for the global branding agency Interbrand Zintzmeyer & Lux in Cologne.

—Nik Thönen is a member of the Vienna-based design collective Re-P.ORG. His work for cultural institutions for the contemporary art sector, film and architecture betrays his interest in functional graphic design reduced to pragmatic language.

Page
107

Promotional pieces for T-Star.

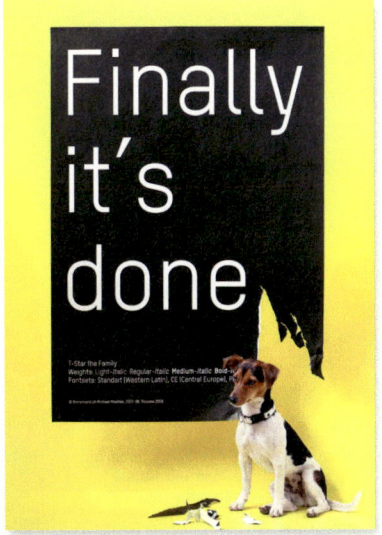

Two specimen posters for Sensaway, designed by Aron Jancso.

| | | | |
|---|---|---|---|
| Typeface | T-Star Pro | Year | 2002 |
| Designer | Mika Mischler | Format | OpenType |

# Aa

Aa Bb Cc Dd Ee Ff Gg Hh Ii Jj Kk Ll Mm Nn Oo Pp Qq Rr Ss Tt Uu Vv Ww Xx Yy Zz
0123456789

T-Star Pro Light 22pt
*T-Star Pro Light Italic 22pt*
T-Star Pro Regular 22pt
*T-Star Pro Italic 22pt*
T-Star Pro Medium 22pt
*T-Star Pro Medium Italic 22pt*
**T-Star Pro Bold 22pt**
***T-Star Pro Bold Italic 22pt***
**T-STAR PRO HEADLINE 22PT**

---

**12/14 — T-Star Pro Light**

The quick brown fox jumps over the lazy dog. Voyez le brick géant que j'examine près du wharf. Zwölf Boxkämpfer jagen Viktor quer über den

**9/12 — T-Star Pro Light**

The quick brown fox jumps over the lazy dog. Voyez le brick géant que j'examine près du wharf. Zwölf Boxkämpfer jagen Viktor quer über den großen Sylter Deich. El veloz murciélago hindú comía feliz cardillo y kiwi. La cigüeña tocaba el

**7/10 — T-Star Pro Light**

The quick brown fox jumps over the lazy dog. Voyez le brick géant que j'examine près du wharf. Zwölf Boxkämpfer jagen Viktor quer über den großen Sylter Deich. El veloz murciélago hindú comía feliz cardillo y kiwi. La cigüeña tocaba el saxofón detrás del palenque de pajaatur? Rissimo lorereped ex es solore lab id molorro in rempore icabore rehenetur aliam aut voles audae dem

**12/14 — T-Star Pro Regular**

The quick brown fox jumps over the lazy dog. Voyez le brick géant que j'examine près du wharf. Zwölf Boxkämpfer jagen Viktor quer über den

**9/12 — T-Star Pro Regular**

The quick brown fox jumps over the lazy dog. Voyez le brick géant que j'examine près du wharf. Zwölf Boxkämpfer jagen Viktor quer über den großen Sylter Deich. El veloz murciélago hindú comía feliz cardillo y kiwi. La cigüeña tocaba el

**7/10 — T-Star Pro Regular**

The quick brown fox jumps over the lazy dog. Voyez le brick géant que j'examine près du wharf. Zwölf Boxkämpfer jagen Viktor quer über den großen Sylter Deich. El veloz murciélago hindú comía feliz cardillo y kiwi. La cigüeña tocaba el saxofón detrás del palenque de pajaatur? Rissimo lorereped ex es solore lab id molorro in rempore icabore rehenetur aliam aut voles audae dem

**12/14 — T-Star Pro Medium**

The quick brown fox jumps over the lazy dog. Voyez le brick géant que j'examine près du wharf. Zwölf Boxkämpfer jagen Viktor quer über den

**9/12 — T-Star Pro Medium**

The quick brown fox jumps over the lazy dog. Voyez le brick géant que j'examine près du wharf. Zwölf Boxkämpfer jagen Viktor quer über den großen Sylter Deich. El veloz murciélago hindú comía feliz cardillo y kiwi. La cigüeña tocaba el

**7/10 — T-Star Pro Medium**

The quick brown fox jumps over the lazy dog. Voyez le brick géant que j'examine près du wharf. Zwölf Boxkämpfer jagen Viktor quer über den großen Sylter Deich. El veloz murciélago hindú comía feliz cardillo y kiwi. La cigüeña tocaba el saxofón detrás del palenque de pajaatur? Rissimo lorereped ex es solore lab id molorro in rempore icabore rehenetur aliam aut voles audae dem

**12/14 — T-Star Pro Bold**

The quick brown fox jumps over the lazy dog. Voyez le brick géant que j'examine près du wharf. Zwölf Boxkämpfer jagen Viktor quer über den großen Sylter Deich. El veloz murciélago hindú comía feliz cardillo y kiwi. La cigüeña tocaba el saxofón detrás del palenque de pajaatur? Rissimo lorereped ex es solore lab id molorro

**9/12 — T-Star Pro Bold**

The quick brown fox jumps over the lazy dog. Voyez le brick géant que j'examine près du wharf. Zwölf Boxkämpfer jagen Viktor quer über den großen Sylter Deich. El veloz murciélago hindú comía feliz cardillo y kiwi. La cigüeña tocaba el saxofón detrás del palenque de pajaatur? Rissimo lorereped ex es solore lab id molorro in rempore icabore rehenetur aliam aut voles audae dem quam, secum eum facesequae consequ aepudam quia voluptiur repel in et faccustibus, nonsenis

**7/10 — T-Star Pro Bold**

The quick brown fox jumps over the lazy dog. Voyez le brick géant que j'examine près du wharf. Zwölf Boxkämpfer jagen Viktor quer über den großen Sylter Deich. El veloz murciélago hindú comía feliz cardillo y kiwi. La cigüeña tocaba el saxofón detrás del palenque de pajaatur? Rissimo lorereped ex es solore lab id molorro in rempore icabore rehenetur aliam aut voles audae dem quam, secum eum facesequae consequ aepudam quia voluptiur repel in et faccustibus, nonsenis aut quisqui rero mi, ipiet lam ant ut maio et hil molupta tustis atatur, consedi tasimol orerem aut volor andipsapis sit, illaut volore officatus alicae dusdaec tatecte cearum qui accatibus restiore nulpa secaerferum, nus dolenim in et quoditat que explam voluptictur? Qui de illuptae.

Typeface  Nautinger
Designer  Moritz Esser
Year  2010
Format  OpenType

# Aa

Aa Bb Cc Dd Ee Ff Gg Hh Ii Jj
Kk Ll Mm Nn Oo Pp Qq Rr Ss
Tt Uu Vv Ww Xx Yy Zz
0123456789
—

Nautinger Thin 22pt
*Nautinger Thin Italic* 22pt
Nautinger Light 22pt
*Nautinger Light Italic* 22pt
Nautinger Regular 22pt
*Nautinger Regular Italic* 22pt
**Nautinger Bold** 22pt
***Nautinger Bold Italic*** 22pt
**Nautinger Heavy** 22pt
***Nautinger Heavy Italic*** 22pt

---

**12/14  Nautinger Thin**

The quick brown fox jumps over the lazy dog. Voyez le brick géant que j'examine près du wharf. Zwölf Boxkämpfer jagen Viktor quer über

**12/14  Nautinger Light**

The quick brown fox jumps over the lazy dog. Voyez le brick géant que j'examine près du wharf. Zwölf Boxkämpfer jagen Viktor

**12/14  Nautinger Regular**

The quick brown fox jumps over the lazy dog. Voyez le brick géant que j'examine près du wharf. Zwölf Boxkämpfer jagen Vik-

**12/14  Nautinger Bold**

The quick brown fox jumps over the lazy dog. Voyez le brick géant que j'examine près du wharf. Zwölf Boxkämpfer jagen Viktor quer über den großen Sylter Deich. El veloz murciélago hindú comía feliz cardillo y kiwi. La cigüeña tocaba el saxofón detrás del palenque de

---

**9/12  Nautinger Thin**

The quick brown fox jumps over the lazy dog. Voyez le brick géant que j'examine près du wharf. Zwölf Boxkämpfer jagen Viktor quer über den großen Sylter Deich. El veloz murciélago hindú comía feliz cardillo y kiwi. La

**9/12  Nautinger Light**

The quick brown fox jumps over the lazy dog. Voyez le brick géant que j'examine près du wharf. Zwölf Boxkämpfer jagen Viktor quer über den großen Sylter Deich. El veloz murciélago hindú comía feliz cardillo y kiwi. La

**9/12  Nautinger Regular**

The quick brown fox jumps over the lazy dog. Voyez le brick géant que j'examine près du wharf. Zwölf Boxkämpfer jagen Viktor quer über den großen Sylter Deich. El veloz murciélago hindú comía feliz cardillo y

**9/12  Nautinger Bold**

The quick brown fox jumps over the lazy dog. Voyez le brick géant que j'examine près du wharf. Zwölf Boxkämpfer jagen Viktor quer über den großen Sylter Deich. El veloz murciélago hindú comía feliz cardillo y kiwi. La cigüeña tocaba el saxofón detrás del palenque de pajaatur? Rissimo lorereped ex es solore lab id molorro in rempore icabore rehenetur aliam aut voles audae dem quam, secum eum

---

**7/10  Nautinger Thin**

The quick brown fox jumps over the lazy dog. Voyez le brick géant que j'examine près du wharf. Zwölf Boxkämpfer jagen Viktor quer über den großen Sylter Deich. El veloz murciélago hindú comía feliz cardillo y kiwi. La cigüeña tocaba el saxofón detrás del palenque de pajaatur? Rissimo lorereped ex es solore lab id molorro in rempore icabore rehenetur aliam

**7/10  Nautinger Light**

The quick brown fox jumps over the lazy dog. Voyez le brick géant que j'examine près du wharf. Zwölf Boxkämpfer jagen Viktor quer über den großen Sylter Deich. El veloz murciélago hindú comía feliz cardillo y kiwi. La cigüeña tocaba el saxofón detrás del palenque de pajaatur? Rissimo lorereped ex es solore lab id molorro in rempore icabore

**7/10  Nautinger Regular**

The quick brown fox jumps over the lazy dog. Voyez le brick géant que j'examine près du wharf. Zwölf Boxkämpfer jagen Viktor quer über den großen Sylter Deich. El veloz murciélago hindú comía feliz cardillo y kiwi. La cigüeña tocaba el saxofón detrás del palenque de pajaatur? Rissimo lorereped ex es solore lab id molorro

**7/10  Nautinger Bold**

The quick brown fox jumps over the lazy dog. Voyez le brick géant que j'examine près du wharf. Zwölf Boxkämpfer jagen Viktor quer über den großen Sylter Deich. El veloz murciélago hindú comía feliz cardillo y kiwi. La cigüeña tocaba el saxofón detrás del palenque de pajaatur? Rissimo lorereped ex es solore lab id molorro in rempore icabore rehenetur aliam aut voles audae dem quam, secum eum facesequae consequ aepudam quia voluptiur repel in et faccustibus, nonsenis aut quisqui rero mi, ipiet lam ant ut maio et hil molupta tustis atatur, consedi tasimol orerem aut volor andipsapis sit, illaut volore officatus alicae

| | | | |
|---|---|---|---|
| Typeface | Maksim | Year | 2011 |
| Designer | Claudia Doms | Format | OpenType |

# Tubeway Quints

Regular

Aa Bb Cc Dd Ee Ff Gg Hh Ii Jj
Kk Ll Mm Nn Oo Pp Qq Rr Ss Tt
Uu Vv Ww Xx Yy Zz 0123456789

| | | | |
|---|---|---|---|
| Typeface | Calcine | Year | 2011 |
| Designer | Mark Frömberg | Format | OpenType |

# Boterham met Kwark

Light
Regular
**Bold**
Condensed Light
Condensed Regular
**Condensed Bold**

Aa Bb Cc Dd Ee Ff Gg Hh Ii Jj Kk Ll
Mm Nn Oo Pp Qq Rr Ss Tt Uu Vv Ww
Xx Yy Zz 0123456789

| | | | |
|---|---|---|---|
| Typeface | Malaussene Translation | Year | 2010 |
| Designer | Laure Afchain | Format | OpenType |

# Royale Babelfisk
## Language University

Roman
*Italic*
**Bold**
**Display**

Aa Bb Cc Dd Ee Ff Gg Hh Ii
Jj Kk Ll Mm Nn Oo Pp Qq
Rr Ss Tt Uu Vv Ww Xx Yy Zz
0123456789

| | | | |
|---|---|---|---|
| Typeface | Treza | Year | 2010 |
| Designer | Benjamin Gomez | Format | OpenType |

# Aa

Treza Thin 18pt
Treza Book 18pt
**Treza Medium 18pt**
**Treza Bold 18pt**
**Treza Black 18pt**

Aa Bb Cc Dd Ee Ff Gg Hh Ii Jj Kk Ll Mm Nn Oo Pp Qq Rr Ss Tt Uu Vv Ww Xx Yy Zz 0123456789
—

9/12   Treza Book

The quick brown fox jumps over the lazy dog. Voyez le brick géant que j'examine près du wharf. Zwölf Boxkämpfer jagen Viktor quer über den großen Sylter Deich. El veloz murciélago hindú comía feliz cardillo y kiwi. La cigüeña tocaba el saxofón detrás del palenque de pajaatur? Rissimo lorereped ex es solore lab id molorro in rempore icabore rehenetur aliam aut voles audae dem quam, secum eum facesequae consequ aepudam quia voluptiur repel in et faccustibus, nonsenis aut quisqui rero

7/10   Treza Book

The quick brown fox jumps over the lazy dog. Voyez le brick géant que j'examine près du wharf. Zwölf Boxkämpfer jagen Viktor quer über den großen Sylter Deich. El veloz murciélago hindú comía feliz cardillo y kiwi. La cigüeña tocaba el saxofón detrás del palenque de pajaatur? Rissimo lorereped ex es solore lab id molorro in rempore icabore rehenetur aliam aut voles audae dem quam, secum eum facesequae consequ aepudam quia voluptiur repel in et faccustibus, nonsenis aut quisqui rero mi, ipiet lam ant ut maio et hil molupta tustis atatur, consedi tasimol orerem aut volor andipsapis sit, illaut volore officatus alicae dusdaec tatecte cearum qui accatibus restiore nulpa secaerferum, nus dolenim in et quoditat que explam

| | | | |
|---|---|---|---|
| Typeface | Sensaway PRO | Year | 2010 |
| Designer | Aron Jancso | Format | OpenType |

# Aa

Sensaway PRO Light 18pt
*Sensaway PRO Light Italic 18pt*
Sensaway PRO Regular 18pt
*Sensaway PRO Regular Italic 18pt*
**Sensaway PRO Heavy 18pt**
***Sensaway PRO Heavy Italic 18pt***

Aa Bb Cc Dd Ee Ff Gg Hh Ii Jj Kk Ll Mm Nn Oo Pp Qq Rr Ss Tt Uu Vv Ww Xx Yy Zz 0123456789
—

9/12   Sensaway PRO Regular

The quick brown fox jumps over the lazy dog. Voyez le brick géant que j'examine près du wharf. Zwölf Boxkämpfer jagen Viktor quer über den großen Sylter Deich. El veloz murciélago hindú comía feliz cardillo y kiwi. La cigüeña tocaba el saxofón detrás del palenque de pajaatur? Rissimo lorereped ex es solore lab id molorro in rempore icabore rehenetur aliam aut voles audae dem quam, secum eum facesequae

7/10   Sensaway PRO Regular

The quick brown fox jumps over the lazy dog. Voyez le brick géant que j'examine près du wharf. Zwölf Boxkämpfer jagen Viktor quer über den großen Sylter Deich. El veloz murciélago hindú comía feliz cardillo y kiwi. La cigüeña tocaba el saxofón detrás del palenque de pajaatur? Rissimo lorereped ex es solore lab id molorro in rempore icabore rehenetur aliam aut voles audae dem quam, secum eum facesequae consequ aepudam quia voluptiur repel in et faccustibus, nonsenis aut quisqui rero mi, ipiet lam ant ut maio et hil molupta tustis atatur, consedi tasimol orerem aut volor andipsapis sit, illaut volore officatus alicae dusdaec

# G

## Grilli Type

Noël Leu,
Thierry Blancpain

Zürich,
Switzerland

Since
2009

Grilli Type is a fiercely independent foundry in Zürich.

## Info

—Why?
We created Grilli Type to build an independent platform for typefaces with an experimental or historical background. We focus on typefaces that make a clear visual statement and distinguish themselves from the mainstream type market.

—People on staff
8

—Type designers on staff
8

—Type families
4 published families
6 unpublished families

—Designers represented
8

—Web shop
www.grillitype.com

—Distributors
Exclusively via grillitype.com

—Webfont services
www.typekit.com

—Basic license
50$ (single font); family packages with discount. Basic license is for 5 computers.

Typeface selection

GT Federal
GT Haptik
GT Lena
GT Walsheim

24pt

## People

—Noël Leu, graphic designer, responsible for the technical side of type-design and mastering. He loves typography and works out hard to look like Arnold Schwarzenegger.

—Thierry Blancpain, graphic designer, responsible for all of the foundry's online activities and communication. He adores curves and shuns meat.

—Daniel Bär, graphic designer based in Zürich, Switzerland.

—Eric Åhnebrink, graphic designer based in London, United Kingdom.

—Erich Brechbühl, graphic designer based in Lucerne, Switzerland.

—Mathis Pfäffli, graphic designer based in Leipzig, Germany.

—Reto Moser and Tobias Rechtsteiner, graphic designers based in Bern, Switzerland.

Famous Macchiavelli quote set in Grilli Type's Haptik.

Promotional poster: two color stone lithography print using GT Walsheim Medium by Noël Leu.

Page
113

Objects and installation made with the Haptik font designed by Tobias Rechsteiner and Reto Moser.

Foundry  Grilli Type

---

Typeface  GT Federal
Designer  Noël Leu
Year  2009
Format  OpenType

# Alpine
## *Slopes*

Regular
*Italic*

Aa Bb Cc Dd Ee Ff Gg Hh
Ii Jj Kk Ll Mm Nn Oo Pp Qq
Rr Ss Tt Uu Vv Ww Xx Yy Zz
0123456789

---

Typeface  GT Haptik
Designers  Reto Moser,
 Tobias Rechtsteiner
Year  2009
Format  OpenType

# Genuine
## *Rotalic*

Regular
*Italic*
**Medium**
***Medium Italic***

Aa Bb Cc Dd Ee Ff Gg Hh Ii
Jj Kk Ll Mm Nn Oo Pp Qq
Rr Ss Tt Uu Vv Ww Xx Yy
Zz 0123456789

---

Typeface  GT Lena
Designer  Eric Åhnebrink
Year  2009
Format  OpenType

# MAG23
## BluePages

Regular

Aa Bb Cc Dd Ee Ff Gg Hh Ii Jj Kk Ll Mm Nn
Oo Pp Qq Rr Ss Tt Uu Vv Ww Xx Yy Zz
0123456789

| | | | |
|---|---|---|---|
| Page | | Foundry | Grilli Type |
| 115 | | | |

| | | | |
|---|---|---|---|
| Typeface | GT Walsheim | Year | 2011 |
| Designer | Noël Leu | Format | OpenType |

# Aa

Aa Bb Cc Dd Ee Ff Gg Hh Ii Jj Kk Ll Mm Nn Oo Pp Qq Rr Ss Tt Uu Vv Ww Xx Yy Zz
0123456789
—

GT Walsheim Ultra Light 14pt
*GT Walsheim Ultra Light Oblique 14pt*
GT Walsheim Thin 14pt
*GT Walsheim Thin Oblique 14pt*
GT Walsheim Light 14pt
*GT Walsheim Light Oblique 14pt*
GT Walsheim Regular 14pt
*GT Walsheim Regular Oblique 14pt*
GT Walsheim Medium 14pt
*GT Walsheim Medium Oblique 14pt*
**GT Walsheim Bold 14pt**
***GT Walsheim Bold Oblique 14pt***
**GT Walsheim Black 14pt**
***GT Walsheim Black Oblique 14pt***
**GT Walsheim Ultra Bold 14pt**
***GT Walsheim Ultra Bold Oblique 14pt***

---

**12/14 — GT Walsheim Light**

The quick brown fox jumps over the lazy dog. Voyez le brick géant que j'examine près du wharf. Zwölf Boxkämpfer jagen Viktor quer über

**12/14 — GT Walsheim Regular**

The quick brown fox jumps over the lazy dog. Voyez le brick géant que j'examine près du wharf. Zwölf Boxkämpfer jagen Viktor quer über den

**12/14 — GT Walsheim Medium**

The quick brown fox jumps over the lazy dog. Voyez le brick géant que j'examine près du wharf. Zwölf Boxkämpfer jagen Viktor quer über

**12/14 — GT Walsheim Bold**

**The quick brown fox jumps over the lazy dog. Voyez le brick géant que j'examine près du wharf. Zwölf Boxkämpfer jagen Viktor quer über den großen Sylter Deich. El veloz murciélago**

---

**9/12 — GT Walsheim Light**

The quick brown fox jumps over the lazy dog. Voyez le brick géant que j'examine près du wharf. Zwölf Boxkämpfer jagen Viktor quer über den großen Sylter Deich. El veloz murciélago hindú comía feliz cardillo y kiwi. La cigüeña

**9/12 — GT Walsheim Regular**

The quick brown fox jumps over the lazy dog. Voyez le brick géant que j'examine près du wharf. Zwölf Boxkämpfer jagen Viktor quer über den großen Sylter Deich. El veloz murciélago hindú comía feliz cardillo y kiwi. La cigüeña

**9/12 — GT Walsheim Medium**

The quick brown fox jumps over the lazy dog. Voyez le brick géant que j'examine près du wharf. Zwölf Boxkämpfer jagen Viktor quer über den großen Sylter Deich. El veloz murciélago hindú comía feliz cardillo y kiwi. La

**9/12 — GT Walsheim Bold**

**The quick brown fox jumps over the lazy dog. Voyez le brick géant que j'examine près du wharf. Zwölf Boxkämpfer jagen Viktor quer über den großen Sylter Deich. El veloz murciélago hindú comía feliz cardillo y kiwi. La cigüeña tocaba el saxofón detrás del palenque de pajaatur? Rissimo lorer-**

---

**7/10 — GT Walsheim Light**

The quick brown fox jumps over the lazy dog. Voyez le brick géant que j'examine près du wharf. Zwölf Boxkämpfer jagen Viktor quer über den großen Sylter Deich. El veloz murciélago hindú comía feliz cardillo y kiwi. La cigüeña tocaba el saxofón detrás del palenque de pajaatur? Rissimo lorereped ex es solore lab id molorro in rempore icabore rehenetur aliam aut

**7/10 — GT Walsheim Regular**

The quick brown fox jumps over the lazy dog. Voyez le brick géant que j'examine près du wharf. Zwölf Boxkämpfer jagen Viktor quer über den großen Sylter Deich. El veloz murciélago hindú comía feliz cardillo y kiwi. La cigüeña tocaba el saxofón detrás del palenque de pajaatur? Rissimo lorereped ex es solore lab id molorro in rempore icabore rehenetur aliam

**7/10 — GT Walsheim Medium**

The quick brown fox jumps over the lazy dog. Voyez le brick géant que j'examine près du wharf. Zwölf Boxkämpfer jagen Viktor quer über den großen Sylter Deich. El veloz murciélago hindú comía feliz cardillo y kiwi. La cigüeña tocaba el saxofón detrás del palenque de pajaatur? Rissimo lorereped ex es solore lab id molorro in rempore icabore rehenetur aliam

**7/10 — GT Walsheim Bold**

**The quick brown fox jumps over the lazy dog. Voyez le brick géant que j'examine près du wharf. Zwölf Boxkämpfer jagen Viktor quer über den großen Sylter Deich. El veloz murciélago hindú comía feliz cardillo y kiwi. La cigüeña tocaba el saxofón detrás del palenque de pajaatur? Rissimo lorereped ex es solore lab id molorro in rempore icabore rehenetur aliam aut voles audae dem quam, secum eum facesequae consequ aepudam quia**

# H

## Hubert Jocham Type

—

Hubert Jocham

—

Lautrach, Germany

—

Since 2007

Hubert Jocham Type is the personal foundry of Hubert Jocham, based in Lautrach, Bavaria (Germany).

## Info

—Why?
Because it enables me to do my own thing.

—People on staff
1

—Type designers on staff
1

—Type families
Approx. 55

—Designers represented
Just me

— Web shop
www.hubertjocham.de

—Distributors
MyFonts

—Webfont services
MyFonts

—Basic license
$39 (for single fonts)

Typeface selection

Madita
Matrona
Mommie
NewJune
Perfetto
VerseSans
VerseSerif

24pt

## People

—In the early 1980s, at the start of his career, Hubert Jocham worked in a print shop with classic metal typesetting. He studied graphic design in Augsburg (Germany) and Preston (England). His graduation project dealt with the history of the italic types of the Renaissance and the relationship between roman and italic.
In 1998 Jocham moved to London to work for Henrion, Ludlow & Schmidt in corporate branding. He designed brandmarks and logotypes for international companies and designed corporate manuals. He got to know the art directors of lifestyle magazines such as *Frank* and *Arena*, where he worked as a type consultant and type designer.

Today Hubert Jocham is a freelance designer. He develops brandmarks and logotypes for leading brand agencies like Interbrand, Landor, The Brand Union and Futurbrand. He designs text and headline systems for international magazines like *GQ* in London, Russian *Vogue*, *L'Officiel* in Paris, *Details* in New York and German publishers like Milchstraße and Gruner & Jahr. He developed corporate typography for Bally in Switzerland, the Kunsthaus Graz in Austria, Agfa Photo and Vattenfall.

Page
117

**Previous page**
Hubert Jocham, pencil sketches for logos. This page: Lettering for a magazine headline. Digital outline art.

Page 118

Foundry  Hubert Jocham Type

Typeface  Mommie
Designer  Hubert Jocham
Year  2004
Format  OpenType

*Reibekuchen*

Regular
Medium
Small

Aa Bb Cc Dd Ee Ff Gg Hh Ii Jj
Kk Ll Mm Nn Oo Pp Qq Rr Ss Tt
Uu Vv Ww Xx Yy Zz 0123456789

Typeface  Madita
Designer  Hubert Jocham
Year  2011
Format  OpenType

Schokoladen brötchen

Light
Book
Regular
Medium
Semibold
Bold

Aa Bb Cc Dd Ee Ff Gg Hh Ii
Jj Kk Ll Mm Nn Oo Pp Qq
Rr Ss Tt Uu Vv Ww Xx Yy Zz
0123456789

Typeface  Matrona
Designer  Hubert Jocham
Year  2010
Format  OpenType

Pfann kuchen

Regular
Medium
Small

Aa Bb Cc Dd Ee
Ff Gg Hh Ii Jj Kk
Ll Mm Nn Oo Pp
Qq Rr Ss Tt Uu
Vv Ww Xx Yy Zz
0123456789

| | | |
|---|---|---|
| Typeface NewJune | Year 1999 | |
| Designer Hubert Jocham | Format OpenType | |

# Aa

Aa Bb Cc Dd Ee Ff Gg Hh Ii Jj Kk Ll Mm Nn Oo Pp Qq Rr Ss Tt Uu Vv Ww Xx Yy Zz 0123456789
—

NewJune Thin 14pt
*NewJune Thin Italic 14pt*
NewJune Fine 14pt
*NewJune Fine Italic 14pt*
NewJune Light 14pt
*NewJune Light Italic 14pt*
NewJune Book 14pt
*NewJune Book Italic 14pt*
NewJune Regular 14pt
*NewJune Italic 14pt*
NewJune Medium 14pt
*NewJune Medium Italic 14pt*
**NewJune Semi Bold 14pt**
***NewJune Semi Bold Italic 14pt***
**NewJune Bold 14pt**
***NewJune Bold Italic 14pt***
**NewJune Heavy 14pt**
***NewJune Heavy Italic 14pt***
**NewJune Extra Bold 14pt**
***NewJune Extra Bold Italic 14pt***
**NewJune Ultra Bold 14pt**
***NewJune Ultra Bold Italic 14pt***

NewJune Serif Regular 14pt
*NewJune Serif Thin Italic 14pt*

**12/14    NewJune Serif Regular**

The quick brown fox jumps over the lazy dog. Voyez le brick géant que j'examine près du wharf. Zwölf Boxkämpfer jagen Vik-

**9/12    NewJune Serif Regular**

The quick brown fox jumps over the lazy dog. Voyez le brick géant que j'examine près du wharf. Zwölf Boxkämpfer jagen Viktor quer über den großen Sylter Deich. El veloz murciélago hindú comía feliz cardillo y kiwi.

**7/10    NewJune Serif Regular**

The quick brown fox jumps over the lazy dog. Voyez le brick géant que j'examine près du wharf. Zwölf Boxkämpfer jagen Viktor quer über den großen Sylter Deich. El veloz murciélago hindú comía feliz cardillo y kiwi. La cigüeña tocaba el saxofón detrás del palenque de pajaatur? Rissimo lorereped ex es solore lab id molorro

---

**12/14    NewJune Regular**

The quick brown fox jumps over the lazy dog. Voyez le brick géant que j'examine près du wharf. Zwölf Boxkämpfer jagen Vik-

**12/14    NewJune Medium**

The quick brown fox jumps over the lazy dog. Voyez le brick géant que j'examine près du wharf. Zwölf Boxkämpfer jagen Vik-

**12/14    NewJune Bold**

**The quick brown fox jumps over the lazy dog. Voyez le brick géant que j'examine près du wharf. Zwölf Boxkämpfer jagen Viktor quer über den großen Sylter Deich. El veloz murciélago**

**9/12    NewJune Regular**

The quick brown fox jumps over the lazy dog. Voyez le brick géant que j'examine près du wharf. Zwölf Boxkämpfer jagen Viktor quer über den großen Sylter Deich. El veloz murciélago hindú comía feliz cardillo y kiwi.

**9/12    NewJune Medium**

The quick brown fox jumps over the lazy dog. Voyez le brick géant que j'examine près du wharf. Zwölf Boxkämpfer jagen Viktor quer über den großen Sylter Deich. El veloz murciélago hindú comía feliz cardillo y kiwi.

**9/12    NewJune Bold**

**The quick brown fox jumps over the lazy dog. Voyez le brick géant que j'examine près du wharf. Zwölf Boxkämpfer jagen Viktor quer über den großen Sylter Deich. El veloz murciélago hindú comía feliz cardillo y kiwi. La cigüeña tocaba el saxofón detrás del palenque de pajaatur? Rissimo lorereped ex**

**7/10    NewJune Regular**

The quick brown fox jumps over the lazy dog. Voyez le brick géant que j'examine près du wharf. Zwölf Boxkämpfer jagen Viktor quer über den großen Sylter Deich. El veloz murciélago hindú comía feliz cardillo y kiwi. La cigüeña tocaba el saxofón detrás del palenque de pajaatur? Rissimo lorereped ex es solore lab id molorro in rempore icabore

**7/10    NewJune Medium**

The quick brown fox jumps over the lazy dog. Voyez le brick géant que j'examine près du wharf. Zwölf Boxkämpfer jagen Viktor quer über den großen Sylter Deich. El veloz murciélago hindú comía feliz cardillo y kiwi. La cigüeña tocaba el saxofón detrás del palenque de pajaatur? Rissimo lorereped ex es solore lab id molorro in rempo-

**7/10    NewJune Bold**

**The quick brown fox jumps over the lazy dog. Voyez le brick géant que j'examine près du wharf. Zwölf Boxkämpfer jagen Viktor quer über den großen Sylter Deich. El veloz murciélago hindú comía feliz cardillo y kiwi. La cigüeña tocaba el saxofón detrás del palenque de pajaatur? Rissimo lorereped ex es solore lab id molorro in rempore icabore rehenetur aliam aut voles audae dem quam, secum eum facesequae consequ aepudam quia**

| | |
|---|---|
| Typeface | Perfetto |
| Designer | Hubert Jocham |
| Year | 2008 |
| Format | OpenType |

Foundry Hubert Jocham Type

# Aa

Aa Bb Cc Dd Ee Ff Gg Hh Ii Jj Kk Ll Mm Nn Oo Pp Qq Rr Ss Tt Uu Vv Ww Xx Yy Zz
0123456789
—

Perfetto Light 14pt
*Perfetto Light Italic 14pt*
Perfetto Book 14pt
*Perfetto Book Italic 14pt*
Perfetto Regular 14pt
*Perfetto Italic 14pt*
Perfetto Medium 14pt
*Perfetto Medium Italic 14pt*
**Perfetto Semi Bold 14pt**
***Perfetto Semi Bold Italic 14pt***
**Perfetto Bold 14pt**
***Perfetto Bold Italic 14pt***
**Perfetto Heavy 14pt**
***Perfetto Heavy Italic 14pt***

PerfettoDis Book 24pt
*PerfettoDis Book Italic 24pt*

---

**12/14 Perfetto Light**

The quick brown fox jumps over the lazy dog. Voyez le brick géant que j'examine près du wharf. Zwölf Boxkämpfer jagen Viktor quer über den

**9/12 Perfetto Light**

The quick brown fox jumps over the lazy dog. Voyez le brick géant que j'examine près du wharf. Zwölf Boxkämpfer jagen Viktor quer über den großen Sylter Deich. El veloz murciélago hindú comía feliz cardillo y kiwi. La cigüeña tocaba el

**7/10 Perfetto Light**

The quick brown fox jumps over the lazy dog. Voyez le brick géant que j'examine près du wharf. Zwölf Boxkämpfer jagen Viktor quer über den großen Sylter Deich. El veloz murciélago hindú comía feliz cardillo y kiwi. La cigüeña tocaba el saxofón detrás del palenque de pajaatur? Rissimo lorereped ex es solore lab id molorro in rempore icabore rehenetur aliam aut voles

**12/14 Perfetto Regular**

The quick brown fox jumps over the lazy dog. Voyez le brick géant que j'examine près du wharf. Zwölf Boxkämpfer jagen Viktor quer

**9/12 Perfetto Regular**

The quick brown fox jumps over the lazy dog. Voyez le brick géant que j'examine près du wharf. Zwölf Boxkämpfer jagen Viktor quer über den großen Sylter Deich. El veloz murciélago hindú comía feliz cardillo y kiwi. La

**7/10 Perfetto Regular**

The quick brown fox jumps over the lazy dog. Voyez le brick géant que j'examine près du wharf. Zwölf Boxkämpfer jagen Viktor quer über den großen Sylter Deich. El veloz murciélago hindú comía feliz cardillo y kiwi. La cigüeña tocaba el saxofón detrás del palenque de pajaatur? Rissimo lorereped ex es solore lab id molorro in rempore icabore rehenetur

**12/14 Perfetto Medium**

The quick brown fox jumps over the lazy dog. Voyez le brick géant que j'examine près du wharf. Zwölf Boxkämpfer jagen Viktor quer über

**9/12 Perfetto Medium**

The quick brown fox jumps over the lazy dog. Voyez le brick géant que j'examine près du wharf. Zwölf Boxkämpfer jagen Viktor quer über den großen Sylter Deich. El veloz murciélago hindú comía feliz cardillo y kiwi. La cigüe-

**7/10 Perfetto Medium**

The quick brown fox jumps over the lazy dog. Voyez le brick géant que j'examine près du wharf. Zwölf Boxkämpfer jagen Viktor quer über den großen Sylter Deich. El veloz murciélago hindú comía feliz cardillo y kiwi. La cigüeña tocaba el saxofón detrás del palenque de pajaatur? Rissimo lorereped ex es solore lab id molorro in rempore icabore rehenetur aliam

**12/14 Perfetto Bold**

**The quick brown fox jumps over the lazy dog. Voyez le brick géant que j'examine près du wharf. Zwölf Boxkämpfer jagen Viktor quer über den großen Sylter Deich. El veloz murciélago hindú comía feliz**

**9/12 Perfetto Bold**

**The quick brown fox jumps over the lazy dog. Voyez le brick géant que j'examine près du wharf. Zwölf Boxkämpfer jagen Viktor quer über den großen Sylter Deich. El veloz murciélago hindú comía feliz cardillo y kiwi. La cigüeña tocaba el saxofón detrás del palenque de pajaatur? Rissimo lorereped ex es solore**

**7/10 Perfetto Bold**

**The quick brown fox jumps over the lazy dog. Voyez le brick géant que j'examine près du wharf. Zwölf Boxkämpfer jagen Viktor quer über den großen Sylter Deich. El veloz murciélago hindú comía feliz cardillo y kiwi. La cigüeña tocaba el saxofón detrás del palenque de pajaatur? Rissimo lorereped ex es solore lab id molorro in rempore icabore rehenetur aliam aut voles audae dem quam, secum eum facsequae consequ aepudam quia voluptiur repel in et faccustibus,**

## Typeface: VerseSans, Serif
**Designer** Hubert Jocham
**Foundry** Hubert Jocham Type
**Year** 2006
**Format** OpenType

# A A

Aa Bb Cc Dd Ee Ff Gg Hh Ii Jj Kk Ll Mm Nn Oo Pp Qq Rr Ss Tt Uu Vv Ww Xx Yy Zz 0123456789

Aa Bb Cc Dd Ee Ff Gg Hh Ii Jj Kk Ll Mm Nn Oo Pp Qq Rr Ss Tt Uu Vv Ww Xx Yy Zz 0123456789

---

VerseSans Regular 14pt
*VerseSans Italic 14pt*
VerseSans Medium 14pt
*VerseSans Medium Italic 14pt*
**VerseSans SemiBold 14pt**
***VerseSans SemiBold Italic 14pt***
**VerseSans Bold 14pt**
***VerseSans Bold Italic 14pt***
**VerseSans Heavy 14pt**
***VerseSans Heavy Italic 14pt***
**VerseSans ExtraBold 14pt**
***VerseSans ExtraBold Italic 14pt***
**VerseSans UltraBold 14pt**
***VerseSans UltraBold Italic 14pt***

VerseSerif Regular 14pt
*VerseSerif Italic 14pt*
VerseSerif Medium 14pt
*VerseSerif Medium Italic 14pt*
**VerseSerif SemiBold 14pt**
***VerseSerif SemiBold Italic 14pt***
**VerseSerif Bold 14pt**
***VerseSerif Bold Italic 14pt***
**VerseSerif Heavy 14pt**
***VerseSerif Heavy Italic 14pt***
**VerseSerif ExtraBold 14pt**
***VerseSerif ExtraBold Italic 14pt***
**VerseSerif UltraBold 14pt**
***VerseSerif UltraBold Italic 14pt***

---

**12/14 VerseSans Regular**

The quick brown fox jumps over the lazy dog. Voyez le brick géant que j'examine près du wharf. Zwölf Boxkämpfer jagen Viktor quer über den

**12/14 VerseSans Medium**

The quick brown fox jumps over the lazy dog. Voyez le brick géant que j'examine près du wharf. Zwölf Boxkämpfer jagen Viktor quer über den

**12/14 VerseSerif Regular**

The quick brown fox jumps over the lazy dog. Voyez le brick géant que j'examine près du wharf. Zwölf Boxkämpfer jagen Viktor quer über den

**12/14 VerseSerif Medium**

The quick brown fox jumps over the lazy dog. Voyez le brick géant que j'examine près du wharf. Zwölf Boxkämpfer jagen Viktor quer über den großen Sylter Deich. El veloz murciélago hindú comía feliz cardillo y kiwi.

**9/12 VerseSans Regular**

The quick brown fox jumps over the lazy dog. Voyez le brick géant que j'examine près du wharf. Zwölf Boxkämpfer jagen Viktor quer über den großen Sylter Deich. El veloz murciélago hindú comía feliz cardillo y kiwi. La cigüeña tocaba el saxofón detrás

**9/12 VerseSans Medium**

The quick brown fox jumps over the lazy dog. Voyez le brick géant que j'examine près du wharf. Zwölf Boxkämpfer jagen Viktor quer über den großen Sylter Deich. El veloz murciélago hindú comía feliz cardillo y kiwi. La cigüeña tocaba el saxofón detrás

**9/12 VerseSerif Regular**

The quick brown fox jumps over the lazy dog. Voyez le brick géant que j'examine près du wharf. Zwölf Boxkämpfer jagen Viktor quer über den großen Sylter Deich. El veloz murciélago hindú comía feliz cardillo y kiwi. La cigüeña tocaba el

**9/12 VerseSerif Medium**

The quick brown fox jumps over the lazy dog. Voyez le brick géant que j'examine près du wharf. Zwölf Boxkämpfer jagen Viktor quer über den großen Sylter Deich. El veloz murciélago hindú comía feliz cardillo y kiwi. La cigüeña tocaba el saxofón detrás del palenque de pajaatur? Rissimo lorereped ex es solore lab id molorro in rempore icabore

**7/10 VerseSans Regular**

The quick brown fox jumps over the lazy dog. Voyez le brick géant que j'examine près du wharf. Zwölf Boxkämpfer jagen Viktor quer über den großen Sylter Deich. El veloz murciélago hindú comía feliz cardillo y kiwi. La cigüeña tocaba el saxofón detrás del palenque de pajaatur? Rissimo lorereped ex es solore lab id molorro in rempore icabore rehenetur aliam aut voles audae dem quam, secum eum

**7/10 VerseSans Medium**

The quick brown fox jumps over the lazy dog. Voyez le brick géant que j'examine près du wharf. Zwölf Boxkämpfer jagen Viktor quer über den großen Sylter Deich. El veloz murciélago hindú comía feliz cardillo y kiwi. La cigüeña tocaba el saxofón detrás del palenque de pajaatur? Rissimo lorereped ex es solore lab id molorro in rempore icabore rehenetur aliam aut voles audae dem quam, secum

**7/10 VerseSerif Regular**

The quick brown fox jumps over the lazy dog. Voyez le brick géant que j'examine près du wharf. Zwölf Boxkämpfer jagen Viktor quer über den großen Sylter Deich. El veloz murciélago hindú comía feliz cardillo y kiwi. La cigüeña tocaba el saxofón detrás del palenque de pajaatur? Rissimo lorereped ex es solore lab id molorro in rempore icabore rehenetur aliam aut voles audae dem

**7/10 VerseSerif Medium**

The quick brown fox jumps over the lazy dog. Voyez le brick géant que j'examine près du wharf. Zwölf Boxkämpfer jagen Viktor quer über den großen Sylter Deich. El veloz murciélago hindú comía feliz cardillo y kiwi. La cigüeña tocaba el saxofón detrás del palenque de pajaatur? Rissimo lorereped ex es solore lab id molorro in rempore icabore rehenetur aliam aut voles audae dem quam, secum eum facesequae consequ aepudam quia voluptiur repel in et faccustibus, nonsenis aut quisqui rero mi,

# H

## HVD Fonts

—

Hannes von Döhren

—

Berlin, Germany

—

Since 2005

HVD Fonts is a type foundry from Berlin, Germany. It was founded in 2005 with the aim of producing high quality typefaces for display as well as text use. Typefaces from the HVD studio (Hannes van Döhren and Livius Dietzel) have been published by Linotype, FSI/FontFont and HVD's own label.

## Info

—Why?
I wasn't really happy with the promotional opportunities the bigger foundries gave me. I wanted more control over what would happen to my fonts after finishing them, I decided to go my own way.

—People on staff
1

—Type designers on staff
1

—Type families
Approx. 20
plus 10+ free fonts

—Designers represented
2

— Web shop
No

—Distributors
MyFonts, Fontshop, Linotype, Monotype, Fontspring, HypeForType, YouWorkForThem, Veer, T26

—Webfont services
Typekit, MyFonts

—Basic license
Approx. $40 (single font), 5 CPUs

Typeface selection

Brevia
Brandon Grotesque
Bumper
Reklame Script
Subway
Supria Sans

24pt

## People

— Born in Berlin, Hannes von Döhren worked in an advertising agency in Hamburg after completing his studies in graphic design. He has run his own type foundry, HVD Fonts, since 2005. Within the last few years he has published several type families like Brevia, Livory, ITC Chino, FF Basic Gothic, Reklame Script and Brandon Grotesque, which became the most successful release at MyFonts in 2010. In 2011 he received a Certificate of Excellence in Type Design from the Type Directors Club NY.

Promotion visuals for HVD's typeface Cowboy Slang.

Page
123

**Above, right and far right**
The HVD *I love type* foldout poster sold out in a few months.

Left: specimen posters for Supria Sans

Page 124 — Foundry HVD Fonts

| Typeface | Subway | Year | 2009 |
| --- | --- | --- | --- |
| Designer | Hannes von Döhren | Format | OpenType |

**¡No More New Bands!**

Berlin
New York
Paris

Aa Bb Cc Dd Ee Ff Gg Hh Ii Jj Kk Ll Mm
Nn Oo Pp Qq Rr Ss Tt Uu Vv Ww Xx Yy Zz
0123456789

| Typeface | Reklame Script | Year | 2010 |
| --- | --- | --- | --- |
| Designer | Hannes von Döhren | Format | OpenType |

**Ultimate Offer!**

Regular
Medium
Bold
Black

Aa Bb Cc Dd Ee Ff Gg Hh Ii Jj Kk Ll Mm Nn Oo
Pp Qq Rr Ss Tt Uu Vv Ww Xx Yy Zz 0123456789

| Typeface | Bumper | Year | 2009 |
| --- | --- | --- | --- |
| Designer | Hannes von Döhren | Format | OpenType |

**Pull up
All the way**

Compressed
Condensed
Regular

Aa Bb Cc Dd Ee Ff Gg Hh Ii Jj Kk Ll
Mm Nn Oo Pp Qq Rr Ss Tt Uu Vv
Ww Xx Yy Zz 0123456789

Page 125

Foundry  HVD Fonts

Typeface  Brevia
Designer  Hannes von Döhren
Year  2009
Format  OpenType

# Aa

Aa Bb Cc Dd Ee Ff Gg Hh Ii Jj
Kk Ll Mm Nn Oo Pp Qq Rr Ss
Tt Uu Vv Ww Xx Yy Zz
0123456789

Brevia Light 20pt
*Brevia Light Italic 20pt*
Brevia Regular 20pt
*Brevia Regular Italic 20pt*
Brevia Medium 20pt
*Brevia Medium Italic 20pt*
**Brevia Semibold 20pt**
***Brevia Semibold Italic 20pt***
**Brevia Bold 20pt**
***Brevia Bold Italic 20pt***
**Brevia Black 20pt**
***Brevia Black Italic 20pt***
**Brevia Extra Black 20pt**
***Brevia Extra Black Italic 20pt***

---

12/14  Brevia Light

The quick brown fox jumps over the lazy dog. Voyez le brick géant que j'examine près du wharf. Zwölf Boxkämpfer

9/12  Brevia Light

The quick brown fox jumps over the lazy dog. Voyez le brick géant que j'examine près du wharf. Zwölf Boxkämpfer jagen Viktor quer über den großen Sylter Deich. El veloz murciélago hindú comía feliz car-

7/10  Brevia Light

The quick brown fox jumps over the lazy dog. Voyez le brick géant que j'examine près du wharf. Zwölf Boxkämpfer jagen Viktor quer über den großen Sylter Deich. El veloz murciélago hindú comía feliz cardillo y kiwi. La cigüeña tocaba el saxofón detrás del palenque de pajaatur? Rissimo lorereped ex es solore lab id

12/14  Brevia Regular

The quick brown fox jumps over the lazy dog. Voyez le brick géant que j'examine près du wharf. Zwölf Boxkämpfer jagen

9/12  Brevia Regular

The quick brown fox jumps over the lazy dog. Voyez le brick géant que j'examine près du wharf. Zwölf Boxkämpfer jagen Viktor quer über den großen Sylter Deich. El veloz murciélago hindú comía feliz car-

7/10  Brevia Regular

The quick brown fox jumps over the lazy dog. Voyez le brick géant que j'examine près du wharf. Zwölf Boxkämpfer jagen Viktor quer über den großen Sylter Deich. El veloz murciélago hindú comía feliz cardillo y kiwi. La cigüeña tocaba el saxofón detrás del palenque de pajaatur? Rissimo lorereped ex es solore lab id

12/14  Brevia Medium

The quick brown fox jumps over the lazy dog. Voyez le brick géant que j'examine près du wharf. Zwölf Boxkämpfer jagen

9/12  Brevia Medium

The quick brown fox jumps over the lazy dog. Voyez le brick géant que j'examine près du wharf. Zwölf Boxkämpfer jagen Viktor quer über den großen Sylter Deich. El veloz murciélago hindú comía feliz car-

7/10  Brevia Medium

The quick brown fox jumps over the lazy dog. Voyez le brick géant que j'examine près du wharf. Zwölf Boxkämpfer jagen Viktor quer über den großen Sylter Deich. El veloz murciélago hindú comía feliz cardillo y kiwi. La cigüeña tocaba el saxofón detrás del palenque de pajaatur? Rissimo lorereped ex es solore lab id

12/14  Brevia Bold

**The quick brown fox jumps over the lazy dog. Voyez le brick géant que j'examine près du wharf. Zwölf Boxkämpfer jagen Viktor quer über den großen Sylter Deich. El veloz**

9/12  Brevia Bold

**The quick brown fox jumps over the lazy dog. Voyez le brick géant que j'examine près du wharf. Zwölf Boxkämpfer jagen Viktor quer über den großen Sylter Deich. El veloz murciélago hindú comía feliz cardillo y kiwi. La cigüeña tocaba el saxofón detrás del palenque de pajaa-**

7/10  Brevia Bold

**The quick brown fox jumps over the lazy dog. Voyez le brick géant que j'examine près du wharf. Zwölf Boxkämpfer jagen Viktor quer über den großen Sylter Deich. El veloz murciélago hindú comía feliz cardillo y kiwi. La cigüeña tocaba el saxofón detrás del palenque de pajaatur? Rissimo lorereped ex es solore lab id molorro in rempore icabore rehenetur aliam aut voles audae dem quam, secum eum facesequae con-**

Typeface Supria Sans  Year 2011
Designer Hannes von Döhren  Format OpenType

# Aa

Aa Bb Cc Dd Ee Ff Gg Hh Ii Jj Kk
Ll Mm Nn Oo Pp Qq Rr Ss Tt Uu
Vv Ww Xx Yy Zz
0123456789
—

Supria Sans Light 14pt
*Supria Sans Light Italic* 14pt
*Supria Sans Light Oblique* 14pt
Supria Sans Regular 14pt
*Supria Sans Regular Italic* 14pt
*Supria Sans Regular Oblique* 14pt
Supria Sans Medium 14pt
*Supria Sans Medium Italic* 14pt
*Supria Sans Medium Oblique* 14pt
**Supria Sans Bold** 14pt
***Supria Sans Bold Italic*** 14pt
***Supria Sans Bold Oblique*** 14pt
**Supria Sans Heavy** 14pt
***Supria Sans Heavy Italic*** 14pt
***Supria Sans Heavy Oblique*** 14pt
**Supria Sans Black** 14pt
***Supria Sans Black Italic*** 14pt
***Supria Sans Black Oblique*** 14pt
Supria Sans Condensed Light → **Black** 14pt

---

12/14  Supria Sans Light

The quick brown fox jumps over the lazy dog. Voyez le brick géant que j'examine près du wharf. Zwölf Boxkämpfer jagen Viktor quer über

12/14  Supria Sans Regular

The quick brown fox jumps over the lazy dog. Voyez le brick géant que j'examine près du wharf. Zwölf Boxkämpfer jagen Viktor quer

12/14  Supria Sans Medium

The quick brown fox jumps over the lazy dog. Voyez le brick géant que j'examine près du wharf. Zwölf Boxkämpfer jagen Vik-

12/14  Supria Sans Bold

**The quick brown fox jumps over the lazy dog. Voyez le brick géant que j'examine près du wharf. Zwölf Boxkämpfer jagen Viktor quer über den großen Sylter Deich. El veloz murciélago**

9/12  Supria Sans Light

The quick brown fox jumps over the lazy dog. Voyez le brick géant que j'examine près du wharf. Zwölf Boxkämpfer jagen Viktor quer über den großen Sylter Deich. El veloz murciélago hindú comía feliz cardillo y kiwi. La cigüe-

9/12  Supria Sans Regular

The quick brown fox jumps over the lazy dog. Voyez le brick géant que j'examine près du wharf. Zwölf Boxkämpfer jagen Viktor quer über den großen Sylter Deich. El veloz murciélago hindú comía feliz cardillo y kiwi. La

9/12  Supria Sans Medium

The quick brown fox jumps over the lazy dog. Voyez le brick géant que j'examine près du wharf. Zwölf Boxkämpfer jagen Viktor quer über den großen Sylter Deich. El veloz murciélago hindú comía feliz cardillo y kiwi.

9/12  Supria Sans Bold

**The quick brown fox jumps over the lazy dog. Voyez le brick géant que j'examine près du wharf. Zwölf Boxkämpfer jagen Viktor quer über den großen Sylter Deich. El veloz murciélago hindú comía feliz cardillo y kiwi. La cigüeña tocaba el saxofón detrás del palenque de pajaatur? Rissimo lorereped ex**

7/10  Supria Sans Light

The quick brown fox jumps over the lazy dog. Voyez le brick géant que j'examine près du wharf. Zwölf Boxkämpfer jagen Viktor quer über den großen Sylter Deich. El veloz murciélago hindú comía feliz cardillo y kiwi. La cigüeña tocaba el saxofón detrás del palenque de pajaatur? Rissimo lorereped ex es solore lab id molorro in rempore icabore rehenetur aliam aut voles

7/10  Supria Sans Regular

The quick brown fox jumps over the lazy dog. Voyez le brick géant que j'examine près du wharf. Zwölf Boxkämpfer jagen Viktor quer über den großen Sylter Deich. El veloz murciélago hindú comía feliz cardillo y kiwi. La cigüeña tocaba el saxofón detrás del palenque de pajaatur? Rissimo lorereped ex es solore lab id molorro in rempore icabore rehenetur aliam

7/10  Supria Sans Medium

The quick brown fox jumps over the lazy dog. Voyez le brick géant que j'examine près du wharf. Zwölf Boxkämpfer jagen Viktor quer über den großen Sylter Deich. El veloz murciélago hindú comía feliz cardillo y kiwi. La cigüeña tocaba el saxofón detrás del palenque de pajaatur? Rissimo lorereped ex es solore lab id molorro in rempore

7/10  Supria Sans Bold

**The quick brown fox jumps over the lazy dog. Voyez le brick géant que j'examine près du wharf. Zwölf Boxkämpfer jagen Viktor quer über den großen Sylter Deich. El veloz murciélago hindú comía feliz cardillo y kiwi. La cigüeña tocaba el saxofón detrás del palenque de pajaatur? Rissimo lorereped ex es solore lab id molorro in rempore icabore rehenetur aliam aut voles audae dem quam, secum eum facesequae consequ aepudam**

Page
127

Foundry   HVD Fonts

Typeface   Brandon Grotesque
Designer   Hannes von Döhren
Year   2010
Format   OpenType

# Aa

Aa Bb Cc Dd Ee Ff Gg Hh Ii Jj Kk Ll
Mm Nn Oo Pp Qq Rr Ss Tt Uu Vv
Ww Xx Yy Zz
0123456789
—

Brandon Grotesque Thin 22pt
*Brandon Grotesque Thin Italic 22pt*
Brandon Grotesque Light 22pt
*Brandon Grotesque Light Italic 22pt*
Brandon Grotesque Regular 22pt
*Brandon Grotesque Regular Italic 22pt*
**Brandon Grotesque Medium 22pt**
***Brandon Grotesque Medium Italic 22pt***
**Brandon Grotesque Bold 22pt**
***Brandon Grotesque Bold Italic 22pt***
**Brandon Grotesque Black 22pt**
***Brandon Grotesque Black Italic 22pt***

---

12/14   Brandon Grotesque Light

The quick brown fox jumps over the lazy dog. Voyez le brick géant que j'examine près du wharf. Zwölf Boxkämpfer jagen Viktor quer über den großen Sylter

9/12   Brandon Grotesque Light

The quick brown fox jumps over the lazy dog. Voyez le brick géant que j'examine près du wharf. Zwölf Boxkämpfer jagen Viktor quer über den großen Sylter Deich. El veloz murciélago hindú comía feliz cardillo y kiwi. La cigüeña tocaba el saxofón detrás del palen-

7/10   Brandon Grotesque Light

The quick brown fox jumps over the lazy dog. Voyez le brick géant que j'examine près du wharf. Zwölf Boxkämpfer jagen Viktor quer über den großen Sylter Deich. El veloz murciélago hindú comía feliz cardillo y kiwi. La cigüeña tocaba el saxofón detrás del palenque de pajaatur? Rissimo lorereped ex es solore lab id molorro in rempore icabore rehenetur aliam aut voles audae dem quam, secum eum facesequae

12/14   Brandon Grotesque Regular

The quick brown fox jumps over the lazy dog. Voyez le brick géant que j'examine près du wharf. Zwölf Boxkämpfer jagen Viktor quer über den großen Sylter

9/12   Brandon Grotesque Regular

The quick brown fox jumps over the lazy dog. Voyez le brick géant que j'examine près du wharf. Zwölf Boxkämpfer jagen Viktor quer über den großen Sylter Deich. El veloz murciélago hindú comía feliz cardillo y kiwi. La cigüeña tocaba el saxofón detrás del

7/10   Brandon Grotesque Regular

The quick brown fox jumps over the lazy dog. Voyez le brick géant que j'examine près du wharf. Zwölf Boxkämpfer jagen Viktor quer über den großen Sylter Deich. El veloz murciélago hindú comía feliz cardillo y kiwi. La cigüeña tocaba el saxofón detrás del palenque de pajaatur? Rissimo lorereped ex es solore lab id molorro in rempore icabore rehenetur aliam aut voles audae dem quam, secum eum facesequae consequ ae-

12/14   Brandon Grotesque Medium

The quick brown fox jumps over the lazy dog. Voyez le brick géant que j'examine près du wharf. Zwölf Boxkämpfer jagen Viktor quer über den großen Sylter

9/12   Brandon Grotesque Medium

The quick brown fox jumps over the lazy dog. Voyez le brick géant que j'examine près du wharf. Zwölf Boxkämpfer jagen Viktor quer über den großen Sylter Deich. El veloz murciélago hindú comía feliz cardillo y kiwi. La cigüeña tocaba el saxofón detrás del palen-

7/10   Brandon Grotesque Medium

The quick brown fox jumps over the lazy dog. Voyez le brick géant que j'examine près du wharf. Zwölf Boxkämpfer jagen Viktor quer über den großen Sylter Deich. El veloz murciélago hindú comía feliz cardillo y kiwi. La cigüeña tocaba el saxofón detrás del palenque de pajaatur? Rissimo lorereped ex es solore lab id molorro in rempore icabore rehenetur aliam aut voles audae dem quam, secum eum facesequae

12/14   Brandon Grotesque Bold

**The quick brown fox jumps over the lazy dog. Voyez le brick géant que j'examine près du wharf. Zwölf Boxkämpfer jagen Viktor quer über den großen Sylter Deich. El veloz murciélago hindú comía feliz cardillo y kiwi. La cigüeña tocaba el**

9/12   Brandon Grotesque Bold

**The quick brown fox jumps over the lazy dog. Voyez le brick géant que j'examine près du wharf. Zwölf Boxkämpfer jagen Viktor quer über den großen Sylter Deich. El veloz murciélago hindú comía feliz cardillo y kiwi. La cigüeña tocaba el saxofón detrás del palenque de pajaatur? Rissimo lorereped ex es solore lab id molorro in rempore icabore rehenetur aliam aut voles**

7/10   Brandon Grotesque Bold

**The quick brown fox jumps over the lazy dog. Voyez le brick géant que j'examine près du wharf. Zwölf Boxkämpfer jagen Viktor quer über den großen Sylter Deich. El veloz murciélago hindú comía feliz cardillo y kiwi. La cigüeña tocaba el saxofón detrás del palenque de pajaatur? Rissimo lorereped ex es solore lab id molorro in rempore icabore rehenetur aliam aut voles audae dem quam, secum eum facesequae consequ aepudam quia voluptiur repel in et faccustibus, nonsenis aut quisqui rero mi, ipiet lam ant ut maio et hil molupta**

# J

Jeremy Tankard Typography

—

Jeremy Tankard

—

Cambridge, Great Britain

—

Since 1998

## Info

—People on staff
1

—Type designers on staff
1

—Type families
Approx. 20

—Designers represented
1

—Web shop
typography.net

—Distributors
typography.net
faces.co.uk

—Basic license
£ 125 for most basic packs (2–5 fonts) for max. 5 devices.

## People

—Since graduating from the Royal College of Art Jeremy Tankard has gained a worldwide reputation for the high quality and unique designs of his typefaces. He initially worked with major consultancies, advising and creating typography for some of the best known international brand names. When Jeremy Tankard Typography was established in 1998, the idea was to design new typefaces and offer a service for typographic design to suit clients' own requirements.
From the outset the aim of the company was to create, manufacture and license high quality digital type, whilst always keeping in touch with current standards and techniques.
The typeface collection from JTT includes many internationally recognized typefaces, which are being used around the world for a variety of editorial, publishing and corporate related work. In addition to the standard collection, some companies are benefiting from specially commissioned typefaces.
Jeremy Tankard is a member of the Wynkyn de Worde Society, iSTD and Letter Exchange and has lectured on typography and given workshops at a number of colleges.

## Typeface selection

Jeremy Tankard established his company in 1998 to market his own type designs. The library of typefaces is always expanding and includes several established types such as Bliss, The Shire Types and Aspect. Commissions include bespoke typefaces for Microsoft, Adobe, Arjowiggins, Telstra, Zurich airport, Epsilon, Gameplay and logotypes for Indesit, Iceland, The FA, Emap and Oxford University.

Kingfisher
Redisturbed
Shaker
Shire Types Pro
Trilogy Egyptian
*Trilogy Fatface*
Trilogy Sans

24pt

Jeremy Tankard, pastiches of 19th and 20th-century typographic styles to demonstrate the stylistic scope and precision of his Trilogy type family.

Page 130  Foundry  Jeremy Tankard Typography

Typeface  Shire Types Pro  Year  2011
Designer  Jeremy Tankard  Format  OpenType

# static

DERBYSHIRE
STAFFORDSHIRE
CHESHIRE
SHROPSHIRE
WARWICKSHIRE
WORCESTERSHIRE

Aa Bb Cc Dd Ee Ff Gg Hh
Ii Jj Kk Ll Mm Nn Oo Pp
Qq Rr Ss Tt Uu Vv Ww Xx
Yy Zz 0123456789

Typeface  Trilogy Egyptian  Year  2009
Designer  Jeremy Tankard  Format  OpenType

# balance

Bold to **Heavy**
Regular to **Expanded**
Roman and *Italic*

Aa Bb Cc Dd Ee Ff Gg Hh Ii
Jj Kk Ll Mm Nn Oo Pp Qq Rr
Ss Tt Uu Vv Ww Xx Yy Zz
0123456789

Typeface  Trilogy Fatface  Year  2009
Designer  Jeremy Tankard  Format  OpenType

# *rhythm*

*Regular*
*Wide*
*Expanded*
*ExtraExpanded*
*UltraExpanded*

*Aa Bb Cc Dd Ee Ff Gg Hh
Ii Jj Kk Ll Mm Nn Oo Pp
Qq Rr Ss Tt Uu Vv Ww Xx
Yy Zz 0123456789*

Typeface Trilogy Sans
Designer Jeremy Tankard
Year 2009
Format OpenType

# Aa

Aaɑ Bb Cc Dd Ee Ff
Ggg Hh Ii Jj Kk Lll Mm
Nn Oo Pp Qqq Rr Ss Tt
Uuu Vv Ww Xx Yy Zz
001123456789

Trilogy Sans Thin Compressed 18pt
*Trilogy Sans Thin Compressed Italic 18pt*
Trilogy Sans Light Condensed 18pt
*Trilogy Sans Light Condensed Italic 18pt*
Trilogy Sans Regular 18pt
*Trilogy Sans Italic 18pt*
**Trilogy Sans Bold 18pt**
***Trilogy Sans Bold Italic 18pt***
**Trilogy Sans ExtraBold Wide 18pt**
***Trilogy Sans ExtraBold Wide Italic 18pt***
**Trilogy Sans Heavy Expanded 18pt**
***Trilogy Sans Heavy Expanded Italic***

---

12/14 Trilogy Sans Condensed

The quick brown fox jumps over the lazy dog. Voyez le brick géant que j'examine près du wharf. Zwölf Boxkämpfer jagen Viktor quer über den großen Sylter Deich.

9/12 Trilogy Sans Condensed

The quick brown fox jumps over the lazy dog. Voyez le brick géant que j'examine près du wharf. Zwölf Boxkämpfer jagen Viktor quer über den großen Sylter Deich. El veloz murciélago hindú comía feliz cardillo y kiwi. La cigüeña tocaba el saxofón detrás del palenque de

7/10 Trilogy Sans Condensed

The quick brown fox jumps over the lazy dog. Voyez le brick géant que j'examine près du wharf. Zwölf Boxkämpfer jagen Viktor quer über den großen Sylter Deich. El veloz murciélago hindú comía feliz cardillo y kiwi. La cigüeña tocaba el saxofón detrás del palenque de pajaatur? Rissimo lorereped ex es solore lab id molorro in rempore icabore rehenetur aliam aut voles audae dem quam, secum eum facesequae consequ aepudam

12/14 Trilogy Sans Wide

The quick brown fox jumps over the lazy dog. Voyez le brick géant que j'examine près du wharf. Zwölf Boxkämpfer jagen Viktor

9/12 Trilogy Sans Wide

The quick brown fox jumps over the lazy dog. Voyez le brick géant que j'examine près du wharf. Zwölf Boxkämpfer jagen Viktor quer über den großen Sylter Deich. El veloz murciélago hindú comía feliz cardillo y kiwi.

7/10 Trilogy Sans Wide

The quick brown fox jumps over the lazy dog. Voyez le brick géant que j'examine près du wharf. Zwölf Boxkämpfer jagen Viktor quer über den großen Sylter Deich. El veloz murciélago hindú comía feliz cardillo y kiwi. La cigüeña tocaba el saxofón detrás del palenque de pajaatur? Rissimo lorereped ex es solore lab id molorro

12/14 Trilogy Sans Regular

The quick brown fox jumps over the lazy dog. Voyez le brick géant que j'examine près du wharf. Zwölf Boxkämpfer jagen Viktor quer über den großen Sylter Deich. El veloz murciélago hindú comía feliz cardillo y kiwi.

9/12 Trilogy Sans Regular

The quick brown fox jumps over the lazy dog. Voyez le brick géant que j'examine près du wharf. Zwölf Boxkämpfer jagen Viktor quer über den großen Sylter Deich. El veloz murciélago hindú comía feliz cardillo y kiwi. La cigüeña tocaba el saxofón detrás del palenque de pajaatur? Rissimo lorereped ex es solore lab id molorro in rempore icabore rehene-

7/10 Trilogy Sans Regular

The quick brown fox jumps over the lazy dog. Voyez le brick géant que j'examine près du wharf. Zwölf Boxkämpfer jagen Viktor quer über den großen Sylter Deich. El veloz murciélago hindú comía feliz cardillo y kiwi. La cigüeña tocaba el saxofón detrás del palenque de pajaatur? Rissimo lorereped ex es solore lab id molorro in rempore icabore rehenetur aliam aut voles audae dem quam, secum eum facesequae consequ aepudam quia voluptiur repel in et faccustibus, nonsenis aut quisqui rero mi, ipiet lam ant

12/14 Trilogy Sans Bold

**The quick brown fox jumps over the lazy dog. Voyez le brick géant que j'examine près du wharf. Zwölf Boxkämpfer jagen Viktor quer über den großen Sylter Deich. El veloz murciélago hindú comía feliz cardillo y kiwi. La cigüeña tocaba el saxofón detrás**

9/12 Trilogy Sans Bold

**The quick brown fox jumps over the lazy dog. Voyez le brick géant que j'examine près du wharf. Zwölf Boxkämpfer jagen Viktor quer über den großen Sylter Deich. El veloz murciélago hindú comía feliz cardillo y kiwi. La cigüeña tocaba el saxofón detrás del palenque de pajaatur? Rissimo lorereped ex es solore lab id molorro in rempore icabore rehenetur aliam aut voles audae dem**

7/10 Trilogy Sans Bold

**The quick brown fox jumps over the lazy dog. Voyez le brick géant que j'examine près du wharf. Zwölf Boxkämpfer jagen Viktor quer über den großen Sylter Deich. El veloz murciélago hindú comía feliz cardillo y kiwi. La cigüeña tocaba el saxofón detrás del palenque de pajaatur? Rissimo lorereped ex es solore lab id molorro in rempore icabore rehenetur aliam aut voles audae dem quam, secum eum facesequae consequ aepudam quia voluptiur repel in et faccustibus, nonsenis aut quisqui rero mi, ipiet lam ant ut maio et hil molupta tustis atatur, consedi**

| | |
|---|---|
| Page | 132 |
| Foundry | Jeremy Tankard Typography |
| Typeface | Shaker |
| Designer | Jeremy Tankard |
| Year | 2000 |
| Format | OpenType |

# Aa

Aa Bb Cc Dd Ee Ff Gg Hh Ii Jj Kk
Ll Mm Nn Oo Pp Qq Rr Ss Tt Uu
Vv Ww Xx Yy Zz
0123456789

Shaker Light Condensed 24pt
*Shaker Light Condensed Italic* 24pt
Shaker Regular 24pt
*Shaker Italic* 24pt
**Shaker Bold** 24pt
***Shaker Bold Italic*** 24pt
**Shaker ExtraBold** 24pt
***Shaker ExtraBold Italic*** 24pt
**Shaker Heavy Wide** 24pt
***Shaker Heavy Wide Italic*** 24pt

---

**12/14 — Shaker Light Condensed**

The quick brown fox jumps over the lazy dog. Voyez le brick géant que j'examine près du wharf. Zwölf Boxkämpfer jagen Viktor quer über den großen Sylter Deich. El veloz murciélago hindú

**12/14 — Shaker Heavy Wide**

**The quick brown fox jumps over the lazy dog. Voyez le brick géant que j'examine près du wharf. Zwölf Boxkämpfer jagen Vik-**

**12/14 — Shaker Regular**

The quick brown fox jumps over the lazy dog. Voyez le brick géant que j'examine près du wharf. Zwölf Boxkämpfer jagen Viktor quer über den großen Sylter Deich. El veloz murciélago hindú comía feliz cardillo y kiwi. La cigüeña tocaba el saxofón

**12/14 — Shaker Bold**

**The quick brown fox jumps over the lazy dog. Voyez le brick géant que j'examine près du wharf. Zwölf Boxkämpfer jagen Viktor quer über den großen Sylter Deich. El veloz murciélago hindú comía feliz cardillo y kiwi. La cigüeña tocaba el saxofón detrás del pa-**

---

**9/12 — Shaker Light Condensed**

The quick brown fox jumps over the lazy dog. Voyez le brick géant que j'examine près du wharf. Zwölf Boxkämpfer jagen Viktor quer über den großen Sylter Deich. El veloz murciélago hindú comía feliz cardillo y kiwi. La cigüeña tocaba el saxofón detrás del palenque de pajaatur? Rissimo lorereped ex es solore lab id

**9/12 — Shaker Heavy Wide**

**The quick brown fox jumps over the lazy dog. Voyez le brick géant que j'examine près du wharf. Zwölf Boxkämpfer jagen Viktor quer über den großen Sylter Deich. El veloz murciélago hindú comía feliz cardillo y kiwi.**

**9/12 — Shaker Regular**

The quick brown fox jumps over the lazy dog. Voyez le brick géant que j'examine près du wharf. Zwölf Boxkämpfer jagen Viktor quer über den großen Sylter Deich. El veloz murciélago hindú comía feliz cardillo y kiwi. La cigüeña tocaba el saxofón detrás del palenque de pajaatur? Rissimo lorereped ex es solore lab id molorro in rempore icabore rehenetur aliam aut voles audae dem

**9/12 — Shaker Bold**

**The quick brown fox jumps over the lazy dog. Voyez le brick géant que j'examine près du wharf. Zwölf Boxkämpfer jagen Viktor quer über den großen Sylter Deich. El veloz murciélago hindú comía feliz cardillo y kiwi. La cigüeña tocaba el saxofón detrás del palenque de pajaatur? Rissimo lorereped ex es solore lab id molorro in rempore icabore rehenetur aliam aut voles audae dem quam, secum eum**

---

**7/10 — Shaker Light Condensed**

The quick brown fox jumps over the lazy dog. Voyez le brick géant que j'examine près du wharf. Zwölf Boxkämpfer jagen Viktor quer über den großen Sylter Deich. El veloz murciélago hindú comía feliz cardillo y kiwi. La cigüeña tocaba el saxofón detrás del palenque de pajaatur? Rissimo lorereped ex es solore lab id molorro in rempore icabore rehenetur aliam aut voles audae dem quam, secum eum facesequae consequ aepudam quia voluptiur repel in et faccustibus, nonsenis aut quisqui rero

**7/10 — Shaker Heavy Wide**

**The quick brown fox jumps over the lazy dog. Voyez le brick géant que j'examine près du wharf. Zwölf Boxkämpfer jagen Viktor quer über den großen Sylter Deich. El veloz murciélago hindú comía feliz cardillo y kiwi. La cigüeña tocaba el saxofón detrás del palenque de pajaatur? Rissimo lorereped ex es solore lab id molorro**

**7/10 — Shaker Regular**

The quick brown fox jumps over the lazy dog. Voyez le brick géant que j'examine près du wharf. Zwölf Boxkämpfer jagen Viktor quer über den großen Sylter Deich. El veloz murciélago hindú comía feliz cardillo y kiwi. La cigüeña tocaba el saxofón detrás del palenque de pajaatur? Rissimo lorereped ex es solore lab id molorro in rempore icabore rehenetur aliam aut voles audae dem quam, secum eum facesequae consequ aepudam quia voluptiur repel in et faccustibus, nonsenis aut quisqui rero mi, ipiet lam ant ut maio et hil molupta tustis atatur, consedi tasimol orerem aut

**7/10 — Shaker Bold**

**The quick brown fox jumps over the lazy dog. Voyez le brick géant que j'examine près du wharf. Zwölf Boxkämpfer jagen Viktor quer über den großen Sylter Deich. El veloz murciélago hindú comía feliz cardillo y kiwi. La cigüeña tocaba el saxofón detrás del palenque de pajaatur? Rissimo lorereped ex es solore lab id molorro in rempore icabore rehenetur aliam aut voles audae dem quam, secum eum facesequae consequ aepudam quia voluptiur repel in et faccustibus, nonsenis aut quisqui rero mi, ipiet lam ant ut maio et hil molupta tustis atatur, consedi tasimol orerem aut volor andipsapis sit, illaut**

Foundry Jeremy Tankard Typography

Typeface Kingfisher
Designer Jeremy Tankard
Year 2005
Format OpenType

# Aa

Aa Bb Cc Dd Ee Ff Gg Hh Ii Jj Kk
Ll Mm Nn Oo Pp Qq Rr Ss Tt Uu
Vv Ww Xx Yy Zz
0123456789

Kingfisher Display 20pt
*Kingfisher Display Italic 20pt*
Kingfisher Regular 20pt
*Kingfisher Italic 20pt*
**Kingfisher Bold 20pt**
***Kingfisher Bold Italic 20pt***
**Kingfisher Heavy 20pt**
***Kingfisher Heavy Italic 20pt***

---

12/14 Kingfisher Regular

The quick brown fox jumps over the lazy dog. Voyez le brick géant que j'examine près du wharf. Zwölf Boxkämpfer jagen Viktor quer über den

9/12 Kingfisher Regular

The quick brown fox jumps over the lazy dog. Voyez le brick géant que j'examine près du wharf. Zwölf Boxkämpfer jagen Viktor quer über den großen Sylter Deich. El veloz murciélago hindú comía feliz cardillo y kiwi. La cigüeña tocaba el saxofón

7/10 Kingfisher Regular

The quick brown fox jumps over the lazy dog. Voyez le brick géant que j'examine près du wharf. Zwölf Boxkämpfer jagen Viktor quer über den großen Sylter Deich. El veloz murciélago hindú comía feliz cardillo y kiwi. La cigüeña tocaba el saxofón detrás del palenque de pajaatur? Rissimo lorereped ex es solore lab id molorro in rempore icabore rehenetur aliam aut voles audae dem

---

Typeface Redisturbed
Designer Jeremy Tankard
Year 2010
Format OpenType

# aa

abcdefghijklmn
opqrstuvwxyz
0123456789

five weights 20pt
two styles 20pt
four optical sizes 20pt

9/12 Redisturbed Regular

the quick brown fox jumps over the lazy dog. voyez le brick géant que j'examine près du wharf. zwölf boxkämpfer jagen viktor quer über den großen sylter deich. el veloz murciélago hindú comía feliz cardillo y kiwi. la cigüeña tocaba el saxofón detrás del palenque de pajaatur? rissimo

9/12 Redisturbed Italic

*the quick brown fox jumps over the lazy dog. voyez le brick géant que j'examine près du wharf. zwölf boxkämpfer jagen viktor quer über den großen sylter deich. el veloz murciélago hindú comía feliz cardillo y kiwi. la cigüeña tocaba el saxofón detrás del palenque de pajaatur? rissimo lorereped ex es*

9/12 Redisturbed Bold

**the quick brown fox jumps over the lazy dog. voyez le brick géant que j'examine près du wharf. zwölf boxkämpfer jagen viktor quer über den großen sylter deich. el veloz murciélago hindú comía feliz cardillo y kiwi. la cigüeña tocaba el saxofón detrás del palenque de pajaatur? rissimo**

9/12 Redisturbed Bold Italic

***the quick brown fox jumps over the lazy dog. voyez le brick géant que j'examine près du wharf. zwölf boxkämpfer jagen viktor quer über den großen sylter deich. el veloz murciélago hindú comía feliz cardillo y kiwi. la cigüeña tocaba el saxofón detrás del palenque de pajaatur? rissimo***

# J

## Just Another Foundry

—

Tim Ahrens,
Shoko Mugikura

—

London, UK

—

Since
2010

Just Another Foundry started off as a one-man project. Recently, JAF has also published fonts designed in collaboration with Brian Jaramillo and with Shoko Mugikura. Since May 2010, JAF has been offering its fonts as one of the first webfont services.

## Info

—Why?
The foundry was started up to publish Tim Ahrens' designs while having full control over font production, marketing and finances. The foundry's size and independence makes it easier to react to new technological developments quickly.

—People on staff
2

—Type designers on staff
2

—Type families
7

—Designers represented
3

—Web shop
www.justanotherfoundry.com/buy

—Distributors
MyFonts, FontShop, Fonts.com

—Webfont services
Just Another Foundry webfont service, Typekit

—Basic license
Single fonts: $29–$49
Families: $99–$349
Basic license for 5 computers

Typeface selection

DOMUS TITLING
Facit
Herß
Lapture

24pt

## People

—Tim Ahrens studied architecture at the University of Karlsruhe, Germany, and holds an MA in Typeface Design from the University of Reading. His first type design, Aroma, was published in 2000 by Linotype. He is also known for his programming projects such as the Font Remix Tools, and research and writing about font related matters. He has given talks at ATypI conferences, Robothon, Typo CPH Copenhagen, Munich Webfontday and Typo Berlin.

—Shoko Mugikura studied Visual Communication Design at Musashino Art University in Tokyo and gained an MA in Book Design from the University of Reading. Her special interest is the historical development of multi script (Japanese and European) typography, on which she has spoken at the ICHILL5 (Oxford University) and the ATypI. Since spring 2010, she has been jointly running JAF, while she continues to work as a graphic designer.

Monika Grzymala, *Up There Up Here*, art catalog, detail of the cover. Designed by Kaune & Hardwig, Berlin, using JAF Facit. Dian Woodner Collection, 2011.

Page 135

Monika Grzymala, *Up There Up Here*, art catalog. Designed by Kaune & Hardwig, Berlin, using JAF Facit. Dian Woodner Collection, 2011.

Foundry  Just Another Foundry

---

Typeface  Lapture
Designer  Tim Ahrens

Year    2004
Format  OpenType

# Aa

Lapture Regular 20pt
*Lapture Italic* 20pt
**Lapture Semi Bold** 20pt
***Lapture Semi Bold Italic*** 20pt
**Lapture Bold** 20pt
***Lapture Bold Italic*** 20pt

Aa Bb Cc Dd Ee Ff Gg Hh Ii Jj Kk Ll Mm Nn Oo Pp Qq Rr Ss Tt Uu Vv Ww Xx Yy Zz
0123456789
—

9/12  Lapture Regular

The quick brown fox jumps over the lazy dog. Voyez le brick géant que j'examine près du wharf. Zwölf Boxkämpfer jagen Viktor quer über den großen Sylter Deich. El veloz murciélago hindú comía feliz cardillo y kiwi. La cigüeña tocaba el saxofón detrás del palenque de pajaatur? Rissimo lorereped ex es solore lab id molorro in rempore icabore rehenetur aliam aut

7/10  Lapture Regular

The quick brown fox jumps over the lazy dog. Voyez le brick géant que j'examine près du wharf. Zwölf Boxkämpfer jagen Viktor quer über den großen Sylter Deich. El veloz murciélago hindú comía feliz cardillo y kiwi. La cigüeña tocaba el saxofón detrás del palenque de pajaatur? Rissimo lorereped ex es solore lab id molorro in rempore icabore rehenetur aliam aut voles audae dem quam, secum eum facesequae consequ aepudam quia voluptiur repel in et faccustibus, nonsenis aut quisqui rero mi, ipiet lam ant ut maio et hil molupta tustis

---

Typeface  Domus Titling
Designer  Shoko Mugikura
          Tim Ahrens

Year    2011
Format  OpenType

ROMAN HOME

EXTRA LIGHT

AA BB CC DD EE FF GG HH II JJ KK LL MM NN OO PP QQ RR SS TT UU VV WW XX YY ZZ 0123456789

---

Typeface  Herb
Designer  Tim Ahrens

Year    2010
Format  OpenType

a bitterer Lager

Regular
Bold
Condensed Regular
Condensed Bold

Aa Bb Cc Dd Ee Ff Gg Hh Ii Jj Kk Ll Mm Nn Oo Pp Qq Rr Ss Tt Uu Vv Ww Xx Yy Zz 0123456789

| | | | |
|---|---|---|---|
| Typeface | Facit | Year | 2005 |
| Designer | Tim Ahrens | Format | OpenType |

# Aa

Aa Bb Cc Dd Ee Ff Gg Hh Ii Jj Kk Ll Mm Nn Oo Pp Qq Rr Ss Tt Uu Vv Ww Xx Yy Zz
0123456789
—

Facit Extra Light 22pt
*Facit ExtraLight Italic 22pt*
Facit Light 22pt
*Facit Light Italic 22pt*
Facit Regular 22pt
*Facit Italic 22pt*
**Facit SemiBold 22pt**
***Facit SemiBold Italic 22pt***
**Facit Bold 22pt**
***Facit Bold Italic 22pt***
**Facit ExtraBold 22pt**
***Facit ExtraBold Italic 22pt***

---

**12/14 Facit Light**

The quick brown fox jumps over the lazy dog. Voyez le brick géant que j'examine près du wharf. Zwölf Boxkämpfer jagen Viktor quer über den

**12/14 Facit Regular**

The quick brown fox jumps over the lazy dog. Voyez le brick géant que j'examine près du wharf. Zwölf Boxkämpfer jagen Viktor quer über den

**12/14 Facit SemiBold**

The quick brown fox jumps over the lazy dog. Voyez le brick géant que j'examine près du wharf. Zwölf Boxkämpfer jagen Viktor quer über den

**12/14 Facit Bold**

The quick brown fox jumps over the lazy dog. Voyez le brick géant que j'examine près du wharf. Zwölf Boxkämpfer jagen Viktor quer über den großen Sylter Deich. El veloz murciélago hindú comía feliz cardillo y

**9/12 Facit Light**

The quick brown fox jumps over the lazy dog. Voyez le brick géant que j'examine près du wharf. Zwölf Boxkämpfer jagen Viktor quer über den großen Sylter Deich. El veloz murciélago hindú comía feliz cardillo y kiwi. La cigüeña tocaba el

**9/12 Facit Regular**

The quick brown fox jumps over the lazy dog. Voyez le brick géant que j'examine près du wharf. Zwölf Boxkämpfer jagen Viktor quer über den großen Sylter Deich. El veloz murciélago hindú comía feliz cardillo y kiwi. La cigüeña tocaba

**9/12 Facit SemiBold**

The quick brown fox jumps over the lazy dog. Voyez le brick géant que j'examine près du wharf. Zwölf Boxkämpfer jagen Viktor quer über den großen Sylter Deich. El veloz murciélago hindú comía feliz cardillo y kiwi. La cigüeña tocaba

**9/12 Facit Bold**

The quick brown fox jumps over the lazy dog. Voyez le brick géant que j'examine près du wharf. Zwölf Boxkämpfer jagen Viktor quer über den großen Sylter Deich. El veloz murciélago hindú comía feliz cardillo y kiwi. La cigüeña tocaba el saxofón detrás del palenque de pajaatur? Rissimo lorereped ex es solore lab id

**7/10 Facit Light**

The quick brown fox jumps over the lazy dog. Voyez le brick géant que j'examine près du wharf. Zwölf Boxkämpfer jagen Viktor quer über den großen Sylter Deich. El veloz murciélago hindú comía feliz cardillo y kiwi. La cigüeña tocaba el saxofón detrás del palenque de pajaatur? Rissimo lorereped ex es solore lab id molorro in rempore icabore rehenetur aliam aut voles

**7/10 Facit Regular**

The quick brown fox jumps over the lazy dog. Voyez le brick géant que j'examine près du wharf. Zwölf Boxkämpfer jagen Viktor quer über den großen Sylter Deich. El veloz murciélago hindú comía feliz cardillo y kiwi. La cigüeña tocaba el saxofón detrás del palenque de pajaatur? Rissimo lorereped ex es solore lab id molorro in rempore icabore rehenetur aliam aut voles

**7/10 Facit SemiBold**

The quick brown fox jumps over the lazy dog. Voyez le brick géant que j'examine près du wharf. Zwölf Boxkämpfer jagen Viktor quer über den großen Sylter Deich. El veloz murciélago hindú comía feliz cardillo y kiwi. La cigüeña tocaba el saxofón detrás del palenque de pajaatur? Rissimo lorereped ex es solore lab id molorro in rempore icabore rehenetur aliam aut voles

**7/10 Facit Bold**

The quick brown fox jumps over the lazy dog. Voyez le brick géant que j'examine près du wharf. Zwölf Boxkämpfer jagen Viktor quer über den großen Sylter Deich. El veloz murciélago hindú comía feliz cardillo y kiwi. La cigüeña tocaba el saxofón detrás del palenque de pajaatur? Rissimo lorereped ex es solore lab id molorro in rempore icabore rehenetur aliam aut voles audae dem quam, secum eum facesequae consequ aepudam quia voluptiur repel in et faccustibus, nonsenis aut quis-

# K

## Kimera Type Foundry

—

Gabriel Martínez Meave

—

Mexico City, Mexico

—

Since 1994

Kimera is the personal type foundry of Mexican type designer, calligrapher, lettering artist and illustrator Gabriel Martínez Meave.

## Info

—Why?
Kimera Type Foundry started as a side business for my graphic design studio Kimera. I have always loved original typography and KTF was a way to develop this passion, and make it a characteristic feature of our work. Since then, we have designed original fonts and wide-ranging custom type projects for many clients.

—People on staff
1

—Type designers on staff
1

—Type families
25

—Designers represented
1

—Web shop
None

—Distributors
Adobe Systems, FontShop

—Webfont services
None

—Basic license
From $25 upwards for a single CPU

## People

—Gabriel Martínez Meave is a Mexican graphic and typographic designer, illustrator, calligrapher and author working in Mexico City. He is the founder and principal of Kimera studio. He has received numerous design awards, including five from the Type Directors Club of New York and two from the Association Typographique Internationale (ATypI). He also won the first prize at the 2001 National Design Biennial in Mexico, as well as the a!Diseño award in Typography in 2002, 2003 and 2008. His work at Kimera has been shown in several exhibitions and reviewed in many international design magazines and books. He was selected as one of 100 important emerging designers for the book *Area2* by Phaidon. Gabriel designed the official type system for the Mexican government, now in use. He has given lectures and workshops in the USA, Latin America and Spain. He is professor at the Universidad Anahuac in Mexico City, and a member of the ATypI and the Type Directors Club of New York.

—Isaías Loaiza and José Luis Acosta, both Mexican graphic and type designers, have collaborated with Gabriel in some KTF type projects.

## Typeface selection

Arcana
**Aztlan**
Darka
Integra
Mexica
Organica
Rondana

24pt

Page 139

Gabriel Martínez Meave,
Neruda Poster

Promotional postcard
Basilica

**Left and right**
Gabriel Martínez Meave,
sketch for Lagarto.

Gabriel Martínez Meave, Futboltecatl.
Poster dedicated to the imaginary
Mexican god of soccer.

Foundry  Kimera Type Foundry

---

Typeface  Arcana
Designer  Gabriel Martínez Meave
Year  1997–2000
Format  OpenType

*La Escritura Personal*

Angular Standard
Curvilinear Alternate

Aa Bb Cc Dd Ee Ff Gg Hh Ii
Jj Kk Ll Mm Nn Oo Pp Qq
Rr Ss Tt Uu Vv Ww Xx Yy Zz
0123456789

---

Typeface  Darka
Designer  Gabriel Martínez Meave
Year  2006
Format  OpenType

*Mi Rubia*

Regular

Aa Bb Cc Dd Ee Ff Gg Hh Ii
Jj Kk Ll Mm Nn Oo Pp Qq
Rr Ss Tt Uu Vv Ww Xx Yy
Zz 0123456789

---

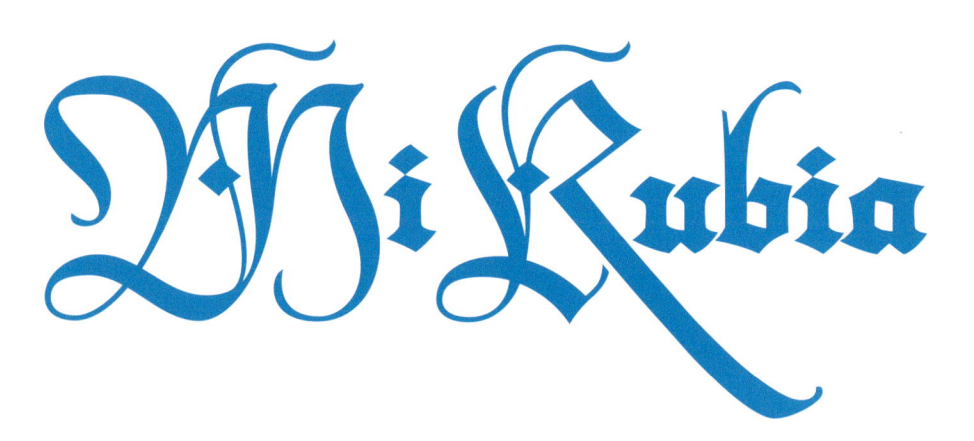

Typeface  Aztlan
Designer  Gabriel Martínez Meave
Year  1996–2002
Format  OpenType

**La Isla Aztlán**

Regular

Aa Bb Cc Dd Ee Ff
Gg Hh Ii Jj Kk Ll
Mm Nn Oo Pp Qq Rr
Ss Tt Uu Vv Ww Xx
Yy Zz 0123456789

Foundry   Kimera Type Foundry

Typeface   Organica
Designer   Gabriel Martínez Meave
Year   1996–2002
Format   OpenType

# Aa

Aa Bb Cc Dd Ee Ff Gg Hh Ii Jj
Kk Ll Mm Nn Oo Pp Qq Rr Ss
Tt Uu Vv Ww Xx Yy Zz
0123456789

Organica Roman 20pt
*Organica Italic 20pt*
**Organica Bold 20pt**
***Organica Bold Italic 20pt***
**Organica Black 20pt**
***Organica Black Italic 20pt***

9/12   Organica Roman

The quick brown fox jumps over the lazy dog. Voyez le brick géant que j'examine près du wharf. Zwölf Boxkämpfer jagen Viktor quer über den großen Sylter Deich. El veloz murciélago hindú comía feliz cardillo y kiwi. La cigüeña tocaba el saxofón detrás del palenque de pajaatur? Rissimo lorereped ex es solore lab id molorro in rempore icabore rehenetur aliam aut voles

7/10   Organica Roman

The quick brown fox jumps over the lazy dog. Voyez le brick géant que j'examine près du wharf. Zwölf Boxkämpfer jagen Viktor quer über den großen Sylter Deich. El veloz murciélago hindú comía feliz cardillo y kiwi. La cigüeña tocaba el saxofón detrás del palenque de pajaatur? Rissimo lorereped ex es solore lab id molorro in rempore icabore rehenetur aliam aut voles audae dem quam, secum eum facesequae consequ aepudam quia voluptiur repel in et faccustibus, nonsenis aut quisqui rero mi, ipiet lam ant ut maio et hil molupta tustis atatur, consedi tasimol orerem aut volor

---

Typeface   Integra
Designer   Gabriel Martínez Meave
Year   1996–2002
Format   OpenType

# Aa

Aa Bb Cc Dd Ee Ff Gg Hh Ii Jj
Kk Ll Mm Nn Oo Pp Qq Rr Ss
Tt Uu Vv Ww Xx Yy Zz
0123456789

Integra Roman 20pt
*Integra Italic 20pt*
**Integra Bold 20pt**
***Integra Bold Italic 20pt***
**Integra Black 20pt**
***Integra Black Italic 20pt***

9/12   Integra Roman

The quick brown fox jumps over the lazy dog. Voyez le brick géant que j'examine près du wharf. Zwölf Boxkämpfer jagen Viktor quer über den großen Sylter Deich. El veloz murciélago hindú comía feliz cardillo y kiwi. La cigüeña tocaba el saxofón detrás del palenque de pajaatur? Rissimo lorereped ex es solore lab id molorro in rempore icabore rehenetur aliam aut voles audae dem quam, secum eum facesequae consequ aepudam quia voluptiur repel in et faccustibus, nonsenis aut quisqui rero mi, ipiet lam ant ut maio et hil molupta tustis atatur, consedi tasimol orerem aut volor

7/10   Integra Roman

The quick brown fox jumps over the lazy dog. Voyez le brick géant que j'examine près du wharf. Zwölf Boxkämpfer jagen Viktor quer über den großen Sylter Deich. El veloz murciélago hindú comía feliz cardillo y kiwi. La cigüeña tocaba el saxofón detrás del palenque de pajaatur? Rissimo lorereped ex es solore lab id molorro in rempore icabore rehenetur aliam aut voles audae dem quam, secum eum facesequae consequ aepudam quia voluptiur repel in et faccustibus, nonsenis aut quisqui rero mi, ipiet lam ant ut maio et hil molupta tustis atatur, consedi tasimol orerem aut volor andipsapis sit, illaut volore officatus alicae dusdaec tatecte cearum qui accatibus restiore nulpa secaerferum, nus dolenim in et quoditat que explam volupictur? Qui de illuptae. Dae nis illiberum volorro ritatis tinullo rerumqu atetur repro eatius asperibus. Rissimo lorereped ex es solore lab id molorro in rempore icabore

Typeface  Mexica
Designer  Gabriel Martínez Meave
Foundry  Kimera Type Foundry
Year  1997–2002
Format  OpenType

# Aa

Mexica Roman 24pt
*Mexica Italic* 24pt
**Mexica Bold** 24pt
***Mexica Bold Italic*** 24pt
**Mexica Black** 24pt
***Mexica Black Italic*** 24pt

Aa Bb Cc Dd Ee Ff Gg Hh Ii Jj Kk Ll Mm Nn Oo Pp Qq Rr Ss Tt Uu Vv Ww Xx Yy Zz
0123456789

---

12/14  Mexica Roman

The quick brown fox jumps over the lazy dog. Voyez le brick géant que j'examine près du wharf. Zwölf Boxkämpfer jagen Viktor quer über den großen Sylter Deich. El veloz murciélago hindú comía feliz cardillo y kiwi. La cigüeña tocaba el saxofón detrás del palenque de pajaatur? Rissimo lorereped ex es solore

9/12  Mexica Roman

The quick brown fox jumps over the lazy dog. Voyez le brick géant que j'examine près du wharf. Zwölf Boxkämpfer jagen Viktor quer über den großen Sylter Deich. El veloz murciélago hindú comía feliz cardillo y kiwi. La cigüeña tocaba el saxofón detrás del palenque de pajaatur? Rissimo lorereped ex es solore lab id molorro in rempore icabore rehenetur aliam aut voles audae dem quam, secum eum facesequae consequ aepudam quia voluptiur repel in et faccustibus, nonsenis aut quisqui rero

7/10  Mexica Roman

The quick brown fox jumps over the lazy dog. Voyez le brick géant que j'examine près du wharf. Zwölf Boxkämpfer jagen Viktor quer über den großen Sylter Deich. El veloz murciélago hindú comía feliz cardillo y kiwi. La cigüeña tocaba el saxofón detrás del palenque de pajaatur? Rissimo lorereped ex es solore lab id molorro in rempore icabore rehenetur aliam aut voles audae dem quam, secum eum facesequae consequ aepudam quia voluptiur repel in et faccustibus, nonsenis aut quisqui rero mi, ipiet lam ant ut maio et hil molupta tustis atatur, consedi tasimol orerem aut volor andipsapis sit, illaut volore officatus alicae dusdaec tatecte cearum qui accatibus restiore nulpa secaerferum, nus dolenim in et quoditat que explam volupic-

12/14  Mexica Bold

**The quick brown fox jumps over the lazy dog. Voyez le brick géant que j'examine près du wharf. Zwölf Boxkämpfer jagen Viktor quer über den großen Sylter Deich. El veloz murciélago hindú comía feliz cardillo y kiwi. La cigüeña tocaba el saxofón detrás del palenque de pajaatur? Rissimo lorereped ex**

9/12  Mexica Bold

**The quick brown fox jumps over the lazy dog. Voyez le brick géant que j'examine près du wharf. Zwölf Boxkämpfer jagen Viktor quer über den großen Sylter Deich. El veloz murciélago hindú comía feliz cardillo y kiwi. La cigüeña tocaba el saxofón detrás del palenque de pajaatur? Rissimo lorereped ex es solore lab id molorro in rempore icabore rehenetur aliam aut voles audae dem quam, secum eum facesequae consequ aepudam quia voluptiur repel in et faccustibus, nonsenis aut quisqui rero**

7/10  Mexica Bold

**The quick brown fox jumps over the lazy dog. Voyez le brick géant que j'examine près du wharf. Zwölf Boxkämpfer jagen Viktor quer über den großen Sylter Deich. El veloz murciélago hindú comía feliz cardillo y kiwi. La cigüeña tocaba el saxofón detrás del palenque de pajaatur? Rissimo lorereped ex es solore lab id molorro in rempore icabore rehenetur aliam aut voles audae dem quam, secum eum facesequae consequ aepudam quia voluptiur repel in et faccustibus, nonsenis aut quisqui rero mi, ipiet lam ant ut maio et hil molupta tustis atatur, consedi tasimol orerem aut volor andipsapis sit, illaut volore officatus alicae dusdaec tatecte cearum qui accatibus restiore nulpa secaerferum, nus dolenim in et quoditat que explam volupic-**

12/14  Mexica Black

**The quick brown fox jumps over the lazy dog. Voyez le brick géant que j'examine près du wharf. Zwölf Boxkämpfer jagen Viktor quer über den großen Sylter Deich. El veloz murcié-**

9/12  Mexica Black

**The quick brown fox jumps over the lazy dog. Voyez le brick géant que j'examine près du wharf. Zwölf Boxkämpfer jagen Viktor quer über den großen Sylter Deich. El veloz murciélago hindú comía feliz cardillo y kiwi. La cigüeña tocaba el saxofón detrás del palenque de pajaatur? Rissimo**

7/10  Mexica Black

**The quick brown fox jumps over the lazy dog. Voyez le brick géant que j'examine près du wharf. Zwölf Boxkämpfer jagen Viktor quer über den großen Sylter Deich. El veloz murciélago hindú comía feliz cardillo y kiwi. La cigüeña tocaba el saxofón detrás del palenque de pajaatur? Rissimo lorereped ex es solore lab id molorro in rempore icabore rehenetur aliam aut voles audae dem quam, secum eum facesequae conse-**

Page
143

Foundry  Kimera Type Foundry

Typeface  Rondana
Designer  Gabriel Martínez Meave
Year  2002
Format  OpenType

# Aa

Aa Bb Cc Dd Ee Ff Gg Hh Ii Jj
Kk Ll Mm Nn Oo Pp Qq Rr Ss Tt
Uu Vv Ww Xx Yy Zz
0123456789

Rondana UltraLight 20pt
*Rondana UltraLight Italic 20pt*
Rondana Light 20pt
*Rondana Light Italic 20pt*
Rondana Roman 20pt
*Rondana Italic 20pt*
**Rondana Bold 20pt**
***Rondana Bold Italic 20pt***
**Rondana Black 20pt**
***Rondana Black Italic 20pt***
**Rondana UltraBlack 20pt**
***Rondana UltraBlack Italic 20pt***

---

12/14  Rondana UltraLight

The quick brown fox jumps over the lazy dog. Voyez le brick géant que j'examine près du wharf. Zwölf Boxkämpfer jagen Viktor

9/12  Rondana UltraLight

The quick brown fox jumps over the lazy dog. Voyez le brick géant que j'examine près du wharf. Zwölf Boxkämpfer jagen Viktor quer über den großen Sylter Deich. El veloz murciélago hindú comía feliz cardillo y kiwi.

7/10  Rondana UltraLight

The quick brown fox jumps over the lazy dog. Voyez le brick géant que j'examine près du wharf. Zwölf Boxkämpfer jagen Viktor quer über den großen Sylter Deich. El veloz murciélago hindú comía feliz cardillo y kiwi. La cigüeña tocaba el saxofón detrás del palenque de pajaatur? Rissimo lorereped ex es solore lab id molorro in rempore icabore

12/14  Rondana Light

The quick brown fox jumps over the lazy dog. Voyez le brick géant que j'examine près du wharf. Zwölf Boxkämpfer jagen Viktor

9/12  Rondana Light

The quick brown fox jumps over the lazy dog. Voyez le brick géant que j'examine près du wharf. Zwölf Boxkämpfer jagen Viktor quer über den großen Sylter Deich. El veloz murciélago hindú comía feliz cardillo y kiwi.

7/10  Rondana Light

The quick brown fox jumps over the lazy dog. Voyez le brick géant que j'examine près du wharf. Zwölf Boxkämpfer jagen Viktor quer über den großen Sylter Deich. El veloz murciélago hindú comía feliz cardillo y kiwi. La cigüeña tocaba el saxofón detrás del palenque de pajaatur? Rissimo lorereped ex es solore lab id molorro in rempore icabore

12/14  Rondana Roman

The quick brown fox jumps over the lazy dog. Voyez le brick géant que j'examine près du wharf. Zwölf Boxkämpfer jagen Viktor

9/12  Rondana Roman

The quick brown fox jumps over the lazy dog. Voyez le brick géant que j'examine près du wharf. Zwölf Boxkämpfer jagen Viktor quer über den großen Sylter Deich. El veloz murciélago hindú comía feliz cardillo y kiwi. La ci-

7/10  Rondana Roman

The quick brown fox jumps over the lazy dog. Voyez le brick géant que j'examine près du wharf. Zwölf Boxkämpfer jagen Viktor quer über den großen Sylter Deich. El veloz murciélago hindú comía feliz cardillo y kiwi. La cigüeña tocaba el saxofón detrás del palenque de pajaatur? Rissimo lorereped ex es solore lab id molorro in rempore icabore

12/14  Rondana Bold

**The quick brown fox jumps over the lazy dog. Voyez le brick géant que j'examine près du wharf. Zwölf Boxkämpfer jagen Viktor quer über den großen Sylter Deich. El veloz murciélago hindú comía**

9/12  Rondana Bold

**The quick brown fox jumps over the lazy dog. Voyez le brick géant que j'examine près du wharf. Zwölf Boxkämpfer jagen Viktor quer über den großen Sylter Deich. El veloz murciélago hindú comía feliz cardillo y kiwi. La cigüeña tocaba el saxofón detrás del palenque de pajaatur? Rissimo lorereped ex es solore**

7/10  Rondana Bold

**The quick brown fox jumps over the lazy dog. Voyez le brick géant que j'examine près du wharf. Zwölf Boxkämpfer jagen Viktor quer über den großen Sylter Deich. El veloz murciélago hindú comía feliz cardillo y kiwi. La cigüeña tocaba el saxofón detrás del palenque de pajaatur? Rissimo lorereped ex es solore lab id molorro in rempore icabore rehenetur aliam aut voles audae dem quam, secum eum facesequae consequ aepudam quia voluptiur repel in et**

# K
## Klim

Kris Sowersby

Wellington, New Zealand

Since 2007

Klim is the one-man foundry of New Zealand type designer Kris Sowersby. Kim's type library has been described as "a succession of finely crafted typefaces that have been as notable for their range and engagement with typographic history as for their immaculate execution." (Mark Thomson in *Eye*)

## Info

—Why?
It was the only real option. Chester at Village offered to retail my fonts, and I've not looked back.

—People on staff
1

—Type designers on staff
1

—Type families
170

—Designers represented
1

—Web shop
None

—Distributors
Village

—Webfont services
None yet

—Basic license
$50 for a single weight to $600 for the complete Founders Grotesk family.

## People

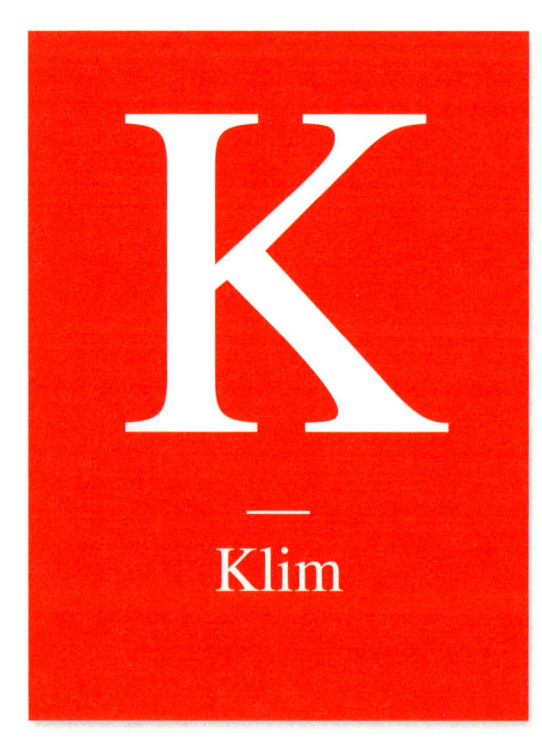

—Kris Sowersby graduated from the Wanganui School of Design in 2003. After brief employment as a graphic designer he started the Klim Type Foundry in 2005, currently based in Wellington, New Zealand. His first retail typeface, Feijoa, was released onto the international market in 2007. National, Sowersby's second retail release, won a Certificate of Excellence from the Type Directors Club, New York in 2008. Since then he has received two more Certificates of Excellence (Serrano, Hardys) and worked on various custom and retail typefaces including FF Meta Serif, the seriffed sibling of the renowned FF Meta. Sowersby's reputation for typeface design has lead to his working with, and for, contemporary typographic luminaries such as Christian Schwartz, Erik Spiekermann, Chester Jenkins, House Industries, DNA Design and Pentagram. In 2010 Sowersby was named an ADC Young Gun. Sowersby's typefaces combine historical knowledge with contemporary craftmanship & finish. The Klim Type Foundry markets its typefaces exclusively through Village.

## Typeface selection

Calibre
Founders Grotesk
Metric
**Tiempos**

24pt

Page
145

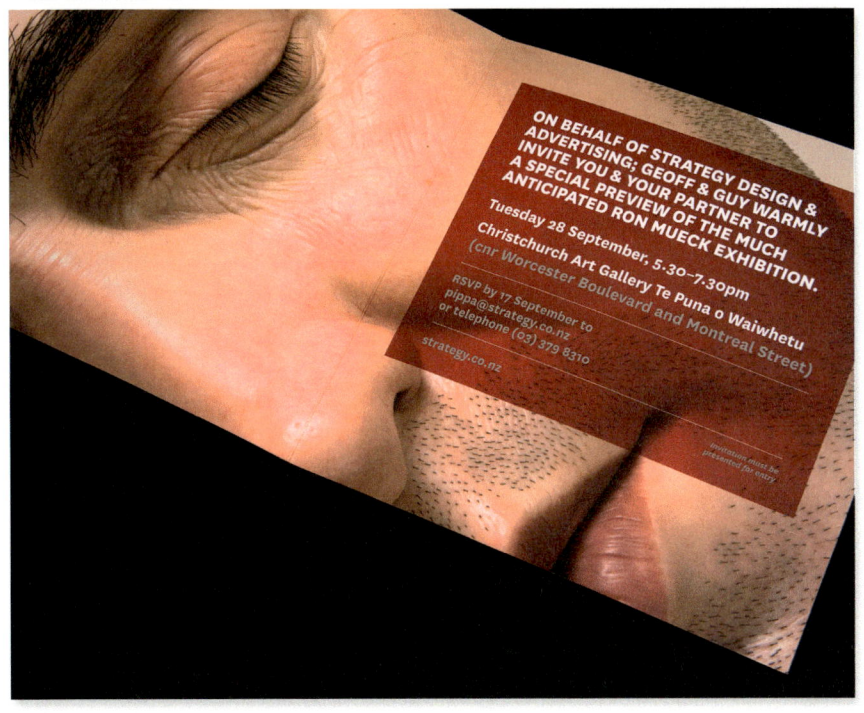

The Christchurch Art Gallery was the only New Zealand venue to host an international exhibition by renowned sculptor Ron Mueck. Christchurch design and advertising agency Strategy created a major publicity campaign using Klim's typeface National. Boldly designed billboards, posters and magazine ads were strategically placed as continual reminders of the show. The campaign helped bring in record numbers with over 135,000 people attending — the gallery's biggest show ever.

| | | | |
|---|---|---|---|
| Typeface | Calibre | Year | 2011 |
| Designer | Kris Sowersby | Format | OpenType |

# Aa

Aa Bb Cc Dd Ee Ff Gg Hh Ii Jj Kk Ll Mm Nn Oo Pp Qq Rr Ss Tt Uu Vv Ww Xx Yy Zz
0123456789

Calibre Thin 22pt
*Calibre Thin Italic 22pt*
Calibre Light 22pt
*Calibre Light Italic 22pt*
Calibre Regular 22pt
*Calibre Regular Italic 22pt*
**Calibre Medium 22pt**
***Calibre Medium Italic 22pt***
**Calibre SemiBold 22pt**
***Calibre SemiBold Italic 22pt***
**Calibre Bold 22pt**
***Calibre Bold Italic 22pt***
**Calibre Black 22pt**
***Calibre Black Italic 22pt***

---

12/14 — Calibre Light

The quick brown fox jumps over the lazy dog. Voyez le brick géant que j'examine près du wharf. Zwölf Boxkämpfer jagen Viktor quer über den großen Sylter Deich.

12/14 — Calibre Regular

The quick brown fox jumps over the lazy dog. Voyez le brick géant que j'examine près du wharf. Zwölf Boxkämpfer jagen Viktor quer über den großen Sylter

12/14 — Calibre Medium

The quick brown fox jumps over the lazy dog. Voyez le brick géant que j'examine près du wharf. Zwölf Boxkämpfer jagen Viktor quer über den großen Sylter

12/14 — Calibre Bold

**The quick brown fox jumps over the lazy dog. Voyez le brick géant que j'examine près du wharf. Zwölf Boxkämpfer jagen Viktor quer über den großen Sylter Deich. El veloz murciélago hindú comía feliz cardillo y kiwi. La**

---

9/12 — Calibre Light

The quick brown fox jumps over the lazy dog. Voyez le brick géant que j'examine près du wharf. Zwölf Boxkämpfer jagen Viktor quer über den großen Sylter Deich. El veloz murciélago hindú comía feliz cardillo y kiwi. La cigüeña tocaba el saxofón detrás del palenque de

9/12 — Calibre Regular

The quick brown fox jumps over the lazy dog. Voyez le brick géant que j'examine près du wharf. Zwölf Boxkämpfer jagen Viktor quer über den großen Sylter Deich. El veloz murciélago hindú comía feliz cardillo y kiwi. La cigüeña tocaba el saxofón detrás del palen-

9/12 — Calibre Medium

The quick brown fox jumps over the lazy dog. Voyez le brick géant que j'examine près du wharf. Zwölf Boxkämpfer jagen Viktor quer über den großen Sylter Deich. El veloz murciélago hindú comía feliz cardillo y kiwi. La cigüeña tocaba el saxofón detrás del

9/12 — Calibre Bold

**The quick brown fox jumps over the lazy dog. Voyez le brick géant que j'examine près du wharf. Zwölf Boxkämpfer jagen Viktor quer über den großen Sylter Deich. El veloz murciélago hindú comía feliz cardillo y kiwi. La cigüeña tocaba el saxofón detrás del palenque de pajaatur? Rissimo lorereped ex es solore lab id molorro in rempore icabore rehene-**

---

7/10 — Calibre Light

The quick brown fox jumps over the lazy dog. Voyez le brick géant que j'examine près du wharf. Zwölf Boxkämpfer jagen Viktor quer über den großen Sylter Deich. El veloz murciélago hindú comía feliz cardillo y kiwi. La cigüeña tocaba el saxofón detrás del palenque de pajaatur? Rissimo lorereped ex es solore lab id molorro in rempore icabore rehenetur aliam aut voles audae dem quam, secum eum facesequae consequ aepudam

7/10 — Calibre Regular

The quick brown fox jumps over the lazy dog. Voyez le brick géant que j'examine près du wharf. Zwölf Boxkämpfer jagen Viktor quer über den großen Sylter Deich. El veloz murciélago hindú comía feliz cardillo y kiwi. La cigüeña tocaba el saxofón detrás del palenque de pajaatur? Rissimo lorereped ex es solore lab id molorro in rempore icabore rehenetur aliam aut voles audae dem quam, secum eum facesequae consequ

7/10 — Calibre Medium

The quick brown fox jumps over the lazy dog. Voyez le brick géant que j'examine près du wharf. Zwölf Boxkämpfer jagen Viktor quer über den großen Sylter Deich. El veloz murciélago hindú comía feliz cardillo y kiwi. La cigüeña tocaba el saxofón detrás del palenque de pajaatur? Rissimo lorereped ex es solore lab id molorro in rempore icabore rehenetur aliam aut voles audae dem quam, secum eum

7/10 — Calibre Bold

**The quick brown fox jumps over the lazy dog. Voyez le brick géant que j'examine près du wharf. Zwölf Boxkämpfer jagen Viktor quer über den großen Sylter Deich. El veloz murciélago hindú comía feliz cardillo y kiwi. La cigüeña tocaba el saxofón detrás del palenque de pajaatur? Rissimo lorereped ex es solore lab id molorro in rempore icabore rehenetur aliam aut voles audae dem quam, secum eum facesequae consequ aepudam quia voluptiur repel in et faccustibus, nonsenis aut quisqui rero mi, ipiet lam ant ut maio et hil molup-**

Page 147

Foundry  Klim

Typeface  Founders Grotesk
Designer  Kris Sowersby
Year  2010
Format  OpenType

# Aa

Aa Bb Cc Dd Ee Ff Gg Hh Ii Jj Kk Ll
Mm Nn Oo Pp Qq Rr Ss Tt Uu Vv Ww
Xx Yy Zz
0123456789
—

Founders Grotesk Light 22pt
*Founders Grotesk Light Italic 22pt*
Founders Grotesk Regular 22pt
*Founders Grotesk Regular Italic 22pt*
**Founders Grotesk Medium 22pt**
***Founders Grotesk Medium Italic 22pt***
**Founders Grotesk SemiBold 22pt**
***Founders Grotesk SemiBold Italic 22pt***
**Founders Grotesk Bold 22pt**
***Founders Grotesk Bold Italic 22pt***

---

12/14  Founders Grotesk Light

The quick brown fox jumps over the lazy dog. Voyez le brick géant que j'examine près du wharf. Zwölf Boxkämpfer jagen Viktor quer über den großen Sylter

12/14  Founders Grotesk Regular

The quick brown fox jumps over the lazy dog. Voyez le brick géant que j'examine près du wharf. Zwölf Boxkämpfer jagen Viktor quer über den großen Sylter

12/14  Founders Grotesk Medium

**The quick brown fox jumps over the lazy dog. Voyez le brick géant que j'examine près du wharf. Zwölf Boxkämpfer jagen Viktor quer über den großen Sylter Deich. El veloz murciéla-**

12/14  Founders Grotesk Bold

**The quick brown fox jumps over the lazy dog. Voyez le brick géant que j'examine près du wharf. Zwölf Boxkämpfer jagen Viktor quer über den großen Sylter Deich. El veloz murciélago hindú comía feliz cardillo y kiwi.**

9/12  Founders Grotesk Light

The quick brown fox jumps over the lazy dog. Voyez le brick géant que j'examine près du wharf. Zwölf Boxkämpfer jagen Viktor quer über den großen Sylter Deich. El veloz murciélago hindú comía feliz cardillo y kiwi. La cigüeña tocaba el saxofón detrás del palenque

9/12  Founders Grotesk Regular

The quick brown fox jumps over the lazy dog. Voyez le brick géant que j'examine près du wharf. Zwölf Boxkämpfer jagen Viktor quer über den großen Sylter Deich. El veloz murciélago hindú comía feliz cardillo y kiwi. La cigüeña tocaba el saxofón detrás del palenque

9/12  Founders Grotesk Medium

**The quick brown fox jumps over the lazy dog. Voyez le brick géant que j'examine près du wharf. Zwölf Boxkämpfer jagen Viktor quer über den großen Sylter Deich. El veloz murciélago hindú comía feliz cardillo y kiwi. La cigüeña tocaba el saxofón detrás**

9/12  Founders Grotesk Bold

**The quick brown fox jumps over the lazy dog. Voyez le brick géant que j'examine près du wharf. Zwölf Boxkämpfer jagen Viktor quer über den großen Sylter Deich. El veloz murciélago hindú comía feliz cardillo y kiwi. La cigüeña tocaba el saxofón detrás del palenque de pajaatur? Rissimo lorereped ex es solore lab id molorro in rempore**

7/10  Founders Grotesk Light

The quick brown fox jumps over the lazy dog. Voyez le brick géant que j'examine près du wharf. Zwölf Boxkämpfer jagen Viktor quer über den großen Sylter Deich. El veloz murciélago hindú comía feliz cardillo y kiwi. La cigüeña tocaba el saxofón detrás del palenque de pajaatur? Rissimo lorereped ex es solore lab id molorro in rempore icabore rehenetur aliam aut voles audae dem quam, secum eum facesequae consequ aepudam quia voluptiur repel in et faccustibus, nonsenis aut quisqui

7/10  Founders Grotesk Regular

The quick brown fox jumps over the lazy dog. Voyez le brick géant que j'examine près du wharf. Zwölf Boxkämpfer jagen Viktor quer über den großen Sylter Deich. El veloz murciélago hindú comía feliz cardillo y kiwi. La cigüeña tocaba el saxofón detrás del palenque de pajaatur? Rissimo lorereped ex es solore lab id molorro in rempore icabore rehenetur aliam aut voles audae dem quam, secum eum

7/10  Founders Grotesk Medium

**The quick brown fox jumps over the lazy dog. Voyez le brick géant que j'examine près du wharf. Zwölf Boxkämpfer jagen Viktor quer über den großen Sylter Deich. El veloz murciélago hindú comía feliz cardillo y kiwi. La cigüeña tocaba el saxofón detrás del palenque de pajaatur? Rissimo lorereped ex es solore lab id molorro in rempore icabore rehenetur aliam aut voles audae dem quam, secum eum**

7/10  Founders Grotesk Bold

**The quick brown fox jumps over the lazy dog. Voyez le brick géant que j'examine près du wharf. Zwölf Boxkämpfer jagen Viktor quer über den großen Sylter Deich. El veloz murciélago hindú comía feliz cardillo y kiwi. La cigüeña tocaba el saxofón detrás del palenque de pajaatur? Rissimo lorereped ex es solore lab id molorro in rempore icabore rehenetur aliam aut voles audae dem quam, secum eum facesequae consequ aepudam quia voluptiur repel in et faccustibus, nonsenis aut quisqui rero**

| | | | |
|---|---|---|---|
| Page | | Foundry | Klim |
| 148 | | | |

| Typeface | Metric | Year | 2011 |
|---|---|---|---|
| Designer | Kris Sowersby | Format | OpenType |

# Aa

Aa Bb Cc Dd Ee Ff Gg Hh Ii Jj Kk Ll Mm Nn Oo Pp Qq Rr Ss Tt Uu Vv Ww Xx Yy Zz
0123456789
—

Metric Thin 22pt
*Metric Thin Italic 22pt*
Metric Light 22pt
*Metric Light Italic 22pt*
Metric Regular 22pt
*Metric Regular Italic 22pt*
**Metric Medium 22pt**
***Metric Medium Italic 22pt***
**Metric SemiBold 22pt**
***Metric SemiBold Italic 22pt***
**Metric Bold 22pt**
***Metric Bold Italic 22pt***
**Metric Black 22pt**
***Metric Black Italic 22pt***

---

12/14 — Metric Light

The quick brown fox jumps over the lazy dog. Voyez le brick géant que j'examine près du wharf. Zwölf Boxkämpfer jagen Viktor quer über den großen Sylter Deich.

12/14 — Metric Regular

The quick brown fox jumps over the lazy dog. Voyez le brick géant que j'examine près du wharf. Zwölf Boxkämpfer jagen Viktor quer über den großen Sylter

12/14 — Metric Medium

The quick brown fox jumps over the lazy dog. Voyez le brick géant que j'examine près du wharf. Zwölf Boxkämpfer jagen Viktor quer über den großen Sylter

12/14 — Metric Bold

**The quick brown fox jumps over the lazy dog. Voyez le brick géant que j'examine près du wharf. Zwölf Boxkämpfer jagen Viktor quer über den großen Sylter Deich. El veloz murciélago hindú comía feliz cardillo y kiwi. La**

9/12 — Metric Light

The quick brown fox jumps over the lazy dog. Voyez le brick géant que j'examine près du wharf. Zwölf Boxkämpfer jagen Viktor quer über den großen Sylter Deich. El veloz murciélago hindú comía feliz cardillo y kiwi. La cigüeña tocaba el saxofón detrás del palenque de

9/12 — Metric Regular

The quick brown fox jumps over the lazy dog. Voyez le brick géant que j'examine près du wharf. Zwölf Boxkämpfer jagen Viktor quer über den großen Sylter Deich. El veloz murciélago hindú comía feliz cardillo y kiwi. La cigüeña tocaba el saxofón detrás del palen-

9/12 — Metric Medium

The quick brown fox jumps over the lazy dog. Voyez le brick géant que j'examine près du wharf. Zwölf Boxkämpfer jagen Viktor quer über den großen Sylter Deich. El veloz murciélago hindú comía feliz cardillo y kiwi. La cigüeña tocaba el saxofón detrás del palenque

9/12 — Metric Bold

**The quick brown fox jumps over the lazy dog. Voyez le brick géant que j'examine près du wharf. Zwölf Boxkämpfer jagen Viktor quer über den großen Sylter Deich. El veloz murciélago hindú comía feliz cardillo y kiwi. La cigüeña tocaba el saxofón detrás del palenque de pajaatur? Rissimo lorereped ex es solore lab id molorro in rempore icabore rehene-**

7/10 — Metric Light

The quick brown fox jumps over the lazy dog. Voyez le brick géant que j'examine près du wharf. Zwölf Boxkämpfer jagen Viktor quer über den großen Sylter Deich. El veloz murciélago hindú comía feliz cardillo y kiwi. La cigüeña tocaba el saxofón detrás del palenque de pajaatur? Rissimo lorereped ex es solore lab id molorro in rempore icabore rehenetur aliam aut voles audae dem quam, secum eum facesequae consequ aepudam

7/10 — Metric Regular

The quick brown fox jumps over the lazy dog. Voyez le brick géant que j'examine près du wharf. Zwölf Boxkämpfer jagen Viktor quer über den großen Sylter Deich. El veloz murciélago hindú comía feliz cardillo y kiwi. La cigüeña tocaba el saxofón detrás del palenque de pajaatur? Rissimo lorereped ex es solore lab id molorro in rempore icabore rehenetur aliam aut voles audae dem quam, secum eum facesequae consequ aepudam

7/10 — Metric Medium

The quick brown fox jumps over the lazy dog. Voyez le brick géant que j'examine près du wharf. Zwölf Boxkämpfer jagen Viktor quer über den großen Sylter Deich. El veloz murciélago hindú comía feliz cardillo y kiwi. La cigüeña tocaba el saxofón detrás del palenque de pajaatur? Rissimo lorereped ex es solore lab id molorro in rempore icabore rehenetur aliam aut voles audae dem quam, secum eum

7/10 — Metric Bold

**The quick brown fox jumps over the lazy dog. Voyez le brick géant que j'examine près du wharf. Zwölf Boxkämpfer jagen Viktor quer über den großen Sylter Deich. El veloz murciélago hindú comía feliz cardillo y kiwi. La cigüeña tocaba el saxofón detrás del palenque de pajaatur? Rissimo lorereped ex es solore lab id molorro in rempore icabore rehenetur aliam aut voles audae dem quam, secum eum facesequae consequ aepudam quia voluptiur repel in et faccustibus, nonsenis aut quisqui rero mi, ipiet lam ant ut maio et hil molupta**

Page
149

Foundry  Klim

Typeface  Tiempos
Designer  Kris Sowersby

Year    2010
Format  OpenType

# Aa

Aa Bb Cc Dd Ee Ff Gg Hh Ii Jj
Kk Ll Mm Nn Oo Pp Qq Rr Ss Tt
Uu Vv Ww Xx Yy Zz
0123456789
—

Tiempos Regular 24pt
*Tiempos Regular Italic* 24pt
Tiempos Medium 24pt
*Tiempos Medium Italic* 24pt
**Tiempos SemiBold** 24pt
***Tiempos SemiBold Italic*** 24pt
**Tiempos Bold** 24pt
***Tiempos Bold Italic*** 24pt

---

12/14  Tiempos Light

The quick brown fox jumps over the lazy dog. Voyez le brick géant que j'examine près du wharf. Zwölf Boxkämpfer jagen Vik-

12/14  Tiempos Regular

The quick brown fox jumps over the lazy dog. Voyez le brick géant que j'examine près du wharf. Zwölf Boxkämpfer jagen Vik-

12/14  Tiempos Medium

The quick brown fox jumps over the lazy dog. Voyez le brick géant que j'examine près du wharf. Zwölf Boxkämpfer jagen Vik-

12/14  Tiempos Bold

**The quick brown fox jumps over the lazy dog. Voyez le brick géant que j'examine près du wharf. Zwölf Boxkämpfer jagen Viktor quer über den großen Sylter Deich. El veloz murcié-**

9/12  Tiempos Light

The quick brown fox jumps over the lazy dog. Voyez le brick géant que j'examine près du wharf. Zwölf Boxkämpfer jagen Viktor quer über den großen Sylter Deich. El veloz murciélago hindú comía feliz cardillo y kiwi. La

9/12  Tiempos Regular

The quick brown fox jumps over the lazy dog. Voyez le brick géant que j'examine près du wharf. Zwölf Boxkämpfer jagen Viktor quer über den großen Sylter Deich. El veloz murciélago hindú comía feliz cardillo y kiwi. La

9/12  Tiempos Medium

The quick brown fox jumps over the lazy dog. Voyez le brick géant que j'examine près du wharf. Zwölf Boxkämpfer jagen Viktor quer über den großen Sylter Deich. El veloz murciélago hindú comía feliz cardillo y

9/12  Tiempos Bold

**The quick brown fox jumps over the lazy dog. Voyez le brick géant que j'examine près du wharf. Zwölf Boxkämpfer jagen Viktor quer über den großen Sylter Deich. El veloz murciélago hindú comía feliz cardillo y kiwi. La cigüeña tocaba el saxofón detrás del palenque de pajaa-**

7/10  Tiempos Light

The quick brown fox jumps over the lazy dog. Voyez le brick géant que j'examine près du wharf. Zwölf Boxkämpfer jagen Viktor quer über den großen Sylter Deich. El veloz murciélago hindú comía feliz cardillo y kiwi. La cigüeña tocaba el saxofón detrás del palenque de pajaatur? Rissimo lorereped ex es solore lab id molorro in rempore

7/10  Tiempos Regular

The quick brown fox jumps over the lazy dog. Voyez le brick géant que j'examine près du wharf. Zwölf Boxkämpfer jagen Viktor quer über den großen Sylter Deich. El veloz murciélago hindú comía feliz cardillo y kiwi. La cigüeña tocaba el saxofón detrás del palenque de pajaatur? Rissimo lorereped ex es solore lab id molorro in rempore

7/10  Tiempos Medium

The quick brown fox jumps over the lazy dog. Voyez le brick géant que j'examine près du wharf. Zwölf Boxkämpfer jagen Viktor quer über den großen Sylter Deich. El veloz murciélago hindú comía feliz cardillo y kiwi. La cigüeña tocaba el saxofón detrás del palenque de pajaatur? Rissimo lorereped ex es solore lab id molorro

7/10  Tiempos Bold

**The quick brown fox jumps over the lazy dog. Voyez le brick géant que j'examine près du wharf. Zwölf Boxkämpfer jagen Viktor quer über den großen Sylter Deich. El veloz murciélago hindú comía feliz cardillo y kiwi. La cigüeña tocaba el saxofón detrás del palenque de pajaatur? Rissimo lorereped ex es solore lab id molorro in rempore icabore rehenetur aliam aut voles audae dem quam, secum eum facesequae consequ**

# K

Kombinat-
Typefounders

—

Hannes Famira

—

Berlin,
Germany

—

Since
2001

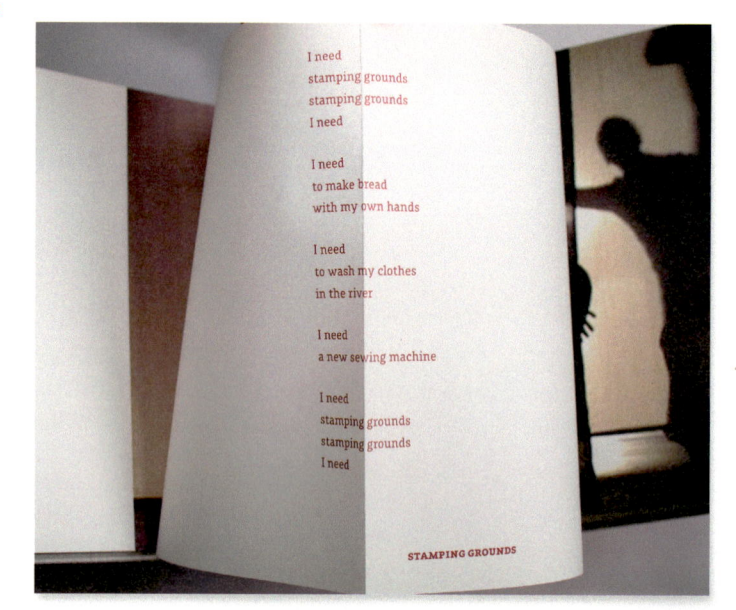

Having been set up as the type founding department of Hannes Famira's design company Kombinat ten years ago, the foundry relaunched in 2011 with a new website and the release of Martin Wenzel's Realist famliy.

## Info

—Why?
After having sold his fonts to friends and acquaintances for a while it occured to Hannes that it might make sense to build a website and do the same thing with a larger pool of clients.

—People on staff
1

—Type designers on staff
1

—Type families
10

—Designers represented
2

— Web shop
www.kombinat-typefounders.com

—Distributors
To be announced

—Webfont services
No webfont service, but the complete retail library is available as webfonts in WOFF and EOT format.

—Basic license
Single styles from €49 (5 devices)

## Typeface selection

Interpol Sans Classic
Interpol Serif Classic
Realist
Realist Narrow
Realist Wide

24pt

## People

—Hannes Famira is founding principal of the Kombinat-Typefounders. He is a graphic designer, a type designer and a teacher of both disciplines. After twenty years in the Netherlands, Switzerland and the United States he now lives in Berlin, Germany, where he freelances part-time for Lucas-Fonts, FontShop International and House Industries. He studied graphic and typographic design at the KABK (Royal Academy of Fine Arts) in The Hague, Netherlands. After apprenticeships at Studio Dumbar and the Font Bureau he worked at Meta Design, at Buro Petr van Blokland + Claudia Mens and House Industries. Hannes started his own design studio, Das Kombinat, in 1999 and Kombinat-Typefounders in 2001. He taught typography and type design classes at the SfG, School for Design in Basel (CH), Cooper Union for the Advancement of Science and Art School of Art, the New Jersey City University and the City University of New York.

—Martin Wenzel had his first typeface (FF Marten) published in the early nineties and has been designing new fonts ever since. In 1993 he moved from his native Berlin to The Hague to study type and communication design at the KABK. His first text typeface, FF Profile, received an award from the Type Directors Club New York in 2000. Besides his type design expertise and teaching he has been working as a communication designer and web developer for clients in Germany, the Netherlands, Denmark, India and the US. After his degree and working in the Netherlands for eight additional years (at Buro Petr van Blokland + Claudia Mens) he moved back to Berlin in 2005. Martin's approach to type design is usually based on the principles of writing with the various writing tools. He has no interest in designing revivals but instead uses basic typographic design and construction principles as inspiration for new designs.

*Out of Silence*, a book on Authentic Movement. Designed by Soup Royale (Judith Haagh and Marjon Stark) using the Interpol Serif typeface.

Eprom consulting company commissioned the popular Flemish writer Herman Brusselmans to write a novel to be published on the occasion of the company's tenth anniversary. Designed by Jeroen Schmit and Hannes Famira for SWA using Interpol Serif.

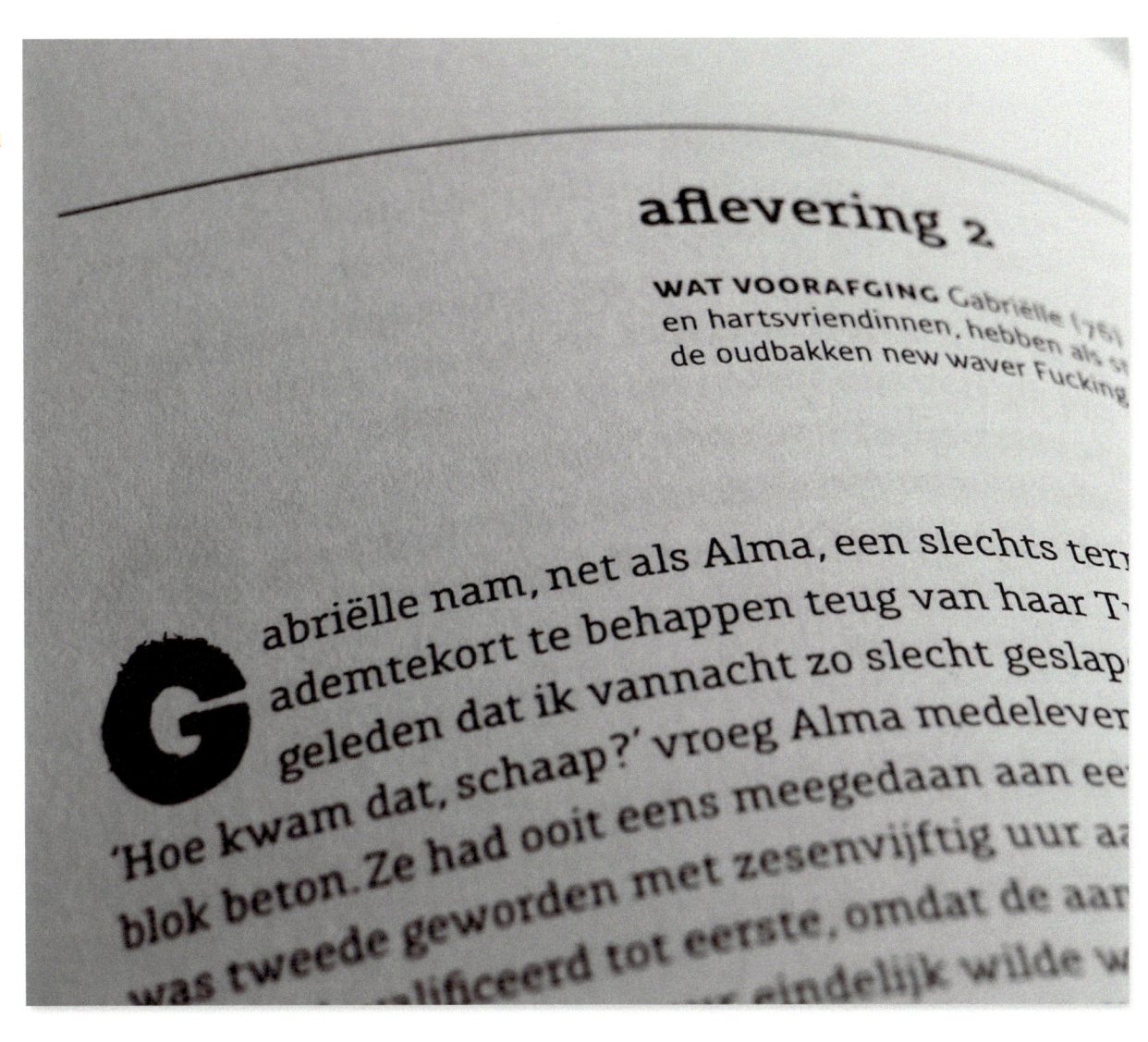

Pages from a series of type specimen brochures designed by Martin Wenzel for his type family Realist.

Foundry   Kombinat-Typefounders

---

Typeface   Interpol Sans Classic
Designer   Hannes Famira
Year       1992
Format     OpenType

# Aa

Interpol Sans Classic Light 18pt
Interpol Sans Classic Book 18pt
Interpol Sans Classic Medium 18pt
**Interpol Sans Classic Semi Bold 18pt**
**Interpol Sans Classic Bold 18pt**
**Interpol Sans Classic Black 18pt**

Aa Bb Cc Dd Ee Ff Gg Hh Ii Jj Kk Ll Mm
Nn Oo Pp Qq Rr Ss Tt Uu Vv Ww Xx Yy Zz
0123456789
-

9/12   Interpol Sans Classic Book

The quick brown fox jumps over the lazy dog. Voyez le brick géant que j'examine près du wharf. Zwölf Boxkämpfer jagen Viktor quer über den großen Sylter Deich. El veloz murciélago hindú comía feliz cardillo y kiwi. La cigüeña tocaba el saxofón detrás del palenque de pajaatur? Rissimo lorereped ex es solore lab id molorro in rempore icabore rehenetur aliam aut voles audae dem quam, secum eum facesequae consequ aepudam quia voluptiur repel in et faccustibus, nonsenis aut quisqui rero mi, ipiet lam ant ut maio et hil molupta tustis atatur, consedi tasimol orerem aut volor andipsapis sit, illaut volore officatus alicae dusdaec tatecte cearum qui accatibus

7/10   Interpol Sans Classic Book

The quick brown fox jumps over the lazy dog. Voyez le brick géant que j'examine près du wharf. Zwölf Boxkämpfer jagen Viktor quer über den großen Sylter Deich. El veloz murciélago hindú comía feliz cardillo y kiwi. La cigüeña tocaba el saxofón detrás del palenque de pajaatur? Rissimo lorereped ex es solore lab id molorro in rempore icabore rehenetur aliam aut voles audae dem quam, secum eum facesequae consequ aepudam quia voluptiur repel in et faccustibus, nonsenis aut quisqui rero mi, ipiet lam ant ut maio et hil molupta tustis atatur, consedi tasimol orerem aut volor andipsapis sit, illaut volore officatus alicae dusdaec tatecte cearum qui accatibus restiore nulpa secaerferum, nus dolenim in et quoditat que explam volupictur? Qui de illuptae. Dae nis illiberum volorro ritatis tinullo rerumqu atetur repro eatius asperibus. Rissimo lorereped ex es solore lab id molorro in rempore icabore rehenetur aliam aut voles audae dem quam, secum eum facesequae consequ

---

Typeface   Interpol Serif Classic
Designer   Hannes Famira
Year       1992
Format     OpenType

# *Aa*

*Interpol Serif Classic Light* 18pt
*Interpol Serif Classic Book* 18pt
*Interpol Serif Classic Medium* 18pt
***Interpol Serif Classic Semi Bold* 18pt**
***Interpol Serif Classic Bold* 18pt**
***Interpol Serif Classic Black* 18pt**

*Aa Bb Cc Dd Ee Ff Gg Hh Ii Jj Kk Ll Mm
Nn Oo Pp Qq Rr Ss Tt Uu Vv Ww Xx Yy Zz
0123456789
-*

9/12   Interpol Serif Classic Book

*The quick brown fox jumps over the lazy dog. Voyez le brick géant que j'examine près du wharf. Zwölf Boxkämpfer jagen Viktor quer über den großen Sylter Deich. El veloz murciélago hindú comía feliz cardillo y kiwi. La cigüeña tocaba el saxofón detrás del palenque de pajaatur? Rissimo lorereped ex es solore lab id molorro in rempore icabore rehenetur aliam aut voles audae dem quam, secum eum facesequae consequ aepudam quia voluptiur repel in et faccustibus, nonsenis aut quisqui rero mi, ipiet lam ant ut maio et hil molupta tustis*

7/10   Interpol Serif Classic Book

*The quick brown fox jumps over the lazy dog. Voyez le brick géant que j'examine près du wharf. Zwölf Boxkämpfer jagen Viktor quer über den großen Sylter Deich. El veloz murciélago hindú comía feliz cardillo y kiwi. La cigüeña tocaba el saxofón detrás del palenque de pajaatur? Rissimo lorereped ex es solore lab id molorro in rempore icabore rehenetur aliam aut voles audae dem quam, secum eum facesequae consequ aepudam quia voluptiur repel in et faccustibus, nonsenis aut quisqui rero mi, ipiet lam ant ut maio et hil molupta tustis atatur, consedi tasimol orerem aut volor andipsapis sit, illaut volore officatus alicae dusdaec tatecte cearum qui accatibus restiore nulpa secaerferum, nus dolenim in et quoditat que explam volupictur? Qui de illuptae. Dae nis illiberum volorro ritatis tinullo rerumqu atetur repro eatius asperibus. Rissimo lorereped ex es*

Page 153

Foundry Kombinat-Typefounders

Typeface Realist, Narrow, Wide
Designer Martin Wenzel
Year 2011
Format OpenType

# Aa

Aa Bb Cc Dd Ee Ff Gg Hh Ii Jj Kk Ll Mm Nn Oo Pp Qq Rr Ss Tt Uu Vv Ww Xx Yy Zz
0123456789
—

Realist Thin 18pt
Realist Light 18pt
Realist Semi Light 18pt
Realist Regular 18pt
Realist Medium 18pt
**Realist Bold 18pt**
**Realist Extra Bold 18pt**
**Realist Black 18pt**
Realist Narrow Thin 18pt
Realist Narrow Light 18pt
Realist Narrow Semi Light 18pt
Realist Narrow Regular 18pt
Realist Narrow Medium 18pt
**Realist Narrow Bold 18pt**
**Realist Narrow Extra Bold 18pt**
**Realist Narrow Black 18pt**
Realist Wide Thin 18pt
Realist Wide Light 18pt
Realist Wide Semi Light 18pt
Realist Wide Regular 18pt
Realist Wide Medium 18pt
**Realist Wide Bold 18pt**
**Realist Wide Extra Bold 18pt**
**Realist Wide Black 18pt**

---

9/12 Realist Regular

The quick brown fox jumps over the lazy dog. Voyez le brick géant que j'examine près du wharf. Zwölf Boxkämpfer jagen Viktor quer über den großen Sylter Deich. El veloz murciélago hindú comía feliz cardillo y kiwi. La cigüeña tocaba el saxofón detrás del palenque de pajaatur? Rissimo lorereped ex es solore lab id molorro in rempore icabore rehenetur aliam aut voles audae dem quam, secum eum facesequae consequ aepudam quia voluptiur repel in et faccustibus, nonsenis

9/12 Realist Narrow Regular

The quick brown fox jumps over the lazy dog. Voyez le brick géant que j'examine près du wharf. Zwölf Boxkämpfer jagen Viktor quer über den großen Sylter Deich. El veloz murciélago hindú comía feliz cardillo y kiwi. La cigüeña tocaba el saxofón detrás del palenque de pajaatur? Rissimo lorereped ex es solore lab id molorro in rempore icabore rehenetur aliam aut voles audae dem quam, secum eum facesequae consequ aepudam quia voluptiur repel in et faccustibus, nonsenis aut quisqui rero mi, ipiet lam ant ut maio et hil

9/12 Realist Wide Regular

The quick brown fox jumps over the lazy dog. Voyez le brick géant que j'examine près du wharf. Zwölf Boxkämpfer jagen Viktor quer über den großen Sylter Deich. El veloz murciélago hindú comía feliz cardillo y kiwi. La cigüeña tocaba el saxofón detrás del palenque de pajaatur? Rissimo lorereped ex es solore lab id molorro in rempore icabore rehenetur aliam aut voles audae dem quam, secum eum facesequae consequ aepudam

# L
## LucasFonts

—

Luc(as) de Groot

—

Berlin, Germany

—

Since 2000

LucasFonts is the foundry established by Dutch designer Luc(as) de Groot in 2000. Today, LucasFonts is a bustling type design studio with a small, international team of designers. LucasFonts aims to produce original typefaces that meet the needs of complex typographic design and multilingual office environments. Many of the foundry's type families were originally designed for specific clients in response to well-defined demands — leading to a very practical and user-oriented approach.

## Info

—Why?
It was important for Luc(as) to have direct contact and communications with the customers.

—People on staff
2

—Type designers on staff
1

—Type families
68+

—Designers represented
1

— Web shop
lucasfonts.com/shop

—Distributors
FontShop, FontHaus, Phil's Fonts, Monotype Imaging, Signum Art, ProType, MyFonts

—Webfont services
Direct from LucasFonts and Typekit (planned)

—Basic license
Starting from 40€ (single font) for 5 CPUs.

—Special Conditions
Font family rebates, e.g. 4 fonts for 5 CPUs = 98€. Possibility of license extensions and upgrades.

## Typeface selection

Floris SP
QuaText
Spiegel
Taz
TheSans
TheSerif
TheMix

24pt

## People

—Luc(as) de Groot, born in Noordwijkerhout, Netherlands, studied at the KABK (Royal Academy of Fine Arts) in The Hague. He then spent four years with the Dutch design group BRS Premsela Vonk, mainly on corporate identity work. In the meantime he taught at the Art Academy in Den Bosch and freelanced before moving to Berlin in 1993 to join MetaDesign for another four years. As typographic director at MetaDesign in Berlin, he worked on a variety of corporate design projects, from logos, magazine concepts and custom typefaces to fine-tuning and implementing type. Luc(as)' first well known type family was Thesis. It grew out of dissatisfaction with the availability of good typefaces for corporate identities. Thesis was first conceived about 1989 and first published in 1994. Since then it has grown into one of the largest and most comprehensive digital type families available on the market. Luc(as)' most widely distributed typeface is Calibri, the new default font in Microsoft Office. In the beginning of 1997 Luc(as) accepted a part-time teaching position in Potsdam. In 1997 he founded FontFabrik, where he has been offering services such as type and logo development and digital implementation to design and advertising agencies. He keeps on designing new and custom typefaces as well as extending his own type families (Thesis, Sun, Taz, Corpid, etc.). He is devoted to type by day and night. In 2000 the font foundry LucasFonts was established, where Luc(as) now sells and distributes his own typefaces directly.

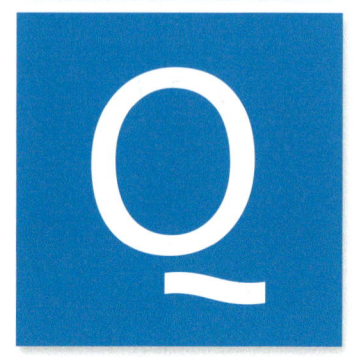

Luc(as) de Groot Qs

Page 155

Examples of the thoroughness of Luc(as) de Groot's design of TheSans. Below: Coordinated stroke thicknesses in TheSans Hairline to obtain equal thickness when setting texts in different point sizes. Right: a wide range of numeral styles.

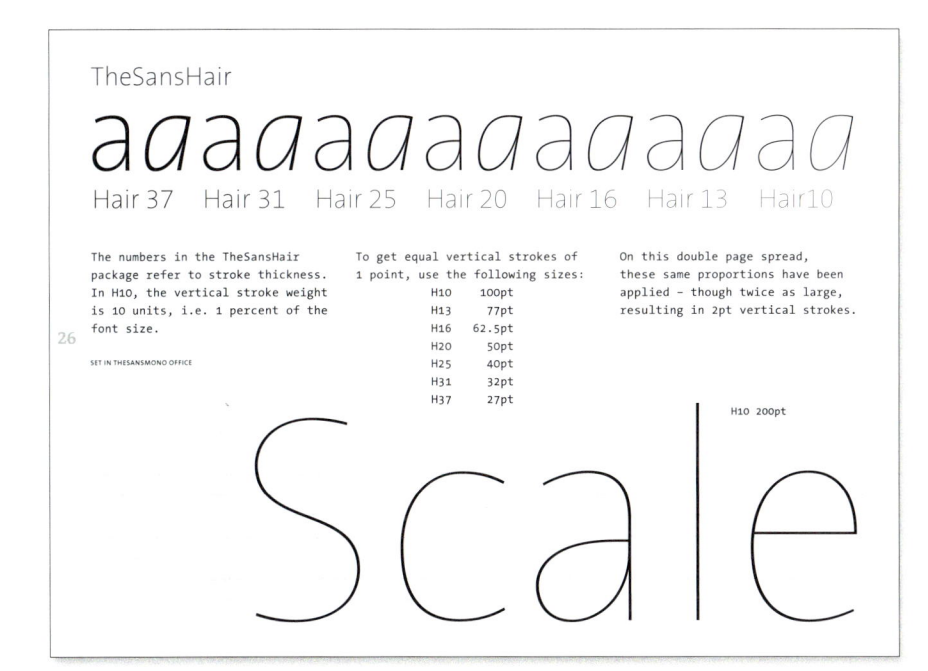

## Hanging figures
efg1234567890
§1.2 $58 37¢

## Lining figures
ABC123456789
§2.5 $112 98¢

## Tabular figures
1234567890
1114135751

## Fraction figures
0⁰1¹2²3³4⁴5⁵6⁶7⁷8⁸9⁹
½₂₀₀ ¼ ¾ $45⁵⁰¢

## Mono figures
1234567890
4512689703

---

**TheSansHair**

aaaaaaaaaa
Hair 37  Hair 31  Hair 25  Hair 20  Hair 16  Hair 13  Hair10

The numbers in the TheSansHair package refer to stroke thickness. In H10, the vertical stroke weight is 10 units, i.e. 1 percent of the font size.

To get equal vertical strokes of 1 point, use the following sizes:
H10  100pt
H13  77pt
H16  62.5pt
H20  50pt
H25  40pt
H31  32pt
H37  27pt

On this double page spread, these same proportions have been applied – though twice as large, resulting in 2pt vertical strokes.

SET IN THESANSMONO OFFICE

Scale   H10 200pt

Equally thick   H20 100pt
& H13 154pt  in different
sizes   H25 80pt
H37 54 pt
Try out a hairy headline
H31 64pt
with caution   H20 100pt

Page
156

Foundry LucasFonts

Typeface TheSans
Designer Lucas de Groot
Year 1994–2011
Format OpenType

# Aa

Aa Bb Cc Dd Ee Ff Gg Hh Ii Jj Kk Ll
Mm Nn Oo Pp Qq Rr Ss Tt Uu Vv
Ww Xx Yy Zz
0123456789
—

TheSans Extra Light 12pt
*TheSans Extra Light Italic 12pt*
TheSans Light 12pt
*TheSans Light Italic 12pt*
TheSans Semi Light 12pt
*TheSans Semi Light Italic 12pt*
TheSans Plain 12pt
*TheSans Plain Italic 12pt*
**TheSans Semi Bold 12pt**
***TheSans Semi Bold Italic 12pt***
**TheSans Bold 12pt**
***TheSans Bold Italic 12pt***
**TheSans Extra Bold 12pt**
***TheSans Extra Bold Italic 12pt***
**TheSans Black 12pt**
***TheSans Black Italic 12pt***

TheSans Cd Extra Light → **Black 12pt**
TheSans Mono Extra Light → **Black 12pt**
TheSans Mono Cd Extra Light → **Black 12pt**

---

**12/14   TheSans Light**

The quick brown fox jumps over the lazy dog. Voyez le brick géant que j'examine près du wharf. Zwölf Boxkämpfer jagen Viktor quer über

**9/12   TheSans Light**

The quick brown fox jumps over the lazy dog. Voyez le brick géant que j'examine près du wharf. Zwölf Boxkämpfer jagen Viktor quer über den großen Sylter Deich. El veloz murciélago hindú comía feliz cardillo y kiwi. La cigüeña tocaba el

**7/10   TheSans Light**

The quick brown fox jumps over the lazy dog. Voyez le brick géant que j'examine près du wharf. Zwölf Boxkämpfer jagen Viktor quer über den großen Sylter Deich. El veloz murciélago hindú comía feliz cardillo y kiwi. La cigüeña tocaba el saxofón detrás del palenque de pajaatur? Rissimo lorereped ex es solore lab id molorro in rempore icabore rehenetur aliam aut voles

**12/14   TheSans Plain**

The quick brown fox jumps over the lazy dog. Voyez le brick géant que j'examine près du wharf. Zwölf Boxkämpfer jagen Viktor quer über den

**9/12   TheSans Plain**

The quick brown fox jumps over the lazy dog. Voyez le brick géant que j'examine près du wharf. Zwölf Boxkämpfer jagen Viktor quer über den großen Sylter Deich. El veloz murciélago hindú comía feliz cardillo y kiwi. La cigüeña tocaba el

**7/10   TheSans Plain**

The quick brown fox jumps over the lazy dog. Voyez le brick géant que j'examine près du wharf. Zwölf Boxkämpfer jagen Viktor quer über den großen Sylter Deich. El veloz murciélago hindú comía feliz cardillo y kiwi. La cigüeña tocaba el saxofón detrás del palenque de pajaatur? Rissimo lorereped ex es solore lab id molorro in rempore icabore rehenetur aliam aut voles

**12/14   TheSans SemiBold**

The quick brown fox jumps over the lazy dog. Voyez le brick géant que j'examine près du wharf. Zwölf Boxkämpfer jagen Viktor quer über Box-

**9/12   TheSans SemiBold**

The quick brown fox jumps over the lazy dog. Voyez le brick géant que j'examine près du wharf. Zwölf Boxkämpfer jagen Viktor quer über den großen Sylter Deich. El veloz murciélago hindú comía feliz cardillo y kiwi. La cigüeña tocaba el

**7/10   TheSans SemiBold**

The quick brown fox jumps over the lazy dog. Voyez le brick géant que j'examine près du wharf. Zwölf Boxkämpfer jagen Viktor quer über den großen Sylter Deich. El veloz murciélago hindú comía feliz cardillo y kiwi. La cigüeña tocaba el saxofón detrás del palenque de pajaatur? Rissimo lorereped ex es solore lab id molorro in rempore icabore rehenetur aliam aut voles

**12/14   TheSans Bold**

**The quick brown fox jumps over the lazy dog. Voyez le brick géant que j'examine près du wharf. Zwölf Boxkämpfer jagen Viktor quer über den großen Sylter Deich. El veloz murciélago hindú comía feliz cardillo y kiwi.**

**9/12   TheSans Bold**

**The quick brown fox jumps over the lazy dog. Voyez le brick géant que j'examine près du wharf. Zwölf Boxkämpfer jagen Viktor quer über den großen Sylter Deich. El veloz murciélago hindú comía feliz cardillo y kiwi. La cigüeña tocaba el saxofón detrás del palenque de pajaatur? Rissimo lorereped ex es solore lab id molorro in**

**7/10   TheSans Bold**

**The quick brown fox jumps over the lazy dog. Voyez le brick géant que j'examine près du wharf. Zwölf Boxkämpfer jagen Viktor quer über den großen Sylter Deich. El veloz murciélago hindú comía feliz cardillo y kiwi. La cigüeña tocaba el saxofón detrás del palenque de pajaatur? Rissimo lorereped ex es solore lab id molorro in rempore icabore rehenetur aliam aut voles audae dem quam, secum eum facesequae consequ aepudam quia voluptiur repel in et faccustibus, nonsenis aut quisqui rero**

Page 157

Foundry LucasFonts

Typeface TheSerif, TheMix
Designer Lucas de Groot

Year 1994–2011
Format OpenType

# Aa

Aa Bb Cc Dd Ee Ff Gg Hh Ii Jj Kk Ll Mm Nn Oo Pp Qq Rr Ss Tt Uu Vv Ww Xx Yy Zz
0123456789

| | |
|---|---|
| TheSerif Extra Light 12pt | TheMix Extra Light 12pt |
| *TheSerif Extra Light Italic 12pt* | *TheMix Extra Light Italic 12pt* |
| TheSerif Light 12pt | TheMix Light 12pt |
| *TheSerif Light Italic 12pt* | *TheMix Light Italic 12pt* |
| TheSerif Semi Light 12pt | TheMix Semi Light 12pt |
| *TheSerif Semi Light Italic 12pt* | *TheMix Semi Light Italic 12pt* |
| TheSerif Plain 12pt | TheMix Plain 12pt |
| *TheSerif Plain Italic 12pt* | *TheMix Plain Italic 12pt* |
| **TheSerif Semi Bold 12pt** | **TheMix Semi Bold 12pt** |
| ***TheSerif Semi Bold Italic 12pt*** | ***TheMix Semi Bold Italic 12pt*** |
| **TheSerif Bold 12pt** | **TheMix Bold 12pt** |
| ***TheSerif Bold Italic 12pt*** | ***TheMix Bold Italic 12pt*** |
| **TheSerif Extra Bold 12pt** | **TheMix Extra Bold 12pt** |
| ***TheSerif Extra Bold Italic 12pt*** | ***TheMix Extra Bold Italic 12pt*** |
| **TheSerif Black 12pt** | **TheMix Black 12pt** |
| ***TheSerif Black Italic 12pt*** | ***TheMix Black Italic 12pt*** |

TheMix Cd Extra Light → **Black 12pt**

9/12 TheSerif Light

The quick brown fox jumps over the lazy dog. Voyez le brick géant que j'examine près du wharf. Zwölf Boxkämpfer jagen Viktor quer über den großen Sylter Deich. El veloz murciélago hindú comía feliz cardillo y kiwi. La cigüe-

9/12 TheSerif Plain

The quick brown fox jumps over the lazy dog. Voyez le brick géant que j'examine près du wharf. Zwölf Boxkämpfer jagen Viktor quer über den großen Sylter Deich. El veloz murciélago hindú comía feliz cardillo y kiwi. La cigüeña

9/12 TheSerif SemiBold

The quick brown fox jumps over the lazy dog. Voyez le brick géant que j'examine près du wharf. Zwölf Boxkämpfer jagen Viktor quer über den großen Sylter Deich. El veloz murciélago hindú comía feliz cardillo y kiwi. La

9/12 TheSerif Bold

**The quick brown fox jumps over the lazy dog. Voyez le brick géant que j'examine près du wharf. Zwölf Boxkämpfer jagen Viktor quer über den großen Sylter Deich. El veloz murciélago hindú comía feliz cardillo y kiwi. La cigüeña tocaba el saxofón detrás del palenque de pajaatur? Rissimo lorereped ex es solore**

9/12 TheMix Light

The quick brown fox jumps over the lazy dog. Voyez le brick géant que j'examine près du wharf. Zwölf Boxkämpfer jagen Viktor quer über den großen Sylter Deich. El veloz murciélago hindú comía feliz cardillo y kiwi. La cigüeña tocaba

9/12 TheMix Plain

The quick brown fox jumps over the lazy dog. Voyez le brick géant que j'examine près du wharf. Zwölf Boxkämpfer jagen Viktor quer über den großen Sylter Deich. El veloz murciélago hindú comía feliz cardillo y kiwi. La cigüe-

9/12 TheMix SemiBold

The quick brown fox jumps over the lazy dog. Voyez le brick géant que j'examine près du wharf. Zwölf Boxkämpfer jagen Viktor quer über den großen Sylter Deich. El veloz murciélago hindú comía feliz cardillo y kiwi. La cigüeña

9/12 TheMix Bold

**The quick brown fox jumps over the lazy dog. Voyez le brick géant que j'examine près du wharf. Zwölf Boxkämpfer jagen Viktor quer über den großen Sylter Deich. El veloz murciélago hindú comía feliz cardillo y kiwi. La cigüeña tocaba el saxofón detrás del palenque de pajaatur? Rissimo lorereped ex es solore**

Page 158

Foundry   LucasFonts

Typeface   Floris SP
Designer   Lucas de Groot
Year       1999
Format     OpenType

# Aa

Aa Bb Cc Dd Ee Ff Gg Hh Ii Jj Kk Ll Mm
Nn Oo Pp Qq Rr Ss Tt Uu Vv Ww Xx Yy Zz
0123456789

Floris SP Extra Light 20pt
*Floris SP Extra Light Italic 20pt*
Floris SP Light 20pt
*Floris SP Light Italic 20pt*
Floris SP Regular 20pt
*Floris SP Regular Italic 20pt*
**Floris SP Semi Bold 20pt**
***Floris SP Semi Bold Italic 20pt***
**Floris SP Bold 20pt**
***Floris SP Bold Italic 20pt***
**Floris SP Black 20pt**
***Floris SP Black Italic 20pt***

---

12/14   Floris Light

The quick brown fox jumps over the lazy dog. Voyez le brick géant que j'examine près du wharf. Zwölf Boxkämpfer jagen Viktor quer über den großen Sylter Deich.

12/14   Floris Regular

The quick brown fox jumps over the lazy dog. Voyez le brick géant que j'examine près du wharf. Zwölf Boxkämpfer jagen Viktor quer über den großen Sylter Deich.

12/14   Floris SemiBold

The quick brown fox jumps over the lazy dog. Voyez le brick géant que j'examine près du wharf. Zwölf Boxkämpfer jagen Viktor quer über den großen Sylter

12/14   Floris Bold

The quick brown fox jumps over the lazy dog. Voyez le brick géant que j'examine près du wharf. Zwölf Boxkämpfer jagen Viktor quer über den großen Sylter Deich. El veloz murciélago hindú comía feliz cardillo y kiwi. La cigüeña tocaba el

---

9/12   Floris Light

The quick brown fox jumps over the lazy dog. Voyez le brick géant que j'examine près du wharf. Zwölf Boxkämpfer jagen Viktor quer über den großen Sylter Deich. El veloz murciélago hindú comía feliz cardillo y kiwi. La cigüeña tocaba el saxofón detrás del palenque de

9/12   Floris Regular

The quick brown fox jumps over the lazy dog. Voyez le brick géant que j'examine près du wharf. Zwölf Boxkämpfer jagen Viktor quer über den großen Sylter Deich. El veloz murciélago hindú comía feliz cardillo y kiwi. La cigüeña tocaba el saxofón detrás del palenque de

9/12   Floris SemiBold

The quick brown fox jumps over the lazy dog. Voyez le brick géant que j'examine près du wharf. Zwölf Boxkämpfer jagen Viktor quer über den großen Sylter Deich. El veloz murciélago hindú comía feliz cardillo y kiwi. La cigüeña tocaba el saxofón detrás del palenque

9/12   Floris Bold

The quick brown fox jumps over the lazy dog. Voyez le brick géant que j'examine près du wharf. Zwölf Boxkämpfer jagen Viktor quer über den großen Sylter Deich. El veloz murciélago hindú comía feliz cardillo y kiwi. La cigüeña tocaba el saxofón detrás del palenque de pajaatur? Rissimo lorereped ex es solore lab id molorro in rempore icabore rehenetur aliam aut voles

---

7/10   Floris Light

The quick brown fox jumps over the lazy dog. Voyez le brick géant que j'examine près du wharf. Zwölf Boxkämpfer jagen Viktor quer über den großen Sylter Deich. El veloz murciélago hindú comía feliz cardillo y kiwi. La cigüeña tocaba el saxofón detrás del palenque de pajaatur? Rissimo lorereped ex es solore lab id molorro in rempore icabore rehenetur aliam aut voles audae dem quam, secum eum facesequae consequ aepudam

7/10   Floris Regular

The quick brown fox jumps over the lazy dog. Voyez le brick géant que j'examine près du wharf. Zwölf Boxkämpfer jagen Viktor quer über den großen Sylter Deich. El veloz murciélago hindú comía feliz cardillo y kiwi. La cigüeña tocaba el saxofón detrás del palenque de pajaatur? Rissimo lorereped ex es solore lab id molorro in rempore icabore rehenetur aliam aut voles audae dem quam, secum eum facesequae consequ aepudam

7/10   Floris SemiBold

The quick brown fox jumps over the lazy dog. Voyez le brick géant que j'examine près du wharf. Zwölf Boxkämpfer jagen Viktor quer über den großen Sylter Deich. El veloz murciélago hindú comía feliz cardillo y kiwi. La cigüeña tocaba el saxofón detrás del palenque de pajaatur? Rissimo lorereped ex es solore lab id molorro in rempore icabore rehenetur aliam aut voles audae dem quam, secum eum facesequae consequ ae-

7/10   Floris Bold

The quick brown fox jumps over the lazy dog. Voyez le brick géant que j'examine près du wharf. Zwölf Boxkämpfer jagen Viktor quer über den großen Sylter Deich. El veloz murciélago hindú comía feliz cardillo y kiwi. La cigüeña tocaba el saxofón detrás del palenque de pajaatur? Rissimo lorereped ex es solore lab id molorro in rempore icabore rehenetur aliam aut voles audae dem quam, secum eum facesequae consequ aepudam quia voluptiur repel in et faccustibus, nonsenis aut quisqui rero mi, ipiet lam ant ut maio et hil molupta

Foundry LucasFonts

Typeface Taz
Designer Lucas de Groot
Year 1997–2010
Format OpenType

# Aa

Aa Bb Cc Dd Ee Ff Gg Hh Ii Jj Kk Ll Mm Nn
Oo Pp Qq Rr Ss Tt Uu Vv Ww Xx Yy Zz
0123456789
—

Taz Ultra Light 18pt
*Taz Ultra Light Italic 18pt*
Taz Ultra Extra Light 18pt
*Taz Ultra Extra Light Italic 18pt*
Taz Ultra Light 18pt
*Taz Ultra Light Italic 18pt*
Taz Semi Light 18pt
*Taz Semi Light Italic 18pt*
**Taz Regular 18pt**
*Taz Italic 18pt*
**Taz Semi Bold 18pt**
***Taz Semi Bold Italic 18pt***
**Taz Bold 18pt**
***Taz Bold Italic 18pt***
**Taz Extra Bold 18pt**
***Taz Extra Bold Italic 18pt***
**Taz Black 18pt**
***Taz Black Italic 18pt***
**Taz Ultra Black 18pt**
***Taz Ultra Black Italic 18pt***

---

12/14  Taz Regular

The quick brown fox jumps over the lazy dog. Voyez le brick géant que j'examine près du wharf. Zwölf Boxkämpfer jagen Viktor quer über den großen Sylter

12/14  Taz SemiBold

**The quick brown fox jumps over the lazy dog. Voyez le brick géant que j'examine près du wharf. Zwölf Boxkämpfer jagen Viktor quer über den großen Sylter**

12/14  Taz Bold

**The quick brown fox jumps over the lazy dog. Voyez le brick géant que j'examine près du wharf. Zwölf Boxkämpfer jagen Viktor quer über den großen Sylter Deich. El veloz murciélago hindú comía feliz cardillo y kiwi. La cigüeña tocaba el**

9/12  Taz Regular

The quick brown fox jumps over the lazy dog. Voyez le brick géant que j'examine près du wharf. Zwölf Boxkämpfer jagen Viktor quer über den großen Sylter Deich. El veloz murciélago hindú comía feliz cardillo y kiwi. La cigüeña tocaba el saxofón detrás del palenque

9/12  Taz SemiBold

**The quick brown fox jumps over the lazy dog. Voyez le brick géant que j'examine près du wharf. Zwölf Boxkämpfer jagen Viktor quer über den großen Sylter Deich. El veloz murciélago hindú comía feliz cardillo y kiwi. La cigüeña tocaba el saxofón detrás del palenque**

9/12  Taz Bold

**The quick brown fox jumps over the lazy dog. Voyez le brick géant que j'examine près du wharf. Zwölf Boxkämpfer jagen Viktor quer über den großen Sylter Deich. El veloz murciélago hindú comía feliz cardillo y kiwi. La cigüeña tocaba el saxofón detrás del palenque de pajaatur? Rissimo lorereped ex es solore lab id molorro in rempore icabore rehenetur aliam aut voles**

7/10  Taz Regular

The quick brown fox jumps over the lazy dog. Voyez le brick géant que j'examine près du wharf. Zwölf Boxkämpfer jagen Viktor quer über den großen Sylter Deich. El veloz murciélago hindú comía feliz cardillo y kiwi. La cigüeña tocaba el saxofón detrás del palenque de pajaatur? Rissimo lorereped ex es solore lab id molorro in rempore icabore rehenetur aliam aut voles audae dem quam, secum eum facesequae consequ

7/10  Taz SemiBold

**The quick brown fox jumps over the lazy dog. Voyez le brick géant que j'examine près du wharf. Zwölf Boxkämpfer jagen Viktor quer über den großen Sylter Deich. El veloz murciélago hindú comía feliz cardillo y kiwi. La cigüeña tocaba el saxofón detrás del palenque de pajaatur? Rissimo lorereped ex es solore lab id molorro in rempore icabore rehenetur aliam aut voles audae dem quam, secum eum**

7/10  Taz Bold

**The quick brown fox jumps over the lazy dog. Voyez le brick géant que j'examine près du wharf. Zwölf Boxkämpfer jagen Viktor quer über den großen Sylter Deich. El veloz murciélago hindú comía feliz cardillo y kiwi. La cigüeña tocaba el saxofón detrás del palenque de pajaatur? Rissimo lorereped ex es solore lab id molorro in rempore icabore rehenetur aliam aut voles audae dem quam, secum eum facesequae consequ aepudam quia voluptiur repel in et faccustibus, nonsenis aut quisqui rero mi, ipiet lam ant ut maio et hil molupta tustis**

Typeface **Spiegel**  
Designer Lucas de Groot  
Year 1994–2011  
Format OpenType

# Aa

Aa Bb Cc Dd Ee Ff Gg Hh Ii Jj Kk Ll Mm Nn Oo Pp Qq Rr Ss Tt Uu Vv Ww Xx Yy Zz
0123456789
—

Spiegel Regular 24pt
*Spiegel Regular Italic 24pt*
**Spiegel Semi Bold 24pt**
***Spiegel Semi Bold Italic 24pt***
**Spiegel Bold 24pt**
***Spiegel Bold Italic 24pt***

---

12/14 Spiegel Regular

The quick brown fox jumps over the lazy dog. Voyez le brick géant que j'examine près du wharf. Zwölf Boxkämpfer jagen Viktor quer über den großen Sylter Deich. El veloz murciélago hindú comía feliz cardillo y kiwi. La cigüeña tocaba el saxofón detrás del palenque de pajaatur? Rissimo lorereped ex es solore lab id molorro in rempore icabore rehenetur aliam

12/14 Spiegel SemiBold

**The quick brown fox jumps over the lazy dog. Voyez le brick géant que j'examine près du wharf. Zwölf Boxkämpfer jagen Viktor quer über den großen Sylter Deich. El veloz murciélago hindú comía feliz cardillo y kiwi. La cigüeña tocaba el saxofón detrás del palenque de pajaatur? Rissimo lorereped ex es solore lab id molorro in rempore icabore rehenetur aliam**

12/14 Spiegel Bold

**The quick brown fox jumps over the lazy dog. Voyez le brick géant que j'examine près du wharf. Zwölf Boxkämpfer jagen Viktor quer über den großen Sylter Deich. El veloz murciélago hindú comía feliz cardillo y kiwi.**

9/12 Spiegel Regular

The quick brown fox jumps over the lazy dog. Voyez le brick géant que j'examine près du wharf. Zwölf Boxkämpfer jagen Viktor quer über den großen Sylter Deich. El veloz murciélago hindú comía feliz cardillo y kiwi. La cigüeña tocaba el saxofón detrás del palenque de pajaatur? Rissimo lorereped ex es solore lab id molorro in rempore icabore rehenetur aliam aut voles audae dem quam, secum eum facesequae consequ aepudam quia voluptiur repel in et faccustibus, nonsenis aut quisqui rero mi, ipiet lam ant ut maio et hil molupta tustis atatur, consedi tasimol orerem aut

9/12 Spiegel SemiBold

**The quick brown fox jumps over the lazy dog. Voyez le brick géant que j'examine près du wharf. Zwölf Boxkämpfer jagen Viktor quer über den großen Sylter Deich. El veloz murciélago hindú comía feliz cardillo y kiwi. La cigüeña tocaba el saxofón detrás del palenque de pajaatur? Rissimo lorereped ex es solore lab id molorro in rempore icabore rehenetur aliam aut voles audae dem quam, secum eum facesequae consequ aepudam quia voluptiur repel in et faccustibus, nonsenis aut quisqui rero mi, ipiet lam ant ut maio et hil molupta tustis atatur, consedi tasimol orerem aut volor**

9/12 Spiegel Bold

**The quick brown fox jumps over the lazy dog. Voyez le brick géant que j'examine près du wharf. Zwölf Boxkämpfer jagen Viktor quer über den großen Sylter Deich. El veloz murciélago hindú comía feliz cardillo y kiwi. La cigüeña tocaba el saxofón detrás del palenque de pajaatur? Rissimo lorereped ex es solore lab id molorro**

7/10 Spiegel Regular

The quick brown fox jumps over the lazy dog. Voyez le brick géant que j'examine près du wharf. Zwölf Boxkämpfer jagen Viktor quer über den großen Sylter Deich. El veloz murciélago hindú comía feliz cardillo y kiwi. La cigüeña tocaba el saxofón detrás del palenque de pajaatur? Rissimo lorereped ex es solore lab id molorro in rempore icabore rehenetur aliam aut voles audae dem quam, secum eum facesequae consequ aepudam quia voluptiur repel in et faccustibus, nonsenis aut quisqui rero mi, ipiet lam ant ut maio et hil molupta tustis atatur, consedi tasimol orerem aut volor andipsapis sit, illaut volore officatus alicae dusdaec tatecte cearum qui accatibus restiore nulpa secaerferum, nus dolenim in et quoditat que explam volupictur? Qui de illuptae. Dae nis illiberum volorro ritatis tinullo rerumqu atetur repro eatius asperibus. Rissimo lorereped ex es solore

7/10 Spiegel SemiBold

**The quick brown fox jumps over the lazy dog. Voyez le brick géant que j'examine près du wharf. Zwölf Boxkämpfer jagen Viktor quer über den großen Sylter Deich. El veloz murciélago hindú comía feliz cardillo y kiwi. La cigüeña tocaba el saxofón detrás del palenque de pajaatur? Rissimo lorereped ex es solore lab id molorro in rempore icabore rehenetur aliam aut voles audae dem quam, secum eum facesequae consequ aepudam quia voluptiur repel in et faccustibus, nonsenis aut quisqui rero mi, ipiet lam ant ut maio et hil molupta tustis atatur, consedi tasimol orerem aut volor andipsapis sit, illaut volore officatus alicae dusdaec tatecte cearum qui accatibus restiore nulpa secaerferum, nus dolenim in et quoditat que explam volupictur? Qui de illuptae. Dae nis illiberum volorro ritatis tinullo rerumqu atetur repro eatius asperibus. Rissimo lorereped ex es solore**

7/10 Spiegel Bold

**The quick brown fox jumps over the lazy dog. Voyez le brick géant que j'examine près du wharf. Zwölf Boxkämpfer jagen Viktor quer über den großen Sylter Deich. El veloz murciélago hindú comía feliz cardillo y kiwi. La cigüeña tocaba el saxofón detrás del palenque de pajaatur? Rissimo lorereped ex es solore lab id molorro in rempore icabore rehenetur aliam aut voles audae dem quam, secum eum facesequae consequ aepudam quia voluptiur repel in et faccustibus, nonsenis aut quisqui**

| | | | |
|---|---|---|---|
| Typeface | QuaText | Year | 1994–2011 |
| Designer | Lucas de Groot | Format | OpenType |

# Aa

**QuaText Regular** 24pt
*QuaText Italic* 24pt
**QuaText Bold** 24pt
***QuaText Bold Italic*** 24pt

Aa Bb Cc Dd Ee Ff Gg Hh Ii Jj Kk Ll Mm Nn Oo Pp Qq Rr Ss Tt Uu Vv Ww Xx Yy Zz
0123456789

---

**12/14 — QuaText Regular**

The quick brown fox jumps over the lazy dog. Voyez le brick géant que j'examine près du wharf. Zwölf Boxkämpfer jagen Viktor quer über den großen Sylter Deich. El veloz murciélago hindú comía feliz cardillo y kiwi. La cigüeña tocaba el saxofón detrás del palenque de pajaatur? Rissimo lorereped ex es solore lab id molorro in rempore icabore

**9/12 — QuaText Regular**

The quick brown fox jumps over the lazy dog. Voyez le brick géant que j'examine près du wharf. Zwölf Boxkämpfer jagen Viktor quer über den großen Sylter Deich. El veloz murciélago hindú comía feliz cardillo y kiwi. La cigüeña tocaba el saxofón detrás del palenque de pajaatur? Rissimo lorereped ex es solore lab id molorro in rempore icabore rehenetur aliam aut voles audae dem quam, secum eum facesequae consequ aepudam quia voluptiur repel in et faccustibus, nonsenis aut quisqui rero mi, ipiet lam ant ut maio et hil molupta

**7/10 — QuaText Regular**

The quick brown fox jumps over the lazy dog. Voyez le brick géant que j'examine près du wharf. Zwölf Boxkämpfer jagen Viktor quer über den großen Sylter Deich. El veloz murciélago hindú comía feliz cardillo y kiwi. La cigüeña tocaba el saxofón detrás del palenque de pajaatur? Rissimo lorereped ex es solore lab id molorro in rempore icabore rehenetur aliam aut voles audae dem quam, secum eum facesequae consequ aepudam quia voluptiur repel in et faccustibus, nonsenis aut quisqui rero mi, ipiet lam ant ut maio et hil molupta tustis atatur, consedi tasimol orerem aut volor andipsapis sit, illaut volore officatus alicae dusdaec tatecte cearum qui accatibus restiore nulpa secaerferum, nus dolenim in et quoditat que explam volupictur? Qui de illuptae. Dae nis illiberum volorro ritatis tinullo rerumqu atetur repro eatius asperibus. Rissimo

**12/14 — QuaText Bold**

**The quick brown fox jumps over the lazy dog. Voyez le brick géant que j'examine près du wharf. Zwölf Boxkämpfer jagen Viktor quer über den großen Sylter Deich. El veloz murciélago hindú comía feliz cardillo y kiwi. La cigüeña tocaba el saxofón detrás del palenque de pajaatur? Rissimo lorereped ex es solore lab id molor-**

**9/12 — QuaText Bold**

**The quick brown fox jumps over the lazy dog. Voyez le brick géant que j'examine près du wharf. Zwölf Boxkämpfer jagen Viktor quer über den großen Sylter Deich. El veloz murciélago hindú comía feliz cardillo y kiwi. La cigüeña tocaba el saxofón detrás del palenque de pajaatur? Rissimo lorereped ex es solore lab id molorro in rempore icabore rehenetur aliam aut voles audae dem quam, secum eum facesequae consequ aepudam quia voluptiur repel in et faccustibus, nonsenis aut quisqui rero mi, ipiet lam ant ut maio et hil molupta**

**7/10 — QuaText Bold**

**The quick brown fox jumps over the lazy dog. Voyez le brick géant que j'examine près du wharf. Zwölf Boxkämpfer jagen Viktor quer über den großen Sylter Deich. El veloz murciélago hindú comía feliz cardillo y kiwi. La cigüeña tocaba el saxofón detrás del palenque de pajaatur? Rissimo lorereped ex es solore lab id molorro in rempore icabore rehenetur aliam aut voles audae dem quam, secum eum facesequae consequ aepudam quia voluptiur repel in et faccustibus, nonsenis aut quisqui rero mi, ipiet lam ant ut maio et hil molupta tustis atatur, consedi tasimol orerem aut volor andipsapis sit, illaut volore officatus alicae dusdaec tatecte cearum qui accatibus restiore nulpa secaerferum, nus dolenim in et quoditat que explam volupictur? Qui de illuptae. Dae nis illiberum volorro ritatis tinullo**

# L

## Ludwig Type

Ludwig Übele

Berlin, Germany

Since 2007

Ludwig Type is the personal foundry of Berlin-based graphic designer and type designer Ludwig Übele.

## Info

—Why?
I never thought much about it. I had designed some fonts, and started to offer them on my webpage. After the release of Marat in 2008 more and more people ordered my fonts, so it became a "serious business".

—People on staff
1

—Type designers on staff
1

—Type families
6

—Designers represented
1

—Web shop
www.ludwigtype.de

—Distributors
MyFonts

—Webfont services
Own webfont service (fonts hosted on Ludwig Type's sever)

—Basic license
29–69€ per font (1-5 CPUs)

## People

—Ludwig Übele studied graphic-design in Germany and Finland and worked for five years in several design agencies. In 2007 he graduated from the postgraduate TypeMedia course at the Royal Academy of Arts (KABK) in The Hague, Netherlands. Today Ludwig Übele works in Berlin as a freelance designer in type design and brand development. He started his own foundry in 2007. He received several awards for his type designs (TDC² 2008, TDC² 2010, MyFonts Top 10 Fonts 2008, Granshan 2009).

## Typeface selection

Augustin
**Daisy**
Helsinki
Marat Pro
Mokka
walhalla
walhalla sans

24pt

Page
163

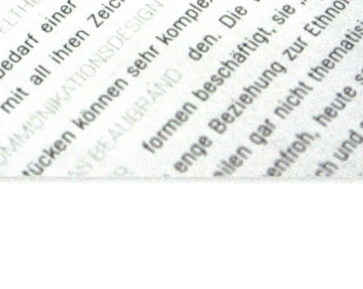

**Opposite page**
Business card designed
by Jürgen Hefele with Daisy.

**Top**
Marat specimen designed
by Ludwig Übele.

**Above and right**
Booklet designed with Helsinki by
Christian Andreas, Maria Arndt,
Clarissa Becker, Christin Ferri, Alex
Katchko and Johannes Nathow.

Foundry  Ludwig Type

Typeface  Augustin           Year     2004
Designer  Ludwig Übele       Format   OpenType

# Aa

Augustin Regular 24pt
*Augustin Italic* 24pt
**Augustin Bold** 24pt
***Augustin Bold Italic*** 24pt

Aa Bb Cc Dd Ee Ff Gg Hh Ii Jj Kk Ll Mm Nn
Oo Pp Qq Rr Ss Tt Uu Vv Ww Xx Yy Zz
0123456789
—

9/12  Augustin Regular

The quick brown fox jumps over the lazy dog. Voyez le brick géant que j'examine près du wharf. Zwölf Boxkämpfer jagen Viktor quer über den großen Sylter Deich. El veloz murciélago hindú comía feliz cardillo y kiwi. La cigüeña tocaba el saxofón detrás del palenque de pajaatur? Rissimo lorereped ex es solore lab id molorro in rempore icabore rehenetur aliam aut voles audae dem quam, secum eum facesequae consequ aepudam quia voluptiur repel in et faccustibus, nonsenis aut quisqui rero mi, ipiet lam ant ut maio et hil molupta tustis atatur, consedi tasimol orerem aut volor andipsapis sit, illaut volore officatus alicae dus-

7/10  Augustin Regular

The quick brown fox jumps over the lazy dog. Voyez le brick géant que j'examine près du wharf. Zwölf Boxkämpfer jagen Viktor quer über den großen Sylter Deich. El veloz murciélago hindú comía feliz cardillo y kiwi. La cigüeña tocaba el saxofón detrás del palenque de pajaatur? Rissimo lorereped ex es solore lab id molorro in rempore icabore rehenetur aliam aut voles audae dem quam, secum eum facesequae consequ aepudam quia voluptiur repel in et faccustibus, nonsenis aut quisqui rero mi, ipiet lam ant ut maio et hil molupta tustis atatur, consedi tasimol orerem aut volor andipsapis sit, illaut volore officatus alicae dusdaec tatecte cearum qui accatibus restiore nulpa secaerferum, nus dolenim in et quoditat que explam volupictur? Qui de illuptae. Dae nis illiberum volorro ritatis tinullo rerumqu atetur repro eatius asperibus. Rissimo lorereped ex es solore lab id molorro in rempore icabore rehenetur aliam aut voles audae dem quam, secum eum facesequae

Typeface  Mokka              Year     2005
Designer  Ludwig Übele       Format   OpenType

# Aa

Mokka Regular 24pt
*Mokka Italic* 24pt
**Mokka Bold** 24pt
***Mokka Bold Italic*** 24pt

Aa Bb Cc Dd Ee Ff Gg Hh Ii Jj Kk Ll
Mm Nn Oo Pp Qq Rr Ss Tt Uu Vv Ww
Xx Yy Zz
0123456789
—

9/12  Mokka Regular

The quick brown fox jumps over the lazy dog. Voyez le brick géant que j'examine près du wharf. Zwölf Boxkämpfer jagen Viktor quer über den großen Sylter Deich. El veloz murciélago hindú comía feliz cardillo y kiwi. La cigüeña tocaba el saxofón detrás del palenque de pajaatur? Rissimo lorereped ex es solore lab id molorro in rempore icabore rehenetur aliam aut voles audae dem quam, secum eum facesequae consequ aepudam quia voluptiur repel in et faccustibus, nonsenis aut quisqui rero mi, ipiet

7/10  Mokka Regular

The quick brown fox jumps over the lazy dog. Voyez le brick géant que j'examine près du wharf. Zwölf Boxkämpfer jagen Viktor quer über den großen Sylter Deich. El veloz murciélago hindú comía feliz cardillo y kiwi. La cigüeña tocaba el saxofón detrás del palenque de pajaatur? Rissimo lorereped ex es solore lab id molorro in rempore icabore rehenetur aliam aut voles audae dem quam, secum eum facesequae consequ aepudam quia voluptiur repel in et faccustibus, nonsenis aut quisqui rero mi, ipiet lam ant ut maio et hil molupta tustis atatur, consedi tasimol orerem aut volor andipsapis sit, illaut volore officatus alicae dusdaec tatecte cearum qui accatibus restiore nulpa secaerferum, nus dolenim in et quoditat que explam volupictur? Qui de illuptae. Dae nis illiberum volorro ritatis tinullo

| | | | |
|---|---|---|---|
| Typeface | Marat Pro | Year | 2008 |
| Designer | Ludwig Übele | Format | OpenType |

# Aa

Aa Bb Cc Dd Ee Ff Gg Hh Ii Jj Kk Ll
Mm Nn Oo Pp Qq Rr Ss Tt Uu Vv Ww
Xx Yy Zz
0123456789
—

Marat Pro Regular 20pt
*Marat Pro Regular Italic 20pt*
**Marat Pro Medium 20pt**
*Marat Pro Medium Italic 20pt*
**Marat Pro Bold 20pt**
***Marat Pro Bold Italic 20pt***
**Marat Pro Black 20pt**
***Marat Pro Black Italic 20pt***
**Marat Pro Fat 20pt**

---

12/14  Marat Pro Regular

The quick brown fox jumps over the lazy dog. Voyez le brick géant que j'examine près du wharf. Zwölf Boxkämpfer jagen Viktor quer über den großen Sylter Deich. El veloz murciélago hindú comía feliz cardillo y kiwi. La cigüeña tocaba el saxofón detrás del palenque de pajaatur? Rissimo lorereped ex es solore lab id molorro in rempore icabore rehenetur aliam aut voles audae dem quam, secum

9/12  Marat Pro Regular

The quick brown fox jumps over the lazy dog. Voyez le brick géant que j'examine près du wharf. Zwölf Boxkämpfer jagen Viktor quer über den großen Sylter Deich. El veloz murciélago hindú comía feliz cardillo y kiwi. La cigüeña tocaba el saxofón detrás del palenque de pajaatur? Rissimo lorereped ex es solore lab id molorro in rempore icabore rehenetur aliam aut voles audae dem quam, secum eum facesequae consequ aepudam quia voluptiur repel in et faccustibus, nonsenis aut quisqui rero mi, ipiet lam ant ut maio et hil molupta tustis atatur, consedi tasimol orerem aut volor andipsapis sit, illaut volore officatus alicae dusdaec

7/10  Marat Pro Regular

The quick brown fox jumps over the lazy dog. Voyez le brick géant que j'examine près du wharf. Zwölf Boxkämpfer jagen Viktor quer über den großen Sylter Deich. El veloz murciélago hindú comía feliz cardillo y kiwi. La cigüeña tocaba el saxofón detrás del palenque de pajaatur? Rissimo lorereped ex es solore lab id molorro in rempore icabore rehenetur aliam aut voles audae dem quam, secum eum facesequae consequ aepudam quia voluptiur repel in et faccustibus, nonsenis aut quisqui rero mi, ipiet lam ant ut maio et hil molupta tustis atatur, consedi tasimol orerem aut volor andipsapis sit, illaut volore officatus alicae dusdaec tatecte cearum qui accatibus restiore nulpa secaerferum, nus dolenim in et quoditat que explam volupictur? Qui de illuptae. Dae nis illiberum volorro ritatis tinullo rerumqu atetur repro eatius asperibus. Rissimo lorereped ex es solore lab id molorro in rempore icabore rehenetur aliam aut voles audae dem quam, secum

12/14  Marat Pro Medium

**The quick brown fox jumps over the lazy dog. Voyez le brick géant que j'examine près du wharf. Zwölf Boxkämpfer jagen Viktor quer über den großen Sylter Deich. El veloz murciélago hindú comía feliz cardillo y kiwi. La cigüeña tocaba el saxofón detrás del palenque de pajaa-**

9/12  Marat Pro Medium

**The quick brown fox jumps over the lazy dog. Voyez le brick géant que j'examine près du wharf. Zwölf Boxkämpfer jagen Viktor quer über den großen Sylter Deich. El veloz murciélago hindú comía feliz cardillo y kiwi. La cigüeña tocaba el saxofón detrás del palenque de pajaatur? Rissimo lorereped ex es solore lab id molorro in rempore icabore rehenetur aliam aut voles audae dem quam, secum eum facesequae consequ ae-**

7/10  Marat Pro Medium

**The quick brown fox jumps over the lazy dog. Voyez le brick géant que j'examine près du wharf. Zwölf Boxkämpfer jagen Viktor quer über den großen Sylter Deich. El veloz murciélago hindú comía feliz cardillo y kiwi. La cigüeña tocaba el saxofón detrás del palenque de pajaatur? Rissimo lorereped ex es solore lab id molorro in rempore icabore rehenetur aliam aut voles audae dem quam, secum eum facesequae consequ aepudam quia voluptiur repel in et faccustibus, nonsenis aut quisqui rero mi, ipiet lam ant ut maio et hil molupta tustis atatur, consedi tasimol orerem aut volor andipsapis sit, illaut volore officatus alicae dusdaec tatecte cearum qui accatibus restiore nulpa**

12/14  Marat Pro Bold

**The quick brown fox jumps over the lazy dog. Voyez le brick géant que j'examine près du wharf. Zwölf Boxkämpfer jagen Viktor quer über den großen Sylter Deich. El veloz murciélago hindú comía feliz cardillo y kiwi. La cigüeña tocaba el saxofón detrás del palenque de pajaatur? Rissimo lorereped ex es solore lab id molorro in rempore icabore rehenetur**

9/12  Marat Pro Bold

**The quick brown fox jumps over the lazy dog. Voyez le brick géant que j'examine près du wharf. Zwölf Boxkämpfer jagen Viktor quer über den großen Sylter Deich. El veloz murciélago hindú comía feliz cardillo y kiwi. La cigüeña tocaba el saxofón detrás del palenque de pajaatur? Rissimo lorereped ex es solore lab id molorro in rempore icabore rehenetur aliam aut voles audae dem quam, secum eum facesequae consequ aepudam quia voluptiur repel in et faccustibus, nonsenis aut quisqui rero mi, ipiet lam ant ut maio et hil mo-**

7/10  Marat Pro Bold

**The quick brown fox jumps over the lazy dog. Voyez le brick géant que j'examine près du wharf. Zwölf Boxkämpfer jagen Viktor quer über den großen Sylter Deich. El veloz murciélago hindú comía feliz cardillo y kiwi. La cigüeña tocaba el saxofón detrás del palenque de pajaatur? Rissimo lorereped ex es solore lab id molorro in rempore icabore rehenetur aliam aut voles audae dem quam, secum eum facesequae consequ aepudam quia voluptiur repel in et faccustibus, nonsenis aut quisqui rero mi, ipiet lam ant ut maio et hil molupta tustis atatur, consedi tasimol orerem aut volor andipsapis sit, illaut volore officatus alicae dusdaec tatecte cearum qui accatibus restiore nulpa secaerferum, nus dolenim in et quoditat que explam volupictur? Qui de illuptae. Dae nis illiberum volorro ritatis tinullo rerumqu atetur repro eatius asperibus. Rissimo lorereped ex es solore lab id molorro**

Foundry  Ludwig Type

Typeface  Daisy
Designer  Ludwig Übele
Year  2010
Format  OpenType

# Funky town

**Regular**
*Kursive*

Aa Bb Cc Dd Ee Ff Gg Hh Ii Jj Kk Ll Mm Nn Oo Pp Qq Rr Ss Tt Uu Vv Ww Xx Yy Zz 0123456789

Typeface  Walhalla
Designer  Ludwig Übele
Year  2003
Format  OpenType

# odin's hall

Regular

Aa Bb Cc Dd Ee Ff Gg Hh ii jj kk ll mm Nn oo pp Qq Rr ss Tt uu vv ww xx yy zz 0123456789

Typeface  Walhalla Sans
Designer  Ludwig Übele
Year  2003
Format  OpenType

# Thor's Anger

Regular

Aa Bb Cc Dd Ee Ff Gg Hh ii jj kk ll mm Nn oo pp Qq Rr ss Tt uu vv ww xx yy zz 0123456789

Page 167

Foundry  Ludwig Type

Typeface  Helsinki
Designer  Ludwig Übele
Year  1998
Format  OpenType

# Aa

Aa Bb Cc Dd Ee Ff Gg Hh Ii Jj Kk
Ll Mm Nn Oo Pp Qq Rr Ss Tt Uu Vv
Ww Xx Yy Zz
0123456789
—

Helsinki Hairline 40pt
Helsinki Light 40pt
Helsinki Book 40pt
Helsinki Regular 40pt
Helsinki Bold 40pt
Helsinki Black 40pt
Helsinki Fat 40pt

---

12/14  Helsinki Light

The quick brown fox jumps over the lazy dog. Voyez le brick géant que j'examine près du wharf. Zwölf Boxkämpfer jagen Viktor quer über den

9/12  Helsinki Light

The quick brown fox jumps over the lazy dog. Voyez le brick géant que j'examine près du wharf. Zwölf Boxkämpfer jagen Viktor quer über den großen Sylter Deich. El veloz murciélago hindú comía feliz cardillo y kiwi. La cigüeña tocaba el

7/10  Helsinki Light

The quick brown fox jumps over the lazy dog. Voyez le brick géant que j'examine près du wharf. Zwölf Boxkämpfer jagen Viktor quer über den großen Sylter Deich. El veloz murciélago hindú comía feliz cardillo y kiwi. La cigüeña tocaba el saxofón detrás del palenque de pajaatur? Rissimo lorereped ex es solore lab id molorro in rempore icabore rehenetur aliam aut voles audae dem

12/14  Helsinki Book

The quick brown fox jumps over the lazy dog. Voyez le brick géant que j'examine près du wharf. Zwölf Boxkämpfer jagen Viktor quer über den großen

9/12  Helsinki Book

The quick brown fox jumps over the lazy dog. Voyez le brick géant que j'examine près du wharf. Zwölf Boxkämpfer jagen Viktor quer über den großen Sylter Deich. El veloz murciélago hindú comía feliz cardillo y kiwi. La cigüeña tocaba el saxofón detrás del

7/10  Helsinki Book

The quick brown fox jumps over the lazy dog. Voyez le brick géant que j'examine près du wharf. Zwölf Boxkämpfer jagen Viktor quer über den großen Sylter Deich. El veloz murciélago hindú comía feliz cardillo y kiwi. La cigüeña tocaba el saxofón detrás del palenque de pajaatur? Rissimo lorereped ex es solore lab id molorro in rempore icabore rehenetur aliam aut voles audae dem quam, secum eum

12/14  Helsinki Regular

The quick brown fox jumps over the lazy dog. Voyez le brick géant que j'examine près du wharf. Zwölf Boxkämpfer jagen Viktor quer über den großen Sylter

9/12  Helsinki Regular

The quick brown fox jumps over the lazy dog. Voyez le brick géant que j'examine près du wharf. Zwölf Boxkämpfer jagen Viktor quer über den großen Sylter Deich. El veloz murciélago hindú comía feliz cardillo y kiwi. La cigüeña tocaba el saxofón detrás del palenque

7/10  Helsinki Regular

The quick brown fox jumps over the lazy dog. Voyez le brick géant que j'examine près du wharf. Zwölf Boxkämpfer jagen Viktor quer über den großen Sylter Deich. El veloz murciélago hindú comía feliz cardillo y kiwi. La cigüeña tocaba el saxofón detrás del palenque de pajaatur? Rissimo lorereped ex es solore lab id molorro in rempore icabore rehenetur aliam aut voles audae dem quam, secum eum

12/14  Helsinki Bold

**The quick brown fox jumps over the lazy dog. Voyez le brick géant que j'examine près du wharf. Zwölf Boxkämpfer jagen Viktor quer über den großen Sylter Deich. El veloz murciélago hindú comía feliz cardillo y kiwi. La cigüeña tocaba el saxofón**

9/12  Helsinki Bold

**The quick brown fox jumps over the lazy dog. Voyez le brick géant que j'examine près du wharf. Zwölf Boxkämpfer jagen Viktor quer über den großen Sylter Deich. El veloz murciélago hindú comía feliz cardillo y kiwi. La cigüeña tocaba el saxofón detrás del palenque de pajaatur? Rissimo lorereped ex es solore lab id molorro in rempore icabore rehenetur aliam aut voles audae dem**

7/10  Helsinki Bold

**The quick brown fox jumps over the lazy dog. Voyez le brick géant que j'examine près du wharf. Zwölf Boxkämpfer jagen Viktor quer über den großen Sylter Deich. El veloz murciélago hindú comía feliz cardillo y kiwi. La cigüeña tocaba el saxofón detrás del palenque de pajaatur? Rissimo lorereped ex es solore lab id molorro in rempore icabore rehenetur aliam aut voles audae dem quam, secum eum facesequae consequ aepudam quia voluptiur repel in et faccustibus, nonsenis aut quisqui rero mi, ipiet lam ant ut maio et hil molupta tustis atatur, consedi tasimol orerem aut**

# M
## MilieuGrotesque

—

Timo Gaessner,
Alexander Meyer

—

Zürich,
Switzerland

—

Since
2010

MilieuGrotesque is an independent publisher and distributor of typefaces and related publications. Set up by graphic designers Alexander Meyer and Timo Gaessner, MilieuGrotesque reflects their ongoing interest and involvement with all things typographical in work and thought.

## Info

—Why?
Well, it's good to know who buys your soul — but mainly we didn't feel well represented by the options we had and felt the urge to do it our own way.

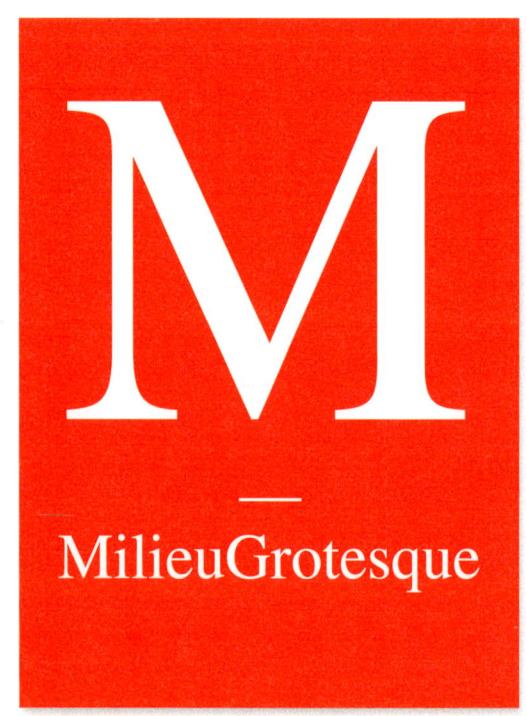

—People on staff
3

—Type designers on staff
3

—Type families
5

—Designers represented
3

—Web shop
milieugrotesque.com

—Distributors
None

—Webfont services
None

—Basic license
99.– CHF (single font for 1–3CPUs)
A 4-weight family is 249.– CHF

## Biographies

—Timo Gaessner, Berlin based graphic designer and typographer, studied at Gerrit Rietveld Academie in Amsterdam and launched studio 123buero after graduating in 2002. The studio's approach is defined by research and analytic thinking, focusing on printed matter, identity programs, exhibition and type design. In 2010, he co-founded Zürich based independent type foundry Milieu-Grotesque, through which he has published most of his recently developed typefaces. Timo has lectured and given workshops at the École nationale supérieure des Arts Décoratifs in Paris, Hochschule für Künste in Bremen and Staatliche Hochschule für Gestaltung in Karlsruhe, among others.

—Alexander Meyer, Zürich based graphic designer and typographer, studied Visual Communication at Zurich University of the Arts and launched studio xyz.ch after graduating in 2003. His work focuses on typography and is influenced by the manual aspects of old typesetting technics. Inspired by vintage typewriters, he started to design the slab-serif typeface family Lacrima and Generika. As result, he co-founded Zürich based independent type foundry MilieuGrotesque in 2010. Alex has lectured at F+F School of Art and Media Design in Zurich and and run letterpress workshops at the Berufsschule für Gestaltung Zürich.

## Typeface selection

Brezel Grotesk
Chapeau
Generika MG
LacrimaMG-Senza
LacrimaMG-Serif

24pt

MilieuGrotesque Logo

Page
169

Lacrima

Brezel Grotesk

Chapeau

Generika MG

Foundry MilieuGrotesque

Typeface  Generika MG
Designer  Alexander Meyer
          (XYZ.ch)
Year      2008
Format    OpenType

# General
# **Motors**

Light
*Light Italic*
Regular
*Italic*
**Bold**
***Bold Italic***

Aa Bb Cc Dd Ee Ff Gg Hh Ii Jj Kk Ll Mm
Nn Oo Pp Qq Rr Ss Tt Uu Vv Ww Xx Yy
Zz 0123456789

Typeface  Chapeau
Designer  Timo Gaessner
          (123Buero.ch)
Year      2010
Format    OpenType

# *Chapeau*
# *Por mi*

Regular
*Italic*

Aa Bb Cc Dd Ee Ff Gg Hh
Ii Jj Kk Ll Mm Nn Oo Pp
Qq Rr Ss Tt Uu Vv Ww Xx
Yy Zz 0123456789

Typeface  Brezel Grotesk
Designer  Stefan Preis
          (Burri-Preis)
Year      2011
Format    OpenType

# ***Laugen***
# Brötchen
# *mit Butter*

Regular
*Italic*
**Bold**
***Bold Italic***

Aa Bb Cc Dd Ee Ff Gg Hh Ii Jj Kk
Ll Mm Nn Oo Pp Qq Rr Ss Tt Uu
Vv Ww Xx Yy Zz 0123456789

Page
171

Foundry  MilieuGrotesque

Typeface  LacrimaMG-Senza, Serif
Designer  Alexander Meyer
(XYZ.ch)

Year  2010
Format  OpenType

# Aa

Aa Bb Cc Dd Ee Ff Gg Hh Ii Jj
Kk Ll Mm Nn Oo Pp Qq Rr Ss
Tt Uu Vv Ww Xx Yy Zz
0123456789
_

LacrimaMG-Senza Light 22pt
LacrimaMG-Senza Regular 22pt
**LacrimaMG-Senza Bold 22pt**

LacrimaMG-Serif Light 22pt
LacrimaMG-Serif Regular 22pt
**LacrimaMG-Serif Bold 22pt**
*LacrimaMG-Italic Light 22pt*
*LacrimaMG-Italic Regular 22pt*
***LacrimaMG-Italic Bold 22pt***

---

12/14  LacrimaMG-Senza Light

The quick brown fox jumps over the lazy dog. Voyez le brick géant que j'examine près du wharf. Zwölf Boxkämpfer jagen Viktor quer über den großen Sylter Deich. El veloz murciélago hindú comía fe-

12/14  LacrimaMG-Senza Regular

The quick brown fox jumps over the lazy dog. Voyez le brick géant que j'examine près du wharf. Zwölf Boxkämpfer jagen Viktor quer über den großen Sylter Deich. El veloz murciélago hindú comía fe-

12/14  LacrimaMG-Senza Bold

**The quick brown fox jumps over the lazy dog. Voyez le brick géant que j'examine près du wharf. Zwölf Boxkämpfer jagen Viktor quer über den großen Sylter Deich. El veloz murciélago hindú comía fe- liz cardillo y kiwi. La cigüeña**

9/12  LacrimaMG-Serif Light

The quick brown fox jumps over the lazy dog. Voyez le brick géant que j'examine près du wharf. Zwölf Boxkämpfer jagen Viktor quer über den großen Sylter Deich. El veloz murciélago hindú comía feliz

9/12  LacrimaMG-Serif Regular

The quick brown fox jumps over the lazy dog. Voyez le brick géant que j'examine près du wharf. Zwölf Boxkämpfer jagen Viktor quer über den großen Sylter Deich. El veloz murciélago hindú comía fe-

9/12  LacrimaMG-Serif Bold

**The quick brown fox jumps over the lazy dog. Voyez le brick géant que j'examine près du wharf. Zwölf Boxkämp- fer jagen Viktor quer über den großen Sylter Deich. El veloz murciélago hindú comía feliz cardillo y kiwi. La cigüeña**

7/10  LacrimaMG-Italic Light

*The quick brown fox jumps over the lazy dog. Voyez le brick géant que j'examine près du wharf. Zwölf Boxkämpfer jagen Viktor quer über den großen Sylter Deich. El veloz murcié- lago hindú comía feliz cardillo*

7/10  LacrimaMG-Italic Regular

*The quick brown fox jumps over the lazy dog. Voyez le brick géant que j'examine près du wharf. Zwölf Boxkämpfer jagen Viktor quer über den großen Sylter Deich. El veloz murcié- lago hindú comía feliz cardillo*

7/10  LacrimaMG-Italic Bold

***The quick brown fox jumps over the lazy dog. Voyez le brick géant que j'examine près du wharf. Zwölf Boxkämpfer jagen Viktor quer über den großen Sylter Deich. El veloz murcié- lago hindú comía feliz cardillo y kiwi. La cigüeña tocaba el***

# N
— Neutura

—

Alexander McCracken

—

San Francisco, USA

—

Since 2003

The Neutura type studio was founded by designer Alexander McCracken, who is joined by type specialist Frank Lawton. They are dedicated to designing and developing high quality typefaces for both independent release as well as bespoke typefaces and customization of existing typefaces in the catalog.

## Info

—Why?
Neutura was formed in 2003 to make fine display typefaces. However, text faces have not been ruled out completely. We have done several exclusive text faces for clients around the world.

—People on staff
2

—Type designers on staff
1

—Type families
26

—Designers represented
2

—Web shop
neutura.org

—Distributors
T26, HypeForType

—Webfont services
None

—Basic license
Prices range from $30 to $100

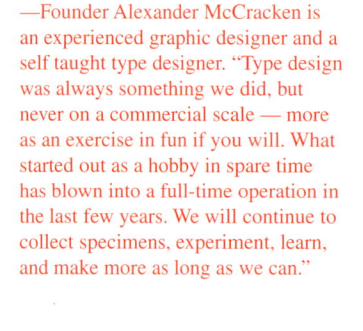

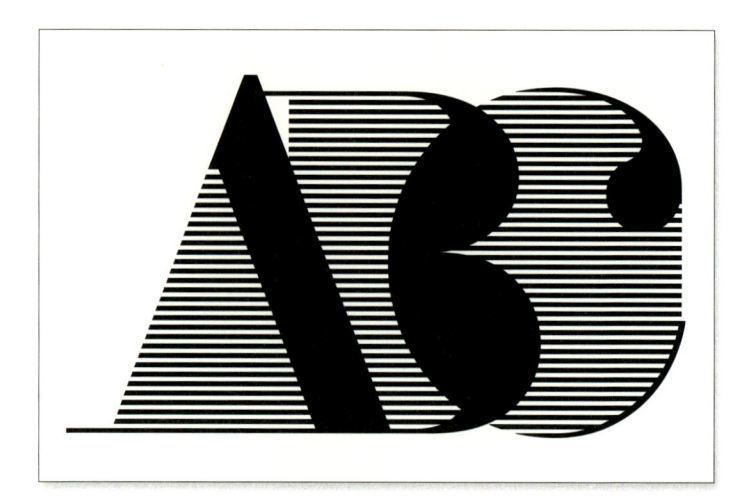

## Typeface selection

NE AIRES
NE Aperture
NE BELFAST
NE DEUCE
NE MAGNUM
NE Sarcophagus

24pt

## People

—Founder Alexander McCracken is an experienced graphic designer and a self taught type designer. "Type design was always something we did, but never on a commercial scale — more as an exercise in fun if you will. What started out as a hobby in spare time has blown into a full-time operation in the last few years. We will continue to collect specimens, experiment, learn, and make more as long as we can."

Bé
Royál
Usé
Royalé

**Top**
This piece of lettering exemplifies Neutura's late-modern op-art esthetics.

**Bottom**
Royalé is a typeface in the nineteenth-century tradition of bold, high-contrast 'modern face' based on the Bodoni model.

**Above**
Aperture Bold, the heaviest weight of a family of three that takes a different look at the concept of the geometric sans-serif.

**Right**
Estrella, another high-contrast, spirited modern face, is one of Neutura's most recent fonts.

**Top**
Dirty words and 19-century esthetics, both elegantly deconstructed.

**Bottom**
Neutrino, an alphabet with no counters. Not ideal for timetables.

Foundry Neutura

| Typeface | NE Aires | Year | 2010 |
| --- | --- | --- | --- |
| Designer | Alexander McCracken, Strahan McMullen | Format | OpenType |

STRETCH UR ARMS WIDELY

LIGHT
REGULAR
**BOLD**

AA BB CC DD EE
FF GG HH II JJ KK
LL MM NN OO PP
QQ RR SS TT UU
VV WW XX YY ZZ
0123456789

| Typeface | NE Aperture | Year | 2010 |
| --- | --- | --- | --- |
| Designer | Alexander McCracken | Format | OpenType |

Big Staple

Light

Regular

**Heavy**

Aa Bb Cc Dd Ee Ff Gg Hh Ii Jj Kk
Ll Mm Nn Oo Pp Qq Rr Ss Tt Uu Vv
Ww Xx Yy Zz 0123456789

| Typeface | NE Sarcophagus | Year | 2002 |
| --- | --- | --- | --- |
| Designer | Alexander McCracken | Format | OpenType |

Tombstone Ornament

Regular
**Bold**

Aa Bb Cc Dd Ee Ff Gg Hh Ii Jj
Kk Ll Mm Nn Oo Pp Qq Rr Ss Tt
Uu Vv Ww Xx Yy Zz 0123456789

Page 175 · Foundry Neutura

| | | | |
|---|---|---|---|
| Typeface | NE Belfast | Year | 2010 |
| Designer | Alexander McCracken, Grant Dickson | Format | OpenType |

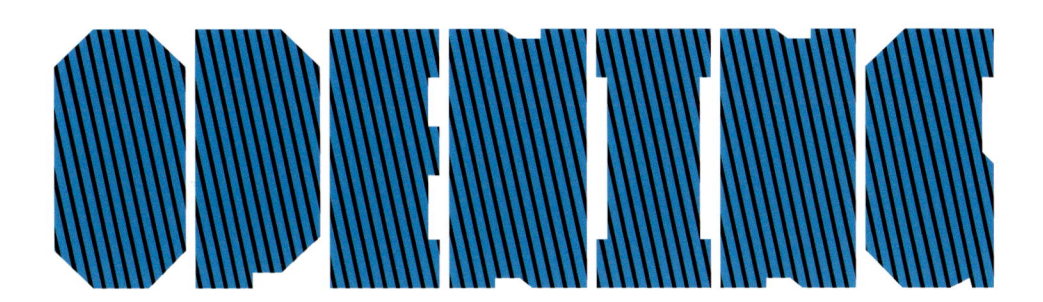

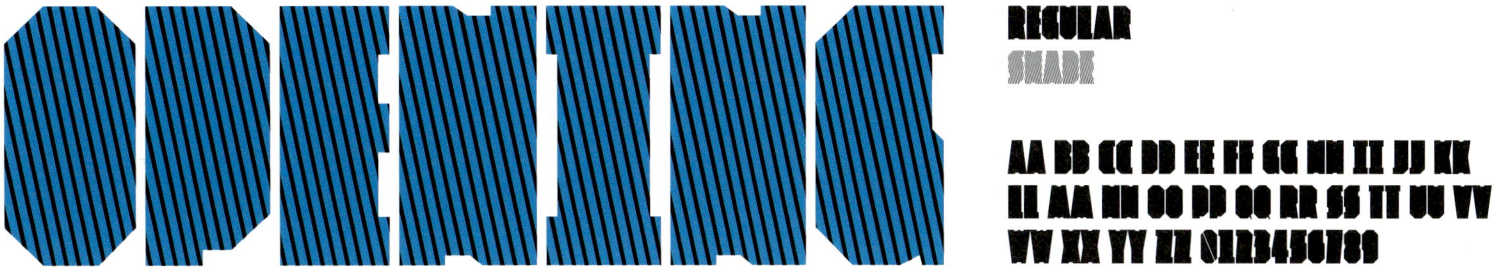

**OPENING**

REGULAR
SHADE

AA BB CC DD EE FF GG HH II JJ KK
LL MM NN OO PP QQ RR SS TT UU VV
WW XX YY ZZ 0123456789

| | | | |
|---|---|---|---|
| Typeface | NE Deuce | Year | 2003 |
| Designer | Alexander McCracken | Format | OpenType |

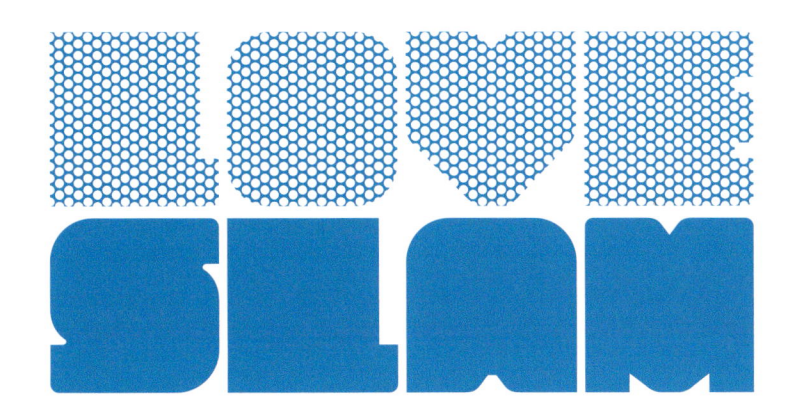

**LOVE SLAM**

BLACK
SCORE
ROUND

AA BB CC DD EE FF
GG HH II JJ KK LL
MM NN OO PP QQ RR SS
TT UU VV WW XX YY ZZ
0123456789

| | | | |
|---|---|---|---|
| Typeface | NE Magnum | Year | 2005 |
| Designer | Alexander McCracken | Format | OpenType |

**PHOTO GRAPHS**

ALTERNATE HEAVY

AA BB CC DD EE FF GG HH II
JJ KK LL MM NN OO PP QQ
RR SS TT UU VV WW XX YY
ZZ 0123456789

# O
## Optimo

David Rust,
Gilles Gavillet

—

Geneva,
Switzerland

—

Since
1998

Optimo is a Swiss foundry publishing original typefaces since 1998. Its principals David Rust and Gilles Gavillet also run Gavillet & Rust, a graphic design studio working for clients in both cultural and commercial fields with a focus on editorial design, brand identities and typeface development. The Optimo library presents a selection of refined typefaces that have continuously appealed to designers across the globe for their unique ability to create iconic design pieces.

## Info

—People on staff
4

—Type designers on staff
2

—Type families
15

—Designers represented
7

—Web shop
optimo.ch

—Distributors
We are the exclusive distributors of our fonts (except for webfonts).

—Webfont services
WebINK

—Basic license
from 100 to 150 CHF for 5 computers
(about $120 to 180)

Typeface selection

**Cargo**
Dada Grotesk
Executive
Hermes
Theinhardt

24pt

## People

François Rappo: Theinhardt, CEO, Didot Elder
deValence (Alexandre Dimos and Gaël Etienne): Dada Grotesk
Julien Gaillardot: Pharma
Niels Wehrspann: Gravostyle Basic

Nicolas Eigenheer: Material
Philipp Hermann: Piek
Philippe Desarzens: Editor

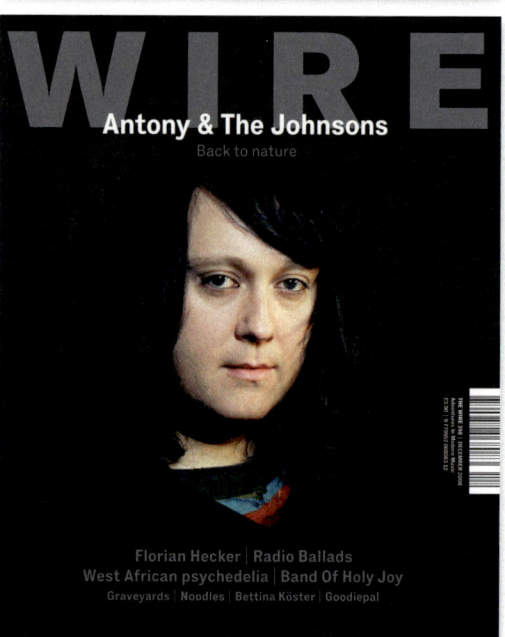

The Executive type family was used throughout Ben Weaver's redesign of British music magazine *Wire*.

Page 177

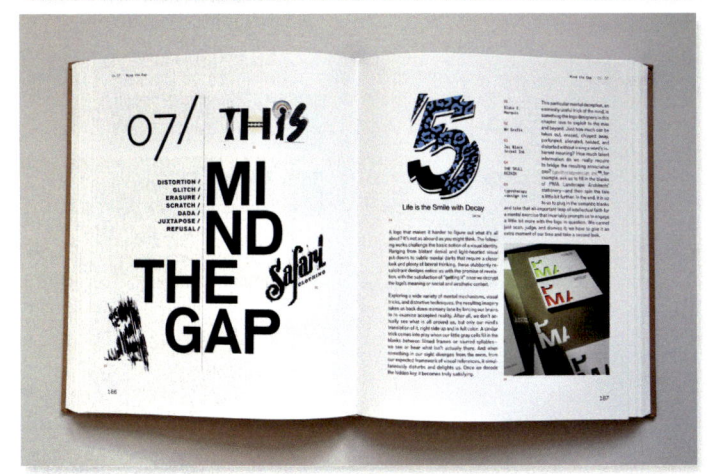

*Los Logos Compass* (Gestalten, 2010). Designed by Adeline Mollard using Optimo's Dada Grotesk.

Since spring 2010, Optimo's Theinhardt typeface has regularly graced covers of the *New York Times Magazine*. Design director: Arem Duplessis. Art director: Gail Bichler. Designer: Hilary Greenbaum.

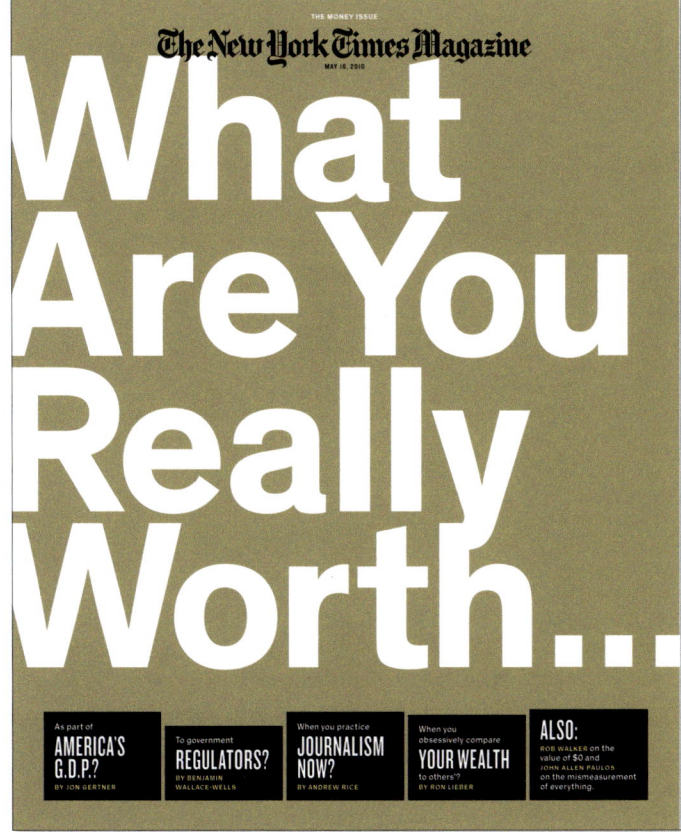

Page 178

Foundry Optimo

Typeface Executive
Designer Gilles Gavillet, David Rust

Year 2007 (remastered 2010)
Format OpenType

# Aa

Aa Bb Cc Dd Ee Ff Gg Hh Ii Jj Kk Ll Mm Nn Oo Pp Qq Rr Ss Tt Uu Vv Ww Xx Yy Zz
0123456789
—

Executive Thin 24pt
*Executive Thin Italic 24pt*
Executive Light 24pt
*Executive Light Italic 24pt*
Executive Regular 24pt
*Executive Regular Italic 24pt*
**Executive Medium 24pt**
***Executive Medium Italic 24pt***
**Executive Bold 24pt**
***Executive Bold Italic 24pt***

---

12/14 Executive Light

The quick brown fox jumps over the lazy dog. Voyez le brick géant que j'examine près du wharf. Zwölf Boxkämpfer jagen Viktor quer über den

12/14 Executive Regular

The quick brown fox jumps over the lazy dog. Voyez le brick géant que j'examine près du wharf. Zwölf Boxkämpfer jagen Viktor quer über

12/14 Executive Medium

The quick brown fox jumps over the lazy dog. Voyez le brick géant que j'examine près du wharf. Zwölf Boxkämpfer jagen Vik-

12/14 Executive Bold

The quick brown fox jumps over the lazy dog. Voyez le brick géant que j'examine près du wharf. Zwölf Boxkämpfer jagen Viktor quer über den großen Sylter Deich. El veloz murciélago

9/12 Executive Light

The quick brown fox jumps over the lazy dog. Voyez le brick géant que j'examine près du wharf. Zwölf Boxkämpfer jagen Viktor quer über den großen Sylter Deich. El veloz murciélago hindú comía feliz cardillo y kiwi. La cigüeña

9/12 Executive Regular

The quick brown fox jumps over the lazy dog. Voyez le brick géant que j'examine près du wharf. Zwölf Boxkämpfer jagen Viktor quer über den großen Sylter Deich. El veloz murciélago hindú comía feliz cardillo y kiwi. La

9/12 Executive Medium

The quick brown fox jumps over the lazy dog. Voyez le brick géant que j'examine près du wharf. Zwölf Boxkämpfer jagen Viktor quer über den großen Sylter Deich. El veloz murciélago hindú comía feliz cardillo y kiwi.

9/12 Executive Bold

The quick brown fox jumps over the lazy dog. Voyez le brick géant que j'examine près du wharf. Zwölf Boxkämpfer jagen Viktor quer über den großen Sylter Deich. El veloz murciélago hindú comía feliz cardillo y kiwi. La cigüeña tocaba el saxofón detrás del palenque de pajaatur? Rissimo lorer-

7/10 Executive Light

The quick brown fox jumps over the lazy dog. Voyez le brick géant que j'examine près du wharf. Zwölf Boxkämpfer jagen Viktor quer über den großen Sylter Deich. El veloz murciélago hindú comía feliz cardillo y kiwi. La cigüeña tocaba el saxofón detrás del palenque de pajaatur? Rissimo lorereped ex es solore lab id molorro in rempore icabore rehenetur aliam

7/10 Executive Regular

The quick brown fox jumps over the lazy dog. Voyez le brick géant que j'examine près du wharf. Zwölf Boxkämpfer jagen Viktor quer über den großen Sylter Deich. El veloz murciélago hindú comía feliz cardillo y kiwi. La cigüeña tocaba el saxofón detrás del palenque de pajaatur? Rissimo lorereped ex es solore lab id molorro in rempore icabore

7/10 Executive Medium

The quick brown fox jumps over the lazy dog. Voyez le brick géant que j'examine près du wharf. Zwölf Boxkämpfer jagen Viktor quer über den großen Sylter Deich. El veloz murciélago hindú comía feliz cardillo y kiwi. La cigüeña tocaba el saxofón detrás del palenque de pajaatur? Rissimo lorereped ex es solore lab id molorro in rempore

7/10 Executive Bold

The quick brown fox jumps over the lazy dog. Voyez le brick géant que j'examine près du wharf. Zwölf Boxkämpfer jagen Viktor quer über den großen Sylter Deich. El veloz murciélago hindú comía feliz cardillo y kiwi. La cigüeña tocaba el saxofón detrás del palenque de pajaatur? Rissimo lorereped ex es solore lab id molorro in rempore icabore rehenetur aliam aut voles audae dem quam, secum eum facesequae consequ aepudam quia

Page
179

Foundry   Optimo

Typeface  Theinhardt
Designer  François Rappo

Year    2009 (remastered 2010)
Format  OpenType

# Aa

Aa Bb Cc Dd Ee Ff Gg Hh Ii Jj Kk
Ll Mm Nn Oo Pp Qq Rr Ss Tt Uu Vv
Ww Xx Yy Zz
0123456789
—

Theinhardt Hairline 16pt
*Theinhardt Hairline Italic 16pt*
Theinhardt Ultra Light 16pt
*Theinhardt Ultra Light Italic 16pt*
Theinhardt Thin 16pt
*Theinhardt Thin Italic 16pt*
Theinhardt Light 16pt
*Theinhardt Light Italic 16pt*
Theinhardt Regular 16pt
*Theinhardt Regular Italic 16pt*
**Theinhardt Medium 16pt**
***Theinhardt Medium Italic 16pt***
**Theinhardt Bold 16pt**
***Theinhardt Bold Italic 16pt***
**Theinhardt Heavy 16pt**
***Theinhardt Heavy Italic 16pt***
**Theinhardt Black 16pt**
***Theinhardt Black Italic 16pt***

---

12/14   Theinhardt Light

The quick brown fox jumps over the lazy dog. Voyez le brick géant que j'examine près du wharf. Zwölf Boxkämpfer jagen Viktor quer über den

12/14   Theinhardt Regular

The quick brown fox jumps over the lazy dog. Voyez le brick géant que j'examine près du wharf. Zwölf Boxkämpfer jagen Viktor quer über den

12/14   Theinhardt Medium

**The quick brown fox jumps over the lazy dog. Voyez le brick géant que j'examine près du wharf. Zwölf Boxkämpfer jagen Viktor quer über den**

12/14   Theinhardt Bold

**The quick brown fox jumps over the lazy dog. Voyez le brick géant que j'examine près du wharf. Zwölf Boxkämpfer jagen Viktor quer über den großen Sylter Deich. El veloz murciélago hindú comía feliz**

---

9/12   Theinhardt Light

The quick brown fox jumps over the lazy dog. Voyez le brick géant que j'examine près du wharf. Zwölf Boxkämpfer jagen Viktor quer über den großen Sylter Deich. El veloz murciélago hindú comía feliz cardillo y kiwi. La cigüeña tocaba el saxofón detrás

9/12   Theinhardt Regular

The quick brown fox jumps over the lazy dog. Voyez le brick géant que j'examine près du wharf. Zwölf Boxkämpfer jagen Viktor quer über den großen Sylter Deich. El veloz murciélago hindú comía feliz cardillo y kiwi. La cigüeña tocaba el

9/12   Theinhardt Medium

**The quick brown fox jumps over the lazy dog. Voyez le brick géant que j'examine près du wharf. Zwölf Boxkämpfer jagen Viktor quer über den großen Sylter Deich. El veloz murciélago hindú comía feliz cardillo y kiwi. La cigüeña tocaba**

9/12   Theinhardt Bold

**The quick brown fox jumps over the lazy dog. Voyez le brick géant que j'examine près du wharf. Zwölf Boxkämpfer jagen Viktor quer über den großen Sylter Deich. El veloz murciélago hindú comía feliz cardillo y kiwi. La cigüeña tocaba el saxofón detrás del palenque de pajaatur? Rissimo lorereped ex es solore**

---

7/10   Theinhardt Light

The quick brown fox jumps over the lazy dog. Voyez le brick géant que j'examine près du wharf. Zwölf Boxkämpfer jagen Viktor quer über den großen Sylter Deich. El veloz murciélago hindú comía feliz cardillo y kiwi. La cigüeña tocaba el saxofón detrás del palenque de pajaatur? Rissimo lorereped ex es solore lab id molorro in rempore icabore rehenetur aliam aut voles audae dem

7/10   Theinhardt Regular

The quick brown fox jumps over the lazy dog. Voyez le brick géant que j'examine près du wharf. Zwölf Boxkämpfer jagen Viktor quer über den großen Sylter Deich. El veloz murciélago hindú comía feliz cardillo y kiwi. La cigüeña tocaba el saxofón detrás del palenque de pajaatur? Rissimo lorereped ex es solore lab id molorro in rempore icabore rehenetur aliam aut voles au-

7/10   Theinhardt Medium

**The quick brown fox jumps over the lazy dog. Voyez le brick géant que j'examine près du wharf. Zwölf Boxkämpfer jagen Viktor quer über den großen Sylter Deich. El veloz murciélago hindú comía feliz cardillo y kiwi. La cigüeña tocaba el saxofón detrás del palenque de pajaatur? Rissimo lorereped ex es solore lab id molorro in rempore icabore rehenetur aliam aut voles**

7/10   Theinhardt Bold

**The quick brown fox jumps over the lazy dog. Voyez le brick géant que j'examine près du wharf. Zwölf Boxkämpfer jagen Viktor quer über den großen Sylter Deich. El veloz murciélago hindú comía feliz cardillo y kiwi. La cigüeña tocaba el saxofón detrás del palenque de pajaatur? Rissimo lorereped ex es solore lab id molorro in rempore icabore rehenetur aliam aut voles audae dem quam, secum eum facesequae consequ aepudam quia voluptiur repel in et faccustibus,**

Foundry　Optimo

Typeface　Dada Grotesk　　Year　　2005–2007
Designer　de Valence　　　Format　OpenType

# Aa

Aa Bb Cc Dd Ee Ff Gg Hh Ii Jj Kk
Ll Mm Nn Oo Pp Qq Rr Ss Tt Uu Vv
Ww Xx Yy Zz
0123456789
—

Dada Grotesk Light 18pt
*Dada Grotesk Light Italic 18pt*
Dada Grotesk Book 18pt
*Dada Grotesk Book Italic 18pt*
**Dada Grotesk Medium 18pt**
*Dada Grotesk Medium Italic 18pt*
**Dada Grotesk Bold 18pt**
***Dada Grotesk Bold Italic 18pt***
**Dada Grotesk Heavy 18pt**
***Dada Grotesk Heavy Italic 18pt***

---

12/14　Dada Grotesk Book

The quick brown fox jumps over the lazy dog. Voyez le brick géant que j'examine près du wharf. Zwölf Boxkämpfer jagen Viktor quer *über den großen Sylter Deich*. El veloz murciélago hindú comía feliz cardillo y kiwi. La cigüeña tocaba el saxofón detrás

9/12　Dada Grotesk Book

The quick brown fox jumps over the lazy dog. Voyez le brick géant que j'examine près du wharf. Zwölf Boxkämpfer jagen Viktor quer *über den großen Sylter Deich*. El veloz murciélago hindú comía feliz cardillo y kiwi. La cigüeña tocaba el saxofón detrás del palenque de pajaatur? *Rissimo lorereped* ex es solore lab id molorro in rempore icabore rehenetur aliam aut voles audae dem quam, secum eum

7/10　Dada Grotesk Medium

The quick brown fox jumps over the lazy dog. Voyez le brick géant que j'examine près du wharf. Zwölf Boxkämpfer jagen Viktor quer *über den großen Sylter Deich*. El veloz murciélago hindú comía feliz cardillo y kiwi. La cigüeña tocaba el saxofón detrás del palenque de pajaatur? *Rissimo lorereped* ex es solore lab id molorro in rempore icabore rehenetur aliam aut voles audae dem quam, secum eum facesequae consequ aepudam quia voluptiur repel in et faccustibus, nonsenis aut quisqui rero mi, ipiet lam ant ut maio et hil molupta tustis atatur, consedi tasimol orerem aut volor andipsapis sit, illaut volore officatus alicae dusdaec tatecte

---

Typeface　Cargo　　　　　　Year　　2002 (remastered 2010)
Designer　Gilles Gavillet,　　Format　OpenType
　　　　　David Rust

# Watch Out!

**Regular**

Aa Bb Cc Dd Ee Ff Gg Hh Ii Jj Kk
Ll Mm Nn Oo Pp Qq Rr Ss Tt Uu
Vv Ww Xx Yy Zz 0123456789

| | | | |
|---|---|---|---|
| Typeface | Hermes | Year | 2003 (updated 2010) |
| Designer | Gilles Gavillet, David Rust | Format | OpenType |

# Aa

Hermes Light 20pt
*Hermes Light Italic 20pt*
Hermes Regular 20pt
*Hermes Regular Italic 20pt*
**Hermes Bold 20pt**
***Hermes Bold Italic 20pt***

Aa Bb Cc Dd Ee Ff Gg Hh
Ii Jj Kk Ll Mm Nn Oo Pp
Qq Rr Ss Tt Uu Vv Ww Xx
Yy Zz
0123456789
—

---

**12/14 — Hermes Light**

The quick brown fox jumps over the lazy dog. Voyez le brick géant que j'examine près du wharf. Zwölf Boxkämpfer jagen Viktor quer über den großen Sylter Deich. El veloz murciélago

**9/12 — Hermes Light**

The quick brown fox jumps over the lazy dog. Voyez le brick géant que j'examine près du wharf. Zwölf Boxkämpfer jagen Viktor quer über den großen Sylter Deich. El veloz murciélago hindú comía feliz cardillo y kiwi. La cigüeña tocaba el saxofón detrás del palenque de pajaatur? Rissimo

**7/10 — Hermes Light**

The quick brown fox jumps over the lazy dog. Voyez le brick géant que j'examine près du wharf. Zwölf Boxkämpfer jagen Viktor quer über den großen Sylter Deich. El veloz murciélago hindú comía feliz cardillo y kiwi. La cigüeña tocaba el saxofón detrás del palenque de pajaatur? Rissimo lorereped ex es solore lab id molorro in rempore icabore rehenetur aliam aut voles audae dem quam, secum eum facesequae consequ aepudam quia voluptiur repel in et

**12/14 — Hermes Regular**

The quick brown fox jumps over the lazy dog. Voyez le brick géant que j'examine près du wharf. Zwölf Boxkämpfer jagen Viktor quer über den großen Sylter Deich. El veloz murciélago

**9/12 — Hermes Regular**

The quick brown fox jumps over the lazy dog. Voyez le brick géant que j'examine près du wharf. Zwölf Boxkämpfer jagen Viktor quer über den großen Sylter Deich. El veloz murciélago hindú comía feliz cardillo y kiwi. La cigüeña tocaba el saxofón detrás del palenque de pajaatur?

**7/10 — Hermes Regular**

The quick brown fox jumps over the lazy dog. Voyez le brick géant que j'examine près du wharf. Zwölf Boxkämpfer jagen Viktor quer über den großen Sylter Deich. El veloz murciélago hindú comía feliz cardillo y kiwi. La cigüeña tocaba el saxofón detrás del palenque de pajaatur? Rissimo lorereped ex es solore lab id molorro in rempore icabore rehenetur aliam aut voles audae dem quam, secum eum facesequae consequ aepudam quia voluptiur

**12/14 — Hermes Bold**

**The quick brown fox jumps over the lazy dog. Voyez le brick géant que j'examine près du wharf. Zwölf Boxkämpfer jagen Viktor quer über den großen Sylter Deich. El veloz murciélago hindú comía feliz cardillo y kiwi. La cigüeña tocaba el saxofón detrás del palenque de pajaatur? Rissimo lorereped ex es solore lab**

**9/12 — Hermes Bold**

**The quick brown fox jumps over the lazy dog. Voyez le brick géant que j'examine près du wharf. Zwölf Boxkämpfer jagen Viktor quer über den großen Sylter Deich. El veloz murciélago hindú comía feliz cardillo y kiwi. La cigüeña tocaba el saxofón detrás del palenque de pajaatur? Rissimo lorereped ex es solore lab id molorro in rempore icabore rehenetur aliam aut voles audae dem quam, secum eum facesequae consequ aepudam quia voluptiur repel in et faccustibus, nonsenis aut**

**7/10 — Hermes Bold**

**The quick brown fox jumps over the lazy dog. Voyez le brick géant que j'examine près du wharf. Zwölf Boxkämpfer jagen Viktor quer über den großen Sylter Deich. El veloz murciélago hindú comía feliz cardillo y kiwi. La cigüeña tocaba el saxofón detrás del palenque de pajaatur? Rissimo lorereped ex es solore lab id molorro in rempore icabore rehenetur aliam aut voles audae dem quam, secum eum facesequae consequ aepudam quia voluptiur repel in et faccustibus, nonsenis aut quisqui rero mi, ipiet lam ant ut maio et hil molupta tustis atatur, consedi tasimol orerem aut volor andipsapis sit, illaut volore officatus alicae dusdaec tatecte cearum qui accatibus restiore nulpa secaerferum, nus doleniim in et quoditat que explam voluupictur? Qui de illuptae. Dae nis**

# O

## OurType

Fred Smeijers,
Corina Cotorobai,
Rudy Geeraerts

De Pinte,
Belgium

Since
2002

Founded in 2002, OurType is managed by three partners: Dutch type designer Fred Smeijers, Corina Cotorobai and Rudy Geeraerts. OurType publishes newly designed fonts that are tailored to contemporary needs, yet it respects traditional values, and strives for the highest quality of product. In the company's own words, "it stands equally apart from those who are enslaved to the new and those who merely try to recreate the past."

## Info

—Why?
For Fred Smeijers flexibility is very important, as the versatility of his oeuvre testifies. The wish to operate in a more open and flexible way encouraged Fred Smeijers and Rudy Geeraerts of FontShop Benelux to launch OurType.

—People on staff
9

—Type designers on staff
4

—Type families
27

—Designers represented
15

—Web shop?
www.ourtype.com

—Distributors
FontShop

—Webfont services
WebINK

—Basic license
Singles ranges from 25€- 115€ for single fonts. Basic license for max. 5 users.

## Typeface selection

Arnhem Pro
Fakt Pro
Fayon Pro
Fresco Pro
Ludwig Pro
Meran Pro

24pt

## People

—Fred Smeijers, co-founder and creative director of OurType, is a type designer specializing in typographic research and development for product manufacturers. Born in the Netherlands, Smeijers studied graphic design at the Academy of Art in Arnhem. In 2000, Smeijers's achievements in the field of practice, research and education were formally recognized with the award of the Gerrit Noordzij Prize. He wrote the influential *Counterpunch*; his second book *Type now* was published in 2003. Smeijers lectures on type design and type history at the leading European type design colleges: Royal Academy of Arts (KABK, The Hague), Hochschule für Grafik und Buchkunst (HGB, Leipzig), University of Reading (Reading, UK), and Ecole cantonale d'art de Lausanne (ECAL).

—Peter Verheul is a first generation digital type designer. His FF NewBerlin (1991), one of the first FontFont releases, was followed by FF Sheriff in 1996. Verheul studied graphic and typographic design at the Royal Academy of Art (KABK) in The Hague, where he has been teaching since 1991. He designed the Dutch government's typefaces Rijksoverheid Serif and Rijksoverheid Sans.

—Merel Matzinger was born in the Netherlands and studied at the Art Center College of Design in Switzerland and the USA, from where she graduated in Graphic & Packaging Design. This led to a year of study at the postgraduate course in Type Design and Typography at the KABK in The Hague.

—André Leonardt studied graphic design in Dessau. Being interested in type, he attended the type design classes given by Lucas de Groot in Potsdam and Fred Smeijers in Leipzig, which led to what is now OurType NeueSans.

—Nikola Djurek, besides being the designer of OurType's Amalia, is the principal of Typonine, one of the other featured foundries in this book. See under Typonine.

—Artur Schmal is a graphic designer born in the Netherlands. He caught the "type fever" when studying at the KABK in The Hague. This led to a Master's degree in typeface design from the Academy's Type & Media course.

—Thomas Thiemich (Alto and Fakt) is a typographic designer, born in Germany. Fascinated by analytics, logic, mathematics and physics, he studied Computational Visualistics and continued his education at the Hochschule für Grafik und Buchkunst in Leipzig, where he obtained a degree in type design; he lectures on type design and technology.

—Maurice Göldner is a typographic designer from Germany. He studied communication and graphic design at Burg Giebichenstein–Hochschule für Kunst und Design in Halle, and type design at the Hochschule für Grafik und Buchkunst in Leipzig, where he graduated in 2009.

—Hendrik Weber is a typographic designer from Germany. He studied at the University of Applied Sciences (FHP) in Potsdam and the Hochschule für Grafik und Buchkunst in Leipzig, from where he holds a degree in Type Design. His graduation thesis *Kursiv*, a study of the italic, was published by Verlag Niggli in 2010. Hendrik currently works and lives in Berlin.

—Peter Mohr is a graphic designer from Germany. He studied at the Academy for Information and Communication Design (AIK) in Dresden and the Hochschule für Grafik und Buchkunst in Leipzig, graduating in Type Design in 2009. During his time at HGB Leipzig Peter has been developing a special interest in historical, economical and technical aspects of Latin printing types. Peter currently lives and works in Leipzig.

—Frederik Berlaen is a typographic designer with a love for programming and scripting. After studying graphic design at Sint-Lucas in Ghent, he went to the KABK in The Hague to study type design, completing his Master's degree in 2006. His final project at KABK was an application — Kalliculator — which studies the broad nib and pointed pen and enables the user to generate thousands of typefaces. Berlaen's multidisciplinary practice TypeMyType is based in Gent, Belgium, where he also teaches.

—Valentin Brustaux from Switzerland graduated from the Ecole des arts décoratifs de Genève in 2000. He went on to work as an independent graphic designer, exploring his passion for graphic design but also increasingly getting involved with type. In 2007 he completed his MA in Typeface Design at the University of Reading, UK.

Page 183

Swiss design company B.ü.L.b grafix (Mathien Christe & Nicholay Baker) used OurType Arnhem in combination with Apex Sans from Village and Maple from Process Type throughout their print and web design for 50JPG (Fifty Days for Photography), an event in Geneva, 2010.

Fresco Sans Light on the cover of Jan Middendorp's *Dutch Type*. Design by Bart de Haas with Peter Verheul, 2004.

The Arnhem typeface was originally designed for the *Staatscourant*, the Dutch government's official newspaper. Redesign proposal by Werkplaats Typografie Arnhem, 1999.

Page 184

Foundry OurType

Typeface Arnhem Pro
Designer Fred Smeijers
Year 2002
Format OpenType

# Aa

Aa Bb Cc Dd Ee Ff Gg Hh Ii Jj Kk
Ll Mm Nn Oo Pp Qq Rr Ss Tt Uu
Vv Ww Xx Yy Zz
0123456789
—

Arnhem Pro Blond 24pt
*Arnhem Pro Blond Italic 24pt*
Arnhem Pro Normal 24pt
*Arnhem Pro Normal Italic 24pt*
**Arnhem Pro Semi Bold 24pt**
***Arnhem Pro Semi Bold Italic 24pt***
**Arnhem Pro Bold 24pt**
***Arnhem Pro Bold Italic 24pt***
**Arnhem Pro Black 24pt**
***Arnhem Pro Black Italic 24pt***

---

12/14 Arnhem Pro Blond

The quick brown fox jumps over the lazy dog. Voyez le brick géant que j'examine près du wharf. Zwölf Boxkämpfer jagen Viktor quer über den

9/12 Arnhem Pro Blond

The quick brown fox jumps over the lazy dog. Voyez le brick géant que j'examine près du wharf. Zwölf Boxkämpfer jagen Viktor quer über den großen Sylter Deich. El veloz murciélago hindú comía feliz cardillo y kiwi. La cigüeña to-

7/10 Arnhem Pro Blond

The quick brown fox jumps over the lazy dog. Voyez le brick géant que j'examine près du wharf. Zwölf Boxkämpfer jagen Viktor quer über den großen Sylter Deich. El veloz murciélago hindú comía feliz cardillo y kiwi. La cigüeña tocaba el saxofón detrás del palenque de pajaatur? Rissimo lorereped ex es solore lab id molorro in rempore icabore rehenetur aliam aut

12/14 Arnhem Pro Normal

The quick brown fox jumps over the lazy dog. Voyez le brick géant que j'examine près du wharf. Zwölf Boxkämpfer jagen Viktor quer über den

9/12 Arnhem Pro Normal

The quick brown fox jumps over the lazy dog. Voyez le brick géant que j'examine près du wharf. Zwölf Boxkämpfer jagen Viktor quer über den großen Sylter Deich. El veloz murciélago hindú comía feliz cardillo y kiwi. La cigüeña to-

7/10 Arnhem Pro Normal

The quick brown fox jumps over the lazy dog. Voyez le brick géant que j'examine près du wharf. Zwölf Boxkämpfer jagen Viktor quer über den großen Sylter Deich. El veloz murciélago hindú comía feliz cardillo y kiwi. La cigüeña tocaba el saxofón detrás del palenque de pajaatur? Rissimo lorereped ex es solore lab id molorro in rempore icabore rehenetur aliam aut

12/14 Arnhem Pro SemiBold

**The quick brown fox jumps over the lazy dog. Voyez le brick géant que j'examine près du wharf. Zwölf Boxkämpfer jagen Viktor quer über den**

9/12 Arnhem Pro SemiBold

**The quick brown fox jumps over the lazy dog. Voyez le brick géant que j'examine près du wharf. Zwölf Boxkämpfer jagen Viktor quer über den großen Sylter Deich. El veloz murciélago hindú comía feliz cardillo y kiwi. La cigüeña to-**

7/10 Arnhem Pro SemiBold

**The quick brown fox jumps over the lazy dog. Voyez le brick géant que j'examine près du wharf. Zwölf Boxkämpfer jagen Viktor quer über den großen Sylter Deich. El veloz murciélago hindú comía feliz cardillo y kiwi. La cigüeña tocaba el saxofón detrás del palenque de pajaatur? Rissimo lorereped ex es solore lab id molorro in rempore icabore rehenetur aliam**

12/14 Arnhem Pro Bold

**The quick brown fox jumps over the lazy dog. Voyez le brick géant que j'examine près du wharf. Zwölf Boxkämpfer jagen Viktor quer über den großen Sylter Deich. El veloz murciélago hindú comía feliz cardillo y**

9/12 Arnhem Pro Bold

**The quick brown fox jumps over the lazy dog. Voyez le brick géant que j'examine près du wharf. Zwölf Boxkämpfer jagen Viktor quer über den großen Sylter Deich. El veloz murciélago hindú comía feliz cardillo y kiwi. La cigüeña tocaba el saxofón detrás del palenque de pajaatur? Rissimo lorereped ex es solore lab id molorro in**

7/10 Arnhem Pro Bold

**The quick brown fox jumps over the lazy dog. Voyez le brick géant que j'examine près du wharf. Zwölf Boxkämpfer jagen Viktor quer über den großen Sylter Deich. El veloz murciélago hindú comía feliz cardillo y kiwi. La cigüeña tocaba el saxofón detrás del palenque de pajaatur? Rissimo lorereped ex es solore lab id molorro in rempore icabore rehenetur aliam aut voles audae dem quam, secum eum facesequae consequ aepudam quia voluptiur repel in et faccustibus, nonsenis aut**

Page
185

Foundry  OurType

Typeface  Fakt Pro         Year    2010
Designer  Thomas Thiemich  Format  OpenType

# Aa

Aa Bb Cc Dd Ee Ff Gg Hh Ii Jj Kk
Ll Mm Nn Oo Pp Qq Rr Ss Tt Uu
Vv Ww Xx Yy Zz
0123456789
—

Fakt Pro Air 16pt
*Fakt Pro Air Italic 16pt*
Fakt Pro Hair 16pt
*Fakt Pro Hair Italic 16pt*
Fakt Pro Thin 16pt
*Fakt Pro Thin Italic 16pt*
Fakt Pro Light 16pt
*Fakt Pro Light Italic 16pt*
Fakt Pro Blond 16pt
*Fakt Pro Blond Italic 16pt*
Fakt Pro Normal 16pt
*Fakt Pro Normal Italic 16pt*
Fakt Pro Medium 16pt
*Fakt Pro Medium Italic 16pt*
**Fakt Pro Bold 16pt**
***Fakt Pro Bold Italic 16pt***
**Fakt Pro Black 16pt**
***Fakt Pro Black Italic 16pt***

---

12/14  Fakt Pro Blond

The quick brown fox jumps over the lazy dog. Voyez le brick géant que j'examine près du wharf. Zwölf Boxkämpfer jagen Viktor quer über den

9/12  Fakt Pro Blond

The quick brown fox jumps over the lazy dog. Voyez le brick géant que j'examine près du wharf. Zwölf Boxkämpfer jagen Viktor quer über den großen Sylter Deich. El veloz murciélago hindú comía feliz cardillo y kiwi. La cigüeña tocaba el

7/10  Fakt Pro Blond

The quick brown fox jumps over the lazy dog. Voyez le brick géant que j'examine près du wharf. Zwölf Boxkämpfer jagen Viktor quer über den großen Sylter Deich. El veloz murciélago hindú comía feliz cardillo y kiwi. La cigüeña tocaba el saxofón detrás del palenque de pajaatur? Rissimo lorereped ex es solore lab id molorro in rempore icabore rehenetur aliam aut voles

12/14  Fakt Pro Normal

The quick brown fox jumps over the lazy dog. Voyez le brick géant que j'examine près du wharf. Zwölf Boxkämpfer jagen Viktor quer über

9/12  Fakt Pro Normal

The quick brown fox jumps over the lazy dog. Voyez le brick géant que j'examine près du wharf. Zwölf Boxkämpfer jagen Viktor quer über den großen Sylter Deich. El veloz murciélago hindú comía feliz cardillo y kiwi. La cigüeña tocaba

7/10  Fakt Pro Normal

The quick brown fox jumps over the lazy dog. Voyez le brick géant que j'examine près du wharf. Zwölf Boxkämpfer jagen Viktor quer über den großen Sylter Deich. El veloz murciélago hindú comía feliz cardillo y kiwi. La cigüeña tocaba el saxofón detrás del palenque de pajaatur? Rissimo lorereped ex es solore lab id molorro in rempore icabore rehenetur aliam aut voles

12/14  Fakt Pro SemiBold

**The quick brown fox jumps over the lazy dog. Voyez le brick géant que j'examine près du wharf. Zwölf Boxkämpfer jagen Vik-**

9/12  Fakt Pro SemiBold

**The quick brown fox jumps over the lazy dog. Voyez le brick géant que j'examine près du wharf. Zwölf Boxkämpfer jagen Viktor quer über den großen Sylter Deich. El veloz murciélago hindú comía feliz cardillo y kiwi.**

7/10  Fakt Pro SemiBold

**The quick brown fox jumps over the lazy dog. Voyez le brick géant que j'examine près du wharf. Zwölf Boxkämpfer jagen Viktor quer über den großen Sylter Deich. El veloz murciélago hindú comía feliz cardillo y kiwi. La cigüeña tocaba el saxofón detrás del palenque de pajaatur? Rissimo lorereped ex es solore lab id molorro in rempore icabore**

12/14  Fakt Pro Bold

**The quick brown fox jumps over the lazy dog. Voyez le brick géant que j'examine près du wharf. Zwölf Boxkämpfer jagen Viktor quer über den großen Sylter Deich. El veloz murciélago hin-**

9/12  Fakt Pro Bold

**The quick brown fox jumps over the lazy dog. Voyez le brick géant que j'examine près du wharf. Zwölf Boxkämpfer jagen Viktor quer über den großen Sylter Deich. El veloz murciélago hindú comía feliz cardillo y kiwi. La cigüeña tocaba el saxofón detrás del palenque de pajaatur? Rissimo lorereped ex**

7/10  Fakt Pro Bold

**The quick brown fox jumps over the lazy dog. Voyez le brick géant que j'examine près du wharf. Zwölf Boxkämpfer jagen Viktor quer über den großen Sylter Deich. El veloz murciélago hindú comía feliz cardillo y kiwi. La cigüeña tocaba el saxofón detrás del palenque de pajaatur? Rissimo lorereped ex es solore lab id molorro in rempore icabore rehenetur aliam aut voles audae dem quam, secum eum facesequae consequ aepudam quia**

Typeface  Fayon Pro        Year    2010
Designer  Peter Mohr       Format  OpenType

# Aa

Aa Bb Cc Dd Ee Ff Gg Hh Ii Jj Kk Ll Mm Nn Oo Pp Qq Rr Ss Tt Uu Vv Ww Xx Yy Zz
0123456789
—

Fayon Pro Normal 20pt
*Fayon Pro Normal Italic* 20pt
Fayon Pro Medium 20pt
*Fayon Pro Medium Italic* 20pt
**Fayon Pro Semi Bold** 20pt
***Fayon Pro Semi Bold Italic*** 20pt
**Fayon Pro Bold** 20pt
***Fayon Pro Bold Italic*** 20pt
**Fayon Pro Extra Bold** 20pt
***Fayon Pro Extra Bold Italic*** 20pt
**Fayon Pro Black** 20pt
***Fayon Pro Black Italic*** 20pt
**Fayon Pro Extra Black** 20pt
***Fayon Pro Extra Black Italic*** 20pt

---

12/14  Fayon Pro Normal

The quick brown fox jumps over the lazy dog. Voyez le brick géant que j'examine près du wharf. Zwölf Boxkämpfer jagen Viktor quer über den

9/12  Fayon Pro Normal

The quick brown fox jumps over the lazy dog. Voyez le brick géant que j'examine près du wharf. Zwölf Boxkämpfer jagen Viktor quer über den großen Sylter Deich. El veloz murciélago hindú comía feliz cardillo y kiwi. La cigüeña tocaba el

7/10  Fayon Pro Normal

The quick brown fox jumps over the lazy dog. Voyez le brick géant que j'examine près du wharf. Zwölf Boxkämpfer jagen Viktor quer über den großen Sylter Deich. El veloz murciélago hindú comía feliz cardillo y kiwi. La cigüeña tocaba el saxofón detrás del palenque de pajaatur? Rissimo lorereped ex es solore lab id molorro in rempore icabore rehenetur aliam aut voles

12/14  Fayon Pro Medium

The quick brown fox jumps over the lazy dog. Voyez le brick géant que j'examine près du wharf. Zwölf Boxkämpfer jagen Viktor quer über den

9/12  Fayon Pro Medium

The quick brown fox jumps over the lazy dog. Voyez le brick géant que j'examine près du wharf. Zwölf Boxkämpfer jagen Viktor quer über den großen Sylter Deich. El veloz murciélago hindú comía feliz cardillo y kiwi. La cigüeña tocaba

7/10  Fayon Pro Medium

The quick brown fox jumps over the lazy dog. Voyez le brick géant que j'examine près du wharf. Zwölf Boxkämpfer jagen Viktor quer über den großen Sylter Deich. El veloz murciélago hindú comía feliz cardillo y kiwi. La cigüeña tocaba el saxofón detrás del palenque de pajaatur? Rissimo lorereped ex es solore lab id molorro in rempore icabore rehenetur aliam aut voles

12/14  Fayon Pro SemiBold

**The quick brown fox jumps over the lazy dog. Voyez le brick géant que j'examine près du wharf. Zwölf Boxkämpfer jagen Viktor quer**

9/12  Fayon Pro SemiBold

**The quick brown fox jumps over the lazy dog. Voyez le brick géant que j'examine près du wharf. Zwölf Boxkämpfer jagen Viktor quer über den großen Sylter Deich. El veloz murciélago hindú comía feliz cardillo y kiwi. La cigüeña tocaba**

7/10  Fayon Pro SemiBold

**The quick brown fox jumps over the lazy dog. Voyez le brick géant que j'examine près du wharf. Zwölf Boxkämpfer jagen Viktor quer über den großen Sylter Deich. El veloz murciélago hindú comía feliz cardillo y kiwi. La cigüeña tocaba el saxofón detrás del palenque de pajaatur? Rissimo lorereped ex es solore lab id molorro in rempore icabore rehenetur aliam aut voles**

12/14  Fayon Pro Bold

**The quick brown fox jumps over the lazy dog. Voyez le brick géant que j'examine près du wharf. Zwölf Boxkämpfer jagen Viktor quer über den großen Sylter Deich. El veloz murciélago hindú comía feliz cardillo y**

9/12  Fayon Pro Bold

**The quick brown fox jumps over the lazy dog. Voyez le brick géant que j'examine près du wharf. Zwölf Boxkämpfer jagen Viktor quer über den großen Sylter Deich. El veloz murciélago hindú comía feliz cardillo y kiwi. La cigüeña tocaba el saxofón detrás del palenque de pajaatur? Rissimo lorereped ex es solore lab id**

7/10  Fayon Pro Bold

**The quick brown fox jumps over the lazy dog. Voyez le brick géant que j'examine près du wharf. Zwölf Boxkämpfer jagen Viktor quer über den großen Sylter Deich. El veloz murciélago hindú comía feliz cardillo y kiwi. La cigüeña tocaba el saxofón detrás del palenque de pajaatur? Rissimo lorereped ex es solore lab id molorro in rempore icabore rehenetur aliam aut voles audae dem quam, secum eum facesequae consequ aepudam quia voluptiur repel in et faccustibus, nonsenis aut quisqui**

Foundry OurType

Typeface Fresco Pro
Designer Fred Smeijers
Year 1998
Format OpenType

# Aa

Aa Bb Cc Dd Ee Ff Gg Hh Ii Jj Kk Ll Mm Nn Oo Pp Qq Rr Ss Tt Uu Vv Ww Xx Yy Zz
0123456789
—

Fresco Pro Light 24pt
*Fresco Pro Light Italic* 24pt
Fresco Pro Normal 24pt
*Fresco Pro Normal Italic* 24pt
Fresco Pro Semi Bold 24pt
*Fresco Pro Semi Bold Italic* 24pt
**Fresco Pro Bold** 24pt
***Fresco Pro Bold Italic*** 24pt
**Fresco Pro Black** 24pt
***Fresco Pro Black Italic*** 24pt

---

12/14 Fresco Pro Light

The quick brown fox jumps over the lazy dog. Voyez le brick géant que j'examine près du wharf. Zwölf Boxkämpfer jagen Viktor quer über den großen Sylter

12/14 Fresco Pro Normal

The quick brown fox jumps over the lazy dog. Voyez le brick géant que j'examine près du wharf. Zwölf Boxkämpfer jagen Viktor quer über den

12/14 Fresco Pro SemiBold

The quick brown fox jumps over the lazy dog. Voyez le brick géant que j'examine près du wharf. Zwölf Boxkämpfer jagen Viktor quer über den

12/14 Fresco Pro Bold

**The quick brown fox jumps over the lazy dog. Voyez le brick géant que j'examine près du wharf. Zwölf Boxkämpfer jagen Viktor quer über den großen Sylter Deich. El veloz murciélago**

9/12 Fresco Pro Light

The quick brown fox jumps over the lazy dog. Voyez le brick géant que j'examine près du wharf. Zwölf Boxkämpfer jagen Viktor quer über den großen Sylter Deich. El veloz murciélago hindú comía feliz cardillo y kiwi. La cigüeña tocaba el saxofón detrás del palenque

9/12 Fresco Pro Normal

The quick brown fox jumps over the lazy dog. Voyez le brick géant que j'examine près du wharf. Zwölf Boxkämpfer jagen Viktor quer über den großen Sylter Deich. El veloz murciélago hindú comía feliz cardillo y kiwi. La cigüe-

9/12 Fresco Pro SemiBold

The quick brown fox jumps over the lazy dog. Voyez le brick géant que j'examine près du wharf. Zwölf Boxkämpfer jagen Viktor quer über den großen Sylter Deich. El veloz murciélago hindú comía feliz cardillo y kiwi. La cigüe-

9/12 Fresco Pro Bold

**The quick brown fox jumps over the lazy dog. Voyez le brick géant que j'examine près du wharf. Zwölf Boxkämpfer jagen Viktor quer über den großen Sylter Deich. El veloz murciélago hindú comía feliz cardillo y kiwi. La cigüeña tocaba el saxofón detrás del palenque de pajaatur? Rissimo**

7/10 Fresco Pro Light

The quick brown fox jumps over the lazy dog. Voyez le brick géant que j'examine près du wharf. Zwölf Boxkämpfer jagen Viktor quer über den großen Sylter Deich. El veloz murciélago hindú comía feliz cardillo y kiwi. La cigüeña tocaba el saxofón detrás del palenque de pajaatur? Rissimo lorereped ex es solore lab id molorro in rempore icabore rehenetur aliam aut voles audae dem quam, secum eum

7/10 Fresco Pro Normal

The quick brown fox jumps over the lazy dog. Voyez le brick géant que j'examine près du wharf. Zwölf Boxkämpfer jagen Viktor quer über den großen Sylter Deich. El veloz murciélago hindú comía feliz cardillo y kiwi. La cigüeña tocaba el saxofón detrás del palenque de pajaatur? Rissimo lorereped ex es solore lab id molorro in rempore icabore rehenetur aliam aut voles

7/10 Fresco Pro SemiBold

The quick brown fox jumps over the lazy dog. Voyez le brick géant que j'examine près du wharf. Zwölf Boxkämpfer jagen Viktor quer über den großen Sylter Deich. El veloz murciélago hindú comía feliz cardillo y kiwi. La cigüeña tocaba el saxofón detrás del palenque de pajaatur? Rissimo lorereped ex es solore lab id molorro in rempore icabore rehenetur aliam aut voles

7/10 Fresco Pro Bold

**The quick brown fox jumps over the lazy dog. Voyez le brick géant que j'examine près du wharf. Zwölf Boxkämpfer jagen Viktor quer über den großen Sylter Deich. El veloz murciélago hindú comía feliz cardillo y kiwi. La cigüeña tocaba el saxofón detrás del palenque de pajaatur? Rissimo lorereped ex es solore lab id molorro in rempore icabore rehenetur aliam aut voles audae dem quam, secum eum facesequae consequ**

Page 188

Foundry  OurType

Typeface  Ludwig Pro   Year    2009
Designer  Fred Smeijers  Format  OpenType

# Aa

Aa Bb Cc Dd Ee Ff Cg Hh Ii Jj Kk Ll
Mm Nn Oo Pp Qq Rr Ss Tt Uu Vv
Ww Xx Yy Zz
0123456789
—

Ludwig Pro Thin 18pt
*Ludwig Pro Thin Italic 18pt*
Ludwig Pro Light 18pt
*Ludwig Pro Light Italic 18pt*
Ludwig Pro Blond 18pt
*Ludwig Pro Blond Italic 18pt*
Ludwig Pro Normal 18pt
*Ludwig Pro Normal Italic 18pt*
**Ludwig Pro Semi Bold 18pt**
*Ludwig Pro Semi Bold Italic 18pt*
**Ludwig Pro Bold 18pt**
***Ludwig Pro Bold Italic 18pt***
**Ludwig Pro Black 18pt**
***Ludwig Pro Black Italic 18pt***
**Ludwig Pro Extra Black 18pt**
***Ludwig Pro Extra Black Italic 18pt***

---

12/14   Ludwig Pro Blond

The quick brown fox jumps over the lazy dog. Voyez le brick géant que j'examine près du wharf. Zwölf Boxkämpfer jagen Viktor quer über den

9/12   Ludwig Pro Blond

The quick brown fox jumps over the lazy dog. Voyez le brick géant que j'examine près du wharf. Zwölf Boxkämpfer jagen Viktor quer über den großen Sylter Deich. El veloz murciélago hindú comía feliz cardillo y kiwi. La cigüeña tocaba

7/10   Ludwig Pro Blond

The quick brown fox jumps over the lazy dog. Voyez le brick géant que j'examine près du wharf. Zwölf Boxkämpfer jagen Viktor quer über den großen Sylter Deich. El veloz murciélago hindú comía feliz cardillo y kiwi. La cigüeña tocaba el saxofón detrás del palenque de pajaatur? Rissimo lorereped ex es solore lab id molorro in rempore icabore rehenetur aliam aut

12/14   Ludwig Pro Normal

The quick brown fox jumps over the lazy dog. Voyez le brick géant que j'examine près du wharf. Zwölf Boxkämpfer jagen Viktor quer über den

9/12   Ludwig Pro Normal

The quick brown fox jumps over the lazy dog. Voyez le brick géant que j'examine près du wharf. Zwölf Boxkämpfer jagen Viktor quer über den großen Sylter Deich. El veloz murciélago hindú comía feliz cardillo y kiwi. La cigüeña

7/10   Ludwig Pro Normal

The quick brown fox jumps over the lazy dog. Voyez le brick géant que j'examine près du wharf. Zwölf Boxkämpfer jagen Viktor quer über den großen Sylter Deich. El veloz murciélago hindú comía feliz cardillo y kiwi. La cigüeña tocaba el saxofón detrás del palenque de pajaatur? Rissimo lorereped ex es solore lab id molorro in rempore icabore rehenetur aliam

12/14   Ludwig Pro SemiBold

**The quick brown fox jumps over the lazy dog. Voyez le brick géant que j'examine près du wharf. Zwölf Boxkämpfer jagen Viktor quer**

9/12   Ludwig Pro SemiBold

**The quick brown fox jumps over the lazy dog. Voyez le brick géant que j'examine près du wharf. Zwölf Boxkämpfer jagen Viktor quer über den großen Sylter Deich. El veloz murciélago hindú comía feliz cardillo y kiwi. La**

7/10   Ludwig Pro SemiBold

**The quick brown fox jumps over the lazy dog. Voyez le brick géant que j'examine près du wharf. Zwölf Boxkämpfer jagen Viktor quer über den großen Sylter Deich. El veloz murciélago hindú comía feliz cardillo y kiwi. La cigüeña tocaba el saxofón detrás del palenque de pajaatur? Rissimo lorereped ex es solore lab id molorro in rempore icabore rehenetur**

12/14   Ludwig Pro Bold

**The quick brown fox jumps over the lazy dog. Voyez le brick géant que j'examine près du wharf. Zwölf Boxkämpfer jagen Viktor quer über den großen Sylter Deich. El veloz murciélago hin-**

9/12   Ludwig Pro Bold

**The quick brown fox jumps over the lazy dog. Voyez le brick géant que j'examine près du wharf. Zwölf Boxkämpfer jagen Viktor quer über den großen Sylter Deich. El veloz murciélago hindú comía feliz cardillo y kiwi. La cigüeña tocaba el saxofón detrás del palenque de pajaatur? Rissimo lorereped ex**

7/10   Ludwig Pro Bold

**The quick brown fox jumps over the lazy dog. Voyez le brick géant que j'examine près du wharf. Zwölf Boxkämpfer jagen Viktor quer über den großen Sylter Deich. El veloz murciélago hindú comía feliz cardillo y kiwi. La cigüeña tocaba el saxofón detrás del palenque de pajaatur? Rissimo lorereped ex es solore lab id molorro in rempore icabore rehenetur aliam aut voles audae dem quam, secum eum facesequae consequ aepudam quia voluptiur repel in et**

Foundry OurType

Typeface Meran Pro
Designer Maurice Göldner
Year 2008
Format OpenType

# Aa

Aa Bb Cc Dd Ee Ff Gg Hh Ii Jj Kk Ll
Mm Nn Oo Pp Qq Rr Ss Tt Uu Vv
Ww Xx Yy Zz
0123456789

Meran Pro Thin 24pt
*Meran Pro Thin Italic 24pt*
Meran Pro Light 24pt
*Meran Pro Light Italic 24pt*
Meran Pro Normal 24pt
*Meran Pro Normal Italic 24pt*
**Meran Pro Semi Bold 24pt**
***Meran Pro Semi Bold Italic 24pt***
**Meran Pro Bold 24pt**
***Meran Pro Bold Italic 24pt***
**Meran Pro Black 24pt**
***Meran Pro Black Italic 24pt***

---

12/14 Meran Pro Light

The quick brown fox jumps over the lazy dog. Voyez le brick géant que j'examine près du wharf. Zwölf Boxkämpfer jagen Viktor quer über den

12/14 Meran Pro Normal

The quick brown fox jumps over the lazy dog. Voyez le brick géant que j'examine près du wharf. Zwölf Boxkämpfer jagen Viktor quer über

12/14 Meran Pro SemiBold

**The quick brown fox jumps over the lazy dog. Voyez le brick géant que j'examine près du wharf. Zwölf Boxkämpfer jagen Viktor quer über den**

12/14 Meran Pro Bold

**The quick brown fox jumps over the lazy dog. Voyez le brick géant que j'examine près du wharf. Zwölf Boxkämpfer jagen Viktor quer über den großen Sylter Deich. El veloz murciélago hindú comía feliz**

---

9/12 Meran Pro Light

The quick brown fox jumps over the lazy dog. Voyez le brick géant que j'examine près du wharf. Zwölf Boxkämpfer jagen Viktor quer über den großen Sylter Deich. El veloz murciélago hindú comía feliz cardillo y kiwi. La cigüeña tocaba el

9/12 Meran Pro Normal

The quick brown fox jumps over the lazy dog. Voyez le brick géant que j'examine près du wharf. Zwölf Boxkämpfer jagen Viktor quer über den großen Sylter Deich. El veloz murciélago hindú comía feliz cardillo y kiwi. La cigüeña tocaba

9/12 Meran Pro SemiBold

**The quick brown fox jumps over the lazy dog. Voyez le brick géant que j'examine près du wharf. Zwölf Boxkämpfer jagen Viktor quer über den großen Sylter Deich. El veloz murciélago hindú comía feliz cardillo y kiwi. La cigüe-**

9/12 Meran Pro Bold

**The quick brown fox jumps over the lazy dog. Voyez le brick géant que j'examine près du wharf. Zwölf Boxkämpfer jagen Viktor quer über den großen Sylter Deich. El veloz murciélago hindú comía feliz cardillo y kiwi. La cigüeña tocaba el saxofón detrás del palenque de pajaatur? Rissimo lorereped ex es solore**

---

7/10 Meran Pro Light

The quick brown fox jumps over the lazy dog. Voyez le brick géant que j'examine près du wharf. Zwölf Boxkämpfer jagen Viktor quer über den großen Sylter Deich. El veloz murciélago hindú comía feliz cardillo y kiwi. La cigüeña tocaba el saxofón detrás del palenque de pajaatur? Rissimo lorereped ex es solore lab id molorro in rempore icabore rehenetur aliam aut voles

7/10 Meran Pro Normal

The quick brown fox jumps over the lazy dog. Voyez le brick géant que j'examine près du wharf. Zwölf Boxkämpfer jagen Viktor quer über den großen Sylter Deich. El veloz murciélago hindú comía feliz cardillo y kiwi. La cigüeña tocaba el saxofón detrás del palenque de pajaatur? Rissimo lorereped ex es solore lab id molorro in rempore icabore rehenetur aliam aut voles

7/10 Meran Pro SemiBold

**The quick brown fox jumps over the lazy dog. Voyez le brick géant que j'examine près du wharf. Zwölf Boxkämpfer jagen Viktor quer über den großen Sylter Deich. El veloz murciélago hindú comía feliz cardillo y kiwi. La cigüeña tocaba el saxofón detrás del palenque de pajaatur? Rissimo lorereped ex es solore lab id molorro in rempore icabore rehenetur aliam**

7/10 Meran Pro Bold

**The quick brown fox jumps over the lazy dog. Voyez le brick géant que j'examine près du wharf. Zwölf Boxkämpfer jagen Viktor quer über den großen Sylter Deich. El veloz murciélago hindú comía feliz cardillo y kiwi. La cigüeña tocaba el saxofón detrás del palenque de pajaatur? Rissimo lorereped ex es solore lab id molorro in rempore icabore rehenetur aliam aut voles audae dem quam, secum eum facesequae consequ aepudam quia voluptiur repel in et**

# P
## P22

---

Richard Kegler,
Carima El-Behairy

---

Buffalo,
NY, USA

---

Since
1994

P22 is a foundry specializing in typefaces related to art and type design history. Its founders, Richard Kegler and Carima El-Behairy, also run a number of labels to accomodate specific typeface collections: IHOF (International House of Fonts), Lanston Type Company, Rimmer Type Foundry, and Sherwood Type. They have published books and music CDs, and are involved in the WNY Book Arts Center in downtown Buffalo.

## Info

—Why?
P22 started as a venue to create digital fonts based on historical lettering styles that may have never been fonts originally. Artists' handwriting became a specialty, but many famous styles of art and design history have been adapted for modern use as well as contemporary designs.

—People on staff
4

—Type designers on staff
1

—Type families
Approx. 275
P22 type foundry: 65
IHOF: 95
Lanston Type Company: 67
Rimmer Type Foundry: 17
Sherwood Collection: 34

—Designers represented
Approx. 36

—Web shop
p22.com

—Distributors
MyFonts, Fonts.com, Linotype, Veer, FontShop, Robert Matton AB, Phil's Fonts, FontHaus, YouWorkForThem, DEX, various gift shops including the Frank Lloyd Wright Foundation and Dard Hunter.

—Webfont services
MyFonts, WebINK, TypeKit, Fontspring

—Basic license
Most fonts are $19.95 US for up to 5 devices at one site. Professional and commercial uses such as branding, broadcast, merchandising, etc., require additional licensing.

## People

—Richard Kegler is the senior partner and founder of P22 type foundry. For years before P22 became a "real" type designing entity, Mr. Kegler had been involved in various aspects of the book arts ranging from hand-binding and hand printing to hypertext. His varied interest in the history and processes of art and design initially seemed to have little in common with interests in up-and-coming technologies, but more and more there seemed to be much common ground that could be found. This meeting of old and new has become the premise of P22's collection of fonts. With so much history overlooked and so much potential for new technologies, Mr. Kegler sees no limit to future projects.

*Stern*
Named in memory of
CHRISTOPHER STERN
1950–2006
Letterpress
Artist
PRINTER

Stern by the late Jim Rimmer (Rimmer Type Foundry) was the first typeface simultaneously created for letterpress and digital use. Its making was the subject of a documentary film directed by Richard Kegler.

## Typeface selection

*P22 Casual Script Pro*
*P22 Cezanne Pro*
P22 Civilite
**P22 Flora Mambo**
P22 Stickley Text
P22 Underground
***P22 Zebra***

18pt

Page
191

Original pattern for the swash capital P of Californian.

**Right**
LTC Caslon CD and specimen (Lanston Type Company). In the 1990s, P22 became known for its elaborate packaging.

**Below**
P22 Zaner by Paul Hunt.

Page 192  Foundry P22

Typeface   P22 Flora Mambo
Designer   Jim Flora
Year       2010
Format     OpenType

# Mambo

Regular A

Aa Bb Cc Dd Ee Ff Gg Hh Ii Jj Kk Ll
Mm Nn Oo Pp Qq Rr Ss Tt Uu Vv
Ww Xx Yy Zz 0123456789

Typeface   P22 Zebra
Designer   Karlgeorg Hoefer, Colin Kahn
Year       2007
Format     OpenType

# Stripe

Zebra A

Live Cut
Stencil
Wedge

Aa Bb Cc Dd Ee
Ff Gg Hh Ii Jj Kk
Ll Mm Nn Oo Pp
Qq Rr Ss Tt Uu
Vv Ww Xx Yy Zz
0123456789

Aa Bb Cc Dd Ee
Ff Gg Hh Ii Jj Kk
Ll Mm Nn Oo Pp
Qq Rr Ss Tt Uu
Vv Ww Xx Yy Zz
0123456789

Foundry P22

Typeface P22 Underground
Designer Paul Hunt,
 Original: Edward Johnston
Year 2007
Format OpenType

# Aa

Aa Bb Cc Dd Ee Ff Gg Hh Ii Jj Kk
Ll Mm Nn Oo Pp Qq Rr Ss Tt Uu
Vv Ww Xx Yy Zz
0123456789
—

P22 Underground Thin 20pt
P22 Underground Thin Petite Caps 20pt
P22 Underground Thin Small Caps 20pt
P22 Underground Light 20pt
P22 Underground Light Petite Caps 20pt
P22 Underground Light Small Caps 20pt
P22 Underground Book 20pt
P22 Underground Book Petite Caps 20pt
P22 Underground Book Small Caps 20pt
P22 Underground Medium 20pt
P22 Underground Medium Petite Caps 20pt
P22 Underground Medium Small Caps 20pt
P22 Underground Demi 20pt
P22 Underground Demi Petite Caps 20pt
P22 Underground Demi Small Caps 20pt
P22 Underground Heavy 20pt
P22 Underground Heavy Petite Caps 20pt
P22 Underground Heavy Small Caps 20pt

P22 Underground Titling A 20pt
P22 Underground Titling B 20pt
P22 Underground Titling C 20pt

---

12/14 P22 Underground Book

The quick brown fox jumps over the lazy dog. Voyez le brick géant que j'examine près du wharf. Zwölf Boxkämpfer jagen Viktor quer über den großen Sylter Deich. El veloz murciélago hindú comía feliz cardillo y kiwi. La cigüeña tocaba el saxofón detrás del palenque de pajaatur? Rissimo lo-

9/12 P22 Underground Book

The quick brown fox jumps over the lazy dog. Voyez le brick géant que j'examine près du wharf. Zwölf Boxkämpfer jagen Viktor quer über den großen Sylter Deich. El veloz murciélago hindú comía feliz cardillo y kiwi. La cigüeña tocaba el saxofón detrás del palenque de pajaatur? Rissimo lorereped ex es solore lab id molorro in rempore icabore rehenetur aliam aut voles audae dem quam, secum eum facesequae consequ aepudam quia voluptiur

7/10 P22 Underground Book

The quick brown fox jumps over the lazy dog. Voyez le brick géant que j'examine près du wharf. Zwölf Boxkämpfer jagen Viktor quer über den großen Sylter Deich. El veloz murciélago hindú comía feliz cardillo y kiwi. La cigüeña tocaba el saxofón detrás del palenque de pajaatur? Rissimo lorereped ex es solore lab id molorro in rempore icabore rehenetur aliam aut voles audae dem quam, secum eum facesequae consequ aepudam quia voluptiur repel in et faccustibus, nonsenis aut quisqui rero mi, ipiet lam ant ut maio et hil molupta tustis atatur, consedi tasimol orerem aut volor andipsapis sit, illaut volore officatus alicae dusdaec tatecte cearum qui accatibus restiore nulpa secaerferum, nus

Page 194
Foundry P22

Typeface P22 Civilite
Designer Colin Kahn,
Richard Kegler,
Milo Kowalski,
Original: Robert Granjon

Year 2009
Format OpenType

Aa

Aa Bb Cc Dd Ee Ff Gg Hh Ii Jj
Kk Ll Mm Nn Oo Pp Qq
Rr Ss Tt Uu Vv Ww Xx Yy Zz
0123456789

P22 Civilite Pro No8 20pt
P22 Civilite Pro No9 20pt
P22 Civilite Pro No11 20pt
P22 Civilite Pro No12 20pt
P22 Civilite Pro No30 20pt
P22 Civilite Pro No14 20pt
P22 Civilite No8 Historic 20pt
P22 Civilite No8 Modern 20pt
P22 Civilite No9 Historic 20pt
P22 Civilite No9 Modern 20pt
P22 Civilite No11 Historic 20pt
P22 Civilite No11 Modern 20pt
P22 Civilite No12 Historic 20pt
P22 Civilite No12 Modern 20pt
P22 Civilite No14 Historic 20pt
P22 Civilite No14 Modern 20pt
P22 Civilite No30 Historic 20pt
P22 Civilite No30 Modern 20pt

12/14   P22 Civilite Pro No8

The quick brown fox jumps over the lazy dog. Voyez le brick géant que j'examine près du wharf. Zwölf Boxkämpfer jagen Viktor quer über den großen Sylter Deich. El veloz murciélago hindú comía feliz cardillo y kiwi. La cigüeña tocaba el saxofón detrás del palenque de pajaatur? Rissimo lorereped ex es solore lab id molorro in rempore icabore rehenetur aliam aut voles audae dem quam, secum eum facesequae consequ aepudam quia voluptiur repel in et faccustibus, nonsenis aut quisqui rero mi, ipiet lam ant ut maio et hil molupta tustis atatur, consedi tasimol orerem aut volor andipsapis sit, illaut volore officatus alicae dusdaec tatecte cearum

12/14   P22 Civilite Pro No9

The quick brown fox jumps over the lazy dog. Voyez le brick géant que j'examine près du wharf. Zwölf Boxkämpfer jagen Viktor quer über den großen Sylter Deich. El veloz murciélago hindú comía feliz cardillo y kiwi. La cigüeña tocaba el saxofón detrás del palenque de pajaatur? Rissimo lorereped ex es solore lab id molorro in rempore icabore rehenetur aliam aut voles audae dem quam, secum eum facesequae consequ aepudam quia voluptiur repel in et faccustibus, nonsenis aut quisqui rero mi, ipiet lam ant ut maio et hil molupta tustis atatur, consedi tasimol orerem aut volor andipsapis sit, illaut volore officatus

12/14   P22 Civilite Pro No11

The quick brown fox jumps over the lazy dog. Voyez le brick géant que j'examine près du wharf. Zwölf Boxkämpfer jagen Viktor quer über den großen Sylter Deich. El veloz murciélago hindú comía feliz cardillo y kiwi. La cigüeña tocaba el saxofón detrás del palenque de pajaatur? Rissimo lorereped ex es solore lab id molorro in rempore icabore rehenetur aliam aut voles audae dem quam, secum eum facesequae consequ aepudam quia voluptiur repel in et faccustibus, nonsenis aut quisqui rero mi, ipiet lam ant ut maio et hil molupta tustis atatur, consedi tasimol orerem aut volor andipsapis sit, illaut volore officatus alicae dusdaec tatecte cearum qui accatibus restiore nulpa secaerferum, nus dolenim in et quoditat que explam

Foundry P22

---

Typeface P22 Stickley Text
Designer Michael Stickley
Year 2009
Format OpenType

# Aa

P22 Stickley Text Regular 20pt
*P22 Stickley Text Italic 20pt*
**P22 Stickley Text Bold 20pt**
***P22 Stickley Text Bold Italic 20pt***

Aa Bb Cc Dd Ee Ff Gg Hh Ii Jj Kk
Ll Mm Nn Oo Pp Qq Rr Ss Tt Uu
Vv Ww Xx Yy Zz
0123456789
—

9/12 Stickley Text Regular

The quick brown fox jumps over the lazy dog. Voyez le brick géant que j'examine près du wharf. Zwölf Boxkämpfer jagen Viktor quer über den großen Sylter Deich. El veloz murciélago hindú comía feliz cardillo y kiwi. La cigüeña tocaba el saxofón

9/12 P22 Stickley Text Bold

**The quick brown fox jumps over the lazy dog. Voyez le brick géant que j'examine près du wharf. Zwölf Boxkämpfer jagen Viktor quer über den großen Sylter Deich. El veloz murciélago hindú comía feliz cardillo y kiwi. La cigüeña tocaba el**

7/10 Stickley Text Regular

The quick brown fox jumps over the lazy dog. Voyez le brick géant que j'examine près du wharf. Zwölf Boxkämpfer jagen Viktor quer über den großen Sylter Deich. El veloz murciélago hindú comía feliz cardillo y kiwi. La cigüeña tocaba el saxofón detrás del palenque de pajaatur? Rissimo lorereped ex es solore lab id molorro in rempore icabore rehenetur aliam aut voles audae dem

7/10 P22 Stickley Text Bold

**The quick brown fox jumps over the lazy dog. Voyez le brick géant que j'examine près du wharf. Zwölf Boxkämpfer jagen Viktor quer über den großen Sylter Deich. El veloz murciélago hindú comía feliz cardillo y kiwi. La cigüeña tocaba el saxofón detrás del palenque de pajaatur? Rissimo lorereped ex es solore lab id molorro in rempore icabore rehenetur aliam aut voles**

---

Typeface P22 Cezanne Pro
Designer Michael Want, James Grieshaber
Year 1996, 2005
Format OpenType

*Les joueurs de cartes*

*Regular*

*Aa Bb Cc Dd Ee Ff Gg Hh Ii
Jj Kk Ll Mm Nn Oo Pp Qq
Rr Ss Tt Uu Vv Ww Xx Yy Zz
0123456789*

---

Typeface P22 Casual Script Pro
Designer Richard Kegler
Year 2011
Format OpenType

*Time off*

*Regular*

*Aa Bb Cc Dd Ee Ff Gg Hh Ii
Jj Kk Ll Mm Nn Oo Pp Qq
Rr Ss Tt Uu Vv Ww Xx Yy
Zz 0123456789*

# P
## PampaType

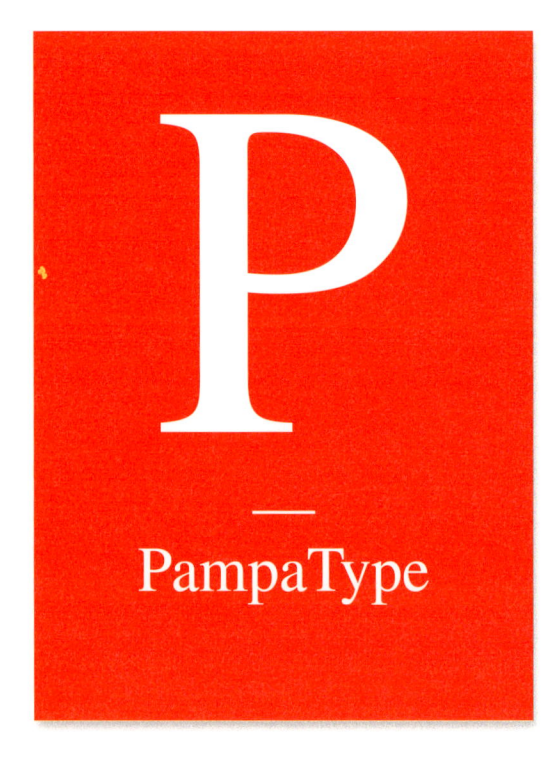

Alejandro Lo Celso

La Plata, Argentina

Since 2001

PampaType is a digital foundry set up in 2001 with the idea of developing high quality typefaces with a Latin flavor. PampaType is run by Argentinian type and information designer Alejandro Lo Celso. After a decade in Mexico the foundry relocated to Argentina in 2010.

## Info

—Why?
To create high quality types with a particularly Latin flavor.

—People on staff
it's a 1 person foundry, though I hire 2 colleagues for OT programming.

—Type designers on staff
1

—Type families
Approx. 10

—Designers represented
1, more to come

—Web shop
None

—Distributors
Fontshop, MyFonts, Veer, Monotype, T26

—Webfont services
Some of the above

—Basic license
It varies

Typeface selection

Perec
Perec Lunatique
Perec Ludique

24pt

## People

—Alejandro Lo Celso is an independent information and type designer born in Cordoba, Argentina. He holds a MA in type design from the University of Reading (UK) and a postgraduate from the Atelier National de Recherche Typographique (Nancy, France). In 2001 he founded the PampaType foundry which pioneered the type design wave in Latin America. His internationally awarded type families are usually large, and they include both text and display fonts. Alejandro is regularly invited to give talks and workshops, and he is a visiting lecturer at a number of schools in Argentina, Mexico, and France. He is a member of ATypI and the Círculo de Tipógrafos in Mexico.

Proofs made during the design process of Lo Celso's typeface Arlt.

Page
197

Promotional material for a series of lectures at the Museum of the Image in Épinal, France. Designed by Cyril Dominger with Arlt.

JOVE XEF, PORTI WHISKY AMB QUINZE GLAÇONS D' HIDROGEN, COI!

LE CŒUR DÉÇU MAIS L'AME PLUTÔT NAÏVE, LOUŸS RÊVA DE CRAPAÜTER EN CANOË AU DELÀ DES ÎLES, PRÈS DU MÄLSTRÖN OÙ BRÛLENT LES NOVÆ

**Above**
Screen shots made as part of the design process of the Arlt typeface.

Promotional material for Perec.

Typeface  Perec
Designer  Alejandro Lo Celso
Year  2009–2011
Format  OpenType
Foundry  PampaType

# Aa

Aa Bb Cc Dd Ee Ff Gg Hh Ii Jj
Kk Ll Mm Nn Oo Pp Qq Rr Ss Tt
Uu Vv Ww Xx Yy Zz
0123456789

Perec SuperBlanca 24pt
*Perec SuperBlanca Italica 24pt*
Perec Blanca 24pt
*Perec Blanca Italica 24pt*
Perec Gris 24pt
*Perec Gris Italica 24pt*
**Perec Negra 24pt**
***Perec Negra Italica 24pt***
**Perec SuperNegra 24pt**
***Perec SuperNegra Italica 24pt***

---

**12/14  Perec SuperBlanca**

The quick brown fox jumps over the lazy dog. Voyez le brick géant que j'examine près du wharf. Zwölf Boxkämpfer jagen Viktor

**12/14  Perec Blanca**

The quick brown fox jumps over the lazy dog. Voyez le brick géant que j'examine près du wharf. Zwölf Boxkämpfer jagen Vik-

**12/14  Perec Gris**

The quick brown fox jumps over the lazy dog. Voyez le brick géant que j'examine près du wharf. Zwölf Boxkämpfer jagen Vik-

**12/14  PerecNegra**

**The quick brown fox jumps over the lazy dog. Voyez le brick géant que j'examine près du wharf. Zwölf Boxkämpfer jagen Viktor quer über den großen Sylter Deich. El veloz murciélago hin-**

**9/12  Perec SuperBlanca**

The quick brown fox jumps over the lazy dog. Voyez le brick géant que j'examine près du wharf. Zwölf Boxkämpfer jagen Viktor quer über den großen Sylter Deich. El veloz murciélago hindú comía feliz cardillo y kiwi. La

**9/12  Perec Blanca**

The quick brown fox jumps over the lazy dog. Voyez le brick géant que j'examine près du wharf. Zwölf Boxkämpfer jagen Viktor quer über den großen Sylter Deich. El veloz murciélago hindú comía feliz cardillo y kiwi. La

**9/12  Perec Gris**

The quick brown fox jumps over the lazy dog. Voyez le brick géant que j'examine près du wharf. Zwölf Boxkämpfer jagen Viktor quer über den großen Sylter Deich. El veloz murciélago hindú comía feliz cardillo y kiwi. La ci-

**9/12  Perec Negra**

**The quick brown fox jumps over the lazy dog. Voyez le brick géant que j'examine près du wharf. Zwölf Boxkämpfer jagen Viktor quer über den großen Sylter Deich. El veloz murciélago hindú comía feliz cardillo y kiwi. La cigüeña tocaba el saxofón detrás del palenque de pajaatur? Rissimo lorer-**

**7/10  Perec SuperBlanca**

The quick brown fox jumps over the lazy dog. Voyez le brick géant que j'examine près du wharf. Zwölf Boxkämpfer jagen Viktor quer über den großen Sylter Deich. El veloz murciélago hindú comía feliz cardillo y kiwi. La cigüeña tocaba el saxofón detrás del palenque de pajaatur? Rissimo lorereped ex es solore lab id molorro in rempore icabore rehenetur

**7/10  Perec Blanca**

The quick brown fox jumps over the lazy dog. Voyez le brick géant que j'examine près du wharf. Zwölf Boxkämpfer jagen Viktor quer über den großen Sylter Deich. El veloz murciélago hindú comía feliz cardillo y kiwi. La cigüeña tocaba el saxofón detrás del palenque de pajaatur? Rissimo lorereped ex es solore lab id molorro in rempore icabore

**7/10  Perec Gris**

The quick brown fox jumps over the lazy dog. Voyez le brick géant que j'examine près du wharf. Zwölf Boxkämpfer jagen Viktor quer über den großen Sylter Deich. El veloz murciélago hindú comía feliz cardillo y kiwi. La cigüeña tocaba el saxofón detrás del palenque de pajaatur? Rissimo lorereped ex es solore lab id molorro in rempore

**7/10  Perec Negra**

**The quick brown fox jumps over the lazy dog. Voyez le brick géant que j'examine près du wharf. Zwölf Boxkämpfer jagen Viktor quer über den großen Sylter Deich. El veloz murciélago hindú comía feliz cardillo y kiwi. La cigüeña tocaba el saxofón detrás del palenque de pajaatur? Rissimo lorereped ex es solore lab id molorro in rempore icabore rehenetur aliam aut voles audae dem quam, secum eum facesequae consequ aepudam quia voluptiur**

Page 199

Foundry  PampaType

Typeface  Perec Lunatique, Ludique
Designer  Alejandro Lo Celso
Year      2010–2011
Format    OpenType

# Aa

Aa Bb Cc Dd Ee Ff Gg Hh Ii Jj
Kk Ll Mm Nn Oo Pp Qq Rr Ss Tt
Uu Vv Ww Xx Yy Zz
0123456789

Perec Lunatique SuperBlanca 20pt
Perec Lunatique Blanca 20pt
Perec Lunatique Gris 20pt
Perec Lunatique Negra 20pt
Perec Lunatique SuperNegra 20pt

PEREC LUDIQUE CUBES 20PT
Perec Ludique Oncle Jacques 20pt
Perec Ludique Pochoir 20pt

---

12/14   Perec Lunatique SuperBlanca

The quick brown fox jumps over the lazy dog. Voyez le brick géant que j'examine près du wharf. Zwölf Boxkämpfer jagen Viktor

12/14   Perec Lunatique Blanca

The quick brown fox jumps over the lazy dog. Voyez le brick géant que j'examine près du wharf. Zwölf Boxkämpfer jagen Viktor

12/14   Perec Lunatique Gris

The quick brown fox jumps over the lazy dog. Voyez le brick géant que j'examine près du wharf. Zwölf Boxkämpfer jagen Vik-

12/14   Perec LunatiqueNegra

**The quick brown fox jumps over the lazy dog. Voyez le brick géant que j'examine près du wharf. Zwölf Boxkämpfer jagen Viktor quer über den großen Sylter Deich. El veloz murciélago hin-**

9/12    Perec Lunatique SuperBlanca

The quick brown fox jumps over the lazy dog. Voyez le brick géant que j'examine près du wharf. Zwölf Boxkämpfer jagen Viktor quer über den großen Sylter Deich. El veloz murciélago hindú comía feliz cardillo y kiwi. La

9/12    Perec Lunatique Blanca

The quick brown fox jumps over the lazy dog. Voyez le brick géant que j'examine près du wharf. Zwölf Boxkämpfer jagen Viktor quer über den großen Sylter Deich. El veloz murciélago hindú comía feliz cardillo y kiwi. La

9/12    Perec Lunatique Gris

The quick brown fox jumps over the lazy dog. Voyez le brick géant que j'examine près du wharf. Zwölf Boxkämpfer jagen Viktor quer über den großen Sylter Deich. El veloz murciélago hindú comía feliz cardillo y

9/12    Perec Lunatique Negra

**The quick brown fox jumps over the lazy dog. Voyez le brick géant que j'examine près du wharf. Zwölf Boxkämpfer jagen Viktor quer über den großen Sylter Deich. El veloz murciélago hindú comía feliz cardillo y kiwi. La cigüeña tocaba el saxofón detrás del palenque de pajaatur? Rissimo lorereped ex**

7/10    Perec Lunatique SuperBlanca

The quick brown fox jumps over the lazy dog. Voyez le brick géant que j'examine près du wharf. Zwölf Boxkämpfer jagen Viktor quer über den großen Sylter Deich. El veloz murciélago hindú comía feliz cardillo y kiwi. La cigüeña tocaba el saxofón detrás del palenque de pajaatur? Rissimo lorereped ex es solore lab id molorro in rempore icabore rehenetur

7/10    Perec Lunatique Blanca

The quick brown fox jumps over the lazy dog. Voyez le brick géant que j'examine près du wharf. Zwölf Boxkämpfer jagen Viktor quer über den großen Sylter Deich. El veloz murciélago hindú comía feliz cardillo y kiwi. La cigüeña tocaba el saxofón detrás del palenque de pajaatur? Rissimo lorereped ex es solore lab id molorro in rempore icabore

7/10    Perec Lunatique Gris

The quick brown fox jumps over the lazy dog. Voyez le brick géant que j'examine près du wharf. Zwölf Boxkämpfer jagen Viktor quer über den großen Sylter Deich. El veloz murciélago hindú comía feliz cardillo y kiwi. La cigüeña tocaba el saxofón detrás del palenque de pajaatur? Rissimo lorereped ex es solore lab id molorro in rempore icabore

7/10    Perec Lunatique Negra

**The quick brown fox jumps over the lazy dog. Voyez le brick géant que j'examine près du wharf. Zwölf Boxkämpfer jagen Viktor quer über den großen Sylter Deich. El veloz murciélago hindú comía feliz cardillo y kiwi. La cigüeña tocaba el saxofón detrás del palenque de pajaatur? Rissimo lorereped ex es solore lab id molorro in rempore icabore rehenetur aliam aut voles audae dem quam, secum eum facesequae consequ aepudam quia voluptiur**

# P
## Parachute

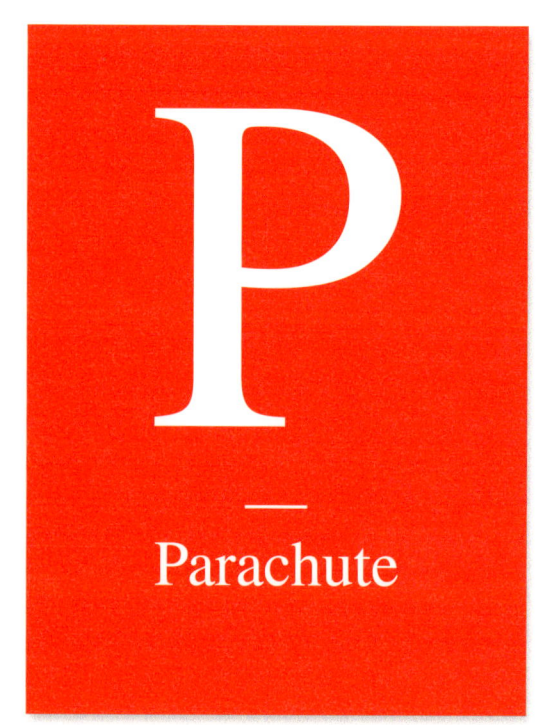

Panos Vassiliou, Charis Tsevis

Greece

Since 2001

The Parachute foundry was set up in 1999 by Panos Vassiliou after he decided to turn his passion for design and typography into a profession. Since then, twelve designers have joined in to form a select group of open-minded, free-spirited individuals. Apart from being the major font supplier to most publishing houses and advertising agencies in Greece, Parachute has built a strong network of valuable relationships with international clients such as Disney, Ikea, MTV Networks, Nike, Penguin Group, PepsiCo, Random House, Samsung, Time Warner and many more.

## Info

—Why?
There was a lack of professional contemporary typefaces in Greece. Combined with a great demand from the advertising and publishing industry, this allowed us to eventually turn a hobby into a profession.

—People on staff
5

—Type designers on staff
2

—Type families
57

—Designers represented
12

—Web shop
Yes

—Distributors
MyFonts, Fonthaus, Fontworks, Paratype, Luth&Co

—Webfont services
Fontdeck, MyFonts

—Basic license
$79–$895 for max. 5 computers

## People

—Panos Vassiliou studied Applied Science and Engineering at the University of Toronto. In the years transitioning from engineering to typography, he became involved with a theater company, founded a design studio and pursued a teaching career. A few years later he started a publishing company. He has designed typefaces since 1993, including commercial fonts as well as custom solutions for national and international companies. He is regularly invited as a guest speaker to conferences and seminars, to speak on typography and related topics. His design work has won him several international awards.

—Charis Tsevis holds a Diploma of Graphic Design from the Akademie für das Grafische Gewerbe, Munich, and an MA in Visual Design from the Scuola Politecnica di Design, Milano. His client list includes Toyota, *Time, Fortune, Los Angeles Times, Panorama, Epoca* and many more. Charis has been an associate professor of Editorial Design and Typography at the AKTO College of Art and Design in Athens since 1996. His awards include ED (Europe), NPSA (USA) and EBGE (Greece).

Parachute merchandising: Defy Rules T-shirt.

## Typeface selection

PF Adamant Pro
PF BeauSans Pro
PF Centro Slab Pro
PF Din Text
PF Encore Sans Pro
PF Regal Finesse Pro
*PF Regal Swash Pro*

24pt

Page
201

Parachute merchandising: left, a set of typographic coasters; above, their first, award-winning type catalog; below, various specimens and promo brochures.

Page
202

Foundry  Parachute

Typeface  PF Adamant Pro
Designer  Vedran Erakovic

Year  2010
Format  OpenType

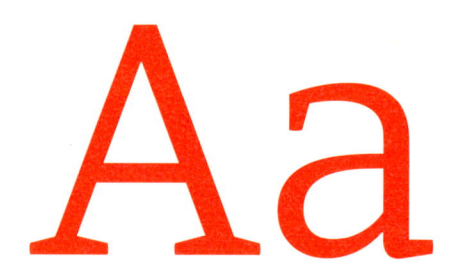

# Aa

Aa Bb Cc Dd Ee Ff Gg Hh Ii Jj
Kk Ll Mm Nn Oo Pp Qq Rr Ss
Tt Uu Vv Ww Xx Yy Zz
0123456789
—

PF Adamant Pro Light 20pt
*PF Adamant Pro Light Italic 20pt*
PF Adamant Pro Regular 20pt
*PF Adamant Pro Italic 20pt*
PF Adamant Pro Medium 20pt
*PF Adamant Pro Medium Italic 20pt*
**PF Adamant Pro Semi Bold 20pt**
***PF Adamant Pro Semi Bold Italic 20pt***
**PF Adamant Pro Bold 20pt**
***PF Adamant Pro Bold Italic 20pt***
**PF Adamant Pro Extra Bold 20pt**
***PF Adamant Pro Extra Bold Italic 20pt***

---

12/14  PF Adamant Pro Regular

The quick brown fox jumps over the lazy dog. Voyez le brick géant que j'examine près du wharf. Zwölf Boxkämpfer jagen

9/12  PF Adamant Pro Regular

The quick brown fox jumps over the lazy dog. Voyez le brick géant que j'examine près du wharf. Zwölf Boxkämpfer jagen Viktor quer über den großen Sylter Deich. El veloz murciélago hindú comía feliz cardillo y

7/10  PF Adamant Pro Regular

The quick brown fox jumps over the lazy dog. Voyez le brick géant que j'examine près du wharf. Zwölf Boxkämpfer jagen Viktor quer über den großen Sylter Deich. El veloz murciélago hindú comía feliz cardillo y kiwi. La cigüeña tocaba el saxofón detrás del palenque de pajaatur? Rissimo lorereped ex es solore lab id

12/14  PF Adamant Pro Medium

The quick brown fox jumps over the lazy dog. Voyez le brick géant que j'examine près du wharf. Zwölf Boxkämpfer jagen

9/12  PF Adamant Pro Medium

The quick brown fox jumps over the lazy dog. Voyez le brick géant que j'examine près du wharf. Zwölf Boxkämpfer jagen Viktor quer über den großen Sylter Deich. El veloz murciélago hindú comía feliz car-

7/10  PF Adamant Pro Medium

The quick brown fox jumps over the lazy dog. Voyez le brick géant que j'examine près du wharf. Zwölf Boxkämpfer jagen Viktor quer über den großen Sylter Deich. El veloz murciélago hindú comía feliz cardillo y kiwi. La cigüeña tocaba el saxofón detrás del palenque de pajaatur? Rissimo lorereped ex es solore lab id

12/14  PF Adamant Pro SemiBold

**The quick brown fox jumps over the lazy dog. Voyez le brick géant que j'examine près du wharf. Zwölf Boxkämpfer**

9/12  PF Adamant Pro SemiBold

**The quick brown fox jumps over the lazy dog. Voyez le brick géant que j'examine près du wharf. Zwölf Boxkämpfer jagen Viktor quer über den großen Sylter Deich. El veloz murciélago hindú comía feliz car-**

7/10  PF Adamant Pro SemiBold

**The quick brown fox jumps over the lazy dog. Voyez le brick géant que j'examine près du wharf. Zwölf Boxkämpfer jagen Viktor quer über den großen Sylter Deich. El veloz murciélago hindú comía feliz cardillo y kiwi. La cigüeña tocaba el saxofón detrás del palenque de pajaatur? Rissimo lorereped ex es solore lab**

12/14  PF Adamant Pro Bold

**The quick brown fox jumps over the lazy dog. Voyez le brick géant que j'examine près du wharf. Zwölf Boxkämpfer jagen Viktor quer über den großen Sylter Deich. El veloz**

9/12  PF Adamant Pro Bold

**The quick brown fox jumps over the lazy dog. Voyez le brick géant que j'examine près du wharf. Zwölf Boxkämpfer jagen Viktor quer über den großen Sylter Deich. El veloz murciélago hindú comía feliz cardillo y kiwi. La cigüeña tocaba el saxofón detrás del palenque de pajaa-**

7/10  PF Adamant Pro Bold

**The quick brown fox jumps over the lazy dog. Voyez le brick géant que j'examine près du wharf. Zwölf Boxkämpfer jagen Viktor quer über den großen Sylter Deich. El veloz murciélago hindú comía feliz cardillo y kiwi. La cigüeña tocaba el saxofón detrás del palenque de pajaatur? Rissimo lorereped ex es solore lab id molorro in rempore icabore rehenetur aliam aut voles audae dem quam, secum eum**

Typeface PF Centro Slab Pro
Designer Panos Vassiliou
Year 2007
Format OpenType

# Aa

Aa Bb Cc Dd Ee Ff Gg Hh Ii Jj Kk Ll
Mm Nn Oo Pp Qq Rr Ss Tt Uu Vv
Ww Xx Yy Zz
0123456789
—

PF Centro Slab Pro Extra Thin 16pt
*PF Centro Slab Pro Extra Thin Italic* 16pt
PF Centro Slab Pro Thin 16pt
*PF Centro Slab Pro Thin Italic* 16pt
PF Centro Slab Pro Light 16pt
*PF Centro Slab Pro Light Italic* 16pt
PF Centro Slab Pro Regular 16pt
*PF Centro Slab Pro Italic* 16pt
**PF Centro Slab Pro Medium** 16pt
*PF Centro Slab Pro Medium Italic* 16pt
**PF Centro Slab Pro Bold** 16pt
***PF Centro Slab Pro Bold Italic*** 16pt
**PF Centro Slab Pro Black** 16pt
***PF Centro Slab Pro Black Italic*** 16pt
**PF Centro Slab Pro Ultra Black** 16pt
***PF Centro Slab Pro Ultra Black Italic*** 16pt

---

12/14    PF Centro Slab Pro Light

The quick brown fox jumps over the lazy dog. Voyez le brick géant que j'examine près du wharf. Zwölf Boxkämpfer jagen Viktor quer über den

9/12    PF Centro Slab Pro Light

The quick brown fox jumps over the lazy dog. Voyez le brick géant que j'examine près du wharf. Zwölf Boxkämpfer jagen Viktor quer über den großen Sylter Deich. El veloz murciélago hindú comía feliz cardillo y kiwi. La cigüeña tocaba el saxofón detrás

7/10    PF Centro Slab Pro Light

The quick brown fox jumps over the lazy dog. Voyez le brick géant que j'examine près du wharf. Zwölf Boxkämpfer jagen Viktor quer über den großen Sylter Deich. El veloz murciélago hindú comía feliz cardillo y kiwi. La cigüeña tocaba el saxofón detrás del palenque de pajaatur? Rissimo lorereped ex es solore lab id molorro in rempore icabore rehenetur aliam aut voles audae dem

12/14    PF Centro Slab Pro Regular

The quick brown fox jumps over the lazy dog. Voyez le brick géant que j'examine près du wharf. Zwölf Boxkämpfer jagen Viktor quer über den

9/12    PF Centro Slab Pro Regular

The quick brown fox jumps over the lazy dog. Voyez le brick géant que j'examine près du wharf. Zwölf Boxkämpfer jagen Viktor quer über den großen Sylter Deich. El veloz murciélago hindú comía feliz cardillo y kiwi. La cigüeña to-

7/10    PF Centro Slab Pro Regular

The quick brown fox jumps over the lazy dog. Voyez le brick géant que j'examine près du wharf. Zwölf Boxkämpfer jagen Viktor quer über den großen Sylter Deich. El veloz murciélago hindú comía feliz cardillo y kiwi. La cigüeña tocaba el saxofón detrás del palenque de pajaatur? Rissimo lorereped ex es solore lab id molorro in rempore icabore rehenetur aliam aut voles

12/14    PF Centro Slab Pro Medium

The quick brown fox jumps over the lazy dog. Voyez le brick géant que j'examine près du wharf. Zwölf Boxkämpfer jagen Vik-

9/12    PF Centro Slab Pro Medium

The quick brown fox jumps over the lazy dog. Voyez le brick géant que j'examine près du wharf. Zwölf Boxkämpfer jagen Viktor quer über den großen Sylter Deich. El veloz murciélago hindú comía feliz cardillo y kiwi. La

7/10    PF Centro Slab Pro Medium

The quick brown fox jumps over the lazy dog. Voyez le brick géant que j'examine près du wharf. Zwölf Boxkämpfer jagen Viktor quer über den großen Sylter Deich. El veloz murciélago hindú comía feliz cardillo y kiwi. La cigüeña tocaba el saxofón detrás del palenque de pajaatur? Rissimo lorereped ex es solore lab id molorro in rempore icabore

12/14    PF Centro Slab Pro Bold

**The quick brown fox jumps over the lazy dog. Voyez le brick géant que j'examine près du wharf. Zwölf Boxkämpfer jagen Viktor quer über den großen Sylter Deich. El veloz murcié-**

9/12    PF Centro Slab Pro Bold

**The quick brown fox jumps over the lazy dog. Voyez le brick géant que j'examine près du wharf. Zwölf Boxkämpfer jagen Viktor quer über den großen Sylter Deich. El veloz murciélago hindú comía feliz cardillo y kiwi. La cigüeña tocaba el saxofón detrás del palenque de pajaatur? Rissimo**

7/10    PF Centro Slab Pro Bold

**The quick brown fox jumps over the lazy dog. Voyez le brick géant que j'examine près du wharf. Zwölf Boxkämpfer jagen Viktor quer über den großen Sylter Deich. El veloz murciélago hindú comía feliz cardillo y kiwi. La cigüeña tocaba el saxofón detrás del palenque de pajaatur? Rissimo lorereped ex es solore lab id molorro in rempore icabore rehenetur aliam aut voles audae dem quam, secum eum facesequae consequ**

Page 204

Foundry Parachute

Typeface PF Encore Sans Pro
Designer Panos Vassiliou
Year 2009
Format OpenType

Aa

Aa Bb Cc Dd Ee Ff Gg Hh Ii Jj Kk Ll
Mm Nn Oo Pp Qq Rr Ss Tt Uu Vv
Ww Xx Yy Zz
0123456789
—

PF Encore Sans Pro Hairline 18pt
*PF Encore Sans Pro Hairline Italic 18pt*
PF Encore Sans Pro Ultra Thin 18pt
*PF Encore Sans Pro Ultra Thin Italic 18pt*
PF Encore Sans Pro Extra Thin 18pt
*PF Encore Sans Pro Extra Thin Italic 18pt*
PF Encore Sans Pro Thin 18pt
*PF Encore Sans Pro Thin Italic 18pt*
PF Encore Sans Pro Light 18pt
*PF Encore Sans Pro Light Italic 18pt*
PF Encore Sans Pro Regular 18pt
*PF Encore Sans Pro Italic 18pt*
**PF Encore Sans Pro Medium 18pt**
***PF Encore Sans Pro Medium Italic 18pt***
**PF Encore Sans Pro Bold 18pt**
***PF Encore Sans Pro Bold Italic 18pt***
**PF Encore Sans Pro Black 18pt**
***PF Encore Sans Pro Black Italic 18pt***
**PF Encore Sans Pro Ultra Black 18pt**
***PF Encore Sans Pro Ultra Black Italic 18pt***

---

12/14 PF Encore Sans Pro Book

The quick brown fox jumps over the lazy dog. Voyez le brick géant que j'examine près du wharf. Zwölf Boxkämpfer jagen Viktor quer über den

9/12 PF Encore Sans Pro Book

The quick brown fox jumps over the lazy dog. Voyez le brick géant que j'examine près du wharf. Zwölf Boxkämpfer jagen Viktor quer über den großen Sylter Deich. El veloz murciélago hindú comía feliz cardillo y kiwi. La cigüeña tocaba el

7/10 PF Encore Sans Pro Book

The quick brown fox jumps over the lazy dog. Voyez le brick géant que j'examine près du wharf. Zwölf Boxkämpfer jagen Viktor quer über den großen Sylter Deich. El veloz murciélago hindú comía feliz cardillo y kiwi. La cigüeña tocaba el saxofón detrás del palenque de pajaatur? Rissimo lorereped ex es solore lab id molorro in rempore icabore rehenetur aliam aut voles

12/14 PF Encore Sans Pro Medium

The quick brown fox jumps over the lazy dog. Voyez le brick géant que j'examine près du wharf. Zwölf Boxkämpfer jagen Viktor quer über

9/12 PF Encore Sans Pro Medium

The quick brown fox jumps over the lazy dog. Voyez le brick géant que j'examine près du wharf. Zwölf Boxkämpfer jagen Viktor quer über den großen Sylter Deich. El veloz murciélago hindú comía feliz cardillo y kiwi. La

7/10 PF Encore Sans Pro Medium

The quick brown fox jumps over the lazy dog. Voyez le brick géant que j'examine près du wharf. Zwölf Boxkämpfer jagen Viktor quer über den großen Sylter Deich. El veloz murciélago hindú comía feliz cardillo y kiwi. La cigüeña tocaba el saxofón detrás del palenque de pajaatur? Rissimo lorereped ex es solore lab id molorro in rempore icabore rehenetur

12/14 PF Encore Sans Pro SemiBold

**The quick brown fox jumps over the lazy dog. Voyez le brick géant que j'examine près du wharf. Zwölf Boxkämpfer jagen Viktor quer über den großen Sylter Deich. El veloz murciélago**

9/12 PF Encore Sans Pro SemiBold

**The quick brown fox jumps over the lazy dog. Voyez le brick géant que j'examine près du wharf. Zwölf Boxkämpfer jagen Viktor quer über den großen Sylter Deich. El veloz murciélago hindú comía feliz cardillo y kiwi. La cigüeña tocaba el saxofón detrás del palenque de pajaatur? Rissimo lorer-**

7/10 PF Encore Sans Pro SemiBold

**The quick brown fox jumps over the lazy dog. Voyez le brick géant que j'examine près du wharf. Zwölf Boxkämpfer jagen Viktor quer über den großen Sylter Deich. El veloz murciélago hindú comía feliz cardillo y kiwi. La cigüeña tocaba el saxofón detrás del palenque de pajaatur? Rissimo lorereped ex es solore lab id molorro in rempore icabore rehenetur aliam aut voles audae dem quam, secum eum facesequae consequ aepudam quia**

Typeface PF Beau Sans Pro    Year   2002–2006
Designer Panos Vassiliou      Format OpenType

# Aa

Aa Bb Cc Dd Ee Ff Gg Hh Ii Jj Kk Ll
Mm Nn Oo Pp Qq Rr Ss Tt Uu Vv
Ww Xx Yy Zz
0123456789
—

PF BeauSans Pro ExtraThin 18pt
*PF BeauSans Pro ExtraThin Italic 18pt*
PF BeauSans Pro Thin 18pt
*PF BeauSans Pro Thin Italic 18pt*
PF BeauSans Pro Light 18pt
*PF BeauSans Pro Light Italic 18pt*
PF BeauSans Pro Regular 18pt
*PF BeauSans Pro Italic 18pt*
PF BeauSans Pro Book 18pt
*PF BeauSans Pro Book Italic 18pt*
PF BeauSans Pro Semi Bold 18pt
*PF BeauSans Pro SemiBold Italic 18pt*
**PF BeauSans Pro Bold 18pt**
***PF BeauSans Pro Bold Italic 18pt***
**PF BeauSans Pro Black 18pt**
***PF BeauSans Pro Black Italic 18pt***

---

12/14  PF BeauSans Pro Light

The quick brown fox jumps over the lazy dog. Voyez le brick géant que j'examine près du wharf. Zwölf Boxkämpfer jagen Viktor quer über den

12/14  PF BeauSans Pro Regular

The quick brown fox jumps over the lazy dog. Voyez le brick géant que j'examine près du wharf. Zwölf Boxkämpfer jagen Viktor quer über den

12/14  PF BeauSans Pro SemiBold

The quick brown fox jumps over the lazy dog. Voyez le brick géant que j'examine près du wharf. Zwölf Boxkämpfer jagen Vik-

12/14  PF BeauSans Pro Bold

**The quick brown fox jumps over the lazy dog. Voyez le brick géant que j'examine près du wharf. Zwölf Boxkämpfer jagen Viktor quer über den großen Sylter Deich. El veloz murciélago**

9/12  PF BeauSans Pro Light

The quick brown fox jumps over the lazy dog. Voyez le brick géant que j'examine près du wharf. Zwölf Boxkämpfer jagen Viktor quer über den großen Sylter Deich. El veloz murciélago hindú comía feliz cardillo y kiwi. La cigüe-

9/12  PF BeauSans Pro Regular

The quick brown fox jumps over the lazy dog. Voyez le brick géant que j'examine près du wharf. Zwölf Boxkämpfer jagen Viktor quer über den großen Sylter Deich. El veloz murciélago hindú comía feliz cardillo y kiwi. La

9/12  PF BeauSans Pro SemiBold

The quick brown fox jumps over the lazy dog. Voyez le brick géant que j'examine près du wharf. Zwölf Boxkämpfer jagen Viktor quer über den großen Sylter Deich. El veloz murciélago hindú comía feliz cardillo y kiwi.

9/12  PF BeauSans Pro Bold

**The quick brown fox jumps over the lazy dog. Voyez le brick géant que j'examine près du wharf. Zwölf Boxkämpfer jagen Viktor quer über den großen Sylter Deich. El veloz murciélago hindú comía feliz cardillo y kiwi. La cigüeña tocaba el saxofón detrás del palenque de pajaatur? Rissimo lorer-**

7/10  PF BeauSans Pro Light

The quick brown fox jumps over the lazy dog. Voyez le brick géant que j'examine près du wharf. Zwölf Boxkämpfer jagen Viktor quer über den großen Sylter Deich. El veloz murciélago hindú comía feliz cardillo y kiwi. La cigüeña tocaba el saxofón detrás del palenque de pajaatur? Rissimo lorereped ex es solore lab id molorro in rempore icabore rehenetur aliam

7/10  PF BeauSans Pro Regular

The quick brown fox jumps over the lazy dog. Voyez le brick géant que j'examine près du wharf. Zwölf Boxkämpfer jagen Viktor quer über den großen Sylter Deich. El veloz murciélago hindú comía feliz cardillo y kiwi. La cigüeña tocaba el saxofón detrás del palenque de pajaatur? Rissimo lorereped ex es solore lab id molorro in rempore icabore rehenetur aliam

7/10  PF BeauSans Pro SemiBold

The quick brown fox jumps over the lazy dog. Voyez le brick géant que j'examine près du wharf. Zwölf Boxkämpfer jagen Viktor quer über den großen Sylter Deich. El veloz murciélago hindú comía feliz cardillo y kiwi. La cigüeña tocaba el saxofón detrás del palenque de pajaatur? Rissimo lorereped ex es solore lab id molorro in rempore

7/10  PF BeauSans Pro Bold

**The quick brown fox jumps over the lazy dog. Voyez le brick géant que j'examine près du wharf. Zwölf Boxkämpfer jagen Viktor quer über den großen Sylter Deich. El veloz murciélago hindú comía feliz cardillo y kiwi. La cigüeña tocaba el saxofón detrás del palenque de pajaatur? Rissimo lorereped ex es solore lab id molorro in rempore icabore rehenetur aliam aut voles audae dem quam, secum eum facesequae consequ aepu-**

Page 206

Foundry  Parachute

Typeface  PF Regal Finesse Pro, PF Regal Swash Pro
Designer  Panos Vassiliou
Year  2010
Format  OpenType

# Aa

Aa Bb Cc Dd Ee Ff Gg Hh Ii Jj
Kk Ll Mm Nn Oo Pp Qq Rr Ss Tt
Uu Vv Ww Xx Yy Zz
0123456789

PF Regal Finesse Pro Regular 18pt
*PF Regal Finesse Pro Italic 18pt*
PF Regal Finesse Pro Medium 18pt
*PF Regal Finesse Pro Medium Italic 18pt*
**PF Regal Finesse Pro Bold 18pt**
***PF Regal Finesse Pro Bold Italic 18pt***
**PF Regal Finesse Pro Black 18pt**
***PF Regal Finesse Pro Black Italic 18pt***
**PF Regal Finesse Pro Ultra Black 18pt**
***PF Regal Finesse Pro Ultra Black Italic 18pt***

*PF Regal Swash Pro Regular 18pt*
*PF Regal Swash Pro Medium 18pt*
***PF Regal Swash Pro Bold 18pt***
***PF Regal Swash Pro Black 18pt***
***PF Regal Swash Pro Ultra Black 18pt***

---

**12/14  PF Regal Finesse Pro Regular**

The quick brown fox jumps over the lazy dog. Voyez le brick géant que j'examine près du wharf. Zwölf Boxkämpfer jagen Viktor quer über den

**12/14  PF Regal Finesse Pro Medium**

The quick brown fox jumps over the lazy dog. Voyez le brick géant que j'examine près du wharf. Zwölf Boxkämpfer jagen Viktor quer über

**12/14  PF Regal Finesse Pro Bold**

The quick brown fox jumps over the lazy dog. Voyez le brick géant que j'examine près du wharf. Zwölf Boxkämpfer jagen Viktor quer über den großen Sylter Deich. El veloz murciélago hindú

**9/12  PF Regal Finesse Pro Regular**

The quick brown fox jumps over the lazy dog. Voyez le brick géant que j'examine près du wharf. Zwölf Boxkämpfer jagen Viktor quer über den großen Sylter Deich. El veloz murciélago hindú comía feliz cardillo y kiwi. La cigüeña tocaba el

**9/12  PF Regal Finesse Pro Medium**

The quick brown fox jumps over the lazy dog. Voyez le brick géant que j'examine près du wharf. Zwölf Boxkämpfer jagen Viktor quer über den großen Sylter Deich. El veloz murciélago hindú comía feliz cardillo y kiwi. La

**9/12  PF Regal Finesse Pro Bold**

The quick brown fox jumps over the lazy dog. Voyez le brick géant que j'examine près du wharf. Zwölf Boxkämpfer jagen Viktor quer über den großen Sylter Deich. El veloz murciélago hindú comía feliz cardillo y kiwi. La cigüeña tocaba el saxofón detrás del palenque de pajaatur? Rissimo lorereped ex

**7/10  PF Regal Finesse Pro Regular**

The quick brown fox jumps over the lazy dog. Voyez le brick géant que j'examine près du wharf. Zwölf Boxkämpfer jagen Viktor quer über den großen Sylter Deich. El veloz murciélago hindú comía feliz cardillo y kiwi. La cigüeña tocaba el saxofón detrás del palenque de pajaatur? Rissimo lorereped ex es solore lab id molorro in rempore icabore rehenetur aliam aut voles

**7/10  PF Regal Finesse Pro Medium**

The quick brown fox jumps over the lazy dog. Voyez le brick géant que j'examine près du wharf. Zwölf Boxkämpfer jagen Viktor quer über den großen Sylter Deich. El veloz murciélago hindú comía feliz cardillo y kiwi. La cigüeña tocaba el saxofón detrás del palenque de pajaatur? Rissimo lorereped ex es solore lab id molorro in rempore icabore rehenetur aliam

**7/10  PF Regal Finesse Pro Bold**

The quick brown fox jumps over the lazy dog. Voyez le brick géant que j'examine près du wharf. Zwölf Boxkämpfer jagen Viktor quer über den großen Sylter Deich. El veloz murciélago hindú comía feliz cardillo y kiwi. La cigüeña tocaba el saxofón detrás del palenque de pajaatur? Rissimo lorereped ex es solore lab id molorro in rempore icabore rehenetur aliam aut voles audae dem quam, secum cum facesequae consequ aepudam quia voluptiur

Foundry   Parachute

Typeface   PF Din Text
Designer   Panos Vassiliou
Year   2002
Format   OpenType

# Aa

Aa Bb Cc Dd Ee Ff Gg Hh Ii Jj Kk Ll Mm Nn Oo Pp Qq Rr Ss Tt Uu Vv Ww Xx Yy Zz
0123456789
—

PF Din Text Extra Thin 18pt
*PF Din Text Extra Thin Italic 18pt*
PF Din Text Thin 18pt
*PF Din Text Thin Italic 18pt*
PF Din Text Light 18pt
*PF Din Text Light Italic 18pt*
PF Din Text Regular 18pt
*PF Din Text Italic 18pt*
**PF Din Text Medium 18pt**
***PF Din Text Medium Italic 18pt***
**PF Din Text Bold 18pt**
***PF Din Text Bold Italic 18pt***
**PF Din Text Extra Black 18pt**
***PF Din Text Extra Black Italic 18pt***

PF Din Stencil Pro Hairline > **Extra Black 18pt**

---

12/14   PF Din Text Regular

The quick brown fox jumps over the lazy dog. Voyez le brick géant que j'examine près du wharf. Zwölf Boxkämpfer jagen Viktor quer über den

12/14   PF Din Text Medium

**The quick brown fox jumps over the lazy dog. Voyez le brick géant que j'examine près du wharf. Zwölf Boxkämpfer jagen Viktor quer über den**

12/14   PF Din Text Bold

**The quick brown fox jumps over the lazy dog. Voyez le brick géant que j'examine près du wharf. Zwölf Boxkämpfer jagen Viktor quer über den großen Sylter Deich. El veloz murciélago hindú comía feliz cardi-**

9/12   PF Din Text Regular

The quick brown fox jumps over the lazy dog. Voyez le brick géant que j'examine près du wharf. Zwölf Boxkämpfer jagen Viktor quer über den großen Sylter Deich. El veloz murciélago hindú comía feliz cardillo y kiwi. La cigüeña tocaba el saxofón detrás

9/12   PF Din Text Medium

**The quick brown fox jumps over the lazy dog. Voyez le brick géant que j'examine près du wharf. Zwölf Boxkämpfer jagen Viktor quer über den großen Sylter Deich. El veloz murciélago hindú comía feliz cardillo y kiwi. La cigüeña tocaba el**

9/12   PF Din Text Bold

**The quick brown fox jumps over the lazy dog. Voyez le brick géant que j'examine près du wharf. Zwölf Boxkämpfer jagen Viktor quer über den großen Sylter Deich. El veloz murciélago hindú comía feliz cardillo y kiwi. La cigüeña tocaba el saxofón detrás del palenque de pajaatur? Rissimo lorereped ex es solore lab id**

7/10   PF Din Text Regular

The quick brown fox jumps over the lazy dog. Voyez le brick géant que j'examine près du wharf. Zwölf Boxkämpfer jagen Viktor quer über den großen Sylter Deich. El veloz murciélago hindú comía feliz cardillo y kiwi. La cigüeña tocaba el saxofón detrás del palenque de pajaatur? Rissimo lorereped ex es solore lab id molorro in rempore icabore rehenetur aliam aut voles audae dem quam, secum eum

7/10   PF Din Text Medium

**The quick brown fox jumps over the lazy dog. Voyez le brick géant que j'examine près du wharf. Zwölf Boxkämpfer jagen Viktor quer über den großen Sylter Deich. El veloz murciélago hindú comía feliz cardillo y kiwi. La cigüeña tocaba el saxofón detrás del palenque de pajaatur? Rissimo lorereped ex es solore lab id molorro in rempore icabore rehenetur aliam aut voles au-**

7/10   PF Din Text Bold

**The quick brown fox jumps over the lazy dog. Voyez le brick géant que j'examine près du wharf. Zwölf Boxkämpfer jagen Viktor quer über den großen Sylter Deich. El veloz murciélago hindú comía feliz cardillo y kiwi. La cigüeña tocaba el saxofón detrás del palenque de pajaatur? Rissimo lorereped ex es solore lab id molorro in rempore icabore rehenetur aliam aut voles audae dem quam, secum eum facesequae consequ aepudam quia voluptiur repel in et faccustibus, nonsenis aut**

# P

## Playtype

—

Jonas Hecksher,
Jens Kajus

—

Copenhagen,
Denmark

—

Since
2002–2010

Playtype is the type foundry set up by e-Types, a Copenhagen agency for brand strategy, graphic design and image campaigns. The font collection is the result of over 20 years of type design, with many typefaces never having been publicly available until recently. Originally formed in 2002 as e-Types' platform for font development, Playtype relaunched in 2010, opening the temporary PLAYTYPE™ concept store in Copenhagen.

## Info

—Why?
Because we love typography. We want to spread the love for type, and we believe there is a need to spread type on platforms that are not just purely functional sites for geeks, but make type attractive, accessible & playful. Typography is a way of living.

—People on staff
2

—Type designers on staff
3

—Type families
110

—Designers represented
4

—Web shop
playtype.com

—Distributors
Playtype

—Webfont services
The site will be re-launched later in 2011, and will include webfonts.

—Basic license
€50 (single font, 1-2 licenses)

Typeface selection

Berlingske Sans
Berlingske Serif
Berlingske Slab
Berlingske Text
JazzHouse
Zetta Round
Zetta Sans
Zetta Serif

18pt

## People

—Jonas Hecksher, partner and creative director of e-Types, holds a degree from Danmarks Designskole (Denmark's School of Design) and École supérieure d'arts graphiques et d'architecture, Paris, where he specialized in graphic and typographic design. He co-founded e-Types in 1997, where he has worked ever since with a wide range of projects within corporate visual identity, typography and editorial design as well as image and branding projects for fashion and luxury brands. He has won numerous awards, and Denmark's leading business weekly has ranked him among Denmark's 100 most talented people under the age of 35.

—Jens Kajus, partner and creative director of e-Types, graduated from Danmarks Designskole (Denmark's School of Design) in 1996, specializing in graphic and typographic design. He joined e-Types in 1998, where he has worked ever since with a wide range of projects within corporate visual identity, typography, newspaper and magazine design as well as art-related projects and catalogs. Recently he has been responsible for a wide range of corporate identity and other large-scale design projects. He has won numerous awards and is one of the few Danish designers that have been nominated for a silver award at the British D&AD.

Poster for the Copenhagen Jazzhouse with the Jazzhouse typeface. Design by Jonas Hecksher, 2010.

For the duration of 2011, Playtype opened the PLAYTYPE™ concept store, selling fonts that came on specially designed USB sticks, as well as oher products and editions designed by e-Types and their friends and colleagues from the design, fashion and art worlds. Interior designed by e-Types / Enok Holsegaard, 2010.

Printed matter for the Danish Broadcasting Corporation – Concert House. Designed by Jens Kajus & Jonas Hecksher with the Nouvel typeface, 2008.

Typeface  Berlingske Sans, Serif, Slab  Year  2010
Designer  Jonas Hecksher  Format  OpenType

# AA

Aa Bb Cc Dd Ee Ff Gg Hh Ii Jj Kk Ll Mm Nn Oo Pp Qq Rr Ss Tt Uu Vv Ww Xx Yy Zz
0123456789
—

Berlingske Sans Light 18pt
Berlingske Sans Regular 18pt
Berlingske Sans Medium 18pt
*Berlingske Sans Medium Italic 18pt*
**Berlingske Sans Bold 18pt**
**Berlingske Sans Extra Bold 18pt**
**Berlingske Sans Heavy 18pt**

Berlingske Serif Regular 18pt
*Berlingske Serif Italic 18pt*
Berlingske Serif Demi Bold 18pt
**Berlingske Serif Bold 18pt**
***Berlingske Serif Bold Italic 18pt***
**Berlingske Serif Extra Bold 18pt**
**Berlingske Serif Heavy 18pt**

Berlingske Slab Regular 18pt
**Berlingske Slab Bold 18pt**
**Berlingske Slab Poster 18pt**

---

12/14 Berlingske Sans Regular

The quick brown fox jumps over the lazy dog. Voyez le brick géant que j'examine près du wharf. Zwölf Boxkämpfer jagen Viktor quer über

12/14 Berlingske Sans Medium

The quick brown fox jumps over the lazy dog. Voyez le brick géant que j'examine près du wharf. Zwölf Boxkämpfer jagen Viktor quer über den

12/14 Berlingske Sans Bold

The quick brown fox jumps over the lazy dog. Voyez le brick géant que j'examine près du wharf. Zwölf Boxkämpfer jagen Viktor quer über den großen Sylter Deich. El veloz murciélago hindú comía feliz cardillo y

12/14 Berlingske Serif Regular

The quick brown fox jumps over the lazy dog. Voyez le brick géant que j'examine près du wharf. Zwölf Boxkämpfer jagen Viktor quer

12/14 Berlingske Serif DemiBold

The quick brown fox jumps over the lazy dog. Voyez le brick géant que j'examine près du wharf. Zwölf Boxkämpfer jagen Viktor quer

12/14 Berlingske Serif Bold

The quick brown fox jumps over the lazy dog. Voyez le brick géant que j'examine près du wharf. Zwölf Boxkämpfer jagen Viktor quer über den großen Sylter Deich. El veloz murciélago hindú comía

12/14 Berlingske Slab Regular

The quick brown fox jumps over the lazy dog. Voyez le brick géant que j'examine près du wharf. Zwölf Boxkämpfer jagen Viktor quer

12/14 Berlingske Slab Bold

The quick brown fox jumps over the lazy dog. Voyez le brick géant que j'examine près du wharf. Zwölf Boxkämpfer jagen Vik-

12/14 Berlingske Slab Poster

The quick brown fox jumps over the lazy dog. Voyez le brick géant que j'examine près du wharf. Zwölf Boxkämpfer jagen Viktor quer über den großen Sylter Deich. El veloz murcié-

Foundry  Playtype

Typeface  Berlingske Text
Designer  Jonas Hecksher
Year  2010
Format  OpenType

# Aa

Aa Bb Cc Dd Ee Ff Gg Hh Ii Jj Kk
Ll Mm Nn Oo Pp Qq Rr Ss Tt Uu
Vv Ww Xx Yy Zz
0123456789
—

Berlingske Text Regular 24pt
*Berlingske Text Italic* 24pt
**Berlingske Text Medium** 24pt
*Berlingske Text Medium Italic* 24pt
**Berlingske Text DemiBold** 24pt
*Berlingske Text DemiBold Italic* 24pt
**Berlingske Text Bold** 24pt
*Berlingske Text Bold Italic* 24pt

---

12/14  Berlingske Text Regular

The quick brown fox jumps over the lazy dog. Voyez le brick géant que j'examine près du wharf. Zwölf Boxkämpfer jagen Viktor quer über den

9/12  Berlingske Text Regular

The quick brown fox jumps over the lazy dog. Voyez le brick géant que j'examine près du wharf. Zwölf Boxkämpfer jagen Viktor quer über den großen Sylter Deich. El veloz murciélago hindú comía feliz cardillo y kiwi. La cigüeña to-

7/10  Berlingske Text Regular

The quick brown fox jumps over the lazy dog. Voyez le brick géant que j'examine près du wharf. Zwölf Boxkämpfer jagen Viktor quer über den großen Sylter Deich. El veloz murciélago hindú comía feliz cardillo y kiwi. La cigüeña tocaba el saxofón detrás del palenque de pajaatur? Rissimo lorereped ex es solore lab id molorro in rempore icabore rehenetur aliam

12/14  Berlingske Text Medium

The quick brown fox jumps over the lazy dog. Voyez le brick géant que j'examine près du wharf. Zwölf Boxkämpfer jagen Viktor quer

9/12  Berlingske Text Medium

The quick brown fox jumps over the lazy dog. Voyez le brick géant que j'examine près du wharf. Zwölf Boxkämpfer jagen Viktor quer über den großen Sylter Deich. El veloz murciélago hindú comía feliz cardillo y kiwi. La cigüe-

7/10  Berlingske Text Medium

The quick brown fox jumps over the lazy dog. Voyez le brick géant que j'examine près du wharf. Zwölf Boxkämpfer jagen Viktor quer über den großen Sylter Deich. El veloz murciélago hindú comía feliz cardillo y kiwi. La cigüeña tocaba el saxofón detrás del palenque de pajaatur? Rissimo lorereped ex es solore lab id molorro in rempore icabore rehenetur aliam

12/14  Berlingske Text DemiBold

The quick brown fox jumps over the lazy dog. Voyez le brick géant que j'examine près du wharf. Zwölf Boxkämpfer jagen Viktor quer

9/12  Berlingske Text DemiBold

The quick brown fox jumps over the lazy dog. Voyez le brick géant que j'examine près du wharf. Zwölf Boxkämpfer jagen Viktor quer über den großen Sylter Deich. El veloz murciélago hindú comía feliz cardillo y kiwi. La cigüeña

7/10  Berlingske Text DemiBold

The quick brown fox jumps over the lazy dog. Voyez le brick géant que j'examine près du wharf. Zwölf Boxkämpfer jagen Viktor quer über den großen Sylter Deich. El veloz murciélago hindú comía feliz cardillo y kiwi. La cigüeña tocaba el saxofón detrás del palenque de pajaatur? Rissimo lorereped ex es solore lab id molorro in rempore icabore rehenetur aliam

12/14  Berlingske Text Bold

The quick brown fox jumps over the lazy dog. Voyez le brick géant que j'examine près du wharf. Zwölf Boxkämpfer jagen Viktor quer über den großen Sylter Deich. El veloz murciélago hindú comía feliz cardi-

9/12  Berlingske Text Bold

The quick brown fox jumps over the lazy dog. Voyez le brick géant que j'examine près du wharf. Zwölf Boxkämpfer jagen Viktor quer über den großen Sylter Deich. El veloz murciélago hindú comía feliz cardillo y kiwi. La cigüeña tocaba el saxofón detrás del palenque de pajaatur? Rissimo lorereped ex es solore lab id mo-

7/10  Berlingske Text Bold

The quick brown fox jumps over the lazy dog. Voyez le brick géant que j'examine près du wharf. Zwölf Boxkämpfer jagen Viktor quer über den großen Sylter Deich. El veloz murciélago hindú comía feliz cardillo y kiwi. La cigüeña tocaba el saxofón detrás del palenque de pajaatur? Rissimo lorereped ex es solore lab id molorro in rempore icabore rehenetur aliam aut voles audae dem quam, secum eum facesequae consequ aepudam quia voluptiur repel in et faccustibus, nonsenis aut

Page 212

Foundry  Playtype

Typeface  JazzHouse
Designer  Jonas Hecksher
Year  2010
Format  OpenType

# Aa

Aa Bb Cc Dd Ee Ff Gg Hh Ii Jj Kk Ll Mm Nn Oo Pp Qq Rr Ss Tt Uu Vv Ww Xx Yy Zz
0123456789
—

JazzHouse Regular 24pt
*JazzHouse Italic* 24pt
**JazzHouse Demi Bold** 24pt
**JazzHouse Bold** 24pt
**JazzHouse Heavy** 24pt
***JazzHouse Heavy Italic*** 24pt

---

12/14  JazzHouse Regular

The quick brown fox jumps over the lazy dog. Voyez le brick géant que j'examine près du wharf. Zwölf Boxkämpfer jagen Viktor quer über den großen Sylter Deich. El veloz murciélago hindú comía feliz cardillo y kiwi. La cigüeña tocaba el saxofón detrás del palenque de pajaatur? Rissimo lorereped ex es solore lab id molorro in rempore icabore rehenetur aliam

9/12  JazzHouse Regular

The quick brown fox jumps over the lazy dog. Voyez le brick géant que j'examine près du wharf. Zwölf Boxkämpfer jagen Viktor quer über den großen Sylter Deich. El veloz murciélago hindú comía feliz cardillo y kiwi. La cigüeña tocaba el saxofón detrás del palenque de pajaatur? Rissimo lorereped ex es solore lab id molorro in rempore icabore rehenetur aliam aut voles audae dem quam, secum eum facesequae consequ aepudam quia voluptiur repel in et faccustibus, nonsenis aut quisqui rero mi, ipiet lam ant ut maio et hil molupta tustis atatur, consedi tasimol orerem aut volor andipsapis sit, illaut volore

7/10  JazzHouse Regular

The quick brown fox jumps over the lazy dog. Voyez le brick géant que j'examine près du wharf. Zwölf Boxkämpfer jagen Viktor quer über den großen Sylter Deich. El veloz murciélago hindú comía feliz cardillo y kiwi. La cigüeña tocaba el saxofón detrás del palenque de pajaatur? Rissimo lorereped ex es solore lab id molorro in rempore icabore rehenetur aliam aut voles audae dem quam, secum eum facesequae consequ aepudam quia voluptiur repel in et faccustibus, nonsenis aut quisqui rero mi, ipiet lam ant ut maio et hil molupta tustis atatur, consedi tasimol orerem aut volor andipsapis sit, illaut volore officatus alicae dusdaec tatecte cearum qui accatibus restiore nulpa secaerferum, nus dolenim in et quoditat que explam volupictur? Qui de illuptae. Dae nis illiberum volorro ritatis tinullo rerumqu atetur repro eatius asperibus. Rissimo lorereped ex es solore lab id molorro in rempore icabore

12/14  JazzHouse DemiBold

**The quick brown fox jumps over the lazy dog. Voyez le brick géant que j'examine près du wharf. Zwölf Boxkämpfer jagen Viktor quer über den großen Sylter Deich. El veloz murciélago hindú comía feliz cardillo y kiwi. La cigüeña tocaba el saxofón detrás**

9/12  JazzHouse DemiBold

**The quick brown fox jumps over the lazy dog. Voyez le brick géant que j'examine près du wharf. Zwölf Boxkämpfer jagen Viktor quer über den großen Sylter Deich. El veloz murciélago hindú comía feliz cardillo y kiwi. La cigüeña tocaba el saxofón detrás del palenque de pajaatur? Rissimo lorereped ex es solore lab id molorro in rempore icabore rehenetur aliam aut voles audae dem quam, secum eum**

7/10  JazzHouse DemiBold

**The quick brown fox jumps over the lazy dog. Voyez le brick géant que j'examine près du wharf. Zwölf Boxkämpfer jagen Viktor quer über den großen Sylter Deich. El veloz murciélago hindú comía feliz cardillo y kiwi. La cigüeña tocaba el saxofón detrás del palenque de pajaatur? Rissimo lorereped ex es solore lab id molorro in rempore icabore rehenetur aliam aut voles audae dem quam, secum eum facesequae consequ aepudam quia voluptiur repel in et faccustibus, nonsenis aut quisqui rero mi, ipiet lam ant ut maio et hil molupta tustis atatur, consedi tasimol orerem aut volor andipsapis sit, illaut volore officatus alicae dusdaec tatecte**

12/14  JazzHouse Bold

**The quick brown fox jumps over the lazy dog. Voyez le brick géant que j'examine près du wharf. Zwölf Boxkämpfer jagen Viktor quer über den großen Sylter Deich. El veloz murciélago hindú comía feliz cardillo y kiwi. La cigüeña tocaba el saxofón detrás**

9/12  JazzHouse Bold

**The quick brown fox jumps over the lazy dog. Voyez le brick géant que j'examine près du wharf. Zwölf Boxkämpfer jagen Viktor quer über den großen Sylter Deich. El veloz murciélago hindú comía feliz cardillo y kiwi. La cigüeña tocaba el saxofón detrás del palenque de pajaatur? Rissimo lorereped ex es solore lab id molorro in rempore icabore rehenetur aliam aut voles audae dem quam, secum eum**

7/10  JazzHouse Bold

**The quick brown fox jumps over the lazy dog. Voyez le brick géant que j'examine près du wharf. Zwölf Boxkämpfer jagen Viktor quer über den großen Sylter Deich. El veloz murciélago hindú comía feliz cardillo y kiwi. La cigüeña tocaba el saxofón detrás del palenque de pajaatur? Rissimo lorereped ex es solore lab id molorro in rempore icabore rehenetur aliam aut voles audae dem quam, secum eum facesequae consequ aepudam quia voluptiur repel in et faccustibus, nonsenis aut quisqui rero mi, ipiet lam ant ut maio et hil molupta tustis atatur, consedi tasimol orerem aut volor andipsapis sit, illaut volore officatus alicae dusdaec tatecte cearum qui accatibus**

Page 213

Foundry  Playtype

Typeface  Zetta Sans, Round, Serif
Designer  Jonas Hecksher
Year  2003–2007
Format  OpenType

# Aa

Aa Bb Cc Dd Ee Ff Gg Hh Ii Jj Kk Ll Mm Nn Oo Pp Qq Rr Ss Tt Uu Vv Ww Xx Yy Zz
0123456789
—

Zetta Sans Ultra Light 14pt
Zetta Sans Light 14pt
Zetta Sans Thin 14p
Zetta Sans Book 14pt
Zetta Sans Regular 14pt
*Zetta Sans Italic* 14pt
Zetta Sans Caps 14pt
Zetta Sans Demi Bold 14pt
**Zetta Sans Bold** 14pt
**Zetta Sans Extra Bold** 14pt
**Zetta Sans Heavy** 14pt
**Zetta Sans Poster** 14pt
Zetta Round Light 14pt
Zetta Round Regular 14pt
**Zetta Round Bold** 14pt

Zetta Serif Ultra Light 14pt
Zetta Serif Light 14pt
*Zetta Serif Light Italic* 14pt
Zetta Serif Thin 14p
Zetta Serif Book 14pt
*Zetta Serif Book Italic* 14pt
Zetta Serif Regular 14pt
*Zetta Serif Italic* 14pt
Zetta Serif Caps 14pt
Zetta Serif Demi Bold 14pt
**Zetta Serif Bold** 14pt
**Zetta Serif Extra Bold** 14pt
**Zetta Serif Heavy** 14pt
**Zetta Serif Poster** 14pt

---

12/14  Zetta Sans Light

The quick brown fox jumps over the lazy dog. Voyez le brick géant que j'examine près du wharf. Zwölf Boxkämpfer jagen Viktor quer über den großen Sylter Deich. El veloz murciélago hindú comía feliz cardillo y kiwi. La cigüeña tocaba el saxofón detrás

12/14  Zetta Round Light

The quick brown fox jumps over the lazy dog. Voyez le brick géant que j'examine près du wharf. Zwölf Boxkämpfer jagen Viktor quer über den großen Sylter Deich. El veloz murciélago hindú comía feliz cardillo y kiwi. La cigüeña tocaba el saxofón detrás

12/14  Zetta Serif Light

The quick brown fox jumps over the lazy dog. Voyez le brick géant que j'examine près du wharf. Zwölf Boxkämpfer jagen Viktor quer über den großen Sylter Deich. El veloz murciélago hindú comía feliz cardillo y kiwi. La cigüeña tocaba el saxofón

12/14  Zetta Sans Regular

The quick brown fox jumps over the lazy dog. Voyez le brick géant que j'examine près du wharf. Zwölf Boxkämpfer jagen Viktor quer über den großen Sylter Deich. El veloz murciélago hindú comía feliz cardillo y kiwi. La cigüeña tocaba el saxofón detrás

12/14  Zetta Round Regular

The quick brown fox jumps over the lazy dog. Voyez le brick géant que j'examine près du wharf. Zwölf Boxkämpfer jagen Viktor quer über den großen Sylter Deich. El veloz murciélago hindú comía feliz cardillo y kiwi. La cigüeña tocaba el saxofón detrás

12/14  Zetta Serif Regular

The quick brown fox jumps over the lazy dog. Voyez le brick géant que j'examine près du wharf. Zwölf Boxkämpfer jagen Viktor quer über den großen Sylter Deich. El veloz murciélago hindú comía feliz cardillo y kiwi. La cigüeña tocaba el sa-

12/14  Zetta Sans Bold

**The quick brown fox jumps over the lazy dog. Voyez le brick géant que j'examine près du wharf. Zwölf Boxkämpfer jagen Viktor quer über den großen Sylter Deich. El veloz murciélago hindú comía feliz cardillo y kiwi. La**

12/14  Zetta Round Bold

**The quick brown fox jumps over the lazy dog. Voyez le brick géant que j'examine près du wharf. Zwölf Boxkämpfer jagen Viktor quer über den großen Sylter Deich. El veloz murciélago hindú comía feliz cardillo y kiwi. La**

12/14  Zetta Serif Bold

**The quick brown fox jumps over the lazy dog. Voyez le brick géant que j'examine près du wharf. Zwölf Boxkämpfer jagen Viktor quer über den großen Sylter Deich. El veloz murciélago hindú comía feliz cardillo y kiwi. La ci-**

# P

## Porchez Typofonderie

Jean François Porchez

Clamart, France

Since 1994

Founded in 1994 by Jean François Porchez, Typofonderie is an independent digital type foundry in France, designing, producing and selling high quality typefaces for adventurous digital typographers. Porchez Typofonderie has been offering font licenses with direct download from its own website since 1999.

## Info

—Why?
I wanted to have total control over my work. I even worked without distributors for almost ten years. But now I've become more open.

—People on staff
3

—Type designers on the team
1: Mathieu Réguer
+ freelance type designers

—Type families
26 families/300 fonts

—Designers represented
1

—Web shop
typofonderie.com
custom-type.com

—Distributors
PTF collection only available at Typofonderie. STD collection also available at FontShop, MyFonts, Veer.

—Webfont services
Typekit, WebINK

—Basic license
€50–€140, 2 devices (STD collection)
€210, 8 devices (PTF collection)

## Typeface selection

ANISETTE
**Ambroise**
Allumi
Costa
**Angie Sans**
Apolline
**Parisine**
AW CONQUEROR

24pt

## People

—Jean François Porchez
As a type designer, then a type director, Jean François Porchez's expertise covers both the design of bespoke typefaces and logotypes as well as the distribution of his fonts. As honorary President of the Association Typographique Internationale, he regularly conducts type design workshops and is a frequent speaker at conferences. He founded the French-language community website Le Typographe in 2003. He was awarded the Prix Charles Peignot in 1998 and has won numerous other prizes for his typefaces.

# Retiro
by Jean François Porchez

GUÍA ¶ FORO ✠ BEBE
aaabbccdddeefffiggkkjj
L·ORCA ✠ A·LL·OA ✱ CALOR
nnappqqrrstssuvyzz
LOS NOVELAS SE LLAMA

Retiro designed to gives a unique voice of the Madriz magazine (2007–09). TYPOFONDERIE

abcdefghijklmnopqrstuvwxyz
RAEILO acdefgjkmnprsyz abnqu
ABCDEFGHIJKLMNOPQRSTUVWXYZ
ACEFGHJKMNSR A AZ AMN
ABCDEFGHIJKLMNOPQRSTUVWXYZ
-@№0123456789 ([{#€¥$¢f£ ¶&!?,.»"-

The Retiro typeface was designed to lend a unique voice to *Madriz*, a city magazine distributed in high class places in Madrid. The layout takes its cues from women's magazines with a touch of Iberian vernacular. Porchez drew a hispanic Didot-style alphabet enhanced by flourishes that recall ornamental styles from Southern Spain. 2006–2009.

Page 215

Different from anything Jean François Porchez has designed in the past, Allumi is a sleek sans-serif designed with technology in mind. Pushed to the extreme, the Allumi shapes are neither perfectly round or geometrically square. It's a human design with a high tech touch. Porchez describes Allumi as "the Eurostyle of the new century, mixed with Frutiger."

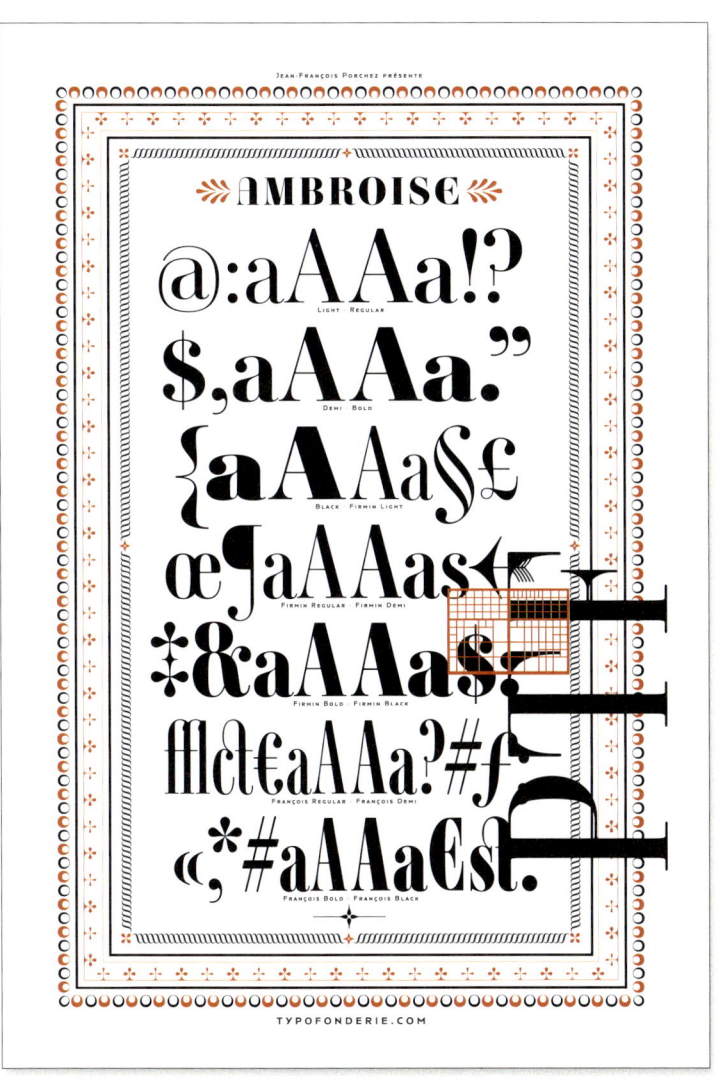

Ambroise is Porchez' interpretation of various types belonging to the late Didot style. It borrows some of its peculiar details from typefaces conceived circa 1830 by the Didots' punchcutter Vibert. Each variation of the typeface carries a name in homage to a member of the illustrious Didot family.

The Apolline typeface family was created in 1993 by Jean François Porchez as a means to study the transition from Renaissance writing to the first printing types. Since its first inception, the family has been updated and expanded more than once.

Foundry  Porchez Typofonderie

---

Typeface  AW Conqueror  Year  2010
Designer  Jean François Porchez  Format  OpenType

# Conqueror CARVED

AW Conqueror Sans
AW Conqueror Didot
AW CONQUEROR SLAB
AW CONQUEROR INLINE
**AW CONQUEROR CARVED**

Aa Bb Cc Dd Ee Ff Gg Hh Ii
Jj Kk Ll Mm Nn Oo Pp Qq
Rr Ss Tt Uu Vv Ww Xx Yy Zz
0123456789

---

Typeface  Anisette  Year  1996
Designer  Jean François Porchez  Format  OpenType

# PASTIS MARSEILLE

ANISETTE THIN
ANISETTE LIGHT
ANISETTE REGULAR
ANISETTE DEMI
**ANISETTE BOLD**
**ANISETTE BLACK**

AA BB CC DD EE FF GG HH
II JJ KK LL MM NN OO PP
QQ RR SS TT UU VV WW
XX YY ZZ 0123456789

---

Typeface  Ambroise  Year  2001
Designer  Jean François Porchez  Format  OpenType

# République Juillet Auguste

Ambroise Light, Firmin, François
Ambroise Regular, Firmin, François
Ambroise Demi, Firmin, François
**Ambroise Bold, Firmin, François**
**Ambroise Black, Firmin, François**

Aa Bb Cc Dd Ee Ff Gg Hh Ii Jj Kk
Ll Mm Nn Oo Pp Qq Rr Ss Tt Uu Vv
Ww Xx Yy Zz 0123456789

| | |
|---|---|
| Typeface Allumi PTF | Year 2009 |
| Designer Jean François Porchez | Format OpenType |

# Aa

Aa Bb Cc Dd Ee Ff Gg Hh Ii Jj
Kk Ll Mm Nn Oo Pp Qq Rr Ss
Tt Uu Vv Ww Xx Yy Zz
0123456789
—

Allumi PTF ExtraLight & *Italic* 20pt
Allumi PTF Light & *Italic* 20pt
Allumi PTF Regular & *Italic* 20pt
Allumi PTF Book & *Italic* 20pt
**Allumi PTF Bold & *Italic* 20pt**
**Allumi PTF ExtraBold & *Italic* 20pt**
**Allumi PTF Heavy & *Italic* 20pt**
**Allumi PTF Black & *Italic* 20pt**
Allumi PTF Ext ExtraLight 20pt
Allumi PTF Ext Regular 20pt
**Allumi PTF Ext Black 20pt**

---

**12/14 Allumi PTF Extended Light**

The quick brown fox jumps over the lazy dog. Voyez le brick géant que j'examine près du wharf. Zwölf Box-

**12/14 Allumi PTF Regular**

The quick brown fox jumps over the lazy dog. Voyez le brick géant que j'examine près du wharf. Zwölf Boxkämpfer jagen Vik-

**12/14 Allumi PTF ExtraLight**

The quick brown fox jumps over the lazy dog. Voyez le brick géant que j'examine près du wharf. Zwölf Boxkämpfer jagen Viktor quer über den

**12/14 Allumi PTF Black**

**The quick brown fox jumps over the lazy dog. Voyez le brick géant que j'examine près du wharf. Zwölf Boxkämpfer jagen Viktor quer über den großen Sylter Deich. El veloz murciélago hindú comía feliz cardillo y kiwi. La cigüeña tocaba el saxofón detrás del**

**9/12 Allumi PTF Italic**

*The quick brown fox jumps over the lazy dog. Voyez le brick géant que j'examine près du wharf. Zwölf Boxkämpfer jagen Viktor quer über den großen Sylter Deich. El veloz murciélago hindú comía feliz cardillo y kiwi.*

**9/12 Allumi PTF Demi**

The quick brown fox jumps over the lazy dog. Voyez le brick géant que j'examine près du wharf. Zwölf Boxkämpfer jagen Viktor quer über den großen Sylter Deich. El veloz murciélago hindú comía feliz cardillo y kiwi.

**9/12 Allumi PTF Extended Bold**

**The quick brown fox jumps over the lazy dog. Voyez le brick géant que j'examine près du wharf. Zwölf Boxkämpfer jagen Viktor quer über den großen Sylter Deich. El**

**9/12 Allumi PTF Book**

The quick brown fox jumps over the lazy dog. Voyez le brick géant que j'examine près du wharf. Zwölf Boxkämpfer jagen Viktor quer über den großen Sylter Deich. El veloz murciélago hindú comía feliz cardillo y kiwi. La cigüeña tocaba el saxofón detrás del palenque de pajaatur? Rissimo lorereped ex es solore lab id molorro in rempore icabore rehenetur aliam aut voles audae dem quam, secum eum facesequae consequ aepudam

**7/10 Allumi PTF Heavy**

**The quick brown fox jumps over the lazy dog. Voyez le brick géant que j'examine près du wharf. Zwölf Boxkämpfer jagen Viktor quer über den großen Sylter Deich. El veloz murciélago hindú comía feliz cardillo y kiwi. La cigüeña tocaba el saxofón detrás del palenque de pajaatur? Rissimo lorereped ex es solore lab**

**7/10 Allumi PTF Bold Italic**

***The quick brown fox jumps over the lazy dog. Voyez le brick géant que j'examine près du wharf. Zwölf Boxkämpfer jagen Viktor quer über den großen Sylter Deich. El veloz murciélago hindú comía feliz cardillo y kiwi. La cigüeña tocaba el saxofón detrás del palenque de pajaatur? Rissimo lorereped ex es solore lab id molor-***

**7/10 Allumi PTF Extra Light**

The quick brown fox jumps over the lazy dog. Voyez le brick géant que j'examine près du wharf. Zwölf Boxkämpfer jagen Viktor quer über den großen Sylter Deich. El veloz murciélago hindú comía feliz cardillo y kiwi. La cigüeña tocaba el saxofón detrás del palenque de pajaatur? Rissimo lorereped ex es solore lab id molorro in rempore icabore rehenetur aliam aut

**7/10 Allumi PTF Extended Regular**

The quick brown fox jumps over the lazy dog. Voyez le brick géant que j'examine près du wharf. Zwölf Boxkämpfer jagen Viktor quer über den großen Sylter Deich. El veloz murciélago hindú comía feliz cardillo y kiwi. La cigüeña tocaba el saxofón detrás del palenque de pajaatur? Rissimo lorereped ex es solore lab id molorro in rempore icabore rehenetur aliam aut voles audae dem quam, secum eum facesequae consequ aepudam quia voluptiur repel in et faccustibus, nonsenis aut quisqui rero mi, ipiet lam ant ut maio et hil molupta

| | | | |
|---|---|---|---|
| Page | | Foundry | Porchez Typofonderie |
| 218 | | | |

| | | | |
|---|---|---|---|
| Typeface | Costa PTF | Year | 1999–2004 |
| Designer | Jean François Porchez | Format | OpenType |

# Aa

Costa PTF Light 24pt
Costa PTF Regular 24pt
*Costa PTF Italic 24pt*
**Costa PTF Demi 24pt**
**Costa PTF Bold 24pt**
**Costa PTF ExtraBold 24pt**

Aa Bb Cc Dd Ee Ff Gg Hh Ii Jj Kk
Ll Mm Nn Oo Pp Qq Rr Ss Tt Uu
Vv Ww Xx Yy Zz
0123456789

---

**12/14 — Costa PTF Regular**

The quick brown fox jumps over the lazy dog. Voyez le brick géant que j'examine près du wharf. Zwölf Boxkämpfer jagen Viktor quer über

**9/12 — Costa PTF Bold**

The quick brown fox jumps over the lazy dog. Voyez le brick géant que j'examine près du wharf. Zwölf Boxkämpfer jagen Viktor quer über den großen Sylter Deich. El veloz murciélago hindú comía feliz cardillo y

**7/10 — Costa PTF Italic**

*The quick brown fox jumps over the lazy dog. Voyez le brick géant que j'examine près du wharf. Zwölf Boxkämpfer jagen Viktor quer über den großen Sylter Deich. El veloz murciélago hindú comía feliz cardillo y kiwi. La cigüeña tocaba el saxofón detrás del palenque de pajaatur? Rissimo lorereped ex es solore lab id molorro in rempore icabore rehenetur aliam aut*

---

| | | | |
|---|---|---|---|
| Typeface | Angie Sans PTF | Year | 1994–2011 |
| Designer | Jean François Porchez | Format | OpenType |

# Aa

Angie Sans PTF Regular *& Italic* 20pt
**Angie Sans PTF Demi** *& Italic* 20pt
**Angie Sans PTF Bold** *& Italic* 20pt

Aa Bb Cc Dd Ee Ff Gg Hh Ii Jj Kk
Ll Mm Nn Oo Pp Qq Rr Ss Tt Uu
Vv Ww Xx Yy Zz
0123456789

---

**9/12 — Angie PTF Regular**

The quick brown fox jumps over the lazy dog. Voyez le brick géant que j'examine près du wharf. Zwölf Boxkämpfer jagen Viktor quer über den großen Sylter Deich. El veloz murciélago hindú comía feliz cardillo y kiwi. La cigüeña tocaba el

**9/12 — Angie PTF Italic**

*The quick brown fox jumps over the lazy dog. Voyez le brick géant que j'examine près du wharf. Zwölf Boxkämpfer jagen Viktor quer über den großen Sylter Deich. El veloz murciélago hindú comía feliz cardillo y kiwi. La cigüeña tocaba el saxofón detrás del palenque de pajaatur? Rissimo lorereped ex es solore lab id molorro in rempore icabore rehenetur*

**7/10 — Angie PTF Bold Italic**

***The quick brown fox jumps over the lazy dog. Voyez le brick géant que j'examine près du wharf. Zwölf Boxkämpfer jagen Viktor quer über den großen Sylter Deich. El veloz murciélago hindú comía feliz cardillo y kiwi. La cigüeña tocaba el saxofón detrás del palenque de pajaatur? Rissimo lorereped ex es solore lab id molorro in rempore icabore rehenetur aliam aut voles***

**7/10 — Angie PTF Demi**

**The quick brown fox jumps over the lazy dog. Voyez le brick géant que j'examine près du wharf. Zwölf Boxkämpfer jagen Viktor quer über den großen Sylter Deich. El veloz murciélago hindú comía feliz cardillo y kiwi. La cigüeña tocaba el saxofón detrás del palenque de pajaatur? Rissimo lorereped ex es solore lab id molorro in rempore icabore rehenetur aliam aut voles audae dem quam, secum eum facesequae consequ aepudam quia voluptiur repel in et faccustibus, nonsenis aut**

Typeface   Apolline PTF
Designer   Jean François Porchez
Year       1993–2011
Format     OpenType

# Aa

Aa Bb Cc Dd Ee Ff Gg Hh Ii Jj Kk
Ll Mm Nn Oo Pp Qq Rr Ss Tt Uu
Vv Ww Xx Yy Zz
0123456789
—

Apolline PTF Regular & *Italic* 24pt
Apolline PTF Book & *Italic* 24pt
Apolline PTF Demi & *Italic* 24pt
**Apolline PTF Bold & *Italic* 24pt**
**Apolline PTF XBold & *Italic* 24pt**

---

**12/14   Apolline PTF Regular**

The quick brown fox jumps over the lazy dog. Voyez le brick géant que j'examine près du wharf. Zwölf Boxkämpfer jagen Viktor quer über den

**12/14   Apolline PTF Italic**

*The quick brown fox jumps over the lazy dog. Voyez le brick géant que j'examine près du wharf. Zwölf Boxkämpfer jagen Viktor quer über den großen Sylter*

**12/14   Apolline PTF Book**

The quick brown fox jumps over the lazy dog. Voyez le brick géant que j'examine près du wharf. Zwölf Boxkämpfer jagen Viktor quer über den

**12/14   Apolline PTF ExtraBold**

**The quick brown fox jumps over the lazy dog. Voyez le brick géant que j'examine près du wharf. Zwölf Boxkämpfer jagen Viktor quer über den großen Sylter Deich. El veloz murciélago hindú comía feliz cardillo y kiwi. La cigüeña tocaba el saxofón detrás del palenque de pajaatur? Rissimo lorer-**

**9/12   Apolline PTF Bold**

**The quick brown fox jumps over the lazy dog. Voyez le brick géant que j'examine près du wharf. Zwölf Boxkämpfer jagen Viktor quer über den großen Sylter Deich. El veloz murciélago hindú comía feliz cardillo y kiwi. La**

**9/12   Apolline PTF Demi**

The quick brown fox jumps over the lazy dog. Voyez le brick géant que j'examine près du wharf. Zwölf Boxkämpfer jagen Viktor quer über den großen Sylter Deich. El veloz murciélago hindú comía feliz cardillo y kiwi. La cigüeña tocaba

**9/12   Apolline PTF Italic**

*The quick brown fox jumps over the lazy dog. Voyez le brick géant que j'examine près du wharf. Zwölf Boxkämpfer jagen Viktor quer über den großen Sylter Deich. El veloz murciélago hindú comía feliz cardillo y kiwi. La cigüeña tocaba el saxofón detrás del palenque de*

**9/12   Apolline PTF Regular**

The quick brown fox jumps over the lazy dog. Voyez le brick géant que j'examine près du wharf. Zwölf Boxkämpfer jagen Viktor quer über den großen Sylter Deich. El veloz murciélago hindú comía feliz cardillo y kiwi. La cigüeña tocaba el saxofón detrás del palenque de pajaatur? Rissimo lorereped ex es solore lab id molorro in rempore icabore rehenetur aliam aut voles audae dem quam, secum eum facesequae consequ aepudam, quia voluptiur repel in et faccustibus,

**7/10   Apolline PTF Book**

The quick brown fox jumps over the lazy dog. Voyez le brick géant que j'examine près du wharf. Zwölf Boxkämpfer jagen Viktor quer über den großen Sylter Deich. El veloz murciélago hindú comía feliz cardillo y kiwi. La cigüeña tocaba el saxofón detrás del palenque de pajaatur? Rissimo lorereped ex es solore lab id molorro in rempore icabore rehenetur aliam aut voles

**7/10   Apolline PTF Book Italic**

*The quick brown fox jumps over the lazy dog. Voyez le brick géant que j'examine près du wharf. Zwölf Boxkämpfer jagen Viktor quer über den großen Sylter Deich. El veloz murciélago hindú comía feliz cardillo y kiwi. La cigüeña tocaba el saxofón detrás del palenque de pajaatur? Rissimo lorereped ex es solore lab id molorro in rempore icabore rehenetur aliam aut voles audae dem quam, secum eum facesequae consequ ae-*

**7/10   Apolline PTF Extra Bold**

**The quick brown fox jumps over the lazy dog. Voyez le brick géant que j'examine près du wharf. Zwölf Boxkämpfer jagen Viktor quer über den großen Sylter Deich. El veloz murciélago hindú comía feliz cardillo y kiwi. La cigüeña tocaba el saxofón detrás del palenque de pajaatur? Rissimo lorereped ex es solore lab id molorro in rempore icabore rehenetur**

**7/10   Apolline PTF Demi Regular**

The quick brown fox jumps over the lazy dog. Voyez le brick géant que j'examine près du wharf. Zwölf Boxkämpfer jagen Viktor quer über den großen Sylter Deich. El veloz murciélago hindú comía feliz cardillo y kiwi. La cigüeña tocaba el saxofón detrás del palenque de pajaatur? Rissimo lorereped ex es solore lab id molorro in rempore icabore rehenetur aliam aut voles audae dem quam, secum eum facesequae consequ aepudam quia voluptiur repel in et faccustibus, nonsenis aut quisqui rero mi, ipiet lam ant ut maio et hil molupta tustis atatur, consedi tasimol orerem aut volor andipsapis sit, illaut volore officatus alicae dusdaec tatecte cearum qui accatibus restiore nulpa secaerferum, nus dolenim in et quoditat que explam

Typeface Parisine PTF  Year 1996–2006
Designer Jean François Porchez  Format OpenType

# Aa

Aa Bb Cc Dd Ee Ff Gg Hh Ii Jj Kk
Ll Mm Nn Oo Pp Qq Rr Ss Tt Uu
Vv Ww Xx Yy Zz
0123456789
—

Parisine PTF Clair Regular & *Italic* 20pt
Parisine PTF Clair **Bold** & ***Italic*** 20pt
Parisine PTF Gris Regular & *Italic* 20pt
Parisine PTF Regular & *Italic* 20pt
Parisine PTF Gris **Bold** & ***Italic*** 20pt
Parisine PTF **Bold** & ***Italic*** 20pt
Parisine PTF Sombre Reg. & *Italic* 20pt
Parisine PTF **Bold** & ***Italic*** 20pt

---

**12/14 — Parisine PTF Regular**

The quick brown fox jumps over the lazy dog. Voyez le brick géant que j'examine près du wharf. Zwölf Boxkämpfer jagen Viktor quer über den

**12/14 — Parisine PTF Clair Italic**

*The quick brown fox jumps over the lazy dog. Voyez le brick géant que j'examine près du wharf. Zwölf Boxkämpfer jagen Viktor quer über den*

**12/14 — Parisine PTF Sombre Bold Italic**

***The quick brown fox jumps over the lazy dog. Voyez le brick géant que j'examine près du wharf. Zwölf Boxkämpfer***

**12/14 — Parisine PTF Bold**

**The quick brown fox jumps over the lazy dog. Voyez le brick géant que j'examine près du wharf. Zwölf Boxkämpfer jagen Viktor quer über den großen Sylter Deich. El veloz murciélago hindú comía feliz cardillo y kiwi. La cigüeña tocaba el saxofón detrás del palenque de pajaatur? Rissi-**

**9/12 — Parisine PTF Italic**

*The quick brown fox jumps over the lazy dog. Voyez le brick géant que j'examine près du wharf. Zwölf Boxkämpfer jagen Viktor quer über den großen Sylter Deich. El veloz murciélago hindú comía feliz cardillo y kiwi. La cigüeña*

**9/12 — Parisine PTF Sombre Regular**

The quick brown fox jumps over the lazy dog. Voyez le brick géant que j'examine près du wharf. Zwölf Boxkämpfer jagen Viktor quer über den großen Sylter Deich. El veloz murciélago hindú comía feliz car-

**9/12 — Parisine PTF Clair Bold**

The quick brown fox jumps over the lazy dog. Voyez le brick géant que j'examine près du wharf. Zwölf Boxkämpfer jagen Viktor quer über den großen Sylter Deich. El veloz murciélago hindú comía feliz cardillo y kiwi. La cigüeña tocaba el

**9/12 — Parisine PTF Bold Italic**

*The quick brown fox jumps over the lazy dog. Voyez le brick géant que j'examine près du wharf. Zwölf Boxkämpfer jagen Viktor quer über den großen Sylter Deich. El veloz murciélago hindú comía feliz cardillo y kiwi. La cigüeña tocaba el saxofón detrás del palenque de pajaatur? Rissimo lorereped ex es solore lab id molorro in rempore icabore rehenetur aliam aut voles audae dem quam, secum eum facesequae consequ aepudam quia voluptiur repel in et faccustibus, nonsenis aut quisqui*

**7/10 — Parisine PTF Sombre Bold**

The quick brown fox jumps over the lazy dog. Voyez le brick géant que j'examine près du wharf. Zwölf Boxkämpfer jagen Viktor quer über den großen Sylter Deich. El veloz murciélago hindú comía feliz cardillo y kiwi. La cigüeña tocaba el saxofón detrás del palenque de pajaatur? Rissimo lorereped

**7/10 — Parisine PTF Clair Italic**

*The quick brown fox jumps over the lazy dog. Voyez le brick géant que j'examine près du wharf. Zwölf Boxkämpfer jagen Viktor quer über den großen Sylter Deich. El veloz murciélago hindú comía feliz cardillo y kiwi. La cigüeña tocaba el saxofón detrás del palenque de pajaatur? Rissimo lorereped ex es solore lab id molorro in rempore icabore rehenetur aliam aut voles audae dem*

**7/10 — Parisine PTF Gris Regular**

The quick brown fox jumps over the lazy dog. Voyez le brick géant que j'examine près du wharf. Zwölf Boxkämpfer jagen Viktor quer über den großen Sylter Deich. El veloz murciélago hindú comía feliz cardillo y kiwi. La cigüeña tocaba el saxofón detrás del palenque de pajaatur? Rissimo lorereped ex es solore lab id molorro in rempore icabore rehenetur aliam aut voles

**7/10 — Parisine PTF Clair**

The quick brown fox jumps over the lazy dog. Voyez le brick géant que j'examine près du wharf. Zwölf Boxkämpfer jagen Viktor quer über den großen Sylter Deich. El veloz murciélago hindú comía feliz cardillo y kiwi. La cigüeña tocaba el saxofón detrás del palenque de pajaatur? Rissimo lorereped ex es solore lab id molorro in rempore icabore rehenetur aliam aut voles audae dem quam, secum eum facesequae consequ aepudam quia voluptiur repel in et faccustibus, nonsenis aut quisqui rero mi, ipiet lam ant ut maio et hil molupta tustis atatur, consedi tasimol orerem aut volor andipsapis sit, illaut volore officatus alicae dusdaec tatecte cearum qui accatibus restiore nulpa secaerferum, nus dolenim in et quoditat que explam voluptictur? Qui de illuptae. Dae nis illiberum volorro ritatis tinullo rerumqu atetur repro

Typeface  Parisine Plus PTF
Designer  Jean François Porchez
Year  1999–2006
Format  OpenType

# Aa

Aa Bb Cc Dd Ee Ff Gg Hh Ii Jj Kk
Ll Mm Nn Oo Pp Qq Rr Ss Tt Uu
Vv Ww Xx Yy Zz
0123456789
—

Parisine PTF Clair Regular 20pt
*Parisine PTF Clair Italic 20pt*
**Parisine PTF Clair Regular Bold 20pt**
***Parisine PTF Clair Bold Bold Italic 20pt***
Parisine PTF Regular 20pt
*Parisine PTF Italic 20pt*
**Parisine PTF Bold 20pt**
***Parisine PTF Bold Italic 20pt***
**Parisine PTF Sombre Regular 20pt**
***Parisine PTF Sombre Italic 20pt***
**Parisine PTF Bold 20pt**
***Parisine PTF Bold Italic 20pt***

---

12/14  Parisine Plus PTF Regular

The quick brown fox jumps over the lazy dog. Voyez le brick géant que j'examine près du wharf. Zwölf Boxkämpfer jagen Viktor quer

12/14  Parisine Plus PTF Bold

**The quick brown fox jumps over the lazy dog. Voyez le brick géant que j'examine près du wharf. Zwölf Boxkämpfer jagen Viktor**

12/14  Parisine Plus PTF Sombre Bold

**The quick brown fox jumps over the lazy dog. Voyez le brick géant que j'examine près du wharf. Zwölf Box-**

12/14  Parisine Plus PTF Clair Italic

*The quick brown fox jumps over the lazy dog. Voyez le brick géant que j'examine près du wharf. Zwölf Boxkämpfer jagen Viktor quer über den großen Sylter Deich. El veloz murciélago hindú comía feliz cardillo y kiwi. La cigüeña tocaba el saxofón detrás del palenque de pajaatur? Rissimo lorereped ex es solore lab id molorro in*

9/12  Parisine Plus PTF Clair Italic

*The quick brown fox jumps over the lazy dog. Voyez le brick géant que j'examine près du wharf. Zwölf Boxkämpfer jagen Viktor quer über den großen Sylter Deich. El veloz murciélago hindú comía feliz cardillo y kiwi. La cigüeña tocaba el saxofón detrás*

9/12  Parisine Plus PTF Italic

*The quick brown fox jumps over the lazy dog. Voyez le brick géant que j'examine près du wharf. Zwölf Boxkämpfer jagen Viktor quer über den großen Sylter Deich. El veloz murciélago hindú comía feliz cardillo y kiwi. La cigüe-*

9/12  Parisine Plus PTF Bold

**The quick brown fox jumps over the lazy dog. Voyez le brick géant que j'examine près du wharf. Zwölf Boxkämpfer jagen Viktor quer über den großen Sylter Deich. El veloz murciélago hindú comía feliz cardillo y kiwi.**

9/12  Parisine Plus PTF Sombre Italic

***The quick brown fox jumps over the lazy dog. Voyez le brick géant que j'examine près du wharf. Zwölf Boxkämpfer Viktor quer über den großen Sylter Deich. El veloz murciélago hindú comía feliz cardillo y kiwi. La cigüeña tocaba el saxofón detrás del palenque de pajaatur? Rissimo lorereped ex es solore lab id molorro in rempore icabore rehenetur aliam aut voles audae dem quam, secum eum facesequae***

7/10  Parisine Plus PTF Sombre Bold Italic

***The quick brown fox jumps over the lazy dog. Voyez le brick géant que j'examine près du wharf. Zwölf Boxkämpfer jagen Viktor quer über den großen Sylter Deich. El veloz murciélago hindú comía feliz cardillo y kiwi. La cigüeña tocaba el saxofón detrás del palenque de pajaatur? Rissimo lorereped ex es***

7/10  Parisine Plus PTF Sombre Regualr

**The quick brown fox jumps over the lazy dog. Voyez le brick géant que j'examine près du wharf. Zwölf Boxkämpfer jagen Viktor quer über den großen Sylter Deich. El veloz murciélago hindú comía feliz cardillo y kiwi. La cigüeña tocaba el saxofón detrás del palenque de pajaatur? Rissimo lorereped ex es solore lab id**

7/10  Parisine Plus PTF Clair Bold

The quick brown fox jumps over the lazy dog. Voyez le brick géant que j'examine près du wharf. Zwölf Boxkämpfer jagen Viktor quer über den großen Sylter Deich. El veloz murciélago hindú comía feliz cardillo y kiwi. La cigüeña tocaba el saxofón detrás del palenque de pajaatur? Rissimo lorereped ex es solore lab id molorro in rempore icabore rehenetur aliam aut voles

7/10  Parisine Plus PTF Clair

The quick brown fox jumps over the lazy dog. Voyez le brick géant que j'examine près du wharf. Zwölf Boxkämpfer jagen Viktor quer über den großen Sylter Deich. El veloz murciélago hindú comía feliz cardillo y kiwi. La cigüeña tocaba el saxofón detrás del palenque de pajaatur? Rissimo lorereped ex es solore lab id molorro in rempore icabore rehenetur aliam aut voles audae dem quam, secum eum facesequae consequ aepudam quia voluptiur repel in et faccustibus, nonsenis aut quisqui rero mi, ipiet lam ant ut maio et hil molupta tustis atatur, consedi tasimol orerem aut volor andipsapis sit, illaut volore officatus alicae dusdaec tatecte cearum qui accatibus restiore nulpa secaerferum, nus dolenim in et quoditat que explam volupictur? Qui de illuptae.

# R

## ReType

Ramiro Espinoza

The Hague, Netherlands

Since 2007

ReType is an independent type foundry run by Ramiro Espinoza. The company has a keen interest in Dutch vernacular alphabets and lettering, and correspondingly, the first typefaces released related to these styles. Since then, more complex and ambitious projects have been completed, and the library has grown with the addition of classic type families oriented to editorial and corporate markets. ReType's philosophy pays tribute to type design traditions, with a hint of humor.

## Info

—People on staff
1

—Type designers on staff
1

—Type families
8

—Designers represented
5

—Web shop
re-type.com

—Distributors
Fontshop, MyFonts

—Webfont services
To be announced

—Basic license
$45 (basic weight)

## Typeface selection

**Barbieri**
Bath Serif
Bath Sans
**Kade**
*Krull*
**KURVERSBRUG**
Lavigne
***Tomate***
Winco

24pt

## People

—Ramiro Espinoza became interested in type design while studying at the Universidad Nacional del Litoral in Santa Fe, Argentina. After graduation he taught Typography at the Universidad de Buenos Aires under the direction of Silvia Gonzalez. In 2003 he moved to the Netherlands and studied at the KABK in The Hague. Since then he has been a contributor to *TipoGráfica* and *Tipo* design magazines, researched vernacular Dutch lettering and worked on numerous freelance assignments for FontShop International. In 2007 he founded the ReType type foundry to market his typefaces.

—David Quay studied graphic communication at Ravensbourne College of Art & Design from 1963-67. For the next seven years he worked in various leading London design companies as a packaging and graphic designer. In 1975 he became a freelance designer specializing in lettering and logotypes. In 1987 he formed his own company David Quay Design to concentrate on graphic and typographic design. He also began to design his first text typefaces which were subsequently released by The International Typeface Corporation in New York and Berthold in Germany. Since 1989 he has worked closely with Freda Sack on a broad range of type projects. In 1990 they co-founded The Foundry to design, manufacture and market their own exclusive typefaces.

David Quay lectures extensively in typography and type design both in the UK and internationally. He now works from his studio in Amsterdam as an independent type and graphic designer.

—Yomar Augusto is one of the brightest stars on the new Latin American graphic design scene. He has a Bachelor's degree from the University of Rio de Janeiro and an MA in Type Design from the KABK in The Hague. He has been involved in two Rojo ArtStorm projects and been published by Taschen in Contemporary Graphic Design, which showcases 100 of the world's most progressive designers. He took part in the Letter Forest art show held at Nanzuka Underground Gallery in Tokyo, Japan, which featured experiments in calligraphy, painting, drawing and printmaking. He runs his studio in Rotterdam and teaches design at the WDKA Academy in the same city.

The Bath type family in use in the recently published official maps for the city of Bath. Design: FWDesign.

Page
223

Cover for *Typographic*, the magazine of the International Society of Typographic Designers ISTD. Design by David Quay featuring Kurversbrug.

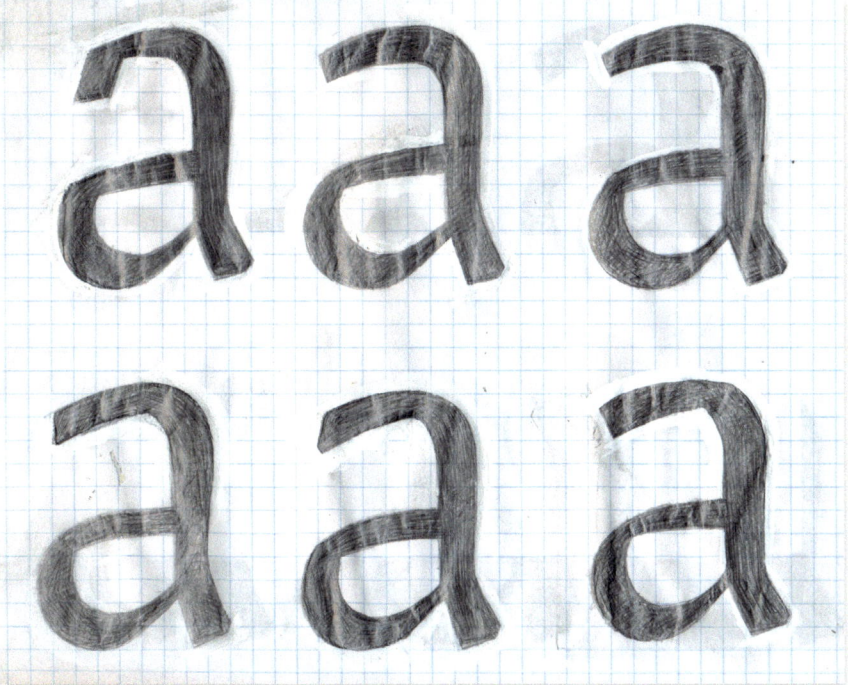

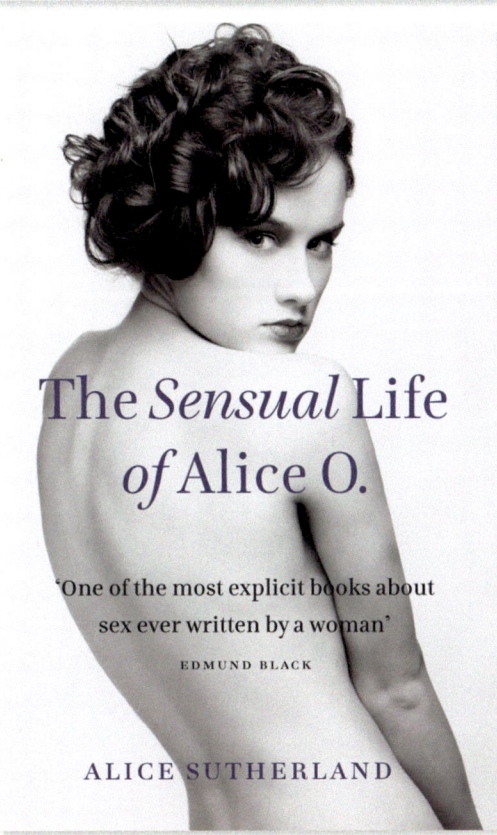

ISTD TypoGraphic 67
'I wonder' issue

Lavigne is a contemporary approach to the classic serif concept and is rather popular for "feminine" subjects.
Photo: Serg Zastavkin/Shutterstock.

**Top**
Sketches for a new roman typeface.
**Center and bottom**
Different stages in the sketching of the Winco family.

Page 224　　　Foundry　ReType

Typeface　Tomate　　　Year　2008
Designer　Ramiro Espinoza　　Format　OpenType

# Milk

Light
Regular
Bold
Black

Aa Bb Cc Dd Ee Ff Gg
Hh Ii Jj Kk Ll Mm Nn
Oo Pp Qq Rr Ss Tt
Uu Vv Ww Xx Yy Zz
0123456789

Typeface　Kurversbrug　　Year　2007
Designer　Ramiro Espinoza　　Format　OpenType

# AMSTERDAM BRUGLETTER

LIGHT
REGULAR
BLACK

ABCDEFGHIJKLMNOPQRS
TUVWXYZ 0123456789

Typeface　Barbieri　　Year　2009
Designer　Ramiro Espinoza　　Format　OpenType

# Psychobilly rampage

Light
Book
Regular
Bold
Heavy
Black

Aa Bb Cc Dd Ee Ff Gg Hh Ii Jj Kk
Ll Mm Nn Oo Pp Qq Rr Ss Tt Uu
Vv Ww Xx Yy Zz 0123456789

Foundry ReType

Typeface Lavigne Text
Designer Ramiro Espinoza
Year 2009
Format OpenType

# Aa

Lavigne Text Regular 22pt
*Lavigne Text Italic* 22pt
**Lavigne Text Bold** 22pt
***Lavigne Text Bold Italic*** 22pt

Aa Bb Cc Dd Ee Ff Gg Hh Ii Jj Kk Ll Mm Nn Oo Pp Qq Rr Ss Tt Uu Vv Ww Xx Yy Zz
0123456789

---

9/10 Lavigne Text Regular

¶ THE QUICK BROWN fox jumps over the lazy dog. Voyez le brick géant que j'examine près du wharf. Zwölf Boxkämpfer jagen Viktor quer über den großen Sylter Deich. El veloz murciélago hindú comía feliz cardillo y kiwi. La cigüeña tocaba el saxofón detrás del palenque

9/10 Lavigne Text Bold

¶ **THE QUICK BROWN fox jumps over the lazy dog. Voyez le brick géant que j'examine près du wharf. Zwölf Boxkämpfer jagen Viktor quer über den großen Sylter Deich. El veloz murciélago hindú comía feliz cardillo y kiwi. La cigüeña tocaba el saxofón detrás del**

9/10 Lavigne Text Italic

¶ *THE QUICK BROWN fox jumps over the lazy dog. Voyez le brick géant que j'examine près du wharf. Zwölf Boxkämpfer jagen Viktor quer über den großen Sylter Deich. El veloz murciélago hindú comía feliz cardillo y kiwi. La cigüeña tocaba el saxofón detrás*

9/10 Lavigne Text Bold Italic

¶ ***THE QUICK BROWN fox jumps over the lazy dog. Voyez le brick géant que j'examine près du wharf. Zwölf Boxkämpfer jagen Viktor quer über den großen Sylter Deich. El veloz murciélago hindú comía feliz cardillo y kiwi. La cigüeña tocaba el saxofón detrás***

---

Typeface Lavigne Display
Designer Ramiro Espinoza
Year 2009
Format OpenType

# Aa

Lavigne Display Light 20pt
*Lavigne Display Light Italic* 20pt
Lavigne Display Regular 20pt
*Lavigne Display Italic* 20pt
**Lavigne Display Bold** 20pt
***Lavigne Display Bold Italic*** 20pt

Aa Bb Cc Dd Ee Ff Gg Hh Ii Jj Kk Ll Mm Nn Oo Pp Qq Rr Ss Tt Uu Vv Ww Xx Yy Zz
0123456789

---

36/38 Lavigne Display Regular

The quick brown fox jumps over the lazy dog.

36/38 Lavigne Display Italic

*The quick brown fox jumps over the lazy dog.*

| | | | |
|---|---|---|---|
| Page | | Foundry | ReType |
| 226 | | | |

| | | | |
|---|---|---|---|
| Typeface | Bath Sans, Serif | Year | 2010 |
| Designer | David Quay, Ramiro Espinoza | Format | OpenType |

# Aa

Bath Sans Regular 22pt
**Bath Sans Bold 22pt**
Bath Serif Regular 22pt
**Bath Serif Bold 22pt**

Aa Bb Cc Dd Ee Ff Gg Hh Ii Jj Kk
Ll Mm Nn Oo Pp Qq Rr Ss Tt Uu
Vv Ww Xx Yy Zz
0123456789
—

12/13 Bath Sans Regular

The quick brown fox jumps over the lazy dog. Voyez le brick géant que j'examine près du wharf. Zwölf Boxkämpfer jagen Viktor quer über den großen Sylter Deich. El veloz murciélago hindú comía feliz cardillo y kiwi.

12/13 Bath Sans Bold

**The quick brown fox jumps over the lazy dog. Voyez le brick géant que j'examine près du wharf. Zwölf Boxkämpfer jagen Viktor quer über den großen Sylter Deich. El veloz murciélago hindú comía feliz**

12/13 Bath Serif Regular

The quick brown fox jumps over the lazy dog. Voyez le brick géant que j'examine près du wharf. Zwölf Boxkämpfer jagen Viktor quer über den großen Sylter Deich. El veloz murciélago hindú comía feliz

12/13 Bath Serif Bold

**The quick brown fox jumps over the lazy dog. Voyez le brick géant que j'examine près du wharf. Zwölf Boxkämpfer jagen Viktor quer über den großen Sylter Deich. El veloz murciélago hindú**

| | | | |
|---|---|---|---|
| Typeface | Krull | Year | 2011 |
| Designer | Ramiro Espinoza | Format | OpenType |

Aa Bb Cc Dd Ff Gg Hh Ii Jj Kk Ll Mm Nn Oo
Pp Qq Rr Ss Tt Uu Vv Ww Xx Yy Zz 0123456789

't Sloefke

Page
227

Foundry  ReType

Typeface  Kade
Designer  David Quay

Year     2010
Format   OpenType

# Snow Storm

Regular
*Italic*
**Medium**
***Medium Italic***
**Bold**
***Bold Italic***

Aa Bb Cc Dd Ee Ff Gg Hh
Ii Jj Kk Ll Mm Nn Oo Pp
Qq Rr Ss Tt Uu Vv Ww
Xx Yy Zz 0123456789

---

Typeface  Winco
Designer  Ramiro Espinoza

Year     2011
Format   OpenType

# Aa

Winco Light 20pt
Winco Regular 20pt
**Winco Bold 20pt**
**Winco Black 20pt**
**Winco Ultra Black 20pt**

Aa Bb Cc Dd Ee Ff Gg Hh Ii Jj Kk Ll Mm Nn Oo Pp Qq Rr Ss Tt Uu Vv Ww Xx Yy Zz 0123456789

30/32  Winco Regular

The quick brown fox jumps over the lazy dog.

30/32  Winco Bold

**The quick brown fox jumps over the lazy dog.**

30/32  Winco Ultra Black

**The quick brown fox jumps over the lazy dog.**

# S

## Shinntype

—

Nick Shinn, Karey Shinn

—

Orangeville, Canada

—

Since 1998

Shinntype is the type foundry run by designer Nick Shinn in close collaboration with his partner, artist Karey Shinn. Besides the collection of retail fonts, Shinntype undertakes custom work, most notably a typeface to commemorate the author Mordecai Richler, and custom types for newspapers such as the *Birmingham News* (Alabama), *Daily Mail* (London), *Chicago Tribune* and *Globe and Mail* (Toronto).

## Info

—Why?
By the mid 1990s, several of my type designs had been published by companies such as FontFont and Agfa (now Monotype), earning a modest sum in royalties which, along with some teaching and writing assignments, supplemented my main income as graphic designer. But I also had a number of rejections, of faces that I considered to be perfectly acceptable. So I determined in 1999 to start my own foundry and publish whatever I saw fit. This was feasible due to two recent inventions, Dreamweaver, which enabled me to design the Shinntype site and establish a web presence, and Makambo, the original online font distributor, which sold licenses for any font I chose to upload (this was before the launch of MyFonts).

—People on staff
2

—Type designers on staff
1

—Type families
27

—Designers represented
2

—Web shop
shinntype.com

—Distributors
Faces, Fonthaus, Fonts.com, FontShop, Fontspring, Fontworks, Linotype, MyFonts, Paratype, Phil's Fonts, Shinntype, Veer, WebINK, YouWorkForThem.

—Webfont services
WebINK

—Basic license
$9 – $79, five CPUs.

## People

—Nick Shinn was born in London, England, and acquired a Dip.AD in Fine Art from Leeds Polytechnic, Yorkshire in 1974. He lived in Toronto from 1976 to 2009, before moving to Orangeville, 60 km north of that city. During the 1980s he was an art director and creative director at a number of advertising agencies, and a founding partner in the environmental marketing company Earthmark from 1988 to 1990. He went digital in 1989 and started the Shinn Design studio, which specialized in publication and marketing design during the 1990s. Between 1980 and 1998 he designed seven type families for a variety of foundries, most notably Fontesque, Merlin and Oneleigh for FontFont. In 1998 he went into the font business full time, launching Shinntype to publish and market his fonts worldwide. Shinn's background as an artist, writer, art director and graphic designer informs his eclectic type designs, which run the gamut from revivals to experimental work exploring new technology.
As a departure from designing original types, Shinn worked from 2004 to 2008 designing the Modern Suite, a set of 19th century revivals extended into the 21st century with massive OpenType features and language support, including Polytonic Greek and Cyrillic.

Shinn has written for magazines such as Applied Arts, Druk, Eye, Graphic Exchange, Marketing and Typographic, has spoken at the ATypI, TypeCon, Graphika and TypoBerlin conferences, and taught at Seneca College, Humber College and York University in Toronto. From 2002 to 2006 he served as a board member of the Society of Typographic Aficionados (SOTA), which puts on the international conference TypeCon every year, helping bring it to Toronto in 2002.

—Karey Shinn (neé Asselstine) has a BA in Fine Art from Leeds Polytechnic, and an MA in Art from Norwich University. She is an artist, designer and environmental activist. Nick and Karey frequently collaborate with their son Eric and daughter Zoë on Karey's art projects, most recently *In Bitu*, a couture/art/dance work that premiered at FAT (Toronto Alternative Arts & Fashion Week) in 2010, which featured couture designed by Karey, graphics and typography by Nick, music by Eric, and choreography by Zoë.

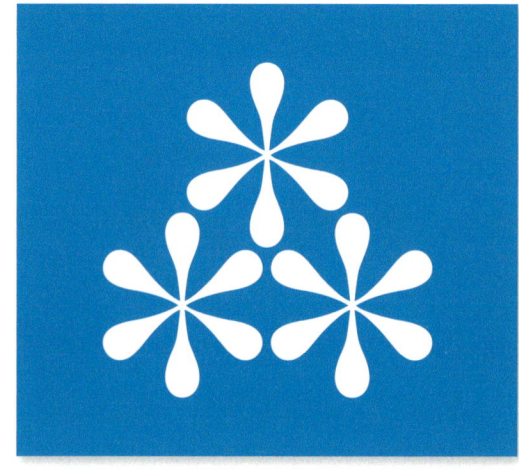

Scotch Modern

## Typeface selection

Bodoni Egyptian Pro

Duffy Script

Figgins Sans

Handsome Pro

Paradigm Pro

Scotch Modern

Sense

Sensibility

Softmachine

24pt

Page
229

Nick Shinn's Panoptica type family is a series of stylisctically diverse fonts based on the same principle — a skeleton that is monospaced as well as unicase. In other words, all fonts have characters which occupy the same width *and* mix upper- and lowercase. The original version of Panoptica was designed for *Diamonds,* a book of concrete poetry by Christian Bök, for which the author needed a monospaced typeface to obtain a regular grid that was vertical as well as horizontal.

Paradigm Pro

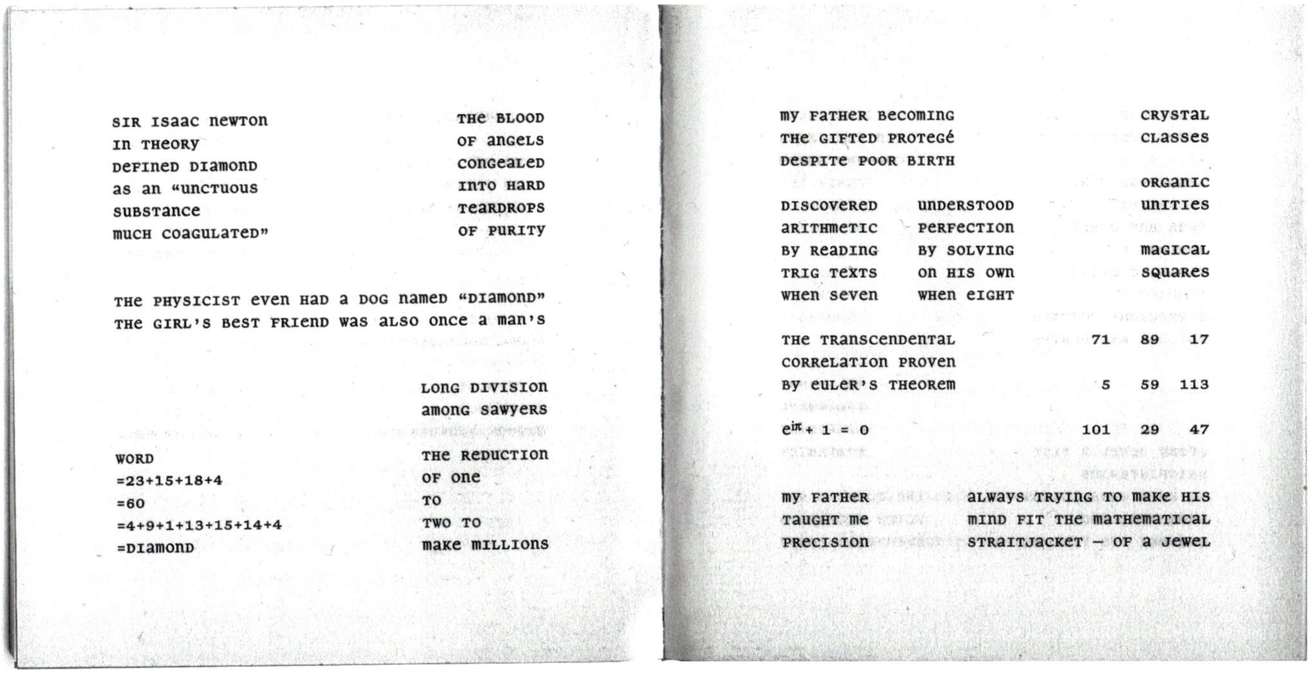

Softmachine

Foundry Shinntype

---

Typeface Figgins Sans  
Designer Nick Shinn  
Year 2008  
Format OpenType

# Aa

Figgins Sans Regular 20pt  
*Figgins Sans Italic 20pt*  
**Figgins Sans Bold 20pt**  
**Figgins Sans Extra Bold 20pt**

Aa Bb Cc Dd Ee Ff Gg Hh Ii Jj Kk Ll Mm Nn Oo Pp Qq Rr Ss Tt Uu Vv Ww Xx Yy Zz  
0123456789

—

9/12 Figgins Sans Regular

The quick brown fox jumps over the lazy dog. Voyez le brick géant que j'examine près du wharf. Zwölf Boxkämpfer jagen Viktor quer über den großen Sylter Deich. El veloz murciélago hindú comía feliz cardillo y kiwi. La cigüeña tocaba el saxofón detrás del palenque de pajaatur? Rissimo lorereped ex es solore lab id molorro in rempore icabore rehenetur aliam aut voles audae dem quam, secum eum

7/10 Figgins Sans Regular

The quick brown fox jumps over the lazy dog. Voyez le brick géant que j'examine près du wharf. Zwölf Boxkämpfer jagen Viktor quer über den großen Sylter Deich. El veloz murciélago hindú comía feliz cardillo y kiwi. La cigüeña tocaba el saxofón detrás del palenque de pajaatur? Rissimo lorereped ex es solore lab id molorro in rempore icabore rehenetur aliam aut voles audae dem quam, secum eum facesequae consequ aepudam quia voluptiur repel in et faccustibus, nonsenis aut quisqui rero mi, ipiet lam ant ut maio et hil molupta tustis atatur, consedi tasimol orerem aut volor andipsapis sit, illaut

---

Typeface Scotch Modern  
Designer Nick Shinn  
Year 2008  
Format OpenType

# Aa

Scotch Modern Regular 20pt  
*Scotch Modern Italic 20pt*  
**Scotch Modern Bold 20pt**  
***Scotch Modern Bold Italic 20pt***

Aa Bb Cc Dd Ee Ff Gg Hh Ii Jj Kk Ll Mm Nn Oo Pp Qq Rr Ss Tt Uu Vv Ww Xx Yy Zz  
0123456789

—

9/12 Scotch Modern Regular

The quick brown fox jumps over the lazy dog. Voyez le brick géant que j'examine près du wharf. Zwölf Boxkämpfer jagen Viktor quer über den großen Sylter Deich. El veloz murciélago hindú comía feliz cardillo y kiwi. La cigüeña tocaba el saxofón detrás del palenque de pajaatur? Rissimo lorereped ex es solore lab id molorro in rempore icabore rehenetur

7/10 Scotch Modern Regular

The quick brown fox jumps over the lazy dog. Voyez le brick géant que j'examine près du wharf. Zwölf Boxkämpfer jagen Viktor quer über den großen Sylter Deich. El veloz murciélago hindú comía feliz cardillo y kiwi. La cigüeña tocaba el saxofón detrás del palenque de pajaatur? Rissimo lorereped ex es solore lab id molorro in rempore icabore rehenetur aliam aut voles audae dem quam, secum eum facesequae consequ aepudam quia voluptiur repel in et faccustibus, nonsenis aut quisqui rero mi, ipiet lam ant ut maio et hil molupta tustis atatur, consedi tasimol orerem

12/14 Scotch Modern Bold

**The quick brown fox jumps over the lazy dog. Voyez le brick géant que j'examine près du wharf. Zwölf Boxkämpfer jagen Viktor quer über den großen Sylter Deich. El veloz murciélago hindú comía feliz cardillo y kiwi. La cigüeña tocaba el saxofón detrás del palenque de pajaatur? Ris-**

9/12 Scotch Modern Bold

**The quick brown fox jumps over the lazy dog. Voyez le brick géant que j'examine près du wharf. Zwölf Boxkämpfer jagen Viktor quer über den großen Sylter Deich. El veloz murciélago hindú comía feliz cardillo y kiwi. La cigüeña tocaba el saxofón detrás del palenque de pajaatur? Rissimo lorereped ex es solore lab id molorro in rempore icabore rehenetur aliam aut voles audae dem quam, secum eum facesequae consequ aepudam**

7/10 Scotch Modern Bold

**The quick brown fox jumps over the lazy dog. Voyez le brick géant que j'examine près du wharf. Zwölf Boxkämpfer jagen Viktor quer über den großen Sylter Deich. El veloz murciélago hindú comía feliz cardillo y kiwi. La cigüeña tocaba el saxofón detrás del palenque de pajaatur? Rissimo lorereped ex es solore lab id molorro in rempore icabore rehenetur aliam aut voles audae dem quam, secum eum facesequae consequ aepudam quia voluptiur repel in et faccustibus, nonsenis aut quisqui rero mi, ipiet lam ant ut maio et hil molupta tustis atatur, consedi tasimol orerem aut volor andipsapis sit, illaut volore officatus alicae dusdaec tatecte cearum qui accatibus restiore**

Typeface  Bodoni Egyptian Pro
Designer  Nick Shinn
Year  1999, 2010
Format  OpenType

# Aa

Aa Bb Cc Dd Ee Ff Gg Hh Ii Jj Kk
Ll Mm Nn Oo Pp Qq Rr Ss Tt Uu
Vv Ww Xx Yy Zz
0123456789
—

Bodoni Egyptian Pro Thin 20pt
Bodoni Egyptian Pro Light 20pt
*Bodoni Egyptian Pro Light Italic* 20pt
Bodoni Egyptian Pro Regular 20pt
*Bodoni Egyptian Pro Italic* 20pt
Bodoni Egyptian Pro Medium 20pt
*Bodoni Egyptian Pro Medium Italic* 20pt
**Bodoni Egyptian Pro Bold** 20pt
***Bodoni Egyptian Pro Bold Italic*** 20pt
**Bodoni Egyptian Pro Black** 20pt

---

12/14  Bodoni Egyptian Pro Light

The quick brown fox jumps over the lazy dog. Voyez le brick géant que j'examine près du wharf. Zwölf Boxkämpfer jagen Viktor quer über den

12/14  Bodoni Egyptian Pro Regular

The quick brown fox jumps over the lazy dog. Voyez le brick géant que j'examine près du wharf. Zwölf Boxkämpfer jagen Viktor quer über den

12/14  Bodoni Egyptian Pro Medium

The quick brown fox jumps over the lazy dog. Voyez le brick géant que j'examine près du wharf. Zwölf Boxkämpfer jagen Viktor quer über den

12/14  Bodoni Egyptian Pro Bold

**The quick brown fox jumps over the lazy dog. Voyez le brick géant que j'examine près du wharf. Zwölf Boxkämpfer jagen Viktor quer über den großen Sylter Deich. El veloz murciélago hindú comía feliz cardillo y kiwi. La cigüeña tocaba el saxofón detrás del palenque de pajaatur? Rissimo lorereped ex es solore lab**

9/12  Bodoni Egyptian Pro Light

The quick brown fox jumps over the lazy dog. Voyez le brick géant que j'examine près du wharf. Zwölf Boxkämpfer jagen Viktor quer über den großen Sylter Deich. El veloz murciélago hindú comía feliz cardillo y kiwi. La cigüeña tocaba el saxofón

9/12  Bodoni Egyptian Pro Regular

The quick brown fox jumps over the lazy dog. Voyez le brick géant que j'examine près du wharf. Zwölf Boxkämpfer jagen Viktor quer über den großen Sylter Deich. El veloz murciélago hindú comía feliz cardillo y kiwi. La cigüeña tocaba el saxofón

9/12  Bodoni Egyptian Pro Medium

The quick brown fox jumps over the lazy dog. Voyez le brick géant que j'examine près du wharf. Zwölf Boxkämpfer jagen Viktor quer über den großen Sylter Deich. El veloz murciélago hindú comía feliz cardillo y kiwi. La cigüeña tocaba el

9/12  Bodoni Egyptian Pro Bold

**The quick brown fox jumps over the lazy dog. Voyez le brick géant que j'examine près du wharf. Zwölf Boxkämpfer jagen Viktor quer über den großen Sylter Deich. El veloz murciélago hindú comía feliz cardillo y kiwi. La cigüeña tocaba el saxofón detrás del palenque de pajaatur? Rissimo lorereped ex es solore lab id molorro in rempore icabore rehenetur aliam aut voles audae dem quam, secum eum facesequae consequ aepudam quia voluptiur repel in et fac-**

7/10  Bodoni Egyptian Pro Light

The quick brown fox jumps over the lazy dog. Voyez le brick géant que j'examine près du wharf. Zwölf Boxkämpfer jagen Viktor quer über den großen Sylter Deich. El veloz murciélago hindú comía feliz cardillo y kiwi. La cigüeña tocaba el saxofón detrás del palenque de pajaatur? Rissimo lorereped ex es solore lab id molorro in rempore icabore rehenetur aliam aut voles audae dem quam,

7/10  Bodoni Egyptian Pro Regular

The quick brown fox jumps over the lazy dog. Voyez le brick géant que j'examine près du wharf. Zwölf Boxkämpfer jagen Viktor quer über den großen Sylter Deich. El veloz murciélago hindú comía feliz cardillo y kiwi. La cigüeña tocaba el saxofón detrás del palenque de pajaatur? Rissimo lorereped ex es solore lab id molorro in rempore icabore rehenetur aliam aut voles audae dem

7/10  Bodoni Egyptian Pro Medium

The quick brown fox jumps over the lazy dog. Voyez le brick géant que j'examine près du wharf. Zwölf Boxkämpfer jagen Viktor quer über den großen Sylter Deich. El veloz murciélago hindú comía feliz cardillo y kiwi. La cigüeña tocaba el saxofón detrás del palenque de pajaatur? Rissimo lorereped ex es solore lab id molorro in rempore icabore rehenetur aliam aut voles

7/10  Bodoni Egyptian Pro Bold

**The quick brown fox jumps over the lazy dog. Voyez le brick géant que j'examine près du wharf. Zwölf Boxkämpfer jagen Viktor quer über den großen Sylter Deich. El veloz murciélago hindú comía feliz cardillo y kiwi. La cigüeña tocaba el saxofón detrás del palenque de pajaatur? Rissimo lorereped ex es solore lab id molorro in rempore icabore rehenetur aliam aut voles audae dem quam, secum eum facesequae consequ aepudam quia voluptiur repel in et faccustibus, nonsenis aut quisqui rero mi, ipiet lam ant ut maio et hil molupta tustis atatur, consedi tasimol orerem aut volor andipsapis sit, illaut volore officatus alicae dusdaec tatecte cearum qui accatibus restiore nulpa secaerferum, nus dolenim in et quoditat que explam volupictur? Qui de illuptae. Dae nis illiberum volorro ritatis tinullo**

Page 234

Foundry  Shinntype

Typeface  Sense
Designer  Nick Shinn
Year  2010
Format  OpenType

# Aa

Aa Bb Cc Dd Ee Ff Gg Hh Ii Jj Kk Ll
Mm Nn Oo Pp Qq Rr Ss Tt Uu Vv Ww
Xx Yy Zz
0123456789
—

Sense Thin 18pt
*Sense Thin Italic 18pt*
Sense Extra Light 18pt
*Sense Extra Light Italic 18pt*
Sense Light 18pt
*Sense Light Italic 18pt*
Sense Regular 18pt
*Sense Regular Italic 18pt*
Sense Medium 18pt
*Sense Medium Italic 18pt*
**Sense Bold 18pt**
***Sense Bold Italic 18pt***
**Sense Extra Bold 18pt**
***Sense Extra Bold Italic 18pt***
**Sense Black 18pt**
***Sense Black Italic 18pt***

---

12/14  Sense Light

The quick brown fox jumps over the lazy dog. Voyez le brick géant que j'examine près du wharf. Zwölf Boxkämpfer jagen Viktor quer über den großen Sylter

12/14  Sense Regular

The quick brown fox jumps over the lazy dog. Voyez le brick géant que j'examine près du wharf. Zwölf Boxkämpfer jagen Viktor quer über den

12/14  Sense Medium

The quick brown fox jumps over the lazy dog. Voyez le brick géant que j'examine près du wharf. Zwölf Boxkämpfer jagen Viktor quer über den

12/14  Sense Bold

**The quick brown fox jumps over the lazy dog. Voyez le brick géant que j'examine près du wharf. Zwölf Boxkämpfer jagen Viktor quer über den großen Sylter Deich. El veloz murciélago hindú comía feliz cardillo y kiwi. La**

9/12  Sense Light

The quick brown fox jumps over the lazy dog. Voyez le brick géant que j'examine près du wharf. Zwölf Boxkämpfer jagen Viktor quer über den großen Sylter Deich. El veloz murciélago hindú comía feliz cardillo y kiwi. La cigüeña tocaba el saxofón detrás del

9/12  Sense Regular

The quick brown fox jumps over the lazy dog. Voyez le brick géant que j'examine près du wharf. Zwölf Boxkämpfer jagen Viktor quer über den großen Sylter Deich. El veloz murciélago hindú comía feliz cardillo y kiwi. La cigüeña tocaba el saxofón detrás del

9/12  Sense Medium

The quick brown fox jumps over the lazy dog. Voyez le brick géant que j'examine près du wharf. Zwölf Boxkämpfer jagen Viktor quer über den großen Sylter Deich. El veloz murciélago hindú comía feliz cardillo y kiwi. La cigüeña tocaba el saxofón detrás

9/12  Sense Bold

**The quick brown fox jumps over the lazy dog. Voyez le brick géant que j'examine près du wharf. Zwölf Boxkämpfer jagen Viktor quer über den großen Sylter Deich. El veloz murciélago hindú comía feliz cardillo y kiwi. La cigüeña tocaba el saxofón detrás del palenque de pajaatur? Rissimo lorereped ex es solore lab id molorro in rempore icabore rehene-**

7/10  Sense Light

The quick brown fox jumps over the lazy dog. Voyez le brick géant que j'examine près du wharf. Zwölf Boxkämpfer jagen Viktor quer über den großen Sylter Deich. El veloz murciélago hindú comía feliz cardillo y kiwi. La cigüeña tocaba el saxofón detrás del palenque de pajaatur? Rissimo lorereped ex es solore lab id molorro in rempore icabore rehenetur aliam aut voles audae dem quam, secum eum

7/10  Sense Regular

The quick brown fox jumps over the lazy dog. Voyez le brick géant que j'examine près du wharf. Zwölf Boxkämpfer jagen Viktor quer über den großen Sylter Deich. El veloz murciélago hindú comía feliz cardillo y kiwi. La cigüeña tocaba el saxofón detrás del palenque de pajaatur? Rissimo lorereped ex es solore lab id molorro in rempore icabore rehenetur aliam aut voles audae dem quam, secum eum

7/10  Sense Medium

The quick brown fox jumps over the lazy dog. Voyez le brick géant que j'examine près du wharf. Zwölf Boxkämpfer jagen Viktor quer über den großen Sylter Deich. El veloz murciélago hindú comía feliz cardillo y kiwi. La cigüeña tocaba el saxofón detrás del palenque de pajaatur? Rissimo lorereped ex es solore lab id molorro in rempore icabore rehenetur aliam aut voles audae dem quam, secum eum

7/10  Sense Bold

**The quick brown fox jumps over the lazy dog. Voyez le brick géant que j'examine près du wharf. Zwölf Boxkämpfer jagen Viktor quer über den großen Sylter Deich. El veloz murciélago hindú comía feliz cardillo y kiwi. La cigüeña tocaba el saxofón detrás del palenque de pajaatur? Rissimo lorereped ex es solore lab id molorro in rempore icabore rehenetur aliam aut voles audae dem quam, secum eum facesequae consequ aepudam quia voluptiur repel in et faccustibus, nonsenis aut quisqui rero mi, ipiet lam ant ut maio et hil molupta**

| | |
|---|---|
| Typeface Sensibility | Year 2010 |
| Designer Nick Shinn | Format OpenType |

# Aa

Aa Bb Cc Dd Ee Ff Gg Hh Ii Jj Kk Ll Mm Nn Oo Pp Qq Rr Ss Tt Uu Vv Ww Xx Yy Zz
0123456789

Sensibility Thin 18pt
*Sensibility Thin Italic* 18pt
Sensibility Extra Light 18pt
*Sensibility Extra Light Italic* 18pt
Sensibility Light 18pt
*Sensibility Light Italic* 18pt
Sensibility Regular 18pt
*Sensibility Regular Italic* 18pt
**Sensibility Medium** 18pt
***Sensibility Medium Italic*** 18pt
**Sensibility Bold** 18pt
***Sensibility Bold Italic*** 18pt
**Sensibility Extra Bold** 18pt
***Sensibility Extra Bold Italic*** 18pt
**Sensibility Black** 18pt
***Sensibility Black Italic*** 18pt

---

**12/14 Sensibility Light**

The quick brown fox jumps over the lazy dog. Voyez le brick géant que j'examine près du wharf. Zwölf Boxkämpfer jagen Viktor quer über den großen Sylter

**9/12 Sensibility Light**

The quick brown fox jumps over the lazy dog. Voyez le brick géant que j'examine près du wharf. Zwölf Boxkämpfer jagen Viktor quer über den großen Sylter Deich. El veloz murciélago hindú comía feliz cardillo y kiwi. La cigüeña tocaba el saxofón detrás del palenque

**7/10 Sensibility Light**

The quick brown fox jumps over the lazy dog. Voyez le brick géant que j'examine près du wharf. Zwölf Boxkämpfer jagen Viktor quer über den großen Sylter Deich. El veloz murciélago hindú comía feliz cardillo y kiwi. La cigüeña tocaba el saxofón detrás del palenque de pajaatur? Rissimo lorereped ex es solore lab id molorro in rempore icabore rehenetur aliam aut voles audae dem quam, secum eum

**12/14 Sensibility Regular**

The quick brown fox jumps over the lazy dog. Voyez le brick géant que j'examine près du wharf. Zwölf Boxkämpfer jagen Viktor quer über den

**9/12 Sensibility Regular**

The quick brown fox jumps over the lazy dog. Voyez le brick géant que j'examine près du wharf. Zwölf Boxkämpfer jagen Viktor quer über den großen Sylter Deich. El veloz murciélago hindú comía feliz cardillo y kiwi. La cigüeña tocaba el saxofón detrás del

**7/10 Sensibility Regular**

The quick brown fox jumps over the lazy dog. Voyez le brick géant que j'examine près du wharf. Zwölf Boxkämpfer jagen Viktor quer über den großen Sylter Deich. El veloz murciélago hindú comía feliz cardillo y kiwi. La cigüeña tocaba el saxofón detrás del palenque de pajaatur? Rissimo lorereped ex es solore lab id molorro in rempore icabore rehenetur aliam aut voles audae dem quam, secum eum

**12/14 Sensibility Medium**

The quick brown fox jumps over the lazy dog. Voyez le brick géant que j'examine près du wharf. Zwölf Boxkämpfer jagen Viktor quer über den

**9/12 Sensibility Medium**

The quick brown fox jumps over the lazy dog. Voyez le brick géant que j'examine près du wharf. Zwölf Boxkämpfer jagen Viktor quer über den großen Sylter Deich. El veloz murciélago hindú comía feliz cardillo y kiwi. La cigüeña tocaba el saxofón detrás

**7/10 Sensibility Medium**

The quick brown fox jumps over the lazy dog. Voyez le brick géant que j'examine près du wharf. Zwölf Boxkämpfer jagen Viktor quer über den großen Sylter Deich. El veloz murciélago hindú comía feliz cardillo y kiwi. La cigüeña tocaba el saxofón detrás del palenque de pajaatur? Rissimo lorereped ex es solore lab id molorro in rempore icabore rehenetur aliam aut voles audae dem quam, secum eum

**12/14 Sensibility Bold**

The quick brown fox jumps over the lazy dog. Voyez le brick géant que j'examine près du wharf. Zwölf Boxkämpfer jagen Viktor quer über den großen Sylter Deich. El veloz murciélago hindú comía feliz cardillo y kiwi.

**9/12 Sensibility Bold**

The quick brown fox jumps over the lazy dog. Voyez le brick géant que j'examine près du wharf. Zwölf Boxkämpfer jagen Viktor quer über den großen Sylter Deich. El veloz murciélago hindú comía feliz cardillo y kiwi. La cigüeña tocaba el saxofón detrás del palenque de pajaatur? Rissimo lorereped ex es solore lab id molorro in rempore icabore rehene-

**7/10 Sensibility Bold**

The quick brown fox jumps over the lazy dog. Voyez le brick géant que j'examine près du wharf. Zwölf Boxkämpfer jagen Viktor quer über den großen Sylter Deich. El veloz murciélago hindú comía feliz cardillo y kiwi. La cigüeña tocaba el saxofón detrás del palenque de pajaatur? Rissimo lorereped ex es solore lab id molorro in rempore icabore rehenetur aliam aut voles audae dem quam, secum eum facesequae consequa aepudam quia voluptiur repel in et faccustibus, nonsenis aut quisqui rero mi, ipiet lam ant ut maio et hil

# S
## Storm Type

— František Štorm —
Prague, Czech Republic —
Since 1993

## Info

—Why?
In 1993 I got my first computer, and the fonts on it were all wrong and I had no budget for buying good new ones. Hence, I had to create my own for my graphic design jobs.

—People on staff
1–2

—Type designers on staff
1

—Type families
Hundreds

—Designers represented
9

—Web shop
www.stormtype.com

—Distributors
MyFonts, FontShop

—Webfont services
Our license is open to self-hosted web solutions within the basic price.

—Basic license
"Very cheap."

—Special conditions
Storm Type provides lifetime warranty on all its fonts.

## People

—František Štorm graduated in 1991 at the Academy of Arts, Architecture and Design in Prague, under professor Jan Solpera. Between 2003–2008 he taught at the same school, and now freelances. Štorm's passion is Baroque Typography (sometimes referred to as "transitional", which is misleading. After spending a decade in libraries studying ancient prints, he designed Regent, Antique Ancienne and Jannon. His later serious projects are based on this initial research and have the same focus: the substantial development of beautiful Latin alphabets finished in the late 18th century — all later "improvements" are only minor technological and esthetic variations.

František Štorm founded the Storm Type foundry with the aim of restoring the values of classical typography for the benefit of digital technologies. "We started by drawing alphabets which could be used in book printing, then we proceeded to alphabets for film- and photosetting and nowadays, in the era of computers, we use the experience we have gained to make digital typefaces more human." When digitizing original Czech typefaces, Storm Type collaborates with experienced designers Otakar Karlas, Jan Solpera and Josef Tyfa.

## Typeface selection

**Header**
*Lokal Script*
Rondka
Walbaum 10&120 Pro
**Vida**
Biblon Pro
**Farao Text**

24pt

František Štorm, griffins (woodcuts). Štorm cut countless variations of this mythical beast, making it an ever-evolving symbol of his foundry.

Page 237

# H P LOVECRAFT

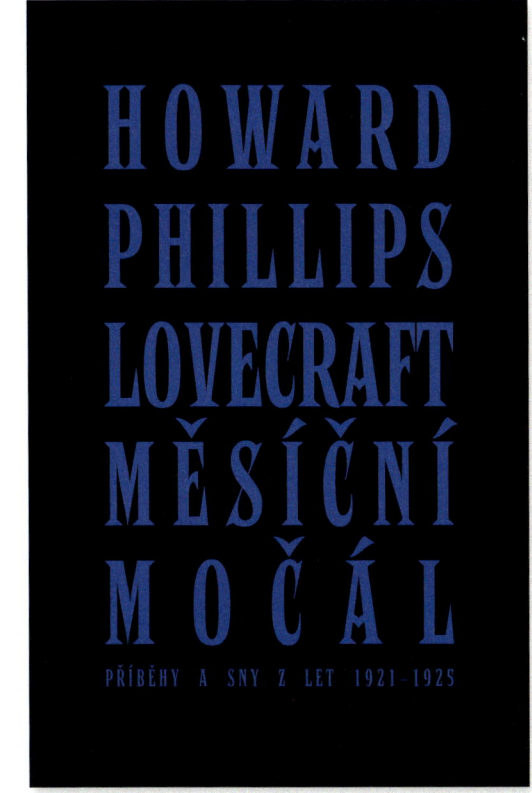

## SPISY 1    HROBKA

PLUS

HOWARD
PHILLIPS
LOVECRAFT
MĚSÍČNÍ
MOČÁL

PŘÍBĚHY A SNY Z LET 1921–1925

Štorm designed and illustrated the covers for the Czech translation of H. P. Lovecraft's complete works. PLUS Publishers, Prague.

František Štorm, gargoyles. Woodcut.

| | | | |
|---|---|---|---|
| Typeface | Header | Year | 2009 |
| Designer | František Štorm | Format | OpenType |

# Skinny Fatman

Header 11
Header 12
**Header 13**
**Header 14**
**Header 15**

Aa Bb Cc Dd Ee Ff Gg Hh Ii Jj Kk Ll Mm
Nn Oo Pp Qq Rr Ss Tt Uu Vv Ww Xx Yy Zz
0123456789

| | | | |
|---|---|---|---|
| Typeface | Lokal Script | Year | 2009 |
| Designer | František Štorm | Format | OpenType |

# *Weinlokal Herrmann*

Lokal Script 11 Regular
*Lokal Script 11 Italic*
Lokal Script 22 Regular
*Lokal Script 22 Italic*
**Lokal Script 22 Bold**
***Lokal Script 22 Bold Italic***
Lokal Script 33 Regular
*Lokal Script 33 Italic*
**Lokal Script 33 Bold**
***Lokal Script 33 Bold Italic***

Aa Bb Cc Dd Ee Ff Gg Hh Ii Jj Kk Ll Mm Nn Oo
Pp Qq Rr Ss Tt Uu Vv Ww Xx Yy Zz 0123456789

| | | | |
|---|---|---|---|
| Typeface | Rondka | Year | 2001 |
| Designer | František Štorm | Format | OpenType |

# Antiquitäten Werner

Regular
**Bold**

Aa Bb Cc Dd Ee Ff Gg Hh Ii Jj Kk
Ll Mm Nn Oo Pp Qq Rr Ss Tt Uu
Vv Ww Xx Yy Zz 0123456789

Page 239

Foundry Storm Type

Typeface Walbaum 10 & 120 Pro
Designer František Štorm
Year 2010
Format OpenType

# Aa

Aa Bb Cc Dd Ee Ff Gg Hh Ii Jj Kk Ll Mm Nn Oo Pp Qq Rr Ss Tt Uu Vv Ww Xx Yy Zz
0123456789
—

Walbaum 10 Pro Regular 18pt
*Walbaum 10 Pro Italic 18pt*
**Walbaum 10 Pro Bold 18pt**
***Walbaum 10 Pro Bold Italic 18pt***
Walbaum 10 XL Pro Regular 18pt
*Walbaum 10 XL Pro Italic 18pt*
**Walbaum 10 XL Pro Bold 18pt**
***Walbaum 10 XL Pro Bold Italic 18pt***
Walbaum 120 Pro Regular 18pt
*Walbaum 120 Pro Italic 18pt*
**Walbaum 120 Pro Bold 18pt**
***Walbaum 120 XL Pro Bold Italic 18pt***
Walbaum 120 XL Pro Regular 18pt
*Walbaum 120 XL Pro Italic 18pt*
**Walbaum 120 XL Pro Bold 18pt**
***Walbaum 120 XL Pro Bold Italic 18pt***

---

12/14 Walbaum 10 Pro Regular

The quick brown fox jumps over the lazy dog. Voyez le brick géant que j'examine près du wharf. Zwölf Boxkämpfer jagen Vik-

12/14 Walbaum 10 Pro Bold

**The quick brown fox jumps over the lazy dog. Voyez le brick géant que j'examine près du wharf. Zwölf Boxkämpfer jagen Vik-**

12/14 Walbaum 120 Pro Regular

The quick brown fox jumps over the lazy dog. Voyez le brick géant que j'examine près du wharf. Zwölf Boxkämpfer jagen Viktor quer

12/14 Walbaum 120 Pro Bold

**The quick brown fox jumps over the lazy dog. Voyez le brick géant que j'examine près du wharf. Zwölf Boxkämpfer jagen Viktor quer über den großen Sylter Deich. El veloz murciélago hin-**

9/12 Walbaum 10 Pro Regular

The quick brown fox jumps over the lazy dog. Voyez le brick géant que j'examine près du wharf. Zwölf Boxkämpfer jagen Viktor quer über den großen Sylter Deich. El veloz murciélago hindú comía feliz cardillo y kiwi. La

9/12 Walbaum 10 Pro Bold

**The quick brown fox jumps over the lazy dog. Voyez le brick géant que j'examine près du wharf. Zwölf Boxkämpfer jagen Viktor quer über den großen Sylter Deich. El veloz murciélago hindú comía feliz cardillo y kiwi. La**

9/12 Walbaum 120 Pro Regular

The quick brown fox jumps over the lazy dog. Voyez le brick géant que j'examine près du wharf. Zwölf Boxkämpfer jagen Viktor quer über den großen Sylter Deich. El veloz murciélago hindú comía feliz cardillo y kiwi. La

9/12 Walbaum 120 Pro Bold

**The quick brown fox jumps over the lazy dog. Voyez le brick géant que j'examine près du wharf. Zwölf Boxkämpfer jagen Viktor quer über den großen Sylter Deich. El veloz murciélago hindú comía feliz cardillo y kiwi. La cigüeña tocaba el saxofón detrás del palenque de pajaatur? Rissimo lorer-**

7/10 Walbaum 10 Pro Regular

The quick brown fox jumps over the lazy dog. Voyez le brick géant que j'examine près du wharf. Zwölf Boxkämpfer jagen Viktor quer über den großen Sylter Deich. El veloz murciélago hindú comía feliz cardillo y kiwi. La cigüeña tocaba el saxofón detrás del palenque de pajaatur? Rissimo lorereped ex es solore lab id molorro in rempore icabore

7/10 Walbaum 10 Pro Bold

**The quick brown fox jumps over the lazy dog. Voyez le brick géant que j'examine près du wharf. Zwölf Boxkämpfer jagen Viktor quer über den großen Sylter Deich. El veloz murciélago hindú comía feliz cardillo y kiwi. La cigüeña tocaba el saxofón detrás del palenque de pajaatur? Rissimo lorereped ex es solore lab id molorro in rempore**

7/10 Walbaum 120 Pro Regular

The quick brown fox jumps over the lazy dog. Voyez le brick géant que j'examine près du wharf. Zwölf Boxkämpfer jagen Viktor quer über den großen Sylter Deich. El veloz murciélago hindú comía feliz cardillo y kiwi. La cigüeña tocaba el saxofón detrás del palenque de pajaatur? Rissimo lorereped ex es solore lab id molorro in rempore icabore

7/10 Walbaum 120 Pro Bold

**The quick brown fox jumps over the lazy dog. Voyez le brick géant que j'examine près du wharf. Zwölf Boxkämpfer jagen Viktor quer über den großen Sylter Deich. El veloz murciélago hindú comía feliz cardillo y kiwi. La cigüeña tocaba el saxofón detrás del palenque de pajaatur? Rissimo lorereped ex es solore lab id molorro in rempore icabore rehenetur aliam aut voles audae dem quam, secum cum facesequae consequ aepudam quia**

Page 240

Foundry  Storm Type

Typeface  Vida
Designer  František Štorm
Year  2005
Format  OpenType

# Aa

Aa Bb Cc Dd Ee Ff Gg Hh Ii Jj Kk Ll Mm Nn Oo Pp Qq Rr Ss Tt Uu Vv Ww Xx Yy Zz 0123456789 —

Vida 21 Pro Regular 20pt
*Vida 21 Pro Italic* 20pt
Vida 22 Pro Regular 20pt
*Vida 22 Pro Italic* 20pt
**Vida 22 Pro Bold** 20pt
***Vida 22 Pro Bold Italic*** 20pt
Vida 23 Pro Regular 20pt
*Vida 23 Pro Italic* 20pt
**Vida 23 Pro Bold** 20pt
***Vida 23 Pro Bold Italic*** 20pt
Vida 31 Pro Regular 20pt
*Vida 31 Pro Italic* 20pt
Vida 32 Pro 🏃 → **Vida 43 Pro**

---

12/14  Vida 21 Pro Regular

The quick brown fox jumps over the lazy dog. Voyez le brick géant que j'examine près du wharf. Zwölf Boxkämpfer jagen Viktor quer über den großen Sylter Deich. El veloz mur-

9/12  Vida 21 Pro Regular

The quick brown fox jumps over the lazy dog. Voyez le brick géant que j'examine près du wharf. Zwölf Boxkämpfer jagen Viktor quer über den großen Sylter Deich. El veloz murciélago hindú comía feliz cardillo y kiwi. La cigüeña tocaba el saxofón detrás del palenque de pajaatur? Rissimo lorereped ex es solo-

7/10  Vida 21 Pro Regular

The quick brown fox jumps over the lazy dog. Voyez le brick géant que j'examine près du wharf. Zwölf Boxkämpfer jagen Viktor quer über den großen Sylter Deich. El veloz murciélago hindú comía feliz cardillo y kiwi. La cigüeña tocaba el saxofón detrás del palenque de pajaatur? Rissimo lorereped ex es solore lab id molorro in rempore icabore rehenetur aliam aut voles audae dem quam, secum eum facesequae consequ aepudam quia voluptiur repel in et faccustibus,

12/14  Vida 22 Pro Regular

The quick brown fox jumps over the lazy dog. Voyez le brick géant que j'examine près du wharf. Zwölf Boxkämpfer jagen Viktor quer über den großen Sylter Deich. El veloz

9/12  Vida 22 Pro Regular

The quick brown fox jumps over the lazy dog. Voyez le brick géant que j'examine près du wharf. Zwölf Boxkämpfer jagen Viktor quer über den großen Sylter Deich. El veloz murciélago hindú comía feliz cardillo y kiwi. La cigüeña tocaba el saxofón detrás del palenque de pajaatur? Rissimo lorereped

7/10  Vida 22 Pro Regular

The quick brown fox jumps over the lazy dog. Voyez le brick géant que j'examine près du wharf. Zwölf Boxkämpfer jagen Viktor quer über den großen Sylter Deich. El veloz murciélago hindú comía feliz cardillo y kiwi. La cigüeña tocaba el saxofón detrás del palenque de pajaatur? Rissimo lorereped ex es solore lab id molorro in rempore icabore rehenetur aliam aut voles audae dem quam, secum eum facesequae consequ aepudam quia voluptiur

12/14  Vida 23 Pro Regular

The quick brown fox jumps over the lazy dog. Voyez le brick géant que j'examine près du wharf. Zwölf Boxkämpfer jagen Viktor quer über den großen Sylter Deich.

9/12  Vida 23 Pro Regular

The quick brown fox jumps over the lazy dog. Voyez le brick géant que j'examine près du wharf. Zwölf Boxkämpfer jagen Viktor quer über den großen Sylter Deich. El veloz murciélago hindú comía feliz cardillo y kiwi. La cigüeña tocaba el saxofón detrás del palenque de

7/10  Vida 23 Pro Regular

The quick brown fox jumps over the lazy dog. Voyez le brick géant que j'examine près du wharf. Zwölf Boxkämpfer jagen Viktor quer über den großen Sylter Deich. El veloz murciélago hindú comía feliz cardillo y kiwi. La cigüeña tocaba el saxofón detrás del palenque de pajaatur? Rissimo lorereped ex es solore lab id molorro in rempore icabore rehenetur aliam aut voles audae dem quam, secum eum facesequae consequ aepudam

12/14  Vida 31 Pro Regular

The quick brown fox jumps over the lazy dog. Voyez le brick géant que j'examine près du wharf. Zwölf Boxkämpfer jagen Viktor quer über den großen Sylter Deich. El veloz murciélago hindú comía feliz cardillo y kiwi.

9/12  Vida 31 Pro Regular

The quick brown fox jumps over the lazy dog. Voyez le brick géant que j'examine près du wharf. Zwölf Boxkämpfer jagen Viktor quer über den großen Sylter Deich. El veloz murciélago comía feliz cardillo y kiwi. La cigüeña tocaba el saxofón detrás del palenque de pajaatur? Rissimo lorereped ex es solore lab id molorro in rempore

7/10  Vida 31 Pro Regular

The quick brown fox jumps over the lazy dog. Voyez le brick géant que j'examine près du wharf. Zwölf Boxkämpfer jagen Viktor quer über den großen Sylter Deich. El veloz murciélago hindú comía feliz cardillo y kiwi. La cigüeña tocaba el saxofón detrás del palenque de pajaatur? Rissimo lorereped ex es solore lab id molorro in rempore icabore rehenetur aliam aut voles audae dem quam, secum eum facesequae consequ aepudam quia voluptiur repel in et faccustibus, nonsenis aut quisqui rero

Foundry Storm Type

Typeface Biblon Pro
Designer František Štorm
Year 2000, 2006
Format OpenType

# Aa

Biblon Pro Regular 20pt
*Biblon Pro Italic* 20pt
**Biblon Pro Bold** 20pt
***Biblon Pro Bold Italic*** 20pt

Aa Bb Cc Dd Ee Ff Gg Hh Ii Jj Kk Ll Mm Nn Oo Pp Qq Rr Ss Tt Uu Vv Ww Xx Yy Zz
0123456789
—

9/12  Biblon Pro Regular

The quick brown fox jumps over the lazy dog. Voyez le brick géant que j'examine près du wharf. Zwölf Boxkämpfer jagen Viktor quer über den großen Sylter Deich. El veloz murciélago hindú comía feliz cardillo y kiwi. La cigüeña tocaba el saxofón detrás del palenque de pajaatur? Rissimo lorereped ex es solore lab id molorro in rempore icabore rehenetur aliam aut voles audae dem quam, secum eum facesequae consequ aepudam quia voluptiur repel in et faccustibus, nonsenis aut quisqui rero mi, ipiet lam ant ut maio et hil molupta tustis atatur, consedi tasimol orerem aut volor andipsapis sit, illaut volore officatus alicae dusdaec tatecte

7/10  Biblon Pro Regular

The quick brown fox jumps over the lazy dog. Voyez le brick géant que j'examine près du wharf. Zwölf Boxkämpfer jagen Viktor quer über den großen Sylter Deich. El veloz murciélago hindú comía feliz cardillo y kiwi. La cigüeña tocaba el saxofón detrás del palenque de pajaatur? Rissimo lorereped ex es solore lab id molorro in rempore icabore rehenetur aliam aut voles audae dem quam, secum eum facesequae consequ aepudam quia voluptiur repel in et faccustibus, nonsenis aut quisqui rero mi, ipiet lam ant ut maio et hil molupta tustis atatur, consedi tasimol orerem aut volor andipsapis sit, illaut volore officatus alicae dusdaec tatecte cearum qui accatibus restiore nulpa secaerferum, nus dolenim in et quoditat que explam voluptictur? Qui de illuptae. Dae nis illiberum voloro ritatis tinullo rerumqu atetur repro eatius asperibus. Rissimo lorereped ex es solore lab id molorro in rempore icabore rehenetur aliam aut voles audae dem quam, secum eum facesequae consequ

Typeface Farao Text
Designer František Štorm
Year 2000
Format OpenType

# Aa

Farao Text Regular 20pt
*Farao Text Italic* 20p
**Farao Text Bold** 20pt
***Farao Text Bold Italic*** 20pt

Aa Bb Cc Dd Ee Ff Gg Hh Ii Jj Kk Ll Mm Nn Oo Pp Qq Rr Ss Tt Uu Vv Ww Xx Yy Zz
0123456789
—

9/12  Farao Text Regular

The quick brown fox jumps over the lazy dog. Voyez le brick géant que j'examine près du wharf. Zwölf Boxkämpfer jagen Viktor quer über den großen Sylter Deich. El veloz murciélago hindú comía feliz cardillo y kiwi. La cigüeña tocaba el saxofón detrás del palenque de pajaatur? Rissimo lorereped ex es solore lab id molorro in rempore icabore rehenetur aliam aut voles audae dem quam, secum eum facesequae consequ aepudam quia voluptiur repel in et faccustibus, nonsenis aut quisqui rero mi, ipiet lam ant ut maio et hil molupta tustis atatur, consedi tasimol orerem aut volor andipsapis sit, illaut volore officatus alicae dusdaec tatecte cearum qui accatibus restiore nulpa secaerferum, nus dolenim in et quoditat

7/10  Farao Text Regular

The quick brown fox jumps over the lazy dog. Voyez le brick géant que j'examine près du wharf. Zwölf Boxkämpfer jagen Viktor quer über den großen Sylter Deich. El veloz murciélago hindú comía feliz cardillo y kiwi. La cigüeña tocaba el saxofón detrás del palenque de pajaatur? Rissimo lorereped ex es solore lab id molorro in rempore icabore rehenetur aliam aut voles audae dem quam, secum eum facesequae consequ aepudam quia voluptiur repel in et faccustibus, nonsenis aut quisqui rero mi, ipiet lam ant ut maio et hil molupta tustis atatur, consedi tasimol orerem aut volor andipsapis sit, illaut volore officatus alicae dusdaec tatecte cearum qui accatibus restiore nulpa secaerferum, nus dolenim in et quoditat que explam voluptictur? Qui de illuptae. Dae nis illiberum voloro ritatis tinullo rerumqu atetur repro eatius asperibus. Rissimo lorereped ex es solore lab id molorro in rempore icabore rehenetur aliam aut voles audae dem quam, secum eum facesequae consequ aepudam quia voluptiur repel in et faccustibus, nonsenis aut quisqui rero mi, ipiet

# S

## Sudtipos

—

Ale Paul,
Diego Giaccone,
Angel Koziupa

—

Buenos Aires,
Argentina

—

Since
2003

Sudtipos was founded in 2003 as a collective type foundry with an attitude. It is a joint venture of professional designers with many years of experience in areas such as branding, packaging design, corporate identity, television, and new media.

## Info

—Why?
We founded Sudtipos shortly after the big Argentinian economical crisis of 2001, as an alternative to our graphic design work for which there was a very low demand.

—People on staff
1

—Type designers on staff
1

—Type families
150+

—Designers represented
12

—Web shop
No

—Distributors
Veer, MyFonts

—Webfont services
MyFonts

—Basic license
$19–$119, up to 7 machines

## People

—Ale Paul is one of the founders of the Sudtipos project, the first Argentinean type foundry collective. Ale's career as an art director landed him in some of Argentina's most prestigious studios, handling such high-profile corporate brands as Arcor, Procter & Gamble, SC Johnson, Danone and others. With the founding of Sudtipos in 2002, Ale shifted his efforts to typeface design, creating fonts and lettering for several top packaging agencies, along with producing retail typefaces.

—Diego Giaccone graduated as a graphic designer from the Architecture Design and Urbanism University of Buenos Aires (FADU-UBA). In 2002 he won the Konex Award, one of Agentina's most prestigious design prizes. Diego also speaks on design, typography and packaging. He was design director at the major Argentinian branding agencies and is currently running his own firm SureBranding.

—Angel Koziupa has been a lettering artist for the past 40 years, creating type and designing dozens of logos. His handiwork is behind nearly every important packaging logotype in Argentina. He worked for McCann Erickson for 35 years and has produced work as a freelancer for other major agencies like Interbrand, Futurebrand and others.

## Typeface selection

Brownstone Sans
Burgues Script
Chocolate
Fan Script
Lady René
Semilla

24pt

Fan Script

Page 243

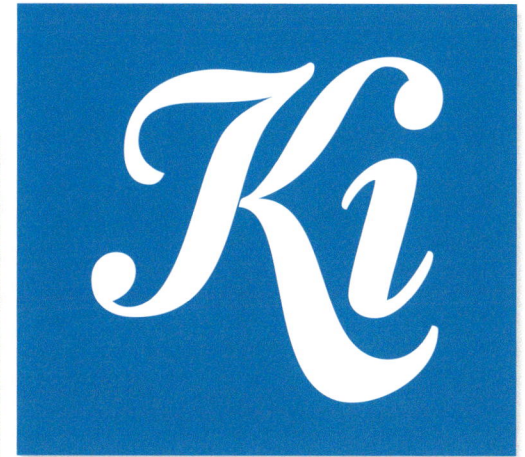

Semilla

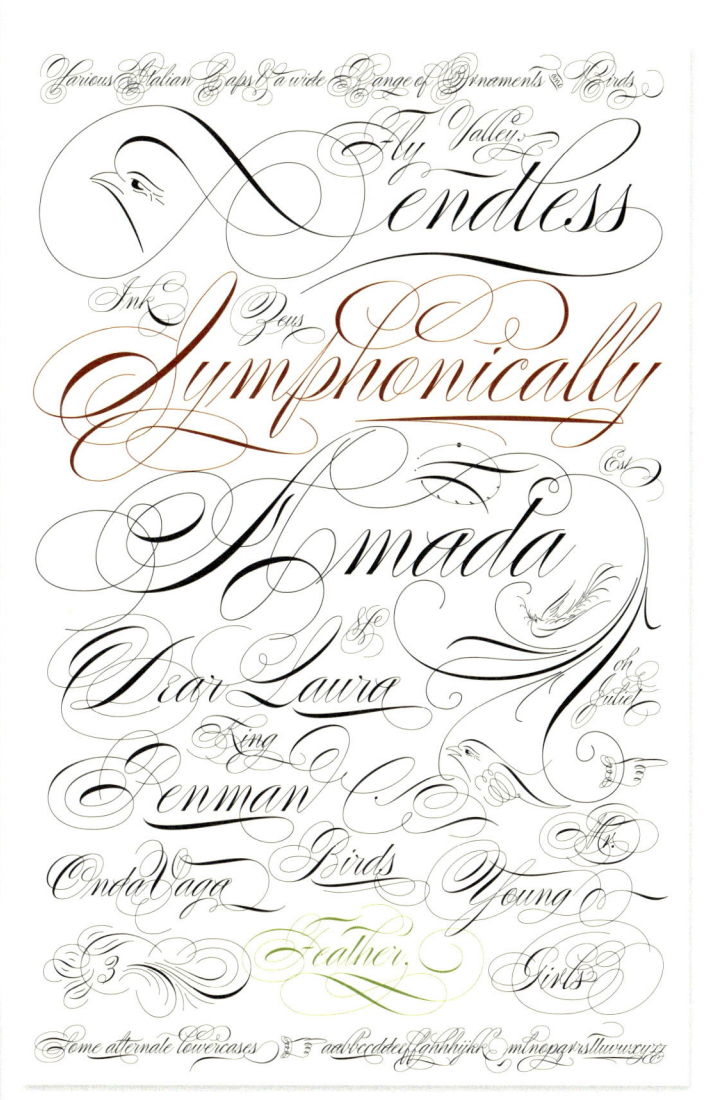

Specimen of Ale Paul's Brownstone.

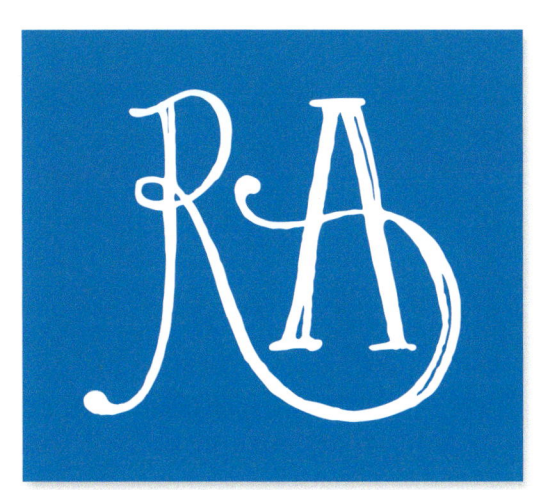

Lady René

**Above**
Specimen of Poem Script, an interpretation of a late nineteenth century American pen script style.
**Left**
Ale Paul designed Piel Script in reaction to requests he received to adapt his earlier script fonts for use in tattoos. The result is a sensitive and stylish script for "personal branding". Piel is Spanish for skin.

Foundry Sudtipos

---

Typeface Brownstone Sans, Frames
Designer Ale Paul
Year 2010
Format OpenType

Inspiration

Thin
Light
Hole

Aa Bb Cc Dd Ee Ff Gg Hh Ii Jj Kk
Ll Mm Nn Oo Pp Qq Rr Ss Tt Uu
Vv Ww Xx Yy Zz 0123456789

---

Typeface Lady René
Designer Laura Varsky, Ale Paul
Year 2010
Format OpenType

LadyKiller

Regular

Aa Bb Cc Dd Ee Ff Gg Hh Ii Jj Kk Ll Mm
Nn Oo Pp Qq Rr Ss Tt Uu Vv Ww Xx Yy Zz
0123456789

---

Typeface Burgues Script
Designer Ale Paul
Year 2007
Format OpenType

Crazy Horse

Regular

Aa Bb Cc Dd Ee Ff Gg Hh Ii
Jj Kk Ll Mm Nn Oo Pp Qq
Rr Ss Tt Uu Vv Ww Xx Yy Zz

0123456789

Foundry   Sudtipos

Typeface   Chocolate
Designer   Angel Koziupa, Ale Paul
Year   2008
Format   OpenType

# Creamy Mandelbrot

**Regular**

Aa Bb Cc Dd Ee Ff Gg Hh Ii
Jj Kk Ll Mm Nn Oo Pp Qq
Rr Ss Tt Uu Vv Ww Xx Yy Zz
0123456789

---

Typeface   Semilla
Designer   Ale Paul
Year   2009
Format   OpenType

# LemonTree

**Regular**

Aa Bb Cc Dd Ee Ff Gg Hh
Ii Jj Kk Ll Mm Nn Oo Pp
Qq Rr Ss Tt Uu Vv Ww Xx
Yy Zz 0123456789

---

Typeface   Fan Script
Designer   Ale Paul
Year   2010
Format   OpenType

# Amy was a huge fan

**Regular**

Aa Bb Cc Dd Ee Ff
Gg Hh Ii Jj Kk Ll Mm
Nn Oo Pp Qq Rr Ss Tt
Uu Vv Ww Xx Yy Zz
0123456789

# S
— Suomi
—
Tomi Haaparanta
—
Helsinki, Finland
—
Since 2004

## Info

—Why?
Originally I licensed my fonts to foundries like T26, Monotype, Linotype and ITC, but then figured that I should sell them myself. But I'm way too lazy to build a site with an online purchasing function, so I've licensed my fonts through sites like MyFonts, YWFT, Fonts.com and FontHouse.

—People on staff
1

—Type families
Approx. 50

—Designers represented
1

—Web shop
None

—Distributors
FontShop, ITC, Monotype, Linotype, MyFonts, Psy/Ops, T26, FontHaus, YouWorkForThem.

—Webfont services
Fontspring, MyFonts

—Basic license
Price range 19$–80$ (single fonts)

## People

—Tomi Haaparanta studied Graphic Design at the University of Industrial Arts in Helsinki, and at the National College of Art and Design in Dublin, where he discovered type design during a short course held by Phil Baines. He still holds a grudge against Baines for that.

Haaparanta has been making typefaces for the past twenty years now, and his computer now holds some three to four hundred typefaces and families, some of which are a great embarrassment to the designer. He has a background as an art director in various agencies, and as a type designer at HEL, where he designed numerous typefaces for Finnish and international clients, including Protokid for Diesel Industries Kids wear department. HEL also produced a few typefaces of their own: the War font set and Denim set are distributed by T26.

Tomi Haaparanta has taught type design at the University of Industrial Arts in Helsinki for the past four years. He works as a graphic designer at Taivas Design, a brand design agency in Helsinki.

Having released typefaces through Linotype, Monotype, ITC, T26 and Psy/Ops, Tomi Haaparanta launched his own foundry in January 2004, naming it after his country — Suomi, Finland. The philosophy of Suomi Type Foundry is to make extensive type families to give users a wide range of weights to choose from. "In order not to exclude any users, we try to keep the range of our type library as versatile as possible, from comfortable types for text setting, to signage type families, to more evocative fonts for brand design. And sometimes stuff just for fun."

## Typeface selection

**Grumpy**
Suomi Sans
Suomi Script
Tang
Taste
**TENNER**

24pt

Tenner

Page
247

*for*

*The*

Suomi Script

# Magazinë
# №37

IN THIS ISSUE:

Drugs, Death & the Fight of His Life

Cat in a Hot Tin Roof!

The Stupid Economy

## And a Special Report on Tom Carnase!

Typographer, type designer, teacher and graphic designer.

Carnase has designed graphics for packaging, exhibitions, corporate identities and logos for numerous clients, including ABC, CBS, Coca-Cola, Condé Nast Publications, Doubleday Publishing and NBC, and partner of the agency Lubalin, Smith, Carnase Inc.

Ficticious magazine cover designed to showcase the Grumpy typeface, 2010.

№ N

Tenner

Foundry Suomi

Typeface Grumpy
Designer Tomi Haaparanta, Tom Carnase
Year 1970, 2011
Format OpenType

Size Specific 48
Size Specific 36
Size Specific 24

Black 24
Black 36
Black 48
Black 72
Black 88
Black 99

Aa Bb Cc Dd Ee Ff Gg Hh Ii
Jj Kk Ll Mm Nn Oo Pp Qq
Rr Ss Tt Uu Vv Ww Xx Yy Zz
0123456789

Typeface Tenner
Designer Tomi Haaparanta
Year 2010
Format OpenType

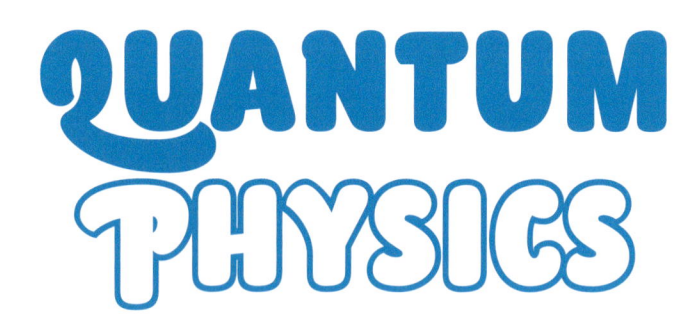

QUANTUM PHYSICS

BOOK
OUTLINE

AA BB CC DD EE FF GG HH II
JJ KK LL MM NN OO PP QQ RR
SS TT UU VV WW XX YY ZZ
0123456789

Typeface Suomi Script
Designer Tomi Haaparanta
Year 2009
Format OpenType

Small Mimicry

Book

Aa Bb Cc Dd Ee Ff Gg Hh Ii Jj Kk
Ll Mm Nn Oo Pp Qq Rr Ss Tt Uu Vv
Ww Xx Yy Zz 0123456789

Page
249

Foundry Suomi

Typeface Taste
Designer Tomi Haaparanta

Year 2010
Format OpenType

# Aa

Aa Bb Cc Dd Ee Ff Gg Hh Ii Jj Kk Ll
Mm Nn Oo Pp Qq Rr Ss Tt Uu Vv Ww
Xx Yy Zz
0123456789
–

Taste Thin 20pt
*Taste Thin Italic 20pt*
Taste Extra Light 20pt
*Taste Extra Light Italic 20pt*
Taste Light 20pt
*Taste Light Italic 20pt*
Taste Book 20pt
*Taste Book Italic 20pt*
**Taste Medium 20pt**
***Taste Medium Italic 20pt***
**Taste Bold 20pt**
***Taste Bold Italic 20pt***
**Taste Black 20pt**
***Taste Black Italic 20pt***

---

12/14 Taste Light

The quick brown fox jumps over the lazy dog. Voyez le brick géant que j'examine près du wharf. Zwölf Boxkämpfer jagen Viktor quer über den großen Sylter Deich. El veloz mur-

12/14 Taste Book

The quick brown fox jumps over the lazy dog. Voyez le brick géant que j'examine près du wharf. Zwölf Boxkämpfer jagen Viktor quer über den großen Sylter Deich. El

12/14 Taste Medium

The quick brown fox jumps over the lazy dog. Voyez le brick géant que j'examine près du wharf. Zwölf Boxkämpfer jagen Viktor quer über den großen Sylter

12/14 Taste Bold

The quick brown fox jumps over the lazy dog. Voyez le brick géant que j'examine près du wharf. Zwölf Boxkämpfer jagen Viktor quer über den großen Sylter Deich. El veloz murciélago hindú comía feliz cardillo y kiwi.

9/12 Taste Light

The quick brown fox jumps over the lazy dog. Voyez le brick géant que j'examine près du wharf. Zwölf Boxkämpfer jagen Viktor quer über den großen Sylter Deich. El veloz murciélago hindú comía feliz cardillo y kiwi. La cigüeña tocaba el saxofón detrás del palenque de pajaatur? Rissimo lorereped ex

9/12 Taste Book

The quick brown fox jumps over the lazy dog. Voyez le brick géant que j'examine près du wharf. Zwölf Boxkämpfer jagen Viktor quer über den großen Sylter Deich. El veloz murciélago hindú comía feliz cardillo y kiwi. La cigüeña tocaba el saxofón detrás del palenque de pajaatur?

9/12 Taste Medium

The quick brown fox jumps over the lazy dog. Voyez le brick géant que j'examine près du wharf. Zwölf Boxkämpfer jagen Viktor quer über den großen Sylter Deich. El veloz murciélago hindú comía feliz cardillo y kiwi. La cigüeña tocaba el saxofón detrás del

9/12 Taste Bold

The quick brown fox jumps over the lazy dog. Voyez le brick géant que j'examine près du wharf. Zwölf Boxkämpfer jagen Viktor quer über den großen Sylter Deich. El veloz murciélago hindú comía feliz cardillo y kiwi. La cigüeña tocaba el saxofón detrás del palenque de pajaatur? Rissimo lorereped ex es solore lab id molorro in rempore icabore

7/10 Taste Light

The quick brown fox jumps over the lazy dog. Voyez le brick géant que j'examine près du wharf. Zwölf Boxkämpfer jagen Viktor quer über den großen Sylter Deich. El veloz murciélago hindú comía feliz cardillo y kiwi. La cigüeña tocaba el saxofón detrás del palenque de pajaatur? Rissimo lorereped ex es solore lab id molorro in rempore icabore rehenetur aliam aut voles audae dem quam, secum eum facesequae consequ aepudam quia voluptiur repel

7/10 Taste Book

The quick brown fox jumps over the lazy dog. Voyez le brick géant que j'examine près du wharf. Zwölf Boxkämpfer jagen Viktor quer über den großen Sylter Deich. El veloz murciélago hindú comía feliz cardillo y kiwi. La cigüeña tocaba el saxofón detrás del palenque de pajaatur? Rissimo lorereped ex es solore lab id molorro in rempore icabore rehenetur aliam aut voles audae dem quam, secum eum facesequae consequ aepudam quia

7/10 Taste Medium

The quick brown fox jumps over the lazy dog. Voyez le brick géant que j'examine près du wharf. Zwölf Boxkämpfer jagen Viktor quer über den großen Sylter Deich. El veloz murciélago hindú comía feliz cardillo y kiwi. La cigüeña tocaba el saxofón detrás del palenque de pajaatur? Rissimo lorereped ex es solore lab id molorro in rempore icabore rehenetur aliam aut voles audae dem quam, secum eum

7/10 Taste Bold

The quick brown fox jumps over the lazy dog. Voyez le brick géant que j'examine près du wharf. Zwölf Boxkämpfer jagen Viktor quer über den großen Sylter Deich. El veloz murciélago hindú comía feliz cardillo y kiwi. La cigüeña tocaba el saxofón detrás del palenque de pajaatur? Rissimo lorereped ex es solore lab id molorro in rempore icabore rehenetur aliam aut voles audae dem quam, secum eum facesequae consequ aepudam quia voluptiur repel in et faccustibus, nonsenis aut quisqui rero mi,

Page 250

Foundry Suomi

Typeface Tang
Designer Tomi Haaparanta
Year 2005
Format OpenType

# Aa

Aa Bb Cc Dd Ee Ff Gg Hh Ii Jj Kk Ll Mm Nn
Oo Pp Qq Rr Ss Tt Uu Vv Ww Xx Yy Zz
0123456789

Tang Thin 20pt
*Tang Thin Italic 20pt*
Tang Ultra Light 20pt
*Tang Ultra Light Italic 20pt*
Tang Light 20pt
*Tang Light Italic 20pt*
Tang Book 20pt
*Tang Book Italic 20pt*
**Tang Medium 20pt**
***Tang Medium Italic 20pt***
**Tang Bold 20pt**
***Tang Bold Italic 20pt***
**Tang Black 20pt**
***Tang Black Italic 20pt***
**Tang Ultra Black 20pt**

---

12/14  Tang Light

The quick brown fox jumps over the lazy dog. Voyez le brick géant que j'examine près du wharf. Zwölf Boxkämpfer jagen Viktor quer über den großen Sylter Deich. El veloz mur-

12/14  Tang Book

The quick brown fox jumps over the lazy dog. Voyez le brick géant que j'examine près du wharf. Zwölf Boxkämpfer jagen Viktor quer über den großen Sylter Deich. El veloz

12/14  Tang Medium

The quick brown fox jumps over the lazy dog. Voyez le brick géant que j'examine près du wharf. Zwölf Boxkämpfer jagen Viktor quer über den großen Sylter Deich.

12/14  Tang Bold

The quick brown fox jumps over the lazy dog. Voyez le brick géant que j'examine près du wharf. Zwölf Boxkämpfer jagen Viktor quer über den großen Sylter Deich. El veloz murciélago hindú comía feliz cardillo y kiwi. La cigüeña tocaba el

9/12  Tang Light

The quick brown fox jumps over the lazy dog. Voyez le brick géant que j'examine près du wharf. Zwölf Boxkämpfer jagen Viktor quer über den großen Sylter Deich. El veloz murciélago hindú comía feliz cardillo y kiwi. La cigüeña tocaba el saxofón detrás del palenque de pajaatur? Rissimo lorereped ex es solo-

9/12  Tang Book

The quick brown fox jumps over the lazy dog. Voyez le brick géant que j'examine près du wharf. Zwölf Boxkämpfer jagen Viktor quer über den großen Sylter Deich. El veloz murciélago hindú comía feliz cardillo y kiwi. La cigüeña tocaba el saxofón detrás del palenque de pajaatur? Rissimo lorereped ex

9/12  Tang Medium

The quick brown fox jumps over the lazy dog. Voyez le brick géant que j'examine près du wharf. Zwölf Boxkämpfer jagen Viktor quer über den großen Sylter Deich. El veloz murciélago hindú comía feliz cardillo y kiwi. La cigüeña tocaba el saxofón detrás del palenque de

9/12  Tang Bold

The quick brown fox jumps over the lazy dog. Voyez le brick géant que j'examine près du wharf. Zwölf Boxkämpfer jagen Viktor quer über den großen Sylter Deich. El veloz murciélago hindú comía feliz cardillo y kiwi. La cigüeña tocaba el saxofón detrás del palenque de pajaatur? Rissimo lorereped ex es solore lab id molorro in rempore icabore rehenetur aliam aut voles

7/10  Tang Light

The quick brown fox jumps over the lazy dog. Voyez le brick géant que j'examine près du wharf. Zwölf Boxkämpfer jagen Viktor quer über den großen Sylter Deich. El veloz murciélago hindú comía feliz cardillo y kiwi. La cigüeña tocaba el saxofón detrás del palenque de pajaatur? Rissimo lorereped ex es solore lab id molorro in rempore icabore rehenetur aliam aut voles audae dem quam, secum eum facesequae consequ aepudam quia voluptiur repel in et faccustibus, nonsenis

7/10  Tang Book

The quick brown fox jumps over the lazy dog. Voyez le brick géant que j'examine près du wharf. Zwölf Boxkämpfer jagen Viktor quer über den großen Sylter Deich. El veloz murciélago hindú comía feliz cardillo y kiwi. La cigüeña tocaba el saxofón detrás del palenque de pajaatur? Rissimo lorereped ex es solore lab id molorro in rempore icabore rehenetur aliam aut voles audae dem quam, secum eum facesequae consequ aepudam quia voluptiur repel

7/10  Tang Medium

The quick brown fox jumps over the lazy dog. Voyez le brick géant que j'examine près du wharf. Zwölf Boxkämpfer jagen Viktor quer über den großen Sylter Deich. El veloz murciélago hindú comía feliz cardillo y kiwi. La cigüeña tocaba el saxofón detrás del palenque de pajaatur? Rissimo lorereped ex es solore lab id molorro in rempore icabore rehenetur aliam aut voles audae dem quam, secum eum facesequae consequ aepudam

7/10  Tang Bold

The quick brown fox jumps over the lazy dog. Voyez le brick géant que j'examine près du wharf. Zwölf Boxkämpfer jagen Viktor quer über den großen Sylter Deich. El veloz murciélago hindú comía feliz cardillo y kiwi. La cigüeña tocaba el saxofón detrás del palenque de pajaatur? Rissimo lorereped ex es solore lab id molorro in rempore icabore rehenetur aliam aut voles audae dem quam, secum eum facesequae consequ aepudam quia voluptiur repel in et faccustibus, nonsenis aut quisqui rero mi, ipiet lam ant ut maio et hil molupta

Foundry Suomi

Typeface Suomi Sans
Designer Tomi Haaparanta
Year 2009
Format OpenType

# Aa

Aa Bb Cc Dd Ee Ff Gg Hh Ii Jj Kk Ll Mm Nn
Oo Pp Qq Rr Ss Tt Uu Vv Ww Xx Yy Zz
0123456789

Suomi Sans Thin 20pt
*Suomi Sans Thin Italic* 20pt
Suomi Sans Light 20pt
*Suomi Sans Light Italic* 20pt
**Suomi Sans Book** 20pt
***Suomi Sans Book Italic*** 20pt
**Suomi Sans Medium** 20pt
***Suomi Sans Medium Italic*** 20pt
**Suomi Sans Bold** 20pt
***Suomi Sans Bold Italic*** 20pt
**Suomi Sans Black** 20pt
***Suomi Sans Black Italic*** 20pt

---

12/14  Suomi Sans Light

The quick brown fox jumps over the lazy dog. Voyez le brick géant que j'examine près du wharf. Zwölf Boxkämpfer jagen Viktor quer über den großen Sylter Deich. El veloz murciélago

9/12  Suomi Sans Light

The quick brown fox jumps over the lazy dog. Voyez le brick géant que j'examine près du wharf. Zwölf Boxkämpfer jagen Viktor quer über den großen Sylter Deich. El veloz murciélago hindú comía feliz cardillo y kiwi. La cigüeña tocaba el saxofón detrás del palenque de pajaatur? Rissimo lorereped ex es solore

7/10  Suomi Sans Light

The quick brown fox jumps over the lazy dog. Voyez le brick géant que j'examine près du wharf. Zwölf Boxkämpfer jagen Viktor quer über den großen Sylter Deich. El veloz murciélago hindú comía feliz cardillo y kiwi. La cigüeña tocaba el saxofón detrás del palenque de pajaatur? Rissimo lorereped ex es solore lab id molorro in rempore icabore rehenetur aliam aut voles audae dem quam, secum eum facesequae consequ aepudam quia voluptiur repel in et faccustibus, nonsenis aut

12/14  Suomi Sans Book

The quick brown fox jumps over the lazy dog. Voyez le brick géant que j'examine près du wharf. Zwölf Boxkämpfer jagen Viktor quer über den großen Sylter Deich. El veloz mur-

9/12  Suomi Sans Book

The quick brown fox jumps over the lazy dog. Voyez le brick géant que j'examine près du wharf. Zwölf Boxkämpfer jagen Viktor quer über den großen Sylter Deich. El veloz murciélago hindú comía feliz cardillo y kiwi. La cigüeña tocaba el saxofón detrás del palenque de pajaatur? Rissimo lorereped ex

7/10  Suomi Sans Book

The quick brown fox jumps over the lazy dog. Voyez le brick géant que j'examine près du wharf. Zwölf Boxkämpfer jagen Viktor quer über den großen Sylter Deich. El veloz murciélago hindú comía feliz cardillo y kiwi. La cigüeña tocaba el saxofón detrás del palenque de pajaatur? Rissimo lorereped ex es solore lab id molorro in rempore icabore rehenetur aliam aut voles audae dem quam, secum eum facesequae consequ aepudam quia voluptiur repel in et

12/14  Suomi Sans Medium

**The quick brown fox jumps over the lazy dog. Voyez le brick géant que j'examine près du wharf. Zwölf Boxkämpfer jagen Viktor quer über den großen Sylter Deich.**

9/12  Suomi Sans Medium

**The quick brown fox jumps over the lazy dog. Voyez le brick géant que j'examine près du wharf. Zwölf Boxkämpfer jagen Viktor quer über den großen Sylter Deich. El veloz murciélago hindú comía feliz cardillo y kiwi. La cigüeña tocaba el saxofón detrás del palenque de**

7/10  Suomi Sans Medium

**The quick brown fox jumps over the lazy dog. Voyez le brick géant que j'examine près du wharf. Zwölf Boxkämpfer jagen Viktor quer über den großen Sylter Deich. El veloz murciélago hindú comía feliz cardillo y kiwi. La cigüeña tocaba el saxofón detrás del palenque de pajaatur? Rissimo lorereped ex es solore lab id molorro in rempore icabore rehenetur aliam aut voles audae dem quam, secum eum facesequae consequ aepudam**

12/14  Suomi Sans Bold

**The quick brown fox jumps over the lazy dog. Voyez le brick géant que j'examine près du wharf. Zwölf Boxkämpfer jagen Viktor quer über den großen Sylter Deich. El veloz murciélago hindú comía feliz cardillo y kiwi. La cigüeña tocaba el**

9/12  Suomi Sans Bold

**The quick brown fox jumps over the lazy dog. Voyez le brick géant que j'examine près du wharf. Zwölf Boxkämpfer jagen Viktor quer über den großen Sylter Deich. El veloz murciélago hindú comía feliz cardillo y kiwi. La cigüeña tocaba el saxofón detrás del palenque de pajaatur? Rissimo lorereped ex es solore lab id molorro in rempore icabore rehenetur aliam aut voles**

7/10  Suomi Sans Bold

**The quick brown fox jumps over the lazy dog. Voyez le brick géant que j'examine près du wharf. Zwölf Boxkämpfer jagen Viktor quer über den großen Sylter Deich. El veloz murciélago hindú comía feliz cardillo y kiwi. La cigüeña tocaba el saxofón detrás del palenque de pajaatur? Rissimo lorereped ex es solore lab id molorro in rempore icabore rehenetur aliam aut voles audae dem quam, secum eum facesequae consequ aepudam quia voluptiur repel in et faccustibus, nonsenis aut quisqui rero mi, ipiet lam ant ut maio et hil molupta**

# T
## TypeTogether

Veronika Burian, José Scaglione

Prague, Czech Republic & Rosario, Argentina

Since 2006

Veronika Burian and José Scaglione, who met at the University of Reading whilst completing their MAs in Type Design, joined forces in 2006 to set up their independent type foundry TypeTogether. Besides their own designs they have published typefaces by Eduardo Berliner, Bart Blubaugh, David Březina, Pilar Cano, Nicolien van der Keur, Gerard Unger and others. In 2010 they launched a side project with David Březina: Rosetta type foundry, specializing in multi-script fonts that include non-Latin scripts such as Arabic and Cyrillic.

## Info

—Why?
TypeTogether developed out of the desire to publish high quality typefaces and work on new type projects together (hence the name). Our main interest was and still is to find innovative and stylish solutions to old problems for the professional market of text typefaces, with a focus on editorial use. This is where the greatest challenges are faced: creating typefaces that perform well in continuous reading, and that also have a high degree of personality.

—People on staff
3

—Type designers on staff
2

—Type families
20

—Designers represented
11

— Webshop
type-together.com

—Distributors
MyFonts, Veer, Fontshop, Linotype, Fontdeck

—Webfont services
Fontdeck, FontsLive, Typekit, WebINK, MyFonts

—Additional services
Custom fonts. Any typography-related consultancy.

—Basic license
€29–€89 per font (1–5 CPUs)

Typeface selection

Abril
Adelle
Athelas
**Bree**
Karmina
Maiola PE
**Ronnia**
Skolar PE

24pt

## People

—Veronika Burian, born in Prague, got her first degree in Industrial Design in Munich, Germany, before she moved on to Austria and Italy to work as a mix between a product and graphic designer. Discovering her true passion for type, she graduated with distinction from the MA in Typeface Design in Reading, UK, in 2003 and started to work as full-time type designer at DaltonMaag in London.
After a 3-year stay in Boulder, Colorado, she is currently living and working in Prague and dedicates her time fully to TypeTogether. She continues to give lectures and workshops at international conferences and universities. Her typeface Maiola received, among others, the TDC Certificate of Excellence in Type Design 2004. Several other typefaces by TypeTogether have also been recognised by international competitions.

—José Scaglione is an Argentinian graphic and multimedia designer, and a graduate from the MA in Typeface Design at the University of Reading, UK. He has been working in branding, editorial design and multimedia projects since 1995. He was co-founder of the Vision Media Design Studio in Argentina and art director at Multiplicity Advertising and The Prepaid Press in USA. In addition to his work for TypeTogether, José runs his own design studio, and consults and lectures on typography and graphic communication matters. He also teaches typography at post-graduate level at the National University of Rosario. José is a board member of ATypI (Association Typographique Internationale) and was appointed Chairman of Letter.2, the second international typeface design competition by ATypI.

Poster from a TypeTogether exhibition, showing the Crete typeface.

Page 253

Euro sign in Bree. 　Abril Display

Skolar

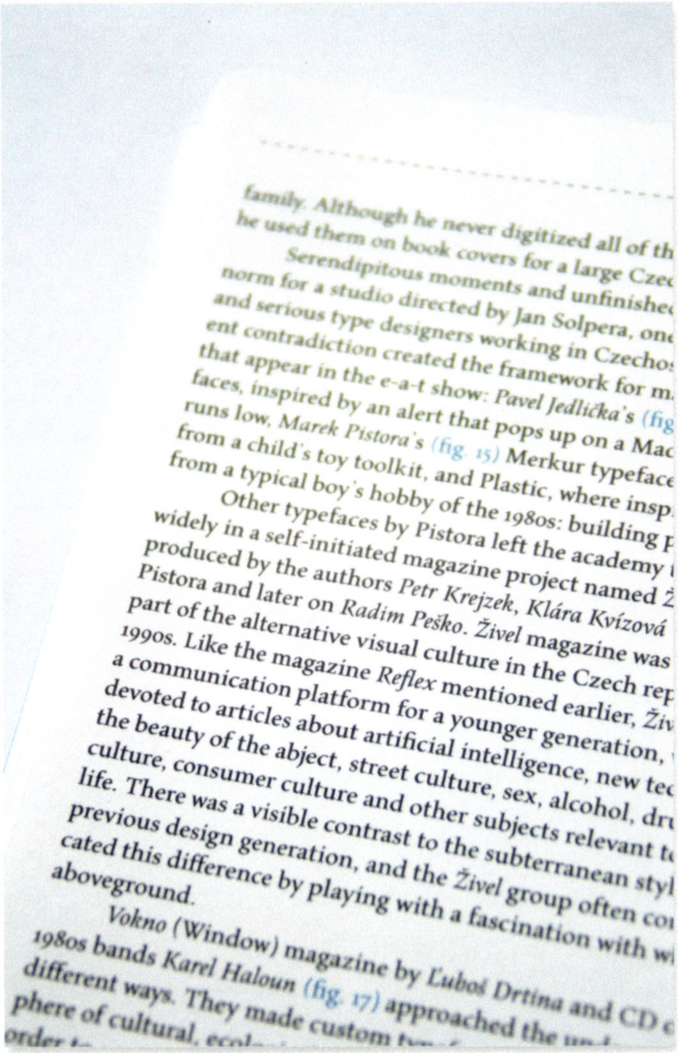

Maiola was used in the catalog of E-a-T (Experiment and Typography), an exhibition on type in the Czech and Slovak Republics.

Specimens of Soleil, Maiol, Skolar and Sirba.

Pilar Cano's Edita in use as body type in the award-winning magazine *komma*, published by the department of design of the Hochschule Mannheim, Germany.

Foundry  TypeTogether

Typeface  Abril
Designer  José Scaglione, Veronika Burian
Year  2011
Format  OpenType

# Aa

## Abril Display Regular 20pt
## **Abril Display Extra Bold 20pt**

Abril Text Regular 12pt
**Abril Text Extra Bold 12pt**

Aa Bb Cc Dd Ee Ff Gg Hh Ii Jj Kk Ll Mm Nn Oo Pp Qq Rr Ss Tt Uu Vv Ww Xx Yy Zz
0123456789
—

9/12  Abril Text Regular

The quick brown fox jumps over the lazy dog. Voyez le brick géant que j'examine près du wharf. Zwölf Boxkämpfer jagen Viktor quer über den großen Sylter Deich. El veloz murciélago hindú comía feliz cardillo y kiwi. La cigüeña tocaba el saxofón detrás del palenque de pajaatur? Rissimo lorereped ex es solore lab id molorro in rempore icabore rehenetur

7/10  Abril Text Regular

The quick brown fox jumps over the lazy dog. Voyez le brick géant que j'examine près du wharf. Zwölf Boxkämpfer jagen Viktor quer über den großen Sylter Deich. El veloz murciélago hindú comía feliz cardillo y kiwi. La cigüeña tocaba el saxofón detrás del palenque de pajaatur? Rissimo lorereped ex es solore lab id molorro in rempore icabore rehenetur aliam aut voles audae dem quam, secum eum facesequae consequ aepudam quia voluptiur repel in et faccustibus, nonsenis aut quisqui rero mi, ipiet lam ant ut maio et hil molupta tustis atatur, consedi tasimol orerem aut volor andipsapis sit, illaut

---

Typeface  Athelas
Designer  José Scaglione, Veronika Burian
Year  2008
Format  OpenType

# Aa

## Athelas Regular 20pt
## *Athelas Italic 20pt*
## **Athelas Bold 20pt**
## ***Athelas Bold Italic 20pt***

Aa Bb Cc Dd Ee Ff Gg Hh Ii Jj Kk Ll Mm Nn Oo Pp Qq Rr Ss Tt Uu Vv Ww Xx Yy Zz
0123456789
—

9/12  Athelas Regular

The quick brown fox jumps over the lazy dog. Voyez le brick géant que j'examine près du wharf. Zwölf Boxkämpfer jagen Viktor quer über den großen Sylter Deich. El veloz murciélago hindú comía feliz cardillo y kiwi. La cigüeña tocaba el saxofón detrás del palenque de pajaatur? Rissimo lorereped ex es solore lab id molorro in rempore icabore rehenetur aliam aut voles audae dem quam, secum eum

7/10  Athelas Regular

The quick brown fox jumps over the lazy dog. Voyez le brick géant que j'examine près du wharf. Zwölf Boxkämpfer jagen Viktor quer über den großen Sylter Deich. El veloz murciélago hindú comía feliz cardillo y kiwi. La cigüeña tocaba el saxofón detrás del palenque de pajaatur? Rissimo lorereped ex es solore lab id molorro in rempore icabore rehenetur aliam aut voles audae dem quam, secum eum facesequae consequ aepudam quia voluptiur repel in et faccustibus, nonsenis aut quisqui rero mi, ipiet lam ant ut maio et hil molupta tustis atatur, consedi tasimol orerem aut volor andipsapis sit, illaut volore officatus alicae dusdaec tatecte

12/14  **Athelas Bold**

**The quick brown fox jumps over the lazy dog. Voyez le brick géant que j'examine près du wharf. Zwölf Boxkämpfer jagen Viktor quer über den großen Sylter Deich. El veloz murciélago hindú comía feliz cardillo y kiwi. La cigüeña tocaba el saxofón detrás del palenque de pajaatur? Rissimo lorereped ex es solore lab**

9/12  **Athelas Bold**

**The quick brown fox jumps over the lazy dog. Voyez le brick géant que j'examine près du wharf. Zwölf Boxkämpfer jagen Viktor quer über den großen Sylter Deich. El veloz murciélago hindú comía feliz cardillo y kiwi. La cigüeña tocaba el saxofón detrás del palenque de pajaatur? Rissimo lorereped ex es solore lab id molorro in rempore icabore rehenetur aliam aut voles audae dem quam, secum eum facesequae consequ aepudam quia voluptiur repel in et faccustibus, nonsenis**

7/10  **Athelas Bold**

**The quick brown fox jumps over the lazy dog. Voyez le brick géant que j'examine près du wharf. Zwölf Boxkämpfer jagen Viktor quer über den großen Sylter Deich. El veloz murciélago hindú comía feliz cardillo y kiwi. La cigüeña tocaba el saxofón detrás del palenque de pajaatur? Rissimo lorereped ex es solore lab id molorro in rempore icabore rehenetur aliam aut voles audae dem quam, secum eum facesequae consequ aepudam quia voluptiur repel in et faccustibus, nonsenis aut quisqui rero mi, ipiet lam ant ut maio et hil molupta tustis atatur, consedi tasimol orerem aut volor andipsapis sit, illaut volore officatus alicae dusdaec tatecte cearum qui accatibus restiore nulpa secaerferum, nus dolenim in et quoditat que explam volupictur? Qui de**

Foundry  TypeTogether

Typeface  Adelle
Designer  José Scaglione, Veronika Burian
Year  2009
Format  OpenType

# Aa

Aa Bb Cc Dd Ee Ff Gg Hh Ii Jj Kk Ll Mm Nn Oo Pp Qq Rr Ss Tt Uu Vv Ww Xx Yy Zz
0123456789

—

Adelle Thin 20pt
*Adelle Thin Italic 20pt*
Adelle Light 20pt
*Adelle Light Italic 20pt*
Adelle Regular 20pt
*Adelle Italic 20pt*
**Adelle Semi Bold 20pt**
***Adelle Semi Bold Italic 20pt***
**Adelle Bold 20pt**
***Adelle Bold Italic 20pt***
**Adelle Extra Bold 20pt**
***Adelle Extra Bold Italic 20pt***
**Adelle Heavy 20pt**
***Adelle Heavy Italic 20pt***

---

12/14  Adelle Light

The quick brown fox jumps over the lazy dog. Voyez le brick géant que j'examine près du wharf. Zwölf Boxkämpfer jagen Viktor quer

12/14  Adelle Regular

The quick brown fox jumps over the lazy dog. Voyez le brick géant que j'examine près du wharf. Zwölf Boxkämpfer jagen Vik-

12/14  Adelle Medium

The quick brown fox jumps over the lazy dog. Voyez le brick géant que j'examine près du wharf. Zwölf Boxkämpfer jagen Vik-

12/14  Adelle Bold

**The quick brown fox jumps over the lazy dog. Voyez le brick géant que j'examine près du wharf. Zwölf Boxkämpfer jagen Viktor quer über den großen Sylter Deich. El veloz murciélago hindú**

9/12  Adelle Light

The quick brown fox jumps over the lazy dog. Voyez le brick géant que j'examine près du wharf. Zwölf Boxkämpfer jagen Viktor quer über den großen Sylter Deich. El veloz murciélago hindú comía feliz cardillo y kiwi. La

9/12  Adelle Regular

The quick brown fox jumps over the lazy dog. Voyez le brick géant que j'examine près du wharf. Zwölf Boxkämpfer jagen Viktor quer über den großen Sylter Deich. El veloz murciélago hindú comía feliz cardillo y kiwi. La

9/12  Adelle Medium

The quick brown fox jumps over the lazy dog. Voyez le brick géant que j'examine près du wharf. Zwölf Boxkämpfer jagen Viktor quer über den großen Sylter Deich. El veloz murciélago hindú comía feliz cardillo y kiwi. La

9/12  Adelle Bold

**The quick brown fox jumps over the lazy dog. Voyez le brick géant que j'examine près du wharf. Zwölf Boxkämpfer jagen Viktor quer über den großen Sylter Deich. El veloz murciélago hindú comía feliz cardillo y kiwi. La cigüeña tocaba el saxofón detrás del palenque de pajaatur? Rissimo lorereped ex**

7/10  Adelle Light

The quick brown fox jumps over the lazy dog. Voyez le brick géant que j'examine près du wharf. Zwölf Boxkämpfer jagen Viktor quer über den großen Sylter Deich. El veloz murciélago hindú comía feliz cardillo y kiwi. La cigüeña tocaba el saxofón detrás del palenque de pajaatur? Rissimo lorereped ex es solore lab id molorro in rempore icabore

7/10  Adelle Regular

The quick brown fox jumps over the lazy dog. Voyez le brick géant que j'examine près du wharf. Zwölf Boxkämpfer jagen Viktor quer über den großen Sylter Deich. El veloz murciélago hindú comía feliz cardillo y kiwi. La cigüeña tocaba el saxofón detrás del palenque de pajaatur? Rissimo lorereped ex es solore lab id molorro in rempore icabore

7/10  Adelle Medium

The quick brown fox jumps over the lazy dog. Voyez le brick géant que j'examine près du wharf. Zwölf Boxkämpfer jagen Viktor quer über den großen Sylter Deich. El veloz murciélago hindú comía feliz cardillo y kiwi. La cigüeña tocaba el saxofón detrás del palenque de pajaatur? Rissimo lorereped ex es solore lab id molorro in rempore icabore

7/10  Adelle Bold

**The quick brown fox jumps over the lazy dog. Voyez le brick géant que j'examine près du wharf. Zwölf Boxkämpfer jagen Viktor quer über den großen Sylter Deich. El veloz murciélago hindú comía feliz cardillo y kiwi. La cigüeña tocaba el saxofón detrás del palenque de pajaatur? Rissimo lorereped ex es solore lab id molorro in rempore icabore rehenetur aliam aut voles audae dem quam, secum eum facesequae consequ aepudam quia voluptiur repel**

Typeface  Karmina
Designer  José Scaglione,
          Veronika Burian

Foundry  TypeTogether
Year     2007
Format   OpenType

# Aa

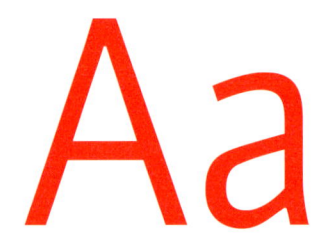

Aa Bb Cc Dd Ee Ff Gg Hh Ii Jj Kk Ll
Mm Nn Oo Pp Qq Rr Ss Tt Uu Vv Ww
Xx Yy Zz
0123456789
—

Karmina Sans Light 18pt
*Karmina Sans Light Italic 18pt*
Karmina Sans Regular 18pt
*Karmina Sans Italic 18pt*
**Karmina Sans Semi Bold 18pt**
***Karmina Sans Semi Bold Italic 18pt***
**Karmina Sans Bold 18pt**
***Karmina Sans Bold Italic 18pt***
**Karmina Sans Extra Bold 18pt**
***Karmina Sans Extra Bold Italic 18pt***
**Karmina Sans Heavy 18pt**
***Karmina Sans Heavy Italic 18pt***
Karmina Regular 18pt
*Karmina Italic 18pt*
**Karmina Bold 18pt**
***Karmina Bold Italic 18pt***

---

12/14  Karmina Light

The quick brown fox jumps over the lazy dog. Voyez le brick géant que j'examine près du wharf. Zwölf Boxkämpfer jagen Viktor quer über den großen Sylter

12/14  Karmina Regular

The quick brown fox jumps over the lazy dog. Voyez le brick géant que j'examine près du wharf. Zwölf Boxkämpfer jagen Viktor quer über den großen Sylter

12/14  Karmina SemiBold

The quick brown fox jumps over the lazy dog. Voyez le brick géant que j'examine près du wharf. Zwölf Boxkämpfer jagen Viktor quer über den großen Sylter

12/14  Karmina Bold

**The quick brown fox jumps over the lazy dog. Voyez le brick géant que j'examine près du wharf. Zwölf Boxkämpfer jagen Viktor quer über den großen Sylter Deich. El veloz murciélago hindú comía feliz cardillo y kiwi. La**

9/12  Karmina Light

The quick brown fox jumps over the lazy dog. Voyez le brick géant que j'examine près du wharf. Zwölf Boxkämpfer jagen Viktor quer über den großen Sylter Deich. El veloz murciélago hindú comía feliz cardillo y kiwi. La cigüeña tocaba el saxofón detrás del palen-

9/12  Karmina Regular

The quick brown fox jumps over the lazy dog. Voyez le brick géant que j'examine près du wharf. Zwölf Boxkämpfer jagen Viktor quer über den großen Sylter Deich. El veloz murciélago hindú comía feliz cardillo y kiwi. La cigüeña tocaba el saxofón detrás del palenque

9/12  Karmina SemiBold

The quick brown fox jumps over the lazy dog. Voyez le brick géant que j'examine près du wharf. Zwölf Boxkämpfer jagen Viktor quer über den großen Sylter Deich. El veloz murciélago hindú comía feliz cardillo y kiwi. La cigüeña tocaba el saxofón detrás del palen-

9/12  Karmina Bold

**The quick brown fox jumps over the lazy dog. Voyez le brick géant que j'examine près du wharf. Zwölf Boxkämpfer jagen Viktor quer über den großen Sylter Deich. El veloz murciélago hindú comía feliz cardillo y kiwi. La cigüeña tocaba el saxofón detrás del palenque de pajaatur? Rissimo lorereped ex es solore lab id molorro in rempore icabore rehene-**

7/10  Karmina Light

The quick brown fox jumps over the lazy dog. Voyez le brick géant que j'examine près du wharf. Zwölf Boxkämpfer jagen Viktor quer über den großen Sylter Deich. El veloz murciélago hindú comía feliz cardillo y kiwi. La cigüeña tocaba el saxofón detrás del palenque de pajaatur? Rissimo lorereped ex es solore lab id molorro in rempore icabore rehenetur aliam aut voles audae dem quam, secum eum

7/10  Karmina Regular

The quick brown fox jumps over the lazy dog. Voyez le brick géant que j'examine près du wharf. Zwölf Boxkämpfer jagen Viktor quer über den großen Sylter Deich. El veloz murciélago hindú comía feliz cardillo y kiwi. La cigüeña tocaba el saxofón detrás del palenque de pajaatur? Rissimo lorereped ex es solore lab id molorro in rempore icabore rehenetur aliam aut voles audae dem quam, secum eum

7/10  Karmina SemiBold

The quick brown fox jumps over the lazy dog. Voyez le brick géant que j'examine près du wharf. Zwölf Boxkämpfer jagen Viktor quer über den großen Sylter Deich. El veloz murciélago hindú comía feliz cardillo y kiwi. La cigüeña tocaba el saxofón detrás del palenque de pajaatur? Rissimo lorereped ex es solore lab id molorro in rempore icabore rehenetur aliam aut voles audae dem quam, secum eum

7/10  Karmina Bold

**The quick brown fox jumps over the lazy dog. Voyez le brick géant que j'examine près du wharf. Zwölf Boxkämpfer jagen Viktor quer über den großen Sylter Deich. El veloz murciélago hindú comía feliz cardillo y kiwi. La cigüeña tocaba el saxofón detrás del palenque de pajaatur? Rissimo lorereped ex es solore lab id molorro in rempore icabore rehenetur aliam aut voles audae dem quam, secum eum facesequae consequ aepudam quia voluptiur repel in et faccustibus, nonsenis aut quisqui rero mi, ipiet lam ant ut maio et hil molupta**

Typeface   Ronnia
Designer   José Scaglione, Veronika Burian

Foundry   TypeTogether
Year   2007
Format   OpenType

# Aa

Aa Bb Cc Dd Ee Ff Gg Hh Ii Jj Kk
Ll Mm Nn Oo Pp Qq Rr Ss Tt Uu
Vv Ww Xx Yy Zz
0123456789
—

Ronnia Condensed Thin 20pt
*Ronnia Condensed Thin Italic* 20pt
Ronnia Thin 20pt
*Ronnia Thin Italic* 20pt
Ronnia Condensed Light 20pt
*Ronnia Condensed Light Italic* 20pt
Ronnia Light 20pt
*Ronnia Light Italic* 20pt
Ronnia Condensed Regular 20pt
*Ronnia Condensed Italic* 20pt
Ronnia Regular 20pt
*Ronnia Italic* 20pt
**Ronnia Condensed Semi Bold** 20pt
***Ronnia Condensed Semi Bold Italic*** 20pt
**Ronnia Semi Bold** 20pt
***Ronnia Semi Bold Italic*** 20pt
**Ronnia Condensed Bold** 20pt
***Ronnia Condensed Bold Italic*** 20pt
**Ronnia Bold** 20pt
***Ronnia Bold Italic*** 20pt
**Ronnia Condensed Extra Bold** 20pt
***Ronnia Condensed Extra Bold Italic*** 20pt
**Ronnia Extra Bold** 20pt
***Ronnia Extra Bold Italic*** 20pt
**Ronnia Condensed Heavy** 20pt
***Ronnia Condensed Heavy Italic*** 20pt
**Ronnia Heavy** 20pt
***Ronnia Heavy Italic* 20pt**

12/14   Ronnia Light

The quick brown fox jumps over the lazy dog. Voyez le brick géant que j'examine près du wharf. Zwölf Boxkämpfer jagen Viktor quer über den

12/14   Ronnia Regular

The quick brown fox jumps over the lazy dog. Voyez le brick géant que j'examine près du wharf. Zwölf Boxkämpfer jagen Viktor quer über den

12/14   Ronnia SemiBold

**The quick brown fox jumps over the lazy dog. Voyez le brick géant que j'examine près du wharf. Zwölf Boxkämpfer jagen Viktor quer über den**

12/14   Ronnia Bold

**The quick brown fox jumps over the lazy dog. Voyez le brick géant que j'examine près du wharf. Zwölf Boxkämpfer jagen Viktor quer über den großen Sylter Deich. El veloz murciélago hindú comía feliz cardillo y**

| Foundry | TypeTogether |

Typeface  Maiola PE
Designer  Veronika Burian
Year      2005–2011
Format    OpenType

# Aa

Maiola PE Book 20pt
*Maiola PE Book Italic 20pt*
Maiola PE Regular 20pt
*Maiola PE Italic 20pt*
**Maiola PE Bold 20pt**
***Maiola PE Bold Italic 20pt***

Aa Bb Cc Dd Ee Ff Gg Hh Ii Jj Kk Ll Mm Nn Oo Pp Qq Rr Ss Tt Uu Vv Ww Xx Yy Zz
0123456789
—

9/12  Maiola PE Regular

The quick brown fox jumps over the lazy dog. Voyez le brick géant que j'examine près du wharf. Zwölf Boxkämpfer jagen Viktor quer über den großen Sylter Deich. El veloz murciélago hindú comía feliz cardillo y kiwi. La cigüeña tocaba el saxofón detrás del palenque de pajaatur? Rissimo lorereped ex es solore lab id molorro in rempore icabore rehenetur aliam aut voles audae dem quam, secum eum facesequae consequ aepudam quia voluptiur repel in et faccustibus, nonsenis aut quis-

7/10  Maiola PE Regular

The quick brown fox jumps over the lazy dog. Voyez le brick géant que j'examine près du wharf. Zwölf Boxkämpfer jagen Viktor quer über den großen Sylter Deich. El veloz murciélago hindú comía feliz cardillo y kiwi. La cigüeña tocaba el saxofón detrás del palenque de pajaatur? Rissimo lorereped ex es solore lab id molorro in rempore icabore rehenetur aliam aut voles audae dem quam, secum eum facesequae consequ aepudam quia voluptiur repel in et faccustibus, nonsenis aut quisqui rero mi, ipiet lam ant ut maio et hil molupta tustis atatur, consedi tasimol orerem aut volor andipsapis sit, illaut volore officatus alicae dusdaec tatecte cearum qui accatibus restiore nulpa secaerferum, nus dolenim in et quoditat que explam volupictur? Qui de illuptae. Dae nis illiberum

Typeface  Skolar PE
Designer  David Březina
Year      2009
Format    OpenType

# Aa

Skolar PE Regular 20pt
*Skolar PE Italic 20pt*
**Skolar PE Semi Bold 20pt**
***Skolar PE Semi Bold Italic 20pt***
**Skolar PE Bold 20pt**
***Skolar PE Bold Italic 20pt***

Aa Bb Cc Dd Ee Ff Gg Hh Ii Jj Kk Ll Mm Nn Oo Pp Qq Rr Ss Tt Uu Vv Ww Xx Yy Zz
0123456789
—

9/12  Skolar PE Regular

The quick brown fox jumps over the lazy dog. Voyez le brick géant que j'examine près du wharf. Zwölf Boxkämpfer jagen Viktor quer über den großen Sylter Deich. El veloz murciélago hindú comía feliz cardillo y kiwi. La cigüeña tocaba el saxofón detrás del palenque de pajaatur? Rissimo lorereped ex es solore lab id molorro in rempore icabore rehenetur aliam aut voles audae dem quam, secum eum facesequae consequ aepudam quia voluptiur repel in et faccustibus, nonsenis aut quisqui rero mi, ipiet lam ant ut maio et hil molupta tustis atatur, consedi tasimol orerem aut volor andipsapis sit, illaut volore officatus alicae dusdaec tatecte cearum qui accatibus

7/10  Skolar PE Regular

The quick brown fox jumps over the lazy dog. Voyez le brick géant que j'examine près du wharf. Zwölf Boxkämpfer jagen Viktor quer über den großen Sylter Deich. El veloz murciélago hindú comía feliz cardillo y kiwi. La cigüeña tocaba el saxofón detrás del palenque de pajaatur? Rissimo lorereped ex es solore lab id molorro in rempore icabore rehenetur aliam aut voles audae dem quam, secum eum facesequae consequ aepudam quia voluptiur repel in et faccustibus, nonsenis aut quisqui rero mi, ipiet lam ant ut maio et hil molupta tustis atatur, consedi tasimol orerem aut volor andipsapis sit, illaut volore officatus alicae dusdaec tatecte cearum qui accatibus restiore nulpa secaerferum, nus dolenim in et quoditat que explam volupictur? Qui de illuptae. Dae nis illiberum volorro ritatis tinullo rerumqu atetur repro eatius asperibus. Rissimo lorereped ex es solore lab id molorro in rempore icabore rehenetur aliam aut voles audae dem quam, secum eum facesequae consequ aepudam quia voluptiur repel in et faccustibus, nonsenis aut quisqui rero

Typeface **Bree**
Designer José Scaglione, Veronika Burian

Foundry **TypeTogether**
Year 2008
Format OpenType

# Aa

Aa Bb Cc Dd Ee Ff Gg Hh Ii Jj Kk Ll Mm Nn Oo Pp Qq Rr Ss Tt Uu Vv Ww Xx Yy Zz
0123456789
—

Bree Thin 24pt
*Bree Thin Oblique* 24pt
Bree Light 24pt
*Bree Light Oblique* 24pt
**Bree Regular** 24pt
*Bree Oblique* 24pt
**Bree Bold** 24pt
***Bree Bold Oblique*** 24pt
**Bree Extra Bold** 24pt
***Bree Bold Oblique*** 24pt

---

12/14  Bree Thin

The quick brown fox jumps over the lazy dog. Voyez le brick géant que j'examine près du wharf. Zwölf Boxkämpfer jagen Viktor quer über den

12/14  Bree Light

The quick brown fox jumps over the lazy dog. Voyez le brick géant que j'examine près du wharf. Zwölf Boxkämpfer jagen Viktor quer über den

12/14  Bree Regular

The quick brown fox jumps over the lazy dog. Voyez le brick géant que j'examine près du wharf. Zwölf Boxkämpfer jagen Viktor quer über den

12/14  Bree Bold

**The quick brown fox jumps over the lazy dog. Voyez le brick géant que j'examine près du wharf. Zwölf Boxkämpfer jagen Viktor quer über den großen Sylter Deich. El veloz murciélago hindú comía feliz cardillo y kiwi.**

---

9/12  Bree Thin

The quick brown fox jumps over the lazy dog. Voyez le brick géant que j'examine près du wharf. Zwölf Boxkämpfer jagen Viktor quer über den großen Sylter Deich. El veloz murciélago hindú comía feliz cardillo y kiwi. La cigüeña tocaba el saxofón detrás

9/12  Bree Light

The quick brown fox jumps over the lazy dog. Voyez le brick géant que j'examine près du wharf. Zwölf Boxkämpfer jagen Viktor quer über den großen Sylter Deich. El veloz murciélago hindú comía feliz cardillo y kiwi. La cigüeña tocaba el saxofón detrás

9/12  Bree Regular

The quick brown fox jumps over the lazy dog. Voyez le brick géant que j'examine près du wharf. Zwölf Boxkämpfer jagen Viktor quer über den großen Sylter Deich. El veloz murciélago hindú comía feliz cardillo y kiwi. La cigüeña tocaba el saxofón

9/12  Bree Bold

**The quick brown fox jumps over the lazy dog. Voyez le brick géant que j'examine près du wharf. Zwölf Boxkämpfer jagen Viktor quer über den großen Sylter Deich. El veloz murciélago hindú comía feliz cardillo y kiwi. La cigüeña tocaba el saxofón detrás del palenque de pajaatur? Rissimo lorereped ex es solore lab id molorro in rempore**

---

7/10  Bree Thin

The quick brown fox jumps over the lazy dog. Voyez le brick géant que j'examine près du wharf. Zwölf Boxkämpfer jagen Viktor quer über den großen Sylter Deich. El veloz murciélago hindú comía feliz cardillo y kiwi. La cigüeña tocaba el saxofón detrás del palenque de pajaatur? Rissimo lorereped ex es solore lab id molorro in rempore icabore rehenetur aliam aut voles audae dem quam, secum eum

7/10  Bree Light

The quick brown fox jumps over the lazy dog. Voyez le brick géant que j'examine près du wharf. Zwölf Boxkämpfer jagen Viktor quer über den großen Sylter Deich. El veloz murciélago hindú comía feliz cardillo y kiwi. La cigüeña tocaba el saxofón detrás del palenque de pajaatur? Rissimo lorereped ex es solore lab id molorro in rempore icabore rehenetur aliam aut voles audae dem

7/10  Bree Regular

The quick brown fox jumps over the lazy dog. Voyez le brick géant que j'examine près du wharf. Zwölf Boxkämpfer jagen Viktor quer über den großen Sylter Deich. El veloz murciélago hindú comía feliz cardillo y kiwi. La cigüeña tocaba el saxofón detrás del palenque de pajaatur? Rissimo lorereped ex es solore lab id molorro in rempore icabore rehenetur aliam aut voles audae dem

7/10  Bree Bold

**The quick brown fox jumps over the lazy dog. Voyez le brick géant que j'examine près du wharf. Zwölf Boxkämpfer jagen Viktor quer über den großen Sylter Deich. El veloz murciélago hindú comía feliz cardillo y kiwi. La cigüeña tocaba el saxofón detrás del palenque de pajaatur? Rissimo lorereped ex es solore lab id molorro in rempore icabore rehenetur aliam aut voles audae dem quam, secum eum facesequae consequ aepudam quia voluptiur repel in et faccustibus, nonsenis aut quisqui rero mi, ipiet**

# T
## TypeTrust

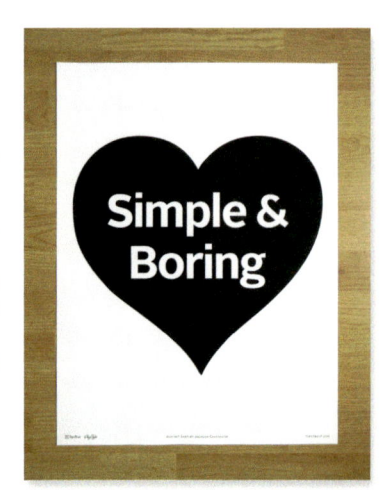

Silas Dilworth,
Neil Summerour

Los Angeles, USA

Since 2005

TypeTrust is both a foundry and a boutique retail platform. It is the label under which Silas Dilworth's fonts are marketed, and it sells fonts by a number of other studios and individual designers, including Neil Summerour's Positype, Jackson Cavanaugh's Okay Type, Marconi Lima's Typefolio, Chris Dickinson's MoreType, and the band REM.

## Info

—Why?
We established TypeTrust as a direct and sustainable channel between the dedicated type designer and the devoted type enthusiast. As type designers, we believe that our audience is best served by our unmediated involvement in the marketing and management of our products and services.

—People on staff
1

—Type designers on staff
2

—Type families
Approx. 20

—Designers represented
15

—Web shop
typetrust.com

—Distributors
MyFonts, Veer, FontShop, TypeTrust

—Prices/Licenses/Conditions:
Visit the TypeTrust website for more information.

Typeface selection

Breuer Condensed
**Breuer Headline**
Breuer Text
**Facebuster**
Vandermark

24pt

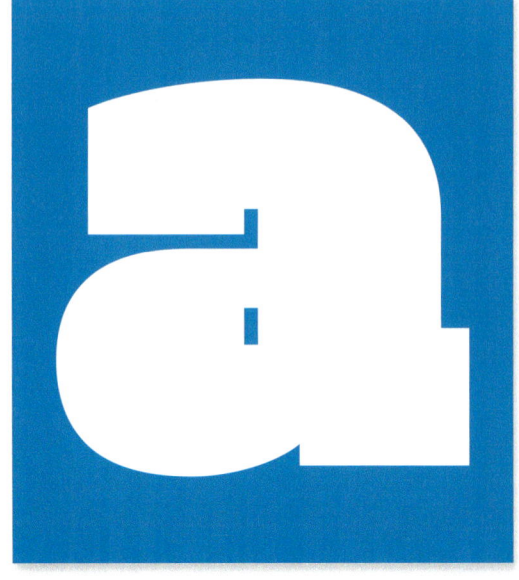

## People

—Silas Dilworth began his typographic career in 2001, as font technician at T26, designing custom fonts and overseeing the production and promotion of hundreds of new releases. Dilworth complements his typographic activities providing graphic design and web development services to artists and entrepreneurs in the contemporary art community.

—Neil Summerour has published over forty typeface families (over 420 fonts) through his foundry, Positype. He has acted as a contributing writer for Typographi.com, has lectured on type design in Japan and the U.S., and served as a professor of Graphic Design at The University of Georgia Lamar Dodd School of Art.

Specimen for Alright Sans by Jackson Cavanaugh of Brooklyn's Okay Type.

Facebuster

Page 261

Specimen posters for Nori by Neil Summerour and for Silas Dilworth's Heroic Condensed.

Vandermark

Breuer Condensed

Page 262　　Foundry　TypeTrust

---

Typeface　Breuer Headline　　Year　　2007
Designer　Silas Dilworth　　Format　OpenType

# Barcelona *Chair*

Regular
*Oblique*

Aa Bb Cc Dd Ee Ff Gg Hh Ii Jj Kk Ll Mm Nn Oo Pp Qq Rr Ss Tt Uu Vv Ww Xx Yy Zz 0123456789

Typeface　Breuer Condensed　　Year　　2009
Designer　Silas Dilworth　　Format　OpenType

# Mies Pavillon

Light
*Light Italic*
Regular
*Regular Italic*
Medium
*Medium Italic*
**Bold**
***Bold Italic***

---

Typeface　Vandermark　　Year　　2005
Designer　Silas Dilworth　　Format　OpenType

# Transatlantic *Cruiser*

Regular
*Oblique*

Aa Bb Cc Dd Ee Ff Gg Hh Ii Jj Kk Ll Mm Nn Oo Pp Qq Rr Ss Tt Uu Vv Ww Xx Yy Zz 0123456789

---

Typeface　Facebuster　　Year　　2009
Designer　Silas Dilworth　　Format　OpenType

# Kartoffel Quark

**Regular**

**Aa Bb Cc Dd Ee Ff Gg Hh Ii Jj Kk Ll Mm Nn Oo Pp Qq Rr Ss Tt Uu Vv Ww Xx Yy Zz 0123456789**

Foundry TypeTrust

Typeface Breuer Text
Designer Silas Dilworth
Year 2007
Format OpenType

# Aa

Aa Bb Cc Dd Ee Ff Gg Hh Ii Jj Kk Ll
Mm Nn Oo Pp Qq Rr Ss Tt Uu Vv Ww
Xx Yy Zz
0123456789

Breuer Text Light 24pt
*Breuer Text Light Italic 24pt*
Breuer Text Regular 24pt
*Breuer Text Regular Italic 24pt*
**Breuer Text Medium 24pt**
***Breuer Text Medium Italic 24pt***
**Breuer Text Bold 24pt**
***Breuer Text Bold Italic 24pt***

---

**12/14 — Breuer Text Light**

The quick brown fox jumps over the lazy dog. Voyez le brick géant que j'examine près du wharf. Zwölf Boxkämpfer jagen Viktor quer über den

**9/12 — Breuer Text Light**

The quick brown fox jumps over the lazy dog. Voyez le brick géant que j'examine près du wharf. Zwölf Boxkämpfer jagen Viktor quer über den großen Sylter Deich. El veloz murciélago hindú comía feliz cardillo y kiwi. La cigüeña tocaba el saxofón detrás

**7/10 — Breuer Text Light**

The quick brown fox jumps over the lazy dog. Voyez le brick géant que j'examine près du wharf. Zwölf Boxkämpfer jagen Viktor quer über den großen Sylter Deich. El veloz murciélago hindú comía feliz cardillo y kiwi. La cigüeña tocaba el saxofón detrás del palenque de pajaatur? Rissimo lorereped ex es solore lab id molorro in rempore icabore rehenetur aliam aut voles audae dem quam, secum

**12/14 — Breuer Text Regular**

The quick brown fox jumps over the lazy dog. Voyez le brick géant que j'examine près du wharf. Zwölf Boxkämpfer jagen Viktor quer über den

**9/12 — Breuer Text Regular**

The quick brown fox jumps over the lazy dog. Voyez le brick géant que j'examine près du wharf. Zwölf Boxkämpfer jagen Viktor quer über den großen Sylter Deich. El veloz murciélago hindú comía feliz cardillo y kiwi. La cigüeña tocaba el saxofón detrás

**7/10 — Breuer Text Regular**

The quick brown fox jumps over the lazy dog. Voyez le brick géant que j'examine près du wharf. Zwölf Boxkämpfer jagen Viktor quer über den großen Sylter Deich. El veloz murciélago hindú comía feliz cardillo y kiwi. La cigüeña tocaba el saxofón detrás del palenque de pajaatur? Rissimo lorereped ex es solore lab id molorro in rempore icabore rehenetur aliam aut voles audae dem quam, secum

**12/14 — Breuer Text Medium**

The quick brown fox jumps over the lazy dog. Voyez le brick géant que j'examine près du wharf. Zwölf Boxkämpfer jagen Viktor quer über den

**9/12 — Breuer Text Medium**

The quick brown fox jumps over the lazy dog. Voyez le brick géant que j'examine près du wharf. Zwölf Boxkämpfer jagen Viktor quer über den großen Sylter Deich. El veloz murciélago hindú comía feliz cardillo y kiwi. La cigüeña tocaba el saxofón detrás

**7/10 — Breuer Text Medium**

The quick brown fox jumps over the lazy dog. Voyez le brick géant que j'examine près du wharf. Zwölf Boxkämpfer jagen Viktor quer über den großen Sylter Deich. El veloz murciélago hindú comía feliz cardillo y kiwi. La cigüeña tocaba el saxofón detrás del palenque de pajaatur? Rissimo lorereped ex es solore lab id molorro in rempore icabore rehenetur aliam aut voles audae dem

**12/14 — Breuer Text Bold**

The quick brown fox jumps over the lazy dog. Voyez le brick géant que j'examine près du wharf. Zwölf Boxkämpfer jagen Viktor quer über den großen Sylter Deich. El veloz murciélago hindú comía feliz cardillo y kiwi.

**9/12 — Breuer Text Bold**

The quick brown fox jumps over the lazy dog. Voyez le brick géant que j'examine près du wharf. Zwölf Boxkämpfer jagen Viktor quer über den großen Sylter Deich. El veloz murciélago hindú comía feliz cardillo y kiwi. La cigüeña tocaba el saxofón detrás del palenque de pajaatur? Rissimo lorereped ex es solore lab id molorro in rempore

**7/10 — Breuer Text Bold**

The quick brown fox jumps over the lazy dog. Voyez le brick géant que j'examine près du wharf. Zwölf Boxkämpfer jagen Viktor quer über den großen Sylter Deich. El veloz murciélago hindú comía feliz cardillo y kiwi. La cigüeña tocaba el saxofón detrás del palenque de pajaatur? Rissimo lorereped ex es solore lab id molorro in rempore icabore rehenetur aliam aut voles audae dem quam, secum eum facesequae consequ aepudam quia voluptiur repel in et faccustibus, nonsenis aut quisqui rero mi, ipiet lam

# T

## Typonine

—

Nikola Djurek

—

Zabok, Croatia
& The Hague,
Netherlands

—

Since
2005

Typonine is a digital type foundry and graphic design studio based in Croatia and the Netherlands. It is run by graphic and type designer Nikola Djurek.

## Info

—Why?
Because

—People on staff
5

—Type designers on staff
3

—Type families
13

—Designers represented
3

—Web shop
www.typonine.com

—Distributors
Typotheque

—Webfont services
Typonine webfont service

—Basic license
49€–95€ per style, with volume discounts. Webfonts prices range from 19€ per style to 100€ per family.

Typeface selection

Delvard Display Pro
Marlene Display Pro
Nota Pro
Tempera Pro
TyStencil Pro

24pt

## People

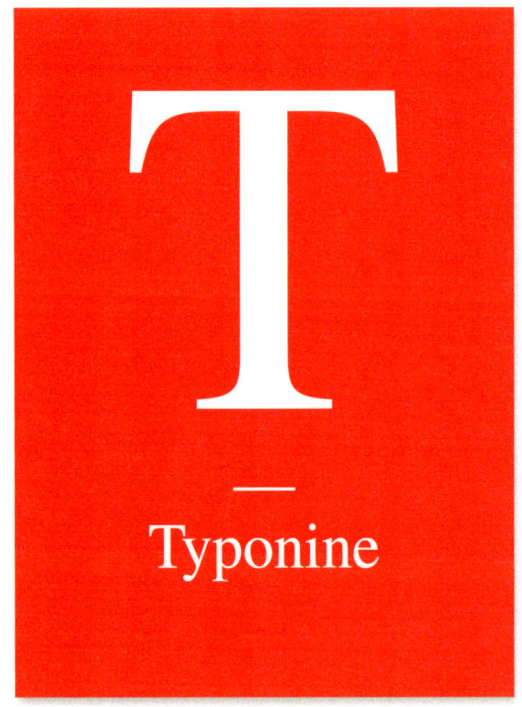

—Nikola Djurek was born in Croatia. He studied in Croatia and Italy, followed by a postgraduate master course in Type & Media, Royal Academy (KABK) in The Hague, Netherlands, finally earning his PhD degree in the graphic and type design fields. He now teaches at DVK Art Academy, University of Split, and the University of Zagreb. Additionally, Nikola is the Croatian country delegate for ATypI (Association Typographique Internationale). He collaborates with Typotheque (Peter and Johanna Bil'ak) on the development of new typefaces.

Notorious
Attention Detail
generalist
Continuously
Fine Tuned
meaningful intent
New Templates

Tempera Biblio is a serif text typeface with a difference. Instead of offering contrasting weights such as Light and Bold, it comes in three variations of the book weight: Book A, Book B and Book C. These are subtly different in color, so that they can be varied according to technical circumstances and point sizes.

Page 265

Marlene Display Pro

## sore
## hands
negotiate

**WRONG NUMBER**

while the unknown voice

*speaks softly over the background*

noise coming from the other side of the wire

Marlene is an elegant, crisp modern face with a distinctive, contemporary calligraphic flourish.

TyStencil

Marlene Stencil is a modern serif that also features an unconventional set of swashes and flourishes available through Titling Alternates and Stylistic Sets.

**difference**
*Usability*
**five weights**
Literature
*independent*
Full grown
friendly & helpful

Marlene Stencil is a contemporary display face to accompany the Marlene family. It boasts a quintet of alternate swashes for each glyph.

Delvard Light

Typonine Sans is an uncomplicated, readable, contemporary humanist sans-serif. It is a part of a larger family that also includes Typonine Sans Condensed, Typonine Sans Monospace & Typonine Sans Hairline.

| | | | |
|---|---|---|---|
| Page | | Foundry | Typonine |
| 266 | | | |

| | | | |
|---|---|---|---|
| Typeface | Marlene Display Pro | Year | 2010 |
| Designer | Nikola Djurek | Format | OpenType |

# Marlene
# Dietrich

Thin
**Dark**

Aa Bb Cc Dd Ee Ff Gg Hh Ii
Jj Kk Ll Mm Nn Oo Pp Qq Rr
Ss Tt Uu Vv Ww Xx Yy Zz
0123456789

| | | | |
|---|---|---|---|
| Typeface | Delvard Display Pro | Year | 2011 |
| Designer | Nikola Djurek | Format | OpenType |

# Humphrey
# Bogart

One
Two
Three
Four
Five

Aa Bb Cc Dd Ee Ff Gg Hh
Ii Jj Kk Ll Mm Nn Oo Pp Qq
Rr Ss Tt Uu Vv Ww Xx Yy Zz
0123456789

| | | | |
|---|---|---|---|
| Typeface | TyStencil Pro | Year | 2008 |
| Designer | Nikola Djurek | Format | OpenType |

# Clark
# Gable

Normal
**Bold**

Aa Bb Cc Dd Ee Ff Gg Hh Ii Jj Kk
Ll Mm Nn Oo Pp Qq Rr Ss Tt Uu
Vv Ww Xx Yy Zz 0123456789

Foundry  Typonine

Typeface  Nota Pro
Designer  Nikola Djurek
Year  2009
Format  OpenType

# Aa

Nota Pro Regular 20pt
*Nota Pro Italic 20pt*
**Nota Pro Bold 20pt**

Aa Bb Cc Dd Ee Ff Gg Hh Ii Jj Kk Ll Mm Nn Oo Pp Qq Rr Ss Tt Uu Vv Ww Xx Yy Zz
0123456789
—

9/12  Nota Pro Regular

The quick brown fox jumps over the lazy dog. Voyez le brick géant que j'examine près du wharf. Zwölf Boxkämpfer jagen Viktor quer über den großen Sylter Deich. El veloz murciélago hindú comía feliz cardillo y kiwi. La cigüeña tocaba el saxofón detrás del palenque de pajaatur? Rissimo lorereped ex es solore lab id molorro in rempore icabore rehenetur aliam aut voles audae dem quam, secum eum facesequae consequ aepudam quia voluptiur repel in et faccustibus, nonsenis aut quisqui rero mi, ipiet lam ant ut maio et hil molupta tustis atatur, consedi tasimol orerem aut volor andipsapis sit, illaut volore officatus alicae

7/10  Nota Pro Regular

The quick brown fox jumps over the lazy dog. Voyez le brick géant que j'examine près du wharf. Zwölf Boxkämpfer jagen Viktor quer über den großen Sylter Deich. El veloz murciélago hindú comía feliz cardillo y kiwi. La cigüeña tocaba el saxofón detrás del palenque de pajaatur? Rissimo lorereped ex es solore lab id molorro in rempore icabore rehenetur aliam aut voles audae dem quam, secum eum facesequae consequ aepudam quia voluptiur repel in et faccustibus, nonsenis aut quisqui rero mi, ipiet lam ant ut maio et hil molupta tustis atatur, consedi tasimol orerem aut volor andipsapis sit, illaut volore officatus alicae dusdaec tatecte cearum qui accatibus restiore nulpa secaerferum, nus dolenim in et quoditat que explam volupictur? Qui de illuptae. Dae nis illiberum volorro ritatis tinullo rerumqu atetur repro eatius asperibus. Rissimo lorereped ex es solore lab id molorro in rempore icabore rehenetur aliam aut voles audae dem

Typeface  Tempera Pro
Designer  Nikola Djurek
Year  2006
Format  OpenType

# Aa

Tempera Pro Normal 20pt
*Tempera Pro Normal Italic 20pt*
**Tempera Pro Bold 20pt**

Aa Bb Cc Dd Ee Ff Gg Hh Ii Jj Kk Ll Mm Nn Oo Pp Qq Rr Ss Tt Uu Vv Ww Xx Yy Zz
0123456789
—

9/12  Tempera Pro Normal

The quick brown fox jumps over the lazy dog. Voyez le brick géant que j'examine près du wharf. Zwölf Boxkämpfer jagen Viktor quer über den großen Sylter Deich. El veloz murciélago hindú comía feliz cardillo y kiwi. La cigüeña tocaba el saxofón detrás del palenque de pajaatur? Rissimo lorereped ex es solore lab id molorro in rempore icabore rehenetur aliam aut voles audae dem quam, secum eum facesequae consequ aepudam quia voluptiur repel in et faccustibus, nonsenis aut quisqui rero mi, ipiet lam ant ut maio et hil molupta tustis atatur, consedi tasimol orerem aut volor andipsapis sit, illaut volore officatus alicae dusdaec tatecte cearum qui accatibus restiore nulpa secaerferum, nus dolenim in et quoditat que explam volupictur? Qui de illuptae. Dae nis illiberum volorro ritatis tinullo rerumqu atetur repro eatius asperibus. Rissimo lorereped ex es solore lab id molorro in rempore icabore rehenetur aliam aut voles audae dem quam, secum eum facesequae consequ aepudam quia voluptiur repel in et faccustibus,

7/10  Tempera Pro Normal

The quick brown fox jumps over the lazy dog. Voyez le brick géant que j'examine près du wharf. Zwölf Boxkämpfer jagen Viktor quer über den großen Sylter Deich. El veloz murciélago hindú comía feliz cardillo y kiwi. La cigüeña tocaba el saxofón detrás del palenque de pajaatur? Rissimo lorereped ex es solore lab id molorro in rempore icabore rehenetur aliam aut voles audae dem quam, secum eum facesequae consequ aepudam quia voluptiur repel in et faccustibus, nonsenis aut quisqui rero mi, ipiet lam ant ut maio et hil molupta tustis atatur, consedi tasimol orerem aut volor andipsapis sit, illaut volore officatus alicae dusdaec tatecte cearum qui accatibus restiore nulpa secaerferum, nus dolenim in et quoditat que explam volupictur? Qui de illuptae. Dae nis illiberum volorro ritatis tinullo rerumqu atetur repro eatius asperibus. Rissimo lorereped ex es solore lab id molorro in rempore icabore rehenetur aliam aut voles audae dem quam, secum eum facesequae consequ aepudam quia voluptiur repel in et faccustibus, nonsenis aut quisqui rero mi, ipiet lam ant ut maio et hil molupta tustis atatur, consedi tasimol orerem aut volor andipsapis sit, illaut volore officatus alicae dusdaec tatecte cearum qui accatibus restiore nulpa secaerferum, nus dolenim in et quoditat que explam volupictur? Qui de illuptae. The quick brown fox jumps over the lazy dog. Voyez le brick géant que j'examine près du wharf. Zwölf Boxkämpfer jagen Viktor quer über den großen Sylter Deich. El veloz murciélago hindú comía feliz cardillo y kiwi. La cigüeña

# T

## Typolar

—

Jarno Lukkarila,
Saku Heinänen

—

Helsinki, Finland
London, UK

—

Since
2006

"The Northern European type collaboration Typolar builds on the Scandinavian tradition of sturdy functionalism. For us it means clever type families built on fresh ideas. Working closely with the publishing industry has made our fonts ideally suited for editorial work. Moreover, many have found them a great fit in branding and identities. And that's how we like it. Besides design, our members also teach, run workshops, and write. At the moment we are based in London and Helsinki."

## Info

—Why?
We evolved from a graphic design studio which was working increasingly on type related issues. Typolar builds on the Scandinavian tradition of sturdy functionalism and hands-in-mud craftsmanship.

—People on staff
2

—Type designers on staff
2

—Type families
6 + several custom type families

—Designers represented
2, soon 3

—Web shop
www.typolar.com

—Distributors
FontShop, MyFonts

—Webfont service
Fontdeck, MyFonts

—Price range fror basic license
40–50€ (single fonts, 2 CPUs)

## People

—Jarno Lukkarila, founder: "My interest in fonts started just from working with type and eventually moved into font design. Somehow there was no turning back for me; it dragged me in. I went to study at the Royal Academy of Art in The Hague where my class was spoiled, for instance with a lettering workshop by Gerrit Noordzij in 2000. After graduation in The Hague and studies in the University of Industrial Arts in Helsinki (now Aalto University), I set up my own studio. With some encouraging push from customers and font users, it has gradually evolved into type designers' collective."

—Saku Heinänen lives in Helsinki and works as a graphic designer and type designer. In the past years, he has been involved in many editorial designs, magazine launches and redesigns. He has created visual identities for companies, organizations and events. Saku has been teaching at the Graphic Design faculty of Aalto University, Helsinki, Finland. His responsibilities are typography, type design and publication design. Saku also lectures and runs workshops elsewhere for educational purposes.

## Typeface selection

Altis
Calypso E
Tanger Serif Medium
Tanger Serif Narrow
Tanger Serif Wide
Vinkel

Economic 1st Class
☑ yeah
QUITE
Modern
angular
Rearranged!
profound & nuanced

Calypso E is an updated interpretation of a Neo-grotesque model Egyptian with a hint of humanist lightness in its forms. This lends the typeface an authoritative tone without an authoritarian tang. Its seriously big x-height, square basic form and sturdy serifs create firm text regardless of the weight.

24pt

Page
269

Transcultural
**swing**
with warm nuances.
TOUCH
& feel guaranteed
**Launching**
new embodiment of a humanist sanserif

Inspired by new transitional and Egyptian fonts, Tanger Serif has elements of a sturdy workhorse text face and finely detailed headline font. A huge variety of widths and weights supports a wide array of uses and text sizes.

Tack!
TANGER SERIF WIDE - ULTRA LIGHT

**Dankjewel**
TANGER SERIF NARROW - SEMI BOLD ITALIC

AČIŪ, DĚKUJI
TANGER SERIF MEDIUM - REGULAR

***Thanks***
TANGER SERIF WIDE - HEAVY ITALIC

Obrigado
TANGER SERIF MEDIUM - BOOK

Altis combines geometric regularity and soulfulness into one font family. It resembles the traditional sans-serif of the early twentieth century, which communicates in a friendly tone and reads extremely well. Altis has been developed to fit present-day editorial conditions and publishing models.

Foundry Typolar

Typeface Tanger Serif Medium
Designer Jarno Lukkarila
Year 2010
Format OpenType

# Aa

Aa Bb Cc Dd Ee Ff Gg Hh Ii Jj Kk Ll Mm Nn Oo Pp Qq Rr Ss Tt Uu Vv Ww Xx Yy Zz
0123456789
—

Tanger Serif Medium UltraLight 18pt
*Tanger Serif Medium UltraLight Italic* 18pt
Tanger Serif Medium Light 18pt
*Tanger Serif Medium Light Italic* 18pt
Tanger Serif Medium Book 18pt
*Tanger Serif Medium Book Italic* 18pt
Tanger Serif Medium Regular 18pt
*Tanger Serif Medium Italic* 18pt
**Tanger Serif Medium SemiBold** 18pt
***Tanger Serif Medium SemiBold Italic*** 18pt
**Tanger Serif Medium Bold** 18pt
***Tanger Serif Medium Bold Italic*** 18pt
**Tanger Serif Medium ExtraBold** 18pt
***Tanger Serif Medium ExtraBold Italic*** 18pt
**Tanger Serif Medium Heavy** 18pt
***Tanger Serif Medium Heavy Italic*** 18pt

---

9/12 Tanger Serif Narrow Light

The quick brown fox jumps over the lazy dog. Voyez le brick géant que j'examine près du wharf. Zwölf Boxkämpfer jagen Viktor quer über den großen Sylter Deich. El veloz murciélago hindú comía feliz cardillo y kiwi. La cigüeña tocaba el saxofón detrás del palenque de pajaatur? Rissimo

9/12 Tanger Serif Narrow Book

The quick brown fox jumps over the lazy dog. Voyez le brick géant que j'examine près du wharf. Zwölf Boxkämpfer jagen Viktor quer über den großen Sylter Deich. El veloz murciélago hindú comía feliz cardillo y kiwi. La cigüeña tocaba el saxofón detrás del palenque de

9/12 Tanger Serif Narrow SemiBold

**The quick brown fox jumps over the lazy dog. Voyez le brick géant que j'examine près du wharf. Zwölf Boxkämpfer jagen Viktor quer über den großen Sylter Deich. El veloz murciélago hindú comía feliz cardillo y kiwi. La cigüeña tocaba el saxofón detrás**

9/12 Tanger Serif Narrow Bold

**The quick brown fox jumps over the lazy dog. Voyez le brick géant que j'examine près du wharf. Zwölf Boxkämpfer jagen Viktor quer über den großen Sylter Deich. El veloz murciélago hindú comía feliz cardillo y kiwi. La cigüeña tocaba el saxofón detrás del palenque de pajaatur? Rissimo lorereped ex es solore lab id molorro in rempore icabore**

9/12 Tanger Serif Medium Light

The quick brown fox jumps over the lazy dog. Voyez le brick géant que j'examine près du wharf. Zwölf Boxkämpfer jagen Viktor quer über den großen Sylter Deich. El veloz murciélago hindú comía feliz cardillo y kiwi. La cigüeña tocaba el saxofón detrás del palen-

9/12 Tanger Serif Medium Book

The quick brown fox jumps over the lazy dog. Voyez le brick géant que j'examine près du wharf. Zwölf Boxkämpfer jagen Viktor quer über den großen Sylter Deich. El veloz murciélago hindú comía feliz cardillo y kiwi. La cigüeña tocaba el saxofón detrás

9/12 Tanger Serif Medium SemiBold

**The quick brown fox jumps over the lazy dog. Voyez le brick géant que j'examine près du wharf. Zwölf Boxkämpfer jagen Viktor quer über den großen Sylter Deich. El veloz murciélago hindú comía feliz cardillo y kiwi. La cigüeña tocaba el**

9/12 Tanger Serif Medium Bold

**The quick brown fox jumps over the lazy dog. Voyez le brick géant que j'examine près du wharf. Zwölf Boxkämpfer jagen Viktor quer über den großen Sylter Deich. El veloz murciélago hindú comía feliz cardillo y kiwi. La cigüeña tocaba el saxofón detrás del palenque de pajaatur? Rissimo lorereped ex es solore lab id**

9/12 Tanger Serif Wide Light

The quick brown fox jumps over the lazy dog. Voyez le brick géant que j'examine près du wharf. Zwölf Boxkämpfer jagen Viktor quer über den großen Sylter Deich. El veloz murciélago hindú comía feliz cardillo y kiwi. La cigüeña tocaba el saxofón

9/12 Tanger Serif Wide Book

The quick brown fox jumps over the lazy dog. Voyez le brick géant que j'examine près du wharf. Zwölf Boxkämpfer jagen Viktor quer über den großen Sylter Deich. El veloz murciélago hindú comía feliz cardillo y kiwi. La cigüe-

9/12 Tanger Serif Wide SemiBold

**The quick brown fox jumps over the lazy dog. Voyez le brick géant que j'examine près du wharf. Zwölf Boxkämpfer jagen Viktor quer über den großen Sylter Deich. El veloz murciélago hindú comía feliz cardillo y kiwi. La**

9/12 Tanger Serif Wide Bold

**The quick brown fox jumps over the lazy dog. Voyez le brick géant que j'examine près du wharf. Zwölf Boxkämpfer jagen Viktor quer über den großen Sylter Deich. El veloz murciélago hindú comía feliz cardillo y kiwi. La cigüeña tocaba el saxofón detrás del palenque de pajaatur? Rissimo lorereped ex**

Typeface  Calypso E
Designer  Jarno Lukkarila

Year    2010
Format  OpenType

# Aa

Aa Bb Cc Dd Ee Ff Gg Hh Ii Jj
Kk Ll Mm Nn Oo Pp Qq Rr Ss
Tt Uu Vv Ww Xx Yy Zz
0123456789
—

Calypso E Hairline 14pt
*Calypso E Hairline Italic 14pt*
Calypso E Thin 14pt
*Calypso E Thin Italic 14pt*
Calypso E ExtraLight 14pt
*Calypso E ExtraLight Italic 14pt*
Calypso E Light 14pt
*Calypso E Light Italic 14pt*
Calypso E Book 14pt
*Calypso E Book Italic 14pt*
Calypso E Regular 14pt
*Calypso E Regular Italic 14pt*
Calypso E Normal 14pt
*Calypso E Normal Italic 14pt*
Calypso E Medium 14pt
*Calypso E Medium Italic 14pt*
Calypso E DemiBold 14pt
*Calypso E DemiBold Italic 14pt*
**Calypso E SemiBold Medium 14pt**
*Calypso E SemiBold Italic 14pt*
**Calypso E Bold 14pt**
***Calypso E Bold Italic 14pt***
**Calypso E ExtraBold 14pt**
***Calypso E ExtraBold Italic 14pt***
**Calypso E Heavy 14pt**
***Calypso E Heavy Italic 14pt***

---

12/14  Calypso E Regular

The quick brown fox jumps over the lazy dog. Voyez le brick géant que j'examine près du wharf. Zwölf Boxkämpfer jagen

12/14  Calypso E Medium

The quick brown fox jumps over the lazy dog. Voyez le brick géant que j'examine près du wharf. Zwölf Boxkämpfer

12/14  Calypso E Bold

**The quick brown fox jumps over the lazy dog. Voyez le brick géant que j'examine près du wharf. Zwölf Boxkämpfer jagen Viktor quer über den großen Sylter**

9/12  Calypso E Regular

The quick brown fox jumps over the lazy dog. Voyez le brick géant que j'examine près du wharf. Zwölf Boxkämpfer jagen Viktor quer über den großen Sylter Deich. El veloz murciélago hindú comía feliz car-

9/12  Calypso E Medium

The quick brown fox jumps over the lazy dog. Voyez le brick géant que j'examine près du wharf. Zwölf Boxkämpfer jagen Viktor quer über den großen Sylter Deich. El veloz murciélago hindú comía

9/12  Calypso E Bold

**The quick brown fox jumps over the lazy dog. Voyez le brick géant que j'examine près du wharf. Zwölf Boxkämpfer jagen Viktor quer über den großen Sylter Deich. El veloz murciélago hindú comía feliz cardillo y kiwi. La cigüeña tocaba el saxofón detrás**

7/10  Calypso E Regular

The quick brown fox jumps over the lazy dog. Voyez le brick géant que j'examine près du wharf. Zwölf Boxkämpfer jagen Viktor quer über den großen Sylter Deich. El veloz murciélago hindú comía feliz cardillo y kiwi. La cigüeña tocaba el saxofón detrás del palenque de pajaatur? Rissimo lorereped ex es solore lab id

7/10  Calypso E Medium

The quick brown fox jumps over the lazy dog. Voyez le brick géant que j'examine près du wharf. Zwölf Boxkämpfer jagen Viktor quer über den großen Sylter Deich. El veloz murciélago hindú comía feliz cardillo y kiwi. La cigüeña tocaba el saxofón detrás del palenque de pajaatur? Rissimo lorereped ex es solore

7/10  Calypso E Bold

**The quick brown fox jumps over the lazy dog. Voyez le brick géant que j'examine près du wharf. Zwölf Boxkämpfer jagen Viktor quer über den großen Sylter Deich. El veloz murciélago hindú comía feliz cardillo y kiwi. La cigüeña tocaba el saxofón detrás del palenque de pajaatur? Rissimo lorereped ex es solore lab id molorro in rempore icabore rehenetur aliam**

Page 272

Foundry  Typolar

Typeface  Altis
Designer  Jarno Lukkarila
Year  2011
Format  OpenType

# Aa

Aa Bb Cc Dd Ee Ff Gg Hh Ii Jj Kk Ll Mm Nn Oo Pp Qq Rr Ss Tt Uu Vv Ww Xx Yy Zz
0123456789

Altis Hairline 24pt
Altis Thin 24pt
Altis Light 24pt
Altis Book 24pt
**Altis Medium 24pt**
**Altis Bold 24pt**
**Altis ExtraBold 24pt**
**Altis Heavy 24pt**
**Altis Black 24pt**

---

12/14  Altis Light

The quick brown fox jumps over the lazy dog. Voyez le brick géant que j'examine près du wharf. Zwölf Boxkämpfer jagen Viktor quer über den

12/14  Altis Book

The quick brown fox jumps over the lazy dog. Voyez le brick géant que j'examine près du wharf. Zwölf Boxkämpfer jagen Viktor quer über den

12/14  Altis Medium

**The quick brown fox jumps over the lazy dog. Voyez le brick géant que j'examine près du wharf. Zwölf Boxkämpfer jagen Viktor quer**

12/14  Altis Bold

**The quick brown fox jumps over the lazy dog. Voyez le brick géant que j'examine près du wharf. Zwölf Boxkämpfer jagen Viktor quer über den großen Sylter Deich. El veloz murciélago hin-**

9/12  Altis Light

The quick brown fox jumps over the lazy dog. Voyez le brick géant que j'examine près du wharf. Zwölf Boxkämpfer jagen Viktor quer über den großen Sylter Deich. El veloz murciélago hindú comía feliz cardillo y kiwi. La cigüeña tocaba el

9/12  Altis Book

The quick brown fox jumps over the lazy dog. Voyez le brick géant que j'examine près du wharf. Zwölf Boxkämpfer jagen Viktor quer über den großen Sylter Deich. El veloz murciélago hindú comía feliz cardillo y kiwi. La cigüeña

9/12  Altis Medium

**The quick brown fox jumps over the lazy dog. Voyez le brick géant que j'examine près du wharf. Zwölf Boxkämpfer jagen Viktor quer über den großen Sylter Deich. El veloz murciélago hindú comía feliz cardillo y kiwi.**

9/12  Altis Bold

**The quick brown fox jumps over the lazy dog. Voyez le brick géant que j'examine près du wharf. Zwölf Boxkämpfer jagen Viktor quer über den großen Sylter Deich. El veloz murciélago hindú comía feliz cardillo y kiwi. La cigüeña tocaba el saxofón detrás del palenque de pajaatur? Rissimo lorereped ex**

7/10  Altis Light

The quick brown fox jumps over the lazy dog. Voyez le brick géant que j'examine près du wharf. Zwölf Boxkämpfer jagen Viktor quer über den großen Sylter Deich. El veloz murciélago hindú comía feliz cardillo y kiwi. La cigüeña tocaba el saxofón detrás del palenque de pajaatur? Rissimo lorereped ex es solore lab id molorro in rempore icabore rehenetur aliam aut voles audae

7/10  Altis Book

The quick brown fox jumps over the lazy dog. Voyez le brick géant que j'examine près du wharf. Zwölf Boxkämpfer jagen Viktor quer über den großen Sylter Deich. El veloz murciélago hindú comía feliz cardillo y kiwi. La cigüeña tocaba el saxofón detrás del palenque de pajaatur? Rissimo lorereped ex es solore lab id molorro in rempore icabore rehenetur aliam aut

7/10  Altis Medium

**The quick brown fox jumps over the lazy dog. Voyez le brick géant que j'examine près du wharf. Zwölf Boxkämpfer jagen Viktor quer über den großen Sylter Deich. El veloz murciélago hindú comía feliz cardillo y kiwi. La cigüeña tocaba el saxofón detrás del palenque de pajaatur? Rissimo lorereped ex es solore lab id molorro in rempore icabore**

7/10  Altis Bold

**The quick brown fox jumps over the lazy dog. Voyez le brick géant que j'examine près du wharf. Zwölf Boxkämpfer jagen Viktor quer über den großen Sylter Deich. El veloz murciélago hindú comía feliz cardillo y kiwi. La cigüeña tocaba el saxofón detrás del palenque de pajaatur? Rissimo lorereped ex es solore lab id molorro in rempore icabore rehenetur aliam aut voles audae dem quam, secum eum facesequae consequ aepudam quia**

Typeface  Vinkel           Year    2010
Designer  Saku Heinänen    Format  OpenType

## Aa

Aa Bb Cc Dd Ee Ff Gg Hh Ii Jj Kk
Ll Mm Nn Oo Pp Qq Rr Ss Tt Uu
Vv Ww Xx Yy Zz
0123456789
—

Vinkel Thin 18pt
*Vinkel Thin Italic 18pt*
Vinkel ExtraLight 18pt
*Vinkel ExtraLight Italic 18pt*
Vinkel Light 18pt
*Vinkel Light Italic 18pt*
Vinkel Regular 18pt
*Vinkel Regular Italic 18pt*
**Vinkel Medium 18pt**
***Vinkel Medium Italic 18pt***
**Vinkel Bold 18pt**
***Vinkel Bold Italic 18pt***
**Vinkel Black 18pt**
***Vinkel Black Italic 18pt***
**Vinkel ExtraBlack 18pt**
***Vinkel ExtraBlack Italic 18pt***

---

12/14  Vinkel Light

The quick brown fox jumps over the lazy dog. Voyez le brick géant que j'examine près du wharf. Zwölf Boxkämpfer jagen Viktor quer

9/12  Vinkel Light

The quick brown fox jumps over the lazy dog. Voyez le brick géant que j'examine près du wharf. Zwölf Boxkämpfer jagen Viktor quer über den großen Sylter Deich. El veloz murciélago hindú comía feliz cardillo y kiwi. La

7/10  Vinkel Light

The quick brown fox jumps over the lazy dog. Voyez le brick géant que j'examine près du wharf. Zwölf Boxkämpfer jagen Viktor quer über den großen Sylter Deich. El veloz murciélago hindú comía feliz cardillo y kiwi. La cigüeña tocaba el saxofón detrás del palenque de pajaatur? Rissimo lorereped ex es solore lab id molorro in rempore icabore rehenetur

12/14  Vinkel Regular

The quick brown fox jumps over the lazy dog. Voyez le brick géant que j'examine près du wharf. Zwölf Boxkämpfer jagen Viktor

9/12  Vinkel Regular

The quick brown fox jumps over the lazy dog. Voyez le brick géant que j'examine près du wharf. Zwölf Boxkämpfer jagen Viktor quer über den großen Sylter Deich. El veloz murciélago hindú comía feliz cardillo y kiwi.

7/10  Vinkel Regular

The quick brown fox jumps over the lazy dog. Voyez le brick géant que j'examine près du wharf. Zwölf Boxkämpfer jagen Viktor quer über den großen Sylter Deich. El veloz murciélago hindú comía feliz cardillo y kiwi. La cigüeña tocaba el saxofón detrás del palenque de pajaatur? Rissimo lorereped ex es solore lab id molorro in rempore

12/14  Vinkel Medium

**The quick brown fox jumps over the lazy dog. Voyez le brick géant que j'examine près du wharf. Zwölf Boxkämpfer jagen**

9/12  Vinkel Medium

**The quick brown fox jumps over the lazy dog. Voyez le brick géant que j'examine près du wharf. Zwölf Boxkämpfer jagen Viktor quer über den großen Sylter Deich. El veloz murciélago hindú comía feliz cardillo y kiwi.**

7/10  Vinkel Medium

**The quick brown fox jumps over the lazy dog. Voyez le brick géant que j'examine près du wharf. Zwölf Boxkämpfer jagen Viktor quer über den großen Sylter Deich. El veloz murciélago hindú comía feliz cardillo y kiwi. La cigüeña tocaba el saxofón detrás del palenque de pajaatur? Rissimo lorereped ex es solore lab id molorro**

12/14  Vinkel Bold

**The quick brown fox jumps over the lazy dog. Voyez le brick géant que j'examine près du wharf. Zwölf Boxkämpfer jagen Viktor quer über den großen Sylter Deich. El veloz murciélago**

9/12  Vinkel Bold

**The quick brown fox jumps over the lazy dog. Voyez le brick géant que j'examine près du wharf. Zwölf Boxkämpfer jagen Viktor quer über den großen Sylter Deich. El veloz murciélago hindú comía feliz cardillo y kiwi. La cigüeña tocaba el saxofón detrás del palenque de pajaatur? Rissimo lorer-**

7/10  Vinkel Bold

**The quick brown fox jumps over the lazy dog. Voyez le brick géant que j'examine près du wharf. Zwölf Boxkämpfer jagen Viktor quer über den großen Sylter Deich. El veloz murciélago hindú comía feliz cardillo y kiwi. La cigüeña tocaba el saxofón detrás del palenque de pajaatur? Rissimo lorereped ex es solore lab id molorro in rempore icabore rehenetur aliam aut voles audae dem quam, secum eum facesequae consequ aepudam quia**

# T
## Typotheque

---

### Peter & Johanna Biľak

---

### The Hague, Netherlands

---

### Since 1999

---

Typotheque is a type foundry based in The Hague, Netherlands, developing and marketing original fonts for Mac and PC. Typotheque aims to continue the tradition of independent type foundries, contributing its tiny bit to the continuous sequence of type history, creating quality typefaces that respond to needs. In addition to developing the retail library, Typotheque specializes in creating custom type solutions for a variety of applications and languages. The Typotheque website is made to inspire and provide valuable information on type, design, and related matters.

## Info

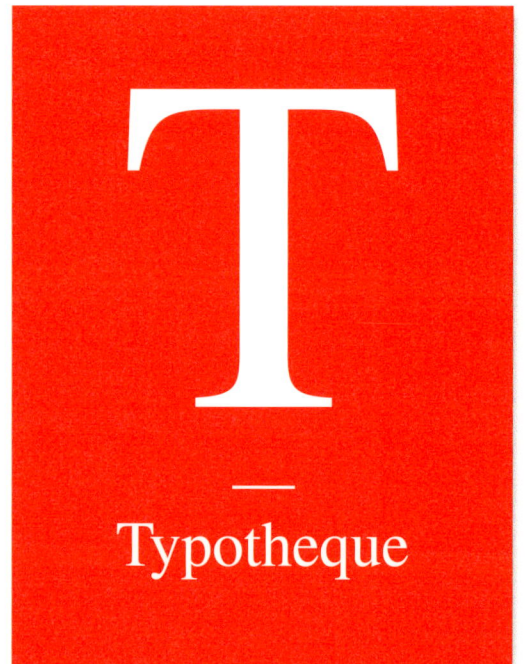

—People on staff
3

—Type designers on staff
2

—Type families
Approx. 25

—Designers represented
6

—Web shop
www.typotheque.com

—Distributors
FontShop, MyFonts

—Webfont services
Typotheque runs its own webfont service

### Typeface selection

**Brioni Std**
Greta Display Std
Greta Text Std
Klimax Std
Nara Std

24pt

## People

—Peter Biľak is a Slovakian graphic designer and type designer based in the Netherlands, and the designer of the Fedra, Greta and Eureka typefaces. In 2000, together with Stuart Bailey, he co-founded *Dot Dot Dot* magazine. He teaches typography part-time at the postgraduate course Type & Media at the Royal Academy of Arts (KABK) in The Hague.

—Johanna Biľak (born Balušíková) is a partner in Typotheque. She has lived in the Netherlands since 1999, and works in the field of graphic and type design with a focus on cultural work. Johanna studied at the Jan van Eyck Akademie (1999–2001), Maastricht; Atelier National de Recherche Typographique (1998–1999), Paris; Ecole des Beaux-arts de Saint-Etienne (1997–1998), France; and Academy of Fine Arts and Design in Bratislava (1992–1998). In 2004 she co-curated an exhibition entitled E-a-T, Experiment and Typography, focusing on the development of typography in the Czech and Slovak Republics over the last twenty years.

Covers for five-part autobiography of Thomas Bernhard. Design by Austrian graphic designer Clemens Theobert Schedler using the Plan Grotesque typeface. The series was awarded the State Award 2010 at the Best Books of Austria.

Page
275

Greta Grande typeface used for *Design Reporter*, an Australian experimental newspaper on what design writing might be. The design by Chase & Galley uses the Greta family exclusively.

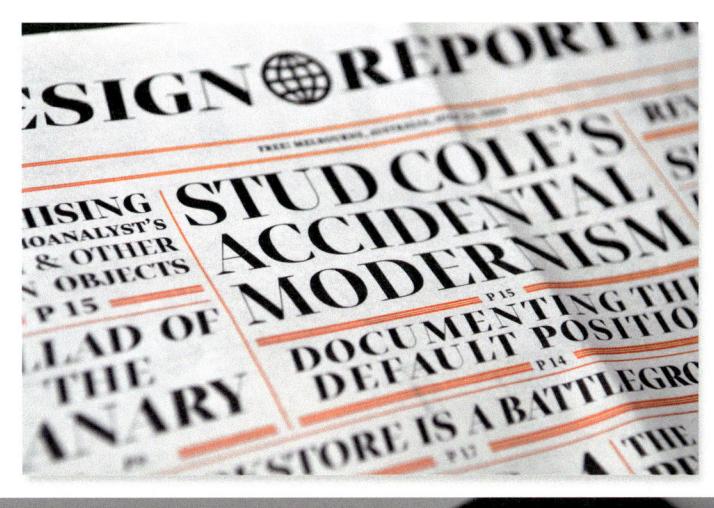

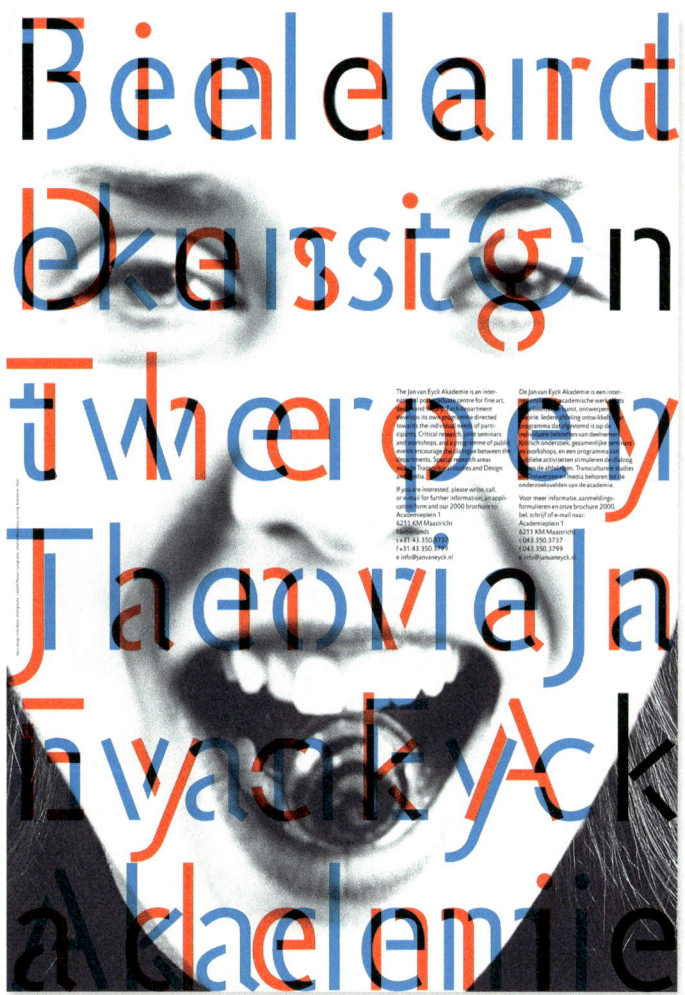

Poster for the Jan van Eyck Academy in Maastricht, Netherlands, using Jigsaw Stencil Light. Poster designed by Irma Boom together with Johanna Bil'ak.

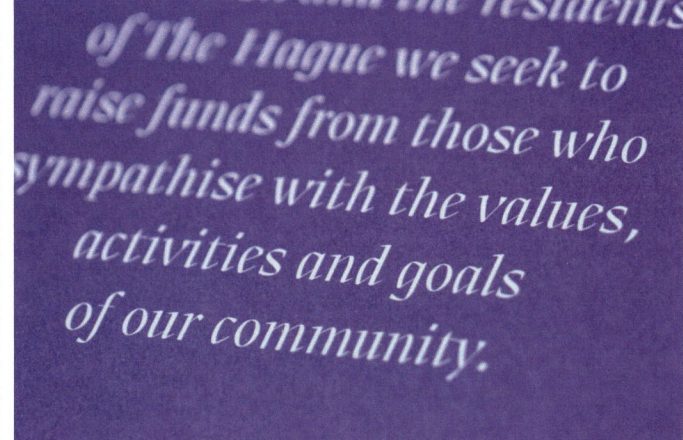

Greta Grande Narrow Light Italic used in a promotional flyer. Anonymous design, 2010.

Klimax font used on the cover of the 2009 Typotheque pocket calendar designed by Peter Bil'ak.

| | | | |
|---|---|---|---|
| Typeface | Greta Display Std | Year | 2007 |
| Designer | Peter Biľak, Nikola Djurek | Format | OpenType |

# Hänsel, *Greta &* Wolfgang

Light
*Light Italic*
Regular
*Regular Italic*
**Medium**
***Medium Italic***
**Bold**
***Bold Italic***

Aa Bb Cc Dd Ee Ff Gg Hh Ii Jj Kk Ll Mm Nn Oo Pp Qq Rr Ss Tt Uu Vv Ww Xx Yy Zz 0123456789

| | | | |
|---|---|---|---|
| Typeface | Klimax Std | Year | 2009 |
| Designer | Ondrej Jób | Format | OpenType |

# Sugar free cakes

Minus
*Minus Italic*
**Plus**
***Plus Italic***

Aa Bb Cc Dd Ee Ff Gg Hh Ii Jj Kk Ll Mm Nn Oo Pp Qq Rr Ss Tt Uu Vv Ww Xx Yy Zz 0123456789

Typeface  Greta Text Std       Year    2007
Designer  Peter Biľak          Format  OpenType

# Aa

Aa Bb Cc Dd Ee Ff Gg Hh Ii Jj Kk Ll Mm Nn Oo Pp Qq Rr Ss Tt Uu Vv Ww Xx Yy Zz
0123456789

Greta Text Std Light 24pt
*Greta Text Std Light Italic* 24pt
Greta Text Std Regular 24pt
*Greta Text Std Regular Italic* 24pt
**Greta Text Std Medium** 24pt
***Greta Text Std Medium Italic*** 24pt
**Greta Text Std Bold** 24pt
***Greta Text Std Bold Italic*** 24pt
**Greta Text Std Black** 24pt
***Greta Text Std Black Italic*** 24pt

---

12/14  Greta Text Std Light

The quick brown fox jumps over the lazy dog. Voyez le brick géant que j'examine près du wharf. Zwölf Boxkämpfer jagen Viktor quer über den

9/12  Greta Text Std Light

The quick brown fox jumps over the lazy dog. Voyez le brick géant que j'examine près du wharf. Zwölf Boxkämpfer jagen Viktor quer über den großen Sylter Deich. El veloz murciélago hindú comía feliz cardillo y kiwi. La cigüeña tocaba el saxofón detrás

7/10  Greta Text Std Light

The quick brown fox jumps over the lazy dog. Voyez le brick géant que j'examine près du wharf. Zwölf Boxkämpfer jagen Viktor quer über den großen Sylter Deich. El veloz murciélago hindú comía feliz cardillo y kiwi. La cigüeña tocaba el saxofón detrás del palenque de pajaatur? Rissimo lorereped ex es solore lab id molorro in rempore icabore rehenetur aliam aut voles audae dem quam, secum eum

12/14  Greta Text Std Regular

The quick brown fox jumps over the lazy dog. Voyez le brick géant que j'examine près du wharf. Zwölf Boxkämpfer jagen Viktor quer über den

9/12  Greta Text Std Regular

The quick brown fox jumps over the lazy dog. Voyez le brick géant que j'examine près du wharf. Zwölf Boxkämpfer jagen Viktor quer über den großen Sylter Deich. El veloz murciélago hindú comía feliz cardillo y kiwi. La cigüeña tocaba el saxofón

7/10  Greta Text Std Regular

The quick brown fox jumps over the lazy dog. Voyez le brick géant que j'examine près du wharf. Zwölf Boxkämpfer jagen Viktor quer über den großen Sylter Deich. El veloz murciélago hindú comía feliz cardillo y kiwi. La cigüeña tocaba el saxofón detrás del palenque de pajaatur? Rissimo lorereped ex es solore lab id molorro in rempore icabore rehenetur aliam aut voles audae dem

12/14  Greta Text Std Medium

**The quick brown fox jumps over the lazy dog. Voyez le brick géant que j'examine près du wharf. Zwölf Boxkämpfer jagen Viktor quer über den**

9/12  Greta Text Std Medium

**The quick brown fox jumps over the lazy dog. Voyez le brick géant que j'examine près du wharf. Zwölf Boxkämpfer jagen Viktor quer über den großen Sylter Deich. El veloz murciélago hindú comía feliz cardillo y kiwi. La cigüeña tocaba el**

7/10  Greta Text Std Medium

**The quick brown fox jumps over the lazy dog. Voyez le brick géant que j'examine près du wharf. Zwölf Boxkämpfer jagen Viktor quer über den großen Sylter Deich. El veloz murciélago hindú comía feliz cardillo y kiwi. La cigüeña tocaba el saxofón detrás del palenque de pajaatur? Rissimo lorereped ex es solore lab id molorro in rempore icabore rehenetur aliam aut voles au-**

12/14  Greta Text Std Bold

**The quick brown fox jumps over the lazy dog. Voyez le brick géant que j'examine près du wharf. Zwölf Boxkämpfer jagen Viktor quer über den großen Sylter Deich. El veloz murciélago hindú comía feliz cardillo y**

9/12  Greta Text Std Bold

**The quick brown fox jumps over the lazy dog. Voyez le brick géant que j'examine près du wharf. Zwölf Boxkämpfer jagen Viktor quer über den großen Sylter Deich. El veloz murciélago hindú comía feliz cardillo y kiwi. La cigüeña tocaba el saxofón detrás del palenque de pajaatur? Rissimo lorereped ex es solore lab id molor-**

7/10  Greta Text Std Bold

**The quick brown fox jumps over the lazy dog. Voyez le brick géant que j'examine près du wharf. Zwölf Boxkämpfer jagen Viktor quer über den großen Sylter Deich. El veloz murciélago hindú comía feliz cardillo y kiwi. La cigüeña tocaba el saxofón detrás del palenque de pajaatur? Rissimo lorereped ex es solore lab id molorro in rempore icabore rehenetur aliam aut voles audae dem quam, secum eum facesequae consequ aepudam quia voluptiur repel in et faccustibus, nonsenis aut quis-**

Typeface   Brioni Std          Year     2008
Designer   Nikola Djurek       Format   OpenType

# Aa

Aa Bb Cc Dd Ee Ff Gg Hh Ii Jj Kk
Ll Mm Nn Oo Pp Qq Rr Ss Tt Uu
Vv Ww Xx Yy Zz
0123456789
—

Brioni Std Light 24pt
*Brioni Std Light Italic 24pt*
**Brioni Std Regular 24pt**
*Brioni Std Regular Italic 24pt*
**Brioni Std Medium 24pt**
***Brioni Std Medium Italic 24pt***
**Brioni Std Bold 24pt**
***Brioni Std Bold Italic 24pt***

---

12/14   Brioni Std Light

The quick brown fox jumps over the lazy dog. Voyez le brick géant que j'examine près du wharf. Zwölf Boxkämpfer jagen Viktor quer über

12/14   Brioni Std Regular

The quick brown fox jumps over the lazy dog. Voyez le brick géant que j'examine près du wharf. Zwölf Boxkämpfer jagen Viktor quer über

12/14   Brioni Std Medium

The quick brown fox jumps over the lazy dog. Voyez le brick géant que j'examine près du wharf. Zwölf Boxkämpfer jagen Vik-

12/14   Brioni Std Bold

The quick brown fox jumps over the lazy dog. Voyez le brick géant que j'examine près du wharf. Zwölf Boxkämpfer jagen Viktor quer über den großjen Sylter Deich. El veloz murciélago hindú

9/12   Brioni Std Light

The quick brown fox jumps over the lazy dog. Voyez le brick géant que j'examine près du wharf. Zwölf Boxkämpfer jagen Viktor quer über den großen Sylter Deich. El veloz murciélago hindú comía feliz cardillo y kiwi. La cigüeña tocaba el

9/12   Brioni Std Regular

The quick brown fox jumps over the lazy dog. Voyez le brick géant que j'examine près du wharf. Zwölf Boxkämpfer jagen Viktor quer über den großen Sylter Deich. El veloz murciélago hindú comía feliz cardillo y kiwi. La

9/12   Brioni Std Medium

The quick brown fox jumps over the lazy dog. Voyez le brick géant que j'examine près du wharf. Zwölf Boxkämpfer jagen Viktor quer über den großen Sylter Deich. El veloz murciélago hindú comía feliz cardillo y kiwi. La

9/12   Brioni Std Bold

The quick brown fox jumps over the lazy dog. Voyez le brick géant que j'examine près du wharf. Zwölf Boxkämpfer jagen Viktor quer über den großen Sylter Deich. El veloz murciélago hindú comía feliz cardillo y kiwi. La cigüeña tocaba el saxofón detrás del palenque de pajaatur? Rissimo lorereped ex es solore

7/10   Brioni Std Light

The quick brown fox jumps over the lazy dog. Voyez le brick géant que j'examine près du wharf. Zwölf Boxkämpfer jagen Viktor quer über den großen Sylter Deich. El veloz murciélago hindú comía feliz cardillo y kiwi. La cigüeña tocaba el saxofón detrás del palenque de pajaatur? Rissimo lorereped ex es solore lab id molorro in rempore icabore rehenetur aliam aut voles au-

7/10   Brioni Std Regular

The quick brown fox jumps over the lazy dog. Voyez le brick géant que j'examine près du wharf. Zwölf Boxkämpfer jagen Viktor quer über den großen Sylter Deich. El veloz murciélago hindú comía feliz cardillo y kiwi. La cigüeña tocaba el saxofón detrás del palenque de pajaatur? Rissimo lorereped ex es solore lab id molorro in rempore icabore rehenetur aliam

7/10   Brioni Std Medium

The quick brown fox jumps over the lazy dog. Voyez le brick géant que j'examine près du wharf. Zwölf Boxkämpfer jagen Viktor quer über den großen Sylter Deich. El veloz murciélago hindú comía feliz cardillo y kiwi. La cigüeña tocaba el saxofón detrás del palenque de pajaatur? Rissimo lorereped ex es solore lab id molorro in rempore icabore

7/10   Brioni Std Bold

The quick brown fox jumps over the lazy dog. Voyez le brick géant que j'examine près du wharf. Zwölf Boxkämpfer jagen Viktor quer über den großen Sylter Deich. El veloz murciélago hindú comía feliz cardillo y kiwi. La cigüeña tocaba el saxofón detrás del palenque de pajaatur? Rissimo lorereped ex es solore lab id molorro in rempore icabore rehenetur aliam aut voles audae dem quam, secum eum facesequae consequ aepudam quia voluptiur repel

Typeface  Nara Std
Designer  Andrej Krátky, Nikola Djurek, Peter Bilak
Year  1989–2009
Format  OpenType

# Aa

Aa Bb Cc Dd Ee Ff Gg Hh Ii Jj Kk Ll Mm Nn Oo Pp Qq Rr Ss Tt Uu Vv Ww Xx Yy Zz
0123456789

Nara Std Light 18pt
Nara Std Light Cursive 18pt
*Nara Std Light Italic 18pt*
Nara Std Regular 18pt
Nara Std Regular Cursive 18pt
*Nara Std Regular Italic 18pt*
Nara Std Medium 18pt
Nara Std Medium Cursive 18pt
*Nara Std Medium Italic 18pt*
**Nara Std Bold 18pt**
**Nara Std Bold Cursive 18pt**
***Nara Std Bold Italic 18pt***
**Nara Std Black 18pt**
**Nara Std Black Cursive 18pt**
***Nara Std Black Italic 18pt***

---

12/14  Nara Std Light

The quick brown fox jumps over the lazy dog. Voyez le brick géant que j'examine près du wharf. Zwölf Boxkämpfer jagen Viktor quer über den

9/12  Nara Std Light

The quick brown fox jumps over the lazy dog. Voyez le brick géant que j'examine près du wharf. Zwölf Boxkämpfer jagen Viktor quer über den großen Sylter Deich. El veloz murciélago hindú comía feliz cardillo y kiwi. La cigüeña tocaba el saxofón detrás

7/10  Nara Std Light

The quick brown fox jumps over the lazy dog. Voyez le brick géant que j'examine près du wharf. Zwölf Boxkämpfer jagen Viktor quer über den großen Sylter Deich. El veloz murciélago hindú comía feliz cardillo y kiwi. La cigüeña tocaba el saxofón detrás del palenque de pajaatur? Rissimo lorereped ex es solore lab id molorro in rempore icabore rehenetur aliam aut voles audae dem quam, secum eum

12/14  Nara Std Regular

The quick brown fox jumps over the lazy dog. Voyez le brick géant que j'examine près du wharf. Zwölf Boxkämpfer jagen Viktor quer über den

9/12  Nara Std Regular

The quick brown fox jumps over the lazy dog. Voyez le brick géant que j'examine près du wharf. Zwölf Boxkämpfer jagen Viktor quer über den großen Sylter Deich. El veloz murciélago hindú comía feliz cardillo y kiwi. La cigüeña tocaba el saxofón detrás

7/10  Nara Std Regular

The quick brown fox jumps over the lazy dog. Voyez le brick géant que j'examine près du wharf. Zwölf Boxkämpfer jagen Viktor quer über den großen Sylter Deich. El veloz murciélago hindú comía feliz cardillo y kiwi. La cigüeña tocaba el saxofón detrás del palenque de pajaatur? Rissimo lorereped ex es solore lab id molorro in rempore icabore rehenetur aliam aut voles audae dem

12/14  Nara Std Medium

The quick brown fox jumps over the lazy dog. Voyez le brick géant que j'examine près du wharf. Zwölf Boxkämpfer jagen Viktor quer über den

9/12  Nara Std Medium

The quick brown fox jumps over the lazy dog. Voyez le brick géant que j'examine près du wharf. Zwölf Boxkämpfer jagen Viktor quer über den großen Sylter Deich. El veloz murciélago hindú comía feliz cardillo y kiwi. La cigüeña tocaba el

7/10  Nara Std Medium

The quick brown fox jumps over the lazy dog. Voyez le brick géant que j'examine près du wharf. Zwölf Boxkämpfer jagen Viktor quer über den großen Sylter Deich. El veloz murciélago hindú comía feliz cardillo y kiwi. La cigüeña tocaba el saxofón detrás del palenque de pajaatur? Rissimo lorereped ex es solore lab id molorro in rempore icabore rehenetur aliam aut voles

12/14  Nara Std Bold

**The quick brown fox jumps over the lazy dog. Voyez le brick géant que j'examine près du wharf. Zwölf Boxkämpfer jagen Viktor quer über den großen Sylter Deich. El veloz murciélago hindú comía feliz cardillo y**

9/12  Nara Std Bold

**The quick brown fox jumps over the lazy dog. Voyez le brick géant que j'examine près du wharf. Zwölf Boxkämpfer jagen Viktor quer über den großen Sylter Deich. El veloz murciélago hindú comía feliz cardillo y kiwi. La cigüeña tocaba el saxofón detrás del palenque de pajaatur? Rissimo lorereped ex es solore lab id**

7/10  Nara Std Bold

**The quick brown fox jumps over the lazy dog. Voyez le brick géant que j'examine près du wharf. Zwölf Boxkämpfer jagen Viktor quer über den großen Sylter Deich. El veloz murciélago hindú comía feliz cardillo y kiwi. La cigüeña tocaba el saxofón detrás del palenque de pajaatur? Rissimo lorereped ex es solore lab id molorro in rempore icabore rehenetur aliam aut voles audae dem quam, secum eum facesequae consequ aepudam quia voluptur repel in et faccustibus, nonsenis aut quis-**

# U
## Underware

Bas Jacobs,
Akiem Helmling,
Sami Kortemäki

—

The Hague &
Amsterdam,
Netherlands
& Helsinki, Finland

—

Since 1999

For more than ten years the pan-European design collective Underware has been creating versatile fonts, surfing the waves, conducting type workshops, running the radio station Typeradio, throwing cannon balls, experimenting with blood, practicing kamikaze chess; but mostly, they gave flowers to their mothers and turned them into cover girls. Which resulted in everlasting smiles on their faces.

## Info

—Why?
Because we wanted to meet the people using our fonts in person.

—People on staff
3

—Type designers on staff
3

—Type families
7

—Designers represented
3

—Web shop
www.underware.nl

—Distributors
Monotype, Veer, Fontshop, MyFonts, Vllg, You work for them + some smaller local ones.

—Webfont services
Typekit

—Basic license
From free to 450€ for the complete Auto family

—Special conditions
Special printed matter will be sent with any order.

## Typeface selection

Auto
Bello Pro
Dolly
Fakir
Fakir Display
Liza Caps Pro
Liza Display Pro
Liza Text Pro
Sauna

18pt

## People

—Bas Jacobs
Born in Wanssum, Netherlands. Studied visual communication at the art academy ABK in Maastricht and followed by the post-graduate course in typography and type design at the KABK, The Hague. Lives in Amsterdam. Still on the lookout for the 5kg jars of Nutella.

—Akiem Helmling was born in Heidelberg, Germany. From 1994 to 1998 he studied graphic design at the Fachhochschule Mannheim, followed postgraduate study at the KABK, The Hague until 2000. He now lives in the Hague and runs Galerie West with his girlfriend Marie-José.

—Sami Kortemäki
Born in Kerava, Finland. Between 1995 and 2001 he studied graphic design at the Lahti Polytechnic/Institute of Design. During 1998 and 1999 he also studied at the KABK in The Hague. Lives with his wife Ulrika and their son in Helsinki, Finland.

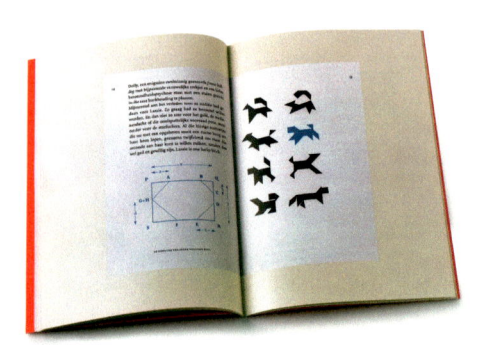

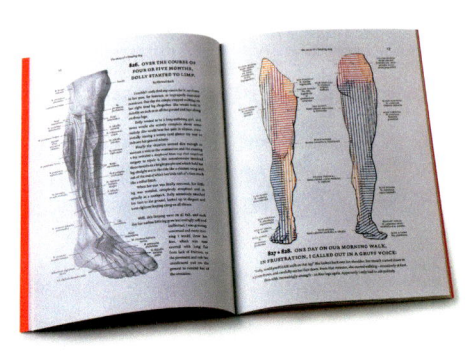

Page
281

Underware invited Orange Sunshine to record a 7-inch rock record, inspired by the typeface Fakir. For the sleeve, designers and rockers were invited to propose a design. Out of 80 entries, an international jury selected Supergabi's design as the official Fakir Rock sleeve winner.

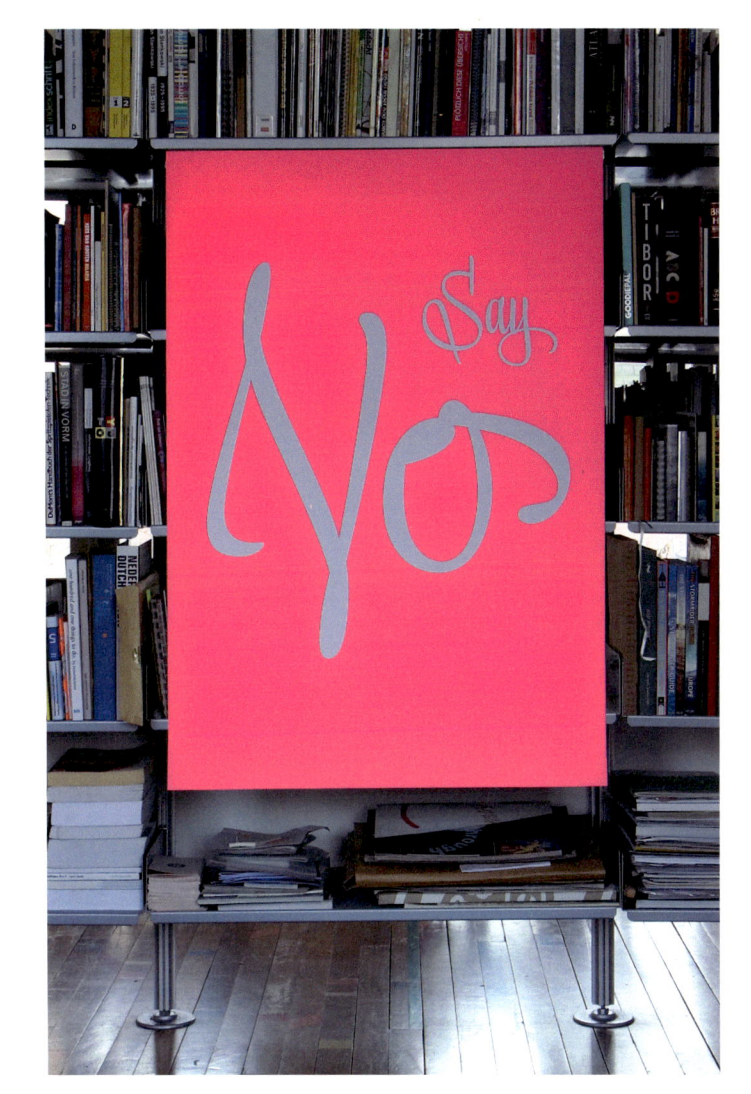

Ambiguity poster (Yes-No) designed using Liza.

Underware had its early specimens designed by renowned Dutch designers Wout de Vringer (Dolly, previous page) and Piet Schreuders (Sauna, above and right).

Page
282

Foundry Underware

Typeface Bello Pro
Designer Bas Jacobs,
Akiem Helmling,
Sami Kortemäki

Year 2004
Format OpenType

# Ciao Bellissima

Regular

Aa Bb Cc Dd Ee Ff Gg Hh Ii Jj Kk Ll Mm Nn Oo Pp Qq Rr Ss Tt Uu Vv Ww Xx Yy Zz 0123456789

The quick brown fox jumps over the lazy dog. Voyez le brick géant que j'examine près du wharf. Zwölf Boxkämpfer jagen Viktor quer über den großen Sylter Deich. El veloz murciélago hindú comía feliz cardillo y kiwi. La cigüeña tocaba el saxofón detrás del palenque de pajaatur? Rissimo lorereped ex es solore lab id molorro in rempore icabore rehenetur aliam aut voles audae dem quam, secum eum facesequae consequ aepudam quia

Typeface Bello Words

# Newsflash

Body Appendix
Shadow
Solo Appendix

Page 283

Foundry  Underware

Typeface   Auto
Designer   Bas Jacobs,
           Akiem Helmling,
           Sami Kortemäki

Year    2004
Format  OpenType

# Aa

Aa Bb Cc Dd Ee Ff Gg Hh Ii Jj Kk Ll
Mm Nn Oo Pp Qq Rr Ss Tt Uu Vv
Ww Xx Yy Zz
0123456789

—

Auto Light 14pt
Auto Light LF 14pt
AUTO LIGHT SMCP 14PT
Auto Regular 14pt
Auto Regular LF 14pt
AUTO REGULAR SMCP 14PT
**Auto Bold** 14pt
**Auto Bold LF** 14pt
**AUTO BOLD SMCP** 14PT
**Auto Black** 14pt
**Auto Black LF** 14pt
**AUTO BLACK SMCP** 14PT

*Auto 1 Light Italic* 14pt
*Auto 1 Light Italic LF* 14pt
*AUTO 1 LIGHT ITALIC SMCP* 14PT
*Auto 1 Italic* 14pt
*Auto 1 Italic LF* 14pt
*AUTO 1 ITALIC SMCP* 14PT
***Auto 1 Bold Italic*** 14pt
***Auto 1 Bold Italic LF*** 14pt
***AUTO 1 BOLD ITALIC SMCP*** 14PT
***Auto 1 Black Italic*** 14pt
***Auto 1 Black Italic LF*** 14pt
***AUTO 1 BLACK ITALIC SMCP*** 14PT

*Auto 2 Light Italic* 14pt
*Auto 2 Light Italic LF* 14pt
*AUTO 2 LIGHT ITALIC SMCP* 14PT
*Auto 2 Italic* 14pt
*Auto 2 Italic LF* 14pt
*AUTO 2 ITALIC SMCP* 14PT
***Auto 2 Bold Italic*** 14pt
***Auto 2 Bold Italic LF*** 14pt
***AUTO 2 BOLD ITALIC SMCP*** 14PT
***Auto 2 Black Italic*** 14pt
***Auto 2 Black Italic LF*** 14pt
***AUTO 2 BLACK ITALIC SMCP*** 14PT

*Auto 3 Light Italic* 14pt
*Auto 3 Light Italic LF* 14pt

*Auto 3 Italic* 14pt
*Auto 3 Italic LF* 14pt

***Auto 3 Bold Italic*** 14pt
***Auto 3 Bold Italic LF*** 14pt

***Auto 3 Black Italic*** 14pt
***Auto 3 Black Italic LF*** 14pt

---

9/12   Auto 1 Regular

THE QUICK BROWN FOX JUMPS over the lazy dog. Voyez le *brick géant* que j'examine près du wharf. Zwölf Boxkämpfer jagen Viktor quer über den großen *Sylter Deich*. El veloz murciélago hindú comía feliz cardillo y kiwi. La cigüeña tocaba el saxofón detrás del palenque de pajaatur? Rissimo lorereped ex es solore lab id molorro in rempore icabore rehen-

9/12   Auto 1 Italic

THE QUICK BROWN FOX JUMPS over the lazy dog. Voyez le brick géant que j'examine près du wharf. Zwölf Boxkämpfer jagen Viktor quer über den großen Sylter Deich. El veloz murciélago hindú comía feliz cardillo y kiwi. La cigüeña tocaba el saxofón detrás del palenque de pajaatur? Rissimo lorereped ex es solore lab id molorro in rempore icabore rehenetur aliam aut voles audae dem quam, secum eum facesequae consequ aepudam quia

9/12   Auto 2 Regular

THE QUICK BROWN FOX JUMPS over the lazy dog. Voyez le *brick géant* que j'examine près du wharf. Zwölf Boxkämpfer jagen Viktor quer über den großen *Sylter Deich*. El veloz murciélago hindú comía feliz cardillo y kiwi. La cigüeña tocaba el saxofón detrás del palenque de pajaatur? Rissimo lorereped ex es solore lab id molorro in rempore icabore rehen-

9/12   Auto 2 Italic

THE QUICK BROWN FOX JUMPS over the lazy dog. Voyez le brick géant que j'examine près du wharf. Zwölf Boxkämpfer jagen Viktor quer über den großen Sylter Deich. El veloz murciélago hindú comía feliz cardillo y kiwi. La cigüeña tocaba el saxofón detrás del palenque de pajaatur? Rissimo lorereped ex es solore lab id molorro in rempore icabore rehenetur aliam aut voles audae dem quam, secum eum facesequae consequ aepudam quia

9/12   Auto 3 Regular

The quick brown fox jumps over the lazy dog. Voyez le *brick géant* que j'examine près du wharf. Zwölf Boxkämpfer jagen Viktor quer über den großen *Sylter Deich*. El veloz murciélago hindú comía feliz cardillo y kiwi. La cigüeña tocaba el saxofón detrás del palenque de pajaatur? Rissimo lorereped ex es solore lab id molorro in rempore icabore rehenetur

9/12   Auto 3 Italic

The quick brown fox jumps over the lazy dog. Voyez le brick géant que j'examine près du wharf. Zwölf Boxkämpfer jagen Viktor quer über den großen Sylter Deich. El veloz murciélago hindú comía feliz cardillo y kiwi. La cigüeña tocaba el saxofón detrás del palenque de pajaatur? Rissimo lorereped ex es solore lab id molorro in rempore icabore rehenetur aliam aut voles audae dem quam, secum eum facesequae consequ aepudam

| | | | |
|---|---|---|---|
| Typeface | Fakir Display | Year | 2006 |
| Designer | Bas Jacobs, Akiem Helmling, Sami Kortemäki | Format | OpenType |

# Fakir Feuershow

Fakir Display Regular
Fakir Display Regular End
**Fakir Display Black**
Fakir Display Black End
FAKIR DISPLAY BLACK SMCP

Aa Bb Cc Dd Ee Ff Gg Hh Ii Jj Kk Ll Mm Nn Oo Pp Qq Rr Ss Tt Uu Vv Ww Xx Yy Zz 0123456789

The quick brown fox jumps over the lazy dog. Voyez le brick géant que j'examine près du wharf. Zwölf Boxkämpfer jagen Viktor quer über den großen Sylter Deich. El veloz murciélago hindú comía feliz cardillo y kiwi. La cigüeña tocaba el saxofón detrás del palenque de pajaatur? Rissimo lorereped ex es solore lab id molorro in rempore icabore rehenetur aliam aut voles audae dem quam, secum eum facesequae consequ aepudam quia voluptiur repel in et faccustibus, nonsenis aut quisqui rero mi, ipiet lam ant ut maio et hil

Fakir Regular
Fakir Italic
FAKIR SMCP
**Fakir Black**
**Fakir Black Italic**

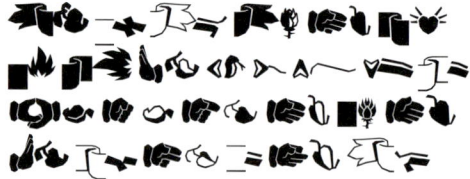

| | | | |
|---|---|---|---|
| Typeface | Liza | Year | 2009 |
| Designer | Bas Jacobs, Akiem Helmling, Sami Kortemäki | Format | OpenType |

# Liza Minelly

Display Pro
Caps Pro
Text Pro

Aa Bb Cc Dd Ee Ff Gg Hh Ii Jj Kk Ll Mm Nn Oo Pp Qq Rr Ss Tt Uu Vv Ww Xx Yy Zz 0123456789

The quick brown fox jumps over the lazy dog. Voyez le brick géant que j'examine près du wharf. Zwölf Boxkämpfer jagen Viktor quer über den großen Sylter Deich. El veloz murciélago hindú comía feliz cardillo y kiwi. La cigüeña tocaba el saxofón detrás del palenque de pajaatur? Rissimo lorereped ex es solore lab id molorro in rempore icabore rehenetur aliam aut voles audae dem quam, secum eum facesequae consequ aepudam quid voluptiur repel in et faccustibus, nonsenis aut quisqui rero mi, ipiet lam ant ut

Foundry  Underware

Typeface  Sauna
Designer  Bas Jacobs,
 Akiem Helmling,
 Sami Kortemäki

Year  2002
Format  OpenType

# Aa

Aa Bb Cc Dd Ee Ff Gg Hh Ii Jj Kk Ll
Mm Nn Oo Pp Qq Rr Ss Tt Uu Vv
Ww Xx Yy Zz
0123456789
—

Sauna Roman 18pt
SAUNA SMALL CAPS 18PT
*Sauna Italic* 18pt
*Sauna Italic Swash* 18pt
**Sauna Bold** 18pt
***Sauna Bold Italic*** 18pt
***Sauna Bold Italic Swash*** 18pt
**Sauna Black** 18pt
***Sauna Black Italic*** 18pt
***Sauna Black Italic Swash*** 18pt

12/14  Sauna Roman

The quick brown fox jumps over the lazy dog. Voyez le brick géant que j'examine près du wharf. Zwölf Boxkämpfer jagen Viktor quer über den großen Sylter Deich. El veloz murciélago hindú comía feliz cardillo y kiwi. La cigüeña tocaba el saxofón detrás del palenque de pajaatur? Rissimo lorereped ex es solore lab id molorro in rempore

9/12  Sauna Roman

The quick brown fox jumps over the lazy dog. Voyez le brick géant que j'examine près du wharf. Zwölf Boxkämpfer jagen Viktor quer über den großen Sylter Deich. El veloz murciélago hindú comía feliz cardillo y kiwi. La cigüeña tocaba el saxofón detrás del palenque de pajaatur? Rissimo lorereped ex es solore lab id molorro in rempore icabore rehenetur aliam aut voles audae dem quam, secum eum facesequae consequ aepudam quia voluptiur repel in et faccustibus, nonsenis aut quisqui

Typeface  Dolly
Designer  Bas Jacobs,
 Akiem Helmling,
 Sami Kortemäki

Year  2001
Format  OpenType

# Aa

Aa Bb Cc Dd Ee Ff Gg Hh Ii Jj Kk Ll
Mm Nn Oo Pp Qq Rr Ss Tt Uu Vv
Ww Xx Yy Zz
0123456789
—

Dolly Roman 20pt
DOLLY SMALL CAPS 20PT
*Dolly Italic* 20pt
**Dolly Bold** 20pt

9/12  Dolly Roman

The quick brown fox jumps over the lazy dog. Voyez le brick géant que j'examine près du wharf. Zwölf Boxkämpfer jagen Viktor quer über den großen Sylter Deich. El veloz murciélago hindú comía feliz cardillo y kiwi. La cigüeña tocaba el saxofón detrás del palenque de pajaatur? Rissimo lorereped ex es solore lab id molorro in rempore icabore rehenetur aliam aut voles audae dem quam, secum eum facesequae consequ aepudam quia voluptiur repel in et faccustibus, nonsenis aut quisqui rero mi, ipiet lam ant ut maio et hil molupta tustis atatur, consedi tasimol orerem aut volor andipsapis sit, illaut volore officatus alicae dusdaec tatecte cearum qui accatibus restiore nulpa secaerferum,

7/10  Dolly Roman

The quick brown fox jumps over the lazy dog. Voyez le brick géant que j'examine près du wharf. Zwölf Boxkämpfer jagen Viktor quer über den großen Sylter Deich. El veloz murciélago hindú comía feliz cardillo y kiwi. La cigüeña tocaba el saxofón detrás del palenque de pajaatur? Rissimo lorereped ex es solore lab id molorro in rempore icabore rehenetur aliam aut voles audae dem quam, secum eum facesequae consequ aepudam quia voluptiur repel in et faccustibus, nonsenis aut quisqui rero mi, ipiet lam ant ut maio et hil molupta tustis atatur, consedi tasimol orerem aut volor andipsapis sit, illaut volore officatus alicae dusdaec tatecte cearum qui accatibus restiore nulpa secaerferum, nus dolenim in et quoditat que explam volupictur? Qui de illuptae. Dae nis illiberum volorro ritatis tinullo rerumqu atetur repro eatius asperibus. Rissimo lorereped ex es solore lab id molorro in rempore icabore rehenetur aliam aut voles audae dem quam, secum eum facesequae consequ aepudam quia voluptiur repel in et faccustibus, nonsenis aut quisqui rero mi, ipiet lam ant

# V

## VetteLetters

—

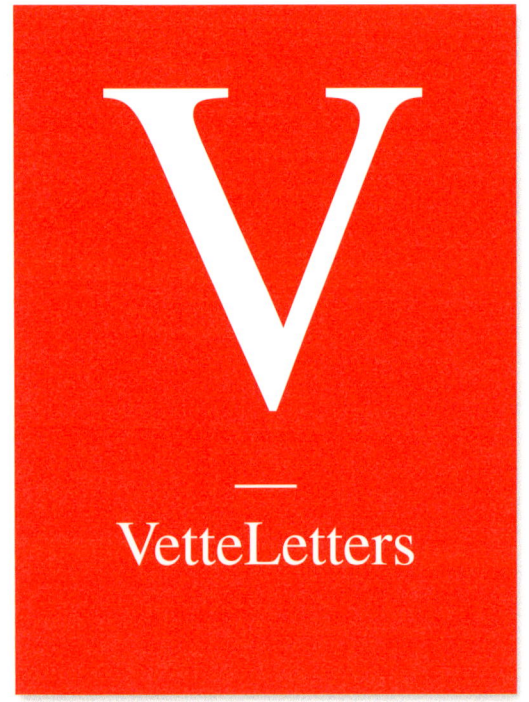

Donald® Roos, Donald Beekman

—

Amsterdam, Netherlands

—

Since 1997

"When I went to the academy in 1997 the idea of a foundry was there when I fell in love with letters, typography and cooking. Officially VetteLetters started selling fonts in 2008." VetteLetters is the greasy spoon café in the world of exclusive typographic haute cuisine.

## Info

—Why?
A long time ago Donald® sold his soul to the devil and went commercial. Donald® started earning big money, as you could tell from his weight, his body becoming fatter and fatter. His love for type designing followed him, caught up with him then brought him back to earth. Inspired by his weight and his fascination for cheap (fast food) restaurants, Donald® founded VetteLetters.

—People on staff
1.5

—Type designers on staff
2

—Type families
20+

—Designers represented
2.5

—Web shop?
Working on it; to open late 2011–early 2012.

—Distributors
MyFonts

—Webfont services
Working on it...

—Basic license
Single weights mostly $35 and $15 for every next weight.

## People

—Donald® Roos (founder/boss)
After a wonderful career as a dishwasher, assistant cook, some kind of designer, and last but not least type designer, Donald is now one of the CEOs of VetteLetters. VetteLetters is the tastiest font foundry in the universe. Donald enjoys working together with the other Donald (also CEO of VetteLetters).

—Donald DBXL Beekman is "the other Donald" as well as the other CEO of VetteLetters. Donald Beekman produces as many typefaces as Prince makes records. Well, maybe not that many, but a lot. Too many to handle for VetteLetters alone. So he has also published fonts at FontFont and Gestalten Fonts, but the big money comes from VetteLetters. That's why he is a partner!

—Jacques "Sardines" Le Bailly, also known as the Baron von Fonthausen. Before becoming a Baron he worked for Linotype designing and implementing the euro sign in over 300 fonts. The Baron likes working on large-scale projects. This is probably why he came up with NeueSardines after Sardines. NeueSardines is the biggest monospaced type family in the world. NeueSardines consists of 11 weights, 4 styles and 42 fonts!

—Martin "Martini" Lorenz is a German designer, working in the lovely climate of Barcelona, Spain. He enjoys paella and other fresh seafood. He also runs a design office called TwoPoints, together with his wife Lupi Asensio. The good thing is, TwoPoints make their own fonts for their projects. The best news is — VetteLetters will release the TwoPoints collection!

VLNL Bonbon in use.

## Typeface selection

**VLNL BINT**
*VLNL Spaghetti Bolognese*
VLNL HOLLANDSCHE NIEUWE
VLNL Knoffel
VLNL BRAK
**VLNL BROKKEN**
VLNL Gaufre
VLNL neuesardines
VLNL TpMartini
VLNL TpHolaBcn

16pt

Page 287

First specimen of the VLNL Spaghetti Bolognese. 14th of June 2000.

VetteLetters Promotion.

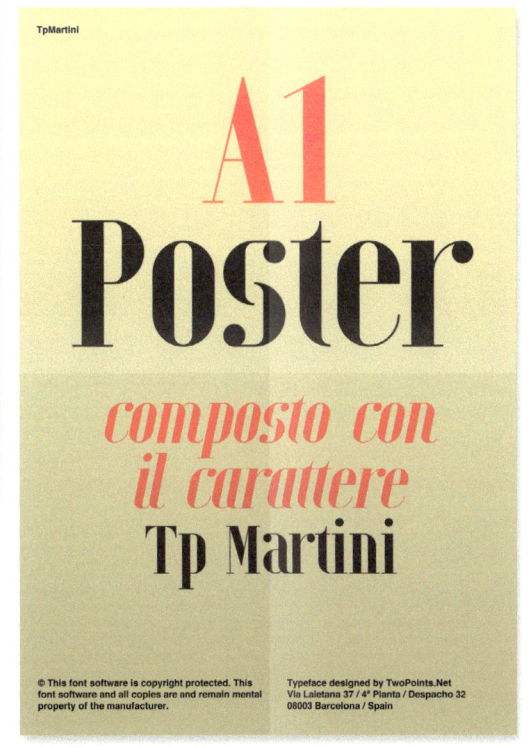

VLNL TpMartini Promotional Poster.

| | | | |
|---|---|---|---|
| Typeface | VLNL Brak | Year | 2004 |
| Designer | Donald DBXL Beekman | Format | OpenType |

# BRAK
# BRAK

REGULAR
**BOLD**

AA BB CC DD EE FF GG HH
II JJ KK LL MM NN OO PP
QQ RR SS TT UU VV WW
XX YY ZZ 0123456789

| | | | |
|---|---|---|---|
| Typeface | VLNL Brokken | Year | 2008 |
| Designer | Donald DBXL Beekman | Format | OpenType |

# HAPKLARE BROKKEN

**REGULAR**

AA BB CC DD EE FF
GG HH II JJ KK LL
MM NN OO PP QQ RR
SS TT UU VV WW XX
YY ZZ 0123456789

| | | | |
|---|---|---|---|
| Typeface | VLNL Hollandsche Nieuwe | Year | 2012 |
| Designer | Donald® Roos | Format | OpenType |

# BROODJE KROKET MET UI

LIGHT
**BOLD**

AA BB CC DD EE FF GG
HH II JJ KK LL MM
NN OO PP QQ RR SS TT
UU VV WW XX YY ZZ
0123456789

Page 289  Foundry VetteLetters

Typeface VLNL Knoffel  Year 2007
Designer Donald® Roos  Format OpenType

# Knoblauch
# Knoblauch

Regular
Outline
Inline

Aa Bb Cc Dd Ee Ff Gg Hh Ii
Jj Kk Ll Mm Nn Oo Pp Qq Rr
Ss Tt Uu Vv Ww Xx Yy Zz
0123456789

---

Typeface VLNL Bint  Year 2005
Designer Donald® Roos  Format OpenType

# LEEST BINT!

REGULAR

AA BB CC DD EE FF GG
HH II JJ KK LL MM
NN OO PP QQ RR SS
TT UU VV WW XX YY ZZ
0123456789

---

Typeface VLNL Gaufre  Year 2005
Designer Donald® Roos  Format OpenType

# Pixie, Jump & Shoot

Regular

Aa Bb Cc Dd Ee Ff Gg Hh Ii
Jj Kk Ll Mm Nn Oo Pp Qq
Rr Ss Tt Uu Vv Ww Xx Yy
Zz 0123456789

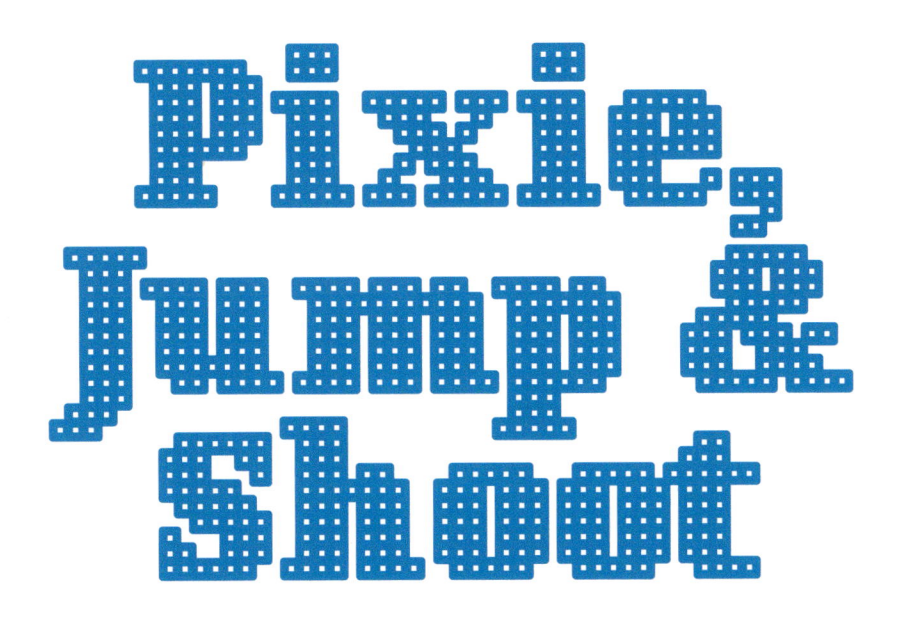

| | | | |
|---|---|---|---|
| Page | 290 | Foundry | VetteLetters |

| | | | |
|---|---|---|---|
| Typeface | VLNL TpMartini | Year | 2006 |
| Designer | Martin "Martini" Lorenz | Format | OpenType |

# Monday Hangover

Regular
*Italic*

Aa Bb Cc Dd Ee Ff Gg Hh Ii
Jj Kk Ll Mm Nn Oo Pp Qq Rr
Ss Tt Uu Vv Ww Xx Yy Zz
0123456789

| | | | |
|---|---|---|---|
| Typeface | VLNL TpHolaBcn | Year | 2006 |
| Designer | Martin "Martini" Lorenz | Format | OpenType |

# Hola!

Regular

Aa Bb Cc Dd Ee Ff Gg Hh
Ii Jj Kk Ll Mm Nn Oo
Pp Qq Rr Ss Tt Uu Vv
Ww Xx Yy Zz 0123456789

| | | | |
|---|---|---|---|
| Typeface | VLNL Spaghetti Bolognese | Year | 2000 |
| Designer | Donald® Roos | Format | OpenType |

# Typo Extra Vergine

Regular

Aa Bb Cc Dd Ee Ff
Gg Hh Ii Jj Kk Ll Mm
Nn Oo Pp Qq Rr Ss Tt
Uu Vv Ww Xx Yy Zz
0123456789

Typeface VLNL Neue Sardines  Year 2009
Designer Jacques "Sardines" Le Bailly  Format OpenType

# Aa

VLNL Neue Sardines One 12pt
VLNL Neue Sardines Two 12pt
VLNL Neue Sardines Three 12pt
VLNL Neue Sardines Four 12pt
VLNL Neue Sardines Five 12pt
VLNL Neue Sardines Six 12pt
VLNL Neue Sardines Seven 12pt
VLNL Neue Sardines Eight 12pt
VLNL Neue Sardines Nine 12pt
VLNL Neue Sardines Ten 12pt
VLNL Neue Sardines Eleven 12pt

Aa Bb Cc Dd Ee Ff
Gg Hh Ii Jj Kk Ll
Mm Nn Oo Pp Qq Rr
Ss Tt Uu Vv Ww Xx
Yy Zz
0123456789
-

VLNL Neue Sardines Condensed One 12pt
VLNL Neue Sardines Condensed Two 12pt
VLNL Neue Sardines Condensed Three 12pt
VLNL Neue Sardines Condensed Four 12pt
VLNL Neue Sardines Condensed Five 12pt
VLNL Neue Sardines Condensed Six 12pt
VLNL Neue Sardines Condensed Seven 12pt
VLNL Neue Sardines Condensed Eight 12pt
VLNL Neue Sardines Condensed Nine 12pt
VLNL Neue Sardines Condensed Ten 12pt

VLNL Neue Sardines Rough One 12pt
VLNL Neue Sardines Rough Two 12pt
VLNL Neue Sardines Rough Three 12pt
VLNL Neue Sardines Rough Four 12pt
VLNL Neue Sardines Rough Five 12pt
VLNL Neue Sardines Rough Six 12pt
VLNL Neue Sardines Rough Seven 12pt
VLNL Neue Sardines Rough Eight 12pt
VLNL Neue Sardines Rough Nine 12pt
VLNL Neue Sardines Rough Ten 12pt
VLNL Neue Sardines Rough Eleven 12pt

VLNL Neue Sardines Rough Condensed One 12pt
VLNL Neue Sardines Rough Condensed Two 12pt
VLNL Neue Sardines Rough Condensed Three 12pt
VLNL Neue Sardines Rough Condensed Four 12pt
VLNL Neue Sardines Rough Condensed Five 12pt
VLNL Neue Sardines Rough Condensed Six 12pt
VLNL Neue Sardines Rough Condensed Seven 12pt
VLNL Neue Sardines Rough Condensed Eight 12pt
VLNL Neue Sardines Rough Condensed Nine 12pt
VLNL Neue Sardines Rough Condensed Ten 12pt

# V

## Village: Incubator

Chester Jenkins, Tracy Jenkins

—

New York

—

Since 2008

Village was founded in 2004 by Tracy Jenkins, graphic designer, and Chester Jenkins, type designer. Launched four years later, the Incubator is the place for promising unpublished designers' work. Several of the types Village is publishing through the Incubator were thesis projects at the type design courses in The Hague or Reading, and needed a little bit of technical tightening and gentle design guidance. Incubator designers receive advice and sometimes collaboration from Village members.

## Info

—Why?
When Tracy was completing her Master's degree in New Haven, Connecticut, we knew we would be moving to New York. It was a perfect time to put together an idea Chester had had several years before for a kind of union of young-ish (sub-35-year-old) independent 1-person foundries. We would be a kind of loose co-operative, with sharing of technical knowledge and decision-making. The Incubator was created to allow us to work with a larger group of upcoming designers within the Village structure.

—People on staff
2

—Type designers on staff
1

—Type families
8

—Designers represented
8

—Web shop
vllg.com/Incubator

—Distributors
None

—Webfont services
We license webfonts to self-host in WOFF, EOT and SVG formats.

—Basic license
$50 (single font, 1–4 computers). Families are priced according to the number of weights, up to US$400

Typeface selection

Agile
**Arrival**
Freya
**Haas**
Kina
Router

24pt

## People

The Incubator designers:

—Hugo d'Alte is a Portuguese-born, Dutch-educated, British-collaborating, Finnish-resident graphic designer.

—Hanno Bennert is a German type and graphic designer.

—Francesca Bolognini is an Italian designer working in London, a graduate of the Type & Media program at the KABK in The Hague, Netherlands.

—Saku Heinänen is a Finnish type and graphic designer specializing in publication design. He also runs Typolar, featured in this book.

—Holger Königsdörfer (Germany) is a German designer, and a graduate of the KABK program in The Hague.

—Jeremy Mickel hails from Ohio, USA, and presently lives and works in Minneapolis, after stints in New York City and Providence, RI.

—Keith Chi-hang Tam is Chinese-Canadian, and is presently teaching at Hong Kong Polytechnic. He is a graduate of the MA in Type Design at the University of Reading, UK.

—Edgar Walthert is a Swiss designer working in the Netherlands, and a graduate of the KABK program.

Francesca Bolognini, sketches for Kina.

Page 293

Edgar Walthert created these packaging mockups to showcase the various weights of his Agile family.

Hugo d'Alte's Kaas typeface.

Francesca Bolognini, sketches for Kina.

Page 294

Foundry  Village: Incubator

Typeface  Freya
Designer  Saku Heinänen

Year    2010
Format  OpenType

# Aa

Freya Medium 20pt
*Freya Medium Italic 20pt*
**Freya Bold 20pt**
***Freya Bold Italic 20pt***

Aa Bb Cc Dd Ee Ff Gg Hh Ii Jj Kk
Ll Mm Nn Oo Pp Qq Rr Ss Tt Uu
Vv Ww Xx Yy Zz
0123456789
—

9/12   Freya Medium

The quick brown fox jumps over the lazy dog. Voyez le brick géant que j'examine près du wharf. Zwölf Boxkämpfer jagen Viktor quer über den großen Sylter Deich. El veloz murciélago hindú comía feliz cardillo y kiwi. La cigüeña tocaba el saxofón detrás del palenque de pajaatur? Rissimo lorereped ex es solore lab id molorro in rempore icabore rehenetur aliam aut voles audae dem quam, secum eum facesequae consequ aepudam

7/10   Freya Medium

The quick brown fox jumps over the lazy dog. Voyez le brick géant que j'examine près du wharf. Zwölf Boxkämpfer jagen Viktor quer über den großen Sylter Deich. El veloz murciélago hindú comía feliz cardillo y kiwi. La cigüeña tocaba el saxofón detrás del palenque de pajaatur? Rissimo lorereped ex es solore lab id molorro in rempore icabore rehenetur aliam aut voles audae dem quam, secum eum facesequae consequ aepudam quia voluptiur repel in et faccustibus, nonsenis aut quisqui rero mi, ipiet lam ant ut maio et hil molupta tustis atatur, consedi tasimol orerem aut volor andipsapis sit, illaut volore officatus alicae dusdaec tatecte cearum qui accatibus restiore nulpa secaerferum,

Typeface  Arrival
Designer  Keith Tam Design

Year    2005
Format  OpenType

# Aa

Arrival Medium 20pt
*Arrival Medium Italic 20pt*
**Arrival ExtraBold 20pt**

Aa Bb Cc Dd Ee Ff Gg Hh Ii Jj Kk
Ll Mm Nn Oo Pp Qq Rr Ss Tt Uu
Vv Ww Xx Yy Zz
0123456789
—

9/12   Arrival Medium

The quick brown fox jumps over the lazy dog. Voyez le brick géant que j'examine près du wharf. Zwölf Boxkämpfer jagen Viktor quer über den großen Sylter Deich. El veloz murciélago hindú comía feliz cardillo y kiwi. La cigüeña tocaba el saxofón detrás del palenque de pajaatur? Rissimo lorereped ex es solore lab id molorro in rempore icabore rehenetur aliam aut voles audae dem quam, secum eum facesequae consequ aepudam quia voluptiur repel in et faccustibus, nonsenis aut quisqui rero mi, ipiet lam ant ut maio et hil molupta tustis atatur, consedi tasimol orerem aut volor andipsapis sit,

7/10   Arrival Medium

The quick brown fox jumps over the lazy dog. Voyez le brick géant que j'examine près du wharf. Zwölf Boxkämpfer jagen Viktor quer über den großen Sylter Deich. El veloz murciélago hindú comía feliz cardillo y kiwi. La cigüeña tocaba el saxofón detrás del palenque de pajaatur? Rissimo lorereped ex es solore lab id molorro in rempore icabore rehenetur aliam aut voles audae dem quam, secum eum facesequae consequ aepudam quia voluptiur repel in et faccustibus, nonsenis aut quisqui rero mi, ipiet lam ant ut maio et hil molupta tustis atatur, consedi tasimol orerem aut volor andipsapis sit, illaut volore officatus alicae dusdaec tatecte cearum qui accatibus restiore nulpa secaerferum, nus dolenim in et quoditat que explam volupictur? Qui de illuptae. Dae nis illiberum volorro ritatis tinullo rerumqu atetur repro eatius asperibus. Rissimo lorereped ex es solore lab id molorro in rempore icabore rehenetur aliam aut voles audae dem

Page
295

Foundry Village: Incubator

Typeface   Agile
Designer   Edgar Walthert
Year       2010
Format     OpenType

# Aa

Aa Bb Cc Dd Ee Ff Gg Hh Ii Jj Kk
Ll Mm Nn Oo Pp Qq Rr Ss Tt Uu
Vv Ww Xx Yy Zz
0123456789
—

Agile Hairline 18pt
*Agile Hairline Italic 18pt*
Agile Thin 18pt
*Agile Thin Italic 18pt*
Agile ExtraLight 18pt
*Agile ExtraLight Italic 18pt*
Agile Light 18pt
*Agile Light Italic 18pt*
Agile Book 18pt
*Agile Book Italic 18pt*
**Agile Medium Regular 18pt**
*Agile Medium Italic 18pt*
**Agile Bold 18pt**
***Agile Bold Italic 18pt***
**Agile ExtraBold 18pt**
***Agile ExtraBold Italic 18pt***
**Agile Black 18pt**
***Agile Black Italic 18pt***
**Agile Fat 18pt**
***Agile Fat Italic 18pt***

---

12/14   Agile Light

The quick brown fox jumps over the lazy dog. Voyez le brick géant que j'examine près du wharf. Zwölf Boxkämpfer jagen Viktor quer über

12/14   Agile Book

The quick brown fox jumps over the lazy dog. Voyez le brick géant que j'examine près du wharf. Zwölf Boxkämpfer jagen Viktor

12/14   Agile Bold

**The quick brown fox jumps over the lazy dog. Voyez le brick géant que j'examine près du wharf. Zwölf Boxkämpfer jagen Viktor quer über den großen Sylter Deich.**

9/12   Agile Light

The quick brown fox jumps over the lazy dog. Voyez le brick géant que j'examine près du wharf. Zwölf Boxkämpfer jagen Viktor quer über den großen Sylter Deich. El veloz murciélago hindú comía feliz cardillo y kiwi. La

9/12   Agile Book

The quick brown fox jumps over the lazy dog. Voyez le brick géant que j'examine près du wharf. Zwölf Boxkämpfer jagen Viktor quer über den großen Sylter Deich. El veloz murciélago hindú comía feliz cardillo y kiwi. La

9/12   Agile Bold

**The quick brown fox jumps over the lazy dog. Voyez le brick géant que j'examine près du wharf. Zwölf Boxkämpfer jagen Viktor quer über den großen Sylter Deich. El veloz murciélago hindú comía feliz cardillo y kiwi. La cigüeña tocaba el saxofón detrás del palenque**

7/10   Agile Light

The quick brown fox jumps over the lazy dog. Voyez le brick géant que j'examine près du wharf. Zwölf Boxkämpfer jagen Viktor quer über den großen Sylter Deich. El veloz murciélago hindú comía feliz cardillo y kiwi. La cigüeña tocaba el saxofón detrás del palenque de pajaatur? Rissimo lorereped ex es solore lab id molorro in rempore icabore rehenetur

7/10   Agile Book

The quick brown fox jumps over the lazy dog. Voyez le brick géant que j'examine près du wharf. Zwölf Boxkämpfer jagen Viktor quer über den großen Sylter Deich. El veloz murciélago hindú comía feliz cardillo y kiwi. La cigüeña tocaba el saxofón detrás del palenque de pajaatur? Rissimo lorereped ex es solore lab id molorro in rempore icabore rehenetur

7/10   Agile Bold

**The quick brown fox jumps over the lazy dog. Voyez le brick géant que j'examine près du wharf. Zwölf Boxkämpfer jagen Viktor quer über den großen Sylter Deich. El veloz murciélago hindú comía feliz cardillo y kiwi. La cigüeña tocaba el saxofón detrás del palenque de pajaatur? Rissimo lorereped ex es solore lab id molorro in rempore icabore rehenetur aliam aut voles audae dem quam, secum eum**

| | | | |
|---|---|---|---|
| Typeface | Kaas | Year | 2005 |
| Designer | Hugo d'Alte | Format | OpenType |

# Patricia Kaasje

**Regular**

Aa Bb Cc Dd Ee Ff Gg Hh Ii
Jj Kk Ll Mm Nn Oo Pp Qq Rr
Ss Tt Uu Vv Ww Xx Yy Zz
0123456789

---

| | | | |
|---|---|---|---|
| Typeface | Kina | Year | 2009 |
| Designer | Francesca Bolognini | Format | OpenType |

## Aa

Aa Bb Cc Dd Ee Ff Gg Hh Ii Jj Kk Ll Mm Nn Oo Pp Qq Rr Ss Tt Uu Vv Ww Xx Yy Zz
0123456789
—

Kina Thin 18pt
*Kina Thin Italic 18pt*
Kina Light 18pt
*Kina Light Italic 18pt*
Kina Book 18pt
*Kina Book Italic 18pt*
Kina Medium Regular 18pt
*Kina Medium Italic 18pt*
**Kina Bold 18pt**
***Kina Bold Italic 18pt***
**Kina Black 18pt**
***Kina Black Italic 18pt***

---

12/14  Kina Light

The quick brown fox jumps over the lazy dog. Voyez le brick géant que j'examine près du wharf. Zwölf Boxkämpfer jagen Viktor quer über den

12/14  Kina Book

The quick brown fox jumps over the lazy dog. Voyez le brick géant que j'examine près du wharf. Zwölf Boxkämpfer jagen Viktor quer über den großen Sylter Deich. El veloz murciélago hindú comía feliz cardillo y kiwi. La cigüeña tocaba el saxofón detrás del palenque de pajaatur? Rissimo lorereped ex es solore lab id molorro in

9/12  Kina Light

The quick brown fox jumps over the lazy dog. Voyez le brick géant que j'examine près du wharf. Zwölf Boxkämpfer jagen Viktor quer über den großen Sylter Deich. El veloz murciélago hindú comía feliz cardillo y kiwi. La cigüeña tocaba el saxofón detrás

9/12  Kina Book

The quick brown fox jumps over the lazy dog. Voyez le brick géant que j'examine près du wharf. Zwölf Boxkämpfer jagen Viktor quer über den großen Sylter Deich. El veloz murciélago hindú comía feliz cardillo y kiwi. La cigüeña tocaba el saxofón detrás del palenque de pajaatur? Rissimo lorereped ex es solore lab id molorro in rempore icabore rehenetur aliam aut voles audae dem quam, secum eum facesequae consequ aepudam quia voluptiur repel in et faccustibus, nonsenis

7/10  Kina Light

The quick brown fox jumps over the lazy dog. Voyez le brick géant que j'examine près du wharf. Zwölf Boxkämpfer jagen Viktor quer über den großen Sylter Deich. El veloz murciélago hindú comía feliz cardillo y kiwi. La cigüeña tocaba el saxofón detrás del palenque de pajaatur? Rissimo lorereped ex es solore lab id molorro in rempore icabore rehenetur aliam aut voles audae dem quam, secum

7/10  Kina Book

The quick brown fox jumps over the lazy dog. Voyez le brick géant que j'examine près du wharf. Zwölf Boxkämpfer jagen Viktor quer über den großen Sylter Deich. El veloz murciélago hindú comía feliz cardillo y kiwi. La cigüeña tocaba el saxofón detrás del palenque de pajaatur? Rissimo lorereped ex es solore lab id molorro in rempore icabore rehenetur aliam aut voles audae dem quam, secum eum facesequae consequ aepudam quia voluptiur repel in et faccustibus, nonsenis aut quisqui rero mi, ipiet lam ant ut maio et hil molupta tustis atatur, consedi tasimol orerem aut volor andipsapis sit, illaut volore officatus alicae dusdaec tatecte cearum qui accatibus restiore nulpa secaerferum, nus dolenim in et quoditat que explam volupictur? Qui de illuptae.

Page
297

Foundry Village: Incubator

Typeface Router
Designer Jeremy Mickel

Year 2008
Format OpenType

# Aa

Aa Bb Cc Dd Ee Ff Gg Hh Ii Jj Kk
Ll Mm Nn Oo Pp Qq Rr Ss Tt Uu
Vv Ww Xx Yy Zz
0123456789
—

Router Thin 18pt
*Router Thin Italic 18pt*
Router ExtraLight 18pt
*Router ExtraLight Italic 18pt*
Router Light 18pt
*Router Light Italic 18pt*
Router Book 18pt
*Router Book Italic 18pt*
**Router Medium Regular 18pt**
***Router Medium Italic 18pt***
**Router Bold 18pt**
***Router Bold Italic 18pt***

---

12/14 Router Thin

The quick brown fox jumps over the lazy dog. Voyez le brick géant que j'examine près du wharf. Zwölf Boxkämpfer jagen Viktor quer über den

12/14 Router Light

The quick brown fox jumps over the lazy dog. Voyez le brick géant que j'examine près du wharf. Zwölf Boxkämpfer jagen Viktor quer über den

12/14 Router Book

The quick brown fox jumps over the lazy dog. Voyez le brick géant que j'examine près du wharf. Zwölf Boxkämpfer jagen Viktor quer über den

12/14 Router Bold

**The quick brown fox jumps over the lazy dog. Voyez le brick géant que j'examine près du wharf. Zwölf Boxkämpfer jagen Viktor quer über den großen Sylter Deich. El veloz murciélago hindú comía feliz cardillo y kiwi. La cigüeña tocaba el saxofón detrás del palenque de pajaatur? Rissimo lorereped ex es**

9/12 Router Thin

The quick brown fox jumps over the lazy dog. Voyez le brick géant que j'examine près du wharf. Zwölf Boxkämpfer jagen Viktor quer über den großen Sylter Deich. El veloz murciélago hindú comía feliz cardillo y kiwi. La cigüeña tocaba el

9/12 Router Light

The quick brown fox jumps over the lazy dog. Voyez le brick géant que j'examine près du wharf. Zwölf Boxkämpfer jagen Viktor quer über den großen Sylter Deich. El veloz murciélago hindú comía feliz cardillo y kiwi. La cigüeña tocaba el

9/12 Router Book

The quick brown fox jumps over the lazy dog. Voyez le brick géant que j'examine près du wharf. Zwölf Boxkämpfer jagen Viktor quer über den großen Sylter Deich. El veloz murciélago hindú comía feliz cardillo y kiwi. La cigüeña tocaba

9/12 Router Bold

**The quick brown fox jumps over the lazy dog. Voyez le brick géant que j'examine près du wharf. Zwölf Boxkämpfer jagen Viktor quer über den großen Sylter Deich. El veloz murciélago hindú comía feliz cardillo y kiwi. La cigüeña tocaba el saxofón detrás del palenque de pajaatur? Rissimo lorereped ex es solore lab id molorro in rempore icabore rehenetur aliam aut voles audae dem quam, secum eum facesequae consequ aepudam quia voluptiur**

7/10 Router Thin

The quick brown fox jumps over the lazy dog. Voyez le brick géant que j'examine près du wharf. Zwölf Boxkämpfer jagen Viktor quer über den großen Sylter Deich. El veloz murciélago hindú comía feliz cardillo y kiwi. La cigüeña tocaba el saxofón detrás del palenque de pajaatur? Rissimo lorereped ex es solore lab id molorro in rempore icabore rehenetur aliam aut voles

7/10 Router Light

The quick brown fox jumps over the lazy dog. Voyez le brick géant que j'examine près du wharf. Zwölf Boxkämpfer jagen Viktor quer über den großen Sylter Deich. El veloz murciélago hindú comía feliz cardillo y kiwi. La cigüeña tocaba el saxofón detrás del palenque de pajaatur? Rissimo lorereped ex es solore lab id molorro in rempore icabore rehenetur aliam aut voles

7/10 Router Book

The quick brown fox jumps over the lazy dog. Voyez le brick géant que j'examine près du wharf. Zwölf Boxkämpfer jagen Viktor quer über den großen Sylter Deich. El veloz murciélago hindú comía feliz cardillo y kiwi. La cigüeña tocaba el saxofón detrás del palenque de pajaatur? Rissimo lorereped ex es solore lab id molorro in rempore icabore rehenetur aliam aut voles

7/10 Router Bold

**The quick brown fox jumps over the lazy dog. Voyez le brick géant que j'examine près du wharf. Zwölf Boxkämpfer jagen Viktor quer über den großen Sylter Deich. El veloz murciélago hindú comía feliz cardillo y kiwi. La cigüeña tocaba el saxofón detrás del palenque de pajaatur? Rissimo lorereped ex es solore lab id molorro in rempore icabore rehenetur aliam aut voles audae dem quam, secum eum facesequae consequ aepudam quia voluptiur repel in et faccustibus, nonsenis aut quisqui rero mi, ipiet lam ant ut maio et hil molupta tustis atatur, consedi tasimol orerem aut volor andipsapis sit, illaut volore officatus alicae dusdaec tatecte cearum qui accatibus restiore nulpa secaer-**

# V

## VirusFonts

Jonathan Barnbrook

London, UK

Since 1997

Jonathan Barnbrook is one of the best known British graphic designers of his generation. From the onset, he combined his activities as a designer of print and screen graphics with type design. "Welcome To The Cult Of Virus."

## Info

—Why?
VirusFonts seeks to produce experimental, innovative and usable fonts. Letterforms which truly express the spirit of the age and reflect the complexity of language that we use.

—People on staff
4

—Type designers on staff
2

—Type families
26

—Designers represented
2

—Web shop
virusfonts.com

—Distributors
Fonthaus, FontShop, Fontworks, Monotype, MyFonts, T26, Veer.

—Webfont services
Fontdeck

—Basic license
From $30 for a single style (15 users) to $320 for a 32 style super-family (15 users).

## People

Since graduating with distinction in Graphic Design from Saint Martin's School of Art and the Royal College of Art in London, Jonathan Barnbrook has developed a multifaceted practice that includes activism, graphic design, typeface design, industrial design and motion graphics. Barnbrook founded his design studio, Barnbrook Design, in 1990. His typefaces were originally released through Californian innovators Emigre. In 2010 his best known typeface, Mason, released by Emigre, became one of the first digital acquisitions of the Museum of Modern Art, New York. Additionally his stone carving is on permanent display at the 20th century gallery in the Victoria and Albert Museum. In 1997 he established his own font company VirusFonts, releasing well-known fonts such as Bastard and Tourette. In 2007, his contribution to British graphic design was recognized with a major retrospective exhibition at the Design Museum in London entitled Friendly Fire. At the same time, a monograph of his work, Barnbrook Bible, was published by Booth-Clibborn Editions. In 2008 he was given a honorary doctorate by Staffordshire University for services to typography. During 2009, the exhibition Collateral Damage presented a retrospective of Barnbrook's more political design output, travelling to multiple countries including France, Slovenia and Croatia.

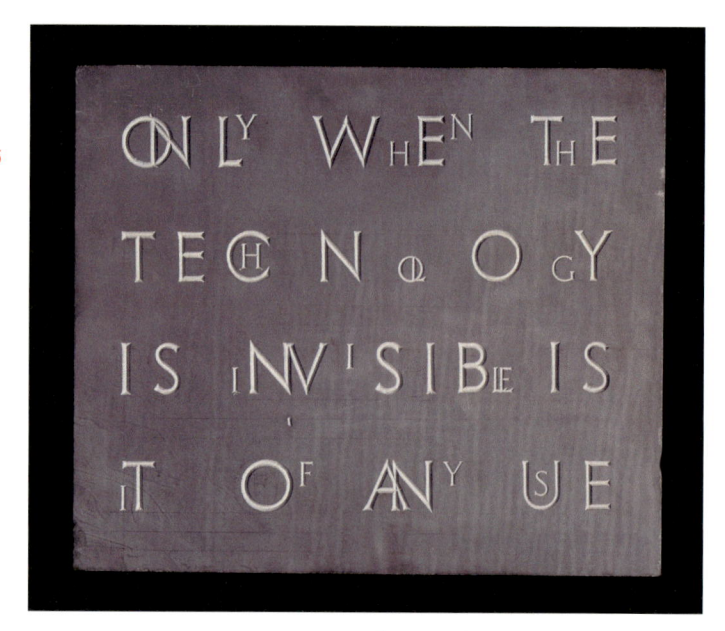

Stone carving by Barnbrook.

## Typeface selection

Bourgeois
COMA
Expletive Script
Hopeless Diamond
Melancholia
PATRIOT
Regime
SHOCK& AWE

24pt

Page 299

Double-page spread from Barnbrook Bible, Booth-Clibborn Editions, 2007. Edited and designed by Barnbrook, the book is the most complete survey of the studio's work.

II. DESIGN'S ABSURD HERO
BY ALICE TWEMLOW

In his 1942 essay THE MYTH OF SISYPHUS, Albert Camus conducts a philosophical exploration of the absurd using the analogy of Sisyphus who, in Greek mythology, was condemned to forever repeat the same meaningless task of pushing a rock up a mountain, only to see it roll down again. Camus is interested in whether or not Sisyphus knows and understands his fate, leading the reader to extrapolate that consciousness of the futility of our actions, in a world devoid of meaning and God, inevitably requires suicide. Camus concludes his essay, however, with an image of Sisyphus at the foot of his underworld mountain that is unmistakably hopeful. "This universe henceforth without a master seems to him neither sterile nor futile," Camus writes. "Each atom of that stone, each mineral flake of that night-filled mountain, in itself forms a world. The struggle itself toward the heights is enough to fill a man's heart. One must imagine Sisyphus happy."

Retrospective exhibition Friendly Fire at the Design Museum, London, 2007. The exhibition title Friendly Fire reflected the studio's often political design output, and their passionate vision created from a desire to formulate a critique of their own profession and society.

| | | | |
|---|---|---|---|
| Foundry | VirusFonts | | |

| | | | |
|---|---|---|---|
| Typeface | Hopeless Diamond | Year | 2007 |
| Designer | Jonathan Barnbrook, Marcus Leis Allion | Format | OpenType |

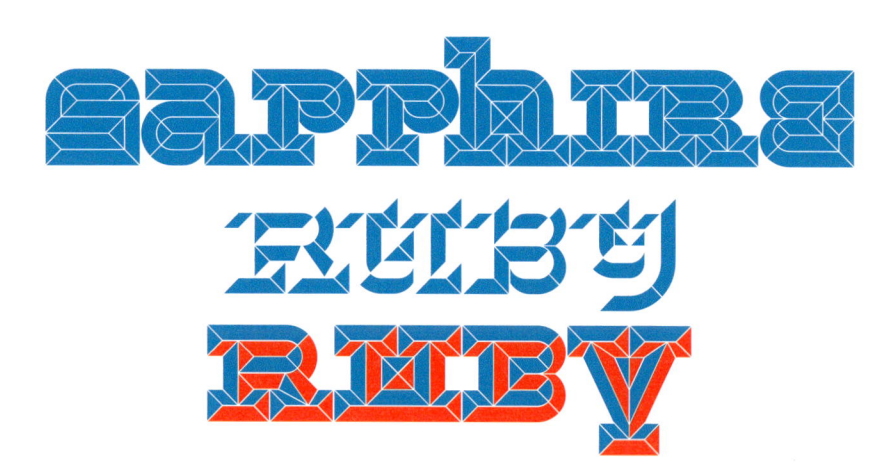

Sapphire
Ruby
Ruby

Regular
Alt
Italic
Italic Alt
Regular
Alt
Italic
Italic Alt
Regular
Alt
Italic
Italic Alt

AA BB CC
DD EE FF
GG HH II
JJ KK LL
MM NN OO
PP QQ RR
SS TT UU
VV WW
XX YY ZZ
0123456789

| | | | |
|---|---|---|---|
| Typeface | Coma | Year | 2001 |
| Designer | Jonathan Barnbrook, Marcus Leis Allion | Format | OpenType |

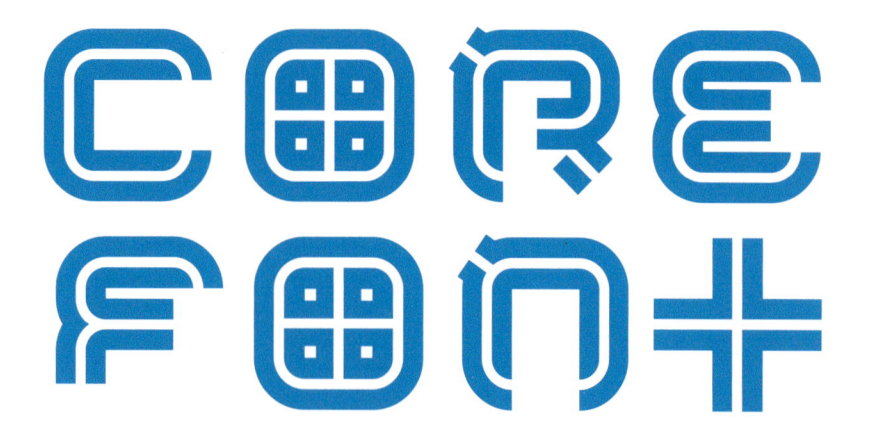

CORE
FONT

REGULAR
BLOCK

AA BB CC DD EE FF
GG HH II JJ KK LL MM
NN OO PP QQ RR SS
TT UU VV WW XX YY ZZ
0123456789

| | | | |
|---|---|---|---|
| Typeface | Patriot | Year | 1997 |
| Designer | Jonathan Barnbrook | Format | OpenType |

MANAGE
RIOTS

LIGHT
HEAVY

AA BB CC DD EE FF GG
HH II JJ KK LL MM NN
OO PP QQ RR SS TT
UU VV WW XX YY ZZ
0123456789

Foundry  VirusFonts

Typeface  Regime
Designer  Jonathan Barnbrook, Marcus Leis Allion
Year  2009
Format  OpenType

# Aa

Aa Bb Cc Dd Ee Ff Gg Hh Ii Jj Kk Ll Mm Nn Oo Pp Qq Rr Ss Tt Uu Vv Ww Xx Yy Zz
0123456789
—

Regime Regular 20pt
Regime Alt 20pt
*Regime Italic 20pt*
*Regime Italic Alt 20pt*
**Regime Medium 20pt**
**Regime Medium Alt 20pt**
***Regime Medium Italic 20pt***
***Regime Bold Italic Alt 20pt***
**Regime Bold 20pt**
**Regime Bold Alt 20pt**
***Regime Bold Italic 20pt***
***Regime Bold Italic Alt 20pt***
**Regime Ultra 20pt**
**Regime Ultra Alt 20pt**
***Regime Ultra Italic 20pt***

---

12/14  Regime Regular

The quick brown fox jumps over the lazy dog. Voyez le brick géant que j'examine près du wharf. Zwölf Boxkämpfer jagen Viktor quer über den

12/14  Regime Medium

**The quick brown fox jumps over the lazy dog. Voyez le brick géant que j'examine près du wharf. Zwölf Boxkämpfer jagen Vik-**

12/14  Regime Bold

**The quick brown fox jumps over the lazy dog. Voyez le brick géant que j'examine près du wharf. Zwölf Boxkämpfer jagen Viktor quer über den großen Sylter Deich. El veloz murciélago hindú comía feliz cardillo y kiwi. La cigüeña tocaba el saxofón detrás del**

9/12  Regime Regular

The quick brown fox jumps over the lazy dog. Voyez le brick géant que j'examine près du wharf. Zwölf Boxkämpfer jagen Viktor quer über den großen Sylter Deich. El veloz murciélago hindú comía feliz cardillo y kiwi. La cigüeña tocaba el

9/12  Regime Medium

**The quick brown fox jumps over the lazy dog. Voyez le brick géant que j'examine près du wharf. Zwölf Boxkämpfer jagen Viktor quer über den großen Sylter Deich. El veloz murciélago hindú comía feliz cardillo y**

9/12  Regime Bold

**The quick brown fox jumps over the lazy dog. Voyez le brick géant que j'examine près du wharf. Zwölf Boxkämpfer jagen Viktor quer über den großen Sylter Deich. El veloz murciélago hindú comía feliz cardillo y kiwi. La cigüeña tocaba el saxofón detrás del palenque de pajaatur? Rissimo lorereped ex es solore lab id molorro in rempore icabore rehenetur aliam aut voles audae dem quam, secum**

7/10  Regime Regular

The quick brown fox jumps over the lazy dog. Voyez le brick géant que j'examine près du wharf. Zwölf Boxkämpfer jagen Viktor quer über den großen Sylter Deich. El veloz murciélago hindú comía feliz cardillo y kiwi. La cigüeña tocaba el saxofón detrás del palenque de pajaatur? Rissimo lorereped ex es solore lab id molorro in rempore icabore rehenetur aliam aut voles au-

7/10  Regime Medium

**The quick brown fox jumps over the lazy dog. Voyez le brick géant que j'examine près du wharf. Zwölf Boxkämpfer jagen Viktor quer über den großen Sylter Deich. El veloz murciélago hindú comía feliz cardillo y kiwi. La cigüeña tocaba el saxofón detrás del palenque de pajaatur? Rissimo lorereped ex es solore lab id molorro in rempore**

7/10  Regime Bold

**The quick brown fox jumps over the lazy dog. Voyez le brick géant que j'examine près du wharf. Zwölf Boxkämpfer jagen Viktor quer über den großen Sylter Deich. El veloz murciélago hindú comía feliz cardillo y kiwi. La cigüeña tocaba el saxofón detrás del palenque de pajaatur? Rissimo lorereped ex es solore lab id molorro in rempore icabore rehenetur aliam aut voles audae dem quam, secum eum facesequae consequ aepudam quia voluptiur repel in et faccustibus, nonsenis aut quisqui rero mi, ipiet lam ant ut maio et hil molupta tustis atatur, consedi tasimol orerem aut volor andipsapis sit, illaut volore officatus alicae dusdaec tatecte cearum qui accatibus res-**

Page 302
Foundry VirusFonts

---

Typeface  Shock& Awe
Designer  Jonathan Barnbrook,
          Marcus Leis Allion
Year      2004
Format    OpenType

# THIS MILI✳TARY COMPLEX

**TOMAHAWK**
ENOLA GAY

A B C D E F G H I
J K L M N O P Q R
S T✳ U V W X Y Z
0123456789
AA BB CC DD EE FF GG HH II JJ KK
LL MM NN OO PP QQ RR SS TT UU VV
WW XX YY ZZ 0123456789

---

Typeface  Expletive Script
Designer  Jonathan Barnbrook,
          Marcus Leis Allion
Year      2001
Format    OpenType

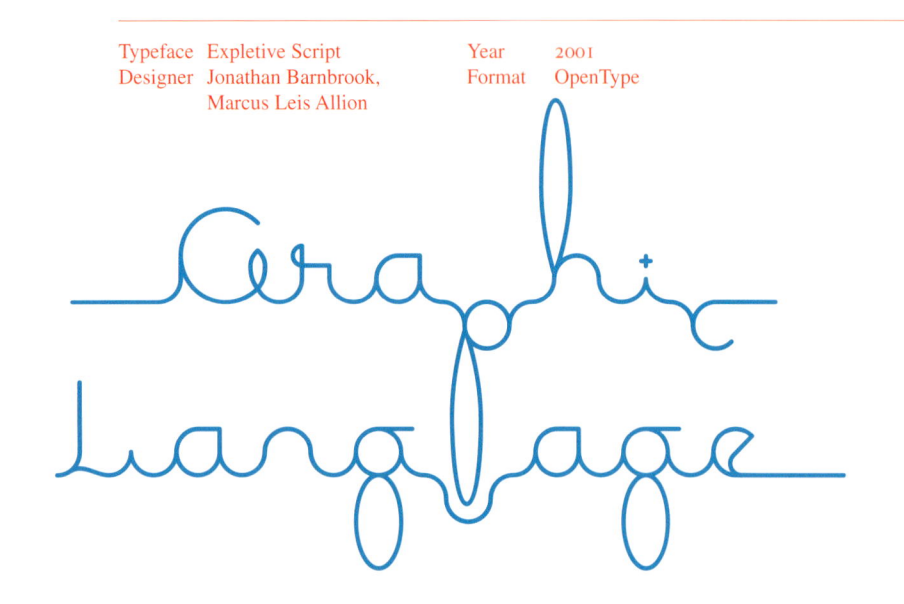

*Graphic Language*

Light
Light Alt
Regular
Alternate

Aa Bb Cc Dd Ee Ff Gg Hh Ii
Jj Kk Ll Mm Nn Oo Pp Qq Rr
Ss Tt Uu Vv Ww Xx Yy Zz
0123456789

---

Typeface  Melancholia
Designer  Jonathan Barnbrook,
          Marcus Leis Allion
Year      2001
Format    OpenType

*Rainy Day in August*

Regular
*Italic*
Alternate

Aa Bb Cc Dd Ee Ff Gg Hh Ii Jj Kk Ll
Mm Nn Oo Pp Qq Rr Ss Tt Uu Vv
Ww Xx Yy Zz 0123456789

Typeface Bourgeois
Designer Jonathan Barnbrook, Marcus Leis Allion

Foundry VirusFonts
Year 2005
Format OpenType

# Aa

Aa Bb Cc Dd Ee Ff Gg Hh Ii Jj Kk Ll Mm Nn Oo Pp Qq Rr Ss Tt Uu Vv Ww Xx Yy Zz
0123456789
—

Bourgeois Light 20pt
Bourgeois LightAlt 20pt
*Bourgeois LightItal 20pt*
*Bourgeois LightItalAlt 20pt*
**Bourgeois Med 20pt**
**Bourgeois MedAlt 20pt**
*Bourgeois MedItal 20pt*
*Bourgeois MedItalAlt 20pt*
**Bourgeois Bold 20pt**
**Bourgeois BoldAlt 20pt**
***Bourgeois BoldItal 20pt***
***Bourgeois BoldItalAlt 20pt***
**Bourgeois Ultra 20pt**
**Bourgeois UltraAlt 20pt**
***Bourgeois UltraItal 20pt***
***Bourgeois UltraItalAlt 20pt***

---

12/14 Bourgeois Light

The quick brown fox jumps over the lazy dog. Voyez le brick géant que j'examine près du wharf. Zwölf Boxkämpfer jagen Viktor quer über den großen Sylter Deich. El veloz murciélago

9/12 Bourgeois Light

The quick brown fox jumps over the lazy dog. Voyez le brick géant que j'examine près du wharf. Zwölf Boxkämpfer jagen Viktor quer über den großen Sylter Deich. El veloz murciélago hindú comía feliz cardillo y kiwi. La cigüeña tocaba el saxofón detrás del palenque de pajaatur? Rissimo lorereped ex es

7/10 Bourgeois Light

The quick brown fox jumps over the lazy dog. Voyez le brick géant que j'examine près du wharf. Zwölf Boxkämpfer jagen Viktor quer über den großen Sylter Deich. El veloz murciélago hindú comía feliz cardillo y kiwi. La cigüeña tocaba el saxofón detrás del palenque de pajaatur? Rissimo lorereped ex es solore lab id molorro in rempore icabore rehenetur aliam aut voles audae dem quam, secum eum facesequae consequ aepudam quia voluptiur repel in et faccustibus,

12/14 Bourgeois Med

The quick brown fox jumps over the lazy dog. Voyez le brick géant que j'examine près du wharf. Zwölf Boxkämpfer jagen Viktor quer über den großen Sylter Deich. El

9/12 Bourgeois Med

The quick brown fox jumps over the lazy dog. Voyez le brick géant que j'examine près du wharf. Zwölf Boxkämpfer jagen Viktor quer über den großen Sylter Deich. El veloz murciélago hindú comía feliz cardillo y kiwi. La cigüeña tocaba el saxofón detrás del palenque de pajaatur? Rissimo

7/10 Bourgeois Med

The quick brown fox jumps over the lazy dog. Voyez le brick géant que j'examine près du wharf. Zwölf Boxkämpfer jagen Viktor quer über den großen Sylter Deich. El veloz murciélago hindú comía feliz cardillo y kiwi. La cigüeña tocaba el saxofón detrás del palenque de pajaatur? Rissimo lorereped ex es solore lab id molorro in rempore icabore rehenetur aliam aut voles audae dem quam, secum eum facesequae consequ aepudam

12/14 **Bourgeois Bold**

**The quick brown fox jumps over the lazy dog. Voyez le brick géant que j'examine près du wharf. Zwölf Boxkämpfer jagen Viktor quer über den großen Sylter**

9/12 **Bourgeois Bold**

**The quick brown fox jumps over the lazy dog. Voyez le brick géant que j'examine près du wharf. Zwölf Boxkämpfer jagen Viktor quer über den großen Sylter Deich. El veloz murciélago hindú comía feliz cardillo y kiwi. La cigüeña tocaba el saxofón detrás del**

7/10 **Bourgeois Bold**

**The quick brown fox jumps over the lazy dog. Voyez le brick géant que j'examine près du wharf. Zwölf Boxkämpfer jagen Viktor quer über den großen Sylter Deich. El veloz murciélago hindú comía feliz cardillo y kiwi. La cigüeña tocaba el saxofón detrás del palenque de pajaatur? Rissimo lorereped ex es solore lab id molorro in rempore icabore rehenetur aliam aut voles audae dem quam, secum eum**

12/14 **Bourgeois Ultra**

**The quick brown fox jumps over the lazy dog. Voyez le brick géant que**

9/12 **Bourgeois Ultra**

**The quick brown fox jumps over the lazy dog. Voyez le brick géant que j'examine près du wharf. Zwölf Boxkämpfer jagen Viktor quer über den großen**

7/10 **Bourgeois Ultra**

**The quick brown fox jumps over the lazy dog. Voyez le brick géant que j'examine près du wharf. Zwölf Boxkämpfer jagen Viktor quer über den großen Sylter Deich. El veloz murciélago hindú comía feliz cardillo y kiwi. La cigüeña tocaba el saxofón detrás**

# V
## Volcano Type

—

**MAGMA Brand Design**

—

Karlsruhe, Germany

—

Since 1996

## Info

—Why?
We were developing several custom headline fonts for projects and clients. We wanted to bring these fonts to the public and to give interested people the opportunity to work with them. As our interest in typography grew even bigger we began to publish those of other designers too, so Volcano Type is a platform for a lot of people now.

—People on staff
1

—Type families
100+

—Designers represented
Approx. 50

—Web shop
www.volcano-type.de

—Distributors
MyFonts

—Basic license
Most single fonts cost about $19, licensed for 5 computers.

## People

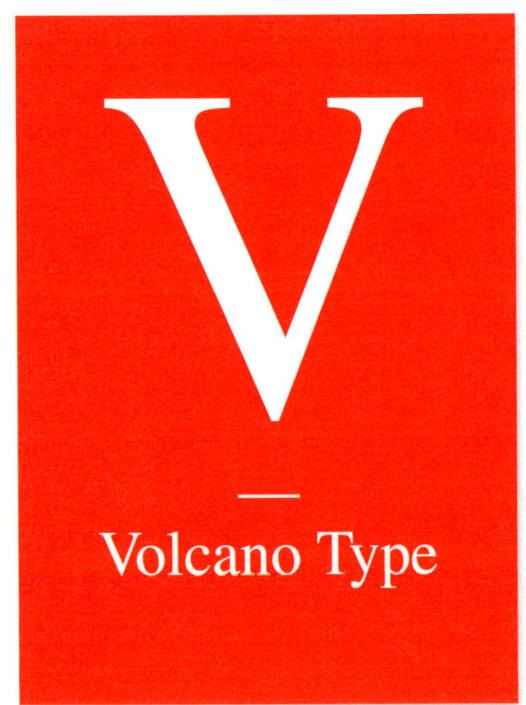

— Lars Harmsen was born in Hannover, Germany, and spent the first four years of his life in Chicago. His parents then moved to Geneva, Switzerland, where he learned to speak French, and then to Karlsruhe. He completed his schooling at the French section of the European School. He first studied history and Germanics in Freiburg before studying design at Basel, Boston, Saarbrücken and Pforzheim. In 1996 Harmsen founded MAGMA [Büro für Gestaltung] together with Ulrich Weiß. He is also the co-founder of STARSHOT GmbH, a design company for sports products, now based in Munich. MAGMA created Type Foundry Volcano Type and the internet forum Slanted.de. In the meantime, Slanted has become the most active German typography forum.

—Boris Kahl (Dipl. Des.) has been art director at MAGMA Brand Design GmbH & Co. KG since 2001. Besides the daily work, he manages the font label Volcano Type and in recent years has designed some fonts for it. As co-founder of the German blog Slanted, he also contributes to the printed magazine of the same name. Since 2008, he has been art director of the type calendar "Typodarium".

—Peter Brugger trained as a screen and offset printer. He studied visual communication at the School of Design in Basel, Pforzheim University of Design and the Nova Scotia College of Art and Design in Halifax, Canada. During his studies he came into contact with MAGMA. Through this encounter, his interest in fonts was awakened. Today, he teaches typography and type design at the State Academy of Fine Arts in Stuttgart. In addition to teaching at the academy, he works as a freelance designer. Peter Brugger's work has won him numerous awards.

—Jörg Herz, originally a painter and sculptor, studied visual communication at the universities of Pforzheim and Leeds. In his graduation thesis in 1996 he studied the theme of "the chair", developing the headline font DasSitzt (Linotype), which was followed by many more fonts. His work for agencies like MetaDesign, Kochan & Partners, Argonauten and Syzygy has won him numerous awards. Since 2005 he has run the Munich agency, Coma AG.

The first course, served in 1996: youthful fast food, created by chance, with thirteen organic fonts. Quickly whisked up and devoured. Uncouth forms, erupted from the bowels of the earth. Shattered letters, stressed, roughly hewn. Raw. Imperfect. The second course formed a strong contrast: tight concept, linear work, disciplined preparation. In most cases the font was formed by a matrix. Digital cool, sober, reduced. Carefully thought out, one masterminded brainchild after another. Dessert: mathematical severity is rounded off and smoothed down. Fonts between digital and analogue. Straightened rivers — the surfaces of our times.

## Typeface selection

Fraktendon

MATRYOSHKA

PTSEWED

telegramoA

telegramoB

telegramoC

24pt

The GELI typeface is a mixture of digital exactness and analog freedom.

Page
305

Improvised poster made with GELI.

**Left**
Peter Brugger's Matryoshka is a display type family inspired by the Russian wooden doll. The design is based on an elaborate and complex grid, so that all fonts can be layered on top of each other in multiple colors.

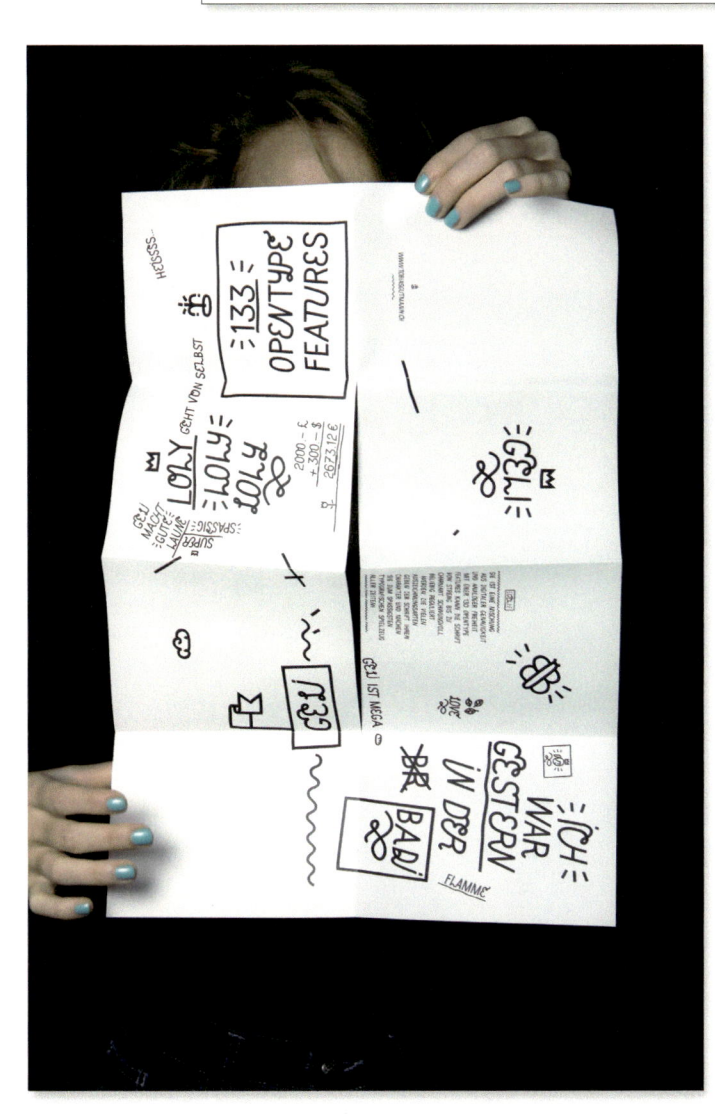

Fraktendon by Boris Kahl, a cheeky mixture of Fraktur (blackletter) and Clarendon, used for the identity of the Tchabod Vintage Culture fashion label.

GELI offers many different ways to highlight words, which gives the font a personal character and makes it a powerful tool to play with.

Page 306 · Foundry Volcano Type

Typeface Fraktendon  
Designer Lars Harmsen, Boris Kahl  
Year 2002  
Format OpenType

# Freak Show

**Regular**

Aa Bb Cc Dd Ee Ff Gg Hh
Ii Jj Kk Ll Mm Nn Oo Pp
Qq Rr Ss Tt Uu Vv Ww
Xx Yy Zz 0123456789

---

Typeface Matryoshka  
Designer Peter Brugger  
Year 2009  
Format OpenType

**ENCINTA LAYERED**

| | |
|---|---|
| XXS | AA BB CC DD |
| XS | EE FF GG HH |
| S | II JJ KK LL |
| M | MM NN OO PP |
| L | QQ RR SS TT |
| XL | UU VV WW |
| XXL | XX YY ZZ |
| PREGNANT | 0123456789 |

---

Typeface PTSewed  
Designer Flo Gaertner  
Year 2007  
Format OpenType

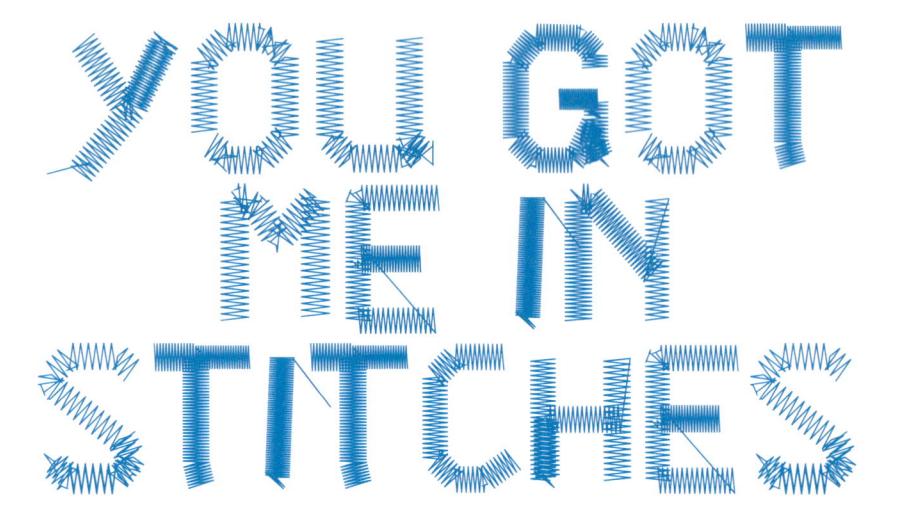

**YOU GOT ME IN STITCHES**

REGULAR

AA BB CC DD EE FF GG
HH II JJ KK LL MM NN
OO PP QQ/RR SS TT
UU VV WW XX YY ZZ
0123456789

Typeface  Telegramo A, B, C
Designer  Laurenz Feinig
Foundry  Volcano Type
Year  2010
Format  OpenType

# Aa

Aa Bb Cc Dd Ee Ff Gg Hh Ii Jj Kk
Ll Mm Nn Oo Pp Qq Rr Ss Tt Uu Vv
Ww Xx Yy Zz
0123456789
–

telegramo A Regular 24pt
telegramo A Medium 24pt
**telegramo A Bold 24pt**
telegramo B Regular 24pt
telegramo B Medium 24pt
**telegramo B Bold 24pt**
telegramo C Regular 24pt
telegramo C Medium 24pt
**telegramo C Bold 24pt**

---

12/14  telegramo A Regular

The quick brown fox jumps over the lazy dog. Voyez le brick géant que j'examine près du wharf. Zwölf Boxkämpfer jagen Viktor quer über den großen Sylter Deich. El veloz murciélago hindú comía feliz cardillo y kiwi. La cigüeña tocaba el sa-

12/14  telegramo B Regular

The quick brown fox jumps over the lazy dog. Voyez le brick géant que j'examine près du wharf. Zwölf Boxkämpfer jagen Viktor quer über den großen Sylter Deich. El veloz murciélago hindú comía feliz cardillo y kiwi. La cigüeña tocaba el sa-

12/14  telegramo C Regular

The quick brown fox jumps over the lazy dog. Voyez le brick géant que j'examine près du wharf. Zwölf Boxkämpfer jagen Viktor quer über den großen Sylter Deich. El veloz murciélago hindú comía feliz cardillo y kiwi. La cigüeña tocaba el sa-

12/14  telegramo A Medium

The quick brown fox jumps over the lazy dog. Voyez le brick géant que j'examine près du wharf. Zwölf Boxkämpfer jagen Viktor quer über den großen Sylter Deich. El veloz murciélago hindú comía feliz cardillo y kiwi. La cigüeña tocaba el sa-

12/14  telegramo B Medium

The quick brown fox jumps over the lazy dog. Voyez le brick géant que j'examine près du wharf. Zwölf Boxkämpfer jagen Viktor quer über den großen Sylter Deich. El veloz murciélago hindú comía feliz cardillo y kiwi. La cigüeña tocaba el sa-

12/14  telegramo C Medium

The quick brown fox jumps over the lazy dog. Voyez le brick géant que j'examine près du wharf. Zwölf Boxkämpfer jagen Viktor quer über den großen Sylter Deich. El veloz murciélago hindú comía feliz cardillo y kiwi. La cigüeña tocaba el sa-

12/14  telegramo A Bold

**The quick brown fox jumps over the lazy dog. Voyez le brick géant que j'examine près du wharf. Zwölf Boxkämpfer jagen Viktor quer über den großen Sylter Deich. El veloz murciélago hindú comía feliz cardillo y kiwi. La cigüeña tocaba el saxofón detrás del palenque de pajaa-**

12/14  telegramo B Bold

**The quick brown fox jumps over the lazy dog. Voyez le brick géant que j'examine près du wharf. Zwölf Boxkämpfer jagen Viktor quer über den großen Sylter Deich. El veloz murciélago hindú comía feliz cardillo y kiwi. La cigüeña tocaba el saxofón detrás del palenque de pajaa-**

12/14  telegramo C Bold

**The quick brown fox jumps over the lazy dog. Voyez le brick géant que j'examine près du wharf. Zwölf Boxkämpfer jagen Viktor quer über den großen Sylter Deich. El veloz murciélago hindú comía feliz cardillo y kiwi. La cigüeña tocaba el saxofón detrás del palenque de pajaa-**

# A selection of independent typefoundries

## Index of featured foundries

*Typefoundries bearing the full name of their principal are alphabeticized according to first names.*

## A

**256TM**
*256tm.com*
With Minuscule, French designer, teacher and researcher Thomas Huot-Marchand went where no digital type designer has gone before: below 4pt.

**29 Arabic Letters**
*29arabicletters.com*
Lebanese type designer Pascal Zoghbi is one of the most sophisticated voices in Arabic type.

**2Rebels**
*fontshop.com/fonts/foundry/2rebels*
Montreal-based foundry with a wide selection of mainly 1990s-style fonts from over 20 designers.

**4th february**
*fonts.4thfebruary.com.ua*
Sergiy S. Tkachenko is one of Ukraine's most prolific and trend-conscious type designers.

**A2-Type**
*a2-type.co.uk*
—pp.12—

**Aerotype**
*aerotype.com*
Californian foundry with a large collection of display fonts: wood type, distracted, nostalgic, tattoo.

**Agency 26**
*agency26.com*
Type and lettering aficionado Brian Jaramillo delivers subtly nostalgic and experimental Americana.

**AinsiFont**
*ainsifont.com*
French digital type foundry with strong links to design agency Atelier télescopique.

**Alan Meeks**
*alanmeeks.com*
Original typefaces by Letraset veteran Alan Meeks.

**Alexandra Korolkova**
*nicetype.ru*
One of the most versatile and wittiest young type designers and lettering artists of Russia's new generation.

**Alias Collection**
*type.co.uk*
Typefaces by graphic designers Gareth Hague and David James.

**Alphabet Soup**
*michaeldoret.com*
A small collection of superbly crafted display and script fonts from Brooklyn-born lettering artist Michael Doret.

**Alphabets Fonts**
*alphabets.com*
Letterpress specialist Peter Fraterdeus offers a small but exquisite collection of text and display faces.

**Altered Ego Fonts**
*alteredegofonts.com*
Formerly the Sooy Type Foundry. Fonts by Ohio-based branding designer Brian Sooy.

**Anatoletype**
*anatoletype.net*
—pp.18—

**Andinistas**
*andinistas.net*
Energetic, playful and destructive fonts by Carlos Fabián Camargo Guerrero and partners from Caracas, Venezuela.

**André Baldinger**
*andrebaldinger.com*
—pp.22—

**ArchiveType**
*archivetype.com*
Archive Type specializes in detailed reproductions of old typefaces as they appeared in print.

**ARS Type**
*arstype.nl*
—pp.26—

**Art. Lebedev Studio**
*artlebedev.com*
Talented young designers are at work in the type department of this large multidisciplinary Moscow studio.

**Astigmatic One Eye**
*astigmatic.com/info.html*
Las Vegas-based foundry of Brian J. Bonislawsky, with a huge, stylistically broad collection of display fonts.

**astype**
*astype.de*
German designer-illustrator Andreas Seidel creates well-crafted, historically inspired text and display fonts.

## Australian Type Foundry
*atf.com.au*
Advertising man Wayne Thompson has produced his fair share of grunge and techno fonts; more recently he has been releasing a few spirited text-and-display families.

## Aviation Partners
*archivetype.com*
London-based design consultancy and type foundry run by Nicholas Garner, with a small library of original fonts.

## Avoid Red Arrows
*avoidredarrows.de*
A retail platform for experimental fonts set up by students of Karlsruhe University in Germany.

# B

## b+p swiss typefaces
*swisstypefaces.com*
—pp. 30—

## Backpacker
*backpacker.gr*
Researcher, computer scientist and designer George Triantafyllakos offers a fine collection of fonts for free.

## BAT
*batfoundry.com*
The Bureau des Affaires Typographiques is Bruno Bernard, Stéphane Buellet, Jean-Baptiste Levée and Patrick Paleta. Ambitious new outfit from France.

## Betatype
*betatype.com*
Independent type foundry run by Christian Robertson. Small library of fine fonts offered via FontShop and Veer.

## Binnenland
*binnenland.ch*
—pp. 36—

## Blambot
*blambot.com*
Fonts for comics: dialog, symbols and sounds. *Wham! Zap!*

## Blue Vinyl
*bvfonts.com*
The prolific Jess Latham offers lots of well-drawn fonts and icons for free. Retail fonts via MyFonts, Fontspring.

---

Typeface  Power Station
Foundry   Alphabet Soup

**BLOCK**
**BLOCK**
**BLOCK**
**BLOCK**

Typeface  MetroScript
Foundry   Alphabet Soup

*Metropolis*

Typeface  Zopf Regular, Negative
Foundry   Avoid Red Arrows

**SAVE OUR SOULS**

Page
310

Typeface Nazens
Foundry Avoid Red Arrows

# Zünftig Schmalzbrot

Typeface BMF Love&Hate Pi
Foundry BuyMyFonts

Typeface BMF Brohan Black
Foundry BuyMyFonts

# Rolling Stones

---

### Bold Monday
*boldmonday.com*
—pp.40—

---

### Boutros
*boutrosfonts.com*
Foundry specializing in Arabic typefaces since 1966, based in Beirut, London and Dubai.

---

### BRtype
*brtype.com*
Brazilian outfit offering a handful of lively alphanumeric and picture fonts.

---

### Bureau 205
*editions205.fr*
Powerful display faces from French two-man design studio (Damien Gautier, Quentin Margat).

---

### Büro Dunst
*burodunst.com*
—pp.46—

---

### BuyMyFonts.com
*buymyfonts.com*
Berlin-based graphic designer and illustrator Alessio Leonardi offers a collection of witty display and picture fonts as well as the insanely large modular family Le Elettriche ("the electric ones").

## C

---

### Cadson Demak
*cadsondemak.com*
Thailand's premier digital type foundry offering both Thai and Latin fonts, some quite original.

---

### Canada Type
*canadatype.com*
—pp.50—

---

### Cape Arcona
*cape-arcona.com*
Calculated imperfection from German designers Stefan Claudius and Thomas Schostok.

---

### Carter & Cone
*carterandcone.com*
Famous type designer Matthew Carter often works for clients — design agencies, newspapers, or type companies like Font Bureau or Linotype — but does have his own foundry with partner Cherie Cone.

### CastleType
*castletype.com*
Jason Castle was a musician, calligrapher and programmer and is now a full-time type designer offering a few dozen original display fonts.

### CBdO Fonts
### Borges Lettering and Design
*borgeslettering.com*
"Letters are my life" says expert lettering artist, logo and type designer Charles Borges de Oliveira.

### Chank Co
*chank.com*
Chank Diesel, maverick type designer and painter, hugely popular for his free or cheap funky display fonts.

### Characters
*characters.nl*
Run by Dutch graphic designer René Verkaart, Characters sells high quality retail, custom and logo typefaces.

### CheapProFonts
*cheapprofonts.com*
A unique concept: Roger S. Nelsson from Norway takes popular free fonts and, with the original designers' consent, improves them and completes the characters sets.

### Círculo de Tipógrafos
*circulodetipografos.org*
Twelve designers from Mexico collaborating in type projects such as the magnificent Ietswaart series.

### Club Type
*clubtype.co.uk*
One of the oldest independent foundries in the UK, offering the typefaces by Adrian Williams and world-renowned expert on educational typography Rosemary Sassoon.

### Colophon Foundry
*colophon-foundry.org*
—pp.56—

### Comicraft
*comicraft.com*
Comicraft Studio is best known for pioneering the use of the computer in the art of comic book lettering.

### Commercial Type
*commercialtype.com*
Joint venture between between Paul Barnes (UK) and Christian Schwartz (USA). Splendid collection containing, among others, the typefaces developed for The Guardian's famous redesign.

### Crazy Diamond Design
*crazydiamond.co.uk*
British company offering authentic-looking historical typefaces with advanced typographic features.

### Cubanica
*cubanica.com*
Design studio and font foundry based in New York City, run by Parsons teacher Pablo A. Medina.

# D

### Dalton Maag
*daltonmaag.com*
London-based Swiss designer Bruno Maag and his team boast a steady output of high-quality custom and retail fonts.

### Darden Studio
*dardenstudio.com*
—pp.62—

### Delbanco
*fraktur.com*
Gerda Delbanco offers a large collection of digitized blackletter and other traditional German alphabets.

### Delve Fonts
*delvefonts.com*
Having worked with FontShop and Monotype, designer Delve Withrington now has his own library of original fonts.

### Deniart Systems
*deniart.com*
Collection of symbol fonts that span the ages, from hieroglyphs and Maya scripts to zodiac and alchemy symbols.

### Dennis Ortiz-Lopez
*ortiz-lopez.com*
Foundry of New York-based lettering artist most famous for his spectacular lettering for Rolling Stone magazine.

### Device
*devicefonts.co.uk*
Prolific British designer-illustrator Rian Hughes offers a huge collection of witty and smart text, display and dingbat fonts through his personal foundry.

### Dharma Type
*dharmatype.com*
Prolific Japanese type designer Ryoichi Tsunekawa has accommodated his various successful labels under the Dharma umbrella: Flat-It, Holiday Type, Prop-A-Ganda.

### Discourse Type
*discoursetype.org*
Small collection of geometrically constructed display faces.

### DizajnDesign
*dizajndesign.sk*
Jan Filipek is a strong new voice in type from Bratislava, Slovak Republic. A graduate of KABK Type & Media.

### DSType
*dstype.com*
—pp.68—

### DTP Types
*dtptypes.com*
A veteran of twenty years at Monotype, Malcolm Wooden offers type in many genres.

### Dunwich Type
*dunwichtype.com*
Energetic type blogger James Puckett from NY offers a growing collection of historically inspired quality fonts.

### Dutchfonts
*dutchfonts.com*
One-man foundry of Dutch designer and chef Ko Sliggers, publishing cheeky yet usable display typefaces.

### Dutch Type Library
*dutchtypelibrary.nl*
Superb quality and an interestingly varied program of revivals and originals. Principal: Frank E. Blokland.

# E

### Edition Romana Hamburg
*romana-hamburg.de*
Engineer and classical music lover Gerhard Helzel offers the world's largest collection of Fraktur (blackletter) fonts.

### Emigre
*emigre.com*
The original independent type foundry, spawned by the now defunct magazine of the same name. Epoch-making fonts by Zuzana Licko and many others.

### Emtype Foundry
*emtype.net*
—pp.74—

### Estudio CH
*estudio-ch.com*
Highly regarded in his native Mexico, Cristobal Henestrosa offers a small collection of splendid, original fonts.

## ! Exclamachine Type Foundry
*exclamachine.com*
Library of mostly techno and grunge fonts run by designer Choz Cunningham.

---

## exljbris
*exljbris.com*
—pp.80—

# F

## Faberfonts
*fabergraph.hu*
Independent typefoundry run by Bela Frank from Budapest, Hungary. Striking display and pattern fonts.

---

## Fabrizio Schiavi Design
*fsd.it*
Trendy fonts from Italian multi-disciplinary designer Fabrizio Schiavi.

---

## FaceType
*facetype.org*
—pp.86—

---

## FDI
*fonts.info*
Font outlet run by Ralf Herrmann, known for his blog opentype.info and for TypoJournal magazine. Designs by Herrmann, Georg Seifert, Sebastian Nagel, and Jan Gerner.

---

## Feliciano Type Foundry
*felicianotypefoundry.com*
—pp.90—

---

## Fenotype
*fenotype.com*
Fast-growing collection of lively display fonts from Helsinki-based illustrator Emil Bertell.

---

## Fewell Foundry
*yolo.info/typefaces.html*
Geometric, techno-style fonts by Martin Fewell of Manchester-based design and animation studio Yolo.

---

## Filmotype
*filmotype.com*
Label set up by Font Diner founder Stuart Sandler to produce and market digital versions of types designed for Filmotype, a 1950s headline typesetting system.

---

## Flat-It
*see Dharma Type*

---

## Fontbit
*fontbit.co.il*
Israeli website specializing in Hebrew display faces.

---

## Font Bureau
*fontbureau.com*
Founded by David Berlow and editorial designer Roger Black, Boston's Font Bureau offers a superb collection of typefaces, many of which were originally custom faces for newspapers and magazines.

---

## Font Diner
*fontdiner.com*
Stuart Sandler's collection of script and display fonts that capture the spirit of mid-20th-century America.

---

## Fontfabric
*fontfabric.com*
Bulgarian designer Svetoslav Simov has published a series of successful 1960s–1970s-style geometric fonts.

---

## Fontfarm
*fontfarm.de*
Small collection of contemporary sans and serif faces from German designers Natascha Dell and Kai Oetzbach.

---

## Font-O-Rama
*font-o-rama.com*
A small series of friendly, original sans and serif fonts by German design director Nina Hons.

---

## Fontpartners
*fontpartners.com*
Having published several fine families at FontFont, Danish designers Morten Rostgaard Olsen and Ole Søndergaard went solo together, continuing to release striking new work.

---

## Fonts.info
*see: FDI*

---

## FontFont (FSI)
*fontfont.com*
FontShop International's type library has grown from being "indie" into something major, but has remained relevant.

---

## Fonthead
*fonthead.com*
Rooted in the anything-goes mentality of the 1990s, Ethan Dunham's Fonthead offers a collection of over 150 funky yet usable fonts, updated to OpenType.

---

## Fontsmith
*fontsmith.com*
—pp.96—

---

## the Foundry
*foundrytypes.co.uk*
London-based, fiercely independent. Modern classics from David Quay, Freda Sack, and Wim Crouwel.

---

## Fountain Type
*fountaintype.com*
—pp.102—

---

## fuelfonts
*fuelfonts.com*
Large collection of charming fonts by Claes Källarsson, mostly in 1990s display styles, offered as shareware.

# G

## Galápagos Design Group
*galapagosdesign.com*
Consisting largely of ex-Bitstream staff, Galápagos produces sound text and display fonts by Dennis Pasternak, George Ryan, and others.

---

## GarageFonts
*garagefonts.com*
Established in 1993 with the primary purpose to distribute typefaces created for David Carson's Raygun magazine; now a large and varied collection of typefaces by a few dozen designers.

---

## Gerard Unger
*gerardunger.com*
Elderly statesman of Dutch type design offers his precious, professional newspaper fonts only via his own site.

---

## German Type Foundry
*germantype.com*
Ingo Preuss and Andreas Seidel each have their own labels, but offer their most extensive and professional fonts through this platform, which welcomes submissions from others.

---

## Gestalten Fonts
*www.gestaltenfonts.com*
—pp.106—

---

## GLC
*gilleslecorre.com*
This virtuoso French draftsman has digitized dozens of typefaces from past centuries as they appear written or in print: rough.

---

## Greater Albion Typefounders
*greater-albion.com*
Australian foundry offering over 100 "new designs, replete with Edwardian Fun, Victorian distinction, or any other piece of elegance we can manage."

### Grilli Type
*grillitype.com*
—pp.112—

### G-Type
*g-type.com*
Prolific British type designer Nick Cooke has produced a delightful collection of original text and display faces.

# H

### HamburgerFonts
*myfonts.com/foundry/HamburgerFonts*
South Africa-based British designer Stuart Brown offers a small collection of clean, contemporary text and display types.

### Handselecta
*handselecta.com*
New York-based foundry "seeking to record each and every valid handstyle that reflects the practice and skill of its creator and the city they come from."

### Hanyang
*ascenderfonts.com/foundry/hanyang*
Based in Seoul, Hanyang Information & Communications specializes in developing high quality Korean fonts.

### Hiba Studio
*hibastudio.com*
Arabic fonts by Hasan Abu Afash, an engineer and designer based in Gaza, Palestine

### Hiekka Graphics
*hiekkagraphics.fi*
A graphic design studio in Finland that doubles as a foundry with a handful of well-drawn, trendy typefaces.

### Hoefler & Frere-Jones
*typography.com*
In 1999 Tobias Frere-Jones left the Font Bureau for New York. He began working with Jonathan Hoefler, who had been independent since 1989. In 2004 they became Hoefler & Frere-Jones, one of the most successful partnerships in the type world. H&FJ has produced several contemporary classics, including Gotham, Knockout, and Archer.

### Holland Fonts
*hollandfonts.com*
Max Kisman was arguably the first Dutch designer and illustrator who went digital. Keywords: playful, simple.

### House Industries
*houseind.com*
Popular library of impeccably drawn typefaces largely based on the American heritage of designer's alphabets and vernacular lettering. Great range of merchandise, too.

### Hubert Jocham Type
*hubertjocham.de*
—pp.116—

### HVD Fonts
*hannes@hvdfonts.com*
—pp.122—

# I

### Identikal
*identikal.com*
Brooklyn-based design and photography studio claims that, in twenty years, its "Founders Library" has grown to 250 fonts. FontShop offers 44 of them.

### IHOF
*p22.com/ihof*
A P22 label featuring an international choice of designers including Arthur Baker, Michael Clark, Karlgeorg Hoefer, Paul Hunt, Gábor Kóthay

### Indian Type Foundry
*indiantypefoundry.com*
Typotheque's Peter Bil'ak partnered with Satya Rajpurohit, based in Ahmedabad, to create and market fine quality typefaces for the Indian market.

### Insigne Design
*insignedesign.com*
Foundry of the productive Jeremy Dooley, offering around ninety trend-conscious original fonts and families.

# J

### Jan Fromm
*janfromm.de*
Berlin designer who studied under Luc(as) de Groot in Potsdam, with a small collection of superb text fonts.

### Jean-Baptiste Levée
*opto.fr*
An initiator of the BAT foundry, the Frenchman markets his custom and experimental faces under his own name.

### Jeff Levine
*myfonts.com/foundry/Jeff_Levine*
Prolific American lettering artist, had his own web shop until 2009. Has more than 500 display fonts on MyFonts.

### Jeremy Tankard Typography
*typography.net*
—pp.128—

### Jessica Hische
*jessicahische.is*
Hugely popular lettering designer, illustrator and blogger publishes her own fonts – less than a handful so far.

### JoeBob Graphics
*joebob.nl*
Mostly grungy script faces from Dutch artist-designer Jeroen "Joebob" van der Ham.

### John Moore
*johnmoore.com.ve*
Well-known Venezuelan designer and lettering artist combines ethnic elements with late-modernist strategies.

### Jonahfonts
*jonahfonts.com*
Based in Mexico, the rather anonymous Jonahfonts foundry offers a huge collection of original text and display faces.

### Jukebox
*jawarts.com*
Energetic, all-American display fonts from lettering and design studio JAW Designs, available from Veer.

### Just Another Foundry
*justanotherfoundry.com*
—pp.134—

# K

### Kimera Type Foundry
*kimeratype.com*
—pp.138—

### Kiosk Fonts
*kiosk-fonts.de*
Experimental shop set up as a student project by Frank Grießhammer, who went on to study at KABK Type & Media and is now at Adobe.

### Klim
*klim.co.nz*
—pp.144—

### KLTF
*kltf.de*
The fonts issued by Karsten Lücke Type Foundry are few, but high in quality. Lücke also provides production assistance to a number of major foundries.

### Kombinat-Typefounders
*kombinat-typefounders.com*
—pp.150—

Page
314

Typeface  Odile
Foundry   Kontour

# Wolpertinger
# Bakonawa
# Vanara
# Amalthea

Typeface  PragmataPro          Designed for coding texts.
Foundry   Fabricio Schiavi

# Designed for coding

Typeface  Billboard
Foundry   Fenotype

# BIGGEST BILLBOARD ON EARTH

---

### Kontour
*kontour.com*
Studio and foundry of Houston-based Swiss designer Sibylle Hagmann, designer of the breathtaking Odile family.

### K-Type
*k-type.com*
Small foundry based in Manchester with dozens of display fonts in many styles. Many are free for personal use.

## L

### La Laiterie
*la-laiterie.com*
Paris-based company offering half a dozen mildly original display fonts.

### Lanston Type Library
*see: P22*

### Latinotype
*latinotype.com*
Foundry in Concepción, Chile, offers fonts with a Latin flavor from Daniel Hernández, Luciano Vergara, and friends.

### Laura Worthington
*checkoutmyportfolio.com*
Lettering artist and illustrator began publishing in 2009 and scored hit after hit with a string of well-made script fonts.

### Lazydogs
*lazydogs.de*
German foundry with half a dozen well-made families and a lot of potential; but things seem to have stalled.

### LetterPerfect
*letterspace.com*
One of the earliest independent foundries, run by Garrett Boge and offering well-crafted typefaces — from loose scripts and display fonts to classical text faces.

### Letterhead
*letterheadfonts.com*
Collection of picturesque, nostalgic display fonts with an early 20th-century Americana flavor.

### LettError
*letterror.com*
Selling retail type is not a priority for Dutch type wizards Just van Rossum and Erik van Blokland, who were involved in developing RoboFab and the WOFF standard. But some of their witty fonts are sold here exclusively.

### Lián Types
*liantypes.com.ar*
Argentinian designer Maximiliano Sproviero has been internationally successful with individualist calligraphic fonts. Separate label Typesenses run with Sabrina Lopez.

### LiebeFonts
*liebefonts.com*
Berlin-based illustrator Ulrike Wilhelm crafts mainly picture fonts but had a hit with her sophisticated "hand-written" alphabetic font LiebeErika.

### Lineto
*lineto.com*
Oldest digital foundry in Switzerland, founded by Stefan Müller and Cornel Windlin, most famous for Laurenz Brunner's Akkurat, the quintessential neo-Swiss face.

### LucasFonts
*lucasfonts.com*
—pp. 154—

### Ludwig Type
*ludwigtype.de*
—pp. 162—

### Lux Typo
*luxtypo.com*
Experienced design director and type designer Greg Lindy (Los Angeles) has joined the Village family with his small collection of smooth, contemporary sans-serifs.

# M

### MAC Rhino Fonts
*macrhino.com*
Swedish designer Stefan Hattenbach produces and sells text and display fonts with a unique sense of style.

### MADType
*madtype.com*
Matthew Aaron Desmond of Minneapolis has developed custom typefaces and logos for the likes of Virgin and Nike. He has made dozens of retail fonts, from grunge to neo-geo.

### Mark Simonson Studio
*ms-studio.com*
Brilliant lettering artist, designer of Proxima Nova and many other fonts inspired by art deco and 1950s styles.

### Media Type Foundry
*mediatypefoundry.com*
Based in Paris, created in 2010 by a Portuguese-French trio of type designers. Thoughtful types rooted in tradition.

### Medieval Unicode Font Initiative
*mufi.info*
A non-profit workgroup of scholars and font designers working on ways to encode and display special characters in Medieval texts written in the Latin alphabet.

### The MicroFoundry
*themicrofoundry.com*
Armenian-American designer Hrant H. Papazian has voiced his strong ideas on letterforms and legibility in numerous online forums and discussion lists.

### MilieuGrotesque
*milieugrotesque.com*
—pp. 168—

### Miller Type Foundry
*millertype.com*
American Richard Miller has recently brought out a nice range of usable yet distinctive text and display types.

### MiniFonts
*minifonts.com*
Collection of miniscule bitmap fonts.

### Misprinted Type
*misprintedtype.com*
Brazilian Eduardo Recife's collection of outrageous fonts that cross the ornamental with the destructive.

### Moretype
*moretype.co.uk*
Having released fonts through T26 and Identikal, Liverpool-based Chris Dickinsonnow has his own collection of well-equipped, stylish sans-serifs.

### Mostardesign
*mostardesign.com*
French designer Olivier Gourvat's graphic design studio offers a handful of cool, clean sans-serifs and display fonts.

### Mota Italic
*motaitalic.com*
Foundry of Berlin-based American type designer Rob Keller, a Reading graduate. Just started, full of promise.

### Munchfonts
*munchfonts.com*
Gary Munch has made superb faces for the likes of Linotype and Microsoft, and has a fine collection of his own; but the Munchfonts site does his work little justice.

### MVB Fonts
*mvbfonts.com*
Mark van Bronkhorst developed typefaces for Adobe, FontShop, ITC, Warner Bros., Disney, and the Bank of America. His personal foundry offers some of his best fonts, including Verdigris, Embarcadero, and Sweet Sans.

# N

### Neufville Digital
*neufville.com*
Once one of the last places where metal type could be ordered, now a collaboration between former Bauer Types in Barcelona and Dutch type technicians Visualogik.

### Neutura
*neutura.org*
—pp. 172—

### Newlyn
*newlyn.com*
Small set from Miles Newlyn in London, who also designed type for David Carson and released fonts at Emigre.

### Nick's Fonts
*nicksfonts.com*
Lettering veteran Nick Curtis has created a collection of over 500 fonts based on vintage type and typography.

### Nonpareil Type
*nonpareiltype.com*
New York-based microfoundry offering a small collection of 20th-century revivals and original faces by Jerry Kelly. Not to be confused with:

### Nonpareille
*nonpareille.net*
Foundry run by Matthieu Cortat, a Swiss type designer living in Lyon, France. Small collection of quality fonts.

### The Northern Block
*thenorthernblock.co.uk*
Jonathan Hill hails from Newcastle, north-east England, and designs "contemporary typefaces that work in the commercial market place."

### Norwegian Fonts
*fontshop.com/fonts/foundry/norwegian_fonts/*
A daughter of former FontShop Norway, founded by designer Jacob Øvergaard in collaboration with several local designers. A popular collection in Scandinavia.

# O

### OldFonts.com
*oldfonts.com*
Fonts based on scanned originals of ancient handwriting and printed types. The name says it all.

### Optimo
*optimo.ch*
—pp. 176—

### Otto Maurer
*myfonts.com/foundry/Otto_Maurer*
German designer and tattoo enthusiast who owns a tattoo info site and has designed dozens of skin

### OurType
*ourtype.com*
—pp.182—

### Outras Fontes
*outrasfontes.com*
Run by Brazilian type/graphic designer and researcher Ricardo Esteves Gomes. A small collection of strikingly original display fonts.

### Outside the Line
*outside-the-line.com*
Rae Kaiser, formerly a high-profile design director, now specializes in witty, wonderfully usable picture fonts and handwritten script fonts.

# P

### P22
*p22.com*
—pp.190—

### PampaType
*pampatype.com*
—pp.196—

### Parachute
*parachute.gr*
—pp.200—

### Paragraph
*paragraph.com.au*
Paragraph is Jan Schmoeger, born in Prague, based in Australia. Spent most of his life as a book designer, now designs quite original text-and-display typefaces.

### ParaType
*paratype.com*
Russia's principal digital type foundry, developing both Cyrillic versions of existing fonts and original typefaces, often with a subtly Russian atmosphere.

### Parkinson Type Design
*typedesign.com*
Jim Parkinson designed the nameplate of Rolling Stone magazine and numerous other newspapers. Published typefaces at Adobe, FontShop, Font Bureau and elsewhere and now markets his striking fonts himself.

### Philatype
*philatype.com*
Small collection of striking display fonts. PhilaType is Kosal Sen from Philadelphia.

### PintassilgoPrints
*pintassilgoprints.com*
Based in Vitória, Brazil, PintassilgoPrints produces effervescent fonts based on hand-rendered alphabets.

### Pizzadude
*pizzadude.dk*
Denmark's answer to Chank Diesel. Real name: Jakob Fischer. Both commercial and free fonts.

### Playtype
*playtype.com*
—pp.208—

### Porchez Typofonderie
*typofonderie.com*
—pp.214—

### Positype
*positype.com*
Foundry of versatile designer Neil Summerour. See also TypeTrust, one of the featured foundries in this book.

### Présence Typo
*myfonts.com/foundry/Presence_Typo*
Sophisticated collection of (mostly) text faces by Thierry Puyfoulhoux, located in the French Alps.

### preussTYPE
*preusstype.com*
The other label of GTF principal Ingo Preuss. A growing collection of well-made text and display faces.

### primetype
*primetype.com*
Ole Schäfer, co-designer of several of Erik Spiekermann's fonts, founded his own library in 2003. Includes designs by some of Berlin's most talented type designers: Verena Gerlach, Andrea Tinnes, Ralph du Carrois, and late GDR designer Karl-Heinz Lange.

### profonts
*profonts.de*
Font label from Hamburg, Germany, run by Peter Rosenfeld of URW++. Includes many revivals of classic German types.

### Process Type Foundry
*processtypefoundry.com*
Minneapolis foundry featuring the typefaces of acclaimed designer Eric Olson. The squarish sans-serif Klavika is their most successful face — a modern classic.

### Protimient
*protimient.com*
Protimient's owner, Ben Jones, has made a series of interesting, slightly quirky variants on well-know type styles.

### p.s.type
*cargocollective.com/pstype*
Both playground and retail platform for some serious type families, p.s.type is the typographic laboratory of pprwrk design studio based in Southern California.

### PSY/OPS
*psyops.com*
Founded by Rodrigo Cavazos in San Francisco in 1995, PSY/OPS carries almost a hundred quality type families by an international selection of designers.

# Q

### Quadrat
*quadrat.com/fonts.html*
Toronto-based microfoundry run by graphic and web designer David Vereschagin.

# R

### Scriptorium
*fontcraft.com*
Hundreds of mostly decorative and calligraphic fonts, based on historical and folk sources.

### Red Rooster Collection
*houseoftype.com*
Steve Jackaman's Red Rooster has been around for two decades and is now part of retail platform House Of Type. Red Rooster is home to 1970s typefaces made by Leslie Usherwood for Toronto outfit Typesettra and for Letraset.

### Resistenza
*resistenza.es*
A small collection of new display fonts by Giuseppe Salerno, an Italian web designer based in Valencia, Spain.

### ReType
*re-type.com*
—pp.222—

### Rosetta
*rosettatype.com*
David Březina set up Rosetta with TypeTogether's José Scaglione and Veronika Burian with the aim to create multi-script typefaces for the global market.

### R-Typography
*r-typography.com*
Talented Portuguese designer Rui Abreu has published most of his fonts at Fountain, but markets his friendly sans-serif Gesta himself. Probably more to come.

## S

### Samuelstype
*samuelstype.com*
Foundry of Stockholm designer Hans Samuelson with a growing collection of well-made, modern typefaces.

### Scholtz Fonts
*design-africa.com*
Anton Scholtz from Durban, South Africa, specializes in "African flavor" fonts and informal scripts.

### SelfBuild Type Foundry
*selfbuildtype.com*
Small foundry based in York, England, specializing in contemporary display and pixel typefaces.

### Sherwood
*see: P22*

### Shinntype
*shinntype.com*
—pp.228—

### ShyFoundry Fonts
*shyfoundry.com*
Having released hundreds of free fonts in the late 1990s, Derek Vogelpohl from Omaha, Nebraska, relaunched in 2008 with a new collection of mostly techno-style fonts.

### Sideshow
*see: Font Diner*

### SMeltery
*smeltery.net*
The typographic lab of Jack Usine, co-owner of GUsto studio in Bordeaux, France. Striking display designs, many of which are free.

### Soneri
*aakashsoneri.com*
Foundry of Aakash Soneri, a graphic and type designer in Ahmedabad, India. His Accord and Sone type families are simple and stylish modern sans-serifs.

### SparkyType
*sparkytype.com*
Based in Wellington, New Zealand, David Buck worked for Chank Co before starting SparkyType in 2003. Specializes in informal and geometric display type.

### St Bride Type Foundry
*stbridetype.com*
A foundry in the making, planning to digitally recreate classic British typefaces as recorded in London's famous St Bride Library.

### Stereo Type Haus
*stereotypehaus.com*
Founded in 2001 by Los Angeles designer RD Granados, Stereo Type Haus creates original typefaces for corporate clients (including The New York Times and Microsoft) as well as retail.

### StereoType
*stereo-type.net*
Type experiments (most of them downloadable for free) by Frenchman Clément Nicolle, who has also operated as Dasklem and Zone Erogene. Not to be confused with:

### Stereotypes
*behance.net/stereotypes*
Although technically still a student, German designer Sascha Timplan has already been hugely successful with his playful display faces.

### Stone Type Foundry
*stonetypefoundry.com*
Sumner Stone, the designer of the popular Stone family, sells his more recent typefaces through his own platform.

### Storm Type
*stormtype.com*
—pp.236—

### Studiocharlie
*studiocharlie.org*
Small studio in northern Italy does product design, graphics, video, and type design. Fonts range from grunge to cool and clean.

### Stylefaces
*stylefaces.de*
Typefaces from Stefan Seifert in Hamburg, Germany. Quirky, spindly forms abound. Curiously expensive.

### Subflux
*subflux.com/Fonts/Fonts.htm*
Free fonts in a range of 1990s and nostalgic styles.

### Subtype
*subtype.org*
Formerly Typisc. Strong, simple display faces from Stockholm concept designer and art director Andreas Pihlström, aka Suprb.

### Sudtipos
*Sudtipos.com*
—pp.242—

### Suitcase Type Foundry
*suitcasetype.com*
Type designer Tomáš Brousil from Prague, Czech Republic, offers a library of excellent, well-equipped typeface families in a wide range of styles.

### Suomi Type Foundry
*type.fi*
—pp.246—

## T

### T26
*t26.com*
Foundry set up by graphic designer Carlos Segura, which became a stepping stone for many young type designers. T26 doubles as a retail platform, selling fonts by several independent foundries featured in this book.

### T4
*t4.se*
While Sweden's T4 is a young foundry, the team behind it has a long history in type design; it includes veteran type designers Bo Berndal and Torbjörn Olsson.

### TeGeType
*gouttenegre.com*
Thierry Gouttenègre is a Belgian type designer currently based in France, offering a growing collection of originals that are idiosyncratic yet rooted in tradition.

### Ten by twenty
*tenbytwenty.com*
Nicely made free fonts and cheap fonts by Ed Merritt, a designer at Headscape, living in Bournemouth, UK.

### Terminal Design
*terminaldesign.com*
James Montalbano is best known as the designer of ClearviewHwy, the only federally approved alternative to the existing US Standard Alphabets for highway signage. His library of quality text faces is impressive.

### Test Pilot Collective
*testpilotcollective.com*
Grunge, pixel and deconstructive fonts by Joe Kral, most of which go back to the late 1990s and early 2000s.

## The Enschedé Font Foundry
*teff.nl*
Digital continuation, under the direction of Peter Matthias Noordzij, of the historical Dutch foundry Enschedé. TEFF has published typefaces by Gerrit and Christoph Noordzij (father and brother of the owner) as well as modern classics by Bram de Does.

## The Type Fetish
*typefetish.com*
Dozens of (mostly grunge-style) fonts by Michael Wallner, located in St. Paul, MN.

## Thirstype
see: Village

## Three Islands Press
*3ipfonts.com*
Platform representing the work of Patricia Lillie, Brian Willson, and 75-year-old Swedish designer Lars Bergquist. Formerly Type Quarry.

## Tilde
*fonts.lv*
The only type-related company in the Baltic States, focusing on Eastern European languages and Cyrillic.

## Tipo
*tipo.net.ar*
Darío Muhafara and Eduardo Tunni from Buenos Aires are the curators of a growing collection of high-quality typefaces by Latin-American designers.

## TipografiaRamis
*myfonts.com/foundry/TipografiaRamis*
Russian-born American designer Ramiz Guseynov creates original typefaces using simple geometric shapes.

## TipoType
*tipotype.com*
Foundry based in Montevideo, Uruguay, with a small collection of highly original Latin-flavored typefaces.

## Tiro Typeworks
*tiro.com*
Vancouver-based designers John Hudson and Ross Mills are best known for their commissioned work; the foundry notably sells Mill's Huronia and the unique Restraint, the only retail face by typographic diva Marian Bantjes.

## Tour de Force Font Foundry
*tourdefonts.com*
Founded by Serbian designers Slobodan and Dusan Jelesijevic in 2009 Tour de Force claims to be "one of the major font foundries on the Balkan Peninsula".

## Treacyfaces
*treacyfaces.com*
Formed in 1984 by Joe Treacy in West Haven, Connecticut. Publishes over 300 of his type designs.

## Trine Rask
*trinerask.dk*
Talented Danish designer who graduated from KABK Type & Media and self-published a small collection of beautifully crafted text and display fonts.

## Typadelic Fonts
*typadelic.com*
Microfoundry run by Ronna Penner, offering her widely admired informal script and display faces.

## Typeco
*typeco.com*
Chicago-based outfit run by James Grieshaber, formerly at P22. A small collection of mostly techno-style, geometrical headline typefaces.

## TypeCulture
*typeculture.com*
Mark Jamra's website is both a platform for his thorough, beautifully drawn fonts and an academic resource for students, educators and professionals seeking information about the history, design, manufacture and use of typefaces.

## typecuts
*typecuts.de*
Graphic designer and teacher Andrea Tinnes has published her fresh text faces at Primetype, but sells her earlier display fonts exclusively via her own label.

## Type Department
*typedepartment.de/typetester.html*
Berlin-based type designer and teacher Jurgen Huber published fonts at FontFont but now runs his own label with promising fonts still in development.

## typedifferent
*typedifferent.com*
Outlet for fonts made at seminal Swiss graphic design studio Büro Destruct since 1995. A large collection of geometric and deconstructivist display faces.

## Typejockeys
*typejockeys.com*
Graphic and type design company based in Vienna, Austria, established in 2008 by Anna Fahrmaier, Thomas Gabriel, and Michael Hochleitner. So far, their handful of published families have been widely acclaimed.

## TypeManufactur
*typemanufactur.com*
German designer Georg Salden has been developing innovative type for five decades, and still has remained relatively unknown. The new site developed by young colleague Ludwig Übele will hopefully change that.

## Type-Ø-Tones
*type-o-tones.com*
Founded by four Barcelona designers, Type-Ø-Tones is one of the oldest independent foundries in Europe. Was recently relaunched, with Laura Meseguer's successful Rumba typeface as their §most impressive new font.

## Typerepublic
*typerepublic.com*
Formerly of Typerware, Barcelona designer Andreu Balius now runs his one-man foundry with a small but exquisite library of beautifully drawn typefaces.

## TypeSETit
*typesetit.com*
Calligrapher-lettegin artist Rob Leuschke is a master of script fonts. He offers dozens through his own foundry.

## TypeTogether
*type-together.com*
—pp. 252—

## TypeTrust
*typetrust.com*
—pp. 260—

## TYPETYPE
*typetype.com*
Based in Essen, Germany, TYPETYPE is run by designer Dirk Uhlenbrock. TYPETYPE currently offers a small set of minimalist neo-geo display fonts.

## Typodermic
*typodermicfonts.com*
Canadian Ray Larabie, former king of free fonts, has built a large library of playful, trendy, usable and highly affordable display fonts.

## Typonine
*typonine.com*
—pp. 264—

## typographies.fr
*typographies.fr*
Collaboration between young French designers Jonathan Perez and Laurent Bourcellier. Their crop is limited so far, but includes a delicious reinterpretation of a little known, 16th-century Flemish upright italic, Joos.

## Typolar
*typolar.com*
—pp. 268—

## Typonauten
*typonauten.com*
Based in Bremen, Germany, Typonauten is a small communications agency with a foundry attached, offering a baker's dozen of colorful display fonts.

**Typotheque**
*typotheque.com*
—pp.274—

## U/V

**Underware**
*underware.nl*
—pp.280—

**Vanarchiv**
*vanarchiv.com*
Portuguese designer Ricardo Santos's foundry, offering a handful of well-made text and display fonts.

**VetteLetters**
*vetteletters.nl*
—pp.286—

**Village: Incubator**
*vllg.com*
—pp.292—

**VirusFonts**
*virusfonts.com*
—pp.298—

**Volcano Type**
*volcano-type.de/*
—pp.304—

## W

**Wiescher Design**
*wiescher-design.de*
Hundreds of fonts from design veteran Gert Wiescher, probably Germany's fastest-working type designer.

**Will-Harris Studios**
*will-harris.com*
American design consultancy offers the font collections of Judith Sutcliff (formerly known as The Electric Typographer), Richard Beatty and David Rakowski.

## Y

**YouWorkForThem**
*youworkforthem.com/fonts*
Type and stock image distributor doubles as a foundry. Most of YouWorkForThem's own fonts were designed by former partner Michael Cina, who left the company in 2009 to start up his own studio.

---

Typeface   Barber
Foundry    Fenotype

*Flowershop*

Typeface   CAPSET
Foundry    Subtype

SPACE TRAVEL

Typeface   Viceroy
Foundry    Typecuts

La Couturière
**Parisienne**

Typeface   YWFT Coltrane
Foundry    YouWorkForThem

GLENN GOULD

**Type Navigator**
*The Independent Foundries Handbook*

Edited by TwoPoints.Net, Jan Middendorp
Text and preface by Jan Middendorp

Cover and layout by TwoPoints.Net
Cover photography by Seber Ugarte
Retouching by Kim Boix Sas
Typeface: Times LT Std

Project management by Julian Sorge for Gestalten
Production management by Martin Bretschneider for Gestalten
Proofreading by transparent Language Solutions
Printed by Optimal Media Production, Röbel
Made in Germany

Readers of Gestalten's *Type Navigator* may also like TypeNavigator, a visual search engine for fonts, developed by Hansjörg and Robert Stulle. Find and identify the font you are envisioning with TypeNavigator. Although it is completely independent from this book, it's a useful tool and a great way to discover fonts for type enthusiasts.
www.typenavigator.com

Published by Gestalten, Berlin 2011
ISBN 978-3-89955-377-2

© Die Gestalten Verlag GmbH & Co. KG, Berlin 2011
All rights reserved. No part of this publication may be reproduced or transmitted in any form or by any means, electronic or mechanical, including photocopy or any storage and retrieval system, without permission in writing from the publisher.

Respect copyrights, encourage creativity!

For more information, please visit www.gestalten.com.

Bibliographic information published by the Deutsche Nationalbibliothek. The Deutsche Nationalbibliothek lists this publication in the Deutsche Nationalbibliografie; detailed bibliographic data are available online at http://dnb.d-nb.de.

None of the content in this book was published in exchange for payment by commercial parties or designers; the inclusion of all work is based solely on its artistic merit.

This book was printed on paper certified by the FSC®.

Gestalten is a climate-neutral company. We collaborate with the non-profit carbon offset provider myclimate (www.myclimate.org) to neutralize the company's carbon footprint produced through our worldwide business activities by investing in projects that reduce $CO_2$ emissions (www.gestalten.com/myclimate).

**myclimate**
Protect our planet